THE ROUTLEDGE HANDBOOK OF INTERNATIONAL LOCAL GOVERNMENT

The Routledge Handbook of International Local Government conducts a rigorous, innovative and distinctive analysis of local government within a comparative, international context.

Examining the subject matter with unrivalled breadth and depth, this handbook shows how different cultures and countries develop different institutions, structures and processes over time, yet that all have some features in common – the most obvious of which is the recognition that some decisions are better made, some services better delivered, and some engagement with the state better organised if there is structured organisational expression of the importance of the *local* dimension of all these factors.

Thematically organised, it includes contributions from international experts with reference to the wider context in terms of geographies, local government modes, recent developments and possible further lines of research. It has a wide academic appeal internationally and will steer a course between the two dimensions of mono-jurisdictional studies and 'cataloguing' forms of comparison.

The Routledge Handbook of International Local Government will be essential reading and an authoritative reference for scholars, students, researchers and practitioners involved in, and actively concerned about, research on local government.

Richard Kerley is emeritus professor of management at Queen Margaret University, UK, having previously been a dean and vice principal over the period the former university college gained full university title. He is chair of the Centre for Scottish Public Policy and on the editorial boards of *Local Government Studies* and the *International Journal of Public Management*.

Joyce Liddle is professor at Newcastle Business School, University of Northumbria, UK. She is a fellow of the British Academy of Social Sciences, fellow of Regional Studies Association, and fellow of Joint University Council. She recently stood down as honorary chair of the UK Joint University Council and was formerly chair of its Public Administration Committee. She is EAB member on seven international journals and researches in local and regional government, public leadership, management and entrepreneurship, and regularly publishes work in noted international journals in the field.

Pamela T. Dunning is associate professor of public administration at Troy University, USA. She is chair of the Section on Public Administration Education within the American Society of Public Administration (ASPA), a previous Hampton Roads Chapter president in ASPA, and is on the editorial board of the Sage journal *Teaching Public Administration*.

'This Handbook will undoubtedly become a key reference source for scholars of local government across the world. The editors are to be congratulated on highlighting in detail many distinctive elements of local government structure and process, across many international boundaries and national cultures . . .'

Tony Bovaird, *Institute of Local Government Studies, University of Birmingham, UK*

'This book fills an important gap in the field of public administration by providing administrators with a wealth of perspectives, knowledge and best practices in local government from around the globe . . .'

John Kiefer, *University of New Orleans, USA*

THE ROUTLEDGE HANDBOOK OF INTERNATIONAL LOCAL GOVERNMENT

Edited by
Richard Kerley, Joyce Liddle and
Pamela T. Dunning

LONDON AND NEW YORK

First published 2019
by Routledge
2 Park Square, Milton Park, Abingdon, Oxon OX14 4RN

and by Routledge
711 Third Avenue, New York, NY 10017

Routledge is an imprint of the Taylor & Francis Group, an informa business

© 2019 selection and editorial matter, Richard Kerley, Joyce Liddle and Pamela T. Dunning; individual chapters, the contributors

The right of Richard Kerley, Joyce Liddle and Pamela T. Dunning to be identified as the authors of the editorial material, and of the authors for their individual chapters, has been asserted in accordance with sections 77 and 78 of the Copyright, Designs and Patents Act 1988.

All rights reserved. No part of this book may be reprinted or reproduced or utilised in any form or by any electronic, mechanical, or other means, now known or hereafter invented, including photocopying and recording, or in any information storage or retrieval system, without permission in writing from the publishers.

Trademark notice: Product or corporate names may be trademarks or registered trademarks, and are used only for identification and explanation without intent to infringe.

British Library Cataloguing in Publication Data
A catalogue record for this book is available from the British Library

Library of Congress Cataloging in Publication Data
Names: Kerley, Richard, editor. | Liddle, Joyce, 1952- editor. | Dunning, Pam, editor.
Title: The Routledge handbook of international local government / edited by Richard Kerley, Joyce Liddle, Pam Dunning.
Other titles: Handbook of international local government
Description: Abingdon, Oxon ; New York, NY : Routledge, 2019. | Includes bibliographical references and index.
Identifiers: LCCN 2018019060| ISBN 9781138234727 (hbk) | ISBN 9781315306278 (ebk)
Subjects: LCSH: Local government. | Local government—Case studies. | Comparative government.
Classification: LCC JS78 .R79 2019 | DDC 320.8—dc23
LC record available at https://lccn.loc.gov/2018019060

ISBN: 978-1-138-23472-7 (hbk)
ISBN: 978-1-315-30627-8 (ebk)

Typeset in Bembo
by Swales & Willis Ltd, Exeter, Devon, UK
Printed and bound by CPI Group (UK) Ltd, Croydon, CR0 4YY

CONTENTS

List of figures ix
List of tables xi
List of contributors xiv

1 Local governments: a global presence? 1
  Richard Kerley, Joyce Liddle and Pamela T. Dunning

PART I
Elected roles and governance **11**

2 Local electoral systems 13
  Michael Cole

3 Local political leadership: the voters or councillors – who chooses who governs? 25
  Colin Copus

4 Traditional leaders and local government in Pacific Island countries 38
  Graham Hassall and Paul Mae

5 The role of the councillor 54
  Neil McGarvey and Fraser Stewart

6 The relationship between politics and administration: from dichotomy to local governance arenas 70
  Alessandro Sancino, Marco Meneguzzo, Alessandro Braga and Paolo Esposito

Contents

7 Institutionalized differences in economic development perspectives: a comparison of city managers, mayors and council members in Texas   82
James Vanderleeuw and Melanie Smith

PART II
Local governments in different jurisdictions   97

8 The political salience of local government in a small state   99
Ann Marie Bissessar

9 Local government in the Pacific Islands   110
Graham Hassall, Matthew Kensen, Rikiaua Takeke, Karibaiti Taoba and Feue Tipu

10 Local government in Latin America: the struggle to overcome social exclusion   131
Andrew Nickson

11 A turbulent past, a turbulent future? Reform and disruption in the local government of New Zealand   149
Michael Reid and Michael Macaulay

12 Constitutional and legislative changes in Caribbean local government   163
Eris Schoburgh

PART III
Range of local government services   181

13 Local government service roles in the USA: consistency and change   183
J. Edwin Benton

14 Public entrepreneurship: is local government necessary to deliver economic development?   203
Lorraine Johnston and John Fenwick

15 The wide range of local government public services   218
Elisabetta Mafrolla

16 Public service delivery in today's Georgia   233
Giorgi Vashakidze

17 The provision of public and personal social services in European countries: between marketisation and the return of the public/municipal and third sector   247
Hellmut Wollmann

PART IV
Citizen engagement   261

18 Practices and challenges of citizen participation in local
    government: case studies of mid-sized cities in Russia and
    the United States   263
    *Sofia Prysmakova-Rivera, Elena Gladun, Thomas Bryer, Andrey Larionov,
    Dmitry Teplyakov, Olga Teplyakova and Natalia Nosova*

19 The urban governance of austerity in Europe   280
    *Adrian Bua, Jonathan Davies, Ismael Blanco, Ioannis Chorianopoulos,
    Mercè Cortina-Oriol, Andrés Feandeiro, Niamh Gaynor, Steven Griggs,
    David Howarth and Yuni Salazar*

20 Redressing the trust deficit: local governments and citizen
    engagement   296
    Jonathan Carr-West

21 Does mode of public outreach matter?   307
    Sheldon Gen and Erika Luger

22 Improving social development in Brazil through an open
    budget perspective: does collaborative stakeholder engagement
    matter?   325
    Welles Abreu and Ricardo Gomes

23 Civic engagement in local politics in Central Europe   344
    Oto Potluka, Judit Kalman, Ida Musiałkowska and Piotr Idczak

PART V
Multi-level governance   361

24 Australia: challenging institutional constraints   363
    Chris Aulich

25 Local government outside local boundaries: rescaling municipalities,
    redesigning provinces and local-level Europeanisation   377
    Koenraad De Ceuninck, Tony Valcke and Tom Verhelst

26 Local government in the European Union's multilevel polity   394
    Marius Guderjan

27 Second thoughts on second-order? Towards a second-tier model
    of local government elections and voting   405
    Ulrik Kjær and Kristof Steyvers

28 The architecture of the local political community: France, Italy,
    Portugal and Spain   418
    Jaume Magre and Esther Pano

PART VI
Getting and spending   **433**

29 Local government anti-corruption initiatives in post-Soviet
    Georgia and Ukraine: another tale of two cities   435
    Terry Anderson

30 Enhancing VFM audit in local government: the Best Value initiative   450
    Michela Arnaboldi and Irvine Lapsley

31 Financing and taxing for local government   467
    Kenneth Gibb and Linda Christie

32 Adapting to the fiscal environment: local governments, revenue
    and taxation powers   482
    Mark Sandford

33 Financing local government in the twenty-first century: local
    government revenues in European Union member states,
    2000–2014   496
    Gerard Turley and Stephen McNena

Index   *518*

FIGURES

6.1	The five stages of the stakeholder management cycle	75
11.1	Rates as a share of GDP	158
13.1	County, municipal, township and special district spending as a percentage of total local government spending, 1962 and 2012	191
13.2	Individual local governments' expenditures as a percentage of all expenditures for traditional, municipal-type and regional services, 1962 and 2012	192
13.3	Municipal-type service expenditure percentages for US, Texas, California and Florida, 2012	195
13.4	County, municipal and special district expenditure percentages for selected regional services, 1962 and 2012	196
13.5	Local government spending percentages, 1962 and 2012	197
13.6	Expenditure percentages for counties, municipalities, townships and special districts, 1962 and 2012	198
16.1	Types of services citizens knew could be received in the centres, 2013	241
16.2	Knowledge about public space available for free in centres, 2013	241
16.3	Types of services citizens are aware municipalities offer and usage of those services by citizens, 2013	242
16.4	How well municipalities perform their functions and how well personnel responds to citizens, 2013	242
16.5	How fairly municipalities treat citizens, 2013	243
16.6	Most commonly used services in the centres, 2016	243
16.7	Knowledge about public space available for free in centres, 2016	244
16.8	Awareness about additional services available in the centres, 2016	244
18.1	Conceptual framework	265
21.1	Modes of public participation	310
21.2	Hypothesized effect of mode of outreach on policy decision	312
22.1	Brazilian budgetary governance model	329
22.2	Structural equation modelling	335

List of figures

22.3	Estimated structural equation modelling: the collaborative budget model	337
22.4	Municipal open budget means	338
23.1	Differences in participation in general elections among European regions	350
23.2	Percentage of people trusting others in Europe (age 16+)	352
23.3	Main features of social capital/civil society in EU and Visegrad countries	353
23.4	Development of advocacy capacity of CSOs in the Visegrad countries	355
27.1	Second-tier elections and voting	410
28.1	Size and local expenditure, 2012	427
29.1	Corruption Perception Index ranking for Georgia and Ukraine, 1999–2015	439
33.1	OECD taxonomy of grants	500

TABLES

2.1	Main electoral systems	15
6.1	Stakeholder management in local governance arenas: the role of different actors	78
7.1	Economic challenges facing your city	88
7.2	Challenges to your office's efforts to attract development	89
7.3	Importance of support from city leaders, business and citizens	89
8.1	Results of the local government elections, 1968	103
8.2	Local government results, 1977	105
8.3	Percentage of persons voting at local government elections, 1999–2016	107
9.1	Pacific Island country populations as at June 2016	110
10.1	Number of municipalities in Latin America, 1994, 2008 and 2017	135
10.2	Latin America: share of regional and local government in national government spending	137
11.1	New Zealand local government functions and responsibilities	152
11.2	Local government income 2015–2016	153
11.3	Recurrent expenditure by local government for the year ending 30 June 2016	154
11.4	Summary of recent local government reforms	157
12.1	Population profile of selected countries in Anglophone Caribbean	165
12.2	Implications of law governing local government financing	174
13.1	Traditional services of local governments	187
13.2	Municipal-type services of local governments	188
13.3	Regional services of local governments	189
13.4	Three types of local government services based on expenditure categories	190
13.5	County government expenditure percentages for selected traditional services, 1962 and 2012	193
13.6	Expenditure percentages for selected municipal-type services, 1962 and 2012	194

List of tables

15.1	The subjective-government classification of health care services in 15 countries	224
19.1	Austerity governance in European cities	283
21.1	Select regression analyses of preferences for specific modes of public outreach	315
21.2	Select regression analyses of preferences for policy options and priorities	316
21.3	Frequency distributions of significant independent variables in 35 regression analyses	317
22.1	Sample of Brazilian municipalities in numbers	335
22.2	Structural equation modelling: statistical summary results	336
22.3	Direct, indirect and total effects of the structural equation modelling	337
23.1	Characteristics of administrative division and election systems at the local level in the Visegrad countries	346
23.2	Opinions about the likelihood of influencing political decision-making in Central Europe	354
24.1	Characteristics of selected Australian councils, 2000–2001	365
24.2	Number of councils in Australia, 1910–2017	366
27.1	Local second-tier elections and voting: premises and hypotheses	414
28.1	Municipalities and population distribution in France, Italy, Portugal and Spain	421
28.2	Municipalities in France, Italy, Portugal and Spain: population and area	422
28.3	Changes in the number of municipalities	422
28.4	Elements of the electoral system	423
28.5	Territorial thresholds and sub-municipal units	425
28.6	Percentage of local expenditure as proportion of GDP	426
28.7	Public expenditure by sub-sector of government, 2012	427
30.1	Key milestones in England's new local government audit	452
30.2	Survey questionnaire structure	455
30.3	Practices before Best Value	455
30.4	Comments on setting and receptivity	456
30.5	Operation of Best Value	457
30.6	Comments on bureaucracy and displacement	457
30.7	Survey response – three-year budgets	459
30.8	Survey response – benchmarking	459
30.9	Survey response – costing practices	460
30.10	Continuous improvement and culture change	461
30.11	Best Value penetration in local authorities	462
30.12	Best Value and other initiatives	462
31.1	Local taxes in OECD countries, 2010	469
31.2	Strategies for property tax reform	475
31.3	Local council tax bands, Scotland, 2013	476
32.1	Own taxes as percentage of local revenue	491
33.1	Local government revenue classifications	502
33.2	Local taxes and user charges	503

List of tables

33.3	Local government current revenue as a share of GDP, 2000–2014	505
33.4	Local government current revenue as a share of general government revenue, 2000–2014	507
33.5	Local government tax revenue as a share of local government current revenue, 2000–2014	508
33.6	Local government grant revenue as a share of local government current revenue, 2000–2014	510
33.7	Local government user charges revenue as a share of local government current revenue, 2000–2014	511
33.8	Local autonomy index, 2014	512

CONTRIBUTORS

Welles Abreu, University of Brasilia, Brazil.

Terry Anderson, Troy University, Alabama, USA.

Michela Arnaboldi, Department of Engineering Management, Polytechnnic of Milan, Spain.

Chris Aulich, University of Canberra, Australia and the University of New South Wales Canberra.

J. Edwin Benton, The School of Interdisciplinary Global Studies, University of South Florida, USA.

Ann Marie Bissessar, University of the West Indies, Trinidad and Tobago.

Ismael Blanco, Autonomous University of Barcelona, Spain.

Alessandro Braga, Faculty of Business and Management, Niccolo' Cusano Italian University of London, UK.

Thomas Bryer, University of Central Florida, USA.

Adrian Bua, De Montfort University, UK.

Jonathan Carr-West, The Local Government Information Unit, UK.

Ioannis Chorianopoulos, University of the Aegean, Greece.

Linda Christie, The University of Glasgow, UK.

Michael Cole, The University of Liverpool, UK.

List of contributors

Colin Copus, De Montfort University, UK.

Mercè Cortina-Oriol, De Montfort University, UK.

Jonathan Davies, De Montfort University, UK.

Koenraad De Ceuninck, Centre for Local Politics, Ghent University, Belgium.

Pamela T. Dunning, Troy University, Alabama, USA.

Paolo Esposito, Department of Law, Economics, Management and Quantitative Methods, University of Sannio, Italy.

Andrés Feandeiro, De Montfort University, UK.

John Fenwick, Newcastle Business School, Northumbria University, UK.

Niamh Gaynor, Dublin City University, Ireland.

Sheldon Gen, San Francisco State University, USA.

Kenneth Gibb, The University of Glasgow, UK.

Elena Gladun, University of Tyumen, Russia.

Ricardo Gomes, University of Brasilia, Brazil.

Steven Griggs, De Montfort University, UK.

Marius Guderjan, Centre for British Studies, Humboldt University of Berlin, Germany.

Graham Hassall, School of Government, Victoria University of Wellington, New Zealand.

David Howarth, University of Essex, UK.

Piotr Idczak, Department of European Studies, Poznań University of Economics and Business, Poland.

Lorraine Johnston, Newcastle Business School, Northumbria University, UK.

Judit Kalman, Hungarian Academy of Sciences, Institute of Economics, Hungary.

Matthew Kensen, University of the West Indies, St. Augustine Campus, Trinidad.

Richard Kerley, Queen Margaret University, Edinburgh, UK.

Ulrik Kjær, Department of Political Science, University of Southern Denmark.

List of contributors

Irvine Lapsley, University of Edinburgh Business School, UK.

Andrey Larionov, University of Tyumen, Russia.

Joyce Liddle, Newcastle Business School, Northumbria University, UK.

Erika Luger, University of California, Berkeley, USA.

Michael Macaulay, Victoria University of Wellington, New Zealand.

Neil McGarvey, University of Strathclyde, UK.

Stephen McNena, J. E. Cairnes School of Business and Economics, National University of Ireland Galway, Ireland.

Paul Mae, The University of the South Pacific, Fiji.

Elisabetta Mafrolla, Department of Economics, The University of Foggia, Italy.

Jaume Magre, The University of Barcelona, Spain.

Marco Meneguzzo, Institute of Economics and Faculty of Economics, University of Italian Switzerland, Switzerland, and University of Rome Tor Vergata, Italy.

Ida Musiałkowska, Department of European Studies, Poznań University of Economics and Business, Poland.

Andrew Nickson, University of Birmingham, UK.

Natalia Nosova, University of Tyumen, Russia.

Esther Pano, The University of Barcelona, Spain.

Oto Potluka, CEPS, University of Basel, Switzerland.

Sofia Prysmakova-Rivera, University of Central Florida, USA.

Michael Reid, Local Government New Zealand, Wellington, New Zealand.

Yuni Salazar, Autonomous University of Barcelona, Spain.

Alessandro Sancino, Department of Public Leadership and Social Enterprise, The Open University Business School, UK.

Mark Sandford, Library, House of Commons, London, UK.

Eris Schoburgh, University of the West Indies, Mona, Jamaica.

List of contributors

Melanie Smith, Park University, Missouri, USA.

Fraser Stewart, Strathclyde University, UK.

Kristof Steyvers, Centre for Local Politics, Ghent University, Belgium.

Rikiaua Takeke, Kiribati Local Government Association, Kiribati.

Karibaiti Taoba, Commonwealth Local Government Forum, Fiji.

Dmitry Teplyakov, University of Tyumen, Russia.

Olga Teplyakova, University of Tyumen, Russia.

Feue Tipu, Commonwealth Local Government Forum, Fiji.

Gerard Turley, J. E. Cairnes School of Business and Economics, National University of Ireland Galway, Ireland.

Tony Valcke, Centre for Local Politics, Ghent University, Belgium.

James Vanderleeuw, Park University, Missouri, USA.

Giorgi Vashakidze, Swiss Graduate School of Public Administration, Université de Lausanne, Switzerland.

Tom Verhelst, Centre for Local Politics, Ghent University, Belgium.

Hellmut Wollmann, Social Science Institute, Humboldt University, Berlin, Germany.

1
LOCAL GOVERNMENTS
A global presence?

Richard Kerley, Joyce Liddle and Pamela T. Dunning

Introduction

As joint editors, we are conscious that this book is ambitiously titled. We set the contributors an enormous challenge; they have more than met that challenge.

Authors were invited to submit contributions of their own research findings and wider work about similar features of local government across different jurisdictions. These were then grouped into relevant sections to create a wide-ranging review of different features of local government internationally.

We have deliberately minimised binary two-country comparisons in favour of a wider-ranging approach. This is because we consider that there are distinctive elements of local government structure, form, and process that can be usefully compared, contrasted and discussed in a number of ways across a number of international boundaries and in the context of a variety of national cultures.

In doing this we wish to prompt readers to think of some research themes and questions that could develop further opportunities for multi-national study and research. All chapters offer the potential for further research opportunities and we discuss these possibilities further below.

Two examples of different aspects of representation will serve to illustrate some of the opportunities we see for further comparative research that could help develop a better understanding of local governments.

Boston, Massachusetts, has a city population of approximately 670,000; the council is governed by 13 councillors and an executive mayor. Liverpool, England, has a population of approximately 490,000; it is governed by 90 councillors and an executive mayor. There is limited work published and available on whether such differences lead to better, worse or simply different forms of governance; even whether such arrangements generate different workloads for the elected representatives involved (McGarvey and Stewart, Chapter 5, this volume).

In a number of countries across (mainly northern) Europe there has been a consistent long-term trend led by central governments to reduce the number of councils and, in doing so, make council areas larger. Sweden has, over several decades, reduced the number of councils from approximately 2,500 to under 300; Holland reduced the number of municipalities from more than a 1,000 to under 400 in the same timescale. In France and Italy there has been much more limited change in the number of councils. Over the past 70 years France has reduced the number of first-tier councils from approximately 38,000 to 35,000; in that same period Italy has *increased* the number of councils from approximately 7,800 to 8,000 (Magre and Pano, Chapter 28, this volume). However, in both France and Italy, there have been major changes applied or discussed in the intermediate tiers of government. In France, regions formally created in the 1980s have recently been merged and reduced in number. In Italy, structural change – a reduction in the number of regions – has been discussed but not implemented, and various regional bodies are proposing ad hoc changes to the already asymmetrical powers possessed by some Italian regions. It would be interesting to further explore why certain forms of institution such as the very many small local councils in France, Italy and Spain have lasted, whereas other forms of intermediate institutions have not been as durable. In some countries the most local and small of councils seem the great survivors; other sub-national institutions wax and wane in their relative status and number (De Ceuninck et al., Chapter 25, this volume).

As editors, our shared observation is that in different countries, within the respective resident academic communities, we often see a focus on a relatively limited range of local governments from an often-limited range of nation states. Two of the editors (Kerley and Liddle) share membership of the editorial board of *Local Government Studies*, published by Taylor & Francis in the United Kingdom. In each volume, the majority of articles are focused on specific local government jurisdictions that tend to be those of the UK, northern Europe, Australasia and North America. A review of similar geographically defined papers from the journal *Lex Localis*, (published in Slovenia) over the past five years, suggests that there is an emphasis on local government across a small number of countries and a particular concentration on Balkan and Eastern European countries. The *Canadian Journal of Local Government* and the *Australian Journal of Public Administration* both signal their editorial focus very clearly through their titles, and this reflects in their contents. Both understandably concentrate on articles related to their particular countries of origin. As Swianiewicz (2018) has recently observed, studies of territorial reform and the impact of that for collaboration between councils have tended to focus on northwestern Europe.

We have therefore not encouraged an over concentration on the most often researched forms of local government systems in a small number of countries, nor have we sought to discuss every form of local government in every nation state in the world. We anticipate this collection will provide a wider focus that can be of value in developing different frameworks of understanding about different aspects of local governments.

What do we mean by 'local'?

As different studies have shown, citizens have different frames of reference describing their sense of community, or place-based allegiance.

People often simultaneously hold more than one geographic place reference in their head and they will use these in different ways to communicate with different agencies and different people. A man might describe himself as coming from 'New York' if speaking to a French colleague; to a fellow New Yorker he might say 'Staten Island'. A woman who says she comes from Manchester is perhaps using the general description labelling the conurbation composed of more than 10 different local governments. That geographic term 'Manchester' is probably globally understood more through the impact of football than any awareness of local governments. These different senses of 'local' are also set against different operational and political/cultural assumptions about the appropriate scale of governments (in terms of landmass, population and local revenues), that have some responsibility for locally delivered and organised functions.

For the various functional responsibilities of local governments globally, there are different assumptions about scale, degree of local discretion that can be exercised within the confines of constitutional or legislative authority, and the manner in which local government units are structured and organised.

The forms of structure and governance are often dependent upon historical legacy and cultural assumptions. In Germany, the states[1] are responsible for most public education, principally as a reaction to events in twentieth-century German history. In most of the constituent states of the USA, school districts, independent of local councils, remain autonomous entities responsible for schooling, with the original motivation of removing universal school education from 'political' influence (Benton, Chapter 13, this volume). In Finland and South Korea, education is managed by agencies of the nation state. In the United Kingdom, education systems are different in each of the four constituent countries.

Whatever the actual form of governance and actual tier of institutional responsibility for public services and decisions on regulation and resources, there are very few nation states where the central governing state alone assumes responsibility for all provision and all decisions in a given geography.

Therefore, the most common reflection of the importance of 'local' is the almost universal extent to which various forms of geographically defined sub-national state administrative or political divisions are found in countries throughout the world. This is regardless of whether these are jurisdictions with large land mass and populations greater than one billion, or the smallest state entities, with populations of fewer than 50,000 (Hassall et al., Chapter 9, this volume). Some form of local entity can be found in almost every nation state in the world; even North Korea has localised arrangements of 'administrative divisions' that are designated in various ways.

The extent, size, formal hierarchy and degree of independence of such localised divisions varies widely. It is apparent that almost every nation state has found some need to create local divisions of some form or another. This has been either as part of historic legacy – 'shires', for example – or is seen as a necessary political development as part of social and institutional development process, sometimes encouraged by international bodies. The creation of such local divisions has happened recently in South Sudan. In Pakistan various changes have occurred over the period since Partition, and the most recent changes to local government have included reservation of some decision making places by gender, religion and social class.

The terminology applied to describe such administrative divisions varies widely.[2] This does however confirm such sub-state divisions – usually referred to as 'local governments' – with various mixtures of authority, responsibilities, and power are a near universal phenomenon (Hassall et al., Chapter 9, this volume). The only nation state that does not appear to have such sub-divisions of any kind is the Vatican City – the smallest state in the world.

Where there are such local divisions across many countries, we can often find a coherence of both structure and terminology; so 'counties' typically encompass a greater area than do 'municipalities'. However, large cities often have distinct forms of government that recognise their sheer scale and economic influence. In some instances, and in some jurisdictions, the term 'city', which most would typically take to denote an urban centre of some population size, has been attached to entities with very small populations. Missouri, for example, has entities described as cities that range from a population of over 500,000 to under 100 people. There are also occasional oddities such as the usage in Alaska of the term 'borough' for local governments, including the mixed and widely distributed non-contiguous areas of 'Unorganized Borough', where more than 80,000 people live.

There is no standard universal form of localised division; one common feature however, is that such divisions, however they are titled, have a major role in delivering a range of public services, providing facilities, and regulating various aspects of social life (Mafrolla, Chapter 15, this volume).

Hesse and Sharpe (1991: 608) observe that 'local governments . . . play a major role in the delivery of fundamental collective public and public and quasi-public goods'. The authors confine their comment to local government in the 'Western industrialised world', but we would argue that this observation now holds more widely and across a wider range of countries than at the time it was first made. Changing patterns of nation state authority and global power have been accompanied by the growth of the varied forms of institution that comprise local governments globally, the services provided and functions fulfilled.

One other significant aspect of the word 'local' is to be found in the extent to which there are variations of organisational architecture and form within the jurisdiction of one nation state. This is not surprising in hard federal jurisdictions, where the structural architecture and processes of local governments would be expected to vary widely as between a number of states or provinces. This is clearly the case in the USA and Germany, for example, where the number of councillors in different councils – and their form of governance – varies widely between different states.

However, many countries have minor variations of governance that depart from the broad norm because of particular historic, geographic, demographic, social and economic features (Schoburgh, Chapter 12, this volume; Bissessar, Chapter 8, this volume). Sometimes such features create forms of local governments that have inherited legacy structural arrangements from previous generations of society and government.

It does seem to be the case that this is often pronounced in nation states that have a legacy of either former imperial power, or quasi-imperial power. The end of empire has often resulted in untidiness (Nickson, Chapter 10, this volume). The Netherlands has three 'special municipalities', which are in the Caribbean. France has departments and communes in the Indian Ocean, in South America, and off the coast of Canada. Spain has two autonomous cities in Morocco, Ceuta and Melilla. Both the US and the UK have complex relationships with a variety of detached island territories. In some long established nation states, even in core geographies, variation has often been historically present, particularly in relation to the capital city. Paris, for example, had no elected mayor between 1793 and 1977 and was directly run by the French government, perhaps because of a continuing residual elite fear of the power of the Paris 'street'. Washington, DC had no mayor until 1973 and no representation up to then in the national legislature. Mexico City and the Australian Capital Territory are similarly located on land areas with governance arrangements unlike that of other states within the two respective countries. London is the capital city of the United Kingdom, and has long been the subject of debate on appropriate forms of governance and the office of Mayor of London was only created in the 1990s. Nested inside the boundaries of London is the City of London, which has a night-time population of around 9,000, and an archaic franchise based on medieval trade arrangements. It does, nevertheless, have extensive powers, including the operation of its own police force (the smallest in the UK). In nation states that have very remote and sparsely populated areas, there are variations of governance, provision of services and control of financial resources (Kitchen and Slack 2004). Canada, Brazil, Australia, and some other countries all have variations of standard structure and organisations in their more remote 'territories'.

While such historic curiosities can arouse intense interest among campaigners and scholars, they appear to be of no great significance to the general population living in such jurisdictions. 'Local' can therefore have many meanings that vary even within nation states and certainly vary across national jurisdictions.

What do we mean by 'government'?

In considering 'local governments' we have assumed that the word 'government' usually implies aspects of two key features that are widely observed.

These are some form of democratic accountability through the periodic election of the ultimate decision makers responsible for governance, and therefore their capacity to reflect views on behalf of those who elect them. The other factor is some degree of local discretion over the exercise of functions that such a body has. Whatever the formal mechanics of representation, we have taken it as axiomatic that the term government implies this periodic election of the ultimate decision makers in those local governments rather than their appointment by others such as a government minister.

However, there are, as we indicate above, always the possibility of localised variation that mediates various features of local government and that are often historically and culturally embedded and broadly accepted, though often the subject of some intermittent discussion about possible change. So in Holland, mayors of local municipalities are appointed by the government, not elected.

The possibility of elected representatives being removed or suspended from office (regardless of the status of that office) is complex in many jurisdictions and often clear provision is not well established, perhaps in the hope that any such necessity will not arise. In some countries, there is provision for recall elections. Elsewhere, the direct removal of elected councillors for no clearly defined legal reason is usually a consequence of some quasi- dictatorial intervention in politics (Hassall and Mae, Chapter 4, this volume).

The other aspect of the power that we associate with government is the extent to which such local governments can be instructed on what actions to take, or to have their actions countermanded through the administrative decision of a superior body or official. This leaves open however, some questions about respective spheres and tiers of government where there is some superordinate responsibility and authority that relates to the decisions of elected representatives.

In France, local communes are often assumed to have considerable autonomy; however, the office of departmental prefect has authority over a range of functions that can, in some cases, directly contradict the intended purpose of the various local councils within the department. He or she is also the official authorised to review the 'legality' of decisions and actions by local governments.

> In the territorial communities of the Republic, the State representative, representing each of the members of the Government, shall be responsible for national interests, administrative supervision and compliance with the law.
> *(Constitution of France, 1958, Article 72)*

In 2017, the Prefecture in Nouvelle Aquitaine prohibited by decree some councils from operating beach showers because of water shortages (Kerley, field observation). More significantly, French prefectural authority was used to relocate refugees in France regardless of the wishes of local mayors (Chrisafis 2016). A similar superordinate process of direction occurred throughout Germany during the refugee inflow of 2015–2016. Local governments in both France and Germany are often cited as autonomous bodies with considerable local discretion by campaigners elsewhere who envy their supposed greater and legally protected autonomy.

In various US states, different state governments appear to exercise such powers most frequently in the suspension of school boards because of continuing poor educational achievements across the jurisdiction. The School District in Philadelphia has been under state control since 2001 (*Economist* 2018). In Italy, some 200 or more councils have been suspended by state decree because of criminal activity.

A further factor that could be considered important is the extent to which local governments have some form of constitutional protection or entrenchment. This is often considered to be an important corollary of democratic provenance and accountability; citizens are confident that they are casting their votes for a body that cannot simply be abolished. Certainly, this matter is often returned to in academic and policy discussions in the different local governments of the United Kingdom. In preparation for the creation of the Scottish Parliament in the late 1990s, one study (Hughes et al. 1998) examined the constitutional status of various local government forms in different nation states. They observed, in relation to France, that the retention of so many small councils was less a matter of constitutional barrier in that:

> In theory the French Parliament does have the power to regulate local government at will. In practice the French communes and departmental councils have a popular 'legitimacy' that few British local authorities would claim.
>
> *(Hughes et al. 1998: 6)*

The same authors also refer in their study to Sweden as a country where any change to the constitutional position of local government (as with other constitutional changes) has to be approved in two parliamentary sessions with a general election intervening. They cite this as an indication that local government has a higher order of constitutional protection than in some other jurisdictions. In contrast, a study by two Swedish authors (Erlingsson and Ödalen 2013) is politely dismissive of this notion of constitutional protection for local government, asserting that if national governments wish to make changes, and have sufficient parliamentary votes, then they can. Whatever the formal position, the reference above to the continuing reduction of the number of Swedish councils suggest that such constitutional protection is, in practice, limited.

In the United States, where public reference to foundational documents appears a near constant feature of daily life, and in Australia (Aulich, Chapter 24, this volume), the Commonwealth constitution is silent on any local government arrangements, as is the case in the USA. The State of New York (2000: iii) argues that:

> It is implicit in the idea of the federal system, however, that the states, in the exercise of the powers reserved to them by the United States Constitution, would provide for local government in ways which would take into account local diversities and needs ... Local governments have become in fact, as well as theory, a third level of the federal system.

Government or administration?

Because of our emphasis on 'government' we have not sought contributions that have exclusively considered local 'administration' in the sense of functions of central government that are operationally provided on a distributed and localised basis. In the case of some changing and developing systems of local government (Vashakidze, Chapter 16, this volume; Hassall and Mae, Chapter 4, this volume), these are sometimes inter-related with the competences of local governments. In other instances, the re-shaping of the overall architecture of a state and the manner in which processes and functions are changing has implications for both local governments and localised forms of operational administration (Anderson, Chapter 29, this volume).

The distinction between the powers, responsibilities, and functions of different tiers and spheres in government and the way that is reflected in operational practice is acknowledged in documents such as European Charter of Local Self-Government (effective from 1988):

> It is not possible to define precisely what affairs local authorities should be entitled to regulate and manage. Expressions such as 'local affairs' and 'own affairs' were rejected as too vague and difficult to interpret. The traditions of member states as to the affairs which are regarded as belonging to the preserve of local authorities differ greatly.
>
> *(Article 3)*

In some fields, such as the provision of various aspects of health care, there clearly are many diverse forms of organisational architecture in different nation states. We can therefore often see a range of arrangements with differing and shared responsibilities and functional overlap (Robertson et al. 2014).

Are local governments important?

There are a number of aspects to the degree of importance we can ascribe to various spheres and tiers of local government in different countries. We might consider political salience to citizens, career options and progression for politicians, policy developments and advancing possible legislative and other changes, in addition to the sheer range of services provided to citizens.

Some years ago, a documentary series about French rural life, broadcast on Channel 4 in the United Kingdom, reported one resident's view about the importance of decisions made at that local level. She compared decisions about elections in her village (one of those 30,000 small communes) to the significance of what is sometimes described as the 'monarchical' presidency that is established in France: 'It's the mayor who affects your life not the President . . . in Presidential elections your vote counts for nothing . . . but in village elections every vote counts' (A French Affair 2003).

Paradoxically, in many countries the importance attached by this resident to voting in village elections is gainsaid by electoral engagement – as indeed it is in France when we assess electoral turnout. Even in countries with a tradition of high electoral turnout, and even where elections to the national parliament and local councils are coterminous (Sweden for example), the votes cast for local government will typically be several points below the national vote. Of course, such levels of electoral engagement and voter turnout vary from country to country, as well as between tiers of government (Potluka et al., Chapter 23, this volume).

Whatever the comparative degree of engagement, and allowing for the reality that voting for local governments is widely seen by many citizens as less electorally important than national elections, local government can be seen as a bellwether for national political trends. During 2017, a shift in local elections in South Africa was seen as significant for the prospects of former President Zuma. In Italy, however previous electoral success of the Five Star movement in local elections in some big cities proved counterproductive, as the newly elected representatives appeared to manage civic affairs very badly.

In the United Kingdom, central government decisions about local government and the possibility of devolution to sub-central government led to the loss an election for the Labour government of James Callaghan in 1979. Decisions about changing local government taxation contributed to the end of the premiership of Margaret Thatcher in 1981.

Sub-central governments have also been important career steps for some leading politicians and, indeed, for the development of some political parties. President Widdodo of Indonesia has been a city mayor and governor of a province; four recent US presidents have been state governors; Prime Minister May of the United Kingdom was a borough councillor; Willi Brandt came to national prominence in Germany as mayor of West Berlin; President Nieto of Mexico has been a state governor; and the prime minister of India, Mr Modi, has been chief minister of Gujarat.

Although success in sub-central government elections has apparently not been that helpful for the Five Star movement, in various countries (notably Germany and Scotland) Green parties have leveraged footholds in local governments and various forms of sub- national governments to build political support. The early breakthrough of the National Front in France was in municipal elections.

In cross national and international networking, politicians in sub - central governments of all forms can advance policy causes they consider important to their jurisdiction and their citizens through their public voice and discretionary authority. In the United States, we have seen cities and states arguing that they will advance preventative environmental measures and remediation of past damage; even President Trump and congress do not intend to. Some cities in the USA have explicitly sought to create 'sanctuary status' to protect people whose residence status is disputed.

City mayors globally and public pension funds such as Calpers (California), one of the largest activist public pension funds, have collectively sought to influence invested companies in matters such as the environment, financial sustainability, and human rights.

In Japan, local governments have, for some time been trying to alter local population flows using financial incentives to attract younger residents into ageing towns and cities (*Economist* 2017).

The basis for such influence remains rooted in the locally representative role that local and sub central governments fulfil on a daily basis, providing services to citizens. In various places, this ranges from maintaining and cleaning streets, educating children, public safety, making provision for older people and those with disabilities, and in most localities, ultimately taking the responsibility for those who die without family or friends to determine and pay for their funeral arrangements.

Such local governments also regulate a wide range of activities and functions for the wellbeing of their residents across a full spectrum of everyday necessities: such as street vendors, taxi drivers, various trades and professions, building codes and land use, and food hygiene. German cities have recently secured constitutional court agreement to institute limitations on diesel cars. Local governments in various countries (using licensing powers) have been central to challenging the Uber growth and operating model.

In all developed countries, and many developing countries, when members of a household go out each morning, their daily activities – from walking on a pavement to buying a coffee, or benefitting from street lighting on their journey home at night – are contingent on the powers and provision of their various local governments.

We hope that readers of the following chapters will get a wider insight into such vital matters as they read the contributions collected here. We also hope that readers will be prompted to develop their own further research ideas and projects.

The structure of this book

This handbook is organised into six sections. Our allocation and grouping of chapters to sections has a degree of 'best fit.' As you will see, some chapters naturally locate themselves, while others could be placed in more than one section.

Elected roles and governance

We start with the core of local governments; election and service as an elected representative. Three of the chapters here consider the relationship between the views of elected representatives and appointed officials or, in relation to communities where traditional roles are still socially and culturally important, the balance between election and the assumption of ultimate decision making power.

Local government jurisdictions

As we suggest above, if readers wish to review a catalogue of local government structures in various countries they might usefully start with a collection such as the *Commonwealth Local Government Handbook 2015/16* (Commonwealth Local Government Forum 2016), or go to the website of the Council of European Municipalities and Regions (www.ccre.org) to obtain coverage of almost 100 countries in all. This section has chapters that review less-noticed groups of local governments or that take an unusual perspective on aspects of local government in more frequently studied countries.

Range of local government services

Local governments globally provide a wide range of public services, either at their own hand, commissioned from other providers, or in some form of partnership with a variety of legal and civic society entities. This range changes over time as societies and governments mature and develop and there is no fixed pattern, even within federal sub-national or national jurisdictional boundaries.

Citizen engagement

The chapters gathered in this section discuss established and emergent forms of citizen participation, with instances examined and reviewed across a total of 16 very different societies and to very different purposes.

Multi-level governance

The yearning expressed by some for a neat and clean division of responsibilities between different spheres and tiers of government appears to be impossible to achieve, even were it desirable to do so. This occurs even in those nation states that have formal written constitutions that appear to provide some specific direction on 'which does what'. However, tensions exist, and responsibilities sometimes shift between different spheres and tiers as partnerships and collaborations mutate and transform.

Getting and spending

These chapters review how some local governments raise money, whether through their own local resources and with some degree of discretion, and monies transferred through some forms of equalisation grant. We also have a chapter that looks at how that expenditure is assessed by other governments, even when quite properly and legitimately spent, and a chapter on challenging corruption in emergent democratic regimes.

We hope you find *all* the chapters interesting.

Richard Kerley, Joyce Liddle and Pamela Dunning

Notes

1 We have used UK English language terminology throughout this collection, with some exceptions. In some chapters a glossary of terms and translations is provided.
2 We have counted in excess of 30 such terms in the English language alone.

References

A French Affair (2003) *A French Affair*. TV documentary, first broadcast 14 July on Channel 4, UK.
Chrisafis, A. (2016) Refugees exchange squalor of Calais for vineyards of Burgundy. *The Guardian* (29 October): 15.
Commonwealth Local Government Forum (2016) *Commonwealth Local Government Handbook 2015/16*. London: Commonwealth Local Government Forum.
Economist, The (2017) Desperately seeking young people. *The Economist* (7 January).
Economist, The (2018) Portfolio theory. *The Economist* (3 March): 35.
Erlingsson, G. and Ödalen, J. (2013) How should local government be organised? Reflections from a Swedish perspective. *Local Government Studies* 39(1): 22–46.
Hesse, J.-J. and Sharpe, L. J. (1991) Local government in international perspective: some comparative observations. In J.-J. Hesse (ed.), *Local Government and Urban Affairs in International Perspective*, 603–621. Baden-Baden: Nomos.
Hughes, M., Clarke, M., Allen, H. and Hall, D. (1998) *The Constitutional Status of Local Government in Other Countries*. Edinburgh: Central Research Unit.
Kitchen, H. and Slack, E. (2004) Providing public services in remote areas. In R. Bird and F. Vaillancourt (eds), *Perspectives on Fiscal Federalism*, 123–140. Washington, DC: World Bank.
Robertson, R., Gregory, S. and Jabbal, J. (2014) *The Social Care and Health Systems of Nine Countries*. London: King's Fund.
State of New York (2000) *Local Government Handbook*, 5th edition. Albany, NY: State of New York.
Swianiewicz, P. (2018) If territorial fragmentation is a problem, is amalgamation a solution? Ten years later. *Local Government Studies* 44: 1–10.

PART I

Elected roles and governance

2
LOCAL ELECTORAL SYSTEMS

Michael Cole

Introduction

This chapter considers a variety of systems used to choose elected local representatives across the globe, initially through four core themes. First, proportionality, the extent to which the proportion of votes and seats obtained by each party equates and the presence or otherwise of mechanisms to facilitate such alignments. Second, magnitude, the number of representatives elected from each division and the implications for the proportionality of the outcomes. Third, capacity to choose between candidates nominated by the same party; for example, through varying the order on party lists or use of primaries to select candidates. Lastly, issues relating to use when executive authority is vested in one individual, often a mayor. This discussion also considers the deployment of run-off elections; an intensification of the focus on the personal qualities of candidates; tendencies for such campaigns to focus on strategic rather than parochial concerns; and the probability that they will diminish the influence of smaller political parties.

These themes are used to illuminate discussion of the main electoral systems deployed for electing local representatives, which are classified as proportional; mixed; and non-proportional. First, two proportional systems, the *single transferable vote* (STV) and party lists, are discussed: the second category is sub-divided into open and closed lists, while variations within both sub-categories, for example the Panachage model, are also addressed. Second, use of the *additional member system* (AMS), which is a mixed model, is considered and variants on the core theme of combining proportional and non-proportional elements are addressed. Third, the analysis encompasses six non-proportional systems. Three of them, *first past the post* (FPTP), the *block vote* (or *multiple non-transferable vote*, MNTV) and the *single non-transferable vote* (SNTV), lack mechanisms to transfer votes between candidates. Alternatively, the other three non-proportional systems, the *alternative vote* (AV); the *supplementary vote* (SV); and the *second ballot*, are preferential systems constructed on the basis of transferring support from unsuccessful candidates to those that are still competitive. This discussion is illustrated through a wide range of international examples, which reference experience in many of the world's most prominent democracies, for example the USA, UK, France, Germany, India and Australia. It also draws on cases from smaller established democracies such as Belgium and Switzerland; and uses examples from less prosperous countries where democracy is often less well entrenched, for example Brazil, Papua New Guinea, Colombia and Zambia.

Discussion of the various electoral models also connects with broader themes of local government management because the choice of an electoral system has important implications for the operation of local governments. Most obviously, decisions to adopt specific systems have political governance effects, particularly through altering the probability of one party or multi-party administrations. There are also (of course) impacts on governance processes in terms of altering the capacity of one political elite to impose agendas and policies. Electoral systems will thus affect the operation and organisational cultures of local government.

There are also significant implications for how precisely the electorate is represented by politicians. Here, a core distinction is through magnitude, for example single member divisions are often praised in terms of creating a direct connection with voters, with one elected politician clearly obliged to represent the electorate in that area. Conversely, multi-member entities can dilute a sense of personal responsibility and accountability among representatives, but give constituents a choice of whom to approach. The capacity of elected politicians to represent distinctive and meaningful territorial communities is typically diminished or removed through the use of list systems.

Selection of electoral systems might additionally be interpreted as indicative of the democratic values and assumptions within which local governments operate. For example, non-proportional models are often justified in terms of facilitating the emergence of *strong* leadership with enhanced capacity to implement difficult decisions. Alternatively, mixed or proportional systems can be interpreted as reflective of aims to facilitate voter choice and promote fairness to both the electorate and political parties. Similarly, allowing voters to cast additional preferences can be perceived as facilitating voter choice and decision-making authority, in terms of ensuring that winning mandates are constructed on the basis of wider electoral support.

Overall, this chapter makes two core contributions to scholarship. First, and primarily, through identifying and assessing the main systems deployed for elections to local governments and illustrating this usage through a diversity of comparative examples from across the globe. Second, in terms of assisting in the development of a genuine comparative understanding of local electoral systems, for example in relation to usage variations and contemporary changes.

Electoral system themes

Proportionality

Electoral systems can be categorised into proportional, mixed and non-proportional groupings (see Table 2.1). Proportional (and mixed) electoral systems strive, at minimum, to ensure a reasonable approximation between the percentage of votes and representatives won by, at least, each of the main parties. Such systems incorporate mechanisms to push outcomes towards proportionality, for example D'Hondt counting procedures to determine allocation of seats among party lists; and regulations for transferring votes from eliminated or elected candidates towards those still engaged with the count. These arrangements have long been advocated on the basis of fairness and as a corrective to the tendency, as documented through Duverger's Law (Cole 2005), of non-proportional systems to disadvantage small parties. Similarly, these electoral systems have been justified through increasing the number of people casting votes, or additional preferences, that contribute towards the election of a candidate.

Perhaps the most well-known non-proportional system is FPTP, where the candidate with the highest number of votes is elected. Alternatively, the process can continue through a *second ballot* run-off between the top two candidates. Similarly, systems such as the AV and SV oblige electors to rank candidates in order of preference so that support can be transferred without

Table 2.1 Main electoral systems

Categories	Specific electoral systems
Proportional	Single transferable vote (STV)
	Party lists
Mixed	Additional member system (AMS)
Non-proportional: non-transfer	First past the post (FPTP)
	Block vote (multiple non-transferable vote, MNTV)
	Single non-transferable vote (SNTV)
Non-proportional: transfer	Alternative vote (AV)
	Supplementary vote (SV)
	Second ballot

staging a second ballot. What these and other non-proportional models (here the MNTV and SNTV) have in common is that voting occurs without recourse to procedures designed to improve alignments between each party's votes and representation.

Limits on proportionality are, however, recognised explicitly in some proportional and mixed systems, particularly through minimum thresholds of support required for parties to secure at least one seat under list systems, which are usually established significantly above the level of mathematical proportionality. Such arrangements are typically justified in terms of preventing parties with allegedly fringe or extremist perspectives from securing representation and or reducing the chance of often maverick individuals obtaining seats and perhaps holding the balance of power between rival parties or coalitions. These thresholds can be substantial: for example, 5% in Germany and New Zealand in parliamentary elections (with an alternative of winning three constituency seats in Germany, or one in New Zealand), which use the mixed AMS model. Significant thresholds also emerge as informal statistical consequences of STV elections, the levels dependent on the number of representatives elected from each division and reflective of local concentrations of support. The electoral backing required to secure even one representative under STV can be substantial. For example, a four member constituency, assuming use of a Droop model, would have an electoral quota of 20% of the vote + 1, although not all winning candidates reach that level, even after the transfers have been completed. Parties with evenly distributed support notably below quota thus struggle to secure representation under STV.

Electoral systems also involve voters in tactical considerations, typically how to stop specific individuals/parties and or secure election of the best realistic option, rather than their preferred candidate. Such considerations are well documented concerning FPTP, for example in UK elections (Johnston and Pattie 2011). Tactical calculations also affect voting decisions under other models, for example through guesses about which candidates have enough support to reach run-off elections or secure AV or SV transfers; estimates regarding who is likely to benefit most from first preferences under STV; or speculation about the probable distribution of list seats and so how an individual's vote might be most effective.

Magnitude

Magnitude concerns the number of representatives allocated to a distinctive geographic area and ranges from single-member divisions to lists covering the whole territory governed by the parliament, assembly or council. Magnitude has significant implications for the proportionality of electoral outcomes and the number of parties securing representation

(Benoit 2001). For example, moving from FPTP to the Block Vote typically diminishes proportionality; in such circumstances dominant parties can often exploit aggregate strength to increase further their share of representatives. In contrast, parties with concentrations of support across smaller geographic areas often find their enclaves overwhelmed and struggle to win seats. Alternatively, under proportional systems, larger magnitudes increase outcome proportionality. As Gallagher (1991: 44) commented: 'as district magnitude approaches infinity, so the outcome produced by every PR formula approaches perfect proportionality'.

Intra-party choice

Electoral systems vary in terms of whether they allow voters to select between candidates of the same party. A notable mechanism of such intra-party choice is the primary contest to choose party nominees for specific offices. For example, in the USA normally all voters registered as Republican or Democrat, and sometimes those designated as Independents, can participate. Elsewhere, as in selecting some Conservative candidates prior to the 2010 and 2015 UK parliamentary elections, the choice involved the whole local electorate (Sparrow 2009); the UK not having electoral registration incorporating party affiliation. Intra-party choice can also occur through, for example, the block vote, where several representatives are chosen for a division at one election. Choice arises specifically from the frequent tendency of some parties to run more than one candidate. However, given the inclination of many voters to identify closely with one party, such choice can seem illusory as many feel an imperative to support all the candidates from their preferred party in order to maximise its representation.

List systems vary in terms of intra-party choice. Many operate as closed arrangements, whereby voters are presented with a pre-determined ranking and invited to endorse the whole list and so the candidates high enough to have a realistic chance of election. Alternatively, open systems enable voters 'to indicate a preference for one candidate (or sometimes several candidates) on their party's list' (Gallagher and Mitchell 2009: 10). STV also allows voters choice between candidates of the same party, albeit within two recurrent constraints. First, parties often encourage supporters to rank candidates in a designated order to prevent unfavourable distributions of first preferences, and subsequent transfers, diminishing their representation. Second, fear of splitting their first preferences, and lack of enthusiasm among some supporters to rank large numbers of candidates, often means that parties stand the maximum number of individuals they might expect to elect rather than contest all the vacancies, thus constraining voter choice. Both of these effects are evident in elections in Northern Ireland and the Republic of Ireland. As Mair and Laver (1975: 492) commented, when 'votes begin to "leak" away from it during the transfer process . . . nomination strategy becomes crucial'.

Executive elections

There are also distinctive issues when the election conveys executive authority on one individual, often a directly elected mayor. Such executive mayors can be contrasted with ceremonial mayors; who lack significant powers and who are often selected on the basis of length of service. As well as having substantive relevance for core governance themes, such as the location of political authority and effectiveness of accountability and scrutiny structures, there are notable implications for the electoral process. First, mayoral elections often involve some form of run-off mechanism, either in terms of an instant process or a second ballot (see, for example, Cole 2001b). Second, vesting executive authority in one individual places an emphasis on the qualities, charisma and profile of the candidates that, for some voters at least, can eclipse policy agendas. Individuals can thus be elected in territories with demographic profiles and psephological records favourable to rival parties. The triumph of Boris Johnson twice (2008 and 2012) in London is a recent example. Similarly, this spotlight on individuals can facilitate election of independents; an effect heightened through contemporary scepticism of, and hostility towards, established political elites. Third, mayoral contests can instinctively draw attention towards themes relevant to the whole authority and away from controversies affecting only parts of the territory. This interpretation implies, therefore, a dynamic favouring articulation of strategic agendas over more parochial matters. Fourth, mayoral elections can diminish substantially the influence exercised by small parties. Vesting executive authority in one individual typically means that power is concentrated into the hands of a politician from one of the larger parties. This reform thus removes, or substantially reduces, the possibility that executive decisions will result from bargains among politicians of different parties operating in a council where no one party has a majority. In other words, the mayoral model places executive authority into the hands of one person.

Some of these themes are also relevant to other cases in which individuals with personal executive authority are chosen, for example police and crime commissioners in England and Wales and a plethora of local contests in the USA. In particular, considerations of the strategic over the parochial are relevant alongside heightened electoral impacts derived from the personal qualities of specific candidates. Such contests routinely use some form of run-off mechanism.

Electoral systems

The single transferable vote

STV elections are conducted through multi-member electoral divisions. Voters are invited to rank each candidate in order of preference; individuals are elected when they reach a quota of votes determined through the number of seats and turnout. Alternatively, candidates are often elected at the end of the counting process without reaching quota provided they cannot be overtaken by a sufficient number of rivals. Each elector has one vote, which is allocated initially to their first preference. When candidates are elected their surplus votes (the number above quota) indicating a preference for a candidate still in the contest are transferred. Similarly, when candidates are eliminated all their votes are transferred unless a preference has not been expressed for any of those candidates still contesting a seat.

STV is advocated in terms of diminishing the alleged quantity of *wasted* votes that do not contribute to the election of any candidate; generating more proportional correlations between votes and seats secured by each party; and enabling voters to exercise intra-party choice. Divisional magnitudes often range from four to perhaps ten; the larger end of the spectrum typically achieves more proportional outcomes. STV is not applicable for elections conveying executive authority on one individual; STV applied to a single member division or office is AV.

Use of STV in local elections is most prevalent where it is also deployed for higher tier authorities. The most obvious case is the Irish Republic, which uses STV throughout its governmental structures. Here, local STV elections are through Local Election Areas (LEAs) which return six to ten councillors. The City of Cork, which also has four and five councillor LEAs, is the exception. In Malta, a tradition of using STV for parliamentary elections since 1921 was reflected in the adoption of STV for local elections following enactment of legislation, in 1993, which enabled local councils to be established.

In New Zealand, contemporary use of STV at local level was reflective of a reform agenda, instituted through the Local Electoral Act (2001), which made STV mandatory for District

Health Boards and enabled local authorities to adopt the system, although few made the shift. In 2016, STV was used by eight out of 78 local councils including Dunedin City, Palmerston North City and Wellington City. Implementation of STV was not, however, inspired by parliamentary elections, which had used FPTP until 1996 and then a mixed (AMS) system. This reform might, however, be interpreted as reflective of a limited tradition of STV in early twentieth century local elections, for example STV was used by Christchurch City Council (1917–1933). Similarly, in Australia STV is deployed for local elections in New South Wales, South Australia, Tasmania and Victoria.

In Northern Ireland, STV was used from 1921 for elections to the Stormont Parliament until 1929, when the Unionist Government introduced FPTP for elections to the House of Commons, a decision intended to reinforce partisan advantage. STV was, however, retained for electing Senators, which occurred through votes in the House of Commons. STV was re-introduced into Northern Ireland in 1973, in response to the re-emergence of armed conflict, and has been deployed for elections to devolved assemblies, the European Parliament and local authorities. UK experience with STV was augmented from 2007 with its implementation for Scottish local elections (Bennie 2006).

Elsewhere, STV has been used in Canadian local elections, specifically in parts of Alberta (Calgary, Edmonton and Medicine Hat) between 1926 and 1955; and Manitoba, for example Winnipeg, from the 1920s until 1958. In the early twentieth century, STV was adopted by over 20 US cities including Cleveland (Ohio), Hamilton (Ohio), Cincinnati (Ohio), Boulder (Colorado), Lowell (Massachusetts), Sacramento (California) and New York City, a reform instrumental in challenging the Tammany Hall political machine. STV had, nevertheless, mostly been abandoned by 1960, although in New York the Community School Boards retained STV until their abolition in 2002.

Currently, STV is restricted to two US municipalities. Since 1941, STV has been used in the City of Cambridge (Massachusetts), currently for elections to the Council and the School Committee, while STV was adopted in 2009 for elections to the Estimate and Taxation; and Park and Recreation Boards of the City of Minneapolis (Minnesota). In recent decades, campaigns to introduce STV elsewhere in cities such as Cincinnati and San Francisco have been unsuccessful. However, experience in Cambridge remains a beacon for US electoral reformers, change, for example, advocated through effectiveness in securing representation for ethnic minorities and women (Douglas 2013).

Party lists

Candidate lists are presented by each party and seats allocated according to vote share, although proportionality is often diminished through minimum vote percentage thresholds below which parties fail to secure representation. There are substantial variations concerning intra-party choice, open systems allow voters to alter candidate rankings; closed models specify a fixed order. Similarly, list magnitudes vary significantly, for example some covering the whole territory, others a quite small geographic segment. Scale variations can affect proportionality. Lists are not suitable for electing one person with executive authority, such as a mayor.

Both open and closed lists are in widespread use, with some countries applying elements of both approaches. For example, in Colombia, municipal councillors are chosen through an optional open list with the parties determining whether their lists are open or closed. Alternatively, in Brazil genuinely open lists are deployed in elections at federal, state and local tiers, although often those lists reflect coalition agreements between two or several parties. A variation on open lists is the Panachage model whereby electors have more than one vote for each contest and are able to distribute them across individuals on contrasting party lists. Panachage was used for Belgium municipal elections until 1976. Similarly, in Switzerland local and other elections give voters a substantial degree of choice. As well as the ability to write the name of candidates from another party onto their preferred list, electors can delete names from that list and or insert names twice. However, amended lists may not contain more names than seats being contested.

Closed lists are in widespread use: for example, in Croatia members of county, city and municipal councils are elected through a closed list the size of the entire territory. However, constitutional obligations to ensure representation of minorities meant that electoral committees are required to determine whether the relevant ethnic quotas have been reached and, if not, to appoint individuals from the appropriate groups to the authority from the pool of defeated candidates. Similarly, closed lists apply for elections to French communes with more than 1,000 inhabitants in a hybrid model that also involves a second ballot if no list wins an absolute majority in the first round. In South Africa, lists, used as components of a mixed member system, contain the party name and a picture of the party leader but not identities of specific candidates. These arrangements deny voters both intra-party choice of candidates and knowledge of candidate identities, but can facilitate election of minority candidates who might struggle under more transparent processes. Closed party lists are also used to elect representatives to councils of the municipalities and communes in Albania and local and county councils in Romania.

Mixed systems

The model combines proportional and non-proportional elements in a two stage process and is often discussed as the additional member system (AMS). Electors have two votes, one for a FPTP constituency representative and one for a party list. List support determines the overall allocation of party representation, and operates as a corrective mechanism to rectify disproportionality derived from the constituency results. Candidates are elected from the lists to secure the overall proportionality of the outcome, procedures that can mean that the most popular parties return few or no list representatives. Reliance on the lists to create broadly proportional outcomes, means that the quantity of representatives selected through those lists is important. For example, election of two-thirds of Welsh Assembly Members (AMs) through FPTP constituencies has meant that the list corrective is too small to effectively counterbalance Labour's disproportionate strength in those FPTP constituencies (Cole 2001a; McAllister and Cole 2014). Alternatively, in South Africa a 50–50 split between list and constituency representation means that its local electoral system has a greater capacity to diminish disproportionality arising from FPTP contests. Individual list magnitudes can be quite substantial in both absolute and percentage terms, for example the single list used in London Assembly elections covers the whole Greater London area and returns 11 members, almost half of the total.

Reflective of arrangements at higher tiers, in German county and municipal elections mixed systems are used. Councillors are elected through FPTP constituencies and as party list representatives. Representation through these lists has not, however, generally been dependent on obtaining minimum thresholds, particularly as the Constitutional Court has been keen to strike them down as constitutional violations, for example in relation to a 5% threshold in Schleswig-Holstein (Kommers and Miller 2012: 262). In some other mixed (AMS) systems minimum list thresholds have not been perceived as desirable or necessary, for example for the London Assembly, despite the election of a British National Party (BNP) AM in 2008. In contrast, Lesotho has used a mixed system at local level since 2005, within the context of a 2004 reform which reserved 30% of the seats in each council for women.

Non-proportional and non-transfer systems

Candidates who obtain the most votes are declared the victor regardless of the proportion of the vote they acquire. Under FPTP and the block vote, the number of votes allocated to each elector reflects the number of representatives to be elected at that specific election. FPTP concerning the election of one representative, block vote contests involving election of two or more individuals. Both FPTP and the block vote can generate highly disproportional outcomes, however intra-party choice is usually possible under the block vote.

These models are used for almost all local elections in England, Wales and the USA. Coverage is also extensive in Canada, where they are deployed to elect single tier and lower tier councillors. However, members of the regional tier, which is inserted between provincial and municipal governments in provinces such as Ontario and Quebec, are seldom directly elected but selected from municipal mayors and councillors. Alternatively, in Cyprus FPTP elections for mayors are an anomaly in an otherwise proportional electoral system (Kolasa-Sikiaridi 2016).

These models have, however, been adopted extensively in many developing Commonwealth countries, for example for parish elections in Jamaica. In Zambia, use for local government was reflective of a uniform approach to the country's elections, contests for the president, MPs and councillors being part of a tripartite process, all held on the same day. India elects all its local councillors through such contests, while institutionalising one-third of reserved seats for women, stipulated through a constitutional amendment and increased to 50% in some states, as well as guaranteeing representation for specific castes and tribes, which is determined on a local basis. In Botswana, local elections use a standardised FPTP system, where all the country's local representatives are chosen from single member wards. Furthermore, in 2003 the block vote was introduced in the smaller Luxembourg municipalities (Van der Kolk 2007: 163).

Despite significant usage, the main narrative surrounding FPTP and Block Vote elections has concerned their deficiencies, for example through alleged *wastage* of votes, negative impacts on representation of women and minorities and distortion of popular preferences (see, for example, Lakeman 1982). Such criticisms have created significant reform movements in some countries, debates conducted on rarefied democratic and technical levels but also within contexts of partisan advantage and operational acceptability. These latter effects can be appreciated through reform in the UK. The introduction of STV for Scottish local elections (Clark and Bennie 2008) can, for example, be explained through a partisan interpretation: a reform reflecting the agenda of the Liberal Democrats and Labour's need to reconstruct the coalition following the 2003 election. The change was also introduced as part of a deal among political elites and without popular endorsement through a referendum.

In contrast, the decision to re-constitute London-wide local government in 2000, after a 14 year hiatus, reflected an assumption that governance incorporating a pluralistic system of AMS was important to gain public assent, in a referendum, for reconstituting a tier of elected politicians. Operational acceptance can also be deployed to interpret the shift to STV in Northern Ireland in 1973; reform reflective of requirements to replace the previous model where gerrymandered ward boundaries and partisan franchise restrictions consolidated unionist dominance. Electoral reform was, therefore, a component of the wider response to the Troubles aimed at persuading at least some nationalists of the legitimacy of governing institutions.

Replacement of FPTP and the block vote has been a recurrent element of institutional and constitutional reform across the globe. For example, in South Africa the mixed (AMS) local electoral model was introduced as part of the negotiation processes that ended Apartheid and created a genuine multi-racial democracy. Similarly, in 1981 reforms in Cyprus meant that FPTP is restricted to mayoral contests, while, as discussed earlier, in 2001 New Zealand passed legislation to compel district heath boards and enable local authorities to switch to STV. A parallel reform occurred in Papua New Guinea which, in 2008, replaced FPTP with limited preferential voting (LPV), a transfer-based non-proportional system which gave voters three preferences.

The third distinctive electoral system is the SNTV. As under FPTP and the block vote, candidates are elected simply on the basis of securing more votes than their opponents. SNTV doesn't, therefore, incorporate any mechanisms to generate proportional electoral outcomes or allow votes to be transferred between candidates. Like the block vote, SNTV relates to divisional magnitudes of greater than one and so potentially facilitates intra-party choice. However, in contrast to FPTP and the Block Vote, SNTV combines one vote with election of several representatives. These arrangements often present voters with major dilemmas concerning how to maximise representation of their favoured party. Similarly, parties can face parallel dilemmas about what strategies they can adopt to get the maximum number of their candidates elected. SNTV typically poses more acute tactical problems than are noted in relation to STV (Grofman et al. 1999), where transfers diminish negative impacts from splitting a party's first preference votes between candidates. Perhaps for such reasons, SNTV is seldom used in local elections; the most prominent contemporary examples are for Japanese prefectural and municipal assemblies.

Non-proportional, transfer systems

These models enable voters to rank more than one candidate and procedures to transfer lower preferences to other candidates are integral to the process. There is no mechanism to compensate for disproportional outcomes accruing from amalgamation of results from many disparate contests and so no guarantee of even a rough equation between the percentage of seats and votes obtained by specific parties. In the three common variants, intra-party choice is absent given restriction to magnitudes of one. Capacity to indicate rankings of candidates and transfer votes, in the absence of proportional mechanisms, mean that these models can also be categorised as non-proportional preferential systems.

The main formats are the alternative vote (AV), the supplementary vote (SV) and the second ballot. Under AV, electors are permitted to vote for one candidate, and allowed to rank the remaining candidates in order of preference. Candidates securing more than 50% of the vote are elected outright, otherwise the candidate with fewest votes is eliminated and their preferences allocated to those that remain. Sometimes, several lowly ranked candidates are simultaneously eliminated provided that the sum total of their votes is less than that of the next lowest ranked candidate.

This process continues until one candidate has passed the 50% threshold or the preferences from all apart from the top two candidates have been re-distributed. SV is a shortened version of AV in which voters indicate only first and second preferences. If no candidate obtains more than 50% of the vote on the basis of first preferences, the leading two candidates proceed to the second stage, the others are eliminated and their support transferred. Alternatively, in some systems voters are allowed to rank a higher but limited number of candidates.

Such preferential models are widely favoured for mayoral elections, where the level of personalised governmental authority being contested facilitates a consensus that victors need to be endorsed (at least through lower preferences) by more than a plurality of those who vote. This logic can be appreciated, for example, in the adoption of SV for choosing directly elected mayors in various English local authorities. Furthermore, SV has been introduced for the directly elected police and crime commissioners, which were established in England and Wales in 2012. Non-proportional preferential voting methods are also used widely in Australian states such as New South Wales, Queensland, South Australia and Victoria to elect both councillors and mayors. Similarly, in Canada, Ontario has legislated to permit its municipalities to allow voters to rank candidates in local elections from 2018 (see, for example, Jones 2016).

AV contests could also emerge as a by-product of STV because AV equates to STV when only one candidate is to be elected. In by-elections for one representative in a multi-member constituency STV systems are, therefore, reconfigured into AV contests. However, co-option of substitutes, to retain the proportional balance from the previous contest, is often preferred, although such appointments can reflect a pre-determined hierarchy of defeated candidates from the relevant party. Co-option of individuals from the same party as the former member has been used to fill vacancies, for example, in local government contests in both Northern Ireland and the Irish Republic. Elsewhere, for example in Cambridge, Massachusetts and Malta, the countback system is deployed. Here, the ballot papers from the previous contest are examined to re-run the count excluding the former member. Alternatively, similar vacancies for one representative in Scottish local authorities and the Irish Dail, which also uses STV, are filled though AV by-elections. In New Zealand, AV is used where one councillor is to be elected in municipalities, such as Kapiti Coast District Council, which have adopted STV for multi-member wards but retain some single-member wards.

Similar electoral systems are deployed in US local government. In 2002, San Francisco passed an initiative establishing a model for most city-wide elections, whereby voters were able to rank three candidates for each position. It was first used in 2004 for selecting the student representative to the city's school board (Hill and Richie 2005). It is now deployed for electing the board of supervisors, the mayor, the sheriff, the district attorney, the city attorney, the treasurer, the assessor-recorder and the public defender. Minneapolis uses a non-proportional preferential voting system to elect, for example, the mayor and the city council, a model introduced in 2009, following the passage of an initiative in 2005. Similarly, in 2008 Telluride (Colorado) adopted similar preferential voting arrangements for three subsequent mayoral elections from 2011 onwards (Slosson 2015).

Second ballot models typically involve voters casting one vote for their favoured candidate and, if nobody obtains an absolute majority of the votes cast, a second ballot is held usually two to three weeks later involving the top two candidates from the first round. This process is similar to AV and SV; however, voters are given more time for reflection than under AV or SV where the run-offs are instant and incorporated within the initial election.

Second ballot elections are deployed in the French communes, through the hybrid model which combines two ballots with party lists. Similarly, Brazil has provisions for second ballots in its municipal elections, however it reserves this option for cities with more than 200,000 inhabitants, which includes every state capital, for example Rio de Janeiro, Sao Paulo and Vitoria, plus 59 other cities. In contrast, Italian mayoral elections in cities with populations over 15,000 are conducted through the second ballot model, which is also used to determine which party or coalition receives a majority-bonus of seats on the council.

A distinctive format of second-ballot voting can be found in US primary elections, which were discussed earlier. A variant is the Louisiana *jungle primary*, through which all candidates for an office run together in one initial plurality contest, a mechanism normally giving Democrats and Republicans intra-party choice. If no candidate wins an absolute majority, the top two candidates, who might represent the same party, contest a second ballot.

Pure second ballot systems lack a proportional mechanism, although, in common with AV and SV, they ensure that the victor has a broader endorsement than, for example, FPTP can guarantee. This system is typically restricted to magnitudes of one, although as the Italian and French hybrids show, alternative scale applications have evolved. It has also been used widely for electing individuals with personal executive authority, but seldom affords intra-party choice, unless primary elections are incorporated.

Conclusions

This chapter has explored some of the core themes relating to the electoral systems used in local elections across the globe, namely their proportionality; the contrasting representational magnitudes, capacity for intra-party choice; and use to elect one individual with personal executive authority, typically a directly elected mayor. Next; various electoral systems have been outlined, related to those themes and discussed in the context of examples from across the world.

This study illustrates the substantive variations in the type of systems used for local electoral contests and, therefore, implies notable divergences in the values and assumptions of local governance among democratic countries. Some models prioritising choice and fairness, others more readily interpreted as facilitating strong authority-wide leadership. Particularly, the analysis illustrates the substantive variations in voter choice, for example contrasts between open and closed lists; and capacity to signify preferences among all the candidates under STV, against ability to cast just one vote without further preferences in FPTP contests. Perhaps a core theme is that while some systems allow voters to choose between candidates of the same party, others only allow voters to choose between lists or individuals representing different political parties.

The chapter also highlights notable variations in the extent to which different electoral systems are deployed, for example while the use of STV is quite restricted, both open and closed lists are operational in a wide range of countries. Furthermore, while non-proportional systems remain widespread for local contests, particularly among countries with a clear Anglo-Saxon inheritance, there is a global reform trend to replace such models. This shift has been identified in countries as diverse as South Africa, Cyprus and New Zealand. It is also evident in the UK, where proportional models have been introduced for local elections in Scotland and Northern Ireland, and the London Assembly, while FPTP has been eschewed in favour of SV for electing directly elected mayors and police and crime commissioners across England and Wales.

In illustrating the variety of contrasting electoral systems in use at local level, this chapter also supplies a potential tool for reformers by illustrating alternatives. Furthermore, by discussing the international trend to replace, in particular, FPTP and the block vote for local electoral contests, the analysis illustrates a significant change agenda. In addition, electoral reform might also be facilitated through evidence, presented here, of co-existence of several local electoral systems within a single country. In summary, this chapter has potential to stimulate debate on electoral reform.

References

Bennie, L. (2006) Transition to STV: Scottish local government elections 2007. *Representation* 42(4): 273–287.
Benoit, K. (2001) District magnitude, electoral formula, and the number of parties. *European Journal of Political Research* 39(2): 203–224.
Clark, A. and Bennie, L. (2008) Electoral reform and party adaptation: the introduction of the single transferable vote in Scotland. *The Political Quarterly* 79(2): 241–251.
Cole, M. (2001a) Elections to the Welsh Assembly: proportionality, continuity and change. *Regional and Federal Studies* 11(2): 147–163.
Cole, M. (2001b) The crowning of Red Ken: the battle for London in 2000. *Talking Politics* 13(2): 97–102.
Cole, M. (2005) Duverger's law: an application to local elections in Britain. *Representation* 41(4): 269–275.
Douglas, A. (2013) Cambridge, Massachusetts elections a model for America. *Fair Vote*. Retrieved from www.fairvote.org/cambridge-massachusetts-elections-a-model-for-america.

Gallagher, M. (1991) Proportionality, disproportionality and electoral systems. *Electoral Studies* 10(1): 33–51.

Gallagher, M. and Mitchell, P. (2009) Introduction to electoral systems. In M. Gallagher and P. Mitchell (eds), *The Politics of Electoral Systems* (2nd edition), 3–23. Oxford: Oxford University Press.

Grofman, B., Sung-Chull, L., Winkler, E. and Woodall, B. (eds) (1999) *Elections in Japan, Korea and Taiwan under the Single Non-Transferable Vote*. Ann Arbor, MI: University of Michigan Press.

Hill, S. and Richie, R. (2005) Success for instant runoff voting in San Francisco. *National Civic Review* 94(1): 65–68.

Johnston, R. and Pattie, C. (2011) Tactical voting at the 2010 British general election: rational behaviour in local contexts? *Environment and Planning A* 43(6): 1323–1340.

Jones, A. (2016) Ontario municipalities allowed to use ranked ballots after legislation passes. Retrieved from https//globalnews.ca/news/2746487/Ontario-municipalities-allowed-to-use-ranked-ballots-after-legislation-passes.

Kolasa-Sikiaridi, K. (2016) Municipal elections in Cyprus: elected mayors pledge to work for the people. *Greek Reporter* (19 December). Retrieved from http://greece.greekreporter.com/2016/12/19/municipal-elections-in-cyprus-elected-mayors-pledge-to-work-for-the-people.

Kommers, D. and Miller, P. (2012) *The Constitutional Jurisprudence of the Federal Republic of Germany* (3rd edition). Durham, NC: Duke University Press.

Lakeman, E. (1982) *Power to Elect*. London: Heinemann.

Mair, P. and Laver, M. (1975) Proportionality, PR and STV in Ireland. *Political Studies* 23(4): 491–500.

McAllister, L. and Cole, M. (2014) The 2011 Welsh general election: an analysis of the latest staging post in the maturing of Welsh politics. *Parliamentary Affairs* 67(1): 172–190.

Slosson, M. (2015) Mayoral election to use instant runoff voting. *Telluride Daily Planet* (29 September). Retrieved from www.telluridenews.com/news/article_43c496a4-66fb-11e5-b159-1bb5c93e91de.html.

Sparrow, A. (2009) The real reason Sarah Wollaston won the Conservatives' Totnes open primary. *The Guardian*, Politics Blog (6 August). Retrieved from www.theguardian.com/politics/blog/2009/aug/06/why-sarah-wollaston-won-totnes.

Van der Kolk, H. (2007) Local electoral systems in western Europe. *Local Government Studies* 33(2): 159–180.

3
LOCAL POLITICAL LEADERSHIP

The voters or councillors – who chooses who governs?

Colin Copus

Introduction

Central and regional governments can rarely resist the temptation to reshape, reformulate and reorganise local government. That temptation is greater when faced with social, economic and political problems stemming from austerity, urbanisation, Europeanisation, globalisation, increasing service demands and public assertiveness (John 2001; Berg and Rao 2005; Denters and Rose 2005; Kuhlmann and Bouckaert 2016). The tendency to respond to such issues by reforming local government structures reflects centralist thinking that exists even in states where local government has constitutional recognition or a degree of constitutional protection (Baldersheim and Rose 2010; Denters et al. 2014). Re-shaping the architecture of local political decision-making is as much about the centre's need to respond to its policy agenda as it is about ensuring local government can respond to the local manifestation of international and national problems. The distribution of territorial power relationships in any national context tells us that facilitating local leaders in taking political action by changing the structure, powers and processes of local leadership must be articulated so as to create a critical mass of support from local elites themselves (Stone 1995; Svara 1987, 1994; Jeffery 2008; Swianiewicz 2010; Loughlin et al. 2011).

Central to the debate about the reformulation of local political leadership are discussions about who should choose that leader and how far the public should be involved in that choice. Related to that point is ensuring the transparency of political decision-making, the visibility and profile of local leaders and enhancing the legitimacy of the local leader to take political action as well as questions about the appropriate role of citizens in local democracy (see Kersting and Vetter 2003; Magre and Bertrana 2007; Elcock 2008; Wollmann 2008). Who chooses the local political leader is condensed into two constituencies: the voting public or councillors. The debate about whether to directly elect the mayor or not is often addressed through different conceptualisations of political leadership to ensure that visibility, transparency and legitimacy fits with those conceptualisations – as well as asking to whom is the local leader accountable (see Steyvers et al. 2008; Loughlin et al. 2011; Rhodes and t'Hart 2014).

In addition to practical and conceptual matters about the characteristics of political systems and the founding principles on which they are based, is the need to accommodate the role and power of political parties in local government particularly the leading national parties. The direct election of the mayor is a challenge to the role of political parties in some local government systems (see Egner 2017; Gendzwill and Swianiewicz 2017). Currently, in England, some 90% of all councillors are members of the three main British national parties: Conservative, Labour and Liberal Democrat. These national parties bring into local council chambers their national rules, their standard operating procedures, their approaches to party discipline and loyalty and their national policy and philosophical differences (Jones 1969; Maor 1997; Copus 2004; Leach 2006) as well as their own approaches to the political recruitment of councillors and local leaders (Brand 1973; Barron et al. 1989; Meadowcroft 2001; Verhelst and Kerrouche 2012; Verhelst et al. 2013).

In countries such as Germany, Greece, Italy, Poland, the US, Canada and Japan elected mayors were introduced to enhance the legitimacy, visibility, openness, transparency, responsiveness and accountability of local government. Yet, the introduction of the potential for the direct election of mayors in England turned out to be one of the most controversial aspects of the Local Government Act 2000. Currently, across the UK only England has directly elected mayors and then only 16 of them sitting within 352 traditional councils. That number does not include the six combined authority elected mayors created by the Cities and Local Government Devolution Act 2016 or the Mayor of London, created under the Greater London Authority Act 1999, and these second-tier offices are not discussed here.

The chapter reviews the arguments deployed by reformers of local political leadership and their opponents as to why the mayor of a council should or should not be directly elected by citizens. It examines why directly elected mayors have had such a sustained interest for policy-makers (Marsh 2012) and why in some countries councillors have displayed such animosity to this office. The next section of the chapter reviews the arguments for and against elected mayors that have been debated by reformers in an international context. The third section explores the introduction of elected mayors in England which has had one of the most protracted and troubled births of mayoral office, despite central governments (of all parties) being willing to otherwise force change on local government (Copus et al. 2017a). The chapter concludes by drawing together the strands of the arguments in favour and opposing direct election to assess whether the number of elected mayors will increase or whether the strength of the collectivist local political decision-making tradition means there may be a ceiling to this number.

Developments in local political leadership: an international context

Direct election of the mayor is not necessarily about whether the mayor is politically strong, as strength of office is not an automatic outcome of direct election (see Stone 1995; Kotter and Lawrence 1974; Svara 1987; Leach and Wilson 2002; Navarro and Sweeting 2015; Copus et al. 2017a). The strength of local political leadership rests on a series of relationships between leaders and those they seek to lead set within varying structural, cultural, political and social contexts which in turn influence the way political leaders operate. Borraz and John (2004) identify four trends to explain the contexts of local political leadership: the development of new, complex and multi-faceted governing networks; the set of political values held by local political leaders and how they develop over time (citing Clark and Hoffmann-Martinot 1998; see also Szucs and Stromberg 2009); the emergence of models of stronger executive local leadership; and the transfer of ideas and views about leadership forms across national boundaries. Indeed, part of the leadership context is the inter-dependence of political actors when taking political action and the need to negotiate, bargain, influence and pressurise others into action the leader wishes to see taken (John and Cole 1999; Borraz and John 2004; Goldsmith and Larsen 2004). Further, local political leadership structures balance hard and soft powers and as a result 'political, cultural and institutional heritage' and traditions of getting things done come at a premium (John and Cole 1999: 106).

Goldsmith and Larsen (2004) suggest that understanding context as well as role and responsibilities is not sufficient to ensure the transformation of the structure and powers of local leaders. Using Nordic local government as the contextual setting they show that change in local political leadership can be successfully resisted by opponents of 'presidentialist' or single executive systems – elected mayors – basing their opposition to change on historical, cultural, political, economic, social and structural arguments (Goldsmith and Larsen 2004: 121; see also Aars 2009). Indeed, they assert that the consensus based, collectivist decision-making of Nordic local government has prevented reforms towards stronger, individualised local political leadership. Similar successful resistance to institutional change has been seen in England (Kukovič et al. 2015) and to a similar extent in Ireland.

Reform of structure and power of the local leader rest for their success as much on the political and personal capabilities of the leader – their skills, capacities, experience, knowledge, abilities and personality – as they do on the leader inhabiting the correct structure and system (Greamion 1976; Lowndes and Leach 2004). Lowndes and Leach (2004: 565) indicate that the ability of local leaders to interpret context as a way of mobilising political support for a set course of action is related to any given institutional environment and that such environments reflect hard and soft aspects of power and power relationships. Thus, for the elected mayor or council leader there are formal and informal rules and settings which provide the contextual boundaries within which they operate, such as: the power relationship between the mayor (or leader) and council; local political and organisational traditions and culture; the framework of legislation within which the political leader operates; the external governance network; and, the profile of the local area, sub-region and region.

So the question for reformers becomes: how much reform do you want? Is the search for powerful local leaders with a direct line of accountability to the voters that can take political action in complex governing networks through the use of hard, legislatively based political powers? Or, do reformers want to simply operationalise principles such as openness, transparency, visibility and accountability, without granting the political leader – directly or indirectly elected – any hard political power which would make local political leadership much easier. In most cases across Europe the answer has been the latter rather than the former (Copus et al. 2016). Thus, expectations can be raised that elected mayors will be able to solve all local problems but may lack the power, functions responsibilities and budgets that would be required to do so. Yet studies in the USA, notably Morgan and Watson (1996), Svara (1990, 1994), and Mouritzen and Svara (2002), have shown that the right local leader with the right political skills can transcend system constraints; this can even include those constraints deliberately designed to prevent the development of powerful local leaders. Local leaders with the right skills can act so as to accumulate extra resources to support their political action.

Individual or collective decision-making and leadership?

The debate about whether citizens or councillors should choose the political head of the council has been a European-wide phenomenon which must reconcile the individualistic or collectivist options – directly elected mayor or council appointed political leader – and address whether or not local political leaders should have hard or soft power (see Kersting and Vetter 2003; Berg and Rao 2005; Denters and Rose 2005; Magre and Bertrana 2007; Elcock 2008; Wollmann 2008).

The debate has reflected concerns about the legitimacy to act, visibility and profile of local leaders, the transparency of political decision-making, the most effective structures and systems for ensuring leadership accountability and the role of citizens in local democracy (see Larsen 2002).

In the former Communist countries of eastern Europe the debate about the direct or indirect election of the mayor has echoed the themes already outlined of visibility, accountability, legitimacy and the desire to adopt an individual or collectivist political decision-making structure. Countries such as Albania, Bosnia and Herzegovina, Bulgaria, Hungary, Macedonia, Moldova, Poland, Romania, Slovakia and Slovenia adopted a system of direct mayoral election. While the powers, resources and functions of the mayor and the national local government context in each of those former Communists states varies, the need for a local leader to enhance legitimacy and gain visibility from public election is a reaction against a dictatorial past. It also indicates that any fear of the concentration of power in one set of hands is diluted by the legitimacy given through a direct public mandate. Further, it points to a reaction against opaque collectivist decision-making taking place outside of a democratic framework. Other former eastern bloc countries however, adopted a more collectivist approach to the appointment of the local political leader, granting that power not to local citizens but the council. Election of the mayor by the council occurs in the Czech Republic, Estonia, Latvia and Lithuania. However the tendency has been for former communist countries to mainly embrace an elected mayor including late adopters such as Croatia.

There is a hybrid alternative to indirect and direct election which finds favour in France and Spain where the leader of the winning party list of candidates becomes the mayor (Borraz and Negrier 2007; Navarro and Sweeting 2015). That system enables the public to know who the mayor will be before the election but keeps the choice of candidates firmly with local party managers who draw up the lists. Even where the mayor is directly elected the local party will decide the party's mayoral candidate. Only in systems where a large number of independents are elected as mayors can the power of the party be diluted – and even then the disguised independent, who is an undeclared member of a party, or who receives endorsement and support from a local branch of a national party, means that large numbers of independent mayors cannot be taken as a signal of the demise of party control (see Kukovič and Haček 2013; Gendzwill and Zołtak 2014; Gendzwill and Swianiewicz 2017).

The debate about the direct election of the mayor has been far from settled across Europe, with countries such as Sweden, the Czech Republic and Spain continuing the debate (Wollmann 2008, 2012; Stevyers et al. 2008; Elcock 2008; Sweeting 2009; Loughlin et al. 2011). Those debates include fundamental questions about the role, purpose, powers and responsibilities of local government and whether local self-government can comfortably continue to exist alongside central governments responding to international political and economic pressures (see Copus et al. 2017a). The US, with a longer, more established experience with directly elected mayors than European nations, has itself seen shifts over time between direct and indirect election (Frederickson and Johnson 2001; Schragger 2006). It is still possible, in some US municipalities, depending on the local charter, to shift governing models from indirect to direct election and vice versa. Elected mayors were seen by some early US reformers as a way of reducing the power of local political parties and party machines (see Allen 1993; Finegold 1995; Burrows and Wallace 1999) echoing contemporary concerns about local party politics (Copus 2004). Any form of powerful local leadership that emerges from reforms however, will be reshaped locally by local political elites with the ability to make sure such reforms accommodate the raw politics of the localities (Svara 1990; Vogelsang-Coombs 2007; Kjear 2014). In systems where central or regional government can impose reforms on local government local political elites can still act to either prevent or distort change in leadership structures (see Copus et al. 2017b). On the other hand, if centrally inspired change to leadership structures suits the purpose of the local political elite, they themselves may drive change locally (see Copus and Dadd 2014).

Where written constitutions exist there well may be some degree of protection for local government from central interference or interference from a region or state. However, Egner and Heinelt (2006) have shown that where constitutional protection for local government exists it does not free it from centrally inspired reforms. Indeed, Loughlin et al. (2011) have identified a pattern across Europe, where relatively strong local government has been reformed or re-organised through pressure by upper-tiers of government or through some form of political pressure or financial inducements (Baldersheim and Rose 2010). The introduction of changes to local leadership structures can be introduced by nationwide reform, such as Italy's adoption of elected mayors in the early 1990s, or it can be successfully resisted, as in the Nordic countries (Goldsmith and Larsen 2004: 121; Aars 2009), and as it has been, to some extent, in England.

Directly elected mayors: the English experience of reforming local political leadership

There has been a 50-year ongoing debate in England on the best form of local political leadership set within the context and constraints of a highly centralised political and governing system. Those constraints mean that any reform of local leadership must take account of and match the existing constitutional position of local government as well as its roles, tasks, functions and purpose. So, when reformulating the office of local political leader, reformers need to reconcile the competing tensions between service delivery and management and the democratic and political role of local government and whether it can indeed govern in the strictest sense – that is, does the structure and powers associated with the leader's office enable effective political action to be taken? Inquiries such as the Herbert Commission (HMSO 1960), the Maud Committee (HMSO 1967), the Redcliffe-Maud Commission (HMSO 1969), the Widdicombe Committee (HMSO 1986) and the Bains Report (Bains 1972) explored those tensions with the consideration of local government as part of the infrastructure of the welfare state. Such centrally inspired inquiries, as these were, shied away from radical reform of the powers and structures of local political leaders and settled for revisions to the committee system. The committee system of political decision-making was not unassailable however, despite the lack of a radical alternatives being proposed.

Individual or collective leadership: the official position

As early as 1967 the Maud Committee recognised the failures of the committee system and the proliferation of committees and sub-committees which it saw as time consuming and causing delays in decision-making. Maud noted the frustration generated by the tendency of committees to involve councillors in administrative detail (Maud 1967: 35). But the solution was to recommend yet another committee, this time a small management board consisting of five to nine councillors. In this can be seen the early development of the Policy and Resources Committee emerging, as the management board would set the principle objectives for the authority, review progress, supervise management and take decisions on behalf of the council beyond the responsibilities of senior officers. It would also be responsible for presenting business to the council. Indeed we can see not only the beginnings of a Policy and Resources Committee but also the beginnings of council cabinets (Maud 1967: 41–42). Maud stopped far short of recommending an elected mayor.

The debate about reforming local political decision-making continued for another twenty years or so when the Widdicombe Committee (HMSO 1986) stressed the advantages of a management committee of senior councillors with a similar role to that which Maud had identified and also shared Maud's aim of improving local accountability and decision-making. However, Widdicombe set out a warning about concentrating power in too few hands within local government and consequently diminishing the role of councillors and that warning set the tone for the arguments that still continue about elected mayors today. The Widdicombe Committee, for example, criticised the personalisation of politics it saw as inherent in directly elected mayors which is more easily accepted, it argued, where a national presidential system operated. The committee made the rather bold claim that such a system would be 'generally disliked in Great Britain'. Concern was expressed that different electoral cycles could result in the mayor and council majority coming from a different party (HMSO 1986: para. 5.26), thus rejecting what could be an important check and balance as an inconvenience for decision-making.

The Widdicombe Committee was concerned at conflict arising between an executive mayor and the council. There was no acceptance of a separation of local powers or of direct election to executive office, rather a fear of political deadlock locally emerging from arguments about who had the strongest mandate – the mayor or council. That concern reflected a traditional and majoritarian view of local politics and an acceptance of national party control of local government. Such concern was both strange and understandable at the same time. Strange because the committee had been set up to investigate what the centre perceived to be problems associated with party political control of local government and that the Widdicombe Committee researched and reported at the time of the mandate wars between the central government of Margaret Thatcher and the urban Labour left in local government. Such a context shaped the committee's thinking. Understandable, because at the time of its formation the intense political conflict between local and national government was unlikely to result in a centrally inspired committee of inquiry recommending stronger, more powerful elected local leadership which could be directed against the government of the day.

A number of factors resulted in these two influential and powerful committees (and Maud and Widdicombe committees) failing to recommend radical reform of local leadership. There was a fear of concentrated local political power and the strongly felt desire to avoid creating a powerful elected mayor; an office could pose a serious challenge to the policies and preferences of central government. There was also historic and long-standing support for a collectivist system of local decision-making and leadership; a reluctance to challenge well-established patterns of national party political control of local government; and reluctance for change expressed by councillors. Little has changed in the opposition expressed by councillors to elected mayors in the 30 years since Widdicombe reported and in the 50 years since Maud reported on such matters.

The debate about how to reform local leadership continued in the 1990s with reports from the Department of the Environment (1991) and the Commission for Local Democracy (1995). The latter being an independent body made up largely of academics. Both these reports made the case for elected mayors more confidently and more forcefully than ever before. Elected mayors at this stage found an enthusiastic supporter in the then Secretary of State for the Environment, Michael Heseltine, who was however unable to convince the government to enforce such a change. What we saw in the 1990s was new thinking about local political leadership. Indeed, the arguments for reform of local leadership were formulated on the basis of following a western European trend of moving towards elected mayors and a local separation of powers. A separation of powers was articulated by reformers as a way of overcoming problems with existing political leadership systems as they sought ways to counter-act the secrecy of leadership activity and opaque and blurred decision-making through committees. Knowing who was responsible for what decisions became a touchstone of the debate, so too did providing clearly identifiable local leadership (Department of the Environment 1991; Commission for Local Democracy 1995).

Elected mayors in England: arguments for reform

The Labour Government elected in 1997 had accepted the arguments of reformers that local leadership needed to become more visible, transparent, accountable, legitimate and responsive. Moreover, that Government began to challenge, cautiously, the role and practices of political parties in local government which it saw as contributing to the secrecy, opaqueness, lack of transparency and visibility about who was responsible for political action. The local government modernisation agenda of the Labour Government and the arguments on which it was based, were set out in a number of publications which laid the ground work for the Local Government Act 2000. It was that Act, while introducing elected mayors into English and Welsh local government, did so remarkably tentatively, given the forceful nature of the arguments set out in the modernisation publications (Labour Party 1995; Blair 1998; DETR 1998a, 1998b; DETR 1999). The reaction from councillors, in opposition to elected mayors, was itself so forceful that it was necessary to continue to present the arguments for change after the 2000 Act (DTLR 2001; ODPM 2004, 2005; see also Copus 2006).

A set of assumptions underpinned the proclaimed modernisation of local government: the need to separate the executive and scrutiny roles of the councillor; the need for a clear source of legitimacy for local leadership because councils were operating in complex networks of public and private players (DETR 1998a); and that political leadership should be visible, open, transparent and responsive to citizens (DETR 1998b, 1999). The committee system failed the test based on these assumptions as it was inefficient and opaque: 'no basis for modern local government', and a 'poor vehicle for developing and demonstrating community leadership' (DETR 1998a: paras 5.1, 5.7). Moreover, the Labour Government's reformers argued that the committee system obscured responsibility for political action and failed to 'foster community leaders and leadership; with local people having 'no direct say over their local leaders' (DETR 1998a). Political leadership and holding of those leaders to account needed different types of councillors and the creation of a political division of labour to produce: 'greater clarity about who is responsible for decisions and who should be held to account for decisions' (DETR 1998a: paras 5.9, 5.11).

Party politics, or at least the behaviour of political party groups, attracted a very concise analysis, linked as it was to the weaknesses of local leadership, thus: 'in most councils it is the political groups, meeting behind closed doors, which make the big and significant decisions' (DETR 1998a: para. 5.4). What is seen here is a challenge to long-standing and well established patterns of political behaviour among councillors, but one which stressed that such practices undermined leadership and the need for leaders to be open and identifiable. As a consequence the government was 'very attracted' to strong executive directly elected mayor:

> *Such a mayor would be a highly visible figure. He or she would have been elected by the people rather than the council or party and would therefore focus attention outwards in the direction of the people rather than inwards towards fellow councillors. The mayor would be a strong political and community leader with whom the electorate could identify. Mayors will have to become well known to their electorate which could help increase interest in and understanding of local government.*
>
> *(DETR 1998a: para. 5.14)*

The introduction of elected mayors was presented as a new era of local political action based on legitimacy, transparency, visibility, openness, accountability and responsiveness. What is surprising given the forceful nature of the government's arguments and articulation of problems associated with the existing system was that rather than legislate to bring elected mayors into all councils the Local Government Act 2000 opted for a voluntary approach. Indeed, the decision to introduce an elected mayor into a locality was placed in the hands of local citizens to decide in a referendum. The lack of a total reform through the introduction of elected mayors across local government was attributable to raw political reality in the shape of overwhelming opposition to it from councillors and the government's reluctance to confront a key part of their activist base on the issue.

In attempting to promote the idea of elected mayors further, the 2007 Local Government and Public Involvement in Health Act enabled councils to resolve to adopt an elected mayor without a referendum. It was as though the government had failed to recognise the opposition from councillors to the idea or believed that certain powerful council leaders would convince reluctant councillors to accept such a model of governance. As should have been expected, this Act did not lead to a widespread adoption of directly elected mayors. So far only Liverpool and Leicester have chosen this route and at the time of writing there are only 16 elected mayors (excluding the mayor of London as the Greater London Authority is not a traditional style of council) in England from a total of 352 councils. But while in traditional local government the reformers' arguments about elected mayors have failed to convince either councillors or the public, the centre has taken a different route into the direct election of a sub-national political executive.

Sub-regional reform: devolution and elected mayors

The devolution agenda started by the 2010 coalition government and continued by the Conservative government of 2015 (which has lately stalled under the current conservative government), has also been based on a similar articulation of the need for visible, high-profile, accountable and legitimate political leadership (HMG 2010). The Government linked the devolution of significant budgets and powers over the public sector to the creation of 'combined authorities' – collections of existing councils which come together as a result of negotiations with central government to receive devolved responsibilities and budgets. The Cities and Local Government Devolution Act (2016) states that, in order for a combined authority to take on additional powers to that granted when they were formed, a metro mayor must be elected for the area.

Thus, the opposition to elected mayors which is a feature of the traditional landscape of local government has been partially by-passed through offering devolution to combinations of existing councils and the creation of a new sub-national system of government headed by an elected mayor. However, that attempt to out-manoeuvre local government opposition has not been totally successful as devolution negotiations across England have floundered on the insistence of an elected mayor for a combined authority. Indeed, some councils have rejected opportunities to extend their control over the local public sector; to receive substantial funding decisions and to have powers long sought by many in local government, because of their opposition to elected mayors. Any acceptance of elected mayors for some is the thin end of the wedge – if the arguments are accepted for combined authorities then this weakens opposition to their arrival in local government which has so far been successfully restrained by local political elites (see Copus 2006; Kukovič et al. 2015).

On 4 May 2017 six English combined authorities held elections for new mayors: Cambridgeshire and Peterborough, Greater Manchester, Liverpool City Region, Tees Valley, West of England and the West Midlands. Together these six combined authority areas account for 9.5 million people, almost 20% of the population of England. In Cambridgeshire and Peterborough, Tees Valley, the West of England and the West Midlands, Conservative Mayors were elected; Labour won the mayoralties of Greater Manchester and Liverpool City Region. Yet, the debate about the need for elected mayors to personify these huge combined authority areas and to provide a face to an artificial area with which few people will have an affinity continues unabated. Negotiations have collapsed in areas such as Hampshire and Yorkshire with potential broader area agreements suffering as a result of local political differences, geographical tensions and the objection to directly elected mayors.

It may be that the objections from councillors to elected mayors in many parts of the country is what has caused the government of Theresa May to retreat on the issue of elected mayors for rural areas and certainly for single county devolution deals. The weight of opposition among councillors who, as in local government, have the most to lose from the arrival of elected mayors, may also defeat this reform of leadership for sub-national, semi-regional government. It could also be that a minority government with Brexit negotiations as a priority simply lacks the time, energy and enthusiasm for a fight with councillors over devolution. One thing is clear though, the arguments about ensuring the legitimacy, visibility and accountability of local political leadership is the same for both local government and combined authorities. Two instances illustrate this point:

The first is Birmingham, the largest traditional unit of local government in England; it currently has 120 councillors, so that 61 councillors are required for a majority on the council, which in turn means that 32 votes are needed in the majority group for a person to become leader of the council. So, although the electorate of Birmingham is approximately 650,000; the effective constituency is only 32 when it comes to choosing the local political leader.

The second case, for comparison is the Greater Manchester Combined Authority which consists of 10 constituent councils with an electorate of 1,845,121. Prior to the first election of the combined authority mayor, the leader of the combined authority was chosen by the 10 council leaders, meeting in private. When the current mayor of Greater Manchester was elected on 4 May 2017 all 1,845,121 residents had the chance to vote for their preferred candidate.

That there are only 16 directly elected mayors across 352 councils in England and while some devolution deals have stalled because of opposition to elected mayors, shows that resistance can be successful in preventing the reform of local political leadership. Yet, the arguments about visibility, openness, transparency, legitimacy and accountability remain. It may be the case, as indicated in the Widdicombe Committee's report, that elected mayors might be disliked in a country without a tradition of directly elected executives. That dislike is certainly apparent among councillors. More worryingly for localists, the lack of enthusiasm among the public for elected mayors may mirror a similar lack of enthusiasm for local government as an institution.

Conclusion

The arguments in favour of shifting to a directly elected local political leader, which echo across Europe, can be crystallised into what has become the reformers mantra: visibility, openness, transparency, legitimacy and accountability. Those factors reflect a presidential style conceptualisation of local leadership and are secured when the mayor has a direct line of accountability to voters, holding office as a result of local citizens making a specific and clear choice about individual candidates. The opponents of elected mayors articulate a more collectivist, though certainly not always consensual, approach to decision-making which rests on the input – normally through committees – of all councillors into policy. Opponents of elected mayors stress the need to diffuse power among many, rather than concentrate it in a single office-holder.

The modernising arguments and the response of the opponents of direct election of the mayor have conceptual starting points that are not as mutually exclusive as they seem. Indirectly elected mayors can be visible, high-profile and accountable to voters, although that is attenuated by their tenure being bound to councillors rather than voters. They can also wield considerable power. Directly elected mayors, especially where they have been in office for some time (see Copus et al. 2017b), can be unresponsive, have weak accountability and act in ways that obfuscate responsibility for political action – although it is harder for an elected mayor to deflect responsibility and accountability than it is for their indirectly elected counterpart. Visibility is generally higher for elected mayors as they come from the obvious starting point of fighting an election as a sole individual and making themselves known to the public in ways that are not required by their indirectly elected counter-parts (see Elcock and Fenwick 2007; Fenwick and Elcock 2014).

The arguments can be condensed on a less conceptual ground to one which reflects the raw realities of local politics. Dahl (1961) asked 'Who governs?'; and a similar question sits at the heart of support or opposition to the direct election of the local political leader: Direct election means the voters make the choice who governs; indirect election means councillors make the choice who governs. Who chooses who governs, in turn, governs. Shifting the choice away from councillors to voters – even if political parties select the candidate – means that the influence over the political leader held by councillors is weakened. If the tenure of the leader in office does not rely on maintaining favour with councillors, or on deals, bargains and agreements made, for whatever reason, between councillors to support a particular leadership candidate that they elect, then the dynamics of council chamber and party group room politics are fundamentally changed.

But no matter how the debate develops, across time and country context, the pressures for reform of local leadership structure are always present and new pressures, as they emerge, will force the pace of change. Whatever the decisions made about the merits or otherwise of direct or indirect election of the mayor, or about any structural change to local leadership all become pointless if the local political leader does not have the power to govern or to take effective political action. The ever present danger is that central and regional government may be tempted to tinker with the way the mayor is chosen while avoiding the big question about the powers with which local leaders should be endowed. By avoiding that question any change could be muted and a new brand of leaders arrives without the powers to deal with intractable local problems. Expectations will then trump reality and that could have dangerous consequences for local government, wherever power is apparently located.

References

Aars, J. (2009) Immune to Reform? The Nordic Mayor. In H. Reynaert, K. Steyvers, P. Delwit and J.-B. Pilet (eds), *Local Political Leadership in Europe. Town Chief, City Boss or Loco President?* Brugge: Vanden Broele.

Allen, O. (1993) *The Tiger: The Rise and Fall of Tammany Hall*. Reading, MA: Addison-Wesley.

Bains, M. (1972) *The New Local Authorities: Management and Structure*. London: HMSO. [Bains Report]

Baldersheim, H. and Rose, L. (2010) *Territorial Choice: The Politics of Boundaries and Borders*. Basingstoke: Macmillan.

Barron, J., Crawley, G. and Wood, T. (1989) Drift and Resistance: Refining Models of Political Recruitment. *Policy and Politics* 17(3): 207–219.

Berg, R. and Rao, N. (2005) (eds) *Transforming Local Political Leadership*. Basingstoke: Palgrave Macmillan.

Blair, T. (1998) *Leading the Way: A New Vision for Local Government*. Institute of Public Policy Research.

Borraz, O. and John, P. (2004) The Transformation of Urban Political Leadership in Western Europe. *International Journal of Urban and Regional Research* 28(1): 107–120

Borraz, O. and Negrier, E. (2007) The End of French Mayors? In J. Garrard (ed.), *Heads of the Local State: Mayors, Provosts and Burgomasters since* 1800, 79–114. New York: Routledge.

Brand, J. (1973) 'Party Organisation and the Recruitment of Councillors', *British Journal of Political Science* 3(4): 473–486.

Burrows, E. and Wallace, M. (1999) *Gotham: A History of New York City to 1898*. New York: Oxford University Press.

Clark, T. N. and Hoffmann-Martinot, V. (eds) (1998) *The New Political Culture*. Boulder, CO: Westview Press.

Commission for Local Democracy (1995) *Taking Charge: The Rebirth Of Local Democracy*. Municipal Journal Books.

Copus, C. (2004) *Party Politics and Local Government*. Manchester: Manchester University Press.

Copus, C. (2006) *Leading the Localities: Executive Mayors in English Local Governance*. Manchester: Manchester University Press.

Copus, C. and Dadd, M. (2014) It's a Proper Job: Process, People and Power in an English City. *Public Money and Management* 34(5): 323–330.

Copus, C., Iglesias, A., Hacek, M., Illner, M. and Lidstrom, A. (2016) Have Mayors Will Travel: Trends and Developments in the Direct Election of the Mayor: A Five-Nation Study. In S. Khulmann and G. Bouckaert (eds), *Local Public Sector Reforms in Times of Crisis: National Trajectories and International Comparisons*, 301–315. Basingstoke: Palgrave Macmillan.

Copus, C., Roberts, M. and Wall, R. (2017a) *Local Government in England: Centralisation, Autonomy and Control*. Basingstoke: Palgrave Macmillan.

Copus, C., Blair, A., Szmigiel-Rawska, K. and Dadd, M. (2017b) New and Established Mayoralties: Lessons for Local Governance in Constructing New Political Institutions: The English and Polish Cases. In D. Sweeting (ed.), *Directly Elected Mayors in Urban Governance: Impact and Practice*, 221–241. Bristol: Policy Press.

Dahl, R. A. (1961) *Who Governs?* New Haven, CT: Yale University Press.

Denters, B. and Rose, L. (2005), *Comparing Local Governance: Trends and Developments*. Basingstoke: Palgrave Macmillan.

Denters, B., Goldsmith, M., Ladner, A., Mouritzen, P. E. and Rose L. (2014) *Size and Local Democracy*. Cheltenham: Edward Elgar.

Department of the Environment (1991) *Local Government Review: The Structure of Local Government in England: A Consultation Paper*. London: Department of the Environment.

DETR (1998a) *Modernising Local Government: Local Democracy and Community Leadership*, London: Department of the Environment, Transport and the Regions.

DETR (1998b) *Modern Local Government: In Touch with the People*, London: Department of the Environment, Transport and the Regions.

DETR (1999) *Local Leadership: Local Choice*, London: Department of the Environment, Transport and the Regions.

DTLR (2001) *Strong Local Leadership: Quality Public Services*, London: Department of Transport Local Government and the Regions.

Egner, B. (2017) Directly Elected mayors in Germany: Leadership and Institutional Context. In D. Sweeting (ed.), *Directly Elected Mayors in Urban Governance: Impact and Practice*, 159–178. Bristol: Policy Press.

Egner, B. and Heinelt, H. (2006) European Mayors and Administrative Reforms. In H. Back, H. Heinelt and A. Magnier (eds), *The European Mayor: Political Leaders in the Changing Context of Local Democracy*, 335–352. Wiesbaden: VS Verlag, fur Sozialwissenschaften.

Elcock, H. (2008) Elected Mayors: Lesson Drawing from Four Countries. *Public Administration* 86(3): 795–811.

Elcock, H. and Fenwick, J. (2007) Comparing Elected Mayors. *International Journal of Public Sector Management* 20(3): 226–238.

Fenwick, J. and Elcock, H. (2014) Elected Mayors: Leading Locally? *Local Government Studies* 40(4): 581–599.

Finegold, K. (1995) *Experts and Politicians: Reform Challenges to Machine Politics in New York, Cleveland, and Chicago*. Princeton, NJ: Princeton University Press.

Frederickson, G. and Johnson, G. (2001) The Adapted American City: A Study of Institutional Dynamics, *Urban Affairs Review* 36(6): 872–884.

Gendzwill, A. and Swianiewicz, P. (2017) Breeding Grounds for Local Independents, Bonus for Incumbents: Directly Elected Mayors in Poland. In D. Sweeting (ed.), *Directly Elected Mayors in Urban Governance: Impact and Practice*, 179–199. Bristol: Policy Press.

Gendzwill, A. and Zołtak, T. (2014) Why Nonpartisans Challenge Parties in Local Politics? The (Extreme) Case of Poland. *Europe and Asia Studies* 66(7): 1122–1145.

Goldsmith, M. and Larsen, H. (2004) Local Political Leadership: Nordic Style. *International Journal of Urban and Regional Research* 28(1): 121–133.

Greamion, P. (1976) *Le pouvoir pearipheariqe*. Paris: Editions du Seuil.

HMG (2010) *The Coalition: Our Programme for Government*. London: HMG.

HMSO (1960) *Report of the Royal Commission on Local Government in Greater London, 1957–60*. Cmnd. 1164. [Herbert Commission]. London: HMSO.

HMSO (1967) *Committee on the Management of Local Government: Report of the Committee, Vol. I*. [Maud Committee]. London: HMSO.

HMSO (1969) *Royal Commission on Local Government: Report, Vol. 1*. Cm 4040. [Redcliffe-Maud Commission]. London: HMSO.

HMSO (1986) *Committee of Inquiry into the Conduct of Local Authority Business: Report of the Committee into the Conduct of Local Authority Business*. Cmnd 9797. [Widdicombe Committee]. London: HMSO.

Jeffery, C. (2008) The Challenge of Territorial Politics. *Policy and Politics* 36(4): 545–557.

John, P. (2001) *Local Governance in Western Europe*. London: Sage.

John, P. and Cole, A. (1999) Political Leadership in the New Urban Governance: Britain and France Compared. *Local Government Studies* 25(4): 98–115.

Jones, G. W. (1969) *Borough Politics: A Study of Wolverhampton Borough Council 1888–1964*. London: Macmillan.

Kersting, N. and Vetter, A. (eds) (2003) *Reforming Local Government in Europe: Closing the gap between Democracy and Efficiency*. Opladen.

Kjear, U. (2014) Local Political Leadership: The Art of Circulating Political Capital. *Local Government Studies* 39(2): 253–272.

Kotter, J. P. and Lawrence, P. R. (1974) *Mayors in Action: 5 Approaches to Urban Governance*. New York: John Wiley & Sons.

Kuhlmann, S. and Bouckaert, G. (eds) (2016) *Local Public Sector Reforms in Times of Crisis: National Trajectories and International Comparisons*. Basingstoke: Palgrave Macmillan.

Kukovič, S. and Haček, M. (2013) The Re-election of Mayors in the Slovenian Local Self-Government. *Lex Localis* 11(2): 87–99.

Kukovič, S., Copus, C., Haček, M. and Blair, A. (2015) Direct Mayoral Elections in Slovenia and England: Traditions and Trends Compared. *Lex Localis* 13(3): 697–718.

Labour Party (1995) *Renewing Democracy, Rebuilding Communities*. London: Labour Party.

Larsen H. O. (2002) Directly Elected Mayors – Democratic Renewal or Constitutional Confusion? In J. Caulfield and H. O. Larsen (eds), *Local Government at the Millennium*, 111–133. Wiesbaden: VS Verlag für Sozialwissenschaften.

Leach, S. (2006) *The Changing Role of Local Politics in Britain*. Bristol: Policy Press.

Leach, S. and Wilson, D. (2002) Rethinking local political leadership. *Public Administration* 80(4): 665–689.

Loughlin, J., Hendricks, F. and Lindstrom, A. (2011) *The Oxford Handbook of Regional Democracy in Europe*. Oxford: Oxford University Press.

Lowndes, V. and Leach, S. (2004) Understanding Local Political Leadership: Constitutions, Contexts and Capabilities. *Local Government Studies* 30(4): 557–575.

Magre, J. and Bertrana, X. (2007) Exploring the Limits of Institutional Change: The Direct Election of Mayors in Western Europe. *Local Government Studies* 33(2): 181–194.

Maor, M. (1997) *Political Parties and Party Systems: Comparative Approaches and the British Experience*. London: Routledge.

Marsh, A. (2012) Is it Time to Put the Dream of Elected Mayors to Bed? *Policy and Poltics* 40(4): 607–611.

Meadowcroft, J. (2001) Political Recruitment and Local Representation: The Case of Liberal Democrat Councillors. *Local Government Studies* 27(1): 19–36.

Morgan, D. and Watson, S. (1996) Mayors of American Cities: An Analysis of Powers and Responsibilities. *American Review of Public Administration* 26(1): 113–125.

Mouritzen, P. E and Svara, J. H. (2002) *Leadership at the Apex: Politicians and administrators in Western Local Government*. Pittsburgh, PA: University of Pittsburgh

Navarro, C and Sweeting, D. (2015) La elcecion directa de alcaldes. Caracterisiticas, experiencias comparadas y el singular caso de los alcaldes quasi-directamente elegidos espanoles. In *Auuario de Derecho Municipal*, 105–126. Madrid: UAM.

ODPM (2004) *The Future of Local Government: Developing a Ten Year Vision*. London: ODPM.

ODPM (2005) *Vibrant Local Leadership*. London: ODPM.

Rhodes, R and t'Hart, P. (2014) *The Oxford Handbook of Political Leadership*. Oxford: Oxford University Press.

Schragger, R. (2006) Can Strong Mayors Empower Weak Cities? On the Power of Local Executives in a Federal System. *Yale Law Journal* 115(9): 2542–2576.

Steyvers, K., Bergström, T., Bäck, H., Boogers, M., De La Fuente, J. and Schaap, L. (2008) From Princeps to President? Comparing Local Political Leadership Transformation. *Local Government Studies* 34(2): 131–146.

Stone, C. N. (1995) Political Leadership in Urban Politics. In D. Judge, G. Stoker, and H. Wolman (eds), *Theories of Urban Politics*, 96–116. London: Sage.

Svara, J. H. (1987) Mayoral Leadership in Council Manager Cities: Preconditions versus Preconceptions. *Journal of Politics* 49(1): 207–227.

Svara, J. H. (1990) *Official Leadership in the City: Patterns of Conflict and Co-operation*. Oxford: Oxford University Press.

Svara, J. H. (ed.) (1994) *Facilitative Leadership in Local Government: Lessons from Successful Mayors and Chairpersons*. San Francisco, CA: Jossey-Bass.

Sweeting, D. (2009) The Institutions of 'Strong' Local Political Leadership in Spain. *Environment and Planning C: Government and Policy* 27(4): 698–712.

Swianiewicz, P. (ed.) (2010) *Territorial Consolidation Reforms in Europe*. Local Government and Public Service Reform Initiative. Budapest: Open Society Institute.

Szucs, S. and Stromberg, L. (2009) The More Things Change, the More They Stay the Same: The Swedish Local Government Elite between 1985 and 2005. *Local Government Studies* 35(2): 251–270.

Verhelst, T. and Kerrouche, E. (2012) Family, Ambition, Locality and Party: A Study of Professionalisation in the Activation and Apprenticeship of Local Councillors in Europe. *Lex Localis* 10(1): 37–62.

Verhelst, T., Reyneart, H. and Steyvers, K. (2013) Political Recruitment and Career Development of Local Councillors in Europe. In B. Egner, D. Sweeting and P.-J. Klok (eds), *Local Councillors in Europe*, 27–49. Wiesbaden: Springer VS.

Vogelsang-Coombs, V. (2007) Mayoral Leadership and Facilitative Governance. *American Review of Public Administration* 37(2): 198–225.

Wollmann, H. (2008) Reforming Local Leadership and Local Democracy: The Cases of England, Sweden, Germany and France in Comparative Perspective. *Local Government Studies* 34(2): 279–298.

Wollmann, H. (2012) Local Government Reforms in (Seven) European Countries: Between Convergent and Divergent, Conflicting and Complementary Developments. *Local Government Studies* 38(1): 41–70.

4
TRADITIONAL LEADERS AND LOCAL GOVERNMENT IN PACIFIC ISLAND COUNTRIES

Graham Hassall and Paul Mae

Introduction: 'traditional' leadership and contemporary governance

The 'call for recognition' of the role of traditional leaders in contemporary governance has been made by a range actors and agencies in the Pacific region. A 2003 Commonwealth Pacific Regional Consultation on Maximising Civil Society's Contribution to Development and Democracy recognized that Pacific indigenous and traditional forms of governance provide authority within their local areas, help maintain Pacific values in the wider society, and provide holistic world views beneficial to the natural environment. A 2004 Regional Symposium on Local Democracy and Good Governance similarly urged commitment by states to develop collaboration with traditional leaders at local level, and highlighted the importance of traditional governance structures in improving governance and reforming local government (Commonwealth Secretariat 2005). While noting the difficulties involved in integrating traditional and modern systems of governance, the Symposium noted the desirability of planners and administrators collaborating with both traditional and modern structures and their associated values: 'Both traditional and modern approaches to conflict resolution, for instance, should be brought together as an assistance to countries in the region.' The 'Auckland Accord' adopted at the 2007 Commonwealth Local Government conference stated:

> Sites of competing authority at the local level are damaging to community wellbeing. The Aberdeen Agenda[1] underscores the importance of inclusive governance with local government acting as first among equals. Effective cooperative governance frameworks that suit the local conditions enable traditional and democratic systems to operate side-by-side or be complementary in the attainment of local development . . . It is essential to have a clearly defined legal framework as . . . the basis for effective cooperation in the local governance context. A sustainable and structured framework for dialogue is needed to ensure genuine communication and provide a peaceful dispute resolution mechanism.
>
> *(University of Technology Sydney 2007: 4)*

A knowledge and understanding of the fundamental cultural groupings prevalent in the Pacific Islands and the differences they display in matters of leadership selection and roles is thus important to understanding local governance in traditional settings. The population of Oceania is approximately 10 million persons, living in tens of thousands of villages, hamlets, settlements, and towns, on thousands of islands, spread across some 20 countries and an ocean area of 550,000 square kilometres. These are some of the 'small island states' of the contemporary era: ten remain dependent on one or other metropolitan power, and the populations of the independent states range from 10,000 (Nauru) to almost 8 million (Papua New Guinea).

Cultural diversity across the Pacific influences styles of leadership and the institutions of government. Sahlins's (1963) anthropological work differentiated Melanesian 'big-man' societies, in which leadership is *achieved*, and Polynesian 'chiefly' titles, which are generally *ascribed* by birthright, but noted that both constituted viable systems of government:

> Almost all of the native peoples of the South Pacific were brought up against intense European cultural pressure in the late eighteenth and the nineteenth centuries. Yet only the Hawaiians, Tahitians, Tongans, and to a lesser extent the Fijians, successfully defended themselves by evolving countervailing, native-controlled states. Complete with public governments and public law, monarchs and taxes, ministers and minions, these nineteenth century states are testimony to the native Polynesian political genius, to the level and the potential of indigenous political accomplishments.
>
> *(Sahlins 1963: 288)*

All traditions are modified over time. What passes as 'traditional' in contemporary times is necessarily a modification of pre-colonial and colonial era practices and could more accurately be termed 'neo-traditional'. In the 1880s, for instance, Fijians were not allowed to revisit or attempt to resurrect the tradition and culture of pre-colonial era, a period called in Fijian 'Daku ni Kuila' (the period before the Union Jack was raised), accompanied by introduction of the Wesleyan Christian Catechism and education system that created the imaginary Trinitarian vanua (tradition), lotu (church) and Matanitu (State). But whereas traditional leadership was based on ascription, and on prowess in war and state-craft, it was 'fossilized' by the British such that traditional leaders became protected government functionaries as part of the colonial administration's 'indirect rule'. After independence was gained in 1970, the role of traditional leaders in contemporary governance became less certain: 'Fijians gradually sensed a drift and purposelessness' (Madraiwiwi 2005), and now the Great Council of Chiefs has been disbanded.

In the case of other Polynesian societies such as Tuvalu, the terms 'tradition' and 'traditional governance' refer to values, beliefs, legends, artefacts, and institutions as filtered and modified by both Samoan pastors of the London Missionary Society and by British colonial government officials.

In some places the very term 'chief' was introduced by colonial authorities or missionaries, keen it identify leadership patterns they could understand and work with. Bolton says of Vanuatu:

> In order to establish points of entry into communities, the Condominium created two categories of person, and appointed community members to them – the categories of chief and assessor. Assessors were established in the Anglo-French protocol of 1911 to act as consultants in cases presented to Native Courts, which were hearings over which District Agents presided. As time passed the role of assessors was modified, and they were given increasing responsibility, being left to settle minor disputes themselves.

> The second category of person introduced by the Condominium was that of chiefs. The Presbyterian chiefly model was taken up and modified by the Condominium Government in order to establish individuals throughout the archipelago who could represent and act for their community in dealings with outsiders.
>
> *(Bolton 1998: 183)*

Studies by Lawson (1990) and White (1992) describe the invention of chiefly categories and traditions in Fiji and Solomon Islands respectively. Maasina Ruru, an anti-colonial political movement among Malaita Workers in the Solomon Islands Labour Corps during the 1930s and 1940s, advocated the creation of an indigenous hierarchy of 'chiefs' to counter the colonial hierarchy of headman and district officers, and to demand political rights and the application of customary law. The chief was the focus of power and meaning in village life, and his formal roles as feast giver, alliance-maker, and warrior, embodied the vitality and integrity of their region. In the case of contemporary Bougainville:

> *kastom* is not the same as the custom of the 'old days', and it is changing, fluid, too. . . . *kastom* refers to the effort to bring institutions and ways that are rooted in indigenous local traditional practices into a modern political realm where both indigenous and exogenous social and cultural forces are at work.
>
> *(Boege 2006: 2)*

Although the passing of long-established leaders Tupou IV of Tonga (in 2006) and Malietoa Tanumafili II of Samoa (in 2007) tested the public's loyalty to notions of paramount rule in those countries, the hold of custom remains strong. Even though these small Pacific countries adopt Western conventions and codes of law, their value systems continue to rely on ancient codes which are acknowledged in society but not in the constitution. In the case of Samoa, for instance:

> Although much has been written about the *fa'asämoa* and *fa'amatai*, most of it has had an institutional, systemic, or procedural focus. Relatively little has been written about the principles that underpin the system. Important concepts such as *pule* (authority, power); *soälaupule* (joint decision making); *'autasi* (consensus); *alofa* (love, compassion, care); *fa'aaloalo* (respect); *mamalu* (dignity); *fa'autaga, töfä,* and *moe* (all refer to wisdom), and many others, have not been defined extensively, and yet they constitute the basis of indigenous Samoan institutions.
>
> *(Huffer and Asofou So'o 2005: 312)*

In Kiribati, social organization maintains some traditional organizational patterns. *Kainga* (hamlets) comprising between twenty and one-hundred family members, remain the foundation of social and residential units. Kainga are usually led by the oldest male, who allocated such tasks as procuring food and other necessities of life in accordance with a clear division of labour based on sex and to a lesser extent, age; assisted with arranging marriages and adoptions; procured the services of specialist canoe builders, house builders and healers; and represented his *kainga* at the district maneaba, a traditional yet continuing institution described by Maude (1977) as 'the focus of the whole social life of the community':

> in it were held all discussions concerning peace or war or any of the other innumerable concerns affecting the common weal; it was the Law Court, where offenders against customary norms were tried, and disputes heard and arbitrated by the Old Men; and

the centre for the many ceremonies and feasts of a formal character, as well as the more dignified community recreations and dances . . . The maneaba was all that to the [I-Kiribati], and much more; the traditional club-house of the aged; a pied á terre for the stranger; and a sanctuary for those in flight. All behavior under its roof had to be seemly, decorous, and in strict conformity with custom, least the maneaba be matauninga (offended) and the culprit maraia (accursed).

(Maude 1977: 34)

Although these roles have been redefined in contemporary Kiribati society, the powers and legitimacy of the *maneaba* still carry weight. The *Laws of Kiribati Act* 1989 recognizes the continued authority of village elders, through the *maneaba*, to lead major community projects and activities.

There are, thus, societal values throughout Pacific Island societies that underpin daily life which draw heavily on social systems of the past but which are in some instances of relatively recent origin. If anything, the notion of 'chief' is not merely undergoing a revitalization, but is being 're-badged' in service of the modern state. Papua New Guinea, for instance, has incorporated chiefly status into its system of public honours. In Samoa, *matai* can be national leaders as well as local, since the Electoral Amendment Act of 1990 only entitles *matai* to stand for election to the 45-member Parliament. In Samoan perspective this is 'faa-Samoa' (in the Samoan tradition), since the Member of Parliament remains answerable to the *matais* of the *nu'u* (village meeting, or *'fono*). Although in theory MPs are those who win at general elections, their tenure is in practice at the pleasure of the nu'u, which determines the 'pre-selection' of candidates.

In Solomon Islands, a proposed review of government in the lead-up to independence recommended that chiefly authority be embedded in local government bodies, and that chiefs hold an annual conference of Elders (British Solomon Islands 1972). In a church-supported initiative for the Island of Santa Ysabel, Anglican Bishop Dudley Tuti was in 1975 installed as paramount chief for the entire island – an arrangement that continues to the present - although nowhere else in the country, since Santa Isabel is Solomons' only island with island-wide traditions.

There is, at the same time a counter-movement, in which chiefly roles are being questioned, especially by youth and women, who regard the inscription of power in senior men as limiting or devaluing. Such tensions between introduced systems of governance and the pre-existing systems are widely reported (Larmour 2005).

But what needs to change: tradition, or modernity? Few now argue that 'traditional' forms of authority should be abolished or allowed to wither away, while some question how appropriate 'modern' forms of democracy are for Pacific societies.

Scope of jurisdiction

Reforms have increasingly sought to restore the role of tradition in local government and to bring together elected officials and traditional elders or even replace the former with the latter. However, while tradition may play an important role in the maintenance of identity, traditional authorities are not necessarily good at delivering services. Moreover, they are not generally able to deliver such services as hospitals, or road maintenance, which require expertise and are subject to economies of scale, or to deliver services that have significant externalities, like immunization. A World Bank report has assessed Pacific Islands' governance as:

. . . national government planning and control that does not involve local authorities in a co-ordinated manner; poor communication among municipal government, rural local authorities, and urban villages in the same metropolitan area; a tax burden to support urban development that falls unevenly on beneficiaries in the urban region; and a lack of capacity to address the needs of the population, which vary greatly across jurisdictions. Equally, traditional forms of governance are also unlikely to respond adequately to these pressures.

(Commonwealth Secretariat 2005: 80)

Leaders whose jurisdictions were geographically bound by the traditional location of their cultural and political community now seek to continue their roles and responsibilities among communities that straddle not only rural and urban environments, but also trans-national ones. For many, the chief personifies aspects of central value and identity that are increasingly seen as being threatened by 'western' values of individualism and materialism.

Constitutional recognition

The extent to which Pacific Island constitutions recognize traditional institutions and norms of leadership and governance was debated during preparations for independence. Constitutional solutions were easiest to discern where such traditions were already acknowledged nation-wide. Where traditional institutions differed by locality, however, entrenchment at national level was more difficult and was usually handled through later legislation, which allowed for localized implementation. For some countries, such as Solomon Islands, this resulted in a situation in which traditional leadership and governance although ignored in the national constitution remains the foundation of decision-making at community level. Pacific Islands' Constitutions thus vary greatly in the extent of their formal recognition of tradition, and the presence of absence of such provisions is not an indicator of the strength of informal traditional authority.

The Constitutions of Marshall Islands and Vanuatu establish Councils of Chiefs and in 2006 Vanuatu passed a *Chiefs Act*. Section 2(a) of the Marshall Islands Constitution (Functions of the Council of Iroij) provides for a council that may consider 'any matter of concern to the Republic of the Marshall Islands, and it may express its opinion thereon to the Cabinet'. The Constitutions of Palau and the Federated States of Micronesia similarly recognize the authority of traditional leaders. Kiribati's Constitutional preamble acknowledges that society's continued adherence to its traditions and heritage. Although the Constitution does not articulate the role that Parliament should play in giving due recognition to customary law and traditional authorities, the *Laws of Kiribati Act* deals recognizes customary law and traditional authorities, and Constitutional Chapter 9 allows the Banaban community to be represented in the Maneaba (Parliament) by a representative (i.e. traditional leader) rather than by an elected member. In Papua New Guinea the Constitution of the Autonomous Province of Bougainville reserves seats in the Provincial Council for traditional leaders.

The Constitution of Solomon Islands gives specific recognition to customary law by virtue of Section 76 and Schedule 3, which recognizes custom as a source of law, but places it below the status of the constitution and statutory law. Parliament can make laws for the application of customary law in the country, and the Constitution directs Parliament to provide a role for traditional chiefs in local governance (Section 114(2)). Attempts had been made under this provision to appoint chiefs in provincial area council assemblies, but the attempt failed, partly because only males can be chiefs, and this norm conflicts with overriding requirements to deliver gender equality. A current draft constitution provides 'church leaders, youth leaders and women's representatives, as well as traditional chiefs' (Nanau 2002: 19) with a role in national legislative processes through membership of a 'Congress of Governors' so as to 'assuage the conflict of traditional and modern laws, and to encourage communities to take ownership of the system' (ibid.).

In the case of Samoa, Constitutional article 111(1) holds that law is 'inclusive of any custom or usage which has acquired the force of law in Samoa or any part thereof under the provisions any Act or under a judgment of a court of competent jurisdiction'. More than two decades passed before Parliament responded to this provision with the *Village Fono Act 1990*, which is discussed in more detail below. There are also Constitutional provisions that deal with land. Clause 103 recognizes customary land as one of the three categories of land ownership in Samoa. By defining 'Customary land' as land held in accordance with Samoan custom and usage the provision recognizes traditional land governance practices. The Constitution also establishes a Land and Titles Court (Clause 103) to deal with land matters and matai titles. Constitutional Article 44 provides that the qualification for a person to stand for election will be determined by statute, and the statute, in turn, declares the determining qualification as being position of matai title, which can only be held through adherence to Samoan custom and usage.

The Constitution of Tonga is silent on the role of customary law. However, at the same time it continues the recognition of the Tongan leadership system first codified in the 1875, Constitution, which recognized the monarchy, and granted land rights and titles to twenty nobles and their families. There are now thirty three nobles. All village affairs and local government is thus subject to a strict hierarchical social order of King, nobles, and commoners.

Vanuatu's independence Constitution of 1980 (Article 95(3)) recognizes customary law, custom practice and traditional authorities. Parliament is authorized to provide for the manner of ascertaining of custom. Article 29 establishes a Council of Chiefs (Malvatumauri), comprising 31 custom chiefs representing Island councils, village councils, and urban councils, entitled to discuss matters relating to custom and tradition, to make recommendations for the preservation and promotion of ni-Vanuatu culture and languages (article 30), and to be consulted on any question, particularly any question relating to tradition and custom, in connection with any bill before Parliament (article 30(2)). Article 49 allows courts to accept people knowledgeable in custom to sit with judges in proceedings with a component on customary law. Courts are authorized to base decisions on custom in instances when no statute is applicable. Although Constitutional Article 95 recognizes customary law as part of the laws of the Republic of Vanuatu, it has not proven easy to practically combine both customary laws the formal legal system. The Great Council of Chiefs has expressed the view that legislation has the effect of eroding customary law.

There are, at the same time, some counter-veiling trends. Although the Constitution of the Federated States of Micronesia (1970) provides for traditional rights, a Constitutional Convention in 2002 specifically excluded traditional leadership from membership. Haglelgam explains that traditional leaders are not fully recognized in the constitution, but remain important:

> the future of traditional governance at the states level in the Federated States of Micronesia is not too rosy. At the national level, it is downright impossible because of opposition from Chuuk and Kosrae. For the Federated States of Micronesia, creating a role for the traditional chiefs to preserve custom and traditional would amount to chasing a phantom because, no matter how one argues it, there is no such thing as national custom and tradition. What the traditional chiefs need to protect and preserve are the various customs and traditions of the four states; so the task would be better handled at the state-level. However, a useful new role of the traditional chiefs might be created

to promote national unity. The traditional leaders might be able to bridge the cultural divides that exist among the states in the Federated States of Micronesia. This new role would be more politically useful and nationally relevant than the role of protecting and preserving customs and traditions that do not exist at the national level.

(Haglelgam undated)

Statutory recognition of traditional rights

Apart from recognition of traditional authority in national constitutions, it can also be provided in subsidiary legislation. In Solomon Islands, Makira-Ulawa Province's *Chiefs Empowerment Act* adds chiefs to the Provincial leadership machinery and to the Provincial Payroll. In 2007 then Prime Minister Manasseh Sogavare attended celebrations and was invested as paramount chief of Makira and Ulawa and Ukinimasi'. The *Customs Recognition Act* (2001) lists criminal and civil matters that courts can deal with in accordance with custom. The *Local Government Act* (1985), however, which provides for the regulation and operation of local area councils, including town councils, is silent on the role of custom and traditional authorities, apart from empowering Councils to determine which forms of custom are good and should be encouraged within council boundaries. The Provincial Government Act (1997), which regulates the operation of provincial governments in Solomon Islands, does not refer to customary law or the use of any form of traditional authority within its governance system. A similar law with no mention of custom and traditional authority is the *Honiara Town Council Act* (1999). Other Acts like the *Islanders Marriage Act* (1945), *Islanders Divorce Act* (1960) and the *Wills, Probate and Administration Act* (1991) provide for the administration of marriage, divorce and administration of estates of Solomon Islanders respectively. Each of these Acts give recognition to custom and the function traditional authorities perform in the ceremonies or roles.

In Vanuatu the Vanuatu Cultural Centre has projects on Traditional Resource Management and the Traditional Ecological Knowledge (TEK) and Traditional Resource Management (TRM) Database Project. Furthermore, the Pentecost-based Melanesian Institute of Philosophy, Science and Technology hosted the Vanuatu Indigenous Peoples' Forum at Lavatmagemu village in north-east Pentecost in April 2007. The Forum brought together 500 participants from all over Vanuatu. The resolutions of the Vanuatu Indigenous Peoples' Forum were finalized as the Lavatmagemu Dekleresen 2007, parts of which were then presented (in the month of May) to the 6th session of the United Nations Permanent Forum on Indigenous Issues in New York. In 2007 Shefa Province was engaged in a 'Year of Traditional Economy' awareness campaign designed to encourage the revitalization of traditional cultural practices and heritage, including resource management and governance practices as the basis for the continuing strength of the traditional economy; and encouraging people who are involved in production within the traditional economy to value their role and to continue expanding the production of traditional foods and wealth items within that economy

Kiribati is one of the few Pacific Islands countries that has provided clear guidelines about customary law as a source of law. The *Laws of Kiribati Act* 1989 declares customary law to be enforceable in all courts, and sets out clearly the different purposes in which custom maybe considered in both criminal and civil matters. In criminal matters custom can be used to determine the existence of a person's state of mind, reasonableness of an act or excuse or to determine a penalty. In civil matters it is used to determine ownership by custom, rights to possession, administration of native land, and the rights of married people and children. Section 6(3)(b) of the Act establishes the hierarchy of laws, stating that where there is conflict between customary law and common law, customary law shall always prevail. This applies to such matters as administration of customary land, custody and guardianship of children, and communal leadership in village projects – thus providing considerable scope for traditional leaders to exert their roles and functions at local level. The *Marriage (Amendment) Act* 2006 recognizes the need to ensure marriage follows the customs and traditions of the Kiribati people. In allows, for instance, marriage to the sixth degree of cousinship as ordered by custom and tradition as compared to second cousins in the previous provision.

The *Island Courts Act* (1983) authorizes island courts to take into account customary law and practices when dealing with criminal cases. This practice was promoted in the courts higher in the court hierarchy by the *Criminal Procedure Code Act* (1981) which promotes reconciliation and dispute settlement in accordance with custom (Section 118). It is a requirement under section 119 for courts to take account of any compensation or reparation made under custom by parties or traditional authorities.

The *Local Government Act* 1984 provides for a local government authority on all the islands in Kiribati in the form of an island council, empowered to amend customary law as it sees fit when making bye-laws. The Act has facilitated a gradual devolution of authority to allow citizens to take charge of their own development at local level (although central government retains a supervisory role over the operation of local government). Island Councils are often assisted by the *Botaki ni Unimwane*, an assembly of older islanders who act as guardians of Kiribati culture and custom, though the role and function is not expressly recognized by any particular legislation.

Finally, the *Electoral Act of Kiribati*, the *Elections Ordinance* 1979 and subsequent amendments still maintain recognition of the mweaka, a customary practice whereby gifts exchanged between traditional leaders during election times are regarded as a traditional practice, rather than a corrupt practice – a recognition that ensures that such traditional practice are protected in the face of modern democratic practice.

In Samoa, custom has remained strong at all levels of society through both the colonial and independent periods. Whereas the *General Laws (No. 2) Ordinance* 1932 declared that certain aspects common law principles pertaining to wills, legitimacy, custody and guidance, could be deemed inapplicable because of the circumstances and lifestyles of the Samoans, such later important legislation as the *Administration Act (No. 23)* of 1975 remained silent on the role of custom. The *Village Fono Act* of 1990, in contrast, has done much to integrate traditional leadership and law into contemporary practice. The Act empowers traditional leaders or village Fonos to deal with matters and residents of the village in accordance with the customs and usages of that respective village. It also allows them to make rules for the maintenance of hygiene, administer the use of village land, direct the allocation of work, and impose punishments on wrong doers.

The Act empowers the village Fono to oversee land ownership and titles to land – although their actions can be challenged by parties in the Land and Titles Court, or further reviewed by the Supreme Court of Samoa. On matrimonial matters, the Matrimonial Act closely follows customary matrimonial law. Marriages in Samoa are monogamous and are solemnized in church and are above the marriageable age because the law and now the culture of the people requires, which is now believed by the people to be proper and a reflection of current customs and beliefs about custom.

Tonga provides an example of a Pacific country in which custom prevails at local level, without necessarily being recognized in law. Although, for instance, the *Marriage and Registration Act* (CAP 61), does not provide for marriages in Tongan custom, Tongan Courts have on numerous occasions accepted custom in proceedings. This is evident in the case of *Tu'iha'ateiho v. Tu'iha'ateiho*, where the court held that the fact that Tonga custom requires a man to give respect and assistance to the widow of the elder brother was a factor which influenced the court In the case *Leota v. Faumuina* the court considered traditional practices such as customary apologies for wrong doing in imposing a reduced punishment. Despite the failure of the *Marriage and Registration Act* to give recognition to marriage in custom, Tongan courts have held that couples who had lived together prior to the enactment of any law pertaining to marriage were presumed married according to Tongan custom and practices prevailing in Tonga.

Laws in Tuvalu also give preference to customary law over common law in such matters as land and waters, rights of succession, dissolution of marriage, and guardianship, custody, and support. The *Laws of Tuvalu Act* 1987 expressly states that customary law shall have effect as part of the laws of Tuvalu: '4(2) In addition to the Constitution, the laws of Tuvalu comprise: (a) every Act; (b) customary law; (c) the common law of Tuvalu; (d) every applied law.' In addition, Schedule 1, paragraph 2 states that 'customary law shall be recognized and enforced by, and may be pleaded in, all courts except so far as in a particular case or in a particular context its recognition or enforcement would result, in the opinion of the court, in injustice or would not be in the public interest'.

Tuvalu's *Local Government (Amendment) Ordinance* 1985 defined the 'maneapa' or 'falekaupule'[2] as 'the traditional assembly of elders which in each island shall have the meaning and composition given to it by local custom and tradition' (sec. 3 of the Ordinance, 1985). Although only a small country, with a population of just 10,000, Tuvalu has been preoccupied politically with the tensions between central government and the eight populated islands. In 1993 the government adopted a policy of decentralization to address such issues as the rapid urbanization of the capital island Funafuti, and a People's Congress in Funafuti in 1995 attended by over 70 delegates from all islands issued a communiqué stating a definitive preference for decentralization and democratization. The subsequent Niutao Forum of 1996 issued 55 resolutions and recommendations that helped shape the revolutionary *Falekaupule Act* of 1997, which re-set the relationship between traditional and 'modern' forms and practices of governance.

The principal functions conferred on the 'Falekaupule' by the Act are the election of the *Pule o Kaupule* (President of Island Council), approval of the Kaupule budget, approval of appointments to Kaupule offices, approval of bye laws, and a few others. The Falekaupule is also responsible for the nation's Falekaupule Trust Fund (FTF) which was established in 1999. The Act enhanced the ability of the Kaupule (Island Executive) and Falekaupule (Island Assembly), to act more independently and more self-reliantly. Traditional leaders and institutions were formally made responsible and accountable for the general well-being of their people (each island community has traditionally had its specialists to assist communities with house building, canoe building, fishing, coconut husbandry, traditional medicine, taro cultivation, fighting, navigation, midwifery, sorcery, divination and curing, tattooing). The Falekaupule and Kaupule also became involved in the provision and delivery of goods and services, capacity building, infrastructural development, education and training, and land management, environment and conservation. They revived traditional methods for resource management, and disaster management. Traditional knowledge concerning tools, zoning, quotas on fish catches, and development of regulations and rules and enforcement mechanisms (punishment and shaming) is increasingly now translated into community programs aimed at preserving and protecting the harvesting of the island's resources.

Yet despite the legal recognition and role given to the Falekaupule in terms of its relationship with the island councils as well as with central government, there still remain a number of irreconcilable differences and continuing power struggle between them. Interestingly, the differences revolved around the conception of the two institutions – the very problem that the Falekaupule Act purports to resolve. Whereas islanders view the Falekaupule as an integral part of their traditions and customs despite its recent origin and a colonial construction, they continue to perceive local government as an alien institution and as an extension of central government.

These tendencies toward the recognition of traditional leaders, decentralization, and recognition of custom law, have also prevailed in Vanuatu. The highest traditional authority in Vanuatu, the National Council of Chiefs was established by the Constitution, and its specific functions, appointments and operation provided for in the *National Council of Chiefs Act* (2006). The *Decentralization of Local Government Regions Act* (1994), which provides for the establishment and operation of local government councils, states that local government council shall consist of elected members and appointed members who may include chiefs, women representatives, youth representatives and church representatives (Section 7).

In the case of Fiji, statutory recognition of custom and traditional authority has shifted markedly over time as a consequence of political conditions in that country. In the modern period governance of the indigenous population was set out in the 1876 Deed of Cession by which Fijian chiefs agreed to the terms of British Annexation. Chiefly authority was entrenched through the establishment of a 'Great Council of Chiefs' and recognition of their authority over their people and land. However the importation to Fiji if indentured labourers from India affected these arrangements, and Fiji came to independence in 1965 with what amounted to dual systems of government – a 'modern' government for all Fiji's citizens, in which a 'Fijian Affairs Board' and other agencies were embedded to administer indigenous Fijian affairs separately. All land remained in under Fijian customary ownership, although the benefits of economic activity were managed by a Native Lands Trust Board on these owners' behalf. A military regime which dismantled Fiji's democratic institutions from late 2006 also dismantled the Great Council of Chiefs while leaving the system of land tenure and the chiefly system in place.

The continuing significance of tradition in contemporary Pacific life

Three areas in which traditional authorities in Pacific Island societies continue to exert considerable influence at local level are in the distribution of land, consent to natural resource development, and dispute resolution. Each of these areas will thus be considered below in brief.

Land distribution

Since most land in Pacific Island countries remains in customary ownership, and has not been formally surveyed, much less alienated or acquired by the state, methods for allocation of ownership and use also remain in customary hands. In Solomon Islands, for instance, the *Land and Titles Act* (1969) states that ownership over customary land is to be in accordance with current customary usage applicable to a respective area. Before any land complaint is brought to the courts all other traditional means of resolving it must be exhausted. This gives authority for traditional authority to deal with land disputes, and if parties disagreed with the outcome, they can take the matter to the local courts. A customary land appeal court (CLAC) includes local chiefs and elders as judges, who deal with cases in accordance with local customary law and practices.

In Tonga, similarly, the *Lands Act* establishes a Land Court but does not expressly spell out whether such a court will consider customary law when making their decisions (recalling the note above that the Tongan Constitution of 1875 provides that all land belongs to the King). In Tuvalu traditional land rights are vested in a 'system of chiefly stewardship' (Brady 1974). The *Native Lands Ordinance* 1957 established a Lands Court which curiously is empowered to deal with child paternity and custody in addition to land boundaries, transfer of title, and usage. The Samoan *Taking of Lands Act* of 1964 recognizes *matai* as head of the pule (family), and as such, as the legitimate authority to forward claims on behalf of a *pule* for compensation and likewise receiving it as well. In Vanuatu, the *Customary Land Tribunal Act* (2001) moved land disputes from the jurisdiction of the judiciary to that of local chiefs, and on the basis of customary law and practice.

Resource consent and community mobilization

Chiefs also play a key role in giving blessing and assent to a range of government projects, which result in the public also giving its broad support. In 2008, for instance Efate Chiefs played a key role in assenting to development of Efate Island's Ring Road, funded by the US' Millennium Challenge Fund. Cooperation with the Ring Road project included facilitating access to quarries. In the Cook Islands, leaders known collectively as the *Koutu Nu* – the custodians of the land and natural resources on the island of Rarotonga – brought their communities together with the private sector and other stakeholders to successfully re-establish the *Raui* system of traditional marine protection, which had not been practiced for over 50 years. They have also, in partnership with NGOs and community stakeholders, pressured the Government to declare the island of Suwarrow, which was being considered for lease to an Australian company for pearl farming, as a Sanctuary for birdlife.

In Samoa, *matai* (chiefs) are nominated by each *'aiga* (family) and sanctioned by the village Fono (assembly, or meeting). The *matai* is trustee of the family's land and property, and empowered to allocate physical, capital, labour and organizational resources for use by family members. The sharing and distribution of food is channelled in accordance with the social hierarchical system of Samoan society. Traditionally, goods flowed to the chiefs, who then redistributed them to the people. The Fono directs all activities related to that village which may include, fishing, housekeeping, preparing feasts, hunting, clearing forests, and in ancient times also included preparation for war. In modern times, *matai* still consider themselves as the rightful and legitimate administrator and coordinator of these family and village activities. Meleisea maintains that the Samoans have consistently pushed that their 'traditions and customs should be the only basis of legitimacy in government' (Meleisea 1987).

In Fiji, there is a hierarchy of *ratus* (chiefs), with the paramount chief of the *Matanitu* (Confederacy) at the apex; with *ratus* at lesser levels graded according to the size of the villages, districts or province under their command. As traditional head of the village, the *ratu* controls and directs all aspects of village life, from development projects, to church activities, and ceremonies. He (although in rare instances she) is responsible for seeing that villagers respect the village; through him village resources are pooled when social occasion demands; he arbitrates in the most serious quarrels between the social units in the village and holds the ultimate authority for correcting misconduct and in general anything requiring the co-operation of the whole village.

In Vanuatu, the cooperative participation of state and community leaders is important in ensuring community development. The state is involving community chiefs and leaders in ensuring and to instigate development at community level. One example is the use of community initiated project areas. On Efate the chiefs are currently the drivers of change and development in the community. They initiate the management of their land and forest resources to ensure its sustainability for the future generation. Councils of Chiefs are becoming increasingly formalized at island level, some now having formal constitutions that define their chiefly status, power and processes. In 2014, fifty-three chiefs on Nguna Island launched a Constitution of nineteen provisions covering such matters as customary land, chiefly title, custom governance, identification of customary land boundaries, customary clan verification, and other customary related issues (Anon 2014).

Dispute resolution and law and order

Traditional leaders play important roles resolving disputes, which often pertain to ownership and use of land, but which also erupt on other issues. In Solomon Islands, the people are of the view that chiefs should decide land matters and the magistrates and high courts should not have power to decide land disputes. Traditional leaders proved a source of stability and continuity during years of crisis. With the decline of government services in many areas between 2000 and 2003, many communities turned to traditional leaders and indigenous modes of organization to carry on with a wide range of such activities as had been the province of government as local courts, to support for teachers and health workers.

In Fiji, the most notable challenges chiefs encountered in the contemporary period were mediating during the coups of 1987, 2000 and 2006 (Appana 2005). Ironically, although the modern chiefly system was constructed to suit British colonial rule, it continues to be drawn on in times of crisis or when political agendas need the stamp of approval. The Great Council of Chiefs (GCC) was always been called upon to find solutions when Fiji faced political uprising. In 1987 it deliberated long and hard before supporting coup leader Rabuka, and in 2000, it worked with the Fijian Military to gain the release of hostages held for several months at parliament. Traditional leadership now plays a significant but diminishing role.

Chiefs and traditional leaders in Vanuatu actively participate in community affairs and have mechanisms in place to try to resolve conflicts at community level. On the island of Tanna, for instance, inter-group conflicts are mediated in the Nakamal by a third group which is invited as neutral observer. Once the dispute is resolved the parties are expected to drink kava together to symbolize that agreement has been sealed and compensation agreed. In Vanuatu's rural areas 'village police' have assisted assist chiefs maintain peace and order since 1994. For example, In the case of Fresh Water, next to Port Vila, chiefs organized themselves at two levels, so that problems were addressed at 'area level' before being referred to a Council of chiefs at a broader level. Chiefs also oversee reconciliation ceremonies (Larmour and Barcham 2005).

In Samoa, the *fono* is the governing body which administers the affairs of the village in accordance with Samoan customs and traditions. Village *fono* have on occasions banished villagers for serious transgressions of custom, although there appears to be some uncertainty as to whether they have this right in law (superior courts have ruled that this power rests with the Land and Titles Court, although this has not stopped villages from using this power).

The *matai* who comprise the village *fono* traditionally enjoy the right to govern village life and punish offenders. Since independence, a number of individual Samoans had challenged the power of the village fonos to regulate village social and economic organization. The legal challenges were mainly to do with the rights of the *matais* to banish offenders from the village and the right to control commerce. The challenges were on the basis that decisions to banish offenders and control commercial activities violated individual rights guaranteed under the constitution. The successful prosecution in certain of these cases against the collective decisions of the village fonos was a major concern to the matais, who saw that as the encroachment of the courts into their domain and jurisdiction (Powles 1986, quoted in Macpherson 1997). Macpherson explains that that was the basis of the debate which led to the enactment of the *Village Fono Act of 1990*.

For Tuvalu, a major point of contention and conflict concerns demarcation of the functions of the *Kaupule* (Island Council) and the *Falekaupule*, especially concerning the relationship between the Falekaupule and such other local government agencies as the island court and lands court. The judicial function traditionally vested together with the other two functions of executive and legislative in traditional leaders and institutions, but which was subsequently subsumed by the colonial government as part of the native island (or local) government system, is a particularly contentious issue. Other conflicts that have cropped up from time to time came about mainly from the discharge of the Falekaupule responsibilities relating to its legislative and executive functions. These can be categorized as management and inter-personal issues which can be tackled through proper training and education.

The Falekaupule had often made decisions on cases that should have rightly and legally come under the purview of the court system. The problem has been long standing and there appears to be no easy solution. Despite the fact there is no legal basis for it, the Falekaupule have continued to hold the idea that they also have legitimate punitive authority to impose decisions on those who wilfully disobey the resolutions of that assembly. Several cases in the past demonstrate the regularity of such incidences. In an incident in the 1990s, the chiefs and the Falekaupule of Vaitupu passed judgment on one individual who repeatedly failed to participate in community projects (community projects normally require the contribution of voluntary labour and there is expectation that everyone without fail must contribute unless a person is sick, or over the retirement age – this varies between the islands – or is an expectant or nursing mother). When the chiefs' decided to banish this man from the island he sought the advice of the police officer on the island. Although then officer pleaded his case on the basis that the chiefs' decision was unconstitutional and illegal this questioning of the chief's authority as being unconstitutional aggravated the situation, and a potential physical confrontation was only avoided when the culprit voluntarily boarded a ship bound for another island.

Such forms of punishment were not uncommon in the past, and continue to be considered legitimate and proper forms of punishment, which are viewed as providing community protection, unity and well-being. Based on that philosophical approach to life any abhorrent and destructive behaviour cannot be tolerated. Additional traditional forms of punishment besides banishment and ostracism include *tolo* in which the offending party would be brought into the *Falekaupule* and a group of strong men – depending on the severity of the offence – would be either hand-picked or simply volunteer to levy punishment by assault. Other forms of punishment included public flogging, which is still a recognized form of traditional punishment in the *Falekaupule* on the island of Nui.

Another important area of conflict relates to the overall customary rights of the Falekaupule vis-á-vis the rights and freedoms of the individual. As noted, customary law under the *Laws of Tuvalu Act 1987* is recognized, enforced by, and pleaded in, all courts – unless its enforcement would result in injustice or is contrary to public interest.

In *Alama v. Tevasa* the precarious nature of the relationship between customary law and the individual rights and freedoms in an election petition was considered by the High Court of Tuvalu. When the petitioner unsuccessfully stood as a candidate in a bye-election on Nukulaelae Island in March 1986 he petitioned the High Court to declare the election results null and void on the ground that the Respondent and his agents, including chiefs and elders, were guilty of corrupt practices in contravention of para. 4(1)(a) of the *Election Provisions (Parliament) Act*. He claimed that the Respondent was present at a large feast organized by the *Falekaupule* and endorsed by the chiefs and elders. The court found that the actions of the traditional leaders were consistent with the customs and traditions of Tuvalu. In making the decisions as they did, the elders were not acting on behalf of the Respondent and it would be very difficult to establish chiefs and elders as acting in a subservient role as agents. In his judgment, Chief Justice Donne observed:

> The authority of [traditional leaders] is founded in the values and culture of Tuvalu. It is the linchpin of the life and laws of Tuvalu protected by the Constitution. The authority of [traditional leaders] requires them to make decisions to guide the people and foster their welfare. This means that . . . in Tuvalu the [traditional leaders] necessarily and legitimately exert great influence and their decisions carry great weight. Their concern with politics . . . is consistent with their role as [traditional leaders] and I am satisfied that what they did was in accordance with the customs and traditions of Tuvalu.

Although the judgment was made in the context of an election petition, it can easily be extended to include a proposition that if traditional leaders and institutions discharge their governmental functions in conformity with the customs and traditions of Tuvalu, the courts may be prepared to acknowledge the validity if not the legality of such decisions (Seluka 2002).

The control of law and order in these communities appears to work best when community-driven, and chiefs are the best drivers of changes at local level. Chiefs in Vanuatu play an important role as dispensers of justice at all the village level. Informal village courts are becoming the most frequently used dispute resolution tribunal in Vanuatu. Although they have no legal powers, village courts also hand down punishments for acts of wrong doing. Chiefs also help maintain stability in times of conflict –notable examples being a 1998 riot fuelled by concerns over the management of the Vanuatu National Provident Fund, and reconciliation ceremonies in 2003 following disagreements over the appointment of the Police Commissioner.

Additionally, local chiefs in Vanuatu are responsible for identifying areas for tourism, industrial development, native reserve, and residential development, and some are also involved in sustainable development initiatives, such as the Efate Land management Area Initiative, a project initiative by the Island's chiefs to conserve land and resources.

In Kiribati, traditionally, the northern islands of Makin-Abemama, Marekei, Abaiang, Tarawa and Maiana including Abemama and its two satellite islands (Kuria and Aranuka) had their respective chieftaincy that were responsible for all matters that affected or might affect the community. The southern islands were traditionally governed by the village elders – representatives of each *kainga* – through the *maneaba* government, a system of gerontocracy rule where the unimane or village elders who were representatives of each kainga, governed and managed the affairs of the community. The maneaba government system had long been greatly changed and weakened with the incursion of the missionaries and the colonial government in the 19th century. Indeed, Macdonald asserts that by 1892, the traditional forms of social and political organization in Kiribati had been significantly modified as a direct result of a number of external forces, notably the missionaries, traders and commercial activities and finally the establishment of the colonial government.

The present local government system which was first introduced in 1894 was the first attempt to rationalize and harmonize traditional systems of governance – the *maneaba* system of government and the chieftaincy with western models of governance. The formalization of local government systems in the respective islands was effected through the enactment of the Native Laws of the Gilbert and Ellice Islands Colony published in 1894. On the islands from Butaritari-Makin to Abemama the King or High Chief was made responsible for the good order of the island. For the central and southern islands of Nonouti, Tabiteuea, Nikunau, Beru, Tamana and Arorae, the *maneaba* governments were given recognition with councils being placed in charge. Native magistrates were also appointed and were given the sole responsibility of adjudicating on criminal and civil cases.

Conclusion

As might be expected, two different systems of governance – the formal and legislation-based, and the traditional – did not and do not sit well together, and tensions and disputes can result from their different philosophical underpinnings. This can vary both between, and within, the different island societies of Oceania. Whereas the western concept of governance emphasizes individualism, the rule of law, and parliamentary democracy, traditional governance systems emphasize principles of egalitarianism and a form of socialism (the collective good). The relationship between traditional authority and local government is still beset by tensions. Island communities have not taken full ownership of local government systems and continue to rely in part on their customs and traditions – some elements of which are accepted by respective governments. While this delivers a strong sense of culture and identity, it has not produced equal opportunities and benefits for all, particularly in the case of women, young people, and, in ranked societies, the majority, who of are of *common* rather than *chiefly* descent.

Notes

1 *Principles on Good Practice for Local Democracy and Good Governance* adopted at the Commonwealth Local Government Conference held in Aberdeen, Scotland, in March 2005
2 The English rendition of the word 'falekaupule' is 'house or council of leaders or elders'.

References

Anon. (2014) Nguna Council of Chiefs Launching Constitution. *Vanuatu Daily Post* (28 November): 1.
Appana, Subhash. (2005) *Traditional Leadership at the Crossroads: The Fijian Chiefly System.* MPA working paper 00-0012. Suva, Fiji: Department of Management and Public Administration, University of the South Pacific.
Boege, Volker. (2006) *Bougainville and the Discovery of Slowness: An Unhurried Approach to State-Building in the Pacific.* Occasional Paper 3. Brisbane: Australian Centre for Peace and Conflict Studies (ACPACS).
Bolton, Lissant. (1998) Chief Willie Bongmatur Maldo and the Role of Chiefs in Vanuatu. *Journal of Pacific History* 33(2): 179–195.
Brady, Ivan. (1974) Land Tenure in the Ellice Islands: A Changing Profile. In Henry P. Lundasgaarde (ed.), *Land Tenure in Oceania,* . Asao Monograph. Honolulu, HI: University Press of Hawaii.
Commonwealth Secretariat. (2005) *Local Democracy and Good Governance in the Pacific: Report of the Regional Symposium Held in Suva, Fiji Islands, December 2004.* London: Commonwealth Secretariat.
Haglelgam, John R. (Undated) Governance in Micronesia: Roles and Influence of Traditional Chiefs.
Huffer, Elise, and Asofou So'o. (2005) Beyond Governance in Sämoa: Understanding Samoan Political Thought. *The Contemporary Pacific* 17(2): 311–333.
Larmour, Peter. (2005) *Foreign Flowers: Institutional Transfer and Good Governance in the Pacific Islands.* Honolulu, HI: University of Hawai'i Press.
Larmour, Peter, and Manuhuia Barcham. (2005) *National Integrity Systems in Small Pacific Island States.* Policy and Governance 05-9. Asia Pacific School of Economics and Government.
Lawson, Stephanie. (1990) The Myth of Cultural Homogeneity and Its Implications for Chiefly Power and Politics in Fiji. *Comparative Studies in Society and History* 32(4) (October): 795–821.
Lini, Lora. (2008) Chief Calls for Independence of Malvatumauri. *Vanuatu Daily Post* (1 November).

Macpherson, Cluny. (1997) The Persistence of Chiefly Authority in Western Samoa. In Geoffrey M. White and Lamont Lindstrom (eds), *Chiefs Today: Traditional Pacific Leadership and the Postcolonial State*, 19–48. Stanford, CA: Stanford University Press.

Madraiwiwi, Joni. (2005) Traditional Leadership and Democracy: Government and Opposition – Roles, Rights and Responsibilities. A workshop organized by the Commonwealth Secretariat and Commonwealth Parliamentary Association, Pacific Islands Forum and Pacific Islands Association of Non-Governmental Organizations, Nadi, 29–31 August.

Maude, Harry E. (1977) *The Evolution of the Gilbertese Boti*. Suva: Institute of Pacific Studies and Gilbert Islands Extension Center, University of the South Pacific.

Meleisea, Malama. (1987) *The Making of Modern Samoa: Traditional Authority and Colonial Administration in the Modern History of Western Samoa*. Suva: Institute of the Pacific Studies of the University of the South Pacific.

Nanau, Gordon Leua. (2002) Uniting the Fragments: Solomon Islands Constitutional Reforms. *Development Bulletin* (December): 17–20.

Sahlins, M. D. (1963) Poor Man, Rich Man, Big Man, Chief: Political Types in Melanesia and Polynesia. *Comparative Studies in Society and History* 5: 3.

Seluka, Albert. (2002) *The Evolution of Traditional Governance in Tuvalu*. Suva: University of the South Pacific.

University of Technology Sydney in association with the Commonwealth Secretariat and Commonwealth Local Government Forum. (2007) *Principles for Effective Local Government Legislation in the Pacific*. Background Paper, Regional Workshop, Suva, 15 November.

White, Geoffrey M. (1992) The Discourse of Chiefs: Notes on a Melanesian Society. *The Contemporary Pacific* 4(1): 73–108.

5

THE ROLE OF THE COUNCILLOR

Neil McGarvey and Fraser Stewart

Introduction

Local councillors play an integral role in the democratic process. Other than nationally elected members of parliament, councils remain in many states the only collective body subject to universal, democratic elections, and exist as a voter's most immediate link to governing power. Functions carried out by councillors, and the role they play within communities and local government, are thus essential to strong, localised democracy, despite claims that councillors are 'amateurish' or local politics incidental to an ever-globalising world (see John 2004; Stone 2005; Trounstine 2009). Indeed, such criticisms habitually ignore the intertwined elements of local, national and international decision-making (Swyngedouw 1997; Sellers 2002; Stoker 2011), and in turn the crucial role councillors play in ensuring citizens and local interests remain represented therein. Without councillors, democracy overall would find itself drastically weakened, and the gulf between citizen and power widened. Local councillors thus provide a first port of call for citizens to have a say in the running of their towns, cities and communities where their voice would be lessened if national legislatures were the only forum of representation.

With the fundamental function local councillors serve, understanding the various roles of the councillor is perhaps more important than ever. How they represent citizens and local interests, how they formulate and scrutinise policy, the work they conduct in their localities and councils, the institutional factors which impact their authority and how other political forces shape and influence their behaviour can all be considered now to be pressing questions for social scientists and politicians alike. Yet research into local councillors remains minimal, with little outside of role perceptions (de Groot et al. 2010; Karlsson 2012; Verhelst et al. 2013a), councillor and ward demographic studies (Improvement and Development Agency 2010; Thrasher et al. 2014; Kerley and McGarvey 2017) and local government reform critiques to build from. We therefore aim here to provide a broad overview of the role and work of local councillors, and some of the political, individual and institutional determinants thereof.

This chapter has five sections. with the first covers the basic roles a councillor must fulfil, focussing primarily on responsibilities of representation and scrutiny, and discuss briefly the professionalisation of the position in recent decades. Second, the specific councillor duties in public, in office and in the party. Building from the first two sections, section three will then delve into the factors which impact councillor workloads, such as electorate-councillor ratio, individual autonomy and political context. Section four will examine the higher institutional and political forces which shape councillor roles and responsibilities, and the authority and influence ultimately wielded thereby. Finally, we review some recommendations for study and the future of the field overall.

The fundamental role of the councillor

Over time and across space, what it means to be a 'local councillor' can vary substantially. Councillors' authority, how they campaign, how they perceive themselves, the ways in which they fulfil certain responsibilities, the influence they have, the amount of time dedicated to council work and how they are incentivised can all be quite different. Institutional format, ward profile, individual traits and political context can all affect the work, authority and autonomy of councillors, shaping the nature of the job in many different ways. Despite these many variances, however, the fundamental ethos of the position remains the same: to represent citizens and their interests in local government.

Councillors are the elected voice of their constituents, wards, and communities, and are above all else responsible for the advocacy for their interests in the local governance process. This responsibility involves not just relaying citizen concerns into the policy cycle, but ensuring the processes by which citizens are represented and power wielded is fair and inclusive. There are hence two fundamentally democratic principles, under which most councillor work can be categorised, that councillors can be expected to uphold: *representation*, and *scrutiny* (Snape and Dodds 2003; de Groot et al. 2010; Karlsson 2012; Heinelt 2013b; Copus 2017). These principles are the ends to which all councillors work. In representation, councillors are responsible for the communication of constituent concerns, serving as a conduit between localities and local government. In scrutiny, councillors are tasked with holding the local executive to account, ensuring the oversight of council conduct, and scrutinising the passing of policy.

Representation

Representation (sometimes referred to as *responsiveness*), is a dynamic concept. Other than parliamentarians, councillors are in many instances the only representatives subject to independent, universal elections. This gives them the democratic legitimacy to act as advocates and leaders within the localities they represent. As a basic responsibility, representation involves the relaying of local interests and concerns to the council, so that these concerns may be reflected in policy and action. How councillors go about representing is changeable, however, based on factors such as a councillors' political orientation (Heinelt 2013a: 649) and whether they see themselves as *trustees* or *delegates*.

In an age-old political debate (see Eulau et al. 1959; McCrone and Kuklinski 1979; Mitchell 1997; Mansbridge 2011), *trustees* consider their primary role to be in the direct representation of their constituents' interests via consultation and citizen interaction, while *delegates* see themselves more as appointed decision-makers on their constituents' behalf. Trustees will typically spend more time consulting with citizens over their concerns and opinions regarding policy and local interests, while delegates will more often use their status as elected leaders to take decisions in line with what they believe is the best course of action. It is estimated that 57% of councillors across Europe consider themselves to be trustees, with the number rising to as high as 77% in Switzerland (Karlsson 2013a: 97). Evidently, most councillors view their democratic mandate as a duty to reflect the interests and concerns of their constituents in the political process, rather than a warrant to act as executive decision-maker therefor. In a cross-national European study of councillors, Heinelt (2013b) notes that those orientated towards the right are more likely to adhere to the liberal democratic model of democracy and be comfortable with the trustee model of representation.

A third way in which councillors perceive their representative role is that of *party soldier*, whereby councillors are not strictly acting as trustees or delegates, but rather place the will and interests of their respective political party as paramount. Verhelst et al. (2013b), in a comparative study of European councillors, note the importance of parties in terms of providing initial motive for seeking election and providing support in doing so. Party soldiers tend to place emphasis on their party duties. In Europe they tend to be more orientated towards the left ideologically (Egner et al. 2013: 262). However, party soldiers tend to be significantly fewer than trustees or delegates overall, although it is worth considering that most councillors today are members of a political party and so their 'party soldier' duties may still be prevalent, even if they are not primary.

Scrutiny

Scrutiny then (sometimes referred to as *accountability*), can be understood broadly as the councillor's responsibility to scrutinise policy design, critically oversee the implementation and delivery of services, and to hold the council and executive to account (Snape and Dodds 2003: 49). Like representation, this responsibility varies dependent on a number of factors, which we can neatly categorise as *formal* and *informal*. Formal factors generally pertain to local councillor responsibilities as outlined in local government acts (LGAs) and other council-specific legislation. LGAs tend to define the scrutiny responsibilities of councillors quite explicitly (see House of Commons 2013; Queensland Government 2016). These can be useful guides in explaining councillor roles and authority, outlining their duties of scrutiny and the jurisdiction thereof, and in settling intra-council disputes.

These formal responsibilities are often somewhat open-ended, however, and can in some cases be undermined by informal factors such as a councillor's position in or outside of the executive, seniority within the council, and relationships with other council members (Karlsson 2013a, 2013b). Research has shown that councillors can often find their *de jure* influence compromised in favour of the popular political clout of directly elected local mayors, for instance, as has been the case notably in recent years in Italy, Germany and Poland (Denters and Rose 2005; de Groot et al. 2010). Whether a councillor belongs to the party of the executive can also impact how effective they are in the policy cycle, and in overseeing the conduct of the executive and council as a whole. Councillors who are members of the executive can expect to have a greater input in the policy cycle than those who are not. Consequently however, they will also find themselves subject of greater behavioural and political scrutiny at the hands of non-executive members, whose sometimes-diminished role in the policy cycle is typically offset against heightened responsibility oversight of the executive and wider council conduct (as well as general opposition roles, such as public debate).

Professionalisation

One further consistency of the job of local councillor across examples, and indeed time, is the general trend toward professionalisation. How councillors go about upholding aforementioned principles and how seriously they do so has shifted considerably in recent decades. In virtually all states, being a councillor was once treated as a mostly voluntary vocation, with minimal attendance allowances paid to compensate councillors for their time commitment and very little formal training involved. Councillor responsibilities now, however, are typically outlined in LGAs, with formal training a necessity of the position in most countries and more generous remuneration provided. The time-series data on councillor working hours tend to suggest that over the decades councillors have committed to ever increasing hours (see, for example, Kerley and McGarvey 2017). Although the amount of time dedicated to the role varies widely across examples – Scottish councillors work on average 35 hours per week, English 23 hours (Improvement and Development Agency 2010) compared with 87% of those in Belgium who work on average 30–60 hours per month, for instance (Verhelst et al. 2013b: 284) – the increasingly professional nature of the role is fairly constant.

Councillor activities

The increasingly professionalised responsibilities of a local councillor can thus vary based on myriad factors, including formal and informal differences, and whether a councillor views herself as a trustee, delegate, or party soldier. We know also that a councillor's responsibilities to democracy involve the pursuit of two key principles: representation of constituents in the political process, and scrutiny of the policy cycle and indeed council conduct. But what is it that councillors actually *do*? Knowing that councillors have common base principles to uphold, what activities and roles do councillors undertake in doing so? Once more, these can vary across examples, although many basic elements of councillor work remain the same. We can thus classify councillor activities neatly under three broad headings: the councillor in public, the councillor in office, and the councillor in the party.

In public

As outlined in the previous section, councillors have traditionally acted as the voice of their constituents in the local governance process, fulfilling first and foremost the role of local representative for respective wards and communities. They are typically better educated than the generality of the population, and act as a conduit representing citizens to a large council bureaucracy. They are the link mechanism between communities and the council, and exist predominantly as the channel through which individual constituents can have some voice in council decision-making. Regardless of whether a councillor considers herself a trustee or delegate, most agree that this most elementary duty to represent constituents is of utmost importance (de Groot et al. 2010; Heinelt 2013a).

Representing constituents naturally requires communicating with constituents, which can take various forms. In the United Kingdom and Ireland, this has taken place historically in *surgeries*, with councillors in most countries employing some version thereof. Surgeries have over time been among the most visible aspects of councillors fulfilling their local representative role, and provide regular opportunity for constituents to meet with their councillor and raise complaints in person. However, there has been a long-term decline in surgery attendance by residents and consequently in surgery provision. Evidence from recent research suggests that even those councillors who still use surgeries find them a less meaningful and useful form of interaction with constituents than perhaps they were years ago (see Wilson and Game 2011; Kerley and McGarvey 2017), and observe that they are being utilised by a declining, ageing segment of their constituents. Surgeries now are thus as much a tool for public visibility as for raising concerns, allowing councillors to demonstrate their local presence, often without actually having to face a member of the public.

Increasingly then, new information and communication technology is superseding face-to-face and other traditional forms of public interaction. Concerns are distinctly more likely to be raised via digital channels than in person, while many councillors are taking to social and new media to relay information back to the public. Outside of the United Kingdom, there have been broad initiatives to capitalise on this technological shift. Local councils in the likes of Sweden and the Netherlands, for example, made a point of pushing digital as a new and versatile means of councillor–constituent communication (Karlsson 2012, 2013a). Even in countries where there no such initiatives have taken place, the transition away from 'old school' forms of councillor–constituent communication toward more modern means has occurred somewhat naturally in line with social and technological shifts.

E-mail is now very much the dominant form of communication, both to and from councillors in most cases. Different social media are still somewhat less consistently employed by councillors, although the utilisation of blogs and online documentation of councillor time is becoming more prevalent. Those who use social media tend to view it as a tool to alert constituents to newsletters, invite them to events and make occasional political comments. Undoubtedly then, the diffusion of easy-to-use channels of communication has reshaped the interaction between councillor and constituent. In the past writing and posting a letter tend to demand time for reflection and thought. Today constituents can send petitions, e-mails and campaigning material instantaneously. They often expect a similarly speedy response.

Beyond communicating with constituents over specific concerns, councillors undertake a variety of public activities. These may include participating in local hustings, attending community events and gatherings, mediating local political discussion and visiting local businesses (see Klok and Denters 2013 for a comparative review of the perceptions and actuality of councillor behaviour). This affords citizens further opportunity to interact with their councillors and raise local concerns, and in turn allowing councillors the chance to keep their finger on the local pulse. As with surgeries, however, many of these activities can serve as exercises in public visibility rather than integral council work, employed to bolster political popularity and future electoral prospects. Hustings will typically only take place today during election campaigns, while the heightened prominence of social media and instant reporting have made photo opportunities of councillors interacting with the public at local events all the more valuable.

In the council

The role of the councillor in public and the role of the councillor within the council are very porous and interrelated. In office, councillors must continue to represent constituents and relay their concerns to council meetings. Day-to-day council organisation may include ward casework based on constituent interaction, which in turn can become a topic for discussion in a committee or debate, for example. Likewise, the oversight and scrutiny of policy will generally be conducted in the interest of the councillor's constituency. When we talk of councillor activities in the council, then, we refer to the formal duties carried out by councillors within specifically within local councils and on council business in the furthering of constituent interests, which we can understand as *internal governance*.

Internal governance is a somewhat catch-all term referring to the activities that all councillors get involved in regarding the organisation of their council. It is any activity that involves debating, administration, formulating policy, approving and overseeing council business, or holding the executive to account. Bernard (2010), for example, talks of Czech councillors in small municipalities as 'politicians, development workers and informal leaders'. Forms of this duty can range widely, from basic casework such as e-mailing constituents and local partners, to acting as council or committee leader. Other activities may include acting as a portfolio holder, serving on a committee or taking part in debates in council meetings. In the most basic sense then, internal activity refers to those duties undertaken by councillors on a day-to-day basis within the council.

Different aspects of internal governance can take precedence over others. Of the key internal governance activities conducted by councillors, *policymaking* naturally stands as significant. Councillors in the vast majority of cases will perform at least some role in the policy cycle. As a base responsibility, councillors generally find themselves attached to one or a few committees relative to specific policy areas. Within these committees, councillors collaborate, debate, scrutinise and formulate policy. This is a continuous cycle, with scrutiny and oversight present at virtually every stage: from conception, to implementation, to service delivery. Councillors are thus not only responsible for designing and passing policy, but for ensuring its effective implementation.

The position of different councillors within the policy cycle can vary. Within local authorities as outlined in the previous section, the influence enjoyed by local councillors over policy can fluctuate dependent on factors such as whether the councillor is a member of the executive or governing party/coalition, how long the councillor has been a member of the council for, and so forth. Yet these factors do not dictate councillor authority in the policy cycle exclusively. To presume so would be to presume that influence over policy and council business is one-dimensional and restricted to directive capacity, which it evidently is not. For example, dissatisfied constituents will approach their local councillor, regardless of their status as an executive or non-executive member, should complaints arise regarding a policy or its delivery. Following directly from duties of representation, all councillors thus have a fundamental role to play in relaying public feedback into the scrutiny and policy process.

More crucially, however, all councillors have a responsibility to provide scrutiny and oversight of the executive and council conduct, which presents another important element of internal governance. Over time, *oversight of the executive* and local government activity has become a councillor duty of markedly greater prominence (de Groot et al. 2010; Wollman 2012). While members of the executive, members of the governing party/coalition, or generally more senior members may boast greater directive influence – that is, influence to set agendas and with more obvious control over policy design – other members maintain substantial responsibility not just in policymaking, but in the scrutiny of conduct and performance of the executive and indeed the council overall. This can be achieved via oversight committees, inquiries and reviews, which are conducted typically by non-executive members. In this role, non-executive members have the authority to hold executive members to account, and to subsequently ensure the effective, efficient, transparent and representative execution of council business.

In the party

Beyond these two primary sets of roles, local councillors undertake various external activities. One of these which can be of significant important is that of party member. While independent candidate numbers remain high compared with national government, most local councils are dominated by one or a coalition of parties. Candidates often stand on party platforms, with party preferences influencing their behaviour once elected. In Spain, 88.2% of members cited that implementing their party programme was of great or upmost importance (Navarro and Sweeting 2013). In Denmark, it was found that party membership was the strongest indicator of a councillor's spending preferences (Serritzlew 2003: 327). Many councillors thus clearly have some interest in advancing party policy at the local level, and partaking in party activity, which may involve things like constituency party meetings, canvassing, attending party conference and the like.

It is worth considering briefly at this point what local party groups are, and what they mean to local democracy. Beyond spending and executive policy decisions, local party groups have a substantial role to play. Colin Copus flatteringly cites these groups as being the 'critical determinants of the vibrancy and health of local democracy' (Copus 2004: 57), despite there still being such a high number of independent local councillors. As with party politics at large, however, parties solve a collective action problem and allow groups of like-minded candidates to form coalitions and govern effectively. Parties increase the predictability and transparency of policy outcomes, and simplify choices for voters and help to aggregate political interests (Dalton and Wattenberg 2000; White 2006; Kölln 2014). They also act as a structure through which councillors are recruited and trained, a proxy where citizens can observe debate (the '*theatre of representation*' as Copus describes it), and provide informational cues to help constituents understand political positions. It is indeed difficult to imagine a functioning democratic polity without them.

With these fundamental tasks as with national politics, then, parties are by now institutionally ingrained in local government, with considerable implications for affiliated councillors. To the local councillor, being a member of a party means working with party colleagues in the pursuit of common goals, which requires a large degree of coordination with the local party group. Involvement with a political party can thus have significant bearing on the amount of time a councillor dedicates to their role, and the way in which that role is fulfilled. In Germany, Egner (2015: 184) found that party activity took up a substantial amount of councillor time; so much so that councillors who were also members of a party registered higher overall working hours than independent candidates. Party infrastructure can also be an invaluable asset to councillors in communicating with constituents, financing and campaigning, while strong party cohesion can help to advance party and indeed constituency interests.

External to the council

Ask a random member of the public what councillors do outside of council hours and they might conjure up an image of one cutting the ribbon on a new community centre, or switching on Christmas lights in the town centre. Out-with party and internal council activities, however, councillors are being asked to fulfil various other important roles, namely representing the council in bodies that involve other organisations in the public, commercial and voluntary sectors. Councillors have a part to play in public and private bodies in areas such as health, planning, community safety, transport and social care. Where councils have privatised services, engaged in inter-municipal co-operation, involved contractors in service provision, or established independent bodies for the purpose of oversight and scrutiny, councillors will often be tasked with liaising with and participating in boards and meetings. Recent local government literature has tended to emphasise that such activities are becoming a more pronounced part of council activity (see Stoker and Wilson 2004; Wilson and Game 2011; McGarvey 2012; Painter 2012). In such arrangements local councillors are merely one actor among many (Plüss and Kübler 2013: 203), albeit often one of few with democratic legitimacy credentials.

These additional duties can also involve procurement and investment activity, such as meeting with developers and planning committees and securing contracts for the council area. We might define these as local economic activities. Managing the local political economy, especially in countries whereby local authorities are responsible for the raising of their own revenue as in France, or where funding has tightened over time as in the UK, can be an important councillor role, with effects ranging well beyond the local setting alone. Local initiatives are markedly crucial links in a much longer chain, with observable effects of local economic activity ranging from community regeneration to national employment and welfare performance to international investment (Cox 1995; Swyngedouw 1997; Wood 1998; Sellers 2002). Economic stimulation is by no means inextricably confined to national or international forums, and nor are local communities necessarily guaranteed to be fully served by generalised national economic policy. As such, councillors play an important role in managing the local economy, which can in turn have much more expansive effect.

Councillor workload

Knowing now the various duties and responsibilities councillors are expected to conduct, and the similarities in these duties evident across examples, it may intuitively seem like councillors everywhere fulfil similar roles that might take up similar amounts of time and effort. Across the literature the trend of professionalisation has been noted, while the base responsibilities over time have remained the same. Indeed, most councillors go about their duties via analogous means and so instinctively this makes sense. As flexible as the role itself, however, councillor workloads can vary substantially for a number of reasons, across examples and indeed within councils themselves. This remains a surprisingly under-researched area: while there have been studies documenting the evolution of councillor roles, few have dissected the underlying factors influencing workload pressure in any great depth.

Within the limited research that exists, some interesting hypotheses have been made. Studies have attempted to show that factors such as deprivation, councillor–electorate ward ratio, party affiliation and time served on the council can all influence councillor workloads to some degree. These relationships are often relatively weak, however, or too heavily caveated to prove generalisable. Ward deprivation, for example, is somewhat shaky in that boundaries change and many wards can have high workloads with relative affluence. There is also the issue that those suffering in deprivation tend to also be politically subdued. Accepting that councillor workloads are at least in part influenced by constituent communication, this hypothesis becomes questionable.

Ward size and ratio

Of the cited determinants of councillor workload, *ward population* and *councillor–electorate ratio* are perhaps the most common. These factors, it is thought, influence councillor workload in that the more people a councillor ultimately represents, the more work they will have to do. This is of course an entirely reasonable hypothesis to make, with research such as that conducted by Rao (1994) seeming to provide support therefor. More recent studies, however, have brought the strength of this relationship into question. Kerley and McGarvey (2017) for example, in their study of councillor workloads in Scotland, find no statistically significant relationship between councillor workload and ward population or councillor–electorate ratio. Rather, it is found that councillor workload can vary within just as much as between Scottish councils (ibid.: 48), exposing a fairly serious methodological issue hidden with the use of average councillor time as a comparative measure; that is, where averages are employed, they can inadvertently mask internal ward and individual councillor differences.

Broad-brush comparisons of average councillor workloads should thus be viewed with some vigilance, although that is not to say that they are always uninformative. Numbers of councillors serving the same population can vary markedly – for example Boston, USA and Glasgow, UK have roughly the same populations (670,000 and 620,000 respectively), Glasgow has 85 councillors, Boston has 13. In US council jurisdictions small numbers of aldermen/councillors in councils are common. Even accounting for the undoubted substantial differences in political culture, council statute and constitutions, representative–executive relationship such a stark difference in number has an inevitable consequence in terms of how councillors in each city see their role.

When we take into account average councillor working hours in the United Kingdom compared with other local councils across Europe, for example, these ratios are quite obviously of some note. The average councillor–electorate ratio in the United Kingdom is approximately 1:2860, while the average hours worked range from 25 in England to 35 in Scotland per week. Contrast this with the average 1:400 ratio in Germany to 30–60 hours per month, or even the 1:800 in Belgium (Wilson and Game 2011: 275) and electorate-councillor ratio appears to be very much an open-and-shut case. But what of the differences between individual councillors, which show no real consistency with macro considerations? We can hence explain the difference in average workload between the anomalous United Kingdom and the rest of Europe in this regard, but we cannot explain differences between UK wards, nor wards in other countries, or differences overall at the individual councillor level.

The same is true when we consider councillor workloads longitudinally. Time-series data on councillor working hours, particularly through the more extensive English studies (see Rao 1994; Purdam et al. 2008), suggests that councillors have committed to increasing hours over time. This has ranged from 52 hours per month in the 1960s to as high as 92 hours per month by the 2000s (Redcliffe-Maud 1969; Robinson 1977; Widdicombe 1986; Improvement and Development Agency 2010). From this we can surmise that councillors overall are expected to commit to bigger workloads today than in the past, but again this presents a very approximate reading of a far more nuanced reality. Again, despite steadily increasing averages, workloads still vary dramatically within councils, across wards and across countries (see Wilson and Game 2011; Karlsson 2012; Verhelst et al. 2013a, 2013b; Egner 2015). Country and ward averages are thus helpful in showing some macro trends, but can often conceal important information regarding internal ward and individual variance.

Self-determination, partisanship and politics

So – how do we get to the root of these individual differences? For this, the most reliable and consistent observation may simply be that 'councillors themselves decide how much energy they put into the representation of their electorate' (Wilson and Game 2011: 274); that is, despite party and council pressures and varying ward profiles, councillors retain a high degree of discretion and agency over their own working hours, both in absolute terms and in focus i.e. which matters they wish to prioritise and the roles they wish to ultimately play (see Glasgow City Council/MORI 2004). This is an important point to emphasise. If councillors have the autonomy and capacity to self-determine their working hours, then institutional pressures such as the size of ward population, its sparsity, deprivation level and other demographic factors will have muted impact on hours worked. With that, personalised factors become distinctly more pressing. Political persuasion or personal belief may very well be more indicative of how much work someone conducts in their ward to combat deprivation, rather than the scale and existence of deprivation itself, for example. The predominance of males in council chambers across the globe becomes very relevant when one considers the differences in importance of policy areas between genders. Women councillors across Europe consistently place social, environmental and (unsurprisingly) equal representation issues above men (Egner et al. 2013: 261).

In this more autonomous vein, other political factors can also have a strong impact on the nature and amount of work councillors choose to do (Thrasher et al. 2012: 1). From the previous section, we know that councillors tied to a party tend to have increased working hours overall than independent members. This is because they have extra party responsibilities to attend to, such as running the local party group, communicating and meeting with party colleagues, and campaigning in party colleague constituencies. But politics does not occur in a party vacuum. Extending this aspect further then, other political factors such as the level of electoral competition in a ward may also influence councillor workloads. Councillors in safe wards, under less immediate electoral pressure, may be less prone to generate higher workloads by responding to contact from citizens or enthusiastically seeking out potential sources of constituent grievance. On the other hand, councillors in highly contested and marginal seats may be inclined to increase their workload, particularly in the public eye, to demonstrate their dedication to constituents and bolster their re-election prospects.

Institutions, multi-level governance and parties

We know now, then, that councillors have reasonable autonomy to determine the amount of work they do, and the ways in which that work is conducted. Yet there are other substantial, external factors which influence the role of the councillor on a more fundamental level; namely, the wider political and institutional contexts in which councillors operate. How a state chooses to organise its democratic and institutional structures can cause significant variance in the autonomy afforded to councillors, the funding they are likely to enjoy, the jurisdictional remit of their position and the formal power held in local councils to affect change. With this, the position of a councillor can differ markedly across examples. The 'millefeuille' multi-level system in France is bound to have serious implications for local councillor duties and remit compared with, say, the very direct central–local relationship in England or Scotland for instance. Thus, where councillors can determine their own workload to a large extent, they cannot dictate their relative position within a state's institutional framework.

Unitary v. federal institutions

Of institutional factors likely to shape the role of the councillor, decentralisation is instinctively most obvious. The extent to which a state is *unitary* or *federal* can have considerable bearing on local powers, authority and responsibilities (Crepaz 1996; Lijphart 1999; McGann 2006; McGann and Latner 2013). Ranging from highly federalised systems as in Germany and the United States, convoluted multi-tier systems as in France and Switzerland, to more direct relationships as in England, the authority granted to local councils, the devolved powers they wield and the funding mechanisms the employ will all have stark impact on how councillors operate, the amount of work they undertake, the official responsibilities they fulfil, and the vitality thereof to the national political context (see Sharpe 1970; Crook 2003).

A cursory glance across cases illustrates this variance well, although perhaps not immediately in line with what we might expect. For instance, under the French system of governance, typified by its numerous layers (national, regional, sub-regional, inter-communal and communal), it would be reasonable to assume that the role of councillors at the smallest commune level would be minimal and jurisdictionally unclear. Compare this with the local government system in England, typified by a direct central–local government relationship and control over larger numbers of citizens, and we could justifiably presume that councillors in England would boast more robustly defined and indeed expansive authority. This is evidently not the case. Where French councillors perhaps have a somewhat smaller remit, the autonomy they have over that remit is arguably stronger than in England. French councillors have almost full control over their raising, spending and policy priorities, protected clearly in legislation, while those in England find themselves heavily dependent on decisions taken at Westminster (Stoker 1997; Rhodes 1997). Councillors in unitary systems, it would seem, tend to be of greater subservience to the centre overall.

One explanation for this may be that, under complex federal systems, councils and councillors are protected from tyranny of national government. National government in these cases has less direct access and input into the affairs of the local council. Local government in Belgium, for example, is intricate and often adversarial – so much so that policy gridlock can become common, with local councils in many instances stifling central government programmes (Happaerts et al. 2012; Happaerts 2015). Germany presents a similar case, in that strongly protected federal rights of *Länder* councils, often referred to as the *principle of subsidiarity* whereby it is held that decisions should be taken at the lowest possible and practical level, can cause fairly staunch embattlement over jurisdiction, responsibility and policy implementation (Kraemer and Schreurs 2007: 7).

We might view this capacity to resist national government as testament to the strong legal respect for local authority and the democratic legitimacy of the local councillor in such systems. Compare this with a unitary state such as England or Finland and we see stark differences. In these mostly unitary systems, a vast majority of power is retained at the centre (Kettunen 2007: 43), with national government reserving the capacity to redefine local council authority and restrict funding should local councils refuse to play ball. In Italy, the constitution allows the national government to pre-empt local councils where they are seen to be failing to perform or meet obligations (Vesperini 2009: 9). Here, gridlock is palpably less common, since central government can adapt the rules of the game to suit their own agenda with relative impunity. Strong federalism can thus provide a safeguard for councillors and their authority from central government, ultimately lending more gravitas to the position itself.

Yet federalism is not always so positive, particularly in cases where political and judicial oversight is found to be lacking. Until now this chapter has been largely concerned with examples from Western systems, reflecting what is often a lack of scope in the literature itself. Venturing further afield, however, the experience of local government and the position of the local councillor in places such as India and across sub-Saharan Africa can be quite different (Crook 2003; Singh 2004; Cali and Sen 2011). Often in these areas there exists a local political culture of clientelism, where patronage and emphasis on social order is more evident.

In some states, convoluted multi-tier governance provides a perfect arena for corruption, patronage, and exploitation. Often this is down to weak scrutiny capacity and political institutions overall allowing unsavoury activity to fester and blossom (North 1990; Acemoglu and Robinson 2012). Councillors can become compromised (or *captured*, to borrow a term from public administration) by corrupt interests. Often they are already members of these interest networks prior to election. They thus cease to fit the traditional representative roles of trustee, delegate or party soldier, instead serving as what we might consider a purveyor of interests for dominant economic, social, and political classes, protected from repercussion by weak institutions and deep-rooted political culture.

Party executives and national government

Multi-level governance is not the only extra-local force with bearing on councillor roles. Party political matters can also be of some significance. We know from previous sections that being a member of a party can increase councillor workload and influence how a councillor behaves in government, while being a party soldier can lead to them being almost entirely subservient to a party machine – yet we have so far only covered the party locally, with little consideration for the party as a national entity controlled by a central executive. At this level, parties shape councillor roles in other ways. Party constitutions, operating practices and culture tend to be designed to induce discipline among elected representatives, councillors included. Being a member of a party, particularly mass parties wherein decision-making is highly centralised (Kirchheimer 1966), will thus have distinct bearing on the autonomy a councillor has not just over policy matters and voting preferences, but over the duties they are expected to fulfil. Party leadership may identify executive and committee roles for councillors, or seek move their voting behaviour and debate contributions in line with their own national priorities. Furthermore, they may encourage councillors to spend more time on activities such as local canvassing and campaigning.

Another, less direct party-related factor which may impact councillor roles and workload is which party or coalition holds power in national government. In the United Kingdom during the 1980s, for instance, Margaret Thatcher's Conservative government was very much in the business of privatising and reducing the responsibility of local councils (see Bulpitt 1986; Buller 1999). With such support for privatisation, typical of conservative parties and not exclusive to the United Kingdom (see for example Bel et al. 2007; Warner and Hebdon 2001), it follows logically that councillors might find themselves with reduced authority and workload. Accepting that conservative parties tend towards privatisation of services and smaller government while social democratic and socialist governments tend towards increased nationalisation and local service provision (see Hicks and Swank 1992), we could hence surmise that the role and workload of the councillor is directly impacted by which party or coalition sits in national government.

Conclusions

The role of the councillor is hence a flexible and multifarious concept. From this chapter, we know the basic responsibilities councillors hold, the roles they play, and the factors which shape the nature, intensity and authority thereof. Where councillors have various duties in the public, in the council, in the party and indeed elsewhere, matters such as formal responsibilities as outlined in LGAs, their position within the local government and the institutional context under which they operate can all impact the role and work of councillors across examples. We understand also the ways in which councillors perceive themselves, and the different drivers and incentives of councillor behaviour.

Councillors today see themselves predominantly as trustees, relaying and representing the will of their local interests and constituents. It is worth taking a moment to reflect on why this is significant. In the modern world, cynical assertions are often made regarding the diminishing role and autonomy of the councillor and local politics under the forces of economic and political globalisation. It is clear, however, that under such forces, the primary democratic roles fulfilled by local councillors provide a vital link between citizens and power, without which democracy overall would be fundamentally weakened. Under such forces – arguably even in spite of them – councillors remain the most direct link to localities and citizens, who might otherwise find themselves marginalised in favour of higher political and economic dealings. The part played by local councillors in representing local, citizen and community interests is thus integral to the political process, and fills an essential need that cannot be achieved by distant central or international governance alone. It is little exaggeration to suggest that councillors, as locally elected representatives, are one of the key building blocks on which democracy is based.

Of course, despite this increasing and fundamental importance, the role of local councillors and local politics overall, often still finds itself sidelined by academics in favour of apparently more significant research areas in field such as global governance and international relations. As such, in the existing literature, there are various questions that remain unanswered, unconvincingly answered or answered in one jurisdiction only. These questions serve as promising avenues for further cross national study. These include, but are by no means restricted to: the impact of central party and partisanship on the local councillor; the role of the councillor in the local economy; the impact of institutions (e.g. elected mayors) on councillor roles and responsibility (i.e. how different institutional structures impact councillor authority and work at local, national and international levels); councillor roles in new networks of focused on service provision; councillors and new media; and councillor workload and role studies beyond the British and European norm. There are hence myriad questions to ask and answer for scholars not just of local politics, but of political parties, democracy and institutions, political economy, globalisation, sociology and beyond. Given the heightened significance of local councillors today, this is perhaps a more important pursuit than ever.

References

Acemoglu, D. and Robinson, J. (2012) *Why Nations Fail? The Origins of Power, Prosperity and Poverty*. New York: Crown.

Bel, G., Hebdon, R. and Warner, M. (2007) Local Government Reform: Privatization and its Alternatives. *Local Government Studies* 33(4): 507–515.

Bernard, J. (2010) The Role of Councillors in Small Municipalities in the Czech Republic – Between Politicians, Development Workers and Informal Leaders. Paper prepared for the ECPR Joint Session, March, Munster.

Buller, J. (1999) A Critical Appraisal of the Statecraft Interpretation. *Public Administration* 77(4): 691–712.

Bulpitt, J. (1986) The Discipline of the New Democracy: Mrs Thatcher's Domestic Statecraft. *Political Studies* 34(1): 19–39.

Cali, M. and Sen, K. (2011) Do Effective State Business Relations Matter for Economic Growth? Evidence from Indian States. *World Development* 39(9): 1542–1557.

Copus, C. (2004) *Party Politics and Local Government*. Manchester: Manchester University Press.

Copus, C. (2017) Could Local Government Govern? Rethinking the Role of Councillors. Retrieved from http://blogs.lse.ac.uk/politicsandpolicy/rethinking-the-role-of-councillors.

Cox, K. R. (1995) Globalisation, Competition and the Politics of Local Development. *Urban Studies* 32(2): 213–224.

Crepaz, M. M. L. (1996) Consensus Versus Majoritarian Democracy: Political Institutions and their Impact on Macroeconomic Performance and Industrial Disputes. *Comparative Political Studies* 29(1): 4–26.

Crook, R. C. (2003) Decentralisation and Poverty Reduction in Africa: The Politics of Local–Central Relations. *Public Administration and Development* 23(1): 77-88.

Dalton, R. and Wattenberg, M. (2000) *Parties without Partisans: Political Change in Advanced Industrial Democracies*. New York: Oxford University Press.

De Groot, M., Denters, B. and Klok, P.-J. (2010) Strengthening the Councillor as a Representative and Scrutiniser: The Effects of Institutional Change on Councillors' Role Orientations in the Netherlands. *Local Government Studies* 36(3): 401–423.

Denters, B. and Rose, L. E. (eds) (2005) *Comparing Local Governance: Trends and Developments*. Basingstoke: Palgrave Macmillan.

Egner, B. (2015) Parliaments in Disguise? How German Councillors Perceive Local Councils. *Local Government Studies* 41(2): 183–201.

Egner, B., Sweeting, D. and Klok, P.-J. (eds) (2013) *Local Councillors in Europe*. Wiesbaden: Springer Fachmedien.

Eulau, H., Wahlke, J. C., Buchanan, W. and Ferguson, L. C. (1959) The Role of the Representative: Some Empirical Observations on the Theory of Edmund Burke. *American Political Science Review* 53(3): 742–756.

Glasgow City Council/Mori (2004) *Councillors in Glasgow: Elected Members Survey*. Glasgow: Glasgow City Council.

Happaerts, S. (2015) Climate Governance in Federal Belgium: Modest Subnational Policies in a Complex Multi-level Setting. *Journal of Integrative Environmental Sciences* 12(4): 285–301.

Happaerts, S., Schunz, S. and Bruyninckx, H. (2012) Federalism and Intergovernmental Relations: The Multi-Level Politics of Climate Change Policy in Belgium. *Journal of Contemporary European Studies* 20(4): 441–458.

Heinelt, H. (2013a) Councillors' Notions of Democracy, and their Role Perception and Behaviour in the Changing Context of Local Democracy. *Local Government Studies* 39(5): 640–660.

Heinelt, H. (2013b) Councillors and Democracy: How Do They Think and How Can Differences in Their Views Be Explained? In B. Egner, D. Sweeting and P.-J. Klok (eds), *Local Councillors in Europe*, 85–96. Wiesbaden: Springer Fachmedien.

Hicks, A. M. and Swank, D. H. (1992) Politics, Institutions and Welfare Spending in Industrialized Democracies, 1960–82. American Political Science Review 86(3): 658–674.

House of Commons (2013) Communities and Local Government Committee Councillors on the Frontline Sixth Report of Session 2012–13 HC 432. London: House of Commons.

Improvement and Development Agency (2010) *Exit Survey of Local Authority Councillors in England*. London: Improvement and Development Agency.

John, P. (2004) *Why Study Urban Politics?* In J. S. Davies and D. L. Imbroscio (eds), *Theories of Urban Politics*, 2nd edition, 17–24. London: Sage.

Karlsson, M. (2012) Participatory Initiatives and Political Representation: The Case of Local Councillors in Sweden. *Local Government Studies* 38(6): 795–815.

Karlsson, D. (2013a) Who Do the Local Councillors of Europe Represent? In B. Egner, D. Sweeting and P.-J. Klok (eds), *Local Councillors in Europe*, 97–119. Wiesbaden: Springer Fachmedien.

Karlsson, M. (2013b) The Hidden Constitutions: How Informal Political Institutions Affect the Representation Style of Local Councils. *Local Government Studies* 39(5): 681–702.

Kerley, R. and McGarvey, N. (2017) *Report: Councillors' Roles and Workload*. Edinburgh: Local Government Boundary Commission for Scotland. Retrieved from www.lgbc-scotland.gov.uk/publications.

Kettunen, P. (2007) EU and the Sub-national Government of Finland: Half-shut Windows of Opportunities. *Politicka misao* XLIV(2): 41–53.

Kirchheimer, O. (1966) The Transformation of Western European Party Systems. In J. Lapalombara and M. Weiner (eds), *Political Parties and Political Development*, 177–200. Princeton, NJ: Princeton University Press.

Klok, P.-J. and Denters, B. (2013) The Roles Councillors Play. In B. Egner, D. Sweeting and P.-J. Klok (eds), *Local Councillors in Europe*, 63–83. Wiesbaden: Springer Fachmedien.

Kölln, A. K. (2014) The Value of Political Parties to Representative Democracy. *European Political Science Review* 7(4): 593–613.

Kraemer, A. R. and Schreurs, M. A. (2007) *Federalism and Environmental Regulation in Germany and the EU*. AICGS Policy Report no. 31. Retrieved from http://ecologic.eu/2095.

Lijphart, A. (1999) *Patterns of Democracy*. New Haven, CT: Yale University Press.

Mansbridge, J. (2011) Clarifying the Concept of Representation. *American Political Science Review* 105(3): 621–630.

McCrone, D. J. and Kuklinski, J. H. (1979) The Delegate Theory of Representation. *American Journal of Political Science* 23(2): 278–300.

McGann, A. (2006) *The Logic of Democracy: Reconciling Equality, Deliberation and Minority Protection*. Ann Arbor, MI: University of Michigan Press.

McGann, A. and Latner, M. (2013) The Calculus of Consensus Democracy: Rethinking Patterns of Democracy Without Veto Players. *Comparative Political Studies* 46(7): 823–850.

McGarvey, N. (2012) Inter-Municipal Co-operation: The United Kingdom Case. Instituzioni del Federalismo 3.12. Retrieved from www.regione.emilia-romagna.it/affari_ist/Rivista_3_2012/McGarvey.pdf.

Mitchell, J. (1997) Representation in Government Boards and Commissions. *Public Administration Review* 57(2): 160–167.

Navarro, C. and Sweeting, D. (2013) Comparing local Councillors in Spain and the UK: Representation, Participation and Party Politics. Paper presented at 63rd Political Studies Association Annual Conference, Cardiff, 26 March. Retrieved from www.psa.ac.uk/sites/default/files/462_227.pdf.

North, D. C. (1990) *Institutions, Institutional Change and Economic Performance*. Cambridge: Cambridge University Press.

Painter, C. (2012) The UK Coalition Government: Constructing public service reform narratives. *Public Policy and Administration* 28(1): 3–20.

Plüss, L. and Kübler, D. (2013) Coordinating Community Governance? Local Councillors in Different Governance Network Arrangements. In B. Egner, D. Sweeting and P.-J. Klok (eds), *Local Councillors in Europe*, 203–219. Wiesbaden: Springer Fachmedien.

Purdam, K., John, P., Greasley, S. and Norman, P. (2008) *How Many Elected Representatives Does Local Government Need? A Review of the Evidence from Europe*. CCSR Working Paper 2008-06. Retrieved from https://s3.amazonaws.com/academia.edu.documents/30770278/2008-06.pdf?AWSAccessKeyId=AKIAIWOWYYGZ2Y53UL3A&Expires=1504805802&Signature=nU%2FIl4kL8bnrhnP%2FdQmL0hkL5dY%3D&response-content-disposition=inline%3B%20filename%3DHow_many_elected_representatives_does_lo.pdf.

Queensland Government (2016) Councillor Responsibilities under the Local Government Act 2009. Retrieved from www.dilgp.qld.gov.au/resources/guideline/local-government/councillor-resource-kit.pdf.

Rao, N. (1994) *The Making and Unmaking of Local Self-Government*. Aldershot: Dartmouth.

Redcliffe-Maud, J. (chair) (1969) *Royal Commission on Local Government in England*. Cmnd 4040. London: HMSO.

Rhodes, R. A. W. (1997) *Understanding Governance: Policy Networks, Governance, Reflexivity and Accountability*. Maidenhead: Open University Press.

Robinson, D. (chair) (1977) *Enquiry into the System of Remuneration of Members of Local Government*. London: HMSO.

Sellers, J. M. (2002) *Governing from Below: Urban Regions and the Global Economy*. Cambridge: Cambridge University Press.

Serritzlew, S. (2003) Shaping Local Councillor Preferences: Party Politics, Committee Structure and Social Background. *Scandinavian Political Studies* 26(4): 327–348.

Sharpe, L. J. (1970) Theories and Values of Local Government. In: *Political Studies* 18(2): 153–174.

Singh, N. (2004) Some Economic Consequences of India's Institutions of Governance: A Conceptual Framework. *India Review* 3(2): 114–146.

Snape, S. and Dodds, L. (2003) The Scrutineer: The Impact of Overview and Scrutiny on Councillor Roles. *Public Policy and Administration* 18(1): 46–62.

Stoker, G. (1997) Local Government in Britain after Thatcher. In J.-E. Lane (ed.), *Public Sector Reform: Rationale, Trends and Problems*. London: Sage.

Stoker, G. (2011) Was Local Governance Such a Good Idea? A Global Perspective. *Public Administration* 89(1): 15–31.

Stoker, G. and Wilson, D. (2004) Conclusions: New Ways of Being Local Government. In G. Stoker and D. Wilson (eds), *British Local Government into the 21st Century*, 225–234. Basingstoke: Palgrave Macmillan.

Stone, C. N. (2005) Looking Back to Look Forward: Reflections on Urban Regime Analysis. *Urban Affairs Review* 40(3): 309–341.

Swyngedouw, E. (1997) Neither Global nor Local: 'Glocalization' and the Politics of Scale. In K. R. Cox (eds), *Spaces of Globalization: Reasserting the Power of the Local*, 137–166. London: Guildford Press.

Thrasher, M, Borisyuk, G., Shears, M and Rallings, C. (2012) The Nature of Local Representation – Councillor Activity and the Pressures of Re-election. Paper presented to Elections, Public Opinion and Parties Conference, University of Oxford, 7–9 September.

Thrasher, M., Borisyuk, G., Shears, M. and Rallings, C. (2014) Councillors in Context: The Impact of Place upon Elected Representatives. *Local Government Studies* 41(5): 713–734.

Trounstine, J. (2009) All Politics is Local: The Reemergence of the Study of City Politics. *Perspectives* 7(3): 611–618.

Verhelst, T., Reynaert, H. and Steyvers, K. (2013a) Necessary Asymmetry or Undemocratic Imbalance? Professionalisation in the Recruitment and Career of Belgian Local Councillors. *Local Government Studies* 39(2): 273–297.

Verhelst, T., Renaert, H. and Steyvers, K. (2013b) Political Recruitment and Career Development of Local Councillors in Europe. In B. Egner, D. Sweeting and P.-J. Klok (eds), *Local Councillors in Europe*, 27–49. Wiesbaden: Springer Fachmedien.

Vesperini, G. (2009) Regional and Local Government in Italy: An Overview. Available at: http://dspace.unitus.it/bitstream/2067/1252/1/regional%20and%20local%20government%20in%20Italy.pdf.

Warner, M. E. and Hebdon, R. (2001) Local Government Restructuring: Privatization and its Alternatives. *Journal of Policy Analysis and Management* 20(2): 315–336.

White, J. K. (2006) What is a Political Party? In R. S. Katz and W. J. Crotty (eds), *Handbook of Party Politics*, 5–15. London: Sage.

Widdicombe, D. (chair) (1986) *The Conduct of Local Authority Business, Volume II: The Local Government Councillor*. London: HMSO.

Wilson, D. and Game, C. (2011) *Local Government in the United Kingdom*, 5th edition. Basingstoke: Palgrave Macmillan.

Wollmann, H. (2012) Local Government Reforms in (Seven) European Countries: Between Convergent and Divergent, Conflicting and Complimentary Developments. *Local Government Studies* 38(1): 41–70.

Wood, A. (1998) Making sense of urban entrepreneurialism. *The Scottish Geographical Magazine* 114(2): 120–123.

6
THE RELATIONSHIP BETWEEN POLITICS AND ADMINISTRATION

From dichotomy to local governance arenas

Alessandro Sancino, Marco Meneguzzo, Alessandro Braga and Paolo Esposito

Introduction

The relationship between politics and administration is a long-standing theme and has been one of the most widely debated issues since the early days of public administration studies (Goodnow 1900; Waldo 1948; Weber 1922; Wilson 1887).

Scholars have developed several models to describe the relationships between elected and tenured officials in public institutions. However, recently the conditions under which politicians and public managers operate have changed a great deal. For example, the shift from government to governance is changing the role of the state in societal regulation. In this context, an array of other actors both at an individual and/or at an organisational level is entering in the democratic governance of public institutions, playing a key role in shaping decision-making processes and in co-creating and co-producing (but potentially also co-destroying) outcomes of public interest (e.g. Bryson et al. 2017; Nabatchi et al. 2017; Sancino 2016).

Thus, politics and administration are currently increasingly situated in settings characterised by both vertical and horizontal multilevel governance arrangements and by various relationships with different actors (Budd and Sancino 2016). Some authors have emphasised the polycentric nature of modern governance processes, pointing out that they are not neutral on the relationships between politics and administration, because (for example) they impact on the role of politicians (Sørensen 2006) and on democratic performance (Mathur and Skelcher 2007).

Against this backdrop, this chapter aims to systematise the main studies on the relationship between politics and administration in local governments and discuss several perspectives for the future research agenda on this topic.

This chapter is organised as follows: the second section pinpoints the dichotomy view of politics and administration; the third section presents the findings of several studies shedding light on the overlapping roles of politicians and public managers across the public policy cycle; the fourth section contextualises our discussion to local governments in the current 'new public governance era'; the fifth section defines the concept of local governance arenas; the sixth section explains what is stakeholder management in local governance arenas; the seventh section provides several case illustrations from Italy; the last section offers some concluding remarks.

The relationship between politics and administration: the dichotomy

Traditionally, relationships between politicians and public managers have been seen as characterised by the concept of strict separation and dichotomy. Weber (1922) has identified six central elements of bureaucracy: (i) clearly defined division of labour and authority, (ii) hierarchical structure of offices, (iii) written guidelines for organising administrative processes, (iv) recruitment procedures based on specialisation and expertise, (v) office holding as a career and/or vocation, and (vi) duties and authority attached to positions, not persons. Embedded in this model is between clear division of roles between politicians and public managers (Pollitt and Bouckaert 2011). The former act as sovereign representatives of political values and interests; define goals and develop strategies, while the latter should implement plans and programs autonomously and neutrally in order to guarantee an efficient running of the government.

The distinction between politics and administration was also conceptualised by Wilson (1887). According to Wilson (1887: 210), the role of politics is 'setting the task for administration' that is a technical instrument devoted to policy execution. This model of division of authority was grounded in the idea – very important at that time – that limiting the interference between politics and administration was beneficial because it would guarantee more accountability and less corruption. This proposition is often referred to as the 'dichotomy model' and it is based on a conception of insulation of public managers from all those activities that are not purely administrative (e.g.: 'formulating mission and policy decisions') and of politicians from activities that are not related to the political mandate and to the process of policy making (e.g. 'administration' and 'management'). In this respect, Overeem (2005) argued about the urgency to rediscover the importance of this model, as the only one that might be able to clearly reaffirm the value of the neutrality of public managers from political interference.

The dichotomy model has influenced not only bureaucratic systems of public administration. Indeed, it has been re-interpreted with some adjustments also by new public management (NPM) reforms. NPM advocates strive to introduce economic rationality into public organisations (Hood 1995) and transform 'classical bureaucrats' (Putnam 1973) into managers with greater autonomy from politics (Rouban 2003). According to this conception of NPM, civil servants in their role of managers are expected to be responsible for the definition and the attainment of goals, as well as for the good management of financial and human resources (e.g. Pierre 2001; Pierre and Peters 2005). In the NPM model, the normative division of roles between politicians and public managers still continues to exist, but it is reinterpreted: the primacy of management replaces the more traditional primacy of politics.

However, the main problem that neither bureaucracy, new public management nor new public governance models can solve is the 'pathological degeneration' of public administration that may occur when authoritarian and/or politicised governments pursue particular instead of general interests (Borgonovi and Esposito 2017; Peters and Pierre 2004).

The relationship between politics and administration: from dichotomy to complementarity

Many contributions in the literature have criticised the dichotomy model pointing out that it does not well depict the more nuanced and complex relationships between politicians and public managers (e.g. Svara 1998, 1999a). Thus, several authors have tried to provide new conceptualisations.

Aberbach et al. (1981) have empirically investigated the relationships between politicians and public managers acting in central governments in seven countries (Italy, France, Germany, Netherlands, Sweden, United Kingdom and the US). The authors proposed four images for representing the relationships between politicians and public managers. Image I (policy/administration) depicts politicians and public managers as separated according to the traditional dichotomy model. Image II (Interests/facts) represents a situation in which both politicians and public managers participate to policy making, but interpreting different rationalities: interests by politicians and facts by public managers. Image III (energy/equilibrium) sees politicians and public managers as respectively energisers and equilibrators in the policy making process. Finally, image IV (pure hybrid) mirrors a situation in which politicians and public managers play overlapping roles in policy making and public management. These authors observed from their empirical findings an increasing prevalence of the Image number four.

Peters (1987) has developed five models of relationships between politicians and public managers along a continuum ranging from the 'formal model', characterised by the subordination of public managers to politicians, to the 'administrative state', where the pivotal role is played by public managers that lead the policy making process because of their strong expertise. The intermediate models are the 'village of life', 'functional village life' and 'adversarial politics'. In the 'village of life', politicians and public managers show strong cohesion, common objectives and shared logics of action and have also a reciprocal convenience in acting for promoting a 'good governance of public institutions', since this may generate positive effects on their careers. The 'functional village of life' model presents similarity with the previous one: politicians and public managers of a specific policy sector build an alliance to get the best allocation of funds and resources against the politicians and public managers of other policy sectors. The 'adversarial model' is opposed to the 'village of life' model since politicians and public managers are in competition for gaining primacy over the policy process.

Svara has developed other typologies of the relationships between politicians and public managers. In his early studies the author adopted a dichotomy-duality model. The governmental process is split in four functions: mission, policy, administration and management. Mission refers to the main underlying philosophy of the organisation, the values that guide its action, the strategic positioning and the portfolio of functions and public services delivered. The mission can be explicit or derived indirectly from the effects of decisions that are not spelled out. Policy concerns all the decision related to the budget and public services. Administration refers to the management of administrative processes that are implemented to achieve the objectives of public policies, as well as the definition of the procedures and administrative regulations. Finally, the function of management is described in residual form and it comprises all the activities undertaken to support the functions of policy and administration, including in particular those related to the management of human resources. Data collected by surveys involving managers and elected officials from local governments (e.g. Svara 1985, 1999b) showed that elected officials and administrators seem to have a dichotomous-like relationship in activities related to mission and management, whereas in policy and administration related activities they seem to play overlapping roles pointing to a duality.

In 2001, Svara developed a new typology that was based on the interplay between two factors; the level of control exerted by elected officials and the level of independence of administrators. Four combinations emerged: (i) political dominance in case of high political control and low administrative independence; (ii) bureaucratic autonomy in case of low political control and high administrative independence; (iii) 'laissez faire', when both control and independence are low; and (iv) complementarity, when both control and independence are high. In this last combination elected officials and administrators play distinctive roles but their functions overlap.

The combination 'laissez faire' includes the dichotomy model, because 'the distance between the two sets of officials does not contribute to real control or real independence, but to coexistence' (Svara 2001: 180).

Combining the degree of distance and differentiation between elected officials and administrators and the level of control of administrators by elected officials – Svara (2006) distinguished four models:

1. Separate roles with subordination of administrators to politicians and separate roles and norms.
2. Autonomous administrator when administrators are involved in the policy role, whereas politicians are separated from the administrative role.
3. Responsive administrator when administrators are subordinates to politicians and political norms dominate over administrative norms.
4. Overlapping roles when reciprocal influence exists between elected officials and administrators and they share roles.

A reference to the empirical reality of the Italian Public Administration system is useful for a better understanding of the models identified by the literature. Italy – and other states as well – has institutionalised the existence of different types of managerial roles which fall within the four main profiles: separate roles is the logic behind general secretaries working in many Italian public agencies across all the levels of government; autonomous administrator resembles the logic of city managers in Italian municipalities with over 100,000 inhabitants and of general directors appointed in Italian Ministries and/or Regions on a fixed term basis for the length of the political term (on Italian city managers, see for example Sancino and Turrini 2009); responsive administrators are managerial staff appointed by Italian politicians to work directly with and for them; overlapping roles is a model clearly illustrated in Italy by the example of many ex-politicians who are then appointed as managers of public corporations, especially at the local and regional level and vice versa by some public managers that who transfer to a political career like in the case of the current Mayor of Milan.

The relationship between politics and administration in the local governance era

In 2006 Svara identified a new frontier for research on political-administrative relations: 'the study of how each set of officials interact with citizens and groups in the community' (Svara 2006: 1086). With other words, but with the same intuition, Skelcher (2007: 61) pointed out how 'the next big step in public management research is to move beyond the question of whether management matters to answer the question: does democracy matter?'

After the development of the bureaucratic and NPM model of public administration, the rise of the new (public) governance model (e.g. Bingham et al. 2005; Rhodes 2000) has drawn attention to the role that citizens and non-government organisations play in pursuing outcomes of public interest. Thus, if the public administration literature rooted in the thought of Wilson (1887) and Weber (1922) was based on the concept of separation between politics and administration and was framed in a context of high politicisation and subordination of public managers to the political will, the present context requires to understand politics and administration through the roles played by new actors and the new domains where politicians and public managers are now operating (Nalbandian and Nalbandian 2003; Nalbandian et al. 2013).

Local governance refers to a practice (or way of governing) implemented by a local government and characterised by the steering and involvement – both formally and informally – of a range of other relevant actors acting within the community (community governance) and beyond the level of the community (multi-level governance) through different forms (e.g. networks and partnerships) and different styles (e.g. coordination and collaboration), with the aim of working with them for the achievement of relevant public and social outcomes (e.g. Rhodes 1996; Benington 2000; Stoker 2003, 2011).

Local governance 'changes how traditional institutions work because they operate in a more protean environment' (John 2001: 17) and it is characterised by the growing attention on network schemes and rules for governing the relationships with stakeholders and by an interactive and collaborative nature, rather than by a hierarchical or contractual nature (Edelenbos 1999, 2005; Denters and Rose 2005; Edelenbos et al. 2010; Torfing et al. 2012). In other words, local governance is enacted in interactive arenas with a variety of stakeholders playing different roles. Several authors have investigated the role played by politicians and/or public managers and their relationships with other actors in governance contexts (e.g. Feldman and Khademian 2007; Hansen 2001; Nalbandian 1999). Sørensen (2006) has extensively written about the implications of governance processes on the roles of politicians, arguing how the role of politicians should evolve towards a meta-governance role. This shift does not necessarily undermine representative democracy as such: in fact, meta-governance opens the door for the development of a new strong model of representative democracy (Sørensen 2006: 99).

If political officials control government processes in the traditional perspective of representative democracy (Edelenbos et al. 2010), something changes in the interactive governance practices (e.g. Sørensen 2002; Sørensen and Torfing 2003, 2005; Torfing et al. 2012) where public managers and political officials have to manage the growing involvement of external stakeholders into the work of government. In this respect, Mathur and Skelcher (2007: 235) argued how (network) governance is reshaping the role of public managers, positioning them as 'responsively competent players in a polycentric system of governance rather than neutrally competent servants of a political executive'.

Local governance arenas

Following Van Damme and Brans (2012: 1047), we define local governance arenas as 'local government organised arrangements of interaction on decision making and/or service delivery with societal parties such as citizens and non-government organizations'. Hirst (2000) and Fung and Wright (2001) clarified how interactive governance arenas bring together governments at different levels in the political system and can promote democracy by improving the exchange of information between them. However, as interactive governance and governance arenas often follow informal rules, they are difficult to hold to account (Katz and Mair 1995; Pierre and Peters 2005).

There are different types of local governance arenas. Local government may engage external stakeholders in doing different things (Svara and Denhardt 2010). Drawing from the work of Alford (2013), we can identify five different functions for engaging external stakeholders in local governance arenas: co-consultation; co-deliberation; co-design; co-delivery; co-evaluation (Borgonovi and Sancino, 2014: 7–8).

The arena of co-consultation refers to situations where the engagement of external stakeholders is aimed at gathering ideas, information and contributions, although the final decision remains in the traditional circuit of representative democracy.

The arena of co-deliberation is characterised by the joint processes of politicians and managers making policy decisions together with external stakeholders. Some examples of these experiences are represented by deliberative arenas like those developed in participatory budgeting experiences.

The arena of co-design describes the processes where public managers engage with external stakeholders for co-designing public services. Examples of practices that fit into this area are, for example, focus groups for co-designing social services that are developed with all the actors of the community active in some welfare-related services. The arena of co-delivery describes the situation where external stakeholders are involved in the concrete delivery of public services. Finally, the last governance arena is represented by the engagement of external stakeholders and citizens for practices of co-evaluation of public services and public policies. Some examples can be found in the popular juries and citizens' evaluation panels of public services (Borgonovi and Sancino, 2014: 7–8).

Stakeholder management in local governance arenas

Stakeholder management can be defined as a series of principles, tools and processes with the aims of identifying, involving, and managing the relationships with stakeholders (Freeman 1984; Frooman 1999; Mitchell et al. 1997). One of the main peculiarity of stakeholder management in the public domain is that it is developed by both politicians and/or managers. Bryson (2004) identified four main categories of activities in stakeholder management: (i) organising participation; (ii) creating ideas for strategic interventions; (iii) building a winning coalition around proposal development, review and adoption; and (iv) implementing, monitoring, and evaluating strategic interventions.

Stakeholder management comprises several stages of activities whose are interlocked and repetitive (Cleland 1998). More specifically, Archer (2003) identified five main stages: (i) identifying; (ii) analysing; (iii) planning and scheduling; (iv) executing; and (v) monitoring. In Figure 6.1, we slightly readapted the stakeholder cycle from Archer (2003), identifying the following five key stages: (1) stakeholder identification; (2) stakeholder mapping; (3) stakeholder engagement design; (4) stakeholder interaction; and (5) stakeholder evaluation.

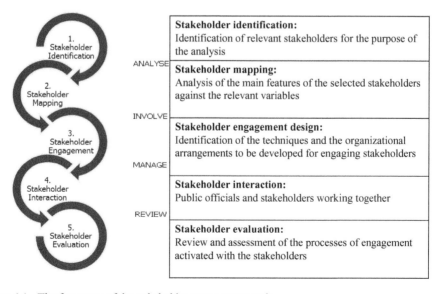

Figure 6.1 The five stages of the stakeholder management cycle

The first phase – *stakeholder identification* – is the identification of relevant stakeholders for the purpose of the engagement; this identification is dynamic (it may change over time) and depends from the issue and from the perspective taken for the analysis. The second phase – *stakeholder mapping* – consists in the analysis of the main features of the relevant stakeholders (identified as such in the previous phase) against the relevant variables for the issue considered. For example, Mitchell et al. (1997) identified three main variables for analysing stakeholders (power, legitimacy, and urgency). Some public agencies have also developed stakeholder profile scorecards for profiling the main features of stakeholders (e.g. Victoria Government 2005). The third phase – *stakeholder engagement design* – aims at identifying the organisational arrangements to be employed for involving stakeholders: examples can be the creation of stakeholder advisory committees, and/or new organisational structures, like associations participated by all the stakeholders engaged. The fourth phase – *stakeholder interaction* – consists in the actual 'management of the interactions' with the stakeholders and this may differ depending on the technique adopted (some examples could be stakeholder meetings, public hearings open to everybody, focus groups, deliberative polling, etc.). The last phase – *stakeholder evaluation* – consists in a review and assessment of the processes of engagement activated with the external stakeholders and it might be based on subjective (perceptions) or objective measures (indicators).

Politicians and public managers managing external stakeholders: case illustrations from Italy

We provide below some concise examples of stakeholder engagement for each local governance arena above mentioned; case examples refer to experiences in Italy. A more detailed analysis of each case using the framework of the stakeholder management cycle is then presented in Table 6.1 below.

Florence: strategic plan

Florence is the capital city of the Tuscany region and it is the most populous city of the region, with approximately 382,000 inhabitants in the Municipality, and over 1,520,000 in the Metropolitan area. The idea to have a strategic plan emerged in the early 2000s on the political initiative of the Mayor Leonardo Domenici following other experience of strategic planning in place in other European cities (e.g. Lille, Barcelona, Turin, etc.). The main goal was to build a shared vision of socio-economic development. The strategic plan was one of the first initiatives where external stakeholders had been involved in a structured way by the municipality for working together on co-planning.

Municipality of Grottammare: participatory budgeting

Grottammare is a small to medium town located in the Centre of Italy. It has almost 16,000 inhabitants. The Municipality of Grottammare has a previous history of about twenty years of inclusive decision-making processes, and it is considered the most exemplary case in Italy for participatory budgeting. Indeed, in 1994 a new political coalition known as 'Participation and Solidarity' organised a system of neighbourhood assemblies as a first attempt at participatory democracy. The main reasons for implementing the citizen involvement schemes were a strong political will to put the citizens (and their rights) at the centre of the policy and the willingness to experiment new innovative forms of participation. A previous study (Fedele et al. 2005) on the experience of Grottammare found as key elements the important role of the Mayor in introducing the participatory budgeting and the political and ideological emphasis that was given to this experience.

Municipality of Lecco: co-design of social services

Lecco is a city of about 50,000 inhabitants in Lombardy region, in the Northern Italy. The Municipality of Lecco has almost ten years of experience in social services co-design. The co-design experience developed for two main reasons: (i) new laws promoting co-design initiatives have been introduced, and (ii) two public managers (the secretary general and the head of the social services) pushed for innovations into the sector.

Municipality of Reggio Emilia: co-delivery of sport services

Reggio Emilia is a city with about 170,000 inhabitants. It is located in the Northern Italy, in the Emilia-Romagna region. Historically the Municipality of Reggio Emilia developed numerous experiences of stakeholder engagement, and it is considered one of the most innovative public sector agencies in Italy with respect to these issues. The main reason to implement co-delivery was to find new forms for sport services delivery in a time of financial crisis.

Municipality of Piacenza: a popular jury

Piacenza is a city of about 100,000 inhabitants, which is located in Northern Italy, in Emilia-Romagna region. In the Municipality of Piacenza other stakeholder engagement experiences had previously been implemented. However, two main reasons prompted the creation of the popular jury in 2011. First, a strong political and managerial will to obtain feedback from citizens about the quality of public policies and services promoted. Second, the municipality leaders wanted to integrate the social reporting system previously activated with the new participating tool of the popular jury.

Conclusions

This chapter has briefly summarised the evolution of the studies on the relationships between politics and administration in public institutions such as local governments from Wilson and Weber to the present day, characterised by networks, collaborations and interactive governance.

Summing up, in contemporary times, politicians and public managers are placed in new relationships with different stakeholders; should play new roles like for example meta-governance for politicians and network design for public managers; and both serve as essential catalysts, conveners, and nurturers of efforts to increase the problem-solving capacity of their communities and improve the quality of their democracies. Accordingly, we are probably in the need to update and to conceptualise the relationships between politics and administration by framing a new complementarity model, characterised by an accountable system of checks and balances and based on politicians, managers and stakeholders together responsible for the pursuing of outcomes of public interests.

We wish to outline five promising research avenues that in our view need to be addressed in the future. First, there is the need to continue to study the new identities and roles played by politicians and managers in current contexts; for example, as Jeffares and Skelcher (2011: 1253) argued: 'how public managers themselves construct their role as actors in a democratic arena and what implications this has for their role in shaping and designing the arrangements for

Table 6.1 Stakeholder management in local governance arenas: the role of different actors

Stakeholder management cycle	Co-planning	Co-deliberation	Co-design	Co-delivery	Co-evaluation
Stakeholder identification	Stakeholders have been identified through snowball sampling by politicians, managers, stakeholders and consultants.	Stakeholders were all citizens resident in a given neighbour. Politicians identified the stakeholders to be engaged.	Open tender to all the organisations working in the welfare sector. Managers identified the stakeholders to be engaged.	Expression of interest addressed to all the voluntary organisations working in the sports sector. Managers and politicians identified the stakeholders to be engaged.	Stratified sampling plus invitation to all the associations operating in the eight neighbour councils. Consultants identified the stakeholders to be engaged.
Stakeholder Mapping	Informal analysis conducted by politicians and consultants. Some stakeholders marked as 'relevant'.	Informal analysis conducted by politicians.	Stakeholders analysed by managers within a formal and explicit procedure.	Informal analysis conducted by managers and politicians.	Informal analysis conducted by consultants and politicians.
Stakeholder engagement design	Ad hoc organising committee, scientific committee and a new organisation has also been created.	Six neighbourhood committees have been created.	An ad hoc organisational structure of the Municipality has been created.	Agreement between local government agency and groups of citizens.	Two public meetings and various working groups.
Stakeholder interaction	Managed and supervised by consultants and stakeholders.	Managed by politicians.	Managed by managers.	Managed by managers.	Managed by consultants.
Stakeholder evaluation	Formal evaluation conducted by consultants and stakeholders.	Informal evaluation conducted by politicians.	Formal evaluation conducted by public managers and stakeholders.	Informal evaluation conducted by public managers.	Informal evaluation conducted by consultants and politicians.

network governance?' Similarly, at what point is the awareness of our politicians of what meta-governance is and how can they do exercise these new roles? And, again, what is the content of the managerial work played by politicians and what is the content of political work played by managers and how are they evolving?

Second, we need to understand the critical skills that public managers and politicians need for operating in the new contexts (e.g. Baddeley 2008; Manzie and Hartley 2013). What are the critical skills for playing meta-governance for politicians and for public managers for designing hard and soft governance structures and processes? What is the role played by public managers as intermediaries between state and civil society?

Third, technology is changing our lives, our social relationships, organisations and societies. So, how are social networks impacting on the relationship between politics and administration in the democratic governance of public institutions?

Fourth, we have argued that the relationship between politics and administration should also integrate different kind of stakeholders. Accordingly, we need to investigate how these relationships are happening in a context of interactive governance paying attention to issues like trust, power structure, and democratic performance. For doing so, it is necessary to employ a more complex and systemic approach for viewing at politicians, managers and other stakeholders. Moreover, if we think about the informality and the interactivity of governance processes, we find that reflections on the role of democracy and of political officials are needed.

Fifth, future studies should recognise the different positions of politicians and public managers in the organisation, better distinguishing among top-, senior-, middle- and street-level managers, as well as in local governments: the mayor, members of the cabinet and city councillors in different institutions.

References

Aberbach, J., Putnam, R. and Rockman, B. (1981) *Bureaucrats and Politicians in Western Democracies*. Cambridge, MA: Harvard University Press.

Alford, J. (2013) Engaging Citizens in Co-producing Service Outcomes. In E. Lindquist and V. Wanna (eds), *Putting Citizens First Engagement in Policy and Service Delivery for the 21st Century*, 75–82. Canberra: Australian National University.

Archer, L. (2003) *Stakeholder Management Guideline*. Retrieved on 13 March 2018 from http://archerid3.com/wp-content/uploads/2017/05/guideline-stakeholder-management.pdf.

Baddeley, S. (2008) Political-Management Leadership. In K. James and J. Collins (eds), *Leadership Perspectives: Knowledge into Action*, 177–192. Basingstoke: Palgrave Macmillan.

Benington, J. (2000) Editorial: The Modernization and Improvement of Government and Public Services. *Public Money and Management* 20(2): 3–8.

Bingham, L., Nabatchi, T. and O'Leary, R. (2005) The New Governance: Practices and Processes for Stakeholder and Citizen Participation in the Work of Government. *Public Administration Review* 65(5): 547–558.

Borgonovi, E. and Esposito, P. (2017) Integrity Management and Policy in Italy. *SYMPHONYA Emerging Issues in Management* 2: 88–102.

Borgonovi, E. and Sancino, A. (2014) Reshaping (Local) Public Management in Turbulent Times: Conceptualizing Domains and Providing Recommendations for Public Managers. Presented at 28th Australian and New Zealand Academy of Management Conference, 3–5 December, Sydney. Retrieved from www.anzam.org/wp-content/uploads/pdf-manager/1675_ANZAM-2014-255.PDF.

Bryson, J. (2004) What to Do When Stakeholders Matter. *Public Management Review* 6(1): 21–53.

Bryson, J., Sancino, A., Benington, J. and Sørensen, E. (2017) Towards a Multi-actor Theory of Public Value Co-creation. *Public Management Review* 19(5): 640–654.

Budd, L. and Sancino, A. (2016) A Framework for City Leadership in Multilevel Governance Settings: The Comparative Contexts of Italy and the UK. *Regional Studies, Regional Science* 3(1): 129–145.

Cleland, D. (1998) Project Stakeholder Management. In D. Cleland and W. King (eds), *Project Management Handbook*, 2nd edn. New York: Van Nostrand in Reinhold.

Denters, B. and Rose, L. (2005) Local Governance in the Third Millennium: A Brave New World? In B. Denters and L. Rose (eds), *Comparing Local Governance Trends and Developments*. Basingstoke: Macmillan.

Edelenbos, J. (1999) Design and Management of Participatory Public Policy Making. *Public Management Review* 1(4): 569–78.

Edelenbos, J. (2005) Institutional Implications of Interactive Governance: Insights from Dutch Practice. *Governance* 18(1): 111–134.

Edelenbos, J., van Schie, N. and Gerrits, L. (2010) Organizing Interfaces between Government Institutions and Interactive Governance. *Policy Sciences* 43(1): 73–94.

Fedele, P., Meneguzzo, M., Plamper, H., and Senese, M. (2005) Participatory Budget in Germany and Italy. Paper presented at 9th Sixth International Research Symposium on Public Sector Management, University L Bocconi, Milan.

Feldman, M. and Khademian, A. (2007) The Role of the Public Manager in Inclusion. *Governance* 20(2): 305–324.

Freeman, R. (1984) *Strategic Management: A Stakeholder Approach*. Boston, MA: Pitman.

Frooman, J. (1999) Stakeholder Influence Strategies. *Academy of Management Review* 24(2): 191–205.

Fung, A. and Wright, E. (2001) Deepening Democracy: Innovations in Empowered Participatory Governance. *Politics and Society* 29(1): 5–42.

Goodnow, F. (1900) *Politics and Administration: A Study in Government*. New York: Russell and Russell.

Hansen, K. (2001) Local Councillors: Between Local Government and Local governance. *Public Administration* 79(1): 105–123.

Hirst, P. (2000) Democracy and Governance. In J. Pierre (ed.), *Debating Governance*, 13–35. Oxford: Oxford University Press.

Hood, C. (1995) The 'New Public Management' in the 1980s: Variations on a Theme. *Accounting, Organizations and Society* 20(2): 93–109.

Jeffares, S. and Skelcher C. (2011) Democratic Subjectivities in Network Governance: A Q Methodology Study of Dutch and English Public Managers. *Public Administration* 89(4): 1253–1273.

John, P. (2001) *Local Governance in Western Europe*. London: Sage.

Katz, R. and Mair, P. (1995) Changing Models of Party Organization and Party Democracy: The Emergence of the Cartel Party. *Party Politics* 1(1): 5–28.

Manzie, S. and Hartley, J. (2013) *Dancing on Ice: Leadership with Political Astuteness by Senior Public Servants in the UK*. Milton Keynes: Open University Business School.

Mathur, N. and Skelcher, C. (2007) Evaluating Democratic Performance: Methodologies for Assessing the Relationship between Network Governance and Citizens. *Public Administration Review* 67(2): 228–237.

Mitchell, R., Agle, B. and Wood, D. (1997) Toward a Theory of Stakeholder Identification and Salience: Defining the Principle of Who and What Really Counts. *Academy of Management Review* 22(4): 853–886.

Nabatchi, T., Sancino, A., and Sicilia, M. (2017) Varieties of Participation in Public Services: The Who, When and What of Coproduction. *Public Administration Review* 77(5): 766–776.

Nalbandian, J. (1999) Facilitating Community, Enabling Democracy: New Roles for Local Government Managers. *Public Administration Review* 59(3): 187–197.

Nalbandian, J. and Nalbandian, C. (2003) Contemporary Challenges in Local Government. *National Civic Review* 92(1): 83–91.

Nalbandian, J., O'Neill, R., Wilkes, J. and Kaufman, A. (2013) Contemporary Challenges in Local Government: Evolving Roles and Responsibilities, Structures, and Processes. *Public Administration Review* 73(4): 567–574.

Overeem, P. (2005) The Value of the Dichotomy: Politics, Administration, and the Political Neutrality of Administrators. *Administrative Theory and Praxis* 27(2): 311–329.

Peters, B. (1987) Politicians and Bureaucrats in the Politics of Policy-Making. In J. Lane (ed.), *Bureaucracy and Public Choice*, 256–282. London: Sage.

Peters, B. and Pierre, J. (2004) Politicization of the Civil Service: Concepts, Causes, Consequences. In B. Peters and J. Pierre (eds), *Politicization of the Civil Service in Comparative Perspective*, 1–13. London: Routledge.

Pierre, J. (2001) Parallel paths? Administrative Reform, Public Policy and Politico-Bureaucratic Relationships in Sweden. In B. Peters and J. Pierre (eds), *Politicians, Bureaucrats and Administrative Reform*, 132–141. London: Routledge.

Pierre, J. and Peters, B. (2005) *Governing Complex Societies: Trajectories and Scenarios*. New York: Springer.

Pollitt, C. and Bouckaert, G. (2011) *Public Management Reform: A Comparative Analysis: New Public Management, Governance, and the Neo-Weberian State*, 3rd edn. Oxford: Oxford University Press.

Putnam, R. (1973) The Political Attitudes of Senior Civil Servants in Western Europe: A Preliminary Report. *British Journal of Political Science* 3(3): 257–290.

Rhodes, R. (1996) The New Governance: Governing without Government. *Political Studies* 44(4): 652–667.

Rhodes, R. (2000) Governance and Public Administration. In J. Pierre (ed.), *Debating Governance*, 54–90. Oxford: Oxford University Press.

Rouban, L. (2003) Politicization of the Civil Service. In B. Peters and J. Pierre (eds), *Handbook of Public Administration*, 310–320. London: Sage.

Sancino, A. (2016) The Meta Coproduction of Community Outcomes: Towards a Citizens' Capabilities Approach. *VOLUNTAS: International Journal of Voluntary and Non Profit Organizations* 27(1): 409–424.

Sancino, A. and Turrini, A. (2009) The Managerial Work of Italian City Managers: An Empirical Study. *Local Government Studies* 35(4): 475–491.

Skelcher, C. (2007) Does Democracy Matter? A Transatlantic Research Design on Democratic Performance and Special Purpose Governments. *Journal of Public Administration Research and Theory* 17(1): 61–76.

Sørensen, E. (2002) Democratic Theory and Network Governance. *Administrative Theory and Praxis* 24(4): 693–720.

Sørensen, E. (2006) Metagovernance: The Changing Role of Politicians in the Process of Democratic Governance. *American Review of Public Administration* 36(1): 98–114.

Sørensen, E. and Torfing, J. (2003) Network Politics, Political Capital and Democracy. *International Journal of Public Administration* 26(6): 609–634.

Sørensen, E. and Torfing, J. (2005) The Democratic Anchorage of Network Governance. *Scandinavian Political Studies* 28(3): 195–218.

Stoker, G. (2003) *Transforming Local Governance*. New York: Palgrave Macmillan.

Stoker, G. (2011) Was Local Governance Such a Good Idea? A Global Comparative Perspective. *Public Administration* 89(1): 15–31.

Svara, J. (1985) Dichotomy and Duality: Reconceptualizing the Relationship between Policy and Administration in Council-Manager Cities. *Public Administration Review* 45(1): 221–232.

Svara, J. (1998) The Politics–Administration Dichotomy Model as Aberration. *Public Administration Review* 58(1): 51–58.

Svara, J. (1999a) Complementarity of Politics and Administration as a Legitimate Alternative to the Dichotomy Model. *Administration and Society* 30(6): 676–705.

Svara, J. (1999b) The Shifting Boundary between Elected Officials and City Managers in Large Council-Manager Cities. *Public Administration Review* 59(1): 44–53.

Svara, J. (2001) The Myth of the Dichotomy: Complementarity of Politics and Administration in the Past and Future of Public Administration. *Public Administration Review* 61(2): 176–183.

Svara, J. (2006) The Search for Meaning in Political–Administrative Relations in Local Government. *International Journal of Public Administration* 29(12): 1065–1090.

Svara, J. (2008) Beyond Dichotomy: Dwight Waldo and the Intertwined Politics–Administration Relationship. *Public Administration Review* 68(1): 46–52.

Svara J. and Denhardt, J. (2010) The Connected Community: Local Governments as Partners in Citizen Engagement and Community Building. In J. Svara and J. Denhardt (eds), *Promoting Citizen Engagement and Community Building*, pp. 4–51. Phoenix, AZ: Arizona State University.

Torfing, J., Peters, B., Pierre, J. and Sørensen, E. (2012) *Interactive Governance: Advancing the Paradigm*. Oxford: Oxford University Press.

Van Damme, J. and Brans, M. (2012) Managing Public Consultation: A Conceptual Framework and Empirical Findings from Belgian Case Studies. *Public Administration* 90(4): 1047–1066.

Victoria Government (2005) *Effective Engagement: Building Relationships with Community and Other Stakeholders, Book 2: The Engagement Planning Workbook*. Victoria: Victoria Government.

Waldo, D. (1948) *The Administrative State*. New York: Ronald Press.

Weber, M. (1922) Bureaucracy. In J. Shafritz and A. Hyde (eds), *Classic of Public Administration*, 4th edition, 63–67. Orlando, FL: Harcourt Brace College Publishers.

Wilson, W. (1887) The Study of Administration. *Political Science Quarterly* 2(2): 197–222.

7
INSTITUTIONALIZED DIFFERENCES IN ECONOMIC DEVELOPMENT PERSPECTIVES

A comparison of city managers, mayors and council members in Texas

James Vanderleeuw and Melanie Smith

Introduction

This chapter examines to what extent economic development perceptions are associated with particular institutional city offices. The answer to this question has relevance for the success of city economic development efforts. Successful economic development efforts are those that increase revenue and/or jobs, among other benefits, and are often dependent upon a united leadership in the local government concerned. A united leadership, in turn, can depend upon the ability to build coalitions in support of economic development initiatives. Economic development activities require commitment of finite city resources, and city leaders may be held accountable by members of an attentive public for poor economic conditions. Coalition building on economic development proposals, therefore, may be instrumental in ensuring not only passage of a given initiative but its success as well. To the extent that economic development perceptions may have some basis in institutional position, resulting in institutionally based differences in attitude between city leaders, coalition building may be a particular challenge.

Our present study employed data from a single state in the United States. We used survey results from city leaders in the state of Texas to determine the extent to which perspectives on economic development differ across three distinct city institutional office-holders – city managers, mayors and council members.

City economic development in the United States

Economic growth is a primary responsibility of city leadership in the United States. A wealth of literature indicates that local economic development policy has been and continues to be a major activity for city leaders (see Kerstein 1993; Rigos and Paulson 1996; Leo, Beavis, Carver and Turner 1998; Ross and Levine 2001; Reese 2006; Reese and Sands 2007; Betz, Partridge, Kraybill and Lobao 2012). We can note several significant reasons for the key role which economic development plays for city leaders. First, the constitutional place of cities in the United States' federal system limits cities' ability to regulate the greater economic environment. Unlike federal or state governments, cities cannot regulate commerce or population movement in and out of their borders (Peterson 1981). Cities can regulate land use, and city leaders, therefore, focus on this single economic growth tool. Through land use policy, cities can determine how land will be developed to increase economic vitality. A second reason city leaders in the United States focus heavily on economic development relates to how cities view developers as 'growth machines' (Molotch 1976, 1988). Developers stand to profit financially from physical development, and this helps ensure that land use policy will move in a specific direction – in the direction of large construction projects, which it is hoped may ultimately benefit the city.

A third reason for an emphasis on economic development projects by city leaders in the United States is similar to the growth machine phenomenon but relates specifically to elected city leaders. There are electoral benefits from development for elected office-holders such as mayors and council members (Feiock and Kim 2001; Feiock, Park, Steinacker and Kim 2005). Elected city leaders can take credit for economic development projects, particularly projects that yield physical structures, as a means of demonstrating positive job performance to their constituents. Development, particularly physical development, produces jobs from the outset.

City leaders in the United States typically pursue supply-side strategies that focus on attracting business by reducing the cost of doing business. These strategies include tax abatements, land clearance, the use of public money to provide infrastructure for private development, an emphasis on downtown business interests, and similar policies with a direct connection to job creation, city revenue generation, and the preferences of local business (see e.g. Grant 1990; Bachelor 1994; Rigos and Paulson 1996; Reese and Rosenfeld 2002; Reese 2006; Reese and Sands 2007; Morgan 2010). While there has been some movement in recent years away from this traditional supply-side approach towards considering more heavily the provision of amenities, such as the arts, as an integral component of economic development strategy (see e.g. Strom 2002; Clark 2011; Vanderleeuw and Sides 2016), city leaders in the United States generally continue to rely on traditional strategies to ensure economic growth and prosperity. A continued reliance on a traditional economic development strategy, with its emphasis on physical construction, benefits the interests of both developers and elected city leaders.

Is there convergence or divergence in economic development perception among institutional city office-holders?

Leadership convergence on economic development issues

An argument can be made that city leaders will tend to be in agreement, or convergence, about the economic choices that need to be made for their city, regardless of their institutional position. In his seminal work, *City Limits*, Paul Peterson (1981) argued that given the placement of cities in the United States' federal system – denied the ability to regulate commerce and the flow of people in and out of their borders – city leaders have little choice but to engage in growth activities that involve land use. Economic growth, therefore, becomes an overriding and unifying challenge for city leaders – a 'unitary interest'.

Several additional factors contribute to a convergence in orientation toward economic development decision making. First, despite differences in job duties, within a given city each institutional office-holder operates in a common context based on a larger cultural milieu (see Reese and Rosenfeld 2002 for a discussion of the relationship between economic development and culture). For example, the orientation toward governance in Texas (the state from which our data were drawn) can be characterized as small government and pro-business. The State Constitution of 1876 reflects skepticism of government and restricts authority by, among other things, limiting the governor's power to formulate the state's budget, which is determined by the Legislative Budget Board composed of state legislators; and by providing for the popular election of top executives. This restricted government authority is accompanied by a business-friendly environment. In 2014, for example, *Chief Executive* ranked Texas as the top state for business, based on a survey of CEOs. This was the tenth consecutive year that Texas was recognized in this manner.

Municipal government in Texas replicates the state's system of restricted government authority and pro-business environment. Mayoral power tends to be limited, with city mayors being of the weak-mayor type – with Houston's use of a strong-mayor system an exception. In keeping with the state's minimal government and pro-business orientation, Texas cities typically have a city manager with a small four- to seven-member part-time council and part-time mayor. This cultural milieu provides the context within which economic development perceptions are molded and decisions made.

In addition, institutional city office-holders experience a push toward convergence in their thinking about economic development because of their service to a common public. Certainly, there can be wide differences in policy preferences among members of the public. Nevertheless, certain communities can attract like-minded individuals or people of a similar socioeconomic standing who share policy preferences. For instance, there is evidence that suburbanites may be more ideologically conservative compared to non-suburbanites and therefore more apt to oppose increased taxes for some types of services (Kruse 2005). Institutional office-holders in the same city, therefore, can be subject to the preferences of a common public, either the direct public pressure experienced by elected leaders or indirect public pressure experienced by those in appointed positions.

Most clearly, elected city leaders have an incentive to claim to be acting in the best economic interests of a citizenry, for example, by promoting activities whereby local government uses its resources to stimulate private development, such as land acquisition and clearance, to promote business interests (to borrow from a point made by Feiock, Park, Steinacker and Kim 2005). However, as Teske and Schneider (1994) argue, appointed leaders such as city managers are not immune from the concerns of citizens. While not overtly engaged in partisan politics, city managers often interact with citizens and citizen groups to explain, if not defend, city policy and to inform the city council regarding citizens attitudes. Further, institutional city position-holders communicate among one another and among a broader set of political, economic, and civic elites. To borrow from Robert Michels (1966), communication across elites tends to foster a shared set of values. This communication may promote a shared vision of what, from a developmental perspective, is in the best interest of the city. In effect, shared interests among city leaders may develop for a number of reasons.

Leadership divergence on economic development issues

However, an argument can be made that a common viewpoint among institutional city office-holders regarding economic development is not something that will necessarily occur.

One argument that runs directly counter to Peterson's unitary interest thesis is that local politics is too politically divisive to allow for the consistent emergence of agree around issues, even the issue of economic growth (see e.g. Stone and Sanders 1987). A very similar argument can be derived from literature that points to severe community divisions over policy that amount to culture wars (Sharp 1999). Cultural divisions – that show up, for example, in political conflict over city policy to provide addicts with needles to dampen the spread of AIDS – can polarize a city's population and leadership. This perspective is consistent with Pfeffer and Salancik's (2003) argument that external constituencies influence the behavior of organizational members beyond what the organization proscribes. When city residents speak with divergent voices, the behavior of those in positions of institutional authority may similarly diverge.

Further, it can be argued that the institutional characteristics associated with the leadership positions under investigation will influence how office-holders view their city's economic development needs. This argument, that the unique characteristics of a city office will influence the office-holder's economic development perspective, is what we investigate in this chapter.

In essence, institutional differences may overpower any influence that drives those in leadership positions to adopt similar viewpoints. For instance, it can be argued that elected position-holders, such as city council members, are 'constituency oriented' (see Svara 1990). This is because their position depends on maintaining an acceptable level of voter approval. Conversely, an appointed position-holder such as a city manager, while not fully insulated from public opinion, is most directly responsible to the appointing body and, as such, may hold a longer-view on city policy compared to elected leaders. While both elected and appointed position-holders may ultimately be accountable to a common citizenry, institutional differences structure how susceptible office-holders may be to public sentiment. Here we refer to models of representation that Pitkin (1967) labels the 'delegate' and 'trustee' models. Publically elected leaders are most proximate to the citizenry and can be expected to act as delegates by according weight to the immediate and specific concerns of their particular constituency. Retaining elected position can depend upon giving such weight. By comparison, appointed office-holders are less proximate to (though not fully insulated from) the citizenry and therefore have greater flexibility to act as trustees for the public interest; they have a greater ability to make decisions without considering public opinion at every turn. As trustees, appointed leaders can rely relatively less on the immediate dictates of the mass citizenry and relatively more on their own training, experience, and judgment.

In addition, because of the duties of their office, appointed position-holders, such as city managers, tend to have high levels of training, experience and education. In their study of Texas city managers, for example, Vanderleeuw, Sides and Williams (2015) reported that the majority of surveyed managers held a Master's degree or above, with most of those in the field of Public Administration. Further, office-holders such as city managers and, depending upon the city, mayors are distinct from city council members because managers and mayors in strong-mayor cities possess an executive function. City councils, by contrast, view issues more from a legislative perspective. Therefore, the institutional duties and responsibilities of offices might be expected to influence perspectives on economic development, as might responsibilities to stake-holders (for example whether the office-holder is responsible to voters or to governmental bodies) and differences in training and education.

The study

According to urban regime theory, a city leadership cohort is composed of a broad spectrum of governmental, business, nonprofit, and community organization actors (see e.g. Stone 1989; May and Jochim 2012). While the particular city leadership mix can vary from city to city and over time, successful local economic development efforts increasingly have come to involve collaboration among a wide set of intra- and inter-community governmental and non-governmental participants (Accordino and Fasulo 2011). While the specific leadership mix of participants can vary depending on the city, the major political institutions of city government in the United States are relatively constant. These common institutional leadership positions are city mayor, council member and city manager.

City government structure in the United States tends to provide for a city council, a mayor and in most cities a city manager. Some cities in the United States use a mayor-council form of government, where formal, institutional power rests with an elected mayor and city council. A strong-mayor form of government may see the mayor have power to veto council ordinances and appoint heads of city departments. In a weak mayor form of government the mayor presides at council meetings but the institutional powers of that office differ little from those of the council as a whole.

A further institutional position across many cities in the United States is that of city manager. Council-manager cities employ a city manager to oversee the day-to-day operations of city government. A city council hires a manager who reports and advises the council. The use of professionally trained, full-time city managers is common. The International City/County Management Association (ICMA) estimates that the council-manager form of government is in fact the most common form of city government in the United States, used by 59% of cities in 2011.

The use of a city manager, however, does not preclude a city from also having a mayor. Council-manager systems will still tend to include the position of mayor, though in these cases the mayor will have reduced responsibilities compared to the strong-mayor system. City councils, of course, can be found across various forms of city government, mayor-council or council-manager.

Our study examined the perceptions of these three city institutional office-holders – city mayors, managers and council members – on a series of economic development-related issues. Prior research points to the influential role in city economic development efforts played by holders of these positions (see e.g. Svara 1987; Zemmering 2008; McCabe, Feiock, Clingermayer and Stream 2009). Our analysis focused on identifying systematic, patterned differences in viewpoint between these three institutional city office-holders. To do so, we mailed surveys to city leaders in the state of Texas: to city managers in 2011, mayors in 2012, and council members in 2013.

Surveys were sent to leaders in home-rule cities in Texas with a population of greater than 5,000. There were 319 home-rule cities that had a manager in 2011, according to the *Texas Municipal League Online Directory*, and this was the list used for the subsequent surveys. The surveys yielded responses from 151 city managers, 136 mayors, and 54 council members. These survey results, of course, measured attitudes and opinions rather than actual decisions. However, given communication skills and experience with community issues as well as prior decision-making regarding community affairs that all three of these institutional office-holders typically engage in, it is reasonable to expect a level of correspondence between the attitudes and opinions of these leaders and their actual decisions.

Our data were drawn one state, Texas. The state is large and diverse, and, despite historic images, is a populous, urban state. With a population of 26 Million is the second most populous state in the United States, and 84.7% of the state's population resides in urban areas, a figure above the national rate of 80.7% (according to the 2010 census). The state includes some of the largest cities in the United States. These include the cities of Austin, Dallas, El Paso, Fort Worth, Houston, and San Antonio.

We investigated economic development perceptions across four dimensions, each of which is posited to influence the type of economic development proposal a given office-holder will likely support. First, we examined the perceived importance of economic development to the city. The importance accorded to economic development will influence the level of urgency that drives city leaders to deal with economic development and adopt economic development proposals. The lower the importance given to economic development by a city leader, the lower that leader's motivation to support any given economic development initiative. Second, we looked at perceived economic challenges facing the city. How a city's economic challenges are viewed will influence the preference for particular economic development strategies. For example, if lack of jobs is considered to be the major economic problem, tax abatements and city land clearing efforts might suffice to attract retail businesses that would provide jobs but at a pay that might be lower than would be desired if the lack of high paying jobs was considered the main problem. Third, we examined city leaders' ideas about resource limitations. How resource limitations are perceived also may influence strategy. The view that the city lacks financial resources necessary to pursue development, for example, may lead officials to oppose initiatives or support inexpensive projects. Fourth, we examined the importance of obtaining support from various others, such as local businesses and citizen groups. The importance accorded support from citizen groups, for instance, may influence a given office-holder to support development proposals that promote quality of life amenities rather than one that provides tax abatements for business without consideration of amenities. The survey questions are listed in the Appendix at end of this chapter.

Perceptions on these four issues – the importance of economic development, economic challenges facing the city, resource limitations, and support from others – are fundamental in shaping the kinds of economic development proposals city leaders are likely to support. For example, if economic development is not considered important to the city, it is unlikely support would be given to any specific proposal. Or, if a lack of high paying jobs is perceived to be the major challenge facing the city, then a proposal to attract a big-box retail store via tax abatements may not receive ready support. As a further example, if support from citizens is considered important, then a proposal to include a quality of life amenity, such as a park, as part of an economic development package may be viewed favorably.

The findings

Importance of economic development

The level of importance accorded economic development was strikingly similar across all three institutional positions. For city managers, mayors and council members, the mean score was 6.6 (out of 7). Despite differences in institutional position, these three types of city leaders considered economic development efforts equally important to their city. There was no reliable institutional difference on this question.

Economic challenges facing the city

Findings on the economic challenges facing their city, reported in Table 7.1, revealed an overall convergence of viewpoint within which there were some notable differences. For comparative purposes, the six items are ordered by importance to city managers. As can be seen, all items were considered an economic challenge; over one-quarter of all respondents identified each item as a challenge. The findings also showed a general consistency in how these challenges are prioritized. Lack of revenue, rising costs, and lack of high paying jobs ranked as the top three challenges for each institutional position-holder.

However, while city managers viewed lack of sufficient revenue as the overriding financial challenge facing their city, mayors and council members viewed rising costs as the more serious

Table 7.1 Economic challenges facing your city

	Managers (n = 151)	Mayors (n = 136)	Council members (n = 54)
Percentage who identified:			
Lack of sufficient revenue	**58**	**38**	**39**
Rising costs (e.g. fuel)	**36**	**49**	48
Lack of high paying jobs	33	41	39
Lack of economic diversity	32	32	30
Lack of jobs	28	26	30
Declining/restrictive state grants	28	28	30

Notes:
Values are the number of responses to a given item expressed as a percentage of returned surveys from a particular city position.
Items are ordered according to city manager responses.
Statistically reliable differences are in bold fo*nt*

financial challenge, though by a plurality and not a majority. A test of means showed the views of city managers to be reliably different from those of the elected officials on this item (significant at the 0.05 level for both – manager v. mayor, $p = 0.001$; manager v. council, $p = 0.018$), while the views of mayors and council members were not reliable different. City managers viewed lack of sufficient city revenue as a greater economic challenge than did mayors or council members. Regarding rising costs, though not reliably different from council members on this item, a test of means showed the views of city managers to be reliable different from those of mayors at the 0.05 level (manager v. mayor, $p = 0.021$). City managers viewed rising costs to be less of an economic problem than do mayors. In all, there were reliable differences between these institutional office-holders regarding city financial challenges related to lack of sufficient revenue and rising costs. Beyond these two items, means tests revealed no reliable difference between the three city office-holders regarding any economic challenge facing the city.

Resource limitations

As was the case with perceptions of economic challenges facing their city, when asked about resource limitations, institutional position-holders exhibited a general convergence of viewpoint punctuated by some divergence. Descriptive findings presented in Table 7.2, ordered by the frequency of responses from city managers, revealed a general consensus that the cost of funding associated with development was the single largest resource challenge, the lack of collaborative partners and city image posed greater limitations than did other listed resources, and the lack of support within city government and other problems with greater priority were not considered resource limitations to the respondent's office. One notable difference was how council members viewed costs associated with development. Council members were reliably less likely than mayors to perceive funding costs associated with development initiatives as a resource challenge compared to mayors (council v. mayor, $p = 0.039$). A second notable difference was that, compared to city managers and mayors, council members were nearly twice as likely to view lack of economic development expertise among employees as a resource challenge faced by their office (at the 0.10 level – council v. manager $p = 0.094$; council v. mayor, $p = 0.091$). Aside from these differences, the three types of office-holders held very similar views on city resource limitations.

Table 7.2 Challenges to your office's efforts to attract development

	Managers (n = 151)	Mayors (n = 136)	Council members (n = 54)
Percentage who identified:			
Funding costs associated with development initiatives	**61**	**66**	**50**
Lack of partners to collaborative with on projects	28	31	26
City's image	28	22	28
Lack of staff committed to development	17	13	13
Lack of expertise in economic development among employees	**11**	**11**	**20**
Inability to communicate with potential new businesses	11	10	9
Lack of political commitment to attracting more development	11	11	7
Lack of support within city government for development initiatives	4	4	4
Other problems have priority among employees	4	5	6

Notes:

Values are the number of responses to a given item expressed as a percentage of returned surveys from a particular city position.

Items are ordered according to city manager responses.

Statistically reliable differences are in bold font.

Importance of support from others

Successful economic development efforts can depend upon broad-based community support. As Table 7.3 reports, city managers, mayors, and council members were in agreement about the level of importance of support from fellow city leaders and citizens in the adoption and implementation of economic development proposals. Each of these institutional city office-holders viewed support from other city leaders as important for an economic development proposal to be adopted and implemented by their city. Support from citizens and citizen groups was considered important, but somewhat less so, and might be labeled as fairly important.

Table 7.3 Importance of support from city leaders, business and citizens

	Managers (n = 151)	Mayors (n = 136)	Council members (n = 54)
Mean score for:			
City leaders	6.6	6.5	6.5
Citizens & citizen groups	5.6	5.8	5.8
Business	**5.6**	**5.7**	**4.3**

Note:

Responses were on a 7 point scale with 1=Unimportant and 7=Important.

Statistically reliable differences are in bold font.

Support from business was also considered less important than support from other city leaders. Regarding business support, however, there was a reliable difference between institutional office-holders. Although there was no reliable difference between city managers and mayors, council members were reliably less likely than their counterparts to view support from business leaders as important (council v. manager, $p = 0.001$; council v. mayor, $p = 0.001$). While the city managers and mayors may be interpreted as viewing business support as fairly important in the adoption and implementation of economic development proposals, council members were decidedly less enthusiastic regarding business support.

Conclusions

Our study was motivated by the following thinking. If the success of an economic development effort depends upon a general consensus among city leaders regarding strategy and necessary resources, then we need to investigate perceptions on resources and economic challenges facing the city and the extent these viewpoints differ systematically across types of city office-holders. To the extent there are patterned differences in economic development perception between types of city leaders, there will be institutionalized differences in opinion regarding appropriate economic development strategies. Therefore, successful city leadership will be a leadership that is able to build coalitions. Successful coalition building, however, will be facilitated by the ability of leadership to recognize the institutionalized nature of varying viewpoints. To address this issue, the guiding question for our study was: To what extent are economic development perceptions associated with particular institutional city offices?

Our study's findings are based on a survey of city mayors, managers and council members in the state of Texas. These findings generally support Peterson's (1981) unitary interest thesis. City leaders in the state of Texas tend to view economic growth as their primary concern. We found a high level of agreement regarding the importance of economic development efforts among city managers, mayors and council members across cities. Regarding perceptions on specific economic development issues, though the findings reveal some level of divergence, for the most part there exists convergence in viewpoint across institutional office-holders and cities. In addition to a high level of congruence in perception regarding the overall importance of economic development efforts, there is general agreement on the economic challenges facing cities, available resources to cities, and the importance of support for specific proposals from various other groups.

The clear implication from our findings is that this level of congruence in perception on economic development issues provides a fundamental context, or starting point, from which coalition building on city economic development proposals can begin. There exists a fundamental perceptual framework that provides the foundation from which specific economic development strategy and policy proposals can be formulated.

Ostensibly, agreement among city leaders becomes easier when there is a broad consensus regarding fundamental orientations and perceptions on an issue, compared to when such consensus is absent. When trying to reach agreement on a specific economic development proposal (for example, land clearance and tax abatements to attract a Walmart) fundamentals in this sense involve perceptions regarding economic challenges facing the city (hypothetically, lack of jobs for city residents, particularly among city youth); fundamentals in this sense also involve ideas about city resources (hypothetically, the city has or can obtain resources to clear land and provide infrastructure to facilitate new retail operations). It is important to note, however, that while our findings support the idea that economic development conversation among those in city leadership positions begins with a general level of consensus regarding fundamentals, coalition building in support of an economic development proposal can still be a challenge. There are numerous factors, such as career ambition and the personalities of the city leaders involved that potentially can make the process of building consensus on a given proposal difficult. Among these factors are any institutional-related differences on specific economic development issues. Our findings indicate an interrupted convergence in economic development viewpoints among institutional city office-holders. Within the context of a general convergence of attitudes, there are occasional institutional-associated differences.

Managers view lack of city revenue as more important than either mayors or council members and tend to view rising costs as less important than do mayors. The views on city finance held by managers may be due to their distinct training – a higher level of education and a specific educational background in the field of public administration (Vanderleeuw, Sides and Williams 2015). While city managers are distinctive regarding city finance items, council members are distinctive regarding resource limitations and support from business. Council members are less likely than mayors to view funding costs associated with development initiatives as important. Though both council members and mayors are elected officials, the greater hesitancy by council members to view funding costs as an impediment to development may stem from their proximity to citizens who might view development as a good thing. In this sense, council members may view funding more from the perspective of a delegate and reflect the immediate concerns of their constituents more than do mayors. While we cannot say with certainty how many of our council member respondents were elected from, and therefore represented, council districts rather than being elected at-large (because this question was not included in the survey instrument), most council members in Texas are elected to represent a unique district. Therefore, in Svara's (1990) terms council members are more constituency-oriented than are mayors.

Further, council members are almost twice as likely to view lack of expertise in economic development among employees as a problem, compared to both city managers and mayors. We suspect this difference reflects the lack of engagement with city bureaucracy on the part of council members by comparison to managers and mayors. Finally, council members are less likely than their institutional counterparts to view support from business as important for an economic development proposal to be adopted and implemented. We speculate this difference is again due to greater proximity to citizens: between those who represent the city at-large (city mayors and managers) and those who represent specific districts (as noted above, for the most part council members represent constituents in districts). Business support for an economic development proposal may be important from an at-large perspective in order to provide jobs and revenue for city residents. However, though the city overall may want business activity, any given council district may not contain many businesses, particular if the pattern of business location is to centralize in one area of the city.

Apart from these several differences in economic development perspective, the overall convergence in viewpoint among the three institutional position-holders – regarding the importance of economic development, economic challenges, resource limitations, and support from city leaders and citizens – is intriguing. Why is there such widespread convergence in viewpoints? While we do not have definitive answers at this point, two explanations are worthy of consideration.

One potential explanation for the wide-spread shared orientation toward economic development found in our study has to do with the fact that city leaders operate in a specific cultural milieu. As noted earlier, Reese and Rosenfeld (2002) argue that culture is instrumental in understanding local economic development. City leaders in the present study were drawn from cities in one state, Texas, where a particular value is placed on small government. Therefore, many city office-holders share a similar orientation toward the importance of city economic development, as opposed to relying on the state or federal government for any assistance.

A second potential explanation involves communication between city leaders. The institutional office-holders that we surveyed operate in the context of an economic development network that can produce similarity in outlook. In this context, city managers and mayors tend to communicate more frequently with each other then they communicate with city council members (Jarmon and Vanderleeuw 2011). This more frequent communication between managers and mayors may explain why in most of the cases of divergence between our surveyed city leaders, the office-holders who differed most from the others were city council members.

While similarity in economic development outlook within any given city is potentially the result of a shared culture and communication between leaders, our findings also point to a high level of consistency in outlook among leaders across different cities. What might account for congruence in economic development perception across cities? Again, while we offer no definitive answers at this point, two potential explanations for a convergence of viewpoint across cities are worthy of consideration.

First, the strategic incentives of city decision-makers, both governmental and nongovernmental, can influence thinking on economic development. In this regard, the financial and electoral motives of developers and local elected officials, as discussed earlier, can play a key role in promoting numerous economic development initiatives (see Molotch 1976; Feiock and Kim 2001). The quest by developers for profits and the desire for local politicians to gain reelection are motivations that cross city boundary lines. Certainly, the financial motives of developers and electoral motives of city office-holders might explain the consistently high value city leaders placed on economic development to the city (responses to the question, 'How important are economic development efforts for your city?').

Second, convergence in economic development perceptions among city leaders across different cities potentially has to do with isomorphic processes. Borrowing from DiMaggio and Powell's (1983) discussion of isomorphic processes, one such process involves the dissemination of information that occurs as the result of attendance at state, regional and national professional conferences, such as the American Society for Public Administration (ASPA). Through this process, a fundamental orientation toward city economic development can spread across leaders of diverse communities. A related isomorphic process involves the city managers' frequent policy-making role relative to city councils. City managers do more than implement policy decided upon by their city council. Rather, a city manager can be relied on by a council for policy advice, and in some instances policy leadership (Teske and Schneider 1994; Zhang and Feiock 2009). Policy involvement by city managers is relevant in that city managers tend to have similar training and educational experiences, with the holding of a Master's in Public Administration (MPA) being common. The MPA educational background for city managers is consistent with a field standard promoted by organizations such as the Network of Schools of Public Policy, Affairs, and Administration (NASPAA). Therefore, a shared orientation about economic development, from manager to mayor and council, may result from the specific training and education obtained by city managers.

Conclusion

Institutional city office-holders such as mayor, council member and manager tend to embrace a common perception regarding city economic development. This common perception likely provides a crucial foundation for coalition building in support of specific economic development proposals. Broad-based support for an economic development proposal is important for its success, and judging from our findings it seems likely that several factors push these city institutional position-holders in the direction of common viewpoints regarding city economic development. These potential factors include a shared culture, the financial and electoral motives of developers and elected city leaders, communication among city officials, and isomorphic processes of information dissemination. Future research might aim to unpack the various potential causes we have identified, to determine why perceptions related to economic development issues might be so similar across different institutional position-holders and across cities.

Future research might also consider addition factors such as the local political context. The level of political competition, for example, has been found to influence a community's economic growth, as has the prevailing political ideology (Besley, Perrson and Sturm 2010; Betz, Partridge, Kraybill and Lobao 2012). City proximity to other communities might also be considered. Holding a leadership position in a geographically isolated community may impact economic development perceptions, in that these types of communities face unique economic development challenges (see e.g. King, Peredo and Chrisman 2009; Stephens and Partridge 2011). Further, city characteristics such as population size and socioeconomic characteristics might influence city leaders' perceptions and might be worthy of consideration.

Finally, the findings reported in this study are drawn from city leaders in one state in the United States – the state of Texas. Though the second most populous state in the United States (behind California) Texas is still one among fifty states. The findings presented in this study could be expanded to include city leaders in other states especially to the extent that cultural milieu has an influence on perceptions. This would allow research to determine the generalizability of the findings presented here (i.e. the breadth of convergence in economic development viewpoint). Future study might also include a wider range of city leaders such as heads of city departments. Their perceptions might tell us something about the depth of similarity in economic development viewpoint among city office-holders.

As a foundation for future research, our present study reveals wide-spread convergence of perception regarding economic development issues among city mayors, managers and council members in the second most populous state in the United States – the state of Texas.

References

Accordino, John and Fabrizio Fasulo. 2011. From Lone Rangers to Collaborative Communities. *Economic Development Journal* 10(1): 5–13.
Bachelor, Lynn. 1994. Regime Maintenance, Solution Sets, and Urban Economic Development. *Urban Affairs Quarterly* 29(4): 596–616.
Besley, Timoth, Torsten Perrson and Daniel Sturm. 2010. Political Competition, Policy and Growth: Theory and Evidence from the US. *Review of Economic Studies* 77: 1329–1352.
Betz, Michael, Mark Partridge, David Kraybill and Linda Lobao. 2012. Why do Localities Provide Economic Development Incentives: Geographic Competition, Political Constituencies, and Government Capacity. *Growth and Change* 43(3): 361–391.
Clark, Terry. 2011. Introduction: Taking Entertainment Seriously. In Terry Clark (ed.), *The City as Entertainment Machine*, 1–17. Lexington Books: New York.
DiMaggio, Paul and Walter Powell. 1983. The Iron Cage Revisited: Institutional Isomorphism and Collective Rationality in Organizational Fields. *American Sociological Review* 48: 147–160.
Feiock, Richard, and Jae-Hoon Kim. 2001. Form of Government, Administrative Organization, and Local Economic Development Policy. *Journal of Public Administration Research and Theory* 11(1): 29–50.
Feiock, Richard, Hyung-Jun Park, Annette Steinacker, and Jae-Hoon Kim. 2005. Institutional Collective Action and Economic Development Joint Ventures. Paper presented at the meeting of the Public Management Research Association in Los Angeles, CA, on October 2.
Grant, Jane. 1990. Making Policy Choices: Local Government and Economic Development. *Urban Affairs Quarterly* 26(2): 148–169.
Jarmon, Christopher and James Vanderleeuw. 2011. City Leaders and Economic Development Networks: The All-Channel Star Network. *Journal of Political Science*, 39: 1–32.

Kerstein, Robert. 1993. Suburban Growth Politics in Hillsborough County: Growth Management and Political Regimes. *Social Science Quarterly* 74(3): 614–630.

King, J. Kirk, Ana Maria Peredo and James Chrisman. 2009. Business Networks and Economic Development in Rural Communities in the United States. *Entrepreneurship Theory and Practice*, January: 171–195.

Kruse, Kevin. 2005. *White Flight: Atlanta and the Making of Modern Conservatism*. Princeton, NJ: Princeton University Press.

Leo, Christopher, Mary Ann Beavis, Andrew Carver and Robyne Turner. 1998. Is Urban Sprawl Back on the Political Agenda? Local Growth Control, Regional Growth Management, and Politics. *Urban Affairs Review* 34(2): 179–212.

May, Peter and Ashley Jochim. 2012. Policy Regime Perspectives: Policies, Politics, and Governing. *Policy Studies Journal* 41(3): 426–452.

McCabe, Barbara, Richard Feiock, James Clingermayer and Christopher Stream. 2009. Turnover among City Managers: The Role of Political and Economic Change. *Public Administration Review* 68(2): 380–387.

Michels, Robert. 1966. *Political Parties: A Sociological Study of the Oligarchical Tendencies of Modern Democracy*. New York: Free Press.

Molotch, Harvey. 1976. The City as a Growth Machine: Toward a Political Economy of Place. *American Journal of Sociology* 82(2): 309–332.

Molotch, Harvey. 1988. Strategies and Constraints of Growth Elites. In Scott Cummings (ed.), *Business Elites and Urban Development: Case Studies and Critical Perspectives*, 25–47. Albany, NY: State University of New York Press.

Morgan, Jonathan. 2010. Governance, Policy Innovation, and Local Economic Development in North Carolina. *Policy Studies Journal* 38(4): 679–702.

Peterson, Paul. 1981. *City Limits*. Chicago, IL: University of Chicago Press.

Pfeffer, Jeffrey and Gerald Salancik. 2003. *The External Control of Organizations: A Resource Dependency Perspective*. Stanford, CA: Stanford University Press.

Pitkin, Hanna. 1967. *The Concept of Representation*. Berkeley, CA: University of California Press.

Reese, Laura. 2006. Do We Really Need Another Typology? Clusters of Local Economic Development Strategies. *Economic Development Quarterly* 20(4): 368–376.

Reese, Laura and Raymond Rosenfeld. 2002. *The Civic Culture of Local Economic Development*. Thousand Oaks, CA: Sage.

Reese, Laura and Gary Sands. 2007. Making the Least of Our Differences? Trends in Canadian and U.S. Local Economic Development, 1990–2005. *Canadian Public Administration* 50(1): 79–99.

Rigos, Platon and Darryl Paulson. 1996. Urban Development, Policy Failure, and Regime Change in a Manager-Council City: The Case of St. Petersburg, Florida. *Urban Affairs Review* 32(2): 244–263.

Ross, Bernard and Myron Levine. 2001. *Urban Politics: Power in Metropolitan America*. Itasca, IL: Peacock.

Sharp, Elaine (ed.). 1999. *Culture Wars and Local Politics*. Lawrence, KS: University Press of Kansas.

Stephens, Heather M. and Mark D. Partridge. 2011. Do Entrepreneurs Enhance Economic Growth in Lagging Regions? *Growth and Change* 42(4): 431–465.

Stone, Clarence. 1989. *Regime Politics*. Lawrence, KS: University Press of Kansas.

Stone, Clarence and Heywood Sanders. 1987. Competing Paradigms: A Rejoinder to Peterson. *Urban Affairs Quarterly* 22: 48–51.

Strom, Elizabeth. 2002. Converting Pork into Porcelain: Cultural Institutions and Downtown Development. *Urban Affairs Review* 38(1): 3–21.

Svara, James. 1987. Mayoral Leadership in Council-Manager Cities: Precondition versus Preconceptions. *The Journal of Politics* 49(1): 207–227.

Svara, James. 1990. *Official Leadership in the City*. New York: Oxford University Press.

Teske, Paul and Mark Schneider. 1994. The Bureaucratic Entrepreneur: The Case of City Managers. *Public Administration Review* 54(4): 331–340.

Vanderleeuw, James and Jason Sides. 2016. Quality of Life Amenities as Contributors to Local Economies: Views of City Managers. *Journal of Urban Affairs* 38(5): 661–675.

Vanderleeuw, James, Jason Sides and Brian Williams. 2015. An Advanced Degree in Public Administration – Is it Valued by City Councils? *Public Administration Quarterly* 39(3): 453–483.

Zemmering, Eric. 2008. Governing Interlocal Cooperation: City Council Interests and the Implications for Public Management. *Public Administration Review* 68(4): 731–741.

Zhang, Yahong and Richard Feiock. 2009. City Managers' Policy Leadership in Council-Manager Cities. *Journal of Public Administration Research and Theory* 20: 461–476.

Appendix

Survey questions

Importance of economic development

How important are economic development efforts for your city?

Important   Unimportant

1   2   3   4   5   6   7

Economic challenges facing the city

What are the specific economic challenges presently facing your city? (You may identify more than one)

Lack of jobs

Lack of high paying jobs

Rising costs (e.g. fuel)

Lack of economic diversity

Lack of sufficient revenue

Declining/restrictive state grants

Resource limitations

What are the primary challenges to your office's efforts to attract more development to your city? (Designate all the apply)

Lack of staff committed to development

City's image

Lack of partners to collaborative with on projects

Funding costs associated with development initiatives

Lack of support within city government for development initiatives

Other problems have priority among employees

Lack of expertise in economic development among employees

Inability to communicate with potential new businesses

Lack of political commitment to attracting more development

Importance of support from others

For an economic development proposal to be adopted and implemented by your city, how important is it that the proposal has support from:

Unimportant	Important
Business leaders in your community	1 2 3 4 5 6 7
Citizens or citizen groups in your city	1 2 3 4 5 6 7
Other city leaders	1 2 3 4 5 6 7

PART II

Local governments in different jurisdictions

8
THE POLITICAL SALIENCE OF LOCAL GOVERNMENT IN A SMALL STATE

Ann Marie Bissessar

Introduction

The basic premise of any democratic society is to expand the 'voice' of its population and to allow citizens, irrespective of race, gender, religion or other differences, some measure of participation in decision making within that society. In other words, the extent of 'democracy' within a society hinges upon the tools or mechanisms introduced in that society to allow for consultation and collaboration. While there is an extensive literature on collaboration in the policy process (Keane 2009; Habermas 1984). Holmes (2011: 1) argues that:

> Genuine engagement in the 'co-production' of policy and services requires major shifts in the culture and operations of government agencies. It demands of public servants' new skills as enablers, negotiators and collaborators. It demands of citizens an orientation to the public good, a willingness to actively engage, and the capabilities needed to participate and deliberate well. These are tall orders, especially if citizens are disengaged and certain groups within the population are marginalised.

In order to foster greater participation and collaboration in decision-making, one mechanism that has been introduced by many developed and developing countries, were systems of local government.

In former colonies of Britain, local government, or 'district or ward administration' as it was then referred to in the early 1900s, focused primarily on the delivery of administrative services and the maintenance of limited infrastructure to areas which were often isolated because of lack of connective structures such as roads and transportation (Bissessar 2003). Later, in the 1960s, as these various colonies attained independence, the system of district administration was conceptually broadened into a system of local government. Included in that system were clear lines of geographical demarcation which later became known as 'boundary lines'. These 'lines' defined the voting constituencies. However, as the concept of local government widened to include not only expanded administrative services that were adaptive to a particular community, but also to include the local population in community as well as central decision-making tensions became apparent. Rather than bringing the population together in a collaborative effort at 'national' decision-making, the boundaries set up under the system of local government established communal territories. It further reinforced the racial divisions within this society. To a large extent, then, in the case of Trinidad and Tobago, local government has remained in a suspended state, one in which a limited measure of 'administration' is the primary focus. Local government has therefore been confined to de-centralisation of basic services at the local level. As it relates to the twin-goals of educating and empowering citizens this has not been achieved. Rather the fragmentation within this society continues to promote the syndrome of 'we' versus 'them'. This communal pull has largely prevented local government from achieving wider goals of participation, collaboration and consensual decision-making. The discussion which follows will accordingly present a brief overview of the county and later discuss the attempts at reforming local government from the 1960s onwards.

Trinidad and Tobago: establishing a society from transplanted groups

In ex-colonial societies such as Trinidad and Tobago, the population is largely a 'transplanted' society comprising mainly of ex-slaves brought from Africa and indentured labourers, the majority of whom were brought from Kolkata, India. The assimilation of these ethnic groups or communities was initially based on the need of the plantation owners for cheap sources of labour. However, with the abolition of slavery, the former slaves, now freed men and women, migrated from the plantations and moved to the townships where they were employed as petty artisans, carpenters or on the railways. The East Indians, on the other hand were mainly domiciled on the cane plantations. While this pattern of settlement of 'groups' existed in many of the ex-colonies, a major difference in how the groups were located was also based on the size of the countries. It is reasonable to assume, for instance, that in large countries where there are many ethnic communities, the method or mechanism for assimilation varied; for example, in the case of Guyana, the African population settled in the coastal areas while the East Indians settled in the interior. In the larger countries, because of the vast geographical distances between the groups, the potential conflict between these groups was understandably limited. In the small countries, however, where the potential for conflict existed, the mechanisms for assimilation of these groups had to take into account the views and expectations of the various ethnic communities and accordingly translate them into what may be reasonable policies for the country as a whole. In other words, the governments had to take a more position that emphasised policy compromise. In doing this, the perceptions a community may have of others was critical in determining the nature of a particular policy or mechanism.

These perceptions of the 'other' may well be what Tonnies (1940) described in his *gemeinschaft* and *gesellschaft* relationships. According to Tonnies, *gemeinshaft* relations are essentially identified with kinship and biological ties, sharing of *place*, as well as common values, ideals and bonds that are expressed through sacred beliefs and represented by sacred places and worshipped deities. *Gesellschaft relationships*, on the other hand, are best represented in states where convention, contract, legislative law and public opinion provide the bases for law, order and morality. In many societies, particularly ex-colonial societies, *gemeinshaft relationships* seem to be the order of the day. It should be recalled, though, that the perception of '*we-ness*' as opposed to '*they-ness*' were constructs that were virtually imposed by the colonial administrators. The policy of what of what has been described as a policy of *divide and rule* was deliberate in order to erect barriers to foster the assimilation of these groups. To further ensure the separation of these groups, in a number of colonial territories, as was noted in the case of Trinidad and Tobago, groups were allocated separate and distinct geographic *spaces*. In some countries, as well, the imposition of colonial political structures, systems and institutions further served to maintain the separation of the various communities. The nature of the accommodation of the various groups is perhaps appropriately summed up by Stavenhagen (1996: 61). He observed that colonial domination created varied different patterns in societies where foreign peoples were brought in, either as slaves or indentured servants or simply as plantation labour. One similarity, he pointed out, was that the struggles that emerged in later years involved ethnic groups whose identities were not linked to early territorial claims (as in Fiji) in regional concentration (as in Nigeria) or to ancient historical markers (Burundi). Rather, these groups or communities were linked to more recent and more visible ethnic markers such as race, religion, and culture and directly related to political competition over the resources of the state.

In the case of the twin-island republic of Trinidad and Tobago, the experience was no different. Even though Trinidad and Tobago are relatively small geographies, the demarcation of the country into divisions, while it did promote awareness of local concerns, led to the establishment of communal territories and erected communal markers. To a large extent, this communal separation has largely been retained and is reflected in the voting trends from 1956 to present. This separation and its continued reinforcement by the two major political parties has been largely responsible for the population perceiving the country along 'communal' rather than national lines. Furthermore, it has led to a major weakness in the management of local government systems within the country.

Independence and the reform of local government

With the limited resource and the wide expanse of territory, under colonial administration, the mandates of the former administrators were limited to law, order, and the maintenance of basic infrastructure. As a result, the mechanism of district administration, the forerunner of local government was limited as well. However, when ministerial government was introduced in 1956 and later in 1962 as the country attained independent status, the newly established government of the People's National Movement (an African-based party) sought to introduce a number of development initiatives. Among these initiatives was a five-year plan, including proposals to decentralise the health systems along with mechanisms to improve the systems of local administration. Accordingly, one local newspaper observed in its editorial:

> The purpose of the extension of local government responsibilities in the counties is to decentralize administrative functions and to provide local people with experience suitable incentives in the management of their affairs.
> (Sunday Guardian, *15 March 1959: 9*)

Singh (1970), an early critic of the systems of local government in the Caribbean, suggested however, that what was actually introduced was a de-concentration of power, rather than decentralisation. He argued that in transplanting local government institutions, even during its inception, the Governors in all the British colonies had 'busied themselves with applying the British forms but failed to give much attention to the spirit and content of political institutions as to their constitutional façade' (Singh 1970: 22). He argued that later attempts to foster the success of this system were thwarted by ambitious and impatient politicians who viewed political power, not training as their aim. To a large extent, this statement has been supported by the minimal reforms attempted to date even though a number of reform committees were established overtime.

For example, in 1965, recommendations for appropriate measures to allow for the shift in local administration away from the former 'ward or district administration' were delegated to a committee, the Sinanan Committee. The head of this committee was Dr Eric Williams, the political leader of the People's National Movement party. The mandate of this Committee was to recommend measures to allow for decentralisation from the central government particularly and to allow for greater empowerment of the local communities. One of the recommendations of this Committee was that the system of Local Government should become one of the major mechanisms to improve democracy within the country. It was believed, in principle, that this introduction would also assist with the movement towards self-determination. In other words, the underlying philosophy was that the country had to be developed by people who lived in the respective communities. The committee gave little attention to the assimilation of the various groups.

Emerging from the recommendations of the Sinanan Committee was the introduction of the County Council Act of 1967. This Act separated local government control into seven distinct and named countries; St Patrick, Victoria, Nariva/Mayaro, St George, St Andrews/St David, Caroni and the smaller island of Tobago. A number of other critical recommendations of the committee were however, ignored and instead of measures to allow for the decentralisation of key functions to local governments in the communities, many of the functions and responsibilities under the control of the municipalities were centralised. For example, the Water and Sewerage Act (1965) established a Statutory Corporation, the Water and Sewerage Authority (WASA), which was given the monopoly position of water sourcing and distribution. Additionally, legislation such as the Statutory Authorities Act (1965) and the Civil Service Act (1966) allowed that the authorities established under these differing pieces of legislation to become the principal agencies with responsibility of staff appointments, transfers and disciplines. The nature of this centralisation, which also included financial centralisation as set out under the Exchequer and Audit Act (1965) seemed counter to the remit of a system of local government. Indeed, the introduction of these authorities and the financial impositions on the county councils were clearly not in keeping with the intent of systems of local government, which by its very term suggested empowerment of the citizenry at the local levels. In interrogating the basic, first level tenets of a system of local government or decentralised administration, it should be noted that this is a broad concept which comprises institutions, systems, processes but essentially focuses on the empowering of its citizenry.

As Shah (2007) observes, local government is usually defined as the formulation and execution of collective action at the local level. Thus, it encompasses the direct and indirect role of formal institutions of local government and government hierarchies as well as the roles of informal norms, networks, community organisations and neighbourhood associations in pursuing collective action by defining the framework for citizen–citizen and citizen–state interactions, collective decision-making and the delivery of local public services. The bottom-line though, is that local government is about 'self-governing' communities. In many countries around the world, local government systems have a number of functions which include planning and monitoring, service delivery at the local level, law-making and enforcement, policy development, representation and advocacy. In other words, the role of the central as opposed to the local government systems are clearly established with the central government having responsibility for policy development as well as for the determination of standards of service and performance while service delivery was to be provided at local government level. Essentially, it was a two tiered system of administration with policy being determined at the centre and delivery at the peripheries. The advantages to be obtained from this kind of arrangement were numerous and included a closer link to customers, timeliness in the delivery of services, and cost effectiveness for the payment of these services. This method of administration also ensured that the voice of the citizen would be heard.

Table 8.1 Results of the local government elections, 1968

Party	Seats won	Votes
People's National Movement	68	49.4%
Democratic Labour Party	28	40.0%
United Country Group, St Andrew-St. David	0	0.8%
Independents	4	9.3%
Rejected		0.0%

Source: www.ebctt.com/elections/local-government-elections.

Yet, while the perception from the outside was that Trinidad and Tobago was a consolidated country subdivided into this two-tiered central and local government structure, within the country it was evident that the country was fractured by two main groups each vying for political power, namely the African-descended population and the East Indian descended population. While it was true that there were other groups within the population, these groups tended to consolidate their power in the business sphere rather than vie for power in the political arena. Thus even before the country attained independence, it was evident that the battle line was drawn between the two majority groups and this was clearly visible from the 1968 local government election results (see Table 8.1).

That it was a two-party race was clear. The People's National Movement (with much of its support drawn from the African-descended population) captured 49.4% of the votes or sixty-eight seats while the East Indian party, the Democratic Labour Party captured 40.0% of the vote or 28 seats.

Given the high level of distrust between the two groups and the contest for power the local government systems in Trinidad and Tobago became confined to the delivery of basic services such as the maintenance of government buildings, the maintenance of public cemeteries, markets, and the maintenance of basic infrastructure

It is not clear why, even at inception, limited powers were actually given to the administrators and local government councillors. Perhaps, one explanation is that offered by Mills (1977). He argued that 'older officials' conditioned by the colonial system and some as heads of departments and who were accustomed to performing roles as policy makers resented the intrusion of elected political heads and found difficultly in adjusting to their new subordinate status. On the other hand, he observed that the ministers were conscious of their newly acquired powers and were determined to dispel any suggestions of inferiority. If his opinion is correct, then perhaps, one of the challenges during this period may have been due to the reluctance of the newly elected and appointed ministers to delegate powers. This suggestion is also supported by Ryan (2002).

Yet other factors may also have been influential. In a newly independent country, issues such as lack of trained staff, inadequate systems to monitor and evaluate agencies, as well the lack of enthusiasm on the part of the general citizenry could also have been relevant to the decision to allow many of the key responsibilities of government to be remain centralised. One salient factor also would have been ideological. While much of the current literature on local government relates to the empowerment of citizenry, it should be recalled that during the period 1960s to 1970s, the focus of governments around the world was primarily on decentralisation as an administrative approach for local-level governance in the post-colonial era. Cohen and Peterson (1996) suggested that during this period the focus was largely on administrative aspects of decentralisation, with particular concern with the legal organisation of centre-field office relationships and the role of local authorities or municipalities within a centrally managed government.

One argument that has never been proffered in an examination of the challenges in delegating power to local government authorities in the case of Trinidad, though, has been the conflicts between the two political parties. Yet, political conflicts between the two majority racial groups cannot be discounted in any discussion about the extent to which power is disbursed in a country or the level of empowerment one allocates to its citizenry. In discussing conflict, perhaps the criteria advanced by Kreps and Wenger (1973) are pertinent. They enlisted four levels of conflict, namely:

- The greater the scope of the conflict, the greater the issues.
- The greater the scope of the conflict, the more important the issues involved in the process.
- The greater the scope of the conflict, the greater the societal polarisation.
- The greater the scope of the conflict, the greater the progress of the partisan and leadership.

In the case of Trinidad and Tobago, the two latter points seem to be extremely relevant. An examination of the composition of the society within specific constituencies would for instance reveal that these formed the bedrock of one of the two major racial groups. Thus, while the constituencies who supported the government virtually enjoyed the 'spoils' those who supported the opposing party complained that they were discriminated and polarised. The idea of 'empowerment' of the rank and file of the citizenry therefore would not have been beneficial to any ruling party at this time. Factors such as the reluctance of the early politicians to delegate power, the lack of capacity, limited resources and racial considerations were undoubtedly responsible for the decisions taken by the government as it related to power-sharing between the centre and the peripheries. In addition, it should be recalled that whenever a party assumes power, it is often accompanied, particularly in societies which are divided along racial lines, with patronage. The creation of authorities, ministries and numerous departments therefore facilitated a number of 'partisan' relationships during the post-independence period.

Further attempts to reform local government

The second attempt at reform of the system of local commenced in 1974 with the appointment of the Hugh Wooding Constitution Commission to address the issue of Constitutional Reform, both at the local and central government levels. Accordingly, This Commission recommended the devolution of significant powers and authority to local governments. These included responsibility for maintenance of schools, specified public buildings, cleaning of beaches, providing facilities for fisheries and greater autonomy to control funds appropriated by Parliament. The central government implemented the recommendation to extend Local Government boundaries, which resulted in the division of County St. George into East and West in 1980. Among other enquiries at this period were the following reports:

- 1975: The Herrera Report – Towards Greater Efficiency in the Existing Local Government System;
- 1976: The Mohammed Report – Report of the Committee on Devolution by Central Government to Local Government;
- 1976: The Allahar Report – Implications of Decentralization/Devolution of Greater Autonomy to Local Government;
- 1977: Report of the Committee appointed to institute discussion on the expanded role and functions of local government.

Table 8.2 Local government results, 1977

Party	Seat won	Votes
Democratic Action Committee	4	6.6%
People's National Movement	69	51.1%
United Labour Front	27	37.8%
Democratic Labour Party	0	1.2%
Tapia House Movement	0	0.3%
Independents	0	2.4%
Rejected		0.7%

Source: Catón (2005)

Many of the recommendations of these various committees were purported to be incorporated in the revised County Council Act No 26 of 1977. A third attempt at reform of the local government system was undertaken with the enactment of the Tobago House of Assembly (THA) Act and subsequent operationalisation of the Assembly in 1982. The THA was in essence a County Council with expanded functions and powers.

During the period 1968–1977, it was evident that the management of local government was one in which the central government assumed the leading role. Local governments within the various constituencies continued to offer basic services. While it was true, that local government boards comprising local councillors or administrators were established in each constituency, to a large extent, if not in nearly in all cases, the racial and political affiliation within the particular constituency reflected either the ruling political (racially based) party or the opposition party. Indeed, the outcome of both the local as well as the general elections were predictive with constituencies, according to ethnic groups, voting for their choice of party and leader (see Table 8.2).

As Table 8.2 indicates, 51.1% of the votes were in favour of the Afro-dominant political party the People's National Movement (PNM) while the East Indian votes were split between the Democratic Action Committee (DAC), Democratic Labour Party (DLP) and the newly formed United Labour Front (ULF) all Indo-based parties.

By the latter half of the 1970s, however, there appeared a shift in the ideological basis of local government to include the citizenry as a primary focus. Thus in 1983, there was a fourth attempt at local government reform by the PNM administration, under the Honourable George Chambers. A Draft Policy Paper on Community Development and Local Government Reform was published for public comment. The language had changed. The manifesto of local government articulated that Local Government Authorities would be a 'partner' in the national development process, through enhanced participation in national policy making, community development and development planning. It also proposed a National and an Area Advisory Committee should be established to accomplish these objectives. However, the plans did not elaborate on meaningful mechanisms to promote greater autonomy of Local Government Authorities, nor did it suggest mechanisms for including all citizens into the decision-making process. No doubt, what the government, under a new leader, had sought to do was to try to appeal to the populace as a way of maintaining some level of stability. Indeed, during the period 1981–1990 the country had experienced an economic downturn as a result of the fall in oil prices, the countries major source of income. The period 1981–1983 was therefore extremely unstable with the threats of shut downs and protests. As it stood, though, the 'good' intentions never materialised as this government lost elections after one term in office and plans to reform local government during the period 1983–1990 was once more deferred.

In 1990, the Municipal Corporations Act was passed. The main achievement of this Act was the splitting of the existing eight counties into 14 municipalities. By the 1990s, it was apparent that although an Act had been introduced very little had changed. Power remained centralised and the local government system exhibited little change from the model that had been introduced in 1965 under the Country Council Act. Accordingly, as part of protest action on the part of a number of groups, a major local government conference was held in 1990. The following weaknesses were identified by the various conference presenters:

- inadequate funding;
- weak management;
- control and discipline of staff;
- tenure of the life of the council;
- remuneration and conditions of service of the representatives;
- interaction between council and other government agencies;
- tendering procedures;
- lack of equipment;
- non-delivery of powers to the Councils as made out by the County Councils Act (e.g. street lighting and school feeding).

Yet even this open display challenging the status quo as it related to the lack of initiatives relating to local government reform did nothing to break the inertia. Reforms were not introduced. Rather, it appeared that the system of local government continued to serve as it did in the 1960s with very few changes. By the end of 2016, then, very few reforms had been introduced in the local government authorities although numerous consultations were held to arrive at mechanisms to allow for reforms. Thus the basic functions of local government continued to be limited.

As it related to the community services these included:

- Provision, maintenance and control of public parks, recreation grounds and other public spaces.
- Provision, maintenance and control of public burial grounds, crematoria and cremation sites.
- Maintenance of state property.
- Provision, maintenance and control of all municipal buildings (such as town halls and community centres).
- Erection and provision of stages and platforms for community events.
- Provision, maintenance and control of public retail markets.
- Distribution of truck-borne water to areas without pipelines.
- Coordination of trade fairs, athletic events, cultural displays and entertainment.
- Management of disaster relief efforts, establishing disaster relief centres, clearing roadways and waterways.

Challenges of local government reform in a small island state

After nearly fifty-five years of stable democratic rule, albeit with oscillation between the two major race-based, political parties, what emerges is that the power relationship between the central government and local government has experienced little or no significant shifts. Policy prescriptions, staffing, funding, and approvals for projects continue to be administered from the

Table 8.3 Percentage of persons voting at local government elections, 1999–2016

Year	Percentage
2016	34.3%
2013	43.6%
2010	39.1%
2003	37.9%
1999	38.7%

Source: www.ebctt.com/elections/local-government-elections.

central ministry. Further to this, with few exceptions, even the collection of taxes is channelled through the government's central fund. In other words, the relationship and the scope of the two agencies of central and the local government remain static.

What accounts for the adherence of this relationship is difficult to unravel since very few data are publicly available as it relates to customer perception of local government, funding irregularities, achievements or lack thereof. What appears from the data, though, is that voter participation at the level of local government continues to be below 50% (Table 8.3).

Conclusion

In the case of Trinidad and Tobago, the challenges first highlighted in the 1960s and 1970s to account for the reluctance to realign the arrangements between the central government and the local government are no longer relevant. Factors such as the lack of capable staff, lack of funding, and general distrust between the newly appointed ministers and civil servants can now be discounted. One factor, however, persists and continues to dominate the discussion, namely the racial composition of the society resulting in polarisation at the levels of the political parties. Again, Kreps and Wenger's (1973: 169) analysis may assist in finding an explanation, from a broader understanding of societal conflict. According to the authors, a number of factors can either facilitate or impede conflict within the community, in this case a small country. The factors identified include:

- a participative political structure;
- the degree of pluralism in the power structures;
- the past history of conflict within the community;
- the degree of structural integration.

Unlike its neighbours such as Suriname or Guyana, in Trinidad and Tobago there is little disturbances during elections, yet it is clear that each government during its term in office has been reluctant to introduce reforms as it relates to local government or to interfere with the existing power-sharing arrangement. While some may suggest that it is due to the lack of political will, this seems a feeble explanation, particularly since there have been many occasions when the respective governments obtained windfalls in their economy.

Rather, what is emerging is that each government, whether African-based or East Indian-based, has paid token attention to decentralisation. Some may suggest that these governments preferred to retain centralised power and exercise control, what some writers may proffer to be a principal–agent arrangement. Yet, another explanation may be, that if further decentralisation or de-concentration of authority was introduced by a government, all groups, irrespective of their race or political affiliation would directly benefit from state resources. Understandably, this new arrangement would result in a major re-alignment in the power relationship between the political directorate and its citizenry.

In a sense, then, one can argue that in keeping the present centre-local arrangement, the principal, in this case, the governing party stands to benefit tremendously not only in the disbursement of funds and resources to those constituencies that support them, but at the same time by creating central agencies they can place their supporters in top and critical decision making positions. In other words in small societies such as Trinidad and Tobago, the avenue for clientelism prevails. As (Brinkerhoff and Goldsmith 2004) suggest, clientelism refers to a complex chain of personal bonds between political patrons and their individual clients or followers. The bonds, they observe are founded on mutual material advantage: the patron furnishes excludable resources to dependents or accomplices in return for their support and cooperation. But as Schedler (undated) notes, and his observation is relevant in the case of Trinidad and Tobago, clientelism is not a blind personal loyalty that creates bonds between patrons and clients. There is rational economic calculation in building this dyadic relationship. To reinforce the concept, Clapham (1985: 56) cites the Mexican case where voters came up with an impressive list: cash, pencils, lighters, bags of basic foodstuff and so forth for the electoral support that the party leaders wanted from them. He summarises the phenomenon as follows:

> Political party leaders at the national level look around for local leaders who command appropriate support within their own areas. They offer the local leader . . . a place in the party, perhaps a candidate in his home constituency. The local leader gets out the vote, essentially through his own contacts and authority, and delivers it to the national party. The national party in turn assuming that it wins power delivers benefits to its local representative, in the form either of economic allocations from the centre to the constituency . . . or of a purely personal pay-off, or of central government support in local political conflicts.
>
> *(Clapham 1985: 56)*

Essentially, then, this also applies in the case of Trinidad and Tobago. The challenge, therefore, is the extent to which the existing relationships between the central body and the local government level can be configured to allow for greater participation by the citizenry. Obviously, the challenge is multi-faceted. Firstly, political and constitutional reform may be necessary since the two party systems have overtime established the polarisation of political parties on lines of race. Secondly, the settlement patterns of the various groups are distinct and thus the separation of the two majority groups remains intact. Finally, one major challenge is the apathy of the citizenry. In the case of Trinidad and Tobago, therefore, it is fair to suggest that the implementation of a system of local government is still to be attained.

References

Bissessar, A. M. (2003) *Colonial Administration: A Reader*. St Augustine: School of Continuing Studies, University of the West Indies.

Brinkerhoff, D. W. and Goldsmith, A. A. (2004) Good Governance, Clientelism and Patrimonialism: A New Perspective on Old Problems. *International Public Management Journal* 7(2): 163–185.

Catón, M. (2005) Trinidad and Tobago. In D. Nohlen (ed.), *Elections in the Americas. A Data Handbook*, 11–56. Oxford: Oxford University Press.

Clapham, C. (1985) *Third World Politics: An Introduction*. London: Routledge.

Cohen, J. M. and Peterson, S. B. (1996) *Methodological Issues in the Analysis of Decentralization*. Development Discussion Paper No 555. Cambridge, MA: Harvard Institute for International Development.

Habermas, J. (1984) *The Theory of Communicative Action*. Boston, MA: Beacon Press.

Holmes, B. (2011) Brenton Holmes Citizen Engagement. Retrieved on 22 May 2017 from www.aph.gov.au/About_Parliament/Parliamentary_Departments/Parliamentary_Library/pubs/rp/rp1112/12rp01.

Keane, J. (2009) *The Life and Death of Democracy*. London: Simon & Schuster.

Kreps, G. A. and Wenger, D. E. (1973) Toward a Theory of Community Conflict: Factors Influencing the Initiation and Scope of Conflict. *The Sociology Quarterly* 14(2): 158–174.

Mills, G. E. (1977) Conflict Between Ministers and Civil Servants. *Sunday Gleaner* (Jamaica), 3 April: 327–347.

Ryan, S. (2002) Political Transitions in Trinidad and Tobago 1986–1992. In R. A. Bissessar (ed.), *Governance in the Caribbean*, 298–297. St Augustine: University of the West Indies.

Schedler, A. (Undated) Clientelism Without Clients: The Incongruent Institutionalization of Electoral Mobilization in Mexico. Paper presented at Conference on Informal Institutions and Politics in the Developing World, Harvard University, Cambridge, MA.

Shah, A. (2007) Role of Local Governments: Lessons from International Practices. Retrieved on 20 July 2017 from Worldbank.org/PSGLP/Resources/Role of Local GovernmentAnwarShah.pdf.

Singh, P. (1970) Problems of Institutional Transplantation: The Case of the Commonwealth Caribbean Local Government System. *Caribbean Studies* 10(1): 22.

Stavenhagen, R. (1996) *Ethnic Conflicts and the Nation-State*. Basingstoke: Macmillan Press.

Tonnies, F. (1940) *Fundamental Concepts of Sociology (Gemeinschaft and Gesellschaft)*. New York: American Book Company.

9
LOCAL GOVERNMENT IN THE PACIFIC ISLANDS

Graham Hassall, Matthew Kensen, Rikiaua Takeke, Karibaiti Taoba and Feue Tipu

Pacific societies and government

The contemporary Pacific Islands region includes 14 independent states and 8 dependent territories, whose combined populations amount to some ten million inhabitants. Approximately one half of all Pacific Islanders live in 100 rapidly expanding towns and cities and are classified as 'urban', while the remainder inhabit villages and settlements. Exact numbers are hard to establish due to the rapid pace of urbanisation. A 2012 report by the Asian Development Bank estimated that the urban population was growing at twice the rate of national population rates. Migration from rural areas and outer-islands thus contributes to declining populations in these areas while fuelling unprecedented population density in urban centres. The approximate populations and land areas of these 22 Pacific nations and territories are indicated in Table 9.1. These regions are classified by the United Nations as 'small island developing states' (SIDS), a designation in which each term is significant.

Table 9.1 Pacific Island country populations as at June 2016

Region/country or territory	Most recent census	Population count at last census	Land area (km²)
MELANESIA			
Fiji	2007	**837,271**	18,333
New Caledonia	2014	**268,767**	18,576
Papua New Guinea	2011	**7,059,653**	462,840
Solomon Islands	2009	**515,870**	28,230
Vanuatu	2009	**234,023**	12,281
		8,915,584	540,260
MICRONESIA			
Federated States of Micronesia	2010	**102,843**	701

Guam	2010	**159,358**	541
Kiribati	2015(p)	**109,693**	811
Marshall Islands	2011	**53,158**	181
Nauru	2011	**10,084**	21
Northern Mariana Islands	2010	**53,883**	457
Palau	2015(p)	**17,661**	444
		506,680	3,156
POLYNESIA			
American Samoa	2010	**55,519**	199
Cook Islands	2011	**14,974**	237
French Polynesia	2012	**268,270**	3,521
Niue	2011	**1,611**	259
Pitcairn Islands	2012	**57**	47
Samoa	2011	**187,820**	2,934
Tokelau	2011	**1,411**	12
Tonga	2011	**103,252**	749
Tuvalu	2012	**10,782**	26
Wallis and Futuna	2013	**12,197**	142
		655,893	8,126
TOTAL		**10,078,157**	**551,542**

Source: http://prism.spc.int/images/Population_Projections_by_PICT.xlsx

First, they are small in population and land area (but in most cases, possessing large maritime exclusive economic zones). Setting aside the remarkably small Pitcairn Island, which has an official population of 57, the smaller dependent states such as Niue and Tokelau have populations under 2,000. Sovereign states such as Nauru and Tuvalu have populations of 50,000 and up. Ten of the states and territories have populations between 100,000 (Federated States of Micronesia, Kiribati, Tonga) and 800,000 (Fiji). Papua New Guinea is by far the largest of the Pacific Island states, with a population of more than 7,000,000.

The archipelagic setting of the Pacific states is a second unique characteristic, which influences the shape of society and government, including local government. Whereas island societies had traditional arrangements for commerce and exchange, most also developed their own distinct language, culture and leadership. Authority was thus more often exercised at local level than across island groups, such that the idea of government administered from a central location only emerged with the development of a main administrative centre during a period of colonial rule. This colonial experience shaped the political and economic circumstances of what are now termed 'developing' countries.

The place of local government in Pacific Island states

Constitutional arrangements across the Pacific – which range from kingdoms to republics – generally focus on delineating government at national and provincial levels, and leave the question of local government to subsidiary legislation or else to the realm of 'customary law'. For this reason, the roles and responsibilities assigned to local government, the levels of fiscal decentralisation, the opportunities (or lack thereof) of autonomous revenue streams, and the complexity of scale vary significantly across the region. There are an estimated 900 sub-national government bodies across the Pacific. Papua New Guinea alone has approximately 6,000 elected or appointed local government councillors, while local level officials in the remaining countries and territories number approximately 900.

Historically, Pacific Islanders governed local communities at village level. The emergence of urban areas, in which local government was established as part of the modern state,[1] is thus a relatively recent phenomenon. In some countries local government has only been established in urban areas and not rural, and there is a tendency for urban populations to replicate traditional patterns of social organisation and leadership in their new settings. Jones has recently commented on the tendency for populations to replicate village formations in their new urban settings:

> In 2012, it was estimated that 800,000–1,000,000 Pacific urban residents lived in native and traditional villages and informal and squatter settlements and, by the end of 2015, this number is likely to have risen to more than 1 million residents.
>
> (Jones 2016)

Pacific cities and urban centres foster regional economic integration and national development. They are focal centres of economic growth, are often seats of government and administration at national or provincial level, national windows and gateways, and centres of higher education, among others. They are also well-placed to be the service and support centres for surrounding rural hinterlands and/or smaller rural towns. However, there are just four designated capital cities in the Pacific – Port Moresby, Port Vila, Honiara, and Suva, the remainder being urban centres on land leased from their traditional owners by national government entities, but remaining, in a formal sense, nothing more than modern urban villages. Tonga's centre of government, for instance, Nuku'alofa, although commonly regarded as one urban area, is actually a fusion of Kolomotua (the old village) and KoloFo'ou (the new village). Samoa's main administrative centre, Apia, has a similar circumstance: both contain their nation's capital, but neither is governed by a local government authority. Papua New Guinea's National Capital District, where Port Moresby is located, exists on land leased long term from the Motu-Koitabu people. Other capitals are similarly located on leased customary land and disputes arise periodically – such as with Vanuatu's Port Vila. In the case of Kiribati, the country is regarded as being 100% urban due to its population density, and has just three declared towns or urban councils: Teinainano Urban, Betio Town and Kiritimati Urban.

Nauru could also be considered 100% urban, now that 169 traditional villages have become slightly more than 100 interconnected communities. Whereas the number of villages in Solomon Islands is not tracked, the number for Samoa is known to be 330, and for Tonga, 170.[2] In the case of Palau, Koro is the only recognised town, although Melekeok has been constructed as the seat of the nation's capital, and there are 21 additional towns and villages.

Papua New Guinea has made the most far-reaching attempts to devolve the legal, financial and administration arrangements between central, provincial and local levels of government. In Vanuatu, Local Governments are responsible for Area Councils, which in turn comprise multiple villages. The size and population of the Area Council is not legally binding and so there is no threshold to how many villages or people can make up an Area Council. In Solomon Islands, Local Governments are responsible for Wards, which likewise are made up of a number of villages and communities. In Tuvalu, 'local government' takes the form of an island council established for each of its eight inhabited islands (Hassall and Tipu 2008).

The scope of local governments thus differs from one Pacific Island Country to the next, and a major challenge concerns the delineation of power, roles, and responsibilities. A few additional examples will demonstrate the variety of constitutional arrangements in place.

Tonga's 1875 constitution established a constitutional monarchy and declared all land as being possessed by the Crown. Land is then managed on the Crown's behalf by the holder of a noble title – whose family is from that region but who may well live in town or abroad rather than in the village. Some villages belong to chiefs, and some belong to the government. In government villages the town officer acts like a chief, and reports to the Ministry of Internal Affairs, which is under the office of the Prime Minister. The size of land available to individual families for cultivation is decreasing. Local government is provided through the District and Town Officers Act (Chapter 43 of Tonga's consolidated laws). Twenty-three district and 155 town councillors are elected every three years in local election to undertake a variety of administrative tasks (there are some seven districts on the main island). These councillors have little autonomy: they report monthly to a district officer, who then reports quarterly to the Office of the Prime Minister. In a sense the town officer acts as an intermediary between the noble, the government and the people. Although town officers receive government salaries, they generally work without a clearly articulated budget or work programme (Bennardo and Cappell 2008). Changes to the system of local government are being considered, albeit very slowly. The government is considering how best to establish a town council (Kolo) in Nukualofa, as there is appreciation of the fact that the current system is not sufficiently responsive to the city's administrative needs.

Vanuatu ('the New Hebrides' prior to independence in 1980) is a unitary state. Local government comprises six provincial councils as well as area councils, and municipalities for the urban townships of Port Vila (the capital, on Efate) and Luganville (on the northern island, Espiritu Santo). There are approximately 2,150 villages in the country. Each province has an executive, and local area councils have a secretary who resides in the villages and who report directly to the secretary-general of the provincial council. Councils are elected through an open constituency system every four years. The mayor is elected by the councillors from among themselves on an annual basis. There are also co-opted members appointed by the minister of internal affairs from such social segments as women, youth, chiefs and churches. Port Vila City Council, the nation's capital, has been suspended on a number of occasions for misconduct or illegality, and there are considerable on-going tensions over land issues. The provincial level government covering the island of Efate, where Port Vila is located, is seeking to address land conservation issues through its 'Efate Land Management Area Initiative'.

Kiribati, a unitary state with a *beretitenti* (president) as both head of state and head of government, is divided, formally, into five districts.[3] Although the Constitution is silent on the matter of local government, three urban and town councils, and 20 island councils have been established on the country's inhabited islands. Councillors are elected for a four year term by a first-past-the post system on the basis of universal adult suffrage. The last council elections in 2016 saw 233 councillors take office. Mayors are elected councillors who can nominate themselves to run in mayoral elections, which take place after council elections, in a similar fashion to elections of MPs. Councillors can determine mayoral candidates through preferential voting when the number of candidates exceeds four. Councils also include 'special members' who are male elders' (*unimwane*) representatives, nominated members selected by the councillors to represent women's, youth's or professional groups, and ex-officio members who are members of parliament. Each council is required by law to have a senior executive officer who is the town clerk (for urban councils) or clerk to the council (for rural councils). The clerk has oversight over government-seconded officials based at the council, schools, clinics and elsewhere, as well as direct control over staff recruited and paid for by the council. From July 2017 all elected councillors receive salaries from central government.

The Kiribati Local Government Association was established in 2012 as an advocacy body through which mayors can speak on local government issues with central government, and with development and other partners. General meetings are held biennially. The association is financed by members' annual contributions of $1000, irrespective of their size, and holds memberships in such international local government bodies as Commonwealth Local Government Forum (CLGF) and United Cities and Local Government, Asia and the Pacific (UCLG ASPAC).

The position of local government in the Republic of Fiji has changed through the impact of national political events. As a result of Britain's importation of indentured labourers from India early in the twentieth century, the country has both an indigenous Fijian population and an Indo-Fijian population. Whereas some Indo-Fijians continue to farm on land leased from iTaukei (indigenous Fijians), a majority live in urban areas or informal settlements. Fiji's two cities (Suva, and Lautoka) and eleven towns were led by democratically elected leaders, and the Fiji had one of the few Local Government Associations in the Pacific region, until the elected bodies were abolished by Fiji's military administrators in 2009 and replaced by appointed administrators.

Prior to 2006, Fiji's cities and towns were administered under two principal laws – the Local Government Act of 1985, and the Rotuma Act of 1978 (applicable for the local council on that island only). In all, there are some 32 pieces of legislation relevant to the functioning of local councils in Fiji (Fiji Local Government Association 2008a). In addition to the municipal councils there are 17 rural local authorities and 14 provincial councils, which link the government to approximately 1200 villages, under a separate governance arrangement known as the iTaukei Affairs Board (formerly the Fijian Affairs Board). The existence of this separate 'Fijian Administration' concerned exclusively with the well-being of indigenous Fijians 'parallel to' the government ministries which administer the affairs of the country as a whole adds an additional level of complexity to local government in Fiji. Whereas a number of reviews have advocated radical changes to this system, and even its dismantlement, separate Fijian institutions have continued to exert considerable influence over public administration at national, provincial and local levels.

Papua New Guinea has a unitary form of government and three tiers of administration: national, provincial, and local. There are 21 provincial governments,[4] plus the National Capital District of Port Moresby, and 326 local-level governments (which include both urban and rural local-level governments). For administrative purposes, the provinces are divided into 89 districts. Local-level governments are further divided into 6003 wards and each ward comprises hamlets, villages and non-traditional villages. Although no official data exists enumerating the number of villages and hamlets, Port Moresby, Lae, and Mount Hagen are categorised as cities and there are at least fifty towns.

Papua New Guinea is the only Pacific Island country that has established a ministry for inter-governmental relations. Local government for all provinces except the Capital District is provided under the 'Organic Law on Provincial and Local Level Government'. Port Moresby, on the other hand, is administered through the National Capital District Commission, which is presided over by a provincial premier. Provincial assemblies comprises members of the national parliament from that province, a representative of the urban local-level governments, one women representative, three representatives of traditional leaders/ chiefs, and up to three further nominees.

The status of local government in Papua New Guinea is in flux. In 2007 the heads of rural local governments (the Presidents of the local governments) were removed from the provincial assemblies through amendment to Section 10 of the Organic Law on Provincial Governments and Local Level Governments, but this was struck down by the courts in 2010, and in 2015 the Constitutional and Law Reform Commission proposed replacing local level governments with a lesser number of 'district development agencies' – a proposal that has been accepted by the O'Neil Government formed following 2017 general elections (Constitutional and Law Reform Commission/Department of Provincial and Local Government Affairs 2015a, 2015b). Given the extent of urbanisation in the country, Papua New Guinea is the one Pacific nation to have developed a national urbanisation policy (for the period 2010–2030), which is overseen by an office of urbanisation.

Samoa has a unitary form of government with a head of state elected by the government every five years. There are only two spheres of government, national and local. There are 11 districts, and local government comprises of all the traditional villages (village councils), of which there are 247, including urban authorities. Under the Local Government Act 1985 the National Minister is empowered to upgrade existing town to city status; create councils, alter boundaries, approve by-laws and regulations, and when deemed necessary, dismiss a council and appoint an administrator to replace it.

The main division in local government is between the village (*fono*) and urban authorities. However, they operate as a single-tier. *Fono* are required to establish executive committees and land boards. The village councils which administer local affairs are composed of '*matais*' who are the heads of extended families. Local councils are wholly responsible for pre-school services, and share responsibility with one or more other spheres of government for policing and civil protection, education, family welfare services, water and sanitation, cemeteries and crematoria, slaughter-houses, sports and leisure, religious facilities, district heating, agriculture, forests and fisheries, economic promotion, trade, and tourism. Much of local government staffing is supplied by the Public Service Commission, which retains the authority to discipline and dismiss staff. Central government staff are also seconded to local authorities. Individual local authorities are not subject to independent scrutiny.

In Solomon Islands, Honiara City Council was established under the Local Government Act, until the Honiara City Council Act of 1999 provided Honiara City with the same 'local government' status as the provincial governments. Noro in Western Province is a Town Council under authority of the Town Council Ordinance 1990. There are other urban areas, but they do not yet have standing as local government entities (although Gizo in Western Province and Auki in Malaita are progressing toward town status). Local communities in the remainder of the country are administered by Provincial governments under the Provincial Government Act 1997. Honiara city council's dissolution in 2004 was the fifth such dissolution since independence in 1978. The city subsequently experienced civil unrest in April 2006 triggered by the politics of post-election formation of the national government but also associated (in the evidence submitted to a Commission of Inquiry into the 2006 riots) with the lack of development and opportunities in and around the capital city (Parker 2010).[5]

Global and regional dimensions to local government

While globalisation undoubtedly creates opportunities for small states such as those in the Pacific, the anticipated integration of markets, when combined with the small scale of island economies, narrow production and export bases, and limited resources and capacity constraints, makes them ever-more vulnerable to external shocks, particularly climate-related shocks, which are likely to increase in frequency and intensity with the impact of global warming and sea-level rise.

In general, local government bodies in Pacific Island states all share these complex characteristics and complex environmental and institutional challenges. UN-Habitat has played an important role in sharing global experience that can benefit the region (UN-Habitat 2007). The future direction of the global agenda for local government development was signalled in the UN Secretary-General's opening remarks to Habitat III in Quito in October 2016:

> Local and regional governments are now seen as key partners for national government to implement their development and economic programmes. Many governments have taken on the principle of subsidiarity. That has required them to strengthen the capacity of local and regional governments, so that decisions can be taken at the most local or immediate level possible.

At regional level, the Pacific Urban Agenda was developed in 2003 through the Pacific Urban Forum, a platform established by regional organisations (including CLGF Pacific, UNESCAP, Pacific Islands Forum Secretariat and UN-Habitat) to coordinate and advocate sustainable urban futures strategies for the region. The Agenda identified the need for greater attention to local planning and management, for linkage between local plans and national plans and priorities, and for responses to the increasing threats to urban community cohesion; it was endorsed by UNESCAP in 2004 and by the Pacific Island Forum leaders in 2005. Although it resulted in the development in 2011 of a regional Pacific Urban framework, the Pacific Urban Agenda never gained solid political support at regional level. It did not succeed in getting onto the annual agenda of the Pacific Islands Forum Leader's meeting – an agenda that sets policy priorities at regional level.

Nevertheless, a Fourth Pacific Urban Forum was convened in 2015 by UN-Habitat and CLGF to develop a NEW Pacific Urban Agenda. Just eight countries participated, together with urban policy makers and practitioners, local government representatives, donors and development partners, academics and representatives from the private sector. Representatives of national ministries of finance and strategic planning agencies, and of national offices responsible for local government and urban management, were invited for the first time.

The 2015 meeting identified three dominant themes: (i) integrated planning and strengthening rural–urban linkages, (ii) peri-urban management, and (iii) ensuring inclusive, safe, resilient and sustainable cities and local authorities. The rapid growth of unplanned informal settlements continued to be a major issue: they are the fastest growing form of urbanisation, but they are not always considered in national urban plans for provision of social services and infrastructure. Other pressing issues are the high population density on the small atolls of Micronesia (in 2013 Betio, Kiribati, had a population of near 13,000 living on a land area of 1.2 square kilometres), and the vulnerability of Pacific Island countries to natural disasters and the impacts of climate change (tropical storms and cyclones, droughts, earthquakes, tsunamis and storm surges). Bearing these and other challenges in mind, the New Pacific Urban Agenda addresses four overarching themes: (i) enhancing social equity, (ii) strengthening resilience, (iii) growing urban economies, and (iv) strengthening urban governance.

Enhancing social equity

It is important that towns and cities be well planned, as this facilitates land use, more affordable housing, and more equitable access to basic services, and encourages urban growth. Such planning implies having greater control over the unplanned and spontaneous emergence and growth informal settlements. These dwellers deserve equal rights and opportunities in regard to access to land and housing, and to such basic services such as water and sanitation. Urban planning, policies and legal framework must become more 'pro-poor' in emphasis, and issues of gender, youth, disability and livelihoods need to be included in urban development initiatives so that wider social equity concerns are given equal and more balanced consideration in programmes and projects. Planning toward these ends requires participatory consultation with urban dwellers and more specifically those in informal settlements, just as it requires support from higher political levels, and from development partners. The agenda accordingly calls for up-scaling and embarking on housing and settlement upgrading programme, and strengthening partnerships across sectors and among national and regional stakeholders.

Strengthening resilience

The impacts of natural hazards and climate change on Pacific Island countries have resulted in unprecedented social, economic and environmental costs, particularly for the most vulnerable communities which lack the means, capability, or infrastructure, to cope with disasters. These risks need to be factored in to urban strategies, planning, and management. Enhancing resilience of infrastructure, enforcement of laws and regulations, and strengthening of institutional capacities need to be built into community preparedness, and response and recovery actions of climate risk planning, in order to adapt to impact of climate change. The integration of cost-efficient green technologies in sustainable infrastructure as well as reducing pollution and energy consumption in urban areas and investing in water and waste management are also important to advancing sustainability and producing economic and social benefits. The New Pacific Urban Agenda recommended four key actions to build urban resilience and environmental sustainability: (i) embark on integrated climate change vulnerability, pollution and greenhouse gas assessments of towns and cities; (ii) develop integrated climate change adaptation, resilience and low emission action plans; (iii) integrate climate change adaptation, resilience and low emission actions into urban policies and plans; and (iv) ensure that climate change adaptation is resilience building and low emission concerns of the Pacific towns and cities are integrated in global climate change negotiations.

Growing urban economies

The 2015 Pacific Urban Agenda suggests that cities be recognised and used as drivers of national economic development. Pacific Urban cities and towns currently account for 60–70% of the national gross domestic product (GDP) in their respective countries, and hence deserve proper planning of urban growth and investment to expand employment opportunities and stimulate economic growth. The potential role of the informal sector in this growth has to be recognised, as does engaging in public-private partnerships that enhance the delivery of basic services. The Agenda recommends four key actions toward the objective of growing urban economies in Pacific Island countries: (i) strengthening understanding of the importance of strong urban economies for national economic development; (ii) developing local economic development projects that are based on Pacific opportunities; (iii) empowering local governments to develop integrated Municipal finance and economic strategies; and (iv) leveraging the private sector as well as the informal economy in local economic development plans.

Strengthening urban governance

The fourth pillar of the Pacific Urban Agenda concerns the strengthening of urban governance. Of the many Pacific Island countries and territories, just Fiji, Papua New Guinea, Samoa and

Tonga, have articulated urban policies and legal frameworks. The challenge of strengthening urban governance requires not only the establishment of good institutional arrangements, but ancillary subsidiary legislation, policies, and work programmes. Building capability for local government in developing countries requires investment in human resources, especially to manage finances and data, but also to communicate with the public and the many stake-holders in other levels of government, the private sector, civil society, and development agencies. To achieve these outcomes, the Agenda recommends seven key actions: (i) develop national urban or urbanisation policies; (ii) periodically review these policies to ensure their alignment with urban priorities; (iii) identify gaps in policies and legislation; (iv) review existing urban and local policies and legislations to ensure that they adequately reflect urban priorities and enable local development and urbanisation; (v) strengthen the capacities of urban professional, policy makers and leaders at national and local levels; (vi) strengthen the capacities of institutions mandated to implement the policies; and (vii) monitor the implementation of such policies with national and local government.

Notwithstanding the recommendations concerning the four themes set out above, all parties to the Pacific Urban Agenda acknowledge its limited status as a non-binding declaration in support of local government which is yet to be fully recognised by national governments or prioritised by the main regional intergovernmental organisations: much additional advocacy is required. The Pacific Urban Agenda is one element of ongoing policy dialogue not only in the Pacific Islands, but in the Asia-Pacific, and at global level. It has been consulted on at the 6th Asia Pacific Urban Forum in October 2015, the CLGF conference in Gaborone, Botswana in June 2015, the Commonwealth Heads of Government Meeting in Malta in November 2015; and at UN-Habitat III in Quito in October 2016. CLGF is working with the Caribbean Urban Agenda (CUA) to establish a SIDS Urban Agenda, in an effort to build stronger representation of small island developing states in international forums. The UN's 'Agenda for Sustainable Development' for the period 2015–2030 includes many goals that are relevant to the goals of improving local government in the Pacific Islands. Goal 11, for instance, which seeks to make 'cities and human settlements inclusive, safe, resilient and sustainable'.

Challenges confronting local government

As already noted, local government bodies in the Pacific are generally shaped by their legal status, which varies across the region from full constitutional recognition to recognition in statutory legislation through an Act of Parliament. Only a handful of local government systems in the Pacific are recognised constitutionally. National efforts to provide local government (both rural and urban), which are supported by international development partners and by the four pillars of the region-wide 'Pacific Urban Agenda', include a number of cross-cutting issues, the most pressing of which include clarity concerning intergovernmental relations; adequacy of financing; and effective decentralisation and service delivery; the place of traditional authority; human and physical infrastructure development; adequate response to climate change adaptation; and the on-going challenges of development coordination. These are discussed below.

Intergovernmental relations

The quality of relations between local government and other levels of government is crucial to how well local governments deliver goods and services and meet other desirable goals (Devas, Alam, Delay, Koranteng and Venkatachalam 2008). The term 'intergovernmental relations' commonly refers to relations between central, regional and local governments, as well as between any of these. Interactions may be 'horizontal' or 'vertical' in as much as they may concern relations between branches of government at a similar level – such as between national departments – or between some departments at national level and others at provincial/island or local level when making plans that span their various jurisdictions.

The lack of distribution of authority to diverse levels of government suggests that many Pacific states continue to adhere to the 'old paradigm' of government that places the 'central government' at the centre of decision-making. This belief that the 'centre' knows more, or is more capable than the 'periphery' in matters of governance is reinforced by the lack of capacity development in outer areas and in 'lower levels' of government. While we presume that this lack of devolution is part of the explanation for the slow pace of economic and social development in the Islands, such an assertion should ideally backed up with empirical research, which is currently lacking. Only further inquiry can identify, for instance, whether those local government authorities that have greater autonomy are giving better service provision than centralised ones.

There is little evidence of systematic 'horizontal' inter-governmental relations (i.e. systematic communication between governmental bodies that share peer relations rather than vertical relations in which one is subordinate to the other). Local Government Associations have only been formed, for instance, in three countries – Fiji, Kiribati and Papua New Guinea, although other neighbouring counties have large numbers of local governments. The lack of systematic procedures for decision-making about provincial and local issues, and the ready acceptance of 'informal' decision-making and dispute resolution procedures that tend to rely on personal acquaintance between government officials at different levels, increases the possibility that these 'familiar' or personal relations become nepotistic or based on biased reasoning and criterion. All these findings suggest that the 'interface' between the modern 'centre' of government and the 'traditional periphery' – as lived in towns, settlements and villages, remains difficult and in need of development in law, policy, and practice.

In Solomon Islands, post-conflict development programmes have addressed some of the challenges for Honiara city, but these do not include the further articulation of intergovernmental arrangements for the overwhelming majority of Solomon Islanders who live in village settings. The foremost informal mechanism is a biennial Provincial Premiers Conference. Some provincial governments have enacted Ordinances to organise, govern, and control village and community affairs (examples include Makira Village Peace Council Ordinance 2006, Temotu Local Governance Ordinance). A Provincial Government Review Committee's 1999 recommendation to remove Provincial Assemblies and introduce constituency governing councils in order to bring national and local government bodies into closer contact was disturbed by ethnic unrest in the country and never fully considered. A draft federal constitution first submitted to parliament in 2004 but still incomplete by the time parliament rose for the 2010 general elections referred to 'local communities', without clarifying the structure, funding, and responsibilities, of government authorities at local level. As at May 2017 the draft constitution proposed adoption of State and Community Government authorities, but left the form of Community government to the decision of the States.

Apart from an extensive literature on decentralisation in Papua New Guinea, and on urbanisation in the Pacific, there are few studies, if any, that focus on intergovernmental relations in the region. This is no doubt due to the highly centralised systems of government that most small states continue to operate. They have not followed the observation by some federalism scholars that societies having significant cultural and political diversity adopt federal systems that allow for expression of this diversity (Kincaid and Elazar 2000). Although the federal ideal has given impetus to constitutional aspirations at different times in Solomon Islands and Vanuatu, only the Federated States of Micronesia is expressly constituted as a federal nation-state. Papua New Guinea remains a unitary state with a degree of devolution in practice – and with the unique arrangements for the 'autonomous' province of Bougainville, constitutionally recognised and entrenched on the basis of the Bougainville Peace Agreement of 2000. Notwithstanding this lack of literature – and indeed, a lack of easily available primary data – the issue of intergovernmental relations is of critical importance to the Pacific states at this time.

The adequacy of a nation's legal framework for inter-governmental relations is fundamental. Legal frameworks establish the extent to which administrative, legislative and adjudicative powers and responsibilities are formally delegated to various levels of government. In the Pacific context, each system of government has inherited a legal framework and tradition from its colonial past and this may account for the endurance of a mentality that favours centralised rule-making and distrusts out-lying areas.[6] Indeed, some of the smaller states see local government as an unnecessary expense; so, for example, Nauru abolished local government in 1996. Fiji's Military government appointed administrators in place of elected councils in 2009.

Another example of such tensions can be found in the Cook Islands. Central government's concern at efficiency and minimising expenditure – particularly in areas where it could identify duplication of effort and responsibilities – has been influenced by the country's struggle with public expenditure deficits over a long period. Although during the decade 1985–1995 Cook Islands' real GDP grew at an average annual rate of 4.5% while population growth was just 1% per annum, government over-expenditure led to the accumulation of debt, and implementation of a structural adjustment programme advised by the Asian Development Bank. A 1993 proposal for development of the 'outer-islands development' was finally implemented in 2000, but in that same year the report of a 'Commission on Political Review', while endorsing the principle of devolution, felt it had been 'taken too far in the case of the Island Councils, which have been given some tasks for which they are not be well equipped and may not become well equipped' (Cook Islands Commission of Political Review 1998).

The central government came to regard local government as a troublesome entity. In 2004 the Woonton Government refused to hold national and local elections at the same time, claiming there would be too much 'social upheaval'. It proceeded with the general election in September that year but only agreed to the outer island local elections in November under the threat of legal action. Then, in 2008 the national government removed the three district councils on the main island, Rarotonga by repeal of the Rarotonga Local Government Act, while retaining local government councils on the outer islands. On Rarotonga, local government responsibilities were handed to members of parliament and to the ministry of internal affairs and social services. The government made this decision – which understandably upset the members of the *vaka* (local councils) of Takitumu, Te-au-o Tonga and Puaikura – on the premise that councils were not fulfilling their responsibilities in cleaning and clearing community roadsides, streams and road drainages, that this task could be undertaken more efficiently by the Ministry of Internal Affairs. For their part, the *vaka* argued that funds made available by the central government were insufficient to undertake these tasks.

Financing

Sub-national governments have key roles in the delivery of many basic services in the Pacific Islands (in health, education, roads, agriculture, etc.). In general, however, they face chronic shortage of revenue, and even though revenue could be increased in the larger centres through enhanced collection capacities, this would not remedy the more general situation in which the demands for services in urban areas are outpacing innovations in governance financing at either central or local level. The financing of local government is thus a concern for all Pacific Island countries and territories. Hassall and Tipu (2008) have noted the critical condition of local government financing in Pacific cities and towns.

For a variety of reasons, few local authorities generate or otherwise receive funding sufficient to meet the growing expectations for service delivery in urban areas. Firstly, national governments face their own fiscal constraints, and do not easily agree to transfer funds to sub-national levels of government. Fiscal decentralisation means that each level of Government has some discretion to make expenditure decisions and raise revenues. With the active encouragement and support of the World Bank, USAID, ADB and others, fiscal decentralisation has become part of a reform agenda to strengthen regional and local governments to meet such challenges as ineffective and inefficient governance, macroeconomic instability, and inadequate economic growth (Kee 2003). The World Bank views fiscal decentralisation and strengthened local government in terms of more discretion in decision-making, along with globalisation, as one of the most important forces shaping governance and development today (World Bank 1999) and at least 62 out of 75 developing countries with populations of five million or more adopted some form of fiscal decentralisation during the mid-1970s (World Bank 1997; Bahl and Wallace 2007).

Whereas most local government systems across the Pacific obtain funding through central government grants, property taxes, and business licenses and taxes, there is great variation in the use of fees for waterfront development, physical planning, vehicle registration, airports, roads, recreational facilities, markets, bus stations, gaming, and domestic animals.

The negligible flow of funds from Fiji's central government to the urban areas has required municipal councils to work within meagre resources derived from their own revenue streams, but these are insufficient to cover the costs of local government (Hassall, Nakagawa and Tipu 2009). In its 2008 submission to the Review-Reform of Local Government Committee, the Fiji Local Government Association re-emphasised the dilemma that the councils 'do not do well in terms of finance' (Fiji Local Government Association 2008b). With minimal fiscal transfers by way of grant, Fiji's municipal councils have to become self-sufficient or otherwise devise new and innovative ways of raising extra capital to finance their several service and work-related projects.

In Samoa the Assembly of Pulenu'u and its executive committee promotes intergovernmental relations, but these conducted through informal as much as through formal mechanisms. The central government makes transfer payments to local authorities for capital development on *ad hoc* basis.

In Tonga the responsibility for revenue collection and expenditure remains a function of Central Government, and there is no separate budget for town administration (e.g. communication costs or transport costs of town councillor). Taxes are collected by Central Government which then provides for capital works, and salaries and wages, for district and town officers. Entrepreneurs start businesses with a permit paid to the ministry of labour and commerce rather than to local authorities. As Tongan society is based on mutual 'self-help', local developments are funded through 'concerti' – entertainment programmes held by committees focused on the church, water, women, sport – as well as by central government inputs and the efforts of the nobles. If a health clinic needs repair the town officer will work with the relevant committee, which can have up to twenty members, and then sub-committees with additional members. The government is moving toward the establishment of village councils, and is looking at how villages can raise revenues. An 'experiment' with citizen participation in local governance is under way in the village of Lapaha, where the community has established committees to take on decision-making responsibilities, in a system that blends Tongan tradition with contemporary practices. They are working with the CLGF Pacific Project on the village council scheme and are watching the progress in Lapaha closely.

In Tuvalu, inter-governmental relations are implicitly guided by the Falekaupule Act 1997, and there are no additional laws covering issues such as fiscal transfers. Severe financial constraints facing Tuvalu and the inability of central government to provide adequate budgetary support to local government led to the creation in 1999 of an innovative financing mechanism for local government in the form of the Falekaupule Trust Fund, as part of a larger decentralisation process specifically to help finance development on the outer islands (Graham 2005). Since its establishment, the Falekaupule Trust Fund has made significant contributions annually by way of block grants to the eight island councils (*kaupules*) for budgetary and development project support. In addition, central government have other grants for the salaries of core staff in the island councils. The nature and size of these grants has remained constant and has not been reviewed since 1997.

Vanuatu does not have a set formula for its intergovernmental fiscal transfer. However, it has been estimated that approximately 70% of the grant is earmarked for administrative expenses and the remaining 30% for small capital projects. A Decentralisation Review Commission reported to parliament in 2001 that the system of provincial and municipal councils in place since independence in 1980 was 'centralized, politicised, expensive and non-participatory . . . confusing, inefficient, and expensive and results in considerable duplication, which is wasteful of Vanuatu's limited resources' (Government of Vanuatu Decentralization Review Commission 2001).

The Commission made 197 recommendations for consideration by the government covering all aspects of planning, financing, staffing, service delivery, and constitutional and legislative reform – a review sufficiently weighty as to earn a place in New Zealand's Development Program Strategy for Vanuatu for the period 2006–2010.

One difficulty encountered when the Area Council Development Plans (ACDP) were drafted for the islands in the southern province (Tafea) concerned lack of clear definitions for the scope of the '*nasara*', 'village' and 'community' – the basic units of society that the plans were to serve. Area council secretaries in Vanuatu mediate between local governments and area councils (which consists of villages and people) but do not have set work plans or job descriptions. They are, furthermore, mostly appointed on the basis of political affiliation, and thus respond to the interests of their party more than to whatever plan exists. Aware of this situation, the national government is currently seeking to apply a 'bottom-up' approach, whereby area councils plans commence with identification of needs at village level, then provincial level, and then national. The government is also seeking to regularise the position of area council secretary, to ensure that the needs of all communities are addressed equally rather than on the basis of political affiliation.

A second challenge to the financing of local government in the Pacific concerns capacity and competency. Local authorities empowered to raise revenues through taxes, levies, and licensing face their own challenges, beginning with administrative competence regarding revenue collection, but also including the small size of the economy under their jurisdiction, especially with the low ratio of rate-payers to non-rate papers is considered (it is common for a town's public facilities to serve many more non-rate paying inhabitants than rate-payers – the squatters who reside informally either within a town's jurisdiction or immediately beyond it).

A third factor affecting local government financing is that few Pacific countries have established in law or policy routine procedures for allocation of resources to sub-national levels of government.

In the case of Papua New Guinea, where financing arrangements for funding provincial governments have been an issue ever since the country gained independence in 1975 (Axline 2008) provincial governments raise funds from three main sources: (i) locally generated revenues such as local taxes, charges and receipts collected by the provincial administration; (ii) transfers of shared nationally collected taxation revenues, such as VAT/GST, and mining and petroleum royalties; and (iii) grant transfers from the national government. They also receive recurrent grants from the national government.

The first post-independence funding formula was based on providing each province an equal amount of kina per head. However, for several reasons this arrangement resulted in highly inequitable resourcing of government at provincial level: firstly, some provinces also received substantial mining royalties and GST (these tax transfers were worth more that the grants received from the national government) but no corresponding downward adjustment to the grant provided by the central government, and secondly, the real cost of service delivery within provinces varied greatly depending on geographic complexity. There were, furthermore, delays with actual transfers of legislated and pledged funds.

Revenues received by local level governments – unlike those of provincial governments – have not varied significantly (although it is known that urban LLGs are better able to collect taxes than are rural ones). There are a few very high-revenue mining and oil-rich local level government areas but the majority are in rural areas, and raise negligible revenue: In 2005 it was estimated that the 286 rural local-level governments had combined revenues of about 1 million kina to offset their costs.

A review of the relevant legislation by the Constitutional and Law Reform Commission in 2009 found local governments:

> ... in the provinces have been either intentionally or unintentionally, subjugated and somewhat made irrelevant or even redundant, in service delivery .... at the great risk of making the people's directly elected government redundant in the eyes and minds of the people themselves ... local governments now are totally ineffective in service delivery and only exist for political reasons – simply as 'window curtains' displaying the presence of government in the remote parts of the country.
>
> *(Kalinoe undated)*

In addition to these conventional mechanisms for raising and distributing revenues, there are two mechanisms that complicate intergovernmental relations in Papua New Guinea, namely the automatic inclusion of politicians at higher levels of government in lower levels, and the disbursement of significant levels of funding through members of parliament for direct project implementation at local (constituency) level.

The first of these arrangements, according to which members of the national parliament automatically become members of government at lower levels, emerged from dissatisfaction with the performance of provincial and local governments over an extended period of time. Unable to have the public service deliver services to satisfactory levels, members of parliament by-passed the traditional lines of responsibility and legislated for themselves via the Provincial Government Reform Act of 1995 a direct role in implementation.

Decentralisation and service delivery

City or municipal entities face the challenge of clarifying of roles and responsibilities with national government. Given the diverse terrain and social histories of the Pacific Island countries and territories, one would presume that establishing effective Local-level government on sound principles of decentralisation and local-level representation would be an ideal way to provide services to isolated villages and scattered islands. In practice, governance in much of the region remains highly centralised, and many villages and communities do not gain the benefits of local government. For some this is due to factors such as geographic isolation, but for others it is due to the absence of effective service delivery mechanisms, capacity, and capability. The failure of local government to deliver the much needed community services is in part due to outdated legislative and policy frameworks including scarcity of resources – finance, capital, and technical/administrative, as well as the absence of robust M&E frameworks. Moreover, the current practices and procedures of local government bodies are not very well aligned with the changing environment.

The Fiji military justified its take-over of the country in December 2006 in terms of poor governance and endemic corruption. Following the dismissal of the government, the dissolution of parliament, the disbandment of the great council of chiefs, and the termination of all permanent secretaries and various senior public servants, the 'interim government' turned its attention to local government. Although a report commissioned to investigate local government operations (Fiji Local Government Association 2008a) recommended that local government be retained despite a range of problems facing the sector, the government proceeded with dismantling elected councils. The challenge facing Fiji's municipalities is provision of council services in the face of high-numbers of non-rate-paying residents (who include both indigenous Fijians and Indo-Fijians).

In Vanuatu most government departments and even NGOs are duplicating their service and responsibilities. Most of the work that is done by one department always overlaps what another department is doing and is responsible of. For example, under the Ministry of Lands and Natural Resources, the Department of Lands has an office responsible for urban planning. This same office can be found under the Department of Local Authorities and their roles and responsibilities are the same. Another is the granting of permission for a development. The developer is always left confused as who he/she should approach, whether the Port Vila Municipal or the Department of Environmental Protection and Conservation (DEPC) or the Department of Geology and Mines to get a permit to develop a land or to extract resources. This leads to the granting of funds by ADB into certain government departments to strengthen their safeguards procedures when it comes to issues related to the delineation of power, roles and responsibilities.

Most government departments in Vanuatu and even in other Pacific Island countries are more reactive than proactive in their daily, monthly and annual operations. For example, the international funding associated with climate change, community resilience and disaster risk reduction attracted much attention and local area councils, so that whereas they are now better informed about the impact of climate change and the increased intensity of natural disasters such as tropical cyclones, but there has as yet been little implementation of adaptation and mitigation measures at area council level. By focusing on projects each time they are offered by development agencies, provincial planners and local area council secretaries risk losing sight of their roles in implementing Vanuatu's existing long-term development goals.

Papua New Guinea's history of service delivery at provincial and district levels has been described as 'chequered' (May 2009). At least 18 provincial administrations[7] and approximately 313 local-level governments provide services through more than 80 district level offices for the 85% of the population who live in rural areas. These services include health centres and aid posts, immunisation and ante-natal care, supervision of deliveries, inspection of primary and elementary schools, agricultural extension patrols to improve crop and food production, fisheries extension; and maintenance of health facilities and schools.

In 2009 the Department of Provincial and Local Government published a 'Determination Assigning Service Delivery Functions and Responsibilities to Provincial and Local-Level Governments' to clearly delineate which services were the responsibility of which level of government. Papua New Guinea's Medium Term Development Strategy (MTDS), the blueprint of the government's development agenda, emphasises the delivery of government services to the sub-national level. Accordingly, the country's three core objectives for undertaking fiscal decentralisation are: providing effective funding of government activities at the same levels they were provided before decentralisation; apportioning funding among provinces to redress the great levels of inequality in service delivery within them, and increasing funding to allow expansion of delivery of services to the population (Axline 2008). These core objectives have been referred to as *stabilisation, equalisation* and *development,* and are somewhat similar to the core objectives for fiscal decentralisation proposed by Richard Musgrave, who refers to the *stabilisation, distribution* and *allocation* functions (Kee undated). Irrespective of plans and the theory, the reality of poor coordination of service delivery in Papua New Guinea is clear and partly discussed above.

Recognising the shortcomings of the arrangements, parliament amended the Organic Law on Provincial Governments and Local-level Governments (OLGPLLG) in 2008 and also passed the Intergovernmental Relations (Functions and Funding) Act. The new arrangements sought to improve both the distribution mechanism and the formula for funding of provincial and local-level governments, and also established the National Economic and Fiscal Commission (NEFC) as an independent Constitutional advisory body to provide independent advice on OLGPLLG grants and other transfers.

Provincial assemblies thus comprises members of the national parliament from that province, a representative of the urban local-level governments, one women representative, three representatives of traditional leaders/chiefs, and up to three further nominees, and the heads of rural local governments.

The second funding mechanism, the 'constituency development funds' administered through the 'District Services Improvement Program' exists in both Papua New Guinea and Solomon Islands. At the current time, each member of Papua New Guinea's national parliament receives an annual 10 million kina allocation for the local constituency – an amount sometimes in excess of the funds available to other government agencies and departments operating in the region. There is growing concern about the use of DISP funds in ways intended to shore up political support, and in ways that perpetuate patronage networks rather than implement public works and services responsibility and transparently, and through coordination with the programmes of line agencies.

In Solomon Islands there has been discussion of federal solutions to the problems of service provision since independence in 1978, with very little action. In Vanuatu, efforts have been made to devolve more responsibility to provincial government level, though not local government.

Traditional authority

One common factor which prevails in almost all Pacific Island countries is the tension between democratic local government systems and traditional/customary governance, which affects both central and local government.[8] This has resulted in experimentation with different local government models in some of the Pacific countries, resulting in recentralisation of powers and functions, with some local governments facing a struggle to maintain their planning and operational roles. Customary law and authority remain strong at local level, and this 'strength of custom' has an impact on how effectively local governments can establish themselves and play a role in governance and development at local level.

The strong position of villages in Samoa, for instance, derives not only from tradition but from their recognition in the Village Fono Act 1990. Village councils (*fonos*) comprise traditional chiefs (*matais*) and every family has a *matai* who is a member of the council. The village mayor (*pulenu'u*) is elected by council members from among themselves for a three year term using a first-past-the-post system. The staffing of the village councils is provided by the central government through the Public Service Commission. A dispute in Vaimoso settled by the Samoan Lands and Titles Court in April 2009 exemplifies the continuing authority of the Samoan village. Former Cabinet Minister Vatu Mutilator Siafausa Vui had been ostracised by the village in 1999 for calling a meeting that he was not authorised to call, and had further antagonised village leaders by participating in the bestowal of a chiefly title in a manner that he was not entitled to. The matai ordered the punishment of *mu le foaga* (the burning of the person's home and belongings) but was thwarted by police and church leaders, and they subsequently rejected the *ifoga* (formal apology) that the court had ordered Vui to make. He was then 'banished' from the village for statements about the dispute made to the media. Vui's appeal to the court was dismissed and he and his immediate family were given one week to leave the village.

In Kiribati, the traditional male elders group, *Unimwane*, have effectively 'abolished' the elected council several times, by various means, including the pressured 'voluntary' resignation of the elected councillors en masse, so that the Mayor, who was the centre of the crisis, had to resign since there was no council.

In Solomon Islands, in contrast, the modern system of government does not recognise traditional leadership roles and responsibilities, despite the fact that chiefs at local level assist their communities in making critical decisions concerning natural resource use, dispute resolution, and other matters. In recognition of this, the Sogovare government announced in 2017 that it has commenced drafting a 'Traditional Governance Bill' that seeks to 'enhance and empower' traditional chiefs and local customary authorities.

Human and physical infrastructure development

Rapid urbanisation growth has brought substantial challenges for urban managers and political leaders in areas of planning, infrastructure provision, employment, human settlements, and the management of climate change among many others. Urbanisation and growth of urban wealth has not been balanced in the region and inequalities remain significant in some areas. This is further compounded by the shortfalls in urban infrastructure investment as experienced in many parts of the region. The local context was expressed succinctly in a report on a workshop for City and Town Managers in Papua New Guinea held in May 2006:

> Local governments in the Pacific region operate in a changing and uncertain social, political and economic environment. Challenges such as rapid urbanization with its inherent increased management responsibilities, decentralization, high expectations from the citizens, resource constraints, service delivery and implementation gaps, good governance, citizen participation and community mobilization, remoteness, political volatility and effective working relationships with traditional structures all add to the strategic management and decision making responsibilities of local leaders.
> *(Commonwealth Local Government Forum 2006)*

Informal settlements and housing

The most evident challenges associated with urbanisation are the increase in the number of peri-urban and informal settlements. Migration from rural areas and outer-islands contribute significantly to the growth of towns and cities and therefore to the challenges posed by urbanisation. This has made it necessary for Pacific Island countries to urgently establish new and innovative mechanisms and structures to respond to these urban challenges. Rapid urban growth has resulted in over-crowding, congestion, and stress on social and economic infrastructures. The impacts are exceptionally great on towns and cities in small islands developing states of the Pacific because their small size and limited capacities and resources. The appearance of informal settlements and their rapid expansion is accompanied by extra demand for better access to basic services and policies to combat the problems of poverty and poor health that are common in such a sector of the community. Max Kep, director of PNG's Office of Urbanization, reported to the Pacific Urban Forum 2015 meeting:

> The vision of a new Settlements Upgrading Strategy was to develop inclusive cities and towns without informal settlements and the goal was to develop affordable and participatory measures for upgrading settlements. A National Settlement Upgrading Strategy was being drafted. Data was being collected for informed decision making.
> (UN-Habitat, Commonwealth Local Government Forum and Alliance 2015: 6)

So, for example, in 2006 the NCDC published its Urban Development Plan to provide a basis for broad land use and service infrastructure planning to 2015 (National Capital District Commission 2006). The plan considered the Capital District's transport needs, and notes in relation to roads a number of inconsistencies between law and practice relating to its 400 kilometres of arterial and minor roads.

Climate change adaptation

The vulnerability of Pacific Islands to adverse weather events has long been known, but in recent decades has developed a language, and a responsive methodology, to the issue, in terms building sustainability, resilience, disaster preparedness, and disaster threat reduction. Ironically, one source of increased vulnerability to natural disasters is the growth of necessary physical infrastructure, such as roads, bridges, high-rise buildings, and communications systems, which are prone to damage if not built to extremely robust specifications. New technology has assisted in reducing threats to life through the use of sirens, radio, internet, and even SMS alerts. However, an additional layer of threat is now posed by climate change and sea level rise (which is manifest in changed agricultural seasons, increased salination of water tables, etc.). The fact that most Pacific communities, whether rural or urban, live in close proximity to the shoreline, adds to the degree of exposure to changed conditions.

Development coordination

The importance of establishing partnerships, alliances and coalitions with the community, the private sector, civil society etc., are increasingly evident; local government bodies need to understand the advantages to be gained from networking, and to developing capacity to work in partnership with others to plan and deliver key local priorities. Intergovernmental relations – both vertical and horizontal – are also an area that needs to be improved and strengthened. The relationship between local and central government is critical to effective institutional strengthening and policy development. The role of local government associations as bodies representing local government in intergovernmental dialogue is growing, and therefore emphasis should be on enhancing the capacity of these embryonic organisations in the region to continue to make sure local government deliver quality and efficient services to the community.

During the Pacific MDG Consultation on the post-2015 agenda held in November 2014, participants expressed concern over the breadth and complexity of the goals and targets. The challenge at the current time is to identify, prioritise and make the post-2015 agenda achievable for Pacific countries. Although each of the goals can be applied to the work of local government, Goal 11, which seeks to make 'cities and human settlements inclusive, safe, resilient and sustainable', and Goal 17, which refers to establishing partnerships to achieve the goals, appear to be the most pertinent.

Key actors in development coordination for the development of local government in Pacific Island countries and territories are UN Habitat and the Commonwealth Local Government Forum.

The goal of ensuring effective intergovernmental relations and central government support to local government is an important component of CLGF's Pacific regional project. Specific activities have included intergovernmental dialogue, particularly involving national/provincial/local government, traditional leaders and civil society in Tuvalu, Kiribati, Vanuatu, Samoa and Fiji; and provision of advice on intergovernmental fiscal relations and fiscal decentralisation, urban development and management. Other developmental activities have included twinning relationships between municipalities in the Pacific and counterparts elsewhere.

UN Habitat's most useful activities in the region, in addition to support for the Pacific Urban Agenda initiative, have been rapid urban assessments and policy support for settlement upgrading in a number of communities Additional support has been given to the Pacific by the Cities Alliance and the United Cities and Local Government for Asia and the Pacific (UCLG ASPAC).

Conclusions

In a number of ways the underlying concept and empirical acceptance of local government is yet to be consolidated in Pacific Island countries and territories. Even though Pacific communities traditionally lived at local level, the small island states and territories have focused in recent decades on the development of government institutions and processes at national level more than at regional or local. Few national constitutions recognise sub-national levels of government, which as a consequence only exist through subsidiary legislation and are easily modified by the government of the day. Notwithstanding this lack of institutional recognition and design, the demands placed on governments by urbanisation cannot be ignored, and have increasingly gained the attention of development agencies as well as the local communities themselves, and many lessons are being learnt. Local government arrangements include villages (mostly rural but also some urban; and mostly traditional but some consciously modernising), informal settlements, and formal municipalities. Adequacy of public sector finding is essential. The urban challenge is significant and complex, and therefore the way cities and towns are managed and urban issues are addressed must take into account these complexities. In order to address this myriad of new challenges, particularly when the emerging disruptions are becoming more difficult to predict, plan for, and adjust to, Pacific local governments will need to be resilient. To do this, they need to apply foresight strategies, be agile, able to evolve and adapt, be responsive and capable of capitalising on opportunities. Urbanisation should not be viewed as a problem but potentially as a powerful tool of democratic governance, economic growth, social inclusion and environmentally sustainability.

Acknowledgements

The authors thank the following colleagues for providing source information or feedback on this chapter: Simon Kunai, Peter Mae, Melanie Phillips, Alotaisi Takai, Pita Vuki and Phillip Tussing.

Notes

1 By 'modern' is meant that which exists in contemporary law – the laws in this part of the world often have their origins in common law, but as the countries are now into their 4th and 5th decade of independent government, they have had opportunities to repeal and replace the most odious of laws from the colonial period. The term 'traditional' is widely used in the region to signal laws, institutions, values, that pre-existed colonial impositions, and some of which continue in modified form today. Hence the term 'traditional leaders' is still accepted for use.
2 See www.clgf.org.uk/resource-centre/clgf-publications/country-profiles.
3 The 'Districts' have been in name only in the recent past, especially when 'District Administrations' phased out after Independence in 1979. Each Council operates for the particular island and the district connection is no longer functional or even referred to. However the term is still applied in some offices; for example, staff of the Ministry of Internal Affairs are grouped into 'districts' to determine the islands they deal with.
4 Nineteen were established at independence, plus Jiwaka and Hela created in 2009.
5 See www.comofinquiry.gov.sb.
6 Pacific Islands' local government legislation is online at the Pacific Local Government Project at the University of Technology Sydney (see www.clg.uts.edu.au/research/paclocgov.html).
7 This does not include the three districts of Bougainville, which is now covered under different funding arrangements in its own Act, or the three districts in the National Capital District.
8 Traditional leadership is discussed in more detail in Chapter 4 of this volume.

References

Axline, W. A. (2008) The Review of Intergovernmental Financing Arrangements and the Restructure of Decentralized Government in PNG. Paper presented at the Reforming Decentralization and Sub-Natinal Fiscal Policy in Papua New Guinea, Port Moresby, Papua New Guinea.

Bahl, R. and Wallace S. (2007) Intergovernmental Transfers: The Vertical Sharing Dimension. In J. Martinez-Vazquez and B. Searle (eds), *Fiscal Equalization*, 205–249. Boston, MA: Springer.

Bennardo, G., and Cappell, C. (2008) Influence Structures in a Tongan Village: Every Villager is not the Same! *Structure and Dynamics: eJournal of Anthropological and Related Sciences* 3(1).

Commonwealth Local Government Forum (2006) *PNG Workshop for City and Town Managers on Effective Management and Leadership in Local Government. Hideaway Hotel, Port Moresby, Papua New Guinea, 24–26 May 2006.* Suva: Commonwealth Local Government Forum.

Constitutional and Law Reform Commission/Department of Provincial and Local Government Affairs (2015a) *Final Report on the Inquiry into the Organic Law on Provincial Governments and Local-Level Governments. Volume 1: Final Report on the Inquiry into the Organic Law on Provincial Governments and Local-Level Governments.* Port Moresby: Constitutional and Law Reform Commission/Department of Provincial and Local Government Affairs.

Constitutional and Law Reform Commission/Department of Provincial and Local Government Affairs (2015b) *Final Report on the Inquiry into the Organic Law on Provincial Governments and Local-Level Governments, Volume 2: Provincial Consultation Report on the Inquiry into the Organic Law on Provincial Governments and Local-Level Governments.* Port Moresby: Constitutional and Law Reform Commission/Department of Provincial and Local Government Affairs.

Cook Islands Commission of Political Review (1998) *Reforming the Political System of the Cook Islands: Preparing for the Challenges of the 21st Century.* Rarotonga: Cook Islands Commission of Political Review.

Devas, N., Alam, M., Delay, S., Koranteng, R. O. and Venkatachalam, P. (2008) *Financing Local Government: Commonwealth Secretariat Local Government Reform Series.* London: Commonwealth Secretariat.

Fiji Local Government Association (2008a) *Submission to Review-Reform of Local Government Committee.* Suva: Fiji Local Government Association.

Fiji Local Government Association (2008b) *Fiji Local Government Association Submission to Review-Reform of Local Government Committee.* Suva: FLGA.

Government of Vanuatu Decentralization Review Commission (2001) *Report, Vol. 1.* Port Vila: Government of Vanuatu.

Graham, B. (2005) *Trust Funds in the Pacific: Their Roles and Future.* Manila.

Hassall, G. and Tipu, F. (2008) Local Government in the Pacific Islands. *Commonwealth Journal of Local Governance* 1 (May): 1–24.

Hassall, G., Nakagawa, H. and Tipu, F. (2009) *Urban Governance Index: Pilot project in Fiji for the Pacific Region: Lami Town Council and Sigatoka Town Council*. Suva: University of the South Pacific.

Jones, P. (2016) *The Emergence of Pacific Urban Villages: Urbanization Trends in the Pacific Islands*. Manila: Asian Development Bank.

Kalinoe, L. (Undated) Conclusion. In *Review of the Organic Law on Provincial Government and Local Level Government*. Port Moresby: Papua New Guinea Constitutional and Law Reform Commission.

Kee, J. E. (2003) Fiscal Decentralization – Theory as Reform. Paper presented at the VIII International Congress of CLAD on State Reform and Public Administration, Panama, 28–31 October, Panama.

Kee, J. E. (Undated) Fiscal Decentralization – Theory as Reform. Working Paper, Center for Latin American Issues, George Washington University, August. Retrieved from www2.gwu.edu/~clai/working_papers.

Kincaid, J., and Elazar, D. (eds). (2000) *From Federal Theology to Modern Federalism*. New York: Lexington Books.

May, R. (2009) Policy Making on Decentralization. In R. J. May (ed.), *Policy-Making and Implementation: Studies from Papua New Guinea*. Canberra: State, Society and Governance in Melanesia Program in association with the National Research Institute, Papua New Guinea.

National Capital District Commission (2006) *National Capital District Urban Development Plan*. Port Moresby: National Capital District Commission.

Parker, T. (2010) Improving institutional and service delivery capacity in conflicted areas: The experience of Honiara City Council, Solomon Islands. *Commonwealth Journal of Local Governance* 6 (July): 132–145.

UN-Habitat. (2007) *Draft Guidelines on Decentralization and the strengthening of Local Authorities*. Nairobi: UN-Habitat.

UN-Habitat, Commonwealth Local Government Forum and Alliance (2015) *Towards a New Pacific Urban Agenda: Harnessing Opportunities in a Post-2015 Environment*. Nairobi: UN-Habitat.

World Bank (1997) *World Bank Report: The State in a Changing World*. Washington DC: World Bank.

World Bank (1999) *India 1998 Macroeconomic Update*. Washington DC: World Bank.

10
LOCAL GOVERNMENT IN LATIN AMERICA
The struggle to overcome social exclusion

Andrew Nickson

Introduction

Latin America is the most urbanised of the developing areas of the world, with around 85% of its 604 million citizens (in 2017) living in cities.[1] The region is marked by the most extreme variation in living standards in the world. Average per capita income in 2016 was US$7,954 but some 28% of the population were still living in multidimensional poverty in 2012. Latin American societies have historically been very exclusionary and are characterised by weak citizenship. The poor are often enmeshed in a subordinated relationship with local political elites through a mechanism of political co-option known as clientelism, under which the client bargains for resources in exchange for favours provided to the patron. There is a growing interest in the contribution that local government can make towards countering these obstacles to more inclusive societies, as exemplified by the promotion of 'local democratic governance' in the region by international development agencies. As in other parts of the world, stronger local government is seen as way to improve the efficiency, equity and effectiveness of public investment, to strengthen citizen trust in the state, and to promote democratic values.

This chapter examines the growing contribution that local government is making to the development process in Latin America and the extent to which it has served to counter social exclusion. It begins by reviewing the history of extreme centralisation of power during and after the colonial period. It then assesses contemporary local government in the region which is examined through seven key aspects of the decentralisation process that began in the late 20th century: size distribution; service delivery; finance; electoral system; political system; administration; and citizen participation. Finally, some conclusions are presented from the analysis.

The colonial legacy

The history of local government in Latin America has been romanticised by modern writers who have often attributed to it powers which it never possessed. Central to this process is the municipal administration during the colonial era, known as the *cabildo*. The heyday of the cabildo was in the immediate aftermath of the conquest and before the Spanish Crown imposed a highly centralist system of imperial administration. During this brief period, the new colonial possessions were effectively ruled by self-governing groups of Spanish conquistadores who established cabildos on conquered territory as an administrative device to ensure a degree of legal protection for activities not specifically authorised by the Crown. The post of *regidor* (councillor) provided many opportunities for financial gain. The cabildo was responsible for distributing the land which the regidores, as settlers, craved, and influenced the administration of indigenous labour, on which they, as land-owners and mine-owners, depended. Before long the Crown began to exert control over its newly acquired territorial possessions, stripping the cabildo of most of its nominal powers.

The new administrative structures consisted of an urban centre and an extensive rural hinterland which invariably extended to the boundary with the adjoining body. This settlement pattern, and the territorial configuration of local government which would derive from it, mirrored the colonial relationship between the Spanish invaders and the indigenous people. In marked contrast to the English settlement of North America, the Spanish colonists congregated in the new urban clusters, and the rural population remained almost exclusively indigenous, providing cheap labour and sustenance for the new urban settlements. In practice, the actions of the cabildo were confined to the urban area of the municipality, where the Spanish resided. As a result, the view was soon established that local government could legitimately abdicate any responsibility for service delivery in rural areas — a perception that remains deeply ingrained in contemporary Latin America.

The essential features of local administration during the colonial era would have a major influence upon the municipal governments established during the post-independence period. The Crown greatly limited the cabildo's powers of taxation and expenditure. But there was little pressure from the regidores to expand its limited functions. This absence of political assertiveness derived from the undemocratic composition of the cabildo. The public auctioning of the lifetime post of regidor and the bequeathing of such proprietary posts to their heirs upon payment of a special tax produced a legacy of graft and corruption that has endured to the present day. It strengthened the oligarchic nature of the cabildo, the membership of which became exclusively drawn from among the creoles, American-born Spaniards.

The overhaul of imperial administration carried out under Charles III (1759–1788), known as the Bourbon Reforms, introduced centralising forces designed to control and modernise the colonial bureaucracy and to increase revenues at the time of a growing threat to Spanish domination of the Americas. This led to a rapid decline in the participation of creoles in the higher echelons of the colonial administration. A system of intendancies was introduced, headed exclusively by Spanish-born *peninsulares*. The intendancies granted greater powers of taxation to the cabildo and pressured it to undertake its neglected responsibilities (Lynch 1958: 210, 211, 288). This produced a new lease of life for the cabildo. By the first decade of the 19th century most cabildos were in dispute with their intendants. The Reforms had provided a vista of economic opportunity through trade, stimulating a new interest for economic advancement and a measure of self-determination. The cabildos were also fast becoming the political conduit for the expression of creole frustrations. They resented their exclusion from high office and the exclusive reliance on Spanish-born administrators in the higher echelons of the colonial administration.

The cabildo had failed dismally as a breeding-ground for democratic values during the colonial period. Nevertheless, it was the only institution in which creoles were well represented, and the only one which retained a small measure of local autonomy. Hence, when the Spanish monarchy collapsed in 1808, separatist sentiments were first articulated through the cabildo, which soon became the midwife of the independence movement. In 1810 cabildos elected revolutionary juntas in towns throughout the sub-continent. The alleged democratic credentials of the cabildo were enhanced by the wider representation of interests through the cabildo *abierto* (open town meeting), which was introduced to garner support for the independence movement.

Post-Independence decline

Spain's legacy to Latin America was a tradition of extreme centralisation in governmental decision-making and an elitist social structure that impeded the implementation of central government policies. Local government was grossly neglected during the post-independence period as governments throughout the region strove to ensure national consolidation. Local government was often suppressed altogether – for example in Argentina (1820–1853), Bolivia (1843–1861), Chile (1830–1861), Mexico (1837–1857) and Paraguay (1824–1882). The centralising tendency was so strong that the capital cities of most Latin American countries were governed directly by the President of the Republic, and two of them (Buenos Aires and Mexico City) still were so as late as in 1994.

From the late 19th century, the growing regional ascendancy of the United States led to the gradual receptivity to Anglo-Saxon liberal philosophy and in many countries idealistic constitutions were promulgated based on the North American model. Local government was granted formal autonomy and widespread powers which were either written directly into the constitution itself, or else were granted through separate municipal codes. Yet from the early decades of the 20th century, a yawning gulf began to emerge between this rhetoric of local government autonomy and the reality of local government's gradual degeneration. Local government lacked the financial resources to implement the wide range of functions to which it was formally committed and the constant abrogation of municipal elections by central government curtailed its political autonomy. At the same time, clientelism and the 'spoils system' of recruitment greatly diminished its administrative capability. During the 1970s a swathe of military regimes came to dominate the political system of Latin America, and by the end of the decade most countries in the region were ruled directly by the armed forces. In fact, the military soon came to personify the centralist tradition, and proceeded to deny the most basic democratic rights to their citizens.

The Decentralisation Process

After more than a century and a half since independence during which local government had played a minimal role in the development process of the region, the democratisation process under way from the mid-1980s saw the emergence of uneasy domestic coalitions in favour of decentralisation and a strengthening of local government. Their main demands were greater political autonomy for local government, the devolution of responsibility for service delivery to the municipal level, and an associated strengthening of municipal finances. Three groups, with very different agendas, saw the decentralisation process as a means to advance their respective aims. First, there were neo-liberals who viewed decentralisation as an essential part of a wider strategy for reducing the role of the public sector as a whole within the economy. Second, there were radical reformers who saw decentralisation as a way of overcoming the non-egalitarian and undemocratic social structures inherited from the preceding period of military rule. Third, there were technocrats who viewed decentralisation primarily as a means to improve the overall efficiency of service delivery through better coordination at the local level. In virtually all cases, these pressures for decentralisation came 'from above' and not from sub-national bodies. The active encouragement of international development agencies was an important support for these domestic coalitions for change (Nickson 1995: 24).

As the influence of this powerful coalition in favour of decentralisation was felt in the public policy-making process, a change began to occur in the relationship of municipalities with both central government and with their own citizens. In 1978 only three countries (Ecuador, Colombia and Venezuela) had democratically elected mayors. By thirty years later, in 2008, all countries in the region except Cuba had free and fair local government elections. This political democratisation was accompanied by the financial and institutional strengthening of local government. However, this reform process has been uneven. Among the federal nations of the region, in Mexico and Venezuela, the main thrust has been to strengthen historically weak state governments rather than local government, while in Argentina and Brazil the strengthening of historically weak local governments was accorded priority over state-level structures. Among the unitary nations, Bolivia, Chile, Colombia and Ecuador experienced considerable strengthening of local government through the transfer of service delivery responsibilities and accompanying fiscal transfers. By comparison progress was more limited and came later in Costa Rica, Honduras, Panama, Paraguay and Uruguay. Nevertheless, by the mid-1990s a clear regional trend had emerged to enhance the role of local government in the development process (Nickson 1995: 25).

The size distribution of local government

Despite the common heritage of Spanish and Portuguese colonialism, there is a surprisingly high degree of diversity with regard to administrative structures within the 19 nations, 350 states and regions and over 15,000 municipalities of the region. Municipal structures have failed to respond to the rapidly changing pattern of human settlement in the region. Rapid rural to urban migration since the 1950s has swelled the populations of historic urban centres while at the same time contributing to the stagnation, if not absolute population decline, of the vast majority of small, rural municipalities. As a result, while a small number of municipalities in the region are the largest cities in the world (e.g. Mexico City, 26 million inhabitants; São Paolo, 24 million inhabitants) around 90% of all municipalities in the region have fewer than 50,000 inhabitants. Yet municipal boundaries have not been reshaped to accommodate the rapidly changing pattern of human settlement.

This unwillingness to contemplate the territorial restructuring of local government in favour of amalgamation has undermined effective and efficient municipal service provision in both large and small municipalities. Most large conurbations in the region have long been formally designated as 'metropolitan' areas although very few have a functioning system of metropolitan government because of the alleged threat that it would pose to the autonomy of municipalities located within their boundaries. The absence of metropolitan government has been responsible for the lack of coordination, rivalry and duplication in service provision between municipalities within large conurbations. This is especially noticeable in the case of solid waste disposal, transportation, and urban planning.

On the contrary, there has been a significant rise in the total number of Latin American municipalities, rising from 13,951 in 1994 to 14,895 in 2008 and to 15,094 in 2017 (Table 10.1). This has been mainly explained by municipal fragmentation in rural areas as expanding colonisation led to the emergence of new urban settlements within the rural hinterland of existing municipalities. They usually lacked adequate political representation and were subordinated to political interests in the municipal headquarters. The prime motive for 'breaking away' has invariably been in order to obtain better access to central government fiscal transfers for basic rural services. The political momentum of this process remains strong. Its effect is to keep most Latin American municipalities well below the critical size needed in order to reap the economies of both scale and scope that would justify the trained personnel and capital investment necessary to provide adequate service provision to its citizens. Local governments in many parts of the region have developed forms of inter-municipal cooperation, known as *mancomunidades*. These voluntary associations seek to achieve economies of scale in service delivery through the sharing of scarce resources, especially for road maintenance, tourism development and environmental protection (Suárez 2014).

Table 10.1 Number of municipalities in Latin America, 1994, 2008 and 2017

Country	Number of municipalities in 1994	Number of municipalities In 2008	Number of municipalities in 2017
Argentina	1,100	1,118	1,129
Bolivia	296	327	339
Brazil	4,974	5,562	5,570
Chile	334	345	345
Colombia	1,034	1,113	1,123
Costa Rica	81	81	82
Dominican Rep.	137	152	158
Ecuador	193	219	221
El Salvador	262	262	262
Guatemala	330	332	340
Honduras	291	298	298
Mexico	2,397	2,439	2,446
Nicaragua	143	153	153
Panama	67	75	76
Paraguay	213	231	254
Peru*	1,798	1,834	1,851
Uruguay	19	19	112
Venezuela	282	335	335
Latin America	13,951	14,895	15,094

Source: Municipal data for 1994 from Nickson (1995: 32); municipal data for 2008 from Nickson (2009:82); municipal data for 2017 from author's own calculations based on individual country data.

*Peru is the only country in the region with a three-tier local government system – comprising 196 provincial municipalities and 1,655 district municipalities, as well as 2,534 rural municipalities at the sub-district level that lack full legal status.

Local government service delivery

The uniform treatment before the law which characterises municipal autonomy in Latin America means that all local governments are granted the same legal mandate for service provision. Despite the enormous differences in population size, hardly anywhere are they classified into size categories, with corresponding differential powers and responsibilities. Yet the capacity of the vast majority of municipalities to carry out those functions mandated to them is severely constrained by lack of financial and human resources. In contrast, a few larger municipalities have far greater access to revenue. This leads, in practice, to enormous differences between large and small municipalities in the range of services that they actually provide (Bland 2011).

Municipal codes usually grant local government a general competence to undertake any service in its jurisdiction which is not assigned to another level of government or which it is not expressly forbidden to do. However, behind the rhetoric of this general competence lies the important legal distinction between so-called discretionary and non-discretionary functions. The point at which the line is drawn between the two is ultimately determined by central government, and reflects the self-imposed limits of its encroachment on municipal terrain.

Non-discretionary functions mandated to local government include few which central government has any interest in undertaking itself. It is these services that the vast majority of municipalities actually provide. But they are obligatory in name only, because no mechanism exists to penalise local government for their non-delivery. These non-discretionary functions fall into four broad categories: (i) elementary powers of regulation carried out on behalf of central government, such as public order, justice of the peace, and civil registration; (ii) essential urban services, such as road maintenance, public lighting, street cleaning, solid waste management, parks and gardens, and basic land use zoning; (iii) essential revenue-generating public services, such as slaughterhouses, cemeteries, public markets and bus terminals; and (iv) basic social services, such as public hygiene, granting of commercial and industrial licenses, and weights and measures.

By contrast, discretionary functions are those which central government has an interest in undertaking. As a result, the role of local government in those functions for which it has been granted a discretionary mandate usually amounts to little more than serving as a junior partner in on-going central government activities at the local level. In several countries, these concurrent powers have led to poor coordination in service delivery between central and local government, producing inefficient duplication in some areas and, in others, gaps where no tier of government takes responsibility for provision. These discretionary functions fall into three broad categories: (i) public utilities (water, sewerage and electricity supply), (ii) social services (primary health care and basic education), and (iii) planning (road transport, zoning) and environmental protection. This unrealistic uniformity in the legal mandate horizontally across municipalities, combined with the blurred allocation of responsibilities vertically between different tiers of government because of the legal ambiguity of discretionary and concurrent powers, has led to a bewildering variety in the range and level of municipalities' service provision within each country.

As a part of the recent decentralisation process there has been a significant devolution of service delivery responsibilities from central to local government. However its scale has often been exaggerated and in most countries its breadth and depth has not matched the concurrent process of fiscal decentralisation. The initiative for the transfer of new service delivery responsibilities has invariably come from central government and has often been resisted by local government. In the federal nations of Mexico and Venezuela, devolution of responsibility for basic education and health has been primarily from central government to state government. By contrast, in Brazil, health and education devolution has proceeded down to the municipal level, accompanied by a growing local government role in administering social welfare and poverty reduction programmes. In some Argentina provinces (states) municipalities share responsibility for basic health care. In almost all the region, local government plays a minimum role in the delivery of basic public services such as electricity and telecom. The major exception is urban water supply and sanitation, where there has been a devolution of responsibility in recent years in several countries from central government (in the form of state water companies) to municipalities.

Municipal services are delivered in one of four main ways. First, they may be directly administered through municipal departments which are directly subordinate to the executive. Second, they may be indirectly administered by municipally owned foundations. Although the chief executive is nominated by the mayor and staff are employed on the same terms as municipal officials, they do allow service deliverers greater budgetary independence. Third, they may be indirectly administered by enterprises which are wholly owned by municipalities or which are joint ventures with the private sector. As private companies, these operate with an even greater degree of flexibility with regard to pay and conditions of service, although their chief executives are still usually nominated by the mayor.

Finally, services may be delivered by private companies that have been granted a concession through a tendering procedure, which is formalised in a contract with the municipality.

This 'contracting out' of service delivery is a well-established practice throughout Latin America, especially for solid waste disposal and street-cleaning, and during the 1990s, under the influence of neo-liberalism, many countries extended the concession of local services, especially to urban water supply. However, the structural weaknesses of municipal administrative systems have militated against the development of the 'relational trust' required for success in private sector participation. Clientelism and corruption have led to a lack of transparency in tendering procedures as well as inadequate mechanisms for monitoring and regulating the performance of the service deliverer (Nickson 2014).

Local government finance

The financial pattern of Latin American local government is similar to that found in many other parts of the world. Municipalities tend to be more important, when measured by their share of gross domestic product, as providers of public services than as collectors of revenues, and in all countries revenue raised by local government from its own sources falls far short of its expenditure obligations. The decentralisation process has had a major impact on strengthening local government finances in the region. The unweighted average of expenditure by regional and local government rose from 11.6% of total national government spending in 1980 to 17.8% in 2005–2013. However, this increase hides considerable intra-regional variation (Table 10.2).

Table 10.2 Latin America: share of regional and local government in national government spending

Country	Regional and local government (%)	Country	National government (%)	Regional government (%)	Local government (%)
Argentina (1980)	22.2	Argentina (2005)	50.1	41.4	8.5
Bolivia (1980)	14.8	Bolivia (2006)	73.4	18.9	7.7
Brazil (1980)	32.4	Brazil (2013)	50.7	30.0	19.3
Chile (1980)	3.7	Chile (2013)	87.6		12.4
Colombia (1982)	26.3	Colombia (2013)	73.0	8.8	18.2
Costa Rica (1980)	4.0	Costa Rica (2013)	95.3		4.7
Dominican Republic (1980)	3.5	Dominican Republic (2012)	95.5		4.5
Ecuador (1980)	18.3	Ecuador (2006)	73.5	5.8	20.7
El Salvador (1978)	5.8	El Salvador (2013)	91.1		8.9
Guatemala (1980)	4.5	Guatemala (2009)	95.6		4.4
Honduras	n.a.	Honduras (2013)	95.5		4.5
Mexico (1980)	22.0	México (2007)	69.3	25.0	5.7
Panama (1980)	2.0	Panamá (2005)	98.3		1.7
Paraguay (1980)	5.5	Paraguay (2013)	91.3	2.1	6.6
Peru (1990)	9.1	Peru (2013)	77.8	13.4	8.8
Uruguay (1980)	8.6	Uruguay (2005)	88.7		11.3
Venezuela (1979)	2.4	Venezuela (2007)	92.0		8.0
Latin America	11.6	Latin America	82.3	8.6	9.2

Source: Nickson (1995: 44); Rosales (2012: 18); IMF (2016).

Own-revenue sources

The financial autonomy of local government is limited by the restrictions on powers of taxation, which are almost everywhere determined either by central government (in unitary nations) or by state governments (in federal nations) although municipalities usually retain the power to decide on the level of fees, user charges and betterment levies. In unitary nations, very few taxes are allocated to intermediate tiers of government. The local tax burden is relatively low throughout the region because of a combination of limited powers of taxation and weak tax administration. The major sources of municipal own-revenue are similar in federal and unitary nations, namely property taxation, vehicle road tax and business and commercial licences. Archaic and complex structures of local taxes influence the low level of tax collection.

In almost all countries, property taxation is the most important local tax. The tariff rate, expressed as a percentage of the capital value, is usually stipulated by municipal finance laws, and central government allows little discretion for municipalities to vary this. Property tax collection is limited by outdated property cadastres, inaccurate assessments, excessive exemptions and a widespread culture of non-payment (Sepulveda and Martínez-Vázquez 2011). Although municipalities in most countries are legally empowered to tax rural as well as urban properties, in practice the latter are usually exempt. This failure to harness a major potential source of locally generated revenue – property tax – is the overwhelming reason for the weak fiscal performance of the vast majority of small municipalities in the region. Because of much larger populations, higher per capita incomes, higher property values and better tax administration, income from own-revenue is much more important in the large urbanised municipalities of the region than in smaller rural municipalities. Consequently, the share of own-revenue in total income is typically above 60% for the former. By contrast, the latter depend heavily on transfers, which typically account for over 90% of total income.

Fiscal transfers and revenue-sharing

Until the 1980s, central government fiscal transfers to local government were on a small-scale, ad hoc basis, and were subject to unpredictable variation. The criteria for allocation between municipalities were shrouded in legal obscurity in order to mask the prevalence of clientelism. This arbitrary arrangement greatly inhibited planning of local service provision because municipalities had no way of forecasting total resources at their disposal over the medium term. The significant increase in intra-governmental fiscal transfers has been a major feature of the decentralisation process in the region (Rezende and Veloso 2012).

These transfers take three major forms – revenue-sharing, sector ear-marked transfers and funding for targeted poverty reduction programmes. Transfers from tax-sharing (either general revenue-sharing or sharing of proceeds from specific national taxes) are increasingly allocated on the basis of transparent formula that incorporate equity variables such as population size, poverty levels and access to services. Examples include Bolivia (20% of national tax revenue), Dominican Republic (10% of national budget) and Ecuador (15% of national tax revenue). Similar legislation exists for allocating a share of the national budget to municipalities in some countries of Central America, such as Guatemala (10%), El Salvador (7%), Nicaragua (10%), Honduras (5%) and Costa Rica (10%). However, governments have often failed to honour these stipulated shares.

Although fiscal resources from such tax-sharing have been allocated on a needs-based criteria rather than the previous origin-based (i.e. derivation) criteria, they have had very limited impact in reducing horizontal inequalities in well-being. This is basically because these transfers have not incorporated a formal equalisation mechanism designed to ensure a standard level of service provision in all municipalities by 'topping up' local revenues in areas of below average fiscal capacity. Instead, transfer formulas usually include equity considerations as only one among several factors in the overall weighting system. As a result, despite the increase in their scale and their greater transparency in recent years, transfers have not diminished the enormous disparities in municipal income per head. Furthermore, even the limited improvements in inter-jurisdictional equity which have taken place in some countries have done little to improve inter-personal equity. This is because the beneficiaries from expenditure carried out by small rural municipalities tend to be highly concentrated among households in mini urban centres.

The second form of intra-governmental fiscal transfer is the earmarked transfers that are used to finance newly decentralised responsibilities, particularly in education and health. The disbursement of these transfers is usually conditional on complicated systems of approval of investment projects. Because they are channelled through a diversity of central government programmes, in many countries it is difficult to estimate the real size and distribution of these transfers. In recent years targeted anti-poverty programmes have emerged in the region. They channel significant volumes of public investment into basic infrastructure and social services. Where conditional cash transfer (CCT) programmes operate through local government, such as Brazil, they may be considered as a third modality of intra-governmental fiscal transfer. However in other cases, such as Peru, these special programmes have by-passed local government altogether and have led to failures in the coordination of local public investment.

Overall, the major thrust of fiscal decentralisation in the region has been an increased level of fiscal transfers via revenue-sharing mechanisms rather than the greater devolution of taxation powers to local government. Furthermore, there is strong evidence of the 'disincentive' effect of these increased transfers on local tax effort and in the smaller, rural and poorer municipalities of many countries in the region income from own-revenue sources has stagnated. Consequently, in the vast majority of municipalities, the annual increase in revenue from fiscal transfers has outstripped that from own-revenue. As a result, there has been a noticeable increase in the share of fiscal transfers in total municipal income in recent years (Martínez-Vázquez 2010).

The local electoral system

Strengthening of the political autonomy of local government has been a major feature of the recent decentralisation process. Until then, non-elected executive heads were the norm, invariably appointed on the basis of political patronage rather than professional competence. From the early 1980s central appointments were increasingly replaced by democratically elected mayors. In Colombia (1988), mayors were elected for the first time for over a century, and in Paraguay (1991) they were elected for the first time ever in the history of the country. In Peru (1981), Bolivia (1985) and Chile (1992), local government elections were held for the first time since 1968, 1950 and 1973 respectively (Nickson 1995: 67). By 2000 the democratic election of mayors had become the norm throughout the region.

The dynamics of the decentralisation process is increasingly understood as a form of political bargaining between presidents, national legislators and sub-national politicians. It has been argued that 'the greater the sensitivity of central level politicians to sub-national political outcomes, the more the decentralised the system is likely to be' (Willis et al. 1999: 9). These authors concluded that the nature of the party system has strongly influenced the pace and extent of decentralisation. Central government will retain greater control over resources in those countries such as Mexico with centralised political parties than in those with a highly fragmented party system such as Brazil. Evidence from Peru suggests that support for decentralisation is also stronger when the parties in the national government believe that support at sub-national levels is more promising than their prospects in national elections (O'Neill 2005).

Throughout the region, the term of office of the elected mayor is now concurrent with that of councillors. Mayors are normally elected by separate election, and this reflects the growing influence of the United States' 'strong mayor' model of local government. This has gradually replaced the 'integrated' French system of indirect election of mayors from among councillors. This system was once widespread in the region, but the method of election changed from indirect to direct in Nicaragua (1995), Venezuela (1989), Costa Rica (2002) and Chile (2004). Indirect election is now only retained in Bolivia and Mexico. Mayors are usually elected by a simple plurality, except in Brazilian municipalities with a population of over 200,000, where they must obtain at least 51% of the votes cast, if necessary by means of a second round run-off. Peru has a hybrid form of mayoral election which spans the 'separate–integrated' divide. Under this arrangement, the candidate heading the winning party list for council membership is automatically selected as the mayor. Voter turnout in municipal elections in the region is relatively high by international standards, although with some evidence of a decline in recent years. In Argentina, Brazil and Uruguay, where voting is obligatory, the turnout exceeds 80% of the electorate. By contrast, the turnout is much lower in the smaller Central America nations, falling to as low as 28% in Costa Rica in 2010.

The recent decentralisation process has made reforms to four features of the electoral system that still militate against accountability to the electorate, as follows:

The democratic deficit

The most striking feature of the electoral system is the very small number of councillors, which range from a minimum of five in most countries to a maximum of only 60 in the case of the Municipality of Buenos Aires. Although this situation is often the legacy of outdated municipal codes promulgated at a time when urban populations were a fraction of what they are today, this 'democratic deficit' has not been corrected through subsequent legislative reform. As a result, political decision-making is now highly concentrated and has led to gross political under-representation especially in larger municipalities where the ratio of citizens per councillor typically ranges between 20,000 and 100,000. North American and European municipalities have much lower councillor/citizen ratios (France, 1:110; Sweden, 1:270; Germany, 1:400; United States, 1:490; Spain, 1:602; Japan, 1:1,600; Britain, 1:1,800) and this gives far greater scope than in Latin America for the political representation of a diversity of interest groups (Norton 1994).

The party list system and absence of territorial representation

Throughout almost all of Latin America, councillors are elected at large rather than on a ward basis, a system which thereby minimises diversity of geographical representation. The only exception is Panama where councillors are elected by the 'first past the post' system based on electoral wards. Elsewhere, the D'Hondt system of proportional representation is the preferred electoral system. As such, elected councillors are not individually accountable to particular territorially defined groups of citizens. This is especially damaging to accountability because of the wide gulf that already separates civil society and the local state, as exemplified by the extremely high ratio of citizens per councillor (see above). Venezuela is the only country to move towards territorial representation as part of its decentralisation reform process, where the 'party list' electoral system was replaced in 1992 by a 'mixed' system, similar to the German model, under which two-thirds of councillors are elected on a ward basis, and the remaining one-third according to party lists.

Furthermore, councillors are elected by party lists that are usually 'closed' (i.e. ranked) and also 'blocked' (i.e. denying the voter the right to select candidates from more than one list). The only exceptions are Brazil and Chile, where voters choose a single candidate instead of a list of candidates. In the Brazilian case, votes are recorded for each polling station so that the geographical locus of support for individual councillors is known. In several countries, notably Peru, the electoral system is not based on full proportional representation, but is according to the 'majority-plus' system, under which the party which wins most votes is automatically granted a majority of council seats and the remaining seats are distributed among other parties on the basis of proportional representation. In the extreme case of El Salvador, the party that wins most votes obtains all council seats and there is consequently no representation of minority parties.

The 'closed' and 'blocked' party list system greatly reduces political accountability to the electorate. Voters are denied the right to rank candidates from within the party of their choice according to their own personal preference. They are also denied the opportunity to select a mix of candidates from different parties. Both features have served to entrench the power of elites within political parties and have thus contributed indirectly to maintaining centralism within Latin American political culture. The system also ensures that intra-party bickering over position on the party list takes precedence over the cultivation of a strong personal relationship between candidates and the electorate. The 'opening up' of the party list system has been noticeably absent from the decentralisation reform process. Venezuela (from 1989) and Chile (from 1992) are the exceptions, where the 'closed and blocked' electoral system was replaced with an open and 'non-blocked' list, *panachage*, preference voting system.

The short term of office and prohibition on re-election

Until recently a short (2–3 years) term of office coupled with prohibition on immediate re-election of the incumbent mayor were common features of the electoral system that reduced accountability to the electorate. This happened because mayors who were elected for short periods without the possibility of re-election did not have the same incentive to maintain standards of probity while in office. The problem was compounded by the fact that where the simple plurality voting system operates, mayors may be elected with a relatively small proportion of the total vote. However, the decentralisation process has seen a significant increase in the length of the municipal term of office. In 1995 seven countries still had terms of three years or less. Yet by 2017 the vast majority had four year terms of office, five others (Bolivia, Paraguay, Panama, Peru and Uruguay) had five-year terms and only Mexico retained a three year term. By 2017 only two countries (Colombia and Mexico) still prohibited consecutive re-election of mayors. Most countries still impose a two-term limit and Chile and Ecuador are the only countries where the unlimited re-election of mayors is permitted.

Linkage with national elections

The practice of holding local government elections at the same time as elections to national political office was once widespread in the region. This meant that local government elections were overshadowed in importance by the national elections, distracting voter attention away from local towards national issues. It also effectively guaranteed that clientelist considerations prevailed in the selection of party candidates for municipal office. Selection was often determined by the electoral support which potential municipal office-holders could mobilise for the party's national politicians rather than by the personal capabilities of the candidates. In exchange for this support, they were 'rewarded' with municipal office. The decentralisation process has brought a gradual decline in this practice as countries such as Venezuela and Colombia have de-linked the timing of local government elections from that of national elections. In three countries (Honduras, Guatemala and Panama) the term of municipal office remains co-terminus with that of national political office and in these cases municipal elections are held concurrently with presidential and congressional elections. In two federal countries (Argentina and Mexico), local government elections usually coincide with the state-level elections (Nickson 1995: 61–68).

The political system of local government

The organisational culture of most municipalities in Latin America is still imbued with the centralist legacy of *caudillismo* ('political bossism'), the 'pork-barrel' political culture whose lifeblood is the absence of job stability and the constant rotation of an overstaffed bureaucracy. In contrast to many parts of the world, municipal office-holders are normally paid salaries rather than attendance allowances. In many countries, financial gain is a major attraction for those seeking municipal office. For this reason, the municipal codes of several countries establish limits on the size of officer remunerations in relation to total municipal income. Despite this, such payments are often excessive in smaller municipalities, where they absorb a disproportionate share of total municipal revenue.

The executive head

Local government in the region has a marked tendency towards unipersonal leadership. This tradition is inherited from the colonial era, as well as from the twin influences of caudillismo and clientelism. It was reinforced by United States foreign aid programmes in the 1950s and 1960s, which transferred to Latin America the 'strong elected, executive mayor – weak council' system that is prevalent in US municipalities. The mayor is the chief executive officer responsible for the day-to-day operations of the municipal administration, determining broad policy and the functioning of municipal services and investment projects. The mayor formulates and controls the execution of the budget and usually initiates municipal legislation. The mayor appoints all confidence post-holders (senior executive assistants who head secretariats, departments and dependent agencies), and in most countries also has the authority to recruit, supervise and dismiss permanent municipal staff, although in some countries such decisions must be endorsed by the council. The mayor also acts as the general agent of central government. This role derives from the delegation of law and order functions but is far less pronounced now than in the past. The major responsibility of this role today involves coordinating local projects with agencies of central or regional government. The mayor is also the ceremonial head of the municipality (e.g. during visits by national political leaders). In the personalist political culture of Latin America, the high visibility of this role has enabled aspiring national politicians to use the mayoral office as an important stepping-stone in their career.

Even in the larger municipalities of the region, management tends to be highly personalised in the figure of the mayor. This style of management is reflected in the de facto nature of the organisational structure, which bears little relation to its de jure design as laid out in organisation charts and accompanying job descriptions. The lack of effective organisational norms and responsibilities means that functional delegation of authority is not complied with. Instead, there is a concentration of decision-making at the highest level and a corresponding lack of it at other levels. Because delegation of responsibility is so limited, a corporate management ethos is generally absent. Instead decisions are taken on the basis of 'orders' from the mayor, which, in the absence of any strategic plan, fluctuate wildly in response to the pressure of competing political interests. In turn, this breeds a lack of initiative within functional departments because of the limited delegation of authority and the absence of long term planning.

The municipal council

As noted above, the municipal council is extremely small by international standards. It elects its own president from among its members and has two major functions – budget approval and oversight. The council also enacts municipal statutes and internal administrative regulations, which are often proposed by the mayor. The other role is to supervise the municipal administration carried out under the executive authority of the mayor. The mayor depends on the council for the approval of key financial decisions such as local fee rates and the annual budget and expenditure program. In practice, however, legislative scrutiny of financial matters is greatly limited by the absence, even in the largest municipalities of the region except Brazil, of any technical support team to give advice to councillors. Instead, debate is often restricted to consideration of the legality or otherwise of budgetary proposals, leaving detailed financial investigation to the Comptroller General's Office. In the larger municipalities, the small size of councils means that councillors are usually fully occupied on municipal business. A proper committee system is unworkable with so few councillors. Instead, individual councillors often oversee a particular area of the municipal administration. This highly personalised system of supervision, when combined with the tradition of clientelism, often gives rise to undue interference by councillors in day-to-day departmental management. In practice, the distinction between supervision and actual executive power is often so blurred that councillors have considerable de facto power to recruit, dismiss, promote and re-grade staff.

Executive–legislature relations at the municipal level have been strongly influenced by the deep-rooted personalist political culture of Latin America and in most countries, the power of the mayor far outweighs that of the council. This happens irrespective of the formal division of responsibilities provided for by municipal legislation. In the past, the power of the executive was such that the mayor often acted as leader of the municipal council, and chaired its meetings. Today that practice is increasingly rare although it is still followed in Chile, Guatemala, Honduras and Peru.

In practice, the power of the legislature vis-à-vis the executive is limited to that of either ratifying municipal legislation or not. In some countries the council even lacks effective power to reject executive action – the municipal codes of Brazil and Colombia still enable the mayor to veto council opposition to executive action. In others, the powers of the legislature are further diminished by the fact that the executive is answerable to it only for some functions and to central government for others. This arrangement derives from the long-standing identification of the municipal executive as the local representative of the president of the republic.

In very many municipalities, the power of the legislature is so weak that the council is often confined to surprisingly trivial matters while important strategic issues regarding the municipality are left in the hands of the mayor. This has contributed to the generally poor public image of the councillor compared with that of the mayor. The unequal power relationship between the executive and the legislature is reflected in the behaviour of individual councillors. Given the relative weakness of the council and the prevalence of clientelism, the power of councillors often derives primarily from their role as a 'broker' between interest groups and the mayor. Their prestige depends on their ability to act as a conduit for such groups to the mayor, and on their ability to obtain favours from the mayor.

The relationship between the executive and the legislature is also affected by the personalist political culture, which is especially strong in smaller, rural municipalities. Although the mayor is usually the party leader at the local level, factional opposition to this leadership usually gels around councillors of the same party. This factionalism often galvanises council opposition to the mayor and expresses itself by the refusal of the council to sanction executive proposals and attempts to use anti-corruption legislation to remove the mayor from office. Such 'blocking' behaviour is motivated by intra-party bickering rather than by the merits of the case and is a major reason for the inertia in municipal decision-making which is common throughout the region (Nickson 1995: 69–72).

Local government administration

The lack of a career civil service in Latin America is particularly pronounced at the local government level. Local government service commissions are absent in the region and the dearth of accurate data on the numbers employed in local government is a striking reflection of the weakness of human resource management. In most countries, the political appointment of senior and middle-management staff, referred to as 'confidence posts', remains the norm, with the resulting rapid rotation of staff as a result of both electoral change and intra-party factional disputes.

In most countries local government permanent staff, usually middle and lower level personnel, are formally covered by national 'civil service career' laws and even some cases by 'municipal career' laws. However, the application of the basic meritocratic norms embodied in these laws (open and competitive recruitment, promotion by performance, disciplinary and dismissal procedures) are rarely implemented. Even when implemented, career progression is usually truncated at the level of departmental head because posts above these are confidence posts. Clientelism ensures that local government personnel systems remain weak and highly fragmented throughout the region. There is no vertical integration between the personnel systems of central and local government. Neither is the local government system unified horizontally between municipalities. Instead each municipality has its own separate personnel system. This absence of vertical and horizontal integration greatly inhibits the mobility of local government personnel and is a major factor obstructing the introduction of a genuine local government career system.

As a result, the 'institutional memory' of local government is weak, as evidenced by the widespread absence of basic features such as open recruitment, job descriptions, filing systems and minutes of meetings. Although some progress has been made towards the introduction of a local government career service in Chile and the southern states of Brazil, the general situation remains woefully inadequate in spite of the recent decentralisation process. This is especially the case in rural areas of the smaller and less developed countries in the region, where the impact of rampant political interference still leads to administrative inefficiency.

Municipal legislation throughout the region almost always imposes a uniform organisational structure on local government and this does not take into consideration the enormous variation in the size of their populations. For the vast majority of small municipalities, each with less than twenty staff members, this structure invariably proves to be unrealistically elaborate. Implementation of the required number of departments presupposes a much larger number of staff, which most municipalities simply cannot afford to recruit. In practice, these organisational norms are ignored, the administrative structure remains very simple, and the mayor takes virtually all decisions.

When combined with the absence of a career-based senior administrative cadre, the highly personalised management style also produces a serious problem of administrative discontinuity.

A major feature of this discontinuity is the tendency for incoming mayors to embark on new, often prestigious, projects, and to reject the continuation of programs initiated by their predecessors, simply in order to stamp their own character on the municipal government. The lack of continuity in policy-making between successive administrations is common even when they belong to the same political party and this hinders strategic direction in municipal management. On the contrary, by making medium-term expenditure planning virtually impossible, it encourages an extreme 'short-termism' in local government and a 'crisis management' approach to day-to-day decision-making. 'Quick yield' projects are given priority because they are capable of delivering rapid political dividends by bolstering the immediate popularity of the mayor.

Overstaffing is a major consequence of clientelism in local government. Even in the larger municipalities of the region, staffing levels are high by international standards, especially in light of the relatively limited range of services that they currently provide. In the small and medium-sized municipalities of the region, wage costs typically absorb over 80% of total expenditure, leaving very little for non-salary recurrent expenditure and virtually nothing for capital expenditure. The accepted norm in many countries is that locally raised revenue is earmarked exclusively for the payment of salaries, leaving capital expenditure entirely dependent upon intra-governmental transfers. Nevertheless, in some countries attempts are made to control overstaffing through financial ratios. In Brazil, the share of salaries must not exceed 65% of total municipal expenditure (Nickson 1995: 72–79).

Citizen participation

The exclusionary style of development has been a major underlying cause of social conflict in Latin America, and opposition to authoritarian rule in the 1970s and 1980s was often expressed through the emergence of vigorous community organisations. These sought to serve as a counterweight to the centralist tradition, by making both national political elites and their clientelist counterparts at the municipal level more accountable to the local electorate. The newly established democratic governments established in the region from the mid-1980s sought to channel this community mobilisation by encouraging greater citizen participation in their own decision-making processes, and this was a major factor in the invigoration of local government in the region. The creation of participatory mechanisms for dialogue and consensus-building at the municipal level became ingredients for strengthening the long-term prospects of democracy and for containing social tensions. Citizen participation was also seen as a way of introducing greater 'rationality' into municipal resource allocation so as to reflect the broad interests of the population. This participation would confront the social problems generated by the exclusionary nature of the development process, in particular the weak access to health care, education and land for housing.

Inspired by the above arguments, the decentralisation process throughout Latin America has incorporated mechanisms for citizen participation in municipal legislation. The most common one is the legal requirement for the municipal executive to consult with citizen organisations and the general public through periodic open meetings, *cabildos abiertos*. While its use remains strong in small municipalities in parts of Central America, elsewhere in the region it has often become a formality with little effort made to publicise it. Legal provision has also been made for municipalities to undertake local referendums and plebiscites, and to accept popular initiatives and the recall of office-holders. However, the allegations of corruption and poor management necessary to trigger a referendum in order to revoke the mayoral mandate are usually so vaguely defined that the mechanism has become open to widespread abuse.

Reforms to promote citizen participation in local governance have been especially strong in Brazil. The 1988 Constitution enshrined the plebiscite, referendum, popular tribune, popular councils, and the right to popular initiative, with the signatures of 5% of those on the electoral register as a requirement to trigger such actions. The 'participatory budget' introduced in the Municipality of Porto Alegre from 1989 to 2004, has provoked worldwide interest as a novel form of citizen participation in the formulation of the municipal budget (Melgar 2014).

The long-term impact of the decentralisation process on the exclusionary nature of Latin American society is the subject of much controversy. International development agencies argue that the introduction of transparent systems of inter-government fiscal transfers, coupled with greater political accountability through electoral reform, will strengthen citizen participation and undermine the basis on which clientelism thrives. Instead, under a decentralised system of government, political elites will be measured by their success in service delivery, because they are now more accountable to the electorate. A contrary view asserts that the growth in central government transfers will unwittingly bolster clientelism and encourage corruption at the local level. According to this view, transferring financial power to local government may simply shift the canker of clientelism from the national to the local arena where it will be even harder to control because of the absence of the strong countervailing regional and sectional interests that are found at the national political level (Finot 2007).

In reality, the upsurge of community organisation in the 1970s and 1980s was intimately linked to the demise of military rule. By the 2010s, a wide gulf had emerged between the rhetoric and reality of citizen participation in local governance, and it impact on local governance was much less than originally envisaged (Rhodes-Purdy 2017). Lack of continuity became a notable feature of community participation throughout the region. Mobilisation was built around specific demands and once these were realised, participation tended to diminish. For this reason, the pressure for citizen participation in local governance may have been primarily a conjunctural phenomenon associated with the transition to democracy in the region (Nickson 2014).

Conclusions

The achievements of the decentralisation process under way in Latin America have contributed somewhat to countering the deep structural inequalities in the direction of greater territorial and social inclusiveness. Political democratisation at the municipal level has been the lynchpin of the process. This is helping to introduce programmatic politics into parties that were hitherto exclusively clientelistic. Constitutional and other legal reforms have transferred new competences and financial resources to sub-national governments. Intra-governmental transfers have risen considerably and sub-national governments now typically account for around one-fifth of total public expenditure, twice the share in the mid-1980s. The new competencies of the local governments translate into progressive— though uneven – institutional development in which some municipalities stand out because of their capacity for innovation, while others still cling to their traditional practices. Nevertheless, following the euphoria of the 1990s when it became a sort of development 'fashion' in the region, by the 2010s there is evidence of a slow-down in the decentralisation process (Bossuyt 2013: 16; Carrera 2013; Tulchin 2012).

There is a rather sterile debate over the extent to which either 'agency' (i.e. political leadership) or 'structure' (i.e. pre-existing levels of social trust and/or economic development) is the major explanatory factor for the degree of success in decentralisation. In this regard, the recent decentralisation process in Latin America offers evidence that supports a more complex yet realistic argument – that the motivations for and outcomes of decentralisation are first and foremost the result of the dynamics of the interaction between local and national political economy

(Angell, Lowden and Thorp 2001; Bossuyt 2013; Eaton 2004; Goldfrank 2007; Montero and Samuels 2003; Nickson 2014). This is not to under-estimate the importance of the dramatic structural changes engineered from above that are profoundly altering intra-governmental relations through fiscal, political and functional devolution. Nor should it demean the importance of advances engineered by the charisma of individual mayors. Rather it is a recognition of the obvious fact that decentralisation 'empowers' local actors (politicians, business leaders and civil society) whose collective impact on local governance had remained muted under the previous centralised system of governance. Hence, as these local actors begin to exercise greater voice through the strengthened structures of local governance, the resulting outcomes necessarily depend – more than anything else – on their respective interests and objectives as well as the 'correlation of forces' between them. As Fauget (2006) shows from an examination of rural municipalities in Bolivia, differences in the local political economy are a major factor in understanding the considerable variation in the outcomes of decentralisation. Given that intra-country variation in the character of this 'local political economy' is so immense, it is therefore hardly surprising that we find such variation in the quality of local governance between municipalities in the same country, even when all have been subjected to the same deep structural reforms (legal, financial and functional).

Note

1 For the purposes of this chapter, Latin America refers to the following countries: Argentina, Bolivia, Brazil, Chile, Colombia, Costa Rica, Dominican Republic, Ecuador, El Salvador, Guatemala, Honduras, Mexico, Nicaragua, Panama, Paraguay, Peru, Uruguay, and Venezuela.

References

Angell, A., Lowden, P. and Thorp, R. (2001) *Decentralizing Development: The Political Economy of Institutional Reform in Colombia and Chile*. Oxford: Oxford University Press.
Bland, G. (2011) Considering Local Democratic Transition in Latin America. *Journal of Politics in Latin America* 3(1): 65–98.
Bossuyt, J. (2013) *Overview of the Decentralisation Process in Latin America*. Maastricht: European Centre for Development Policy Management.
Carrera, A. (2013) Descentralización y gobiernos locales: 30 años de la experiencia en Latinoamérica. *Carta Económica Regional* 25: 112–133.
Eaton, K. (2004) *Politics Beyond the Capital: The Design of Subnational Institutions in South America*. Stanford, CA: Stanford University Press.
Fauget, J. P. (2006) Decentralizing Bolivia: Local Government in the Jungle. In P. Bardhan and D. Mookherjee (eds), *Decentralization and Local Governance in Developing Countries. A Comparative Perspective*, 125–151. Cambridge, MA: MIT Press.
Finot, I. (2007) Los procesos de descentralización en América Latina. *Investigaciones Regionales* (Madrid) 10: 173–205.
Goldfrank, B. (2007) The Politics of Deepening Local Democracy: Decentralization, Party Institutionalization and Participation. *Comparative Politics* 39(2): 147–167.
IMF (2016) *Government Finance Statistics Yearbook*. Washington DC: International Monetary Fund.
Lynch, J. (1958) *Spanish Colonial Administration, 1782–1810*. London: University of London, Athlone Press.
Martínez-Vázquez, J. (2010) Latin America. In UCLG (ed.), *Local Government Finance: The Challenges of the 21st Century. Second Global Report on Decentralization and Local Democracy*. Barcelona: United Cities and Local Governments.
Melgar, T. (2014) A Time of Closure? Participatory Budgeting in Porto Alegre, Brazil after the Workers' Party Era. *Journal of Latin American Studies* 46: 121–149.
Montero, A. and. Samuels, D. (eds) (2003) *Decentralization and Democracy in Latin America*. Notre Dame, IN: University of Notre Dame Press.

Nickson, A. (1995) *Local Government in Latin America*. Boulder, CO: Lynne Rienner.

Nickson, A. (2009) The Local Governance Reforms in Latin America. In J. Kersting et al. (eds), *Local Governance Reforms in Global Perspective*, 76–126. Wiesbaden: VS Verlag für Sozialwissenschaften.

Nickson, A. (2014) Where is Local Government Going in Latin America? In J. Ojendal and A. Dellnas (eds), *The Imperative of Good Local Government: Challenges for the Next Decade of Decentralization*. Tokyo: United Nations University.

Norton, A. (1994) *International Handbook of Local and Regional Government: A Comparative Analysis of Advanced Democracies*. Aldershot: Edward Elgar.

O'Neill, K. (2005) *Decentralizing the State: Elections, Parties and Local Power in the Andes*. Cambridge: Cambridge University Press.

Rezende, F. and Veloso, J. (2012) Intergovernmental Transfers in Subnational Finances. In G. Brosio and J. Jiménez (eds), *Decentralisation and Reform in Latin America: Improving Intergovernmental Relations*. Cheltenham: Edward Elgar.

Rhodes-Purdy, M. (2017) Participatory Governance in Latin America: Promises and Limitations. *Latin American Politics and Society* 59(3): 122–131.

Rosales, M. (2012) *Descentralización del Estado y finanzas municipales en América Latina*. México, D.F: Instituto Nacional para el Federalismo y el Desarrollo Municipal.

Sepulveda, J. and Martínez-Vázquez, J. (2011) *Explaining Property Tax Collections in Developing Countries: The Case of Latin America*. Atlanta, GA: Andrew Young School of Policy Studies, Georgia State University.

Suárez, M. (2014) El asociativismo municipal en América Latina – análisis comparado. Universidad de Quilmes, Argentina. Retrieved from www.academia.edu/19636650/ASOCIATIVISMO_MUNICIPAL_EN_AMERICA_LATINA.

Tulchin, J. (2012) Decentralization and its Discontents. *Latin American Research Review* 47(2): 191–199.

Willis, E., Garman, C. and Haggard, S. (1999) The Politics of Decentralization in Latin America. *Latin American Research Review* 34(1): 7–56.

11

A TURBULENT PAST, A TURBULENT FUTURE?

Reform and disruption in the local government of New Zealand

Michael Reid and Michael Macaulay

Introduction: a fight for legitimacy?

The 2017 general election in New Zealand was arguably the most significant for local government since 1876, which saw the abolition of provincial government and the creation of the local government structure that lasted until 1989.[1] A key issue in 2017 was the very nature of local government itself, and the future of local democracy. Although it was rarely articulated as such, the election presented a choice between a conception of local government as the 'government' of New Zealand's towns, cities and localities and a conception of local government as little more than a service provider with relatively minimal ability to act in the interest of their various publics. Neither of the major New Zealand political parties, National or Labour, went into the election with stand-alone local government policies, but over the last two decades they have each clearly signalled quite different preferences for the roles that local government should play. The full ramifications of the election result will need to be worked through, but it is clear that the future of local government and local democracy in New Zealand will be heavily influenced by the voting preferences of those who voted in October 2017.

In many respects New Zealand has been viewed as an international leader in public sector reform over the last few decades (Reid 2016a; Cheyne 2002), and a comparable situation can be seen in terms of local government. In the aftermath of the reform and reorganisation of local government that took place in 1989, the number of local bodies was reduced from 852 to 87 and the radical changes to the way in which councils worked were introduced, which mirrored central government's obsessions with what has been characterised as New Public Management (NPM) (Boston et al. 1996). Other countries were following similar paths to reform The elements underpinning much of the New Zealand approach to NPM (e.g. contractualism, a focus on scale and efficiency, etc.) also influenced the nature of local government reform in many countries, particularly given the endorsement of international agencies like the OECD and World Bank, both of which have strongly endorsed decentralisation as a critical development strategy (OECD 2017; Wollman 2004).

New Zealand local government issues have come under the spotlight a number of times recently. A local governance national dialogue was launched in 2015 by Victoria University of Wellington to look specifically at a number of aspects of central–local relations.[2] Entire special issues of journals have bene dedicated to charting the new research terrain for local government (see Reid and Macaulay 2016); whereas some researchers have been calling for radical reforms to local democracy, along the Swiss model (Krupp 2016).

Such reforms potentially make the case that turbulence is perhaps just the natural state of play for local government. We can see this at a global level. As this book goes to press for example, there are potentially huge changes ongoing with local government systems in countries as diverse as Finland, Wales and the state of Victoria in Australia. There is an extensive literature on the subject of local government reform and the factors that cause or 'drive' change in local government (Dollery and Robotti 2008) and while the nature of local government change in each country will be driven by factors specific to that country, that is, reform has a major 'path-dependent' nature, there are some underlying themes. Perhaps the most important concerns the tension between changes that are designed to promote efficiency and those designed to promote democracy, and how this tension plays out on the ground, which is the very distinction that was central to debate in the New Zealand 2017 general election.

Underpinning this tension is a more fundamental issue: how local government itself is understood. Is it a legitimate and 'organic' expression of a community of people or is it simply an instrument for meeting the objectives of higher level governments. Current discussions in New Zealand, then, do not simply revolve around the *limits* of local government power and influence, but the *legitimacy* of local government itself. This chapter will explore these tensions further and will pose the question as to the impact of reforms on the electoral enthusiasm for local government in New Zealand.

The New Zealand local government model

The origins of local government in New Zealand are frequently traced back to British colonisation in 1840, although a more accurate reading acknowledges New Zealand's indigenous history in which sovereignty belonged to multiple tribal systems of the Māori which were essentially forms of local government. The creation of conventional local government resulted from a combination of settler pressure and the influence of the British Colonial Office (Bush 1995) which sought to replicate the outcomes of the Municipal Reform Act, 1835 in the new colony. For the first 35 years or so of its existence the new colony was a federation in which provincial government held considerable authority and was responsible for establishing local governments. Unlike other local government systems which evolved more organically, the New Zealand system exists as the result of the decisions of it parliaments. This relationship was clear from early on, as the provinces were abolished in 1876 and a national system of county and municipal government established to take their place. It was a system of local government that remained relatively intact until reform and modernisation in 1989.

The current New Zealand model consists of a single tier system of local government consisting of three types of local authority; territorial, unitary and regional. There are 61 territorial authorities (average population is 49,253, excluding Auckland), known as cities or districts, which provide a broad range of local services, such as local roads, parks and libraries. There are also 11 regional councils which tend to have specific environmental and resource management responsibilities with boundaries that largely match water catchment areas. In addition there are six unitary councils (cities or districts) which combine both territorial and regional council functions and responsibilities. In some instances such arrangements have been varied because of relative remoteness and population distribution. Reflecting a growing acceptance of this approach a new unitary authority, Auckland Council which was previously a metropolitan area consisting of seven territorial councils and one regional council, was created by Parliament in 2010. Not only is Auckland Council the largest local authority in New Zealand, representing nearly one third of the country's total population, but it is also a new and bespoke approach involving a stronger mayor and a shared governance approach with local boards responsible for neighbourhood services. It also placed responsibility for major infrastructure activities and metropolitan services, such as water, transport and economic development, with corporate type bodies (council-controlled organisations) – a move that was to provide a template for later reforms.

Unlike many other local government systems, where the relationship between local and regional government is hierarchical, the relationship in the New Zealand model was designed to be complementary rather than hierarchical. Emphasising this complementarity regional councils were initially given a narrow range of functions that were outside the responsibilities of territorial councils, except for district and city planning. This reflected the objective, important in the late 1980s, which was to create an institutional environment in which regulatory activities were separate to operational activities (to avoid the 'gamekeepers turned poacher' issue). Regional councils, for example, were given responsibility for water quality standards while those activities that use, or pollute, waterways were located with territorial authorities, which were required to seek regional council approval before agreeing ting discharges into waterways or establishing new landfills. The growth in unitary councils, particularly Auckland Council, highlights a shift away from that early policy objective (see Duncan 2016).

The New Zealand local government system also contains community boards and local boards which are types of elected sub-municipal bodies. Approximately 45 cities and districts have 109 *community* boards which have a number of mandatory responsibilities prescribed in the Local Government Act 2002 (hereafter LGA 2002). These are to:

- represent and act as an advocate for the interests of its community;
- consider and report on all matters referred to it by the territorial authority, or any matter of interest or concern to the community boards;
- maintain and overview of services provided by the territorial authority within the community;
- prepare an annual submission to the territorial authority for expenditure within the community;
- communicate with community organisations and special interest groups with the community; and
- undertake any other responsibilities that are delegated to it by the territorial authority (LGA 2002: §52).

While the primary roles of community boards are representation and advocacy many councils have delegated additional responsibilities to their boards, through a process of internal devolution.

At the time of writing, *local* boards are only found in Auckland which has a co-governing arrangement between a governing body and 21 local boards. Local boards are similar to community boards but have a much larger operational role, which involves budgetary control of neighbourhood services within their jurisdictions such as local parks, libraries and recreation services. Local boards are also required by statute to prepare three year plans and develop funding agreements with their governing body of the Auckland Council. The members of Auckland's local boards are elected and have a range of responsibilities in relation to local services, such as local parks, facilities, libraries and community activities. Each board is required to prepare a three year strategic plan and negotiates an annual funding agreement with the governing body.

New Zealand has a council manager model of local administration with governing bodies restricted to the direct employment of a single staff member, the chief executive, who is

Table 11.1 New Zealand local government functions and responsibilities

Territorial council functions		Regional council functions
Rural fire protection	Town planning and	Public transport
Emergency management	Environmental management	Port ownership
Crime prevention	Museums	Marine regulations
After-school care*	Libraries	Bio-diversity
Crèches	Economic development	Bulk water supply*
Voluntary sector grants	Tourism promotion	Pest management
Public health protection	Airport ownership	Regional environmental
Community Housing	Events	planning and policy
Community centres	Sports facilities	(air and water quality)
Refuse collection and disposal	Parks and open spaces	Environmental protection
Drainage	Public health regulation	
Cemeteries	Local roads	
Cultural facilities	Local regulations, including:	
Drinking water		
Waste water	• Dog control	
Storm water	• Building control	
Citizens' advisory services	• Noise control	
Citizenship ceremonies	• Food premises	
Town planning	• Psychoactive substances	
	• Gaming machines	
	• Sale and supply of alcohol	
	• Location of brothels	
	• Freedom camping	

*Only provided by two regional councils; Wellington Regional Council and the former Auckland Regional Council (now Auckland Council).

responsible for the employment of all staff on their behalf. Chief executives are employed on contracts and the positions must be re-advertised every five years, although a process is available to extend the original contract for additional two years. Mayors have no executive authority, other than being the presiding member and may have a casting vote at council meetings. The exception, as noted above, is the Mayor of Auckland Council who has a broader range of powers, including a mayoral office with a guaranteed number of staff. In 2012 the Government amended the LGA 2002 to make it clear that a mayor's role is to lead the members of a council, the community and the development of plans, policies and budgets as a way of strengthening the role of mayors outside Auckland Council.

New Zealand local government has a relatively narrow range of functions and responsibilities. Most social policy responsibilities (e.g. health, welfare and education) sit with central government, although key areas such as housing remain with local governments. The functions of New Zealand local government are outlined in Table 11.1.

Councils are also major providers of local and regional regulations, such as the regulation of dogs, responsibility for bio-security, the location of gaming machines, licensing food premises, building control and the location of premises selling alcohol. Regulatory regimes vary from those that provide councils with minimal discretion to fully decentralised regulatory responsibilities which have extensive discretion.

The financial and constitutional model of New Zealand local government

Reflecting its narrow task profile local government expenditure constitutes less than 4% of gross domestic product and 9.8% of all public expenditure, a figure well down on the share of public expenditure in 1930 which as approximately 50% (Cookson 2007). Consequently central government expenditure is approximately 90% of all public expenditure compared with 72.3% in the United Kingdom, 63% in Australia and 14% in Switzerland (OECD 2011). Despite its small share of public expenditure recent governments have begun to look closely at local government's functions and responsibilities with a view to driving efficiency, including a greater interest in national steering and direction setting, a tendency not unique to New Zealand (see Vakkala and Leinonen 2016). Although local government expenditure reflects a low level of fiscal decentralisation it is also one of the most fiscally autonomous systems in the world with high levels of political and administrative decentralisation (Reid 2015). New Zealand local government raises approximately 90% of its own income and has full capacity to spend that income according to local preferences although constrained by councils' reliance on a single tax base, which is on land and/or improvements. Rates are the largest source of local government revenues (see Table 11.2).

Property rates are the sector's exclusive tax base with councils required by law to operate a balanced budget on an accrual basis. Draft budgets and work programmes must be prepared before the start of each financial year and councils must provide a least a month for citizens and businesses to provide comment and feedback on the draft. Rates are normally set to fill the gap once income from user charges, regulatory fees, interest, dividend income, and government subsidies has been estimated. Depending upon external sources the proportion of income from property rates can be as high as 75% or as low as 35% of a council's total revenue. Property rates are distributed across residential and business properties on the basis of the land or capital value of each property. Councils can also apply uniform general charges and targeted rates, based on a feature of a property. Valuation is undertaken by independent valuers at least once every three years.

An important aspect of the New Zealand framework is the requirement on councils to prepare a Long Term Plan (LTP) incorporating a ten-year financial forecast and a 30 year infrastructure strategy. LTPs must be reviewed every three years and include a councils financial strategy, which provides, among other information, the forecast levels of rates and debt for the next ten years. The LTP, the original version of which was introduced in 1996, reflects the New Zealand preference for a social accountability approach (community steering), although, as the paper will show, the use of top-down accountability measures is increasing.

Table 11.2 Local government income 2015–2016

Source	NZ$ thousands	Percentage
Rates (property taxes)	5,317,234	60
Regulatory income and petrol tax	580,839	6.5
Grants and subsidies income	1,029,893	11.6
Total investment income	540,882	6.1
Sales and other operating income	1,396,582	15.8
Total operating revenue	**8,865,430**	100

Source: www.localcouncils.govt.nz

Table 11.3 Recurrent expenditure by local government for the year ending 30 June 2016

Economic classification		Functional classification	
Employee costs	22%	Governance	9%
Interest	7.5%	Culture, recreation and sport	14%
Depreciation	21%	Regulation and planning	9.1%
Grants and subsidies	11.5%	Solid waste management	4%
Goods and Services	38%	Water & wastewater	12%
		Environmental protection	4%
		Roads and transportation	28%
		Emergency management	0.6%
		Other*	15.9%
Total	100.0%	**Total**	100.0%

Source: www.localcouncils.govt.nz

*Includes economic development, community development, property and support services.

One feature that distinguishes the New Zealand system from many other local government systems is the relatively small proportion of transfers (grants and subsidies) allocated by central government. Grants and subsidies are primarily used for the construction, renewal and maintenance of local roads, which make up 13% of council income. Local government owns nearly 90% of all roads and transport is funded by a hypothecated tax consisting of road user charges and fuel taxes. Councils receive approximately 45% of the fund which is allocated on a matched funding basis with contributions weighted to acknowledge socio-economic status of the each community. Another relatively unusual feature of the New Zealand system is the absence of any formal equalisation funding. The expenditure pattern of councils highlights the minor role they play in social services. In contrast, roads, transport, water and waste water make up nearly 44% of total expenditure, indicating that their major focus is infrastructure (see Table 11.3).

A key feature of the shift towards corporatisation, privatisation and outsourcing has been the reduced share of expenditure allocated to employee costs – a share that has fallen from nearly 25% in 1998 to 21% in 2012. Since the early 1990s there has also been an increase in expenditure on depreciation which has grown from under 8% in 1995 to 21% in 2016. This is related to the requirement for councils to balance budgets on an accrual basis which treats depreciation (or the loss in asset value) as an actual cost. There has also been an increase in the level of local government debt although the average cost of debt-servicing continues to be modest at 6% and well below the thresholds set by the government through its financial prudence benchmarks. In 2016 the sector's liabilities sat at $18 billion set against total equity of $113 billion (www.localcouncils.govt.nz).

Local-central relations are frequently approached through a constitutional lens: local government systems that have constitutional status are seen to be qualitatively different from those that are not. Arguably this creates a false dichotomy, however, as constitutions themselves are social constructs and in most cases, although the existence of a local government system may be guaranteed constitutionally, the systems' powers and responsibilities will be left to legislation and regulation by state or provincial governments. Yet the constitutional position of New Zealand's levels of government is, we suggest, crucially important.

Like very few other countries New Zealand does not have a codified constitution, nor a constitutional court. Consequently, local government has no effective constitutional status: its status, powers and even its existence are entirely dependent upon the wishes of the executive and parliament. And in the absence of an upper house the executive has considerable authority

(Drage 2016). Consequently the central–local relationship is markedly asymmetrical which goes some way to explaining New Zealand's high level of fiscal centralisation and the frequency with which the rules under which councils operate tend to be changed. In place of a consolidated constitution New Zealand's constitutional status is found in a number of statutes, such as the New Zealand Constitution Act 1986. Some commentators arguing that the core local government statutes should be seen as part of this constitutional framework (Reid 2011). The three core local government statutes are:

- the LGA 2002, which sets out the purpose, powers and accountability requirements of councils;
- the Local Government (Rating Act) Act 2002 which allows councils to levy a property tax; and
- the Local Electoral Act 2001, which sets out local government's electoral rules.

There are in addition numerous statutes that provide councils with specific powers and duties or define accountability requirements, such as the Local Government Official Information Act 1986 which guarantees public access to information. At least 30 statutes provide councils with specific regulatory powers, including the power to regulate land use.

A whirlwind of reform

The one-sided relationship, politically, financially and constitutionally, has also resulted in the substantial turbulence to which the title of this chapter refers. Changes in government have often resulted in wholesale reform of local government, even within the last thirty years. The 'modern' period of local government reform began with the Local Government Act Amendment Act (no. 2) 1989, with 828 local bodies replaced with 86 multi-purpose local authorities. It was this legislation that also introduced some NPM measures designed to modernise the way in which local governments worked, including the introduction of private sector management techniques, such as contracting and performance management; the creation of local authority trading enterprises which were exposed to market competition; a clear separation of governance and management, with chief executive contracts for limited periods; and the introduction of accrual accounting. The massive restructuring of local government bodies led to warnings 'not to equate size of authority with efficiency' (Ellwood 1995: 311) and there were frequent concerns that while efficiency was one of the reform objectives, that it should not be achieved at the expense of democracy. It was a view shared by many:

> The social, economic and environmental problems confronting New Zealand are not capable of being solved by central government alone. . . . The legislation needs to give local government sufficient scope for it to be able to work in partnership with central government, and with community and business . . .
> *(Department of Internal Affairs 2000: 3)*

This continuing debate between democracy and efficiency meant that with the election of a Labour-led government, that a new local government regime was enshrined in law.

Addressing the concerns about the loss of local democracy, the LGA 2002 essentially 'repurposed' local government as an active player in the governance and leadership of communities. Local authorities were granted the power of general competence (which replaced the principle of *ultra vires*) and gave local government the new purpose as enabling democratic local decision-making and action by, and on behalf of, communities; and the promotion of the social, economic, environmental and cultural well-being of communities, in the present and for the future (see LGA 2002: §10).

In addition, LGA 2002 instituted evolution from the requirement to develop Long Term Financial Strategies (LTFS) into a requirement to develop Long Term Council Community Plans (LTCCPs), a form of community strategic planning. There was also a requirement to establish a community based process for defining community outcomes and an obligation to report to citizens on those pre-identified outcomes. Finally there was a move towards increasingly acknowledging the views of diverse communities and to provide opportunities for the Māori to participate in decision-making processes.

This approach did not endure. The notion of local government as a community enabler and proactive facilitator came to an end shortly after the election of a national-led government in 2008. Once again for the drive was to subordinate local to central government, which instituted a series of major legislative changes that removed the LGA 2002 provisions for engaged community governance and simultaneously diminished the autonomy of local governments through the diminution of the policy space in which councils were permitted to operate. The most important policy drivers came to be those of accountability, technical (rather than allocative) efficiency and scale.

The national government reforms embodied an explicitly expedient approach. The reasons given for dismantling the LGA 2002's community governance orientation were ultimately driven by an apparent need to improve local government accountability and improve efficiency, on the view that the LGA 2002 had encouraged councils to expand into services that Ministers considered were inappropriate for local government. Ministers believed that local government accountability was too weak, despite accountability reforms enacted since 1989, and that councils were too willing engage in 'non-core' activities due to a lack of fiscal discipline. Within a year of the election the government released a reform package entitled 'Improving Transparency, Accountability and Fiscal Management', which, among other measures, argued the need for core services to be defined. Consequently the 2010 amendment to the LGA 2002 included a list of so called core services including network infrastructure; public transport services; and, libraries, museums, reserves, and other recreational facilities and community amenities (LGA 2002: §11A).

Still unsatisfied with the level of accountability the then-Minister, Nick Smith, developed a reform programme he called 'Better Local Government' (BLG), which he described as 'an eight point programme to improve the legislative framework for New Zealand's 78 councils. It will provide better clarity about councils' roles, improved efficiency and more' (Smith 2012: 2).

The BLG programme was given effect through LGA amendments in 2012 and 2014, both of which were completed by the Minister Smith's successors, and resulted in significant change to the original LGA 2002, including a new purpose for local government that removed the focus on community well-being and replaced it with requirement to provide local infrastructure and services. Yet these changes were not considered sufficient and a further LGA 2002 amendment was prepared in 2016. This bill was designed to give the Local Government Commission (LGC) the ability to compulsorily establish multiply owned council controlled organisations to operate council services, without any right of a council or its community to object. If enacted it would also greatly increase the power of the Minister of Local Government to decide which areas of New Zealand should be subject to local government reorganisation and set performance measures for council services. While the Local Government and Environment Select Committee made significant changes to many aspects of the Bill, such as making the transfer of activities to multiply owned CCOs subject to council agreement, it still signalled a major increase in the powers available to central government to intervene in local affairs.[3]

An unexpected change of government in October 2017 brought a Labour-led coalition to power which, while it failed to publish a local government manifesto, quickly began work on drafting legislation to reverse some of what it saw as the egregious changes introduced by its predecessor since 2009. At the time of writing work had begun on a Bill to re-instate the previous purpose of local government, to promote social, economic, cultural and environmental well-being, which was removed in 2012.

Recent amendments and their impacts are summarised in Table 11.4.

Table 11.4 Summary of recent local government reforms

LGA 2002 Amendment Act 2010	1 Changed name of the Long Term Council Community Plan to Long Term Plan (LTP).
	2 Removed any reference to coordination and participation in the purpose of the LTP.
	3 Removed the requirement to involve citizens directly in the identification of desired community outcomes.
	4 Removed the requirement to report on achievement of outcomes.
	5 Introduced a list of core services.
	6 Introduced non-financial benchmarks for infrastructure services.
LGA 2002 Amendment Act 2012	1 Replaced the obligation to promote wellbeing in s. 10, (the purpose of local government) and replaced it with a requirement to deliver good quality local infrastructure, public services and regulation;
	2 Defined the leadership roles of mayors and allowed them to access additional powers;
	3 Changed the rules governing council re-organisation to favour establishment of unitary councils;
	4 Added s.17A which requires regular reviews of the way in which councils deliver services;
	5 Introduced significant ministerial intervention powers where there is a 'problem';
	6 Also introduced fiscal benchmarks and gave the Minister of Local Government new intervention powers.
LGA 2002 Amendment Act 2014	1 Required the adoption (without consultation) of Significance and Engagement policies.
	2 Reduced the requirement to consult on annual plans and budgets to one where significant change is proposed.
	3 Introduced a new duty to review efficiency of the way in which services are delivered.
	4 Introduced prudent financial benchmarks.
LGA 2002 Amendment Bill* 2016	Proposes a new re-organisation framework that includes:
	1 The ability of the Local Government Commission (LGC) and councils to establish multiply owned CCOs.
	2 Greater discretion for the LGC to develop reorganisations on its own volition.
	3 Powers for the Minister of Local Government to direct the LGC.**
Local Government (Community Well-being) Bill 2018	Designed to reinstate the purpose of local government set out in 2002 and removed by the LGA Amendment Act 2012.

*Currently waiting for a decision by the Labour-led Government, elected in late 2017, as to whether the Bill will be amended or withdrawn.

**Multiply owned CCOs can be established by the LGC but the agreement of affected councils is required before they can be established.

Implications and impact

By anybody's standard, the programme of legislation outlined above embodies substantial change over time. Yet they are far from a coherent policy approach: for example, much of the LGA Amendment Bill 2016 simply replaces the local government reorganisation provisions of the 2014 Act. The government decision to change the LGA 2002 and remove the key elements that constituted the community governance approach was based on the view that the Act, with its general powers and broader purpose, had caused councils to expand into new areas of policy and operations consequential significant increases in local taxation, necessary to pay for them. The arguments were a combination of anecdote and highly aggregated data and the use of both, in all cases, was problematic.

One notable example was the misleading argument that:

> Rates have increased by 6.8% per annum since 2002; more than double the rate of inflation. If rates had been kept to the rate of inflation the economy would have spent $1 billion per year less ($500 per year for each average household)
>
> *(Smith 2012)*

While households might have been better off if rates were capped to the rate of inflation, a substantial amount of infrastructure investment ($1 billion per annum according to the Minister of Local Government) would not have occurred which would have had a disastrous impact on social and economic investment (Dollery 2017). The justifications given to show that council expenditure was out of control and measures were required to constrain the scope of local government activity were crude at best, often relying on simple comparisons between increases in rates and household inflation. Yet the 2007 Local Government Rates Inquiry which considered among other matters the fiscal impact of the LGA 2002 concluded: 'the panel does not consider that this empowerment [the LGA 2002] has been a significant driver of increased

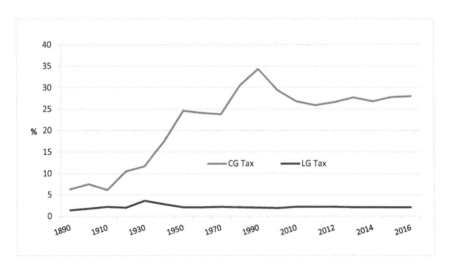

Figure 11.1 Rates as a share of GDP

Source: www.treasury.govt.nz/government/financialstatements/yearend/jun16snapshot/fsgnz-snap-jun16.pdf and Local Government Financial Statistics New Zealand

expenditures ... there is little that local government is now doing that it has not previously been doing' (Local Government Rates Inquiry 2007: 78).

In fact, a commonly used measure of fiscal prudence that Ministers could have taken note of, and one that paints a very different picture, is the relationship of rates to gross domestic product (GDP). In local government's case there has been very little change over the last century (see Figure 11.1).

Despite the lack of a sound evidence base and incoherent nature of the successive reforms, a number of implications can be discerned. Many of the changes have had the effect of reducing the discretion of elected members, such as the amended §10 of LGA 2002, which removed the references to promoting community well-being in the purpose of local government. The autonomy of local councils has been further eroded by giving increased powers of intervention to both the Minister of Local Government and other Ministers, such as the Minister for the Environment following changes to the Resource Management Act 1991. And democratic decision-making has been clearly diminished by shifting activities into corporate style arms-length delivery arrangements away from the direct democratic oversight of citizens. In attempting to strengthen accountability, the reforms have overlooked the key point that accountability in local democracy must be for local citizens.

The shift of accountability and local democratic principles have been keenly felt in local elections, and the latest data suggests another set of implications that must be taken seriously in the continued battle for the soul of New Zealand local government.

Local elections are held by universal suffrage every three years according to provisions set in statute which allow some variation in forms of election. So, for example, elections can be by ward or at large, with plurality voting or Single Transferable Vote; the number of councillors can be varied; and online voting is currently being explored Territorial authorities have directly elected mayors while regional councils are led by chairs elected from and by councillors. The maximum number of elected members on regional councils is 14 while territorial authorities can have as many as 30 elected members, however, the average number per council is less than 12. As a result New Zealand's representation ratios are considerably higher than in other jurisdictions, with one councillor per 5056 citizens, as opposed to France's 1:120 ratio or even Scotland's 1:4229 (Reid 2016b). Auckland Council, the largest, has a governing body of 21 members, including the Mayor with a representation ratio of approximately one member to 76,000 citizens (it also has a framework of local boards for local matters). Following the 2016 local authority elections the proportion of elected members who are women reached its highest level at 38% of all elected members. There are approximately 880 councillors and mayors and more than 500 sub-municipal elected members (community and local board members) (Reid 2016b).

Recent research sheds light on some of the potential electoral impacts of reform in the 2016 New Zealand local elections. Two surveys were undertaken using a common methodology and a similar set of questions: the first was a survey of Auckland residents involving a sample size of 1,259; the second was a survey of the rest of the New Zealand with a sample size of 1,054. The surveys were conducted in October and November 2016, respectively.

The turnout for the 2016 local elections throughout New Zealand, including Auckland, was 43 per cent, which reflects a downward trend over the last thirty years (in the late 1980s local election turnout was approximately 60%). This cannot be attributed to local awareness: 93% respondents stated that they knew the elections were taking place; over 80% had received information through advertising; and 58% recognised the 'Vote 2016' logo, which had been designed specifically to raise awareness (Macaulay and Weinhold 2016).

Respondents clearly evinced principles of democracy for both their reasons *for* voting and for *not* voting. In an open-ended questions respondents commonly identified 'to have my say', 'civic duty' and 'for a better future' as common reasons for voting (Macaulay and Weinhold 2016). Perhaps even more interestingly, ennui and lack of interest were not important factors for respondents. Only 10% stated that they had not voted because they were not interested in politics; whereas a mere 2.6% of non-voters did not do so because they felt their vote would not have made a difference (Macaulay and Weinhold 2016).

Conclusion: looking out from the eye of the storm

This chapter has argued that the current turbulence facing New Zealand's local government sector is not new: far from it, the last three decades alone have seen almost continual reform. Yet it does feel that the sector is facing a genuine crossroads in perceptions as to its place in the political realm: is it simply to be seen as a delivery arm for services or does it have a genuine democratic future? There are a number of reasons for this.

First and perhaps most obviously, current debate can be seen as the logical end to the longer period of reforms, starting with NPM and the 1989 legislation. Ever-growing privatisation and managerialism has shunted democratic accountability to one side, bringing in other forms that do not necessarily reflect the public view. The latest research on the 2016 elections clearly demonstrates that as far as local citizens are concerned, local government maintains its emotional and civic hold on people. In fact it goes further; respondents argued that local government is part of democratic and civic culture in New Zealand.

A second reason must be the lack of constitutional status afforded local government in New Zealand, which has allowed such sweeping and contradictory reforms to be imposed. These in themselves have a very negative trade-off for local democracy. The more time local government needs to spend in responding to such changes, the less time it capacity and capability it has to enact its democratic mandate. The process of continual reform effectively undermines local government's ability to perform, which creates a vicious circle whereby it faces increased accusations of poor performance. A further issue is that local government in New Zealand is not the instigator of its own discord: in fact it has never stepped beyond its duties or its boundaries. Even in the Local Government Act 1974, which predates the 'modern' era of reform its freedoms were clearly legislated:

> The Council may . . . undertake, promote, and encourage the development of such services and facilities as it considers necessary in order to maintain and promote the general well-being of the public and may promote or assist in promoting co-operation in and co-ordination of welfare activities in the district.
>
> *(Local Government Act 1974: §598(1))*

Each subsequent wave of reform played on this theme: the autonomy and political independence of local governments to serve their communities. Yet each wave of proposed change also challenged the extent to which these powers and roles needed to be calibrated. The current challenge is over the principle of local democracy itself. The extent to which local government in New Zealand would have thrived if it had not been subjected to the enforcement of decades of central government direction is, of course, a moot point. But the stakes are now for the future of the New Zealand local government system itself – indeed, for the degree to which it would be able to be described as local *government* in the future. What is crucial is that political leaders at all levels acknowledge democratic desires rather than ideological orientations. There remains strong support from New Zealand citizens for local democracy, one that is linked with notions of civic duty and citizenship rather than just receipt and consumption of services. As a result of the change of government in October 2017 there is every indication that citizen engagement will once again come to the fore with an expectation that local government should play a more active role in creating more positive well-being outcomes.

Notes

1 After a number of unsuccessful attempts to establish local government, beginning with the Municipal Corporations Act 1842 passed by the then Legislative Council, a system of provincial government was established in 1852, with provinces empowered to establish local councils although with no national consistency. Parliament abolished the provincial governments in 1876 and replaced them with a national local government system consisting of municipalities for urban areas and counties for rural areas, a system that remained until 1989.
2 See http://igps.victoria.ac.nz/2014%20+/Local%20Governance%20National%20Dialogue.html.
3 While the bill remains on parliament's order paper it is not expected to proceed in its current form.

References

Boston, J., Martin, J., Pallot, J. and Walsh, P. (1996) *Public Management: The New Zealand Model*. Oxford: Oxford University Press.
Bush, G. (1995) *Local Government and Politics in New Zealand*, second edition. Auckland: Auckland University Press.
Cheyne, C. (2002) Public Involvement in Local Government in New Zealand: A Historical Account. In J. Drage (ed.), *Empowering Communities: Representation and Participation in New Zealand's Local Government*, 116–155. Wellington: Victoria University Press.
Cookson, J. (2007) How British? Local Government in New Zealand to c1930. *New Zealand Journal of History* 41(2): 143–160.
Department of Internal Affairs (2000) *Statement of Policy Direction for the Review of the Local Government Act 1974*. Wellington: Department of Internal Affairs.
Dollery, B. (2017) *An Empirical Assessment of the Impact of Rate-Pegging on South Australian Local Government*. Retrieved in September 2017 from www.lga.sa.gov.au/contentFile.aspx?filename=Impact%20of%20rate%20Pegging%20on%20South%20Australian%20local%20government,%20Professor%20Dollery.pdf.
Dollery, B. and Robotti, L. (2008) *The Theory and Practice of Local Government Reform*. Cheltenham: Edward Elgar.
Drage, J. (2016) Do We Underestimate the Political Strength of New Zealand's Local Government? *Policy Quarterly* 12(4): 17–19.
Duncan, G. (2016) Auckland Council: Is It Too Big to Last? *Policy Quarterly* 12(4): 54–59.
Ellwood, B. (1995) From Theory to Practice: The New Zealand Experience. In P. McDermott, V. Forgie and R. Howell (eds), An Agenda for Local Government: Proceedings from the New Local Government Conference 1995, 158–171. Palmerston North: Massey University.
Krupp, J. (2016) The Local Benchmark. Retrieved from https://nzinitiative.org.nz/insights/reports/the-local-benchmark.
Local Government Rates Inquiry (2007) Funding Local Government. Retrieved in September 2017 from www.dia.govt.nz/Decommissioned-websites---Rates-Inquiry.
Macaulay, M. and Weinhold, M. (2016) *New Zealand Local Elections 2016 Survey: Quantitative Data Presentation*. Wellington: IGPS.
OECD (2011) *Government at a Glance*. Paris: OECD.
OECD (2017) *Multi-level Governance Reforms: Overview of OECD Country Experiences OECD*. Paris: OECD.
Reid, M. (2011) Local Government's Search for Constitutional Status, in *Along A Fault-Line: New Zealand's Changing Local Government Landscape*, (eds) Drage, J., McNeill, J., and Cheyne, C., Dunmore Publishing 2011
Reid, M. (2015) Decentralisation: Does the New Zealand Local Government System Measure Up? *Policy Quarterly* 11(2): 45–53.

Reid, M. (2016a) Contemporary Local Government Reform in New Zealand: Efficiency or Democracy. In U. Sadioglu and K. Dede (eds), *Theoretical Foundations and Discussions on the Reformation Process in Local Governments*, 205–236. Hershey, PA: IGI Global.

Reid, M. (2016b) Local Authority Turnout: What's the Story? *Policy Quarterly* 12(4): 3–9.

Reid, M. and Macaulay, M. (eds) (2016) Special Issue: Local Government. *Policy Quarterly* 12(4). Retrieved from https://ojs.victoria.ac.nz/pq/issue/view/542.

Smith, N. (2012) *Better Local Government*. Retrieved in September 2017 from www.dia.govt.nz/better-local-government.

Vakkala, H. and Leinonen, J. (2016) Current Features and Developments of Local Governance in Finland: The Changing Roles of Citizens and Municipalities. In U. Sadioglu and K. Dede (eds), *Theoretical Foundations and Discussions on the Reformation Process in Local Governments*, 304–327. Hershey, PA: IGI Global.

Wollman, H. (2004) Local Government Reforms in Great Britain, Sweden, Germany and France: Between Multi-Function and Single-Purpose Organisations. *Local Government Studies* 30(4): 639–665.

12

CONSTITUTIONAL AND LEGISLATIVE CHANGES IN CARIBBEAN LOCAL GOVERNMENT

Eris Schoburgh

Introduction

The Caribbean is a combination of small island states and continental land forms that have an unusual socio-political history of domination and colonialism, which in large measure have contributed to the ascribed status of developing countries. Though the economies of these countries vary in size, they generally are categorised as 'small', making their integration into the global economy quite tenuous. Importantly, the nomenclature 'Caribbean' masks critical geo-political divisions. For instance, the Anglophone Caribbean or Commonwealth Caribbean[1] are English-speaking countries once ruled predominantly by Britain; the Francophone areas are French-speaking, the majority of which have remained *departments* of France[2] with the exception of Haiti. The Hispanophone Caribbean islands are Spanish-speaking[3] and as the description implies were colonies of Spain. Finally, the group of islands that are now autonomous countries, but which were once known as the Netherland Antilles,[4] still maintain political and economic links with Holland. The history of the region has also been shaped by Portugal and the United States. The Anglophone Caribbean remains the largest grouping in the region with the majority being independent nations that have established intergovernmental arrangements to facilitate economic harmonisation and integration. The Caribbean Community (CARICOM) and the Caribbean Single Market and Economy (CSME), established under the Treaty of Chaguaramas 1973, and the Organisation of the Eastern Caribbean States (OECS) formed in 1981 are examples.

The Commonwealth Caribbean countries are relatively stable democracies due to a degree of political and administrative decentralisation that facilitated the political socialisation of local political elites in Westminster philosophy and values (Dominguez, Pastor and Worrell 1993; Ryan 1999; Sutton 1999; Anckar 2000). Political decentralisation denotes a form of power-sharing between levels of government in which local elected representatives are given a degree of power to facilitate democratic and accountable decision-making, and a closer fit between citizens' preferences and service delivery. Political decentralisation is usually associated with some form of constitutional or statutory change to create the framework for devolution of power and authority. Administrative decentralisation is the transfer of authority and responsibility from central government to field agencies as well as other levels of government and may take the form of deconcentration – transfer of functional responsibility minus authority; delegation – transfer of responsibility with proscribed authority; and devolution – transfer of significant power and authority. Fiscal decentralisation, the assignment of tax-raising and discretionary spending powers, is usually categorised as the third type, and is a key consideration in devolution of powers to local government. Privatisation which describes a change in the structure of ownership of an economic unit, has emerged as a criterion of good governance in the contemporary period of decentralising reforms and is frequently associated with the empowerment of local government (UNDP 1999; Shah 2004; Schoburgh 2006; Lora 2007). The practice of decentralisation irrespective of the form, is not without controversy as outcomes have differed from those theorised (see e.g. Wolman 1990; Prud'homme 1995; Ter-Minassian 1997; Shah 2004). This chapter explores these various strands of change in the Commonwealth Caribbean, focusing in particular on three countries: Jamaica, Trinidad and Tobago, and Guyana.

During the colonial period, political and administrative decentralisation produced a prototype system of semi-autonomous local government that oversaw remote colonies. The hegemonic character and extended period of British rule did not inhibit indigenous political organising and competitive elections. Political administrative turn-over occurred during the colonial period in these countries and although unusual, might have contributed to their resilience as democracies later on. The fidelity of the Anglophone Caribbean political structures to Westminster institutions and practices, that is, parliamentary government, majoritarian rule, and cabinet dominance after independence is notable. It also derives from the motivation of post-independence leaders operating albeit in a 'controlled' decentralised context. Political independence has meant the replacement of the prototype local government system with intra-jurisdictional structures that vary in geographic expanse but which are appropriately subnational in nature, exemplars of which are regional, municipal and city governments.

The socio-economic character of the Anglophone Caribbean is similarly complex. Population profiles signify a racial composition of varying levels of African, East Indian, Amerindian, Asian and European origins illustrated by the largest countries in terms of population size. Table 12.1 shows that the Anglophone Caribbean is ethnically heterogeneous but with a clear dominance of persons of African descent. However, unlike the political changes through which the region has transitioned relatively smoothly, economic development has been characterised by greater degrees of variability from one period to the next and among the different countries. The region remains important in geopolitical relations evidenced by the United States (US) Congress passing the United States–Caribbean Strategic Engagement Act 2016 aimed at strengthening partnership between the US and the region. Similarly, the US$197.9 million support of the United Nations Multi-country Sustainable Development Framework in the Caribbean in June 2016 represents a recent major investment in the region. The Caribbean faces existential threats in 'new wicked problems' not the least of which is terrorism. Because Bretton Woods Institutions such as the World Bank (WB) and the International Monetary Fund (IMF) have been active participants in shaping the economic futures of a few of these countries some commentators question whether notions of sovereignty or 'independence' apply in reality to these political systems.

Decentralisation figures prominently in new paradigms of governmental reorganisation. The new socio-economic and political order in which post-modern and neoliberal ideas contend has compelled an appreciation for re-definition and re-specification of roles of actors whether as institutions or as individuals. At various points reform practice must confront new perspectives on the shift from local government to local governance and finally to developmental local governance (Schoburgh, Martin and Gatchair 2016) which brings into focus the nature of the constitutional and legislative enactments associated with local government reform in the

Table 12.1 Population profile of selected countries in Anglophone Caribbean

Country	Census year/ population	African/ Black	Amerindian	Asian/ Chinese	Creole	East Indian	Garifuna	Maya	Mennonite	Mestizo	Mixed	White/ Caucasian
Barbados	(2010) 277,821	92.4	–	–	–	1.3	–	–	–	–	3.1	2.7
Belize	(2010) 312,971	–	–	0.9	21.0	2.1	4.5	10.0	3.6	50.0	6.0	1.0
Guyana	(2012) 746,955	29.2	10.5	0.18	–	39.8	–	–	–	–	19.9	–
Jamaica	(2011) 2.7 mil.	90.9	–	0.2	–	0.2	–	–	–	–	7.3	0.2
Trinidad and Tobago	(2011) 1.3 mil.	34.2	–	–	–	35.4	–	–	–	–	22.8	–

Caribbean. The questions of how, and to what extent have these enactments facilitated local government change inform this chapter that is divided into four sections: the nature of legislative and constitutional change; the vacillation between continuity and change in constituting and legislating local government; the outcomes of legislative change in specific case studies; a concluding analysis of the findings.

The logic of legislative and constitutional change

Public policies establish norms, values and principles that influence the behaviour of actors and agents in society. By that token public policies are behavioural in nature deriving their organisational relevance from being embedded in an institutional framework in order to effect social influence or achieve the conformity desired through implementation. Policy reform of any type or duration, has one fundamental goal in common, social transformation. Social transformation occurs wherever social interactions, whether in loosely coupled social systems like groups, or in more formal collectives like organisations do one of two things – make a complete break with the past or improve on what existed previously. Policy reform is therefore institutional reform, a perspective that is elaborated by Goodin and Klingemann (1996), Goodin (1996), Marsh and Stoker (2002) and Barzelay and Gallego (2006). Critical components of institutions are rules and laws, making legislative change the nucleus of public decision-making.

Seidman, Seidman and Abeyesekere (2001: 13) confirm the importance of legislative change in policy reform:

> government officials invariably must translate seriously-intended, publicly-avowed policies into laws: to promulgate the necessary rules to channel the manifold behaviours that comprise not only societies, but the way itself government works, and to maintain the government's legitimacy.

Legislation has certain functions: laws allocate rights and duties, provide for the settlement of disputes; prescribe the values that are considered important for society; and determine perhaps figuratively what or who counts in society. In relation to policy reforms legislation compels new behaviours (Seidman, Seidman and Abeyesekere 2001: 15) and depending on the scope and depth of reforms, legislative change can be elevated to become constitutional change.

A constitution, as fundamental legislation evinces norms about the authority and legitimacy of government. Three theoretical perspectives have emerged as explanatory frames for constitutionalism. Initial conservatism, reflected a preference for strong and stable political systems at the core of which was governmental restraint. At an early period in the evolution of this perspective constitutionalism aimed at social harmony among three primary actors: monarchy, aristocracy and the church. Secular authority had a symbiotic relationship with religious authority and as a consequence the latter preceded the former in the influence on political life. Modern conservatism is more secular in nature and interpretation and application of the attendant core values vary between political systems given the emphasis on tradition and continuity that are contextually defined. Importantly the constitutional ideals of modern conservatism surround limited governmental intervention. Liberalism, the second perspective promotes ideals that are diametrically opposed to conservatism although early adherents such as Hobbes and Locke had opposing interpretations of constitutionalism. Liberalism advocates freedoms and rights and thus constitutionalism from this perspective is both a means to, and the end-state of these goals. Finally a Marxist theoretical perspective on constitutionalism is in opposition to liberal ideals. The central argument is that the constitution, rather than limiting the powers of government should instead expand them, to facilitate the emergence of a new type of state that is proletarian in character. Constitutionalism in an era of neoliberalism values various forms of autonomy. Neoliberalism may have had its greatest impact on the constitutions of transitioning democracies mostly in Eastern Europe more so than Western democracies that appeared to have adopted the ideology of the supremacy of the markets with no major constitutional change.

Constitutionalism in the Commonwealth

The constitutions of the English-speaking Caribbean favour modern conservatism even though the values of neoliberalism have occasioned enactment of some new laws. More than anything constitutionalism in the English-speaking Caribbean conforms to the western hypothesis of a constitutional state whose political system adheres to the rule of law, ensures liberty and equality for all, freedom of the press and a plurality of interests. The three arms of government – legislature, executive, judiciary – are theorised to be independent, reflecting the 'separation of powers' principle. However there are marked differences in the degree to which there is separation of powers between the Westminster Parliamentary System to which the Commonwealth Caribbean is aligned and the Presidential system, argued to be closer to the ideal than the former. Importantly the principle of peaceful and orderly change is a feature of Western constitutionalism that is reinforced through a democratic process to reduce shocks and strains on the political system. Westminster influenced constitutional traditions in the English-speaking Caribbean are conservative in that their durability suggests that constitutional reform translates into revisions rather than outright change. Of the twelve countries that display this institutional heritage, nine are parliamentary democracies with the head of government being accountable to the legislature. The exceptions are the semi-presidential regimes of Dominica, Guyana, and Trinidad and Tobago, whose constitutions provide for a directly elected head of state. The indistinctiveness between parliamentary and presidential political practices in the region has led some commentators to think of the political systems as hybrids of the two. A Report of the Conflict Prevention and Peace Forum 2011 contends that constitutions in the English-speaking Caribbean depart from 'the typical parliamentary model, if not the Westminster model' (Constitutional Design Group 2011). With respect to 'the powers *as stipulated* in the constitution', political practice in actuality 'deviates from these hard-wired provisions' (p. 8). McIntosh (2002) provides a more expansive discussion of constitutionalism in the Commonwealth Caribbean.

Traditionalism v. modernism

Support for the proposition that constitutionalism in the Commonwealth Caribbean is conservative in orientation is best illustrated in the character of intergovernmental relations. The Westminster model of government to which the Commonwealth Caribbean subscribes is a transplant model but core values have been transferred in the process of adaptation. Features such as parliamentary sovereignty, majority party control of the executive, strong cabinet government, accountability through elections and institutionalised opposition are well established. And so too is the primacy of the national (central) government in shaping political and policy processes derived from the concept of the *unitary state*, which means that power resides in a single national authority (see e.g. Lijphart 1999). The act of governing in a unitary state is monolithic in orientation where government 'speaks with one voice'. Parliamentary sovereignty is the guiding principle underpinning the Westminster model of government and in translation 'there is no other higher authority than parliament . . . and no other national body can question the legitimacy of its decisions' (McAnulla 2006: 13). This is the institutional setting for intergovernmental relations, where relationships between spheres and tiers of government are structured.

The philosophy of *government speaks with one voice* plays out in local government operations that are the subject of central government coordination. Caribbean local governments in the majority of instances do not have constitutional status. Constitutional status gives local government its own identity and authority and can be seen as one precondition for local autonomy. Arguably the constitutional status of local government adds, in theory, an important veto point in any decision by central government to controvert the system, and thus reduces central government's influence over local affairs. However, constitutional status for local government is neither compatible with the region's institutional heritage nor modern political philosophy about intergovernmental relations which as demonstrated in practice in the Caribbean is antagonistic to power-sharing.

The foregoing argument finds support in Jamaica's reform experience where intense debate ensued between reformers and elected representatives at the national level about the virtues of *ordinary v. deep* entrenchment of local government in the Jamaican Constitution. Finally, local government was entrenched in the Jamaican Constitution in 2015, twenty-two years after the commencement of local government reform, a complementary aspect of which was a programme of constitutional reform. Entrenchment in the Constitution of Jamaica is on the assumption that local government will be protected from adverse decisions on the part of central government. The website of the Ministry of Local Government and Community Development under whose portfolio local government falls in Jamaica published online what might be considered to be a rationale for the constitutional amendment. Accordingly:

> It will no longer be the singular remit of the Minister to dissolve Local Government in whole or in part. It will demonstrate the commitment of the Administration to local government as a critical ingredient of the national governance process by providing it with constitutional protection.
>
> *(MLGCD undated)*

The antecedent in this regard is Guyana, which, on a path to socialism, repealed its 1966 independence constitution and adopted in 1980 the Constitution of the Cooperative Republic of Guyana (amended in 1996). In that new constitution local government is accorded the fourth highest priority after 'sovereignty of the people; the right to form political parties and their freedom to act; and the entitlement of cooperatives, trade unions and other socio-economic organisations to participate in policy management' (Chapter 2).

The Constitution designates local government as 'an integral part of the democratic organisation of the State'. It goes further in Chapter 7 to designate local government as, 'a vital aspect of socialist democracy' that 'shall be organised . . . to involve as many people as possible in the task of managing and developing the communities in which they live' (Paragraph 71(1)).

Local government in Guyana represents the third tier in a hierarchy of government at the apex of which is central government and immediately below is an intermediary level composed of ten administrative regions. Local government in Guyana is formed of regional democratic councils (RDCs), municipal councils (MCs) and neighbourhood democratic councils (NDCs). Chapter 7.72(1) of the Constitution empowers parliament to provide for 'sub-regions and other subdivisions as it may deem for the purpose of organising local democratic organs' and consequently there are over 70 Amerindian village councils (AVCs) with similar constitutional status as the NDCs. The Constitution further provides for role and responsibilities of all local democratic organs but specified election procedures, revenue raising and utilisation authority and decision-making powers of the NDCs. The most far-reaching provision in the Constitution is the developmental orientation of local government and the direct linkage it made with national development.

Constitutional status for local government is one thing but the political willingness to translate this into devolution of power to, or on a lesser scale greater autonomy for local government, is another. In the fragile political environment of Guyana during the run-up to the 1992 parliamentary and presidential elections, the local government system was barely functional. Opposition parties accused the ruling People National Congress (PNC) of electoral fraud. Importantly the 1980 Constitution of the Cooperative Republic of Guyana enacted by the PNC concentrated significant powers in the Office of the Presidency emasculating the legislature on the one hand, and local government on the other. Municipal and local elections were held for the first time in 1994 after a twenty-four year suspension, on account of frequent protests and boycotts by opposition parties. Central government influence in local government was not lessened with the adoption of a socialist ideology; mayors and district councillors were appointed from the centre (central government); the system of district, village, country and rural government was non-functional. Local government institutions were unable to provide basic services unless dictated by the centre. Although defined in the 1980 Constitution as a critical dimension of local democracy, its treatment by central government has not substantiated this constitutional principle. Constitutional status has not improved local government's position in intergovernmental relations which in practice is structured along lines similar to other countries in the region in which a central government ministry assumes policy oversight of local government and serves as the institutional linkage between local and central governments. Central government's disregard for the constitutional status of local government in Guyana is evident in that from 1994 local elections were suspended until March 2016.

There are three other cases of constitutional mention of another typology of 'local government' in the region. These 'local governments' are considered distinct in that they are individual islands (non-contiguous) that each forms a part of separate countries. The first is, the Tobago House of Assembly (THA) created by Act 39 of 1996 to administer the island of Tobago, that forms one-half of the twin island Republic of Trinidad and Tobago. Chapter 11A of the Constitution of the Republic of Trinidad and Tobago is dedicated to outlining key features of the THA but has not attributed special powers to it; instead declaring in Chapter 11A.141B that 'the Assembly shall have such powers and functions in relation to Tobago as may be prescribed' implying that some other organ of the state, most likely Parliament has that discretion. The Constitution provides for the creation of the THA Fund to be financed from two sources – appropriations from Parliament and revenues earned by the THA (Chapter 11A.141D). Interestingly, the larger island of Trinidad has a system of local government which is not named in its Constitution.

The second is the Nevis Island Legislature and Assembly (NIL/A) described in the 1983 Constitution of the Federation of St Kitts and Nevis. Like Tobago, 'local government' merely describes the administration of the island of Nevis. The NIL/A has significant powers and authority for example to make laws and raise taxes, unlike the THA and therefore has conferred on it a degree of local autonomy. Importantly the Constitution includes a provision for secession of the island of Nevis from St. Kitts were Nevis's independence to become a goal. The third is represented by Antigua and Barbuda where the Barbuda Council enacted by the Barbuda Local Government Act 1976 is assigned responsibility for the island of Barbuda, one half of the Republic of Antigua and Barbuda. The Constitution provides for no direct powers for the

Barbuda Council leaving the assignment of powers to Parliament (Chapter 10.2). Like Trinidad, local government on the Antigua half of the island-state has no constitutional provision.

Local government in the Commonwealth Caribbean is at different stages of development with respect to its embeddedness in the institutional framework that forms the superstructure of government as outlined in the constitution. Constitutional status signifies variations in the scope of local autonomy. Even where a modicum of local autonomy is granted to local government by the constitution this autonomy is derivative of parliamentary procedures and action. The instances in which local government, irrespective of its manifestation, whether as island-form (e.g. Tobago) or the traditional-form (e.g. Jamaica), has constitutional status one could hardly consider this status to be exceptional as the *de jure* position of local government in intergovernmental relations remains substantially unchanged. Reformers appear daunted by the idea of moving beyond the status of local government as a subordinate of central government, which action validates Chandler's (1996: 89) position that 'it is impossible to seriously consider local government as an entity autonomous from the centre'. The cautious approach to constitutional change is a factor. The Report of the Conflict Prevention and Peace Forum 2016 found that across the world constitutions last for nineteen years on an average before they are replaced with modern versions. Constitutions in the Commonwealth have longer life-span and since 1962 only four countries – Barbados, Guyana, Jamaica and Trinidad and Tobago – account for approximately seventy percent of all constitutional events. Constitutional longevity is touted as an indicator of democratic stability. That might be so but it does not augur well for the type of decentralisation that is required for local government to improve its prospects and assume its position as a significant actor in multi-level governance and ultimately as an enabler of local (economic) development (Schoburgh et al. 2016).

Reformers' efforts to constitute local government as an unequivocal dimension of governing in the Commonwealth Caribbean have been at best exploratory. The conservative character of the institutional superstructure that shapes intergovernmental relations is a more significant determinant in this regard than a lack of political will to devolve power and authority to local government. Central government's fear of power-sharing is a definitive variable in whether to entrench local government in the constitution, but might not be as influential as the compulsion felt by Caribbean constitutionalists to retain Westminster traditions that have contributed to relative political stability. The fact that the Commonwealth Caribbean has experienced long periods of economic volatility but which have not triggered fundamental constitutional change is evidence of the *resilience* of the institutional framework or the *adaptive* nature of it. The contradiction in all of this is that, in comparison to the constitutional reform agenda, the legislative agenda in general, and specific to local government operations demonstrates a higher level of activism in the region, and might offer other explanations for reformers' acquiescence to the status quo.

New paradigms – old practice

After nearly two decades of implementation, local government reform in the Commonwealth Caribbean has entered a new era; one marked by new laws. The belief is that modernising laws and regulations will enable the multi-level governance framework desired. The abiding concern has been the value of local government to the political system and the role it should play in the political economy. Two countries, Jamaica and The Republic of Trinidad and Tobago, are furthest along this path of the modernisation and will be examined in the ensuing sections. Two questions that will guide the evaluation of legislative developments are: What are the underlying intentions of the new laws? What have been the outcomes?

Jamaica's three strategic laws

The 2003 Report of the National Advisory Council (NAC) on local government reform saw a modern legal framework as an essential pre-requisite for successful implementation. New legislation is more likely, arguably, to incorporate and give expression to the concepts and principles of the paradigm of participatory local governance articulated in Ministry Paper 8/1993 and 7/2003 (p. 12). Local autonomy and local self-management; citizen participation; fiscal decentralisation; accountability, transparency and high ethical standards in the conduct of public affairs; and local sustainable development are values emphasised in the discourse on a modern local government.

There is an acknowledgment that adjustments to existing power relations are required to create 'partnerships for change', a crucial step in which is rationalisation and modernisation of local government legislation for greater responsiveness to the new context. The legislative infrastructure is composed historically of approximately eighty principal laws and several hundred subsidiary legislation that are archaic. Legislation considered to be strategic to the attainment of reform goals were reviewed leading to the promulgation in 2016 of three 'strategic laws': The Local Governance Act; The Local Government Financing and Financial Management Act; The Local Government (Unified Services and Employment Act). It must be noted that these laws were preceded by an amendment to the Parochial Rates and Finance Act to establish the Parochial Revenue Fund (PRF) in 1996.

The Local Governance Act 2016

The Local Governance Act 2016 is be the most expansive institutional infrastructure governing local government operations to date and results from a consolidation of The Parish Councils Act (1887), The Kingston and St. Andrew Corporation Act (1923), The Parochial Elections (Modifications) Act (1979) and The Municipalities Act (2003). The Local Governance Act 2016 is claimed to be a means to a political ethos in which local government's value to the political economy, its role and responsibilities and the relationships in support of these are delineated. That political ethos according to the preamble to the Act are 'local authorities having greater scope and autonomy in the management of local affairs, an expanded and a more holistic mandate for good governance, sustainable development and good civic order' (p. 1).

Perhaps the most critical distinction between the 2016 Act and the legislation from which it is derived is that it signifies a new paradigm of governing at the local level, illustrated by the replacement of local government with local governance in the title. Local governance in both concept and practice emphasises relationships in the process of governing against the backdrop of a redefinition of the role of the state and government and a change in the behaviour of citizens. Deployment of the concept of local governance is the first stage in ensuring realisation of the vision of a multi-level governance framework in which local government is one actor among a complex array of actors participating in co-regulation and co-production of local services and local sustainable development. The 2016 Act is explicit in this regard:

> A local authority . . . is responsible for encouraging and facilitating effective coordination and collaboration between bodies or entities that are within the public, private, and non-governmental sectors and that exist or operate within the area of its jurisdiction to ensure greater or better synergy, service delivery and responsiveness to the needs, concerns and priorities of inhabitants within the area of its jurisdiction.
>
> *(Local Governance Act 2016: Section 21[g])*

Notably the political role signified in the past by a preoccupation with electoral procedures and structure of local authorities, now calls attention to a participatory ethos. Section 22.1 states:

> Each local authority shall promote, establish and utilize appropriate mechanisms to facilitate participation of, and collaboration or networking with, all relevant stakeholders who exist or operate within the area of its jurisdiction.

The developmental role of local government forms part of its expanded mandate and thus 'development' irrespective of the kind, (e.g. community, local economic or sustainable) is deemed a functional responsibility of all local authorities as seen in Section 21.1:

> [b] ... promoting, spearheading and coordinating local sustainable development
>
> [e] ... spearheading, fostering and promoting economic and social development, cultural advancement, alleviation of poverty and environmental protection ...

Other sections of the 2016 Act stipulates the strategies that local authorities are to implement to give effect to the developmental role of local government, among which are: local sustainable development plans (LSDPs); urban renewal, rural and community development; poverty alleviation programmes. The most far-reaching stipulation debatably, is the link made between local and national development as local authorities are to contribute to, and coordinate national development plans. One inference from the developmental role of local government is its responsibility for the economic governance of local jurisdictions. Citizen participation is conjoined with a socio-economic role, establishing two important criteria for good local governance. Local actors with which the local authority must now interact for effective economic governance and which hitherto were not adequately integrated into the institutional framework of local governance are development committees (parish development committees, development area committees and community development committees), business improvement districts, and special improvement districts.[5] Local economic governance will thus be an essential dimension of the functional scope of local governance in Jamaica.

The new Act is *demand-driven* as the evolving needs of each geographic space will be met via a rational framework that provides for different types of local authorities categorised as municipal corporations (first-tier structures that have replaced parish councils), city municipalities (second-tier structures) and town municipalities (third-tier structures). A layered system of local governance exhibiting degrees of fragmentation with jurisdictions of varying sizes in response to rapid urbanisation is one outcome of the Act. The criteria for establishing second- and third-tier structures, are outlined in Section 5 of the Act, three of which are: the area must be an urban centre or group of urban centres; population size cannot be less than 50,000; and, there should be income generating or revenue potential.

What's in a name?

Many commentators question the rationale for the change from parish council to municipal corporation. Apart from the distinctive elements discussed previously one could argue that the change is symbolic; it is a marketing strategy to generate citizens' interest in the operations of local authorities who will then demand that the provisions of the new law are enforced. With increased pressure from citizens the process of transformation can begin within the local authority thereby fulfilling reform goals. The change in name serves to silence the critics; it is a therapeutic means to an instrumental end. The other side to this argument is that there *is* substantive difference between a council and a corporation. A council is a political and an administrative organisation while a corporation balances the political and administrative dimensions of the local authority with a business-orientation which then suggests a rejection of the existing organisational status quo for a new paradigm of local political and policy management. Municipal corporation is more in synchrony with the provisions of the new Act and the new name sends a message that it is not business as usual. In fact a *Jamaica Gleaner* columnist links the change in name to positive impact on political participation: 'if the shiny new municipal corporations can break with the depressing history of their predecessor parish councils we may yet see more voters turning out next time' (Martin Henry, *Jamaica Gleaner*, 11 December 2016).

All perspectives on the change in name are valid. If the change is to be significant however, much depends on the capacity endowments of the local authority. This perhaps is the worth of the two other supporting pieces of legislation.

The Local Government (Financing and Financial Management) Act 2016

Any new law that is dedicated to local government financing in Jamaica must be revolutionary. Or so it would appear in light of a direct correlation between effective decentralisation and the state of local government financing. Moreover, there is a history of public agitation for adequate and sustainable financing for local government in Jamaica hence the establishment of the PRF, but to which concern the new law is expected to be more responsive. The claim is that insufficiency in financial resources has slowed the pace of transformation of local authorities. The Report of the National Advisory Council (NAC) on Local Government Reform 2009 views local government financing the most influential aspect of reform:

> A primary objective of local government reform is to ensure that local authorities have **access to adequate and independent sources of revenues,** and that these revenues are properly managed, so that municipalities are better able to undertake projects to improve the social and economic welfare of their constituents.

The NAC Report proposed *fiscal decentralisation* to achieve this objective. Fiscal decentralisation describes the devolution of taxing and spending powers to lower levels of government. Besides political decentralisation that sets the framework for the allocation of authority and responsibility between levels of government, fiscal decentralisation gives effect to devolution of powers. The pros and cons of fiscal decentralisation have been a source of ongoing debate but as an imperative of governance reforms it is an important part of local government reform.

For the NAC Report fiscal decentralisation requires: (a) intergovernmental transfers design that matches expenditure with responsibilities and that gives local authorities control over the Parish Revenue Fund; (b) measures to increase the revenue flow to local government that includes simplifying property tax rates and/or re-introduction of local/municipal rates for specified services or municipal improvement works; and (c) maintenance of databases on revenue and cost structure of all services and periodic cost-benefit analyses of such services. The extent to which the Local Government (Financing and Financial Management) Act 2016 reflects the building blocks of fiscal decentralisation or responds to the recommendations of the NAC Report are assessed in Table 12.2. Evidently the law has made provisions for more predictable sources of funding for local government services but stops short in the powers that it devolves. Overall the Act is strong on financial management and traditional sources of revenue but weak

Table 12.2 Implications of law governing local government financing

Building-blocks of fiscal decentralisation	Jamaica's interpretation based on NAC Report	Local Government (Financing and Financial Management) Act 2016	Policy implications
Assignment of expenditure responsibilities	Expenditure and responsibilities match	Provides for: 1 Parochial Revenue Fund 2 Equalisation Fund	Ambiguous about expenditure and responsibilities match
Allocation of revenue sources	Measures to increase the revenue flow: 1 Simplify property tax 2 Reintroduce municipal rates	Provides for: 1 90% of property tax revenue for local government 2 25% of motor vehicle licence revenue for local government 3 Accrual of local rates, fees, charges and income from investments to local government	Level and proportion subject to approval from Minister with responsibility for finance
Design of intergovernmental transfers	Local authorities control Parish Revenue Fund	Provides for: 1 Ministerial control of Parish Revenue Fund 2 90% property tax directly to local authorities; 10% property tax to Equalisation Fund 3 25% motor vehicle licence directly to local authorities; 75% to Equalisation Fund	1 Permanent Secretary in Ministry and NOT Chief Executive Officer of Municipal Corporation is the Accountable Officer 2 Minister allocates 10% on needs basis 3 Minister allocates 75% on basis of mileage of parochial roads
Structuring subnational borrowing/debt		Provides for local authority borrowing/debt with approval of, but not guaranteed by, Minister with responsibility for finance	Local authority's status similar to a department in the Jamaican public service

in devolution of powers for revenue generation or providing for innovative sources of local revenue, even with a provision for local investment. The boldest provision might be that which delegates responsibility for borrowing/debt to local government. Fiscal decentralisation is therefore not a priority of local government reform in Jamaica.

The Local Government (Unified Service and Employment) Act 2016

The 'quality' of the human resource is arguably the most indispensable dimension of complete transformation of local authorities in Jamaica. With an expanded mandate in reform come questions about the capacity of local government especially in light of a legacy of underperformance in local service provision and representation. Local government's unsatisfactory performance is believed to be a function of *low* quality human resource, weak management and accountability systems and poor administrative and political leadership. Perception is not always reality; the truth is somewhere in the mix. A capacity audit (CAPAUD) of a sample of local authorities in Jamaica carried out by this researcher in 2010 revealed that *administrative leaders in local authorities are equipped for their posts based on educational entry requirements and training* (Schoburgh 2014: 16–17). However, local government systems are devoid of an effective human resource strategy in which performance- and results-orientation are at a premium. Educational qualifications and competencies are lesser factors in local government performance levels than the character of the system and organisational ethos that militate against efficiency and effectiveness. The CAPAUD 2010 found that: the extent to which educational qualifications and training are converted into leadership competencies was unclear; there was lack of will on the part of senior managers to institute measures that could lead to higher organisational performance; and innovation in local authorities was negligible evidenced by the absence of a clear organisational strategy in response to Ministry Papers 8 of 1993 and 7 of 2003 (Schoburgh 2014: 16–17). The CAPAUD 2010 described 'the capacity of the local authority for self-renewal and sustainability in light of limited expressions in organisational operations of foresight, innovativeness and autonomy even with strong endowments of education and training' (Schoburgh 2014: 17). These deficiencies are the remit of the new Act, which resolves to 'provide a comprehensive framework for the employment, management and regulation of personnel employed by local government authorities' (p. 1).

The Act espouses critical themes that align appropriately with its purpose. The constitution of a Services Commission is given ample coverage in Sections 3–6 and 9–11, implicitly responding to the existing human resource strategy gap in local government. The *unified* in title of the Act signals a break from the disjointed approach to conditions of employment. The immediate impact of Act 2016 is the repeal of the Municipal Service Commission Act; the Parish Council Unified Service Act; and the Poor Relief Officers Unified Service Act that provided for differential treatment of each of these staff establishments causing conundrum in the areas of setting and meeting performance and accountability standards; ensuring fairness; and dispensing discipline, with adverse effect on staff morale. What obtained previously could not fulfil the human resource capacity requirements of a modern developmental local government. The Commission is thus empowered to cultivate a workforce that, according to Section 5[1]:

(a) possesses the requisite skills, competencies and outlook to achieve good governance and sustainable development at the local level; and
(b) is strongly oriented to innovation, problem solving and responsiveness to customer needs.

Among the list of functions of the Commission, the Act provides for the development of a human resource policy framework for local authorities; adoption of standards for recruitment, deployment and development of staff; manpower planning and human resource management information system (HRMIS).

Jamaica's strategic laws are commendable efforts towards meeting long-held objectives of local government reform. They respond to institutional deficiencies that have the potential to stymie the transformation of local government into an agent of development.

Trinidad and Tobago's law and bill

The Tobago House of Assembly (THA) Act 1980 precipitated a flow of structural changes to local government in the Republic of Trinidad and Tobago and importantly a recognition that local self-government is a necessary pathway to growth and development of a geographic area. The central concern has been to elevate local government to the position of partner in national development, which became the core theme of the draft policy paper on Community Development and Local Government Reform 1983. The plan was to establish Area and National Advisory Committees to foster citizen participation in local and national planning and development. Although, the ruling People's National Movement (PNM) under whose portfolio these perspectives were advocated lost the 1986 national elections and the ideas in the draft policy paper never got to the stage of implementation, the new government, the National Alliance for Reconstruction (NAR) might have been convinced by the value of local government and proposed its own version of reform in a draft policy paper, titled *The Decentralization Process, Regional Administration and Regional Development Proposals for Reform 1989–1990*. How the debate unfolded is discussed here.

Municipal Corporations Act 1990/1991

Local government reform in the twin-island republic was marked by the promotion of a policy of decentralisation and drafting of a municipal corporations bill. The Municipal Corporations Act 1990/1991 consolidated all existing pieces of legislation pertaining to local government in Trinidad. Its significance lies in (a) transformation of the structure of local government, creating thirteen regions (that were reduced to nine in 1992), two cities and three boroughs; and (b) expansion of the functional responsibilities of local government.

There was a disconnect between the 1983 vision of local government as a development partner and the Municipal Corporations Act 1990/1991 which focused on restructuring local government and consolidating laws. The constitution of Municipal Corporations was laid out, viz., internal structures and procedures, electoral matters and functional scope. It did not clarify the role of local government in the broader frame of governance. The 1990/91 Act intended to be catalytic, providing for greater local autonomy, financial self-sufficiency, efficiency and effectiveness in service delivery, and facilitating the emergence of high performing corporate entities that operate within a participatory ethos. However many of the provisions of the Act and subsequent amendments were not enforced.

Local Government Bill 2009

During the 2000s The Republic of Trinidad and Tobago entered another period of policy activism on local government reform that yielded: a Draft Green Paper on Local Government

Reform 2004; a Draft White Paper on Local Government Reform 2006; a Green Paper on Roles and Responsibilities of Local Government Bodies 2008; and a Draft White Paper on Local Government Reform 2009. The 2009 Draft White Paper was dubbed 'an agenda for change' as local government reform was attached to the auspicious goal of developed country status by 2020, referred to as *Vision 2020*. Among the measures identified for implementation are (a) legislation that introduces a new management system and provides for citizen engagement; (b) institutional restructuring and human resource development; and (c) monitoring and evaluation.

The 2009 Bill followed the draft policy paper with a more expansive mandate than the Municipal Corporations Act 1990/1991. It specified reform and modernisation of local government in Trinidad with an immediate consequence in the repeal of the Municipal Corporations Act (Chapter 25:04). It provides for: establishment, classification, delineation and continuation of municipalities, policy and administrative leadership, and roles and responsibilities.

The 2009 Bill, when and if finally enacted, would further rationalise the number of municipalities. Each municipality is to be governed by a municipal corporation that is a body corporate. The municipal corporation will be governed internally by an executive council and externally, by a consortium of municipal corporations designated central administrative districts (CADs).

The Municipal Corporations Act 1990/1991 was narrowly focused; the Local Government Bill 2009 was more comprehensive. Local government reform in Trinidad started out on a mantra of decentralisation. Yet the 2009 Bill has proposed a degree of centralisation in the concept of CADs. And in practice there might be some ambiguity in the role of CADs vis-a-vis the Ministry with responsibility for local government, even though the responsibility of both is defined in the Bill. Perhaps the Draft Policy, Transitioning of Local Government 2016 will rectify these deficiencies. For among the impediments to effective functioning of local government bodies in Trinidad it listed: political interference and manipulation; inadequate funding; and inadequacy of the current legislation. The 2009 Bill has not been enacted so it is anticipated that a new law or at the least amendments to the 2009 Bill may emerge. Apart from new local governance arrangements there has been little fundamental change to the position of local government in Trinidad.

The bigger picture in the Caribbean

So what does new legislation on local government in some countries of the Commonwealth Caribbean say about the intentions of reformers? Clearly reformers desire change, even though there is sometimes another motivation, of political manipulation of the process. If the policy prescriptions for local government change are purely symbolic as in the view of some commentators, there needs to be serious accounting for the commitment of resources invested in designing instruments that are purported to be facilitators of change. Undoubtedly the discourse is populated by the 'appropriate' contemporary concepts suggesting a shift in policy perspective on the position and role of local government in Caribbean political systems.

The legislative changes enacted in the Caribbean promote values that lay the foundation for institutional change and social transformation. The 'indicators of policy shift' – local sustainable development, local autonomy, citizen/stakeholder participation – resonate with the normative principles of successful local government reform (Andrews and Shah 2005; Shah 2006; Dollery and Robotti 2008; Schoburgh et al. 2016). As it stands their interpretation in law might not be as radical as advocates of reform desired. Legislation in both Jamaica and Trinidad associates sustainable development with local government but its role in poverty reduction and the broader issue of social inequality needs to be more explicit (see e.g. Schoburgh et al. 2016).

Also in this period of technologically-driven solutions the legislation has not provided for the integration of information and communications technology (ICT) into local government operations. This represents a missed opportunity to demonstrate a strategic move towards business process reengineering in local government that would be in alignment with the new image that the *name* Municipal Corporation proclaims. Local government reform in these various Caribbean countries is thus incremental in nature.

Constitutional status and fiscal decentralisation are viewed as panaceas for effective local government reform. A degree of fiscal decentralisation has been granted but not fiscal empowerment which is activated through full tax-raising powers and discretionary spending. McIntosh's (2002) interpretation of constitutional reform is enlightening:

> Constitutional reform . . . is not a revolutionary act; it does not seek a radical transformation of the character of the constitution and of the political society. Neither does it seek 'to deconstitute and reconstitute' the constitutional order, or abandon its primary principles. . . . constitutional reform places itself in a continuity of the temporal development of the legal order. It is a process of better realizing the substantive values already present in the legal order.
>
> *(McIntosh 2002: 55)*

Citizens of the Commonwealth Caribbean along with their political representatives must contemplate and answer one fundamental question: What is the value of local government to the society and the political economy? The response will be the basis for social transformation in the roles of actors and agents in the new spirit of multi-level governance that the legislation heralds.

Conclusion

Caribbean local government systems have been the object of reform for more than three decades. Although the process has been characteristically episodic, local government reform responds to domestic and international pressures imposed on the modern state to be productive and competitive. These pressures are embodied in the social forces of globalisation and technological developments which combined with citizens' demand for greater responsiveness have occasioned questions about *roles* of actors in both the public and private spheres. Local government specifically, and the subnational sphere generally, have come into focus as the case for decentralisation gains traction despite the disparity between the positive outcomes theorised and actual practice of decentralising reforms. Irrespective of the motive, reform is an empirical matter and therefore reform processes and outcomes are shaped by contextual factors. Constitutional and legislative changes define this stage of local government reform in the Commonwealth Caribbean given the auspicious goal of institutionalisation of new norms and values in support of a multilevel governance framework. But the shift from local government to local governance and ultimately to developmental local governance although reflected in the provisions of legal enactments, is challenged in a fundamental way by the high degree of conservatism that defines the political systems. So, in as much as local government in the Commonwealth Caribbean is now assigned, through the different pieces of legislation a developmental role, there is no guarantee of a rapid transformation of this system of government. For once conservatism translates into incremental changes which further favour the political status quo in which national priorities retain dominance. Constitutional and legislative changes promote decentralisation, non-enforcement of the provisions suggests continued centralisation. This is the dilemma within the countries studied.

If there is a lesson here it is that, constitutional status for local government needs a strong dose of political capital found in citizens' understanding and appreciation for the new value of local government. Otherwise the constitution of local government as a principal actor in governance and sustainable development in the Commonwealth Caribbean will remain at the stage of experimentation.

Notes

1 Anguilla, Antigua and Barbuda, The Bahamas, Barbados, Belize, British Virgin Islands, Dominica, Grenada, Guyana, Jamaica, St. Kitts and Nevis, St, Lucia, St. Vincent and the Grenadines, Trinidad and Tobago, and Turks and Caicos.
2 Guadeloupe, Martinique, Saint-Barthélemy, Saint Martin and French Guiana.
3 Cuba, Dominican Republic and Puerto Rico.
4 Aruba, Bonaire, Curaçao, Sint Eustatius, Saba and Sint Maarten.
5 The special improvement district is an association of residents, businesses or other interests constituted to benefit members within a particular jurisdiction.

References

Anckar, D. 2000. Westminster Democracy: A Comparison of Small Island States Varieties in the Pacific and the Caribbean. *Pacific Studies* 23(3/4): 57–76.
Andrews, M. and A. Shah. 2005. Citizen-Centered Governance: A New Approach to Public Sector Reform. In A. Shah (ed.), *Public Expenditure Analysis*, 153–175. Washington, DC: World Bank.
Barzelay, M. and R. Gallego. 2006. From 'New Institutionalism' to 'Institutional Processualism': Advancing Knowledge about Public Management Policy Change. *Governance* 19(4): 531–557.
Chandler, J. A. 1996. *Local Government Today*. Manchester: Manchester University Press.
Constitutional Design Group (2011) Constitutional Reform in the English speaking Caribbean: Challenges and Prospects. Social Sciences Research Council. Retrieved on 25 May 2017 from www.comparativeconstitutionprojects.org.
Dollery, B. and L. Robotti. 2008. *The Theory and Practice of Local Government Reform*. Cheltenham: Edward Elgar.
Dominguez, J. I., R. A. Pastor and R. D. Worrell (eds). 1993. *Democracy in the Caribbean*. Baltimore, MD: Johns Hopkins University Press.
Goodin, R. E. (ed.). 1996. *The Theory of Institutional Design*. Cambridge: Cambridge University Press.
Goodin, R. E. and H. D. Klingemann (eds). 1996. *A New Handbook of Political Science*. Oxford: Oxford University Press.
Lijphart, A. 1999. *Patterns of Democracy: Government Forms and Performance in Thirty-Six Countries*. New Haven, CT: Yale University Press.
Lora, E. (ed.). 2007. *The State of State Reforms in Latin America*. Stanford, CA: Stanford University Press.
Marsh, D. and G. Stoker (ed.). 2002. *Theory and Methods in Political Science* (2nd edition). Basingstoke: Palgrave Macmillan.
McAnulla, S. 2006. *British Politics: A Critical Introduction*. London: Continuum.
McIntosh, S. C. R. 2002. *Caribbean Constitutional Reform: Rethinking the West Indian Polity*. Kingston: Caribbean Law.
MLGCD. Undated. Local Government Reform 2013 Onward. Retrieved from www.localgovjamaica.gov.jm/localgovernmentreform.aspx?c=acheivement.
Prud'homme, R. 1995. The Dangers of Decentralisation. *The World Bank Research Observer* 10(2): 201–220.
Ryan, S. 1999. *Winner Takes All: The Westminster Experience in the Anglophone Caribbean*. St Augustine: ISER.
Schoburgh, E. D. 2006. *Local Government Reform: The Prospects for Community Empowerment in Jamaica*. Mona: SALISES.
Schoburgh, E. D. 2014. Does Local Government Have Capacity for Enabling Local Economic Development? Lessons from Jamaica. *Commonwealth Journal of Local Governance* 14 (June). Retrieved from http://epress.lib.uts.edu.au/ojs/index.php/cjlg.

Schoburgh, E. D., J. Martin and S. Gatchair. 2016. *Developmental Local Governance: A Critical Discourse in 'Alternative' Development*. Basingstoke: Palgrave Macmillan.

Seidman, A., R. B. Seidman and N. Abeyesekere. 2001. *Legislative Drafting for Democratic Social Change*. Dordrecht: Kluwer Law International.

Shah, A. 2004. *Fiscal Decentralization in Developing and Transition Economies: Progress, Problems and Promise*. Working Paper no. 3282. Washington, DC: World Bank.

Shah, A. 2006. *Local Governance in Developing Countries*. Washington, DC: World Bank.

Sutton, P. 1999. Democracy in the Commonwealth Caribbean. *Democratization*. 6(1): 67–86.

Ter-Minassian, T. 1997. Intergovernmental Fiscal Relations in a Macroeconomic Perspective: An Overview. In T. Ter-Minassian (ed.), *Fiscal Federalism in Theory and Practice* (3–24). Washington, DC: IMF.

UNDP. 1999. *Decentralisation: A Sampling of Definitions*. Working Paper. UNDP. Retrieved from www.undp.org/eo/documents/decentralisation_working_report.PDF.

Wollmann, H. 1990. Decentralisation: What It Is and Why We Should Care. In R. J. Bennett (ed.), *Decentralization, Local Government and Markets: Towards a Post-Welfare Agenda* (29–43). Oxford: Clarendon Press.

PART III

Range of local government services

13
LOCAL GOVERNMENT SERVICE ROLES IN THE USA
Consistency and change

J. Edwin Benton

Introduction

Local governments in the United States have an interesting history and existence. The U.S. Constitution is silent on the subject of local governments and legally recognizes only two levels of government—the national government and the states. Nonetheless, almost immediately after the United States came into existence, the states established local governments and vested them with a variety of responsibilities, with an expectation that they would provide a range of services to their residents. Actually, the states really did not do much more than permit local governments, which were already in existence during Colonial America, to continue in their familiar role of delivering a wide variety of vital services to local residents. To the extent that states did more, it was to give constitutional sanction to the existence of local governments and grant them legal authority to perform a number of functions and deliver state-level services (e.g., public welfare, health care, judicial functions, and so forth), to state citizens within local jurisdictions; and purely local-type services (e.g., streets, sidewalks, fire protection, garbage collection, etc.) to these same persons.

From their genesis local governments have been and continue to be legal creatures of the respective states and exist in a dependent relationship with them. This means that the power to create local governments also implies that states have the power to abolish them. Concomitantly, it also means that local governments have only those powers expressly granted to them, and, at the discretion of the states, those powers may be modified or rescinded. Over the years, most states have slowly lessened their control over local governments through grants of home rule, giving them more decision-making authority in determining their government structure, deciding what functions to perform and services to provide, and choosing sources of revenue. Nevertheless, Dillon's Rule, promulgated in 1868 (deriving from the case of *Merriam* v. *Moody's Executors* (25 Iowa 1868),[1] reinforces the settled legal principle that local governments were granted limited powers. In elaborating on the narrow scope of local government powers, Dillon concluded that they can exercise the following powers: (1) those granted in express words; (2) those necessarily or fairly implied in or incident in the powers expressly granted; and (3) those essential to the accomplishment of the declared objects and purposes of the corporation—not simply convenient, but indispensable (Dillon 1911: 448).

Succinctly put, this judicial decision emphatically stated that, if a local government has not been expressly granted a certain power in its state's constitution, then the interpretation should be that it does not have that power.

Despite the limited nature of their powers, local governments nonetheless are entrusted with significant service responsibilities that require considerable financial resources. Local governments in total typically spend more money that do their state governments. In Fiscal Year 2016, direct expenditures of local governments to deliver a range of services to local residents amounted to $1.81 trillion (www.census.gov/gov/index.html). This compares to $1.66 trillion which was spent by the fifty states (www.census.gov/gov/index.html).

Given the vast number and variety of services that local governments provide in the U.S. as well as the amounts of money spent to deliver them, the purpose of this chapter is to conduct a comparative analysis of the service roles played by four types of local governments—counties, municipalities, townships, and special districts[2]—over the last fifty years. First, attention focuses on the part played by each of the four types of local governments to provide three major categories of services (traditional, municipal-type, and regional). This is determined by examining the proportion of total local government expenditures accounted for in each of the three service areas. Second, consideration shifts to the priority that each type of local government assigns to the provision of services in the three service areas. This is measured by the proportion of each local government's expenditures allotted to the delivery of services grouped in the traditional, municipal-type, and regional categories.

Before turning to the analysis sections of this chapter, it is instructive to provide a brief overview of the five types of local governments in the U.S. (counties, municipalities, townships, special districts, and school districts) and a context for the evolution of local government service roles and the subsequent three categories of services (traditional, municipal-type, and regional) that are synonymous with local governments.

Types of U.S. local governments

Local governments in the U.S. can be divided into two distinct types—general-purpose governments (i.e., counties, municipalities, and townships) and single-purpose governments (i.e., special districts and school districts).

County governments are the result of states dividing up their territory into 3,031 distinct, general-purpose subunits (except in Louisiana, where counties are called parishes, and Alaska, where they are referred to as boroughs).[3] States created counties to function as their agents. In other words, counties were expected to manage activities of statewide concern or deliver basically state services at the local level. In this sense, counties sometimes can be viewed as "branch" or "satellite" offices of the state and, in this role, their customary set of functions traditionally have included such things as property tax assessment and collection, law enforcement, elections, rudimentary recordkeeping (concerning matters like land transaction, births, and deaths) and road maintenance. Due, however, to the dual pressures of modernization and population growth, additional demands have been placed on county governments. As a consequence, their service offerings have expanded. In addition to their traditional service responsibilities, counties presently handle health and hospitals, pollution control, mass transit, industrial development, social services, and consumer protection (Bowman and Kearney 2008).

Municipal governments are specific, populated territories usually operating under a charter from the state. Municipalities differ from counties in terms of how they were created and what they do. The process for an area to become a municipality begins with residents of that area petitioning the state for incorporation. The area designed for incorporation must satisfy certain criteria, like population and density minimums. In most instances, a referendum (where residents are permitted to vote on whether they wish to become an incorporated municipality) is required. Sometimes, residents are also asked to vote on the name of the proposed municipality and its form of government. If the incorporation referendum is successful, then a charter is granted by the state, and the newly created municipality has the legal authority to elect officials, levy taxes and fees, and provide services to its residents. Not all municipalities, however, have charters, as California municipalities, for example, function under general state law.

Unlike counties, however, municipalities usually have greater decision making authority and discretion. Almost all states have enacted home rule provisions for municipalities, although in some states, only municipalities which have reached a certain population size can exercise this option. Moreover, municipalities typically provide a larger menu of services to their residents than most counties do. Standard services delivered by municipalities include: police and fire, public works, parks and recreation, garbage and trash collection, water and sewer, streets and sidewalks, and traffic signals. In addition, some municipalities supplement these services with facilities such as publicly maintained cemeteries, city-operated marinas, convention centers, and sports stadiums, museums, municipal-owned and -operated housing, restaurant inspections, economic development, urban renewal, performing arts centers, swimming pools, and government access television and radio.

Townships, which exist in only twenty states, are also general-purpose local governments but are distinct from county and municipal governments. Created by their states, townships are actually subdivisions of counties and may have some of the same responsibilities as county governments and perform many of the functions of county government at the grassroots level. In some states (primarily in New England, along with those in New Jersey, Pennsylvania, and to some degree, Michigan, New York, and Wisconsin), townships typically are vested with broad powers and offer the kinds of services linked to municipalities and counties in other states. In the rest of the township states (Illinois, Indiana, Kansas, Minnesota, Missouri, Nebraska, North Dakota, Ohio, and South Dakota), the character of township government is more rural and the services they provide are usually limited to roads and law enforcement. However, the nearer these rural townships are to large urban areas, the more likely they are to provide a larger menu of services to their residents (Bowman and Kearney 2008: 278).

Special districts are presumed to do what other local governments (that is, counties and municipalities) cannot or will not do and thereby are established to satisfy services needs in a specific area. In some instances, special districts can be viewed as the governments of last resort because counties and municipalities do not have the legal authority to provide a service or sometimes are forbidden to do so. In other instances, they may have no interest in providing a particular service for various reasons, including not having the fiscal resources to do so. Special districts can be established in three different ways: (1) states can create them through special enabling legislation; (2) general purpose local governments (that is, counties and municipalities) may adopt a resolution creating them; and (3) citizens may initiate districts by petition, which is often followed by a referendum on the question (Bowman and Kearney 2008: 279). Once they are created, special districts may finance their operations by levying taxes, charging user fees, receiving intergovernmental grants, and using private revenue bonds.

Unlike general-purpose governments, most special districts (over ninety percent of them) provide a single service, although the functions vary. Natural resources management, housing and community development, fire protection, and water and sewer service are the most common (Bowman and Kearney 2008: 280). Most states have other state-specific districts, such as Colorado's mine drainage districts and tunnel districts or Florida's beach and shore preservation districts, water management districts, and mobile home park recreation districts.

School districts are a type of single-purpose local government that can also be regarded as a distinct kind of special district. They are distinct is the sense that they provide only one service—education. The decision to create a separate and independent governmental entity to be responsible for the administration and operation of public schools was rooted in Americans' strongly held belief that "free quality public education is a core societal value" and even a "fundamental right" (see Donovan, Mooney, and Smith 2009). Taking no chances that education could become politicized or have to compete with other interests for attention and funding, Americans, for the most part, were insistent that education not be one among the many services provided by either a county or municipal government. Nevertheless, four states (Alaska, Maryland, North Carolina, and Tennessee) have assigned responsibility for the provision of public education to county governments. In addition, there are a number of large U.S. cities (New York, Chicago, and Philadelphia, among others) that have been granted permission by their states to create their own school districts, while all public schools in Hawaii are operated by the state government.

As noted in the introduction, the analysis of trends and patterns in local government services conducted in this chapter will be confined to counties, municipalities, townships, and special districts.

Context for understanding local government service roles

Over the years, scholars and practitioners have devised and utilized a number of practical terms to identify and capture the essence of the service roles played by local governments (see Benton 2002). Each term was designed to convey what it was that local governments do when providing services to their residents. For convenience sake and organizational purposes, similar types of services were grouped into three categories—that is, traditional, municipal-type, and regional (sometimes referred to as urban-type).

Traditional services are unquestionably the oldest type of services that local government deliver. When providing these kinds of services, local governments are oftentimes assisting the state government in providing what are essentially state-level services to people living within a local government's jurisdiction and thereby function as administrative arms of the state. These services are provided to residents in both incorporated and unincorporated areas. In addition, traditional services are commonly ones that the state mandates that local governments provide. As such, local governments have no choice but to provide these services; however, in the case of many of these kinds of services, the state usually provides a considerable amount of financial assistance to underwrite the cost of service delivery (good examples are public welfare and health care services). Some of the more widely visible traditional services provided by local governments are listed in Table 13.1.

Municipal-type services are services that one ordinarily associates with city or municipal governments. Oftentimes, these services have been referred to as "optional" services that local governments, at their discretion, might be able to provide. However, county governments have always been less likely to provide "optional" services like fire protection, utilities (e.g., water, electric power, and natural gas supply), and sewage collection/disposal because they were either not granted state authority to do so or did not have the tax base or large population concentrations to make delivery of these type services cost efficient. Therefore, cities and sometimes townships have been more inclined to offer their residents municipal-type

Table 13.1 Traditional services of local governments

Finance/other administration	Public health	Police protection/ corrections/public safety	Judicial and legal services	Social Services	Other	Transportation
Property tax assessment	Mosquito control	patrol	Criminal prosecution	Income maintenance	Property/auto records/titling	Road/bridge maintenance
Property and other tax collection	Home health	Detective investigation	General jurisdiction courts	Emergency medical assistance	Vital statistics	Road/bridge construction
Personnel services	Maternal and child health	Forensic investigation	Limited jurisdiction courts	Food stamps	Elections	Traffic control
Purchasing	Commutable disease control	Criminal records	Indigent defense	Family social services	Agricultural extension services	Snow removal
Data processing	Dental health	Detention facilities	Juvenile/family court	Individual social services	Veteran's affairs	Sidewalks
		Work release program	Legal/civil services	Children welfare services	Cemeteries	Street/road signage
		Adult probation/ parole program		Children/senior daycare services		
		Juvenile probation/ parole program		Human resource planning		
		Coroner's services		General welfare assistance		
				Meals-on-wheel program		

Table 13.2 Municipal-type services of local governments

Public safety	Public health	Public utilities	Parks/recreation	Other
Fire prevention	Garbage collection	Water supply	Neighborhood parks	Libraries
Fire protection	Sewer collection	Power supply	Neighborhood recreational facilities	Public information services
Emergency medical service	Sanitation inspection	Natural gas supply		Museums/arts/cultural affairs
				Parking facilities
				Auditoriums
				Marinas
				Consumer protection services
				Cable television
				Sidewalks/stormwater management

or "optional" services. In fact, the desire for these kinds of services is what usually prompted residents of densely populated areas to petition their state legislature for permission to incorporate—in other words, to create a new municipality. Table 13.2 contains a list of some of the most common and recognizable municipal-type services

Regional services are ones that are designed to address pressing service needs and issues of an "urban" or "metropolitan" character and usually transcend or know no traditional political boundaries. Like traditional services, regional services are provided to residents of both the incorporated and unincorporated area. Urbanization, suburbanization, and metropolitan fragmentation have been primarily responsible for ratcheting up demands for regional services, and unorganized or chaotic development patterns known as "urban sprawl" have tended to exacerbate the underlying problem requiring a solution. Given the regional or urban area-wide nature of the problem, it is usually not possible for a municipality or a township and sometimes even a county to adequately service needs like water and air pollution, solid waste and sewage disposal, natural resource conservation, economic development, urban deterioration, and traffic congestion. Table 13.3 contains some of the more common regional services.

As desirable as it is to be able to definitively sort local government services into three distinct categories, that is not always possible. Some services could logically fall into two or all three categories. One example would be solid waste and sewer services. While the collection of solid waste (garbage) and sewage could be classified as municipal-type services, solid waste disposal (management) and sewage disposal (treatment) could fall into the regional service category. Likewise, parks and recreational services could also be placed in these same two service categories. That is, parks and recreational facilities that are funded and operated by municipalities would logically fit into the municipal-types service category, while parks and recreational facilities located in both incorporated and unincorporated areas and funded and operated by a county government or a special district could conceivably be classified as regional services. A third example is that of emergency medical services (EMS). At one time, municipalities were the only governmental entities to provide EMS services, and as such these services could be

Table 13.3 Regional services of local governments

Transportation	Land use	Culture and recreation
Public parking facilities	Comprehensive land use planning	Recreational services
Mass transit	Zoning	Fairgrounds
Airports	Growth management	Stadiums
Highway safety	Open space control	Convention centers
Bikeways	Subdivision control	Marinas
Natural resources	**Community development/housing**	Swimming pools
Flood control/drainage	Building code enforcement	Museums
Irrigation	Housing code enforcement	Performing arts
Soil conservation	Convention public housing	**Public utility**
Coastal zoning	Leased public housing	Sewage collection and disposal
Energy conservation	Rural housing programs	**Other**
Energy management	Industrial development	Central emergency number (911)
Solid waste disposal	**Parks**	Emergency medical services (EMS)
Water pollution control	Park acquisition	Emergency medical services (EMS)
Air pollution control	Park development	Disaster preparedness
Noise control	Park maintenance	Job training
	County parks	Work experiences programs
		Public service employment

categorized as municipal-type services. With more and more county governments assuming financial and operational responsibility for EMS services, they could be reasoned pigeonholed into all three services categories.

Another service that is difficult to assign to anyone of the three service categories is education. There are several large cities in the U.S. (for example, New York, Philadelphia, and Chicago) and counties in four states (Alaska, Maryland, North Carolina, and Tennessee) that operate public schools, Furthermore, some cities and counties operate junior/community colleges and four-year universities. The question therefore becomes: In which of the three service categories should education be placed?

Methodology

As mentioned early on, the focal point of this chapter is to investigate the role that county governments, municipal governments, townships, and special districts have usually played in the provision of three categories of local government services (traditional, municipal-type, and regional). This focus will also entail an analysis of a number of trends and patterns so as to determine what has stayed the same or what has changed over time.

To accomplish the goals laid out here will require us to examine the spending behavior of each type of local government. First, a comparison of the proportion of total local government spending in each of the three service categories accounted for by counties, municipalities, townships, and special districts will reveal which government is playing a greater or less role in service provision. Second, a comparison of the proportion of a local government's expenditures allocated to traditional, municipal-type, and regional services will show the priority that these governments place on delivering services in each of the three service categories.

Table 13.4 Three types of local government services based on expenditure categories

Traditional	Municipal-type	Regional
Corrections	Fire protection	Air transportation
Financial administration	Libraries	Housing and urban
General public buildings	Protective inspections	Development
Health	Utilities	Natural resources
Highways		"Other transportation
Hospitals		Parking facilities
Judicial/legal		Parks and recreation
"Other" general government		Sewage
"Other" social services		Solid waste
Police		Management
Public welfare		

Data to conduct these analyses will be derived from the U.S. Bureau of the Census, Census of Governments, *Compendium of Government Finances* series, which is published every five years in years ending in "2" and "7." The time frame for the analyses will be 1962–2012, since 1962 marks the first year that expenditure data for all of the specific local government services needed for this study was available and 2012 is the year of the most recent publication of these data. This fifty-year time frame should provide a well-defined picture from which to draw significant conclusions about the service roles played by each of the four types of local governments.

For the most part, the expenditure data reported in the Census of Governments surveys closely align with the services that are clustered into the traditional, municipal-type, and regional categories in Tables 13.1, 13.2, and 13.3. These expenditure groupings are located in Table 13.4. While not a perfect fit in every instance, they nonetheless are the best facsimile that can be produced, given the way in which the U.S. Census Bureau collects and reports these spending figures.

Provision of three kinds of services: what part does each local government play?

Before turning our attention to the part that each local government plays in the provision of three categories of services, it is important to develop an understanding of the bigger picture. That is, how much of total local government spending for all types of local services do counties, municipalities, townships, and special districts account for? Figure 13.1 assists in answering this question.

As can be plainly seen from the figure, municipalities have always outdistanced all other local governments in accounting for the largest proportion of spending for all local government services. In 1962, municipalities accounted for around 80 percent of total local government monies spent to deliver all types of local government services. Nevertheless, it is useful to note that, while municipalities were still accounting for a larger percentage of all local government expenditures made for all local government services some fifty years later, the municipal share has dropped to about 55 percent. This means that other local governments—but especially special districts and, to a lesser extent, counties—are more involved today in delivering a wider menu of services than ever before. In short, municipalities no longer hold a monopoly over the provision of most local government services. In addition, it is important to note that the size of

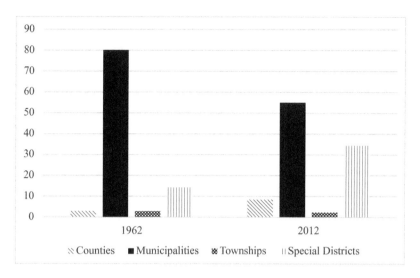

Figure 13.1 County, municipal, township and special district spending as a percentage of total local government spending, 1962 and 2012

Source: Figures derived from Table 48 of the U.S. Bureau of the Census, 1962 Census of Governments, *Compendium of Government Finances* (Washington, D.C.: U.S. Government Printing Office) and Table 2 of the U.S. Bureau of the Census, 2012 Census of Governments, *State & Local Finances* located at census. gov//govs/local/historical_data_2012.html. Accessed on April 26, 2017.

the service role of townships, while never rivaling that of counties and municipalities and even special districts, has declined over time, but especially for those that are located in rural areas.

Besides this important observation about local government service delivery, other points of interest come to light in the analysis that follows. For instance, from perusal review of the kinds of services that each type of local government provides, certain patterns and truisms emerge. In particular, it appears that states have engaged in a calculated and logical assignment of functional responsibilities. In addition, it is obvious that there has been a conscious and calculated effort on the part of local governments and their officials to satisfy the service needs and expectations of the citizens and businesses within their jurisdictions. This is confirmed in the examination below of the proportion of total local government expenditures in each of our three service categories accounted for by counties, municipalities, townships, and special districts.

Traditional services

From an inspection of the first panel of Figure 13.2, it is evident that county governments are the dominant providers of traditional kinds of services. In 1962, counties accounted for around 47 percent of all local government spending for these services. Little had changed by 2012, as counties still accounted for slightly over one-half of such spending. However, we can observe a notable decrease in the percentage of expenditures made by municipalities (a drop of about 8 percent), while the proportion accounted for by townships also decreased slightly from 1962 to 2012. Moreover, it can be seen that there was a clear increase (roughly 8 percent) in the special district share of traditional service expenditures from about 3 percent in 1962 to nearly 11 percent in 2012. Finally, townships have had a relatively small part to play in the provision of traditional kinds of services.

J. Edwin Benton

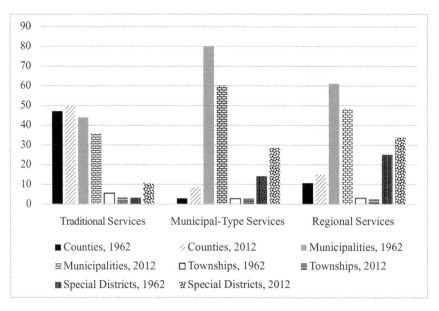

Figure 13.2 Individual local governments' expenditures as a percentage of all expenditures for traditional, municipal-type and regional services, 1962 and 2012

Source: Figures derived from Table 48 of the U.S. Bureau of the Census, 1962 Census of Governments, *Compendium of Government Finances* (Washington, D.C.: U.S. Government Printing Office) and Table 2 of the U.S. Bureau of the Census, 2012 Census of Governments, *State & Local Finances* located at census.gov//govs/local/historical_data_2012.html. Accessed on April 26, 2017.

These data confirm the expectation that counties would be the primary providers of traditional services, since it is a well-known fact that most states mandate that county governments provide several of the major and most costly services included in this category (e.g., heath care, public welfare, judicial/legal, and corrections) that, in 2012, constituted roughly one-third of all local government spending for traditional types of services.

An examination of county spending for these four services reveals several noteworthy patterns (see Table 13.5). First, county government dominance in spending for welfare has been quite pronounced, with these governments consistently accounting for about three-fourths of all local governments expenditures in this area. Second, county government expenditures made for judicial/legal and corrections increased by 23 and 15 percentage points, respectively between 1962 and 2012 due to states mandating that more of the cost of providing these services be borne by states' administrative arms or subdivisions (that is, counties). In addition, the county proportion of health care spending rose by around 19 percentage points from 1962 to 2012 because of the tremendous increase in Medicaid funds flowing from the Federal government to the states and ultimately passed onto counties in their time-honored and mandated role to be the primary providers of this service.

Municipalities, while doing less in the area of traditional services overall in recent years, was still accounting for a considerable proportion (close to one-half) of all local government expenditures in roads and highways. Conspicuous decreases, however, in expenditures for hospitals (18 percent in 2012 versus 38 percent in 1962) and welfare (20 percent in 2012 compared to 43 percent in 1962) point to a declining role for cities in providing these two traditional kinds of services.

Table 13.5 County government expenditure percentages for selected traditional services, 1962 and 2012

	Welfare	Judicial/legal	Corrections	Health
1962	71	54	70	51
2012	75	77	85	69

Source: Figures derived from Table 48 of the U.S. Bureau of the Census, 1962 Census of Governments, *Compendium of Government Finances* (Washington, D.C.: U.S. Government Printing Office) and Table 2 of the U.S. Bureau of the Census, 2012 Census of Governments, *State & Local Finances* located at census.gov//govs/local/historical_data_2012.html. Accessed on April 26, 2017.

The increase in the expenditure percentage of traditional services accounted for by special districts that occurred over the last 50 years can be attributed to the markedly greater role that they were playing in providing hospital services. By 2012, special district expenditures for hospitals made up 40 percent of total local government spending for this service compared to only 15 percent in 1962. Two factors can be offered for the enlarged role of special districts. One, states were creating more hospital special district authorities at the urging of both counties and municipalities that were becoming increasingly concerned that their governments' financial security was being threatened by the tremendous rise in medical malpractice lawsuits. Two, municipalities, which historically had constructed and operated hospitals primarily from taxes levied on city residents, complained that a growing number of hospital users were residents of the unincorporated area who did not pay city taxes—an unfair situation from a city's perspective that is often referred to as a "freeloader" problem.

Municipal-type services

Looking again at Figure 13.2 (see second panel), it is clear that municipalities have always been the principal providers of municipal-types services. Nevertheless, the municipal government share of total municipal-type service expenditures declined substantially from 80 percent in 1962 to 55 percent in 2012. Picking up the slack for the reduced role played by cities in recent years have been special districts, as their share of spending for these type services increased significantly from 14 percent in 1962 to 34 percent in 2012. To a lesser extent, counties have assumed additional responsibility for the delivery of these services as evidenced by the increase in their share of total local government monetary allocations (that is, from 3 to 8 percent) over this same period of time. The part played by townships in the delivery of these kinds of services, however, has been minimal over the last 50 years. The greater role played by special districts and counties is inevitably due to the significant increase in the number of people and businesses choosing to reside or locate in unincorporated areas and who desire and expect the delivery of a number of services historically associated with living in a city. With municipalities often being reticent about providing these services beyond their borders, counties have been agreeable to provide these services if economies of scale can be achieved; alternatively, state legislatures have been persuaded to create special service districts to satisfy unmet service demand.

A review of Table 13.6 provides insight into the role played by counties, municipalities, and special districts for the provision of two of the primary specific services in the municipal-type services category—utilities (e.g., water supply, sewer collection, electric power, natural gas, etc.) and fire protection. Like what was found for municipal-type services generally, one can see that the huge role that municipal governments played at one time in providing utilities and fire protections is no longer the case. More specifically, the proportion of total local government

Table 13.6 Expenditure percentages for selected municipal-type services, 1962 and 2012

	1962			2012		
	County governments	Municipal governments	Special districts	County governments	Municipal governments	Special districts
Utilities	2	79	17	5	54	40
Fire Protection	3	88	4	16	63	15

Source: Figures derived from Table 48 of the U.S. Bureau of the Census, 1962 Census of Governments, *Compendium of Government Finances* (Washington, D.C.: U.S. Government Printing Office) and Table 2 of the U.S. Bureau of the Census, 2012 Census of Governments, *State & Local Finances* located at census.gov//govs/local/historical_data_2012.html. Accessed on April 26, 2017.

spending for utilities and fire protection substantially dropped between 1962 and 2012 from 79 to 54 percent for the former and from 88 to 63 percent for the latter. Concomitantly, note the marked increase in the special district proportion for both services and a moderate increase for counties for fire protection. These trends are undoubtedly the consequence of the rapid increase in the unincorporated area population of the last five decades.

But, do these findings for the provision of municipal-type services, in general, and for fire protection and utilities, in particular, accurately depict the role played by local governments in states that are experiencing rapid growth and also exhibit major differences in the percentage of people residing in unincorporated areas and possess varying degrees of home rule authority? To answer this question, the analysis will be directed to an examination of municipal-type expenditures for counties and special districts in the nation's fastest-growing states—Florida, California, and Texas. These states were selected for separate analysis not only because of their rapid untypical population growth but also because two other characteristics, which set them apart, could have a significant effect on the role played by their local governments as providers of municipal-type services.

First, let's consider the differences in the size of the unincorporated area population in these states as a factor in the provision of municipal-type services in 2012. From Figure 13.3, it can be seen that counties play a much greater role in the provision of these services in Florida than is the case for counties in either California or Texas (or even counties, generally). This is probably because there is a much greater proportion of incorporated area residents in Florida (49 percent compared to 27 and 16 percent in Texas and California, respectively). Since Texas has a larger unincorporated area population than California, one would logically expect that there would be a greater need for the delivery of municipal-type services to Texans living outside a municipality. However, Figure 13.3 indicates that counties are not playing that role. Therefore, if counties are not playing the role of service provider, then who is? Another look at the far-right side of Figure 13.3 reveals that special districts are assuming this responsibility because Texas does not grant a great deal of home rule authority to its counties. It should also be mentioned that special districts in Florida play an important role—although not as much as counties—in the delivery of municipal-type services. While counties in Florida have more home rule authority than counties in Texas and California[4] (and even more so than counties in other states), their ability to raise additional revenue to fund the growing demand for municipal-type services is still quite limited. Suffice it to say, similar patterns (data is not shown here) were observed for the two major services in the municipal-type services category—fire protection and utilities.

Local government service roles in the USA

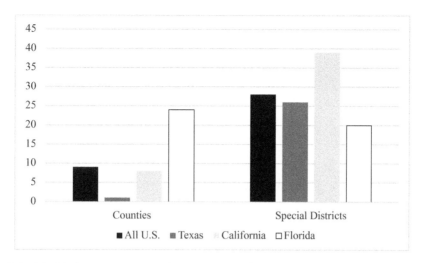

Figure 13.3 Municipal-type service expenditure percentages for U.S., Texas, California, and Florida, 2012

Source: Figures derived from Table 48 of the U.S. Bureau of the Census, 1962 Census of Governments, *Compendium of Government Finances* (Washington, D.C.: U.S. Government Printing Office) and Table 2 of the U.S. Bureau of the Census, 2012 Census of Governments, *State & Local Finances* located at census.gov//govs/local/historical_data_2012.html. Accessed on April 26, 2017.

In addition, these findings suggest that the responsibility that local governments in other states (but especially, counties and special districts) have for providing these kinds of services can also be dictated by the size of the their unincorporated population and the scope of home role authority.

Regional services

Returning once again to Figure 13.2 (see third panel), it is obvious that municipalities historically have been the major providers of regional services, although these governments' share of total local government spending for these kinds of services dropped by about 13 percentage points over the 1962–2012 time period. At the same time, counties and special districts, for the most part, have filled the void left by the diminished role played by municipalities, as their share of total local government expenditures increased by 4 and 9 percentage points, respectively. The role played by townships in providing these type services, however, remained negligible from 1962 to 2012.

The changes observed for the service roles played by municipalities, counties, and special districts are probably the result of several key factors. On the one hand, the reordering of service responsibility for many regional services has been brought about by discernable shifts in the U.S. population from large central cities to suburbia, which includes unincorporated places and satellite cities surrounding the core/major city of metropolitan statistical areas (MSAs). Such population swings have underscored the realization that service needs in areas like solid waste and sewage disposal, natural resource conservation/environmental protection, cultural amenities, parks and recreational facilities, economic development and redevelopment, housing for the poor, and airports are increasingly viewed as region-wide issues and concerns that require an area-wide or county-wide response. On the other hand, municipalities have been becoming

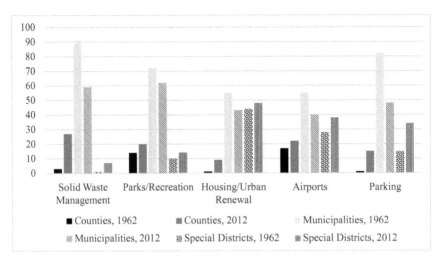

Figure 13.4 County, Municipal and Special District Expenditure Percentages for selected regional Services, 1962 and 2012

reluctant to continue to provide some services (e.g., social amenities, parks and recreational facilities, and airports) that are seen as a "free-loader" phenomenon as referred to above. Over the last several decades, large central cities and their citizens have taken the position that they will no longer "go it alone" in funding services, in which residents of metropolitan satellite cities in the MSA and unincorporated parts of the county increasingly utilize but pay little or nothing in the way to finance them.

The most conspicuous changes in fiscal responsibility between 1962 and 2012 occurred in five regional service areas (see Figure 13.4). In each area, the municipal government share of total local government expenditures declined, with it being particularly pronounced for solid waste management and parking. It can also be seen that county governments and special districts were accounting for a larger part of regional service spending by 2012. This was most evident for counties in those areas where municipalities were doing less (solid waste management and parking), while the special districts role had expanded most noticeably in parking and airports. Furthermore, it is important to note that special districts have always been an important provider of housing and urban redevelopment services and even rival the role played by municipalities.

Another service area that warrants separate consideration is transit. While transit was not listed as an expenditure category in 1962 by the Census of Governments in its *Compendium of Government Finances*, provision of this service has been the primary responsibility of special districts. By 2012, special districts accounted for over one-half of all local government spending for this service (58 percent), while municipalities accounted for another 35 percent of the money spent for this service. Counties accounted for almost all of the remaining 8 percent of transit funding (township contributed only 0.1 percent).

Natural resources conservation also deserves mention as well as a special case since counties and special districts have always accounted for the bulk of spending in area. In 2012, these two governments' spending for conservation efforts constituted around 84 percent of all local government expenditures for this purpose (that is, 39 percent for counties and 45 percent for special districts.

To varying degrees, all regional services have region- or area-wide implications. As such, municipal government usually do not have the legal or moral responsibility to address these kinds of service needs. Sometimes, the service need requires a county-wide response and, at other times, a multi-county response. Many times, service needs emanating from environmental degradation, conservation consciousness, urban decay, metropolitan sprawl, traffic gridlock, recreational and social amenity desires, and inadequate/substandard housing defy a simple or parochial solution where each government in a metropolitan area tries to craft its own response. Put, differently, the service needs mentioned above and the issues that give rise to them know no political boundaries, as pollution and urban decay, for example, do not stop at the city limits or even county lines. This means that governments such as counties and special districts, which typically possess area-wide authority and coordinating abilities, are the best equipped to respond adequately.

County, municipal, township, and special district spending priorities

Another important way to view the service provision roles played by the four types of local governments is to consider the importance or priority that each assigns to the delivery of traditional, municipal-type, and regional services. Looking at Figure 13.5, it is clear that local governments have a history of assigning the greatest importance and thereby have allocated the largest proportion of their collective resources to the provision of traditional kinds of services—roughly 50 percent or greater. This includes not only mandated services like health, welfare, and judicial/legal services but also staple services like roads and highways, police, financial and other administrative (collection of vital statistics, supervision of elections, agricultural advice, etc.) functions, and construction and maintenance of public buildings and allied facilities. Still, a closer look at Figure 13.5 shows that local governments were dedicating a somewhat smaller percentage of their budgets to traditional services over the last fifty years—that is, 50 percent in 2012 versus 54 percent in 1962. It appears that this reduction in the emphasis on traditional services coupled with a slight decrease in emphasis on municipal-type services has meant that local governments

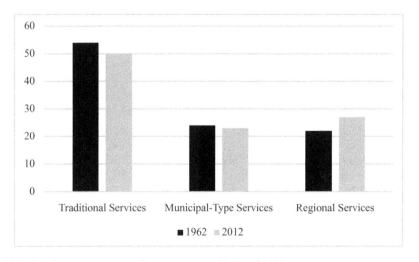

Figure 13.5 Local government spending percentages, 1962 and 2012

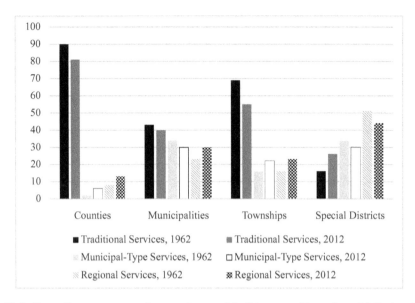

Figure 13.6 Expenditure percentages for counties, municipalities, townships and special districts, 1962 and 2012

have been able to redirect a fairly larger proportion of their resources to urban-type services (27 percent in 2012 compared to 22 percent in 1962).

Beyond these general observations about expenditure priorities, what priority does each type of local government assign to the provision of traditional, municipal-type, and regional services? Figure 13.6 will be helpful in answering this question.

County governments

Given our earlier discussion about the rationale for the creation of county governments as well as the findings in the first analytical section, it is not surprising to see that counties have assigned the greatest priority to the provision of traditional kinds of services, but especially to those services that the state mandates them to provide in counties' role as administrative arms or satellite offices of the state government. As the first panel in Figure 13.6 indicates, counties have allotted 80 percent or greater of their money to deliver these kinds of services since 1962. This means that counties place much less emphasis on providing both municipal-type and regional services, although they have been directing a little more attention to both of these services areas in recent years. The finding that counties place a much greater emphasis on traditional services probably has always been the case and is supported by some historical accounts. However, we cannot confirm this assumption, since the U.S. Census Bureau did not publish these data prior to 1962.

As could be predicted, the specific traditional services that are assigned the high priority by counties in 2012 (as evidenced by the proportion of the total resources allocated to them) are ones that are mandated. These include judicial/legal/corrections (15 percent), public welfare (14 percent), hospitals (14 percent), and health (11 percent). Other important but non-mandated staple services that local citizens have come to expect from their county governments are police (10 percent), highways and roads (8 percent), and financial and other administration (6 percent).

Municipal governments

Further inspection of Figure 13.6 (second panel) reveals that municipal governments have a more balanced set of priorities. Like county governments, municipalities make the delivery of traditional services their highest priority but not nearly to the degree that counties do; the proportion of municipal spending for traditional services have hovered between 43 (1962) and 40 (2012) percent. The provision of municipal-type services is a close second in their priority rankings, with the proportion of municipal expenditures devoted to them ranging from 34 (1962) to 30 percent (2012). The slight decrease in the percentage of municipal government resources allocated to both traditional and municipal-type services over the 1962–2012 period means that these governments were able to devote a somewhat larger proportion of their money to provide regional services. In other words, municipalities were spending 30 percent of their resources on urban-type services by 2012 compared to 23 percent in 1962.

The highest municipal government priorities among traditional services in 2012 include police (14 percent) and highways and roads (8 percent), while the top municipal-type service priorities are utilities (21 percent) and fire protection (7 percent). Between 1962 and 2012, municipalities were assigning a slightly higher priority to two regional services—transit (up from 0 to 5 percent) and sewage (up from 6 to 8 percent).

Townships

The priority given by townships to each of our three service areas is consistent with their purpose and role assigned to them when they were established by the various states. Simply put, special districts, being subdivisions of counties, were created primary for the purpose of assisting county governments in the performance of their duties—both mandated and non-mandated. As the data in Figure 13.6 suggests, townships assign the greatest priority to traditional services, even though the proportion of funds they allot to these kinds of services dropped from 69 percent in 1962 to 55 percent in 2012. As a consequence, townships began to place a somewhat higher priority on the provision of both municipal-type and regional services (note the proportion increases from 16 to 22 percent and 16 to 23 percent, respectively) between 1962 and 2012. This was most likely the result of the greater spending for services in these two areas for townships that were located in highly urbanized areas or on the fringe of a major MSA.

Like county governments, townships place a high priority on the provision of traditional services such as highways and roads and police that made up 22 and 16 percent, respectively, of their expenditures in 2012. Township spending priorities also signify the importance that they attach to two municipal-type services—utilities and fire protection (each being allotted 9 percent of their budgets in 2012). Moreover, given the increasing urban character of some townships, it is logical that they were allocating a somewhat larger proportion of their resources in 2012 versus 1962 to three regional services—sewage (up from 7 to 9 percent) and solid waste management and parks and recreation (each up from 4 to 6 percent).

Special districts

Owing to the fact that special districts are commonly established for a variety of purposes and have flexibility in service boundaries, it is reasonable to find that they still assign the greatest importance to the provision of regional services. In 2012, special districts devoted the largest proportion of their expenditures (44 percent) to deliver these kind of services; however, this is considerably less what they allocated in 1962 (51 percent). Special districts make the delivery of municipal-type services their second highest priority, with a little less than one-third of all of their expenditures allotted for these kinds of services over the last 50 years. While the provision of traditional services is the lowest priority for special districts, there was a noticeable jump in the proportion of these governments' resources dedicated to them in recent years (26 percent 2012 compared to 17 percent in 1962). This can be interpreted as special districts increasingly being called upon to help provide services normally delivered by counties or municipalities.

Among regional services, special districts in 2012 devoted the largest proportion of expenditures to transit (16 percent), housing and urban redevelopment (12 percent), and sewage (6 percent), while utilities (25 percent) was the biggest spending item among municipal-type services. The increase in the proportion of special district spending for traditional services from 1962 to 2012 was driven largely by the doubling of the resources (from 10 to 20 percent allotted to hospitals.

Conclusions

The familiar and important role played by U.S. local governments in the provision of various services at a local level will probably continue unabated. Nevertheless, the service and spending patterns and trends highlighted in this chapter are always subject to change in both the near and distant future. In point of fact, several ongoing situations/events and others gaining force over the horizon could be the harbingers of change and thus pose a significant challenge to local governments' ability to sustain current service levels. These challenges can be both externally- and internally-driven.

One external challenge appears to be the lingering aftermath of the most recent Great Recession (see Gordon 2012). Local governments, but especially counties, municipalities, and townships, continue to grapple with the loss of revenue from their most plentiful and reliable source (property tax), as real estate assessed values that plummeted during the Great Recession have yet to rebound back to pre-recession levels in many areas. Compounding the problem was the massive number of home foreclosures and people abandoning their homes due to their mortgages "being underwater." Current reports indicate that property tax revenues for local governments are still lagging behind what they were prior to the onset of the Great Recession (see Fisher and Wassmer 2016; Dadayan 2012). In fact, some scholars and practitioners have raised the question as to whether it would be prudent for local officials to rethink current reliance on the property tax (Alm, Buschman, and Sjoquist 2012).

To make matters worse, local governments in states like California, Florida, Michigan, Wisconsin, and Massachusetts, among others, have also had to deal with the backlash of citizens who demand tax relief because local governments have had to raise property tax rates on fewer homeowners and business owners to make up for the loss of property tax revenue due to declining property values. Such citizens have been aided in their cause by politically sensitive state legislatures that have mandated local governments rollback property tax rates (for example, the Florida legislature required local governments in 2007 to reset tax rates to 2006 levels). In other instances, state legislatures have been in partnership with constituents to facilitate voter referenda that have added exemptions that further reduce property tax yields.

A second external challenge posed to local governments comes more recently and is in the form of federal budget cuts proposed by the Trump administration for Fiscal Year 2018. This could potentially result in the loss of billions of dollars of federal funding that local as well as state governments have depended on for several decades (see Parrott, Reich, and Shapiro 2017; Harkness 2017). Major areas projected for cuts include: health care (primarily Medicaid but also protection against infectious diseases) and welfare (covers such things as child care assistance to low- and moderate-income families, job training, and SNAP—formerly known as food stamps). As is shown above, health and welfare are two of the costliest traditional services usually provided by counties. Federal aid cuts are also proposed for Community Development Block Grants that fund urban renewal and community redevelopment (including massive infrastructure) projects and public housing for low- to moderate-income families. Congress is also considering the elimination of federal income tax exemptions for taxes paid to state and local governments, as well as taxing interest earnings from state and local government bonds.

Related to the proposed reductions in federal aid and congressional actions that could reduce state revenues is the possibility that local governments could also be the victim of cuts in state aid and revenue sharing. In the past when states' revenues have been squeezed, there has been a clear pattern of them cutting back on aid and shared revenues to their local governments (see Benton 2018). A number of observers of state and local finances have used the metaphor "fend-for-yourself" federalism to explain this phenomenon (e.g., see Shannon 1987; Wright 1988).

Another external challenge is long-standing: local government officials, but particularly those at the county and municipal levels, often complain that they are not given enough latitude in fiscal decision making and therefore lobby for greater home rule authority Their position is that their constituents and not the legislature is enough of a safeguard over the public purse. While over 40 states have given their counties and municipalities greater home rule authority in recent years, these governments' ability to maintain service levels during downturns in the economy and cuts in federal fiscal assistance is sometimes pushed to the limit and fiscal stress and distress is commonplace (see Benton 2010, 2012, 2018).

A final challenge is the burgeoning, omnipresent threat of severe fiscal instability—even insolvency—due to burdensome pension obligations. Entities that regularly monitor localities' underfunded pension plans (for example, Center for State and Local Government Excellence, Rockefeller Institute of Government, and the Pew Institute) argue this cannot continue for much longer without their being serious repercussions for local governments. The result could be that local governments will have to shift funds away from vital programs and services to meet current and future pension obligations unless these governments are able to address this.

All of these conditions, situations, and factors will present significant tests to the ability of local governments in their efforts to continue to deliver a large menu of services that the public views as essential while revenue sources, at a minimum, are threatened or, at the worst, declining. Several scenarios are possible. One could entail a reordering of the service priorities of various local governments (but most likely for counties and municipalities) so as to provide an optimum level of services with less expenditure. A second scenario could involve the eventual transfer or change in functional assignment of some services from one local government to another or from a local government to the state government. A third possibility is for local governments to contract out certain services where cost efficiencies can be realized. Then, there is the option of co-producing services in those situations where economies of scale can be achieved. These are possible options if local governments are forced to change their expenditure behavior in light of the realities of their changing environment.

Notes

1 Dillon's Rule was first written in the case of *City of Clinton v. Cedar Rapids and Missouri Railroad Company* (1868).
2 School districts are not included in this analysis because they provide only one service—education, while the other types of local governments deliver a large numbers and variety of services, but this is especially the case for counties and municipalities.

3 Counties exist in 48 states, with Rhode Island and Connecticut abolishing them in 1842 and 1958, respectively; Massachusetts has abolished 11 of its original 16 counties since 1997.
4 Currently, 20 of Florida's 67 counties have achieved charter status, which means that they have more home rule authority than other counties. However, more latitude has been granted them in the area of structure of government than in fiscal flexibility.

References

Alm, James, Robert D. Buschman, and David L. Sjoquist. 2012. *Rethinking Local Government Reliance on the Property Tax*. Tulane Economic Working Paper Series, Working Paper 1215. New Orleans, LA: Tulane University.

Benton, J. Edwin. 2002. *Counties as Service Delivery Agents: Changing Expectations and Roles*. Westport, CT: Praeger.

Benton, J. Edwin. 2010. Trends in Local Government Revenues: The Old, the New, and the Future. In Gregory K. Ingram and Yu-Hung Hong (eds), *Municipal Revenues and Land Policies*, 81–112. Cambridge, MA: Lincoln Land Institute of Land Policy.

Benton, J. Edwin. 2012. State–City and State–County Fiscal Relations: A Look at the Past and Present and a Glimpse at the Future. In Jack W. Meek and Kurt Thurmaier (eds), *Networked Governance: The Future of Intergovernmental Management*, 39–63. Washington, DC: CQ Press.

Benton, J. Edwin. 2018. Intergovernmental Relations in the Early 21st Century: Lingering Images of Earlier Phases or Emergence of a New Phase? In Carl W. Stenburg and David Hamilton (eds), *Intergovernmental Relations in the United States: Reflections and Directions*, 15–36. New York: Routledge.

Bowman, Ann O'M., and Richard C. Kearney. 2008. *State and Local Government*, 7th edition. Boston, MA: Houghton Mifflin.

Dadayan, Lucy. 2012. *The Impact of the Great Recession on Local Property Taxes*. Albany, NY: Nelson A. Rockefeller Institute of Government.

Dillon, John F. 1911. *Commentaries on the Laws of Municipal Corporations*, 5th edition. Boston, MA: Little, Brown, and Company.

Donovan, Todd, Christopher Z. Mooney, and Daniel A. Smith. 2009. *State and Local Politics: Institutions and Reform*. Belmont, CA: Wadsworth/Cengage Learning.

Fisher, Ronald C., and Robert W. Wassmer. 2016. State–Local Government Fiscal Conditions after the Great Recession. *State Tax Notes* (July): 23–25.

Gordon, Tracy. 2012. *State and Local Budgets and the Great Recession*. Washington, DC: Brookings Institute.

Harkness, Peter A. 2017. Trump-Watching from City Hall. *Governing* 30 (May): 16–17.

Parrott, David Reich, and Isaac Shapiro. 2017. *Trump's Skinny Budget Will Be Short on Details, But Troubling Fiscal Agenda Is Emerging*. Washington, DC: Center on Budget and Policy Priorities.

Shannon, John. 1987. The Return to Fend-For-Yourself Federalism: The Reagan Mark. *Intergovernmental Perspective* (Summer–Fall): 34–37.

U.S. Bureau of the Census. 2014. Annual Surveys of State and Local Government Finances, Table 1. Retrieved on 8 April 2017 from www.census.gov/govs/local.

Wright, Deil S. 1988. *Understanding Intergovernmental Relations*, 3rd edition. Belmont, CA: Brooks/Cole.

14
PUBLIC ENTREPRENEURSHIP

Is local government necessary to deliver economic development?

Lorraine Johnston and John Fenwick

Introduction

This chapter is concerned with the role of local government in initiating and supporting public entrepreneurship, a role which is increasingly important in times of austerity but simultaneously more difficult to achieve due to constraints on public resources. Public entrepreneurship may underpin the innovation necessary in troubled times, requiring different skills on the part of public managers than those traditionally possessed by bureaucratic actors. Innovation may also be secured through local government functioning as a collaborator in enterprising public/private institutions, bounded by place and community as local government, throughout Europe and elsewhere, remains territorially defined. The question arises of whether entrepreneurship is ultimately assisted or hindered by the received structures and cultures of local government.

Bartlett and Dibben (2002) refer to local government as 'champions' and 'sponsors' of entrepreneurship. In his recent update of his article, Bartlett (2017) argues that much is unchanged since the first paper was written, with the significant exception that there is now more emphasis upon 'open innovation' wherein entrepreneurship is based upon open-ended collaboration between actors and institutions manifested, for instance, in local authority shared services. Conceivably this 'opens up' entrepreneurship but it also raises potentially problematic issues, particularly those linked with the governance and co-ordination of collaborative partnerships (Fenwick, Johnston Miller and McTavish 2012) and place-making (Hambleton 2015b).

The chapter begins with a detailed consideration of the nature of public entrepreneurship, its relationship to innovation and the importance of tribal governance. We then go on to consider local authority enterprises in more detail, in particular focussing upon the importance of place to the local community. The discussion is then positioned in an international context of public entrepreneurship before offering overall conclusions.

What is public entrepreneurship?

A synthesis of public entrepreneurship

Public entrepreneurship is synonymous with innovation policy and attempts to introduce entrepreneurship into the public sector (Leyden and Link 2015; Audretsch and Link 2016). These ideas reflect an emergent international theoretical literature (see for example, Zerbinati and Souitaris 2005). Seminal authors equate public entrepreneurship with 'collective action' (Olsen 1965; Ostrom 1990, 2014) and efforts to create a 'public value' mission (Moore 1994) enacted through strategic management processes that enhance government competition. Klein et al. (2010: 1) express public entrepreneurship as a nebulous term which they argue is 'enabled and constrained by a political system and institutional context'.

An assortment of ideas constructs public entrepreneurship as multi-method and multi-dimensional (Schnellenbach 2007). The recent resurgence of the public entrepreneurship term, driven to some extent by technological expansion (Leyden and Link 2015) and new global uncertainties, has driven government institutions to focus attention towards the supposition that entrepreneurial belief systems can enable innovation strategies that boost service delivery mechanisms and, in effect, to 'do more with less'. Klein et al. (2010) call for greater responsiveness to the constraints of public entrepreneurship. Similarly, Liddle (2016) questions the oversight of public entrepreneurship from within the mainstream entrepreneurship literature. The public entrepreneurship discourse is fortified by historical economic, political and management influences and underpinned by state-centred (Swyngedouw 2006) 'urban entrepreneurialism' in policy-making (Pike et al. 2017: 52).

Conversely, an upsurge in public entrepreneurship studies that focus on local government has sought to enhance the scope of public value through knowledge transactions and innovation-led local economic development (Benington and Moore 2011; Leyden and Link, 2015). Yet the challenge of public entrepreneurship is that it remains an assortment of categorisations, divergences, fads and polemic (Llewellyn and Jones 2003). Edwards et al. (2002: 252) distinguish public entrepreneurship through far-reaching features of 'service innovation'; 'new venture creation' and 'innovation in service delivery'. In contrast to this, Swyngedouw (2006, 1991) depicts competing paradigms and intersectional concepts as diverse as 'new governmentability', 'governance-beyond-the-state' and 'social innovation'. He argues these 'institutional fixes' operate at the core of theories of public entrepreneurship (ibid.). Public entrepreneurship in local government pursues opportunities beyond 'top down' policy-making towards more pragmatic 'outside in' tactics. Scholars point to dimensions of reciprocity, cohesiveness and creativity in public entrepreneurship relationships. The multidimensional nature of public entrepreneurship exemplifies the struggle of its peculiarity and eccentricity to evolve innovative, if untried, methods of doing 'what matters'.

Exploratory studies locate public entrepreneurship practice at the intersection of ambiguity and risk-taking. As Boyett (1996: 49) sums the matter up, public entrepreneurship

> occurs in the public sector where there is an uncertain environment, a devolution of power, and at the same time re-allocation of resource ownership, to unit management level. It is driven by those individuals, particularly susceptible to the 'manipulation' of their stakeholders and with a desire for a high level social 'self-satisfaction', who have the ability to spot market opportunities and who are able through follower 'manipulation' to act on them.

New public entrepreneurship thinking is a kaleidoscopic paradigm that seeks to transfer entrepreneurship to the public sector. Prevailing Schumpeterian notions imagine that innovation characteristics exist in a continuous process of 'creative destruction' (Schumpeter 1934). Acting as responsive 'agents for change' (Schneider et al. 1995), and 'alert' to the economic function in the market through 'opportunity recognition' (Kirzner 1973, 1997, 2000), these accepted wisdoms perceive that innovation is driven by 'public entrepreneurs' (Schneider et al. 1995; Ács et al. 2014) embedded in a 'national system of entrepreneurship' (Ács et al. 2014: 477). Here, Ács et al. (ibid.: 476) challenge the quandary of 'entrepreneurship' as a 'silent' accessory in the collective 'systems of innovation' (Edquist and Johnson 1997; Lundvall 1999). As a result, public entrepreneurship is a contested space (Mintrom 1997). Studies overlook the distinctive roles of public entrepreneurs in entrepreneurship as characterised by Joseph Schumpeter (1934) in fashioning the evolution of economic development strategies beyond the market (Feldman et al. 2016).

Correspondingly, the public–entrepreneurship synthesis also draws on Adam Smith's (1976) earlier classical liberalist ideas in the *Theory of Moral Sentiments* and *The Wealth of Nations*, which interpret public value to be a distinctive characteristic in contrast to 'trickle down' modes of entrepreneurship. Drawing on Phillipson (2010), characteristics of public value are intrinsic in normative visualisations of outdated top-down hierarchical 'command and control' public policy mechanisms. In response to Smith, Phillipson (ibid.) invokes 'human beings who inhabit the types of society about which he writes are driven by moral, intellectual and aesthetic as well as material needs'. To some extent, the above sentiments paved the way for a new wave of innovative policy studies, resolute in their interpretation that public entrepreneurship matters for local government (Bernier 2014).

More contemporary studies observe the influence of public entrepreneurship in enterprising partnerships and are informed by the co-evolution of mutual public-private values (Mazzucato, 2015). These studies involve ideas of self-governance, co-creation and collaborative innovation in partnerships as a means to restructure socio-political and social-economic interactions. Fundamentally, these interpretations show the capacity of socio-political systems to impact upon innovation. In addition, endogenous and exogenous factors influence rational decision making in policy communities. This point of divergence confirms that socio-economic innovation systems can disrupt exogenous economic development (Myerson 1991). Wider studies indicate that purposeful interaction habitually employs game theory in an effort to grasp the features of cooperation when exposed to rational decision making. Such choices guide how actors operate in uncertainty contexts. Here, risk taking is an element of enterprising behaviour. In particular, it proves by what means conflict and uncertainty in decision-making informs a process of brokering at the interface of enterprising places (Crowley et al. 2012) and interactive forms of co-operative strategic partnerships.

Smith's (2014) inductive Swedish study alerts us to the challenge of public entrepreneurship and the need to maintain institutional distinctiveness in public and private partnership, perhaps exposing 'public entrepreneurship' as a contradiction. Notwithstanding this, Boyett (1996) asserts that the private sector through necessity can learn from public entrepreneurship to create 'public value'. Despite this, studies understate the multifaceted nature of public entrepreneurship. In making sense of the embeddedness and intricacies of public entrepreneurship relations, Jessop (1999: 390) drew attention to these strategic relationships through his account of 'reinventing government' towards enterprising 'governance' in public services (see also Osborne 1993). By the same token, Tilly's (1999: 418–419) research alerts us to the 'repertoires of contention' in an attempt to validate the strategic-relational approach she depicts as a 'place of culture in state-linked social processes'. Tilly is persuasive in her consideration of strategic-relational policies which, she argues, display aspects of conflict together with skirmishes that crucially bond distinctive social characteristics. Her four-stage typology exemplifies:

- First, 'embeddedness in complex networks among multiple parties having competing interests'.
- Second, 'engagement in communication among those parties and coordination of their interactions'.
- Third, the 'use of compressed codes whose comprehension depends heavily on prior experience and previous interaction with the same parties',
- Finally, 'activation of previously negotiated agreements, implicit and explicit, concerning the conditions and limits of different sorts of interaction among the parties' (Tilly 1999: 418–419).

Public entrepreneurship and innovation

Hartley (2005: 27) identifies public entrepreneurship as a process of open innovation in public services (see also Moore and Hartley 2008). Consistent with this, public entrepreneurship studies view open innovation as rooted in entrepreneurial governance mechanisms and the political arrangements of local government. Similarly, local government studies concerned with collective action (Olsen 1965; Ostrom 1990, 1998, 2014) personify enterprise as a detectable capital resource that originates from open innovation. Significant institutional studies recognise aspects such as cross fertilisation, rational choice, trust, reciprocity and reputation (Ostrom 1998) to be important. In particular, original studies present 'public entrepreneurs' as 'heroic' with a capacity to adapt the 'rules of the game' (Mintrom 1997; Ostrom 1998; Klein et al. 2010). This judgement clarifies the symbolic nature of public entrepreneurs as 'agents for change' (Schneider et al. 1995). In consequence, as Cantillon's (1973) earlier classification reveals, capitalists in pursuit of profit espouse capabilities that exploit human and capital resources. More exclusively 'added value' that inspires innovative simulations leads to success in revenue terms. In turn, 'entrepreneurial profits' are gained by the accomplishments of public entrepreneurs (ibid.). Moreover, this demonstrates that public entrepreneurs play a key role in risk-taking. Of course, risk-taking opportunities may be depleted in a context of limited resources. This may be countered by efforts toward multi-level governance: Hartley (2005), for instance, contends that public entrepreneurs are competitive when they co-exist in a process of 'networked' governance to deliver public services (Rhodes 1996). This point clearly reveals the limitations of local government acting alone: something it simply cannot do in the light of ever-diminishing resources.

We now consider the relevance of 'tribal governance' in framing our understanding of public entrepreneurship and, indeed, governance as a whole.

Tribal governance and local government sovereignty

Tribal governance is a feature of indigenous communities seeking state sovereignty and self-governance (Niezen 2003; Hibbard 2006; Shaw 2008). From this perspective, local government is sovereign and its autonomy is representative of community governance through devolved powers. Ortiz (2002: 466) regards sovereignty as a 'feudal system of medieval Europe'. In the same vein, he contends sovereignty 'is a right of self-government' (ibid.: 460). Further, he claims tribes are 'stepchildren in the family of government' due to their capability to assume 'many powers equal to the states but remain subordinate to the federal government and that government is the trustee of tribal lands but more often acts as the taker of tribal lands and therefore raises a potential conflict of interest'. In Ortiz's (2002: 459) study he posits American Indian and Alaskan native tribal governance to be traditionally rooted in an 'awareness of tribes'. Conversely, as Papillon (2011) explains, an alertness to intrinsic tribal characteristics such as past tribal histories, tribal cultures and tribal social values can be beneficial in progressing tribal governance. Of fundamental importance in how tribal governance works is the extraordinary ongoing academic debate, which draws attention to the inherent struggle in ambiguous local government and local community relations. This characteristic illustrates the rigidity in intergovernmental interactions and demonstrates the problematic nature of state-tribe collaborative dealings.

Extensive and more critical European studies draw attention to multi-level governance and a wealth of rich culture in tribal communities (Nelles and Alcantara 2011; Marks and Hooge 2004; Ongaro et al. 2010). Multi-level governance studies assert that the characteristics of tribal governance support the spread of creativity and knowledge in the advancement of tribal governance developments, particularly in multi-level governance regimes (Nelles and Durand 2014). Explicitly international scholars annotate a plethora of ground-breaking legal challenges and exploits in case studies – as demonstrated in the legal action of Canada, the United States, Australia and New Zealand federal governments in direct competition with indigenous tribes (Alcantara and Nelles 2013). Case studies portray the consequences of futile intergovernmental state-tribe indecisiveness. Moreover, indecisiveness was a central motive in the failure of intergovernmental inaction in state-tribal disagreements (Papillon 2011; Nelles and Alcantara 2011). These divergences illustrate the fiasco which impacts upon state-tribe collaborations, particularly when faced with obligatory governance regimes. On the contrary, multi-level governance studies observe that enforced state-tribe interactions also demonstrate the capability of actors to revert to ideal types – conflict administration, arbitration and resolution of purpose are renowned characteristics and the outcomes of unstable and unbalanced leadership positions, which as Papillon (2011) explains, if left undetected can unsettle marginal boundaries. Correspondingly, the consequences of forced state-tribal interfaces are testament to reciprocal interactions that transpire in an assigned space (Marks and Hooge 2004). Conversely, European studies illustrate that substitute strategies counteract more dominant state-tribe behaviours. In the same way, as Papillon (2011) stresses, the close examination of state-tribe traits observes that primary personas imitate contradictory characteristics – scepticism, mistrust and the vulnerability of tribes. Fluctuating traits are an essential component of fluctuating path dependencies particularly those that seek to overcome institutional, political and cultural restraints. Moreover, as Papillon (2011: 293) argues 'institutional layering' can adapt behaviours and is a useful mechanism in which 'actors position themselves *within* and *in relation* to the existing institutional framework' to change planning tactics.

Moreover, state-tribal scholars elucidate that collaborative relationships evolve over time. Thus far, these studies chart the danger of overlooking vital facets – context, diversity and histories. These studies contend that a cautious approach in conjunction with reflexivity is a way forward. Similarly, the preservation of these aforementioned prerequisites is essential to gain trust in state-tribe interactions prior to evolving reciprocal solutions between – enterprise, state and local government. Broome and Christakis (1988) report 'conflict' is characteristic when tribal governance is deficient in community consensus. They caution the need to pay attention to cultural tribal governance concerns as 'a lack of intentional efforts to build consensus; poor communication; differing perceptions in the distribution of power, resources, recognition . . . and inadequate institutions to deal with problems' (Broome and Christakis 1988: 111).

Hitherto, Foucault (1991; see also Lindroth 2011) found characteristics of both power and resistance feature within indigenous communities in their struggle between tribal governance and the State. Latterly, the policy trend towards community self-governance and autonomy necessitates the expansion of local government sovereignty to collect local taxes. Similarly, this rapid shift devolved decision making responsibilities for economic development from the State to local enterprise partnerships, generating compliant local government within national State actor relationships. As mentioned above, public entrepreneurship can be traced back to transformations in local government and the dynamic bond between state and locality. Thus the idea appears increasingly fashionable in the social sciences. Notable studies exemplify a series of factors that influence this progressive trend.

- First, the drive towards public entrepreneurship is embedded in theories that reject the administrative nation state in favour of decentralised power through a denationalised, deregulated and self-governed state.
- Second, the legitimacy of the welfare state's role and function exemplifies a shift from 'government to governance' (Harvey 1989; Rhodes 1996).
- Third, neoliberal governments exhibit the sporadic nature of 'new public management' policy reforms, leading to fragmented policies (Rhodes 1996).

Consistent throughout the public entrepreneurship discourse are attempts towards decentralised decision making powers, often anticipated through collective action, trust and mutuality in partnerships: all critical for self-governance. This is extensive in Perkmann's (2007: 861) comparative study of cross-border governance in European city regions of EUREGIO (Germany/Netherlands), Viadrina (Poland/Germany) and Tyrol Euro (Austria/Italy). He found administrative and institutional aspects exist in multi-level governance structures and these relationships influence city regions' absorptive capacity. Essentially, diversity is a fundamental characteristic of cross border institutional governance. As a result, diversity impacts on public entrepreneurship and the motivation for policy entrepreneurship. Correspondingly, as Nelles and Durand's (2014: 104–105) study of the progressive city regions of Lille and Luxembourg show, de-bordering city regions can steer them towards the 'intensification of functional interdependencies and the institutionalisation of informally defined cross-border metropolitan spaces'. Moreover, they reason that liberal cross border structures require time to foster territorial and political capabilities. At this juncture, more sustainable cities necessitate the 'coordination of policies at multiple scales and across institutionally diverse territories' (ibid.: 120). Furthermore, they concede that adaptations of new institutional forms and innovative political space may be interpreted as 'political rescaling' (ibid.).

In summary, the concept of public entrepreneurship presented so far in this chapter represents a multifaceted notion that is embedded in past historical representations that have emerged over time. These diverse influences, including academic disciplines and policy debates, illustrate the wide-ranging opinions and often conflicting archetypical views that emerge from studies of public entrepreneurship and its relationship with local government. Moreover, the diversity inherent in public entrepreneurship is evocative of a more holistic approach in which to view and understand broader interpretations of the idea. These interpretations offer investigative methodologies associated with our focus on more public modes of entrepreneurial governance (Harvey 1989). Moreover, the review of extant public entrepreneurship theories presented here offers a conceptual framework in which to depict the essential characteristics of more entrepreneurial forms of local government, enriching our understanding of public entrepreneurship.

We now consider the importance of place in the understanding of local entrepreneurship.

Local partnerships and place-making

Local governments throughout Europe, as elsewhere, are bounded by territory and defined by place: the leaders of our great cities and small municipalities alike are linked to the area they serve. On one level this is unremarkable: even if only for pragmatic reasons the scope of local administration must by definition by linked to locality. On another level however the nature of 'place' is both more important and more problematic. Place offers the opportunity to examine more closely the remit of local partnership and of local governance.

Hambleton and Sweeting (2014) consider the practice of local leadership in Europe, with a particular focus on directly elected mayors in urban areas. This includes the institutional design of local government, the 'outward facing' nature of leadership, the relationships between elected figures and paid officials, and the links between leaders and followers (Hambleton and Sweeting 2014: 316–317). This emphasis upon 'place-based leadership' (Hambleton 2015a, 2015b) raises the question of how partnerships and collaboration are to be managed – and by whom. The 'outward facing' nature of local urban leadership echoes the call for 'open collaboration' discussed above. Yet the focus of Hambleton and Sweeting upon executive mayors creates some problems, in particular the question of how far such individuals represent real 'places' (rather than artificial administrative areas) at all (Fenwick and Elcock 2016).

How then might we approach the links between place and local entrepreneurship? Hambleton (2015b) has examined the 'new civic leadership' in Germany and Australia and we may consider the extent to which such leadership characterises attempts at local entrepreneurship. This particularly involves consideration of local actors brought together to achieve economic development. To some degree elected executive mayors may succeed in doing this but experience is highly uneven in England (Elcock and Fenwick 2012) and in Germany (Wollmann 2014). The real issue is the extent to which (and how) place-based leadership may play a role in 'releasing energies' – especially the entrepreneurial energies with which we are concerned – even in the light of financial constraints (Hambleton and Howard 2013).

Releasing entrepreneurial dynamism has a direct link to modes of governance and this takes us back to the role of local government and its basis in indigenous communities. There is a time lag in this relationship. Modes of local governance in Europe were largely forged at a time of confident public spending. Local authorities served to distribute public funds and to raise funds locally and directly (albeit decreasingly so in the UK) but as austerity has become the normal climate for raising and spending money so the local link with entrepreneurship has become ever stronger.

International examples of public entrepreneurship in local government

Pike, Rodríguez-Pose and Tomaney (2017) have reviewed the international practice of local and regional development and the evolution of competing theoretical perspectives. From their discussion it is significant to point to the relevance of governance, whether through mayors or other institutional arrangements. 'Well-functioning institutions enable human flourishing in cities and regions, but they can also facilitate regressive and unproductive forms of development' (Pike et al. 2017: 52). This is important for it casts doubt on many of the debates about governance of the local area such as whether the mayoral system works or not. It depends. The local government level is crucial: Graute (2016) points out, for instance, that the UN Sustainable Development goals adopted in 2015 'cannot be achieved without being implemented at a local level'. But the manner of implementation can vary widely. The solution is to find local ways of leading 'economic development' that fit the circumstances of the country and the locality. For the purpose of this chapter we adopt Feldman et al.'s definition of economic development:

> the expansion of capacities that contribute to the advancement of society through the realization of individuals', firms' and communities' potential.
> *(Feldman et al. 2016: 8)*

Likewise:

> Economic development is a sustained increase in prosperity and quality of life realized through innovation, lowered transaction costs, and the utilizations of capabilities towards the responsible production and diffusion of goods and services. Economic development requires effective institutions grounded in norms of openness, tolerance for risk, appreciation for diversity, and confidence in the realisation of mutual gain for the public and the private sector. Economic development is essential to creating the conditions for economic growth and ensuring our economic future.
> *(Feldman et al. 2016: 10)*[1]

Furthermore, they argue that economic development 'occurs when individual agents have the opportunity to develop the capacities that allow them to actively engage and contribute to the economy' (ibid.: 7).

Lee (2016) refers to local authorities with similar objective characteristics being likely to work together in economic development, and she perhaps significantly suggests that this tends to happen in closed network relationships – in contrast to the open collaboration we refer to above.

Unlike closed network relationships, open collaboration is characteristic of collective and networked community governance and, as local government studies illustrate, is more useful in the development of cross boundary independencies particularity those embedded in intergovernmental and inter-institutional practices in network relationships (Stoker 2005). For example, in a Canadian context, Johns et al.'s (2006) collaborative study of federal provincial territorial structures articulates how unforeseen intergovernmental interactions in policy innovations enhanced technical committee relations. By contrast, the OECD discourse on entrepreneurship networks distinguishes between horizontal and vertical interdependencies (Rodrigo et al. 2009). Here, Casson (1982: 119) states, vertical networks connect physical networks and service societies. In contrast, community horizontal networks bond individuals through dispersed knowledge. In turn, horizontal networks can usefully influence economic development. Of practical importance in open collaboration network relationships is the facility to take on social processes within spatial parameters (Johnston et al. 2010). Similarly, Johnston and Blenkinsopp's (2017) empirical study on hybrid local enterprise partnerships report the haphazard and unstructured nature of collective voices in governance regimes as a feature of public entrepreneurship. In local government, economic development policies are also confronted by the fragmented governance in states undergoing stark financial severity. These case studies illustrate the collapse of global fragmented governance in liberal regimes and the complex challenges and causalities in states as dissimilar as Ireland, Greece and Spain (Dellepiane-Avellaneda and Hardiman 2015). For example, Ó Riain (2014) sequences the fragmented governance catastrophe of the Irish boom-and-bust 'Celtic Tiger' initiative.

Swyngedouw et al. (2002: 561) demonstrated that enterprising local governments' contribution to public/private partnerships may have served to implement neoliberal socio-economic development policies and redefined and proliferated local government entrepreneurial roles toward 'steering' economic development. In turn, emergent forms of enterprising government began to inspire 'pluralistic governance' (ibid.: 561) and regulatory governance innovations began to boost economic activity and partnership at multiple levels of government. For example, in the UK, public entrepreneurship flagship studies are exemplified by the Urban Development Community (UDCs) projects of the 1970s and 1980s (Castells 1977; Lawless 1981; Loney 1983) and the UDCs that subsequently emerged in the 1990s (Imrie and Thomas 1999). The innovative potential of public entrepreneurship experiments was consistent with decentralised urban development policies that continue to impact on the enterprise activity of local governments. In particular, auxiliary trials were deemed to be a failure (Loney 1983) due to the constraints of macro level political structures (Catney and Henneberry 2016), and the challenge of social-economic disparities (Crowley et al. 2012) left their mark on what were seen at that time to be entrepreneurial local governments.

Governance and its problems

Considering these transitions, Swyngedouw (2006) draws on Greek tradition to depict the 'Janus face of governance beyond the state'. These relationships illustrate the inherent complexities in the effect of horizontal and vertical social interactions between UDCs and urban renewal policy. Earlier, in a 1997 comparative study of Urban Restructuring and Social Polarization in European Cities (URSPIC), Swyngedouw et al. (2002: 547) drew on the findings of thirteen European cities to express these dichotomies (see also Moulaert et al. 2003). The study states that six European cities – Berlin, Bilbao, Brussels, Dublin, Naples and Vienna – sponsored public entrepreneurship strategies through the 'indirect promotion of entrepreneurship' (Swyngedouw et al., 2002: 547). Fundamentally the findings show competitive strategies that resist entrepreneurial distinctiveness inform a process of so called 'selective deregulation, stripping away red tape, and investment 'partnerships'' (ibid.: 552). According to the OECD, good practice public governance models show 'the shared goal should be the reduction of costs for citizens and businesses and the improvement of service delivery in an efficient way and without additional burden on bureaucracy' (Rodrigo et al. 2009: 10).

Significantly, Swyngedouw's et al. (2002: 547) portrayal of large-scale urban development projects and new forms of entrepreneurial governance in urban policy exemplify how uncertainty and local government prototypes remain misunderstood. Congruent in these studies is the view that competitive European capital cities can reimagine and reconstruct urban space and place-making through outside competition for economic development impact (ibid.). On one hand, the findings validate the need to raise political and cultural aspects in place-making. And on the other, the limitations of flagship urban development corporations (UDPs) to wield decision-making power and influence in local economic development policies to generate innovation in local communities are evident. Further, the study argues that mainstream UDP growth plans simply fragmented territorial governance. Moreover, against this backdrop, the 'functional and physical separation' of authorities create 'limited', 'ambiguous' and 'negative' local impacts (ibid.: 567–568).

The ideas and debates behind 'reinventing government' have been replaced by 'enterprising governments' (Osborne 1993). As mentioned earlier, Rhodes (1996) depicts the comprehensive paradigm of local government in transformation as a shift from government to governance. International exemplars of effective representative democracy illustrate examples of bottom-up enterprising governance in major cities of Brazil, Mexico, United States and India. These case studies draw on Ackerman's (2004) accounts of 'co-governance' for democracy undertaken through: 'participatory budgeting' in Porto Alegre, Brazil; 'accountability' in Mexico; 'beat teams' in the Chicago Police reform; and grass roots 'anti-corruption' in India. Ackerman's (2004: 452) message is clear for institutional activists: 'governments need to take civil society into account in the design of the participative mechanisms'.

Here citizens influence local government policy making from the outside (Ackerman 2004). As suggested above, local governments with innovative capability to transmute public services can also mobilise risk-taking – a local government powerhouse – of what Rhodes (1996) argues to be 'self-organising' and 'inter-organisational networks'. Wider appraisals of enterprising local government show that 'public value', performance and impact are embedded in 'regional innovation systems' (Asheim and Isaksen 1997; Cooke and Morgan 1998; Morgan 2016), and resilient local governments as Rodriguez-Pose and Di Cataldo (2015) found in their study of the Basque Country. Yet for local government to succeed, as Travers (2012: 23) spells out, 'blockages' must be removed, alongside the negotiation of a 'new settlement' (Travers 2015).

Similarly, an increase in innovative performance management studies demonstrates the effects of path-dependent local government economic policies and the power dynamics required to prove local government capabilities in transformations of regional competitiveness (Valdaliso et al. 2014). For example, Vecchi et al. (2014) from an Italian context, demonstrate management enactment in policy activities is vital to focus collaborative effort and can affect enterprise competitiveness in economic development. Similarly, Uyarra (2008) simplified how the process of path-dependency in evolutionary local government economic policies can stimulate smart specialisation. In contrast, benefactors of 'collaborative entrepreneurship' have considered the effects of give-and-take two-way collaboration and innovation in economic development policies in regional collaborative learning (Morgan 2016). In Morgan's study of the Basque Country, he reflects on the collaborative entrepreneurship consequences in regional innovation systems (ibid.: 1544).

Moreover, he posits that past economic development capabilities can inform future prospective policy intricacies. His study exemplifies the perplexing nature of economic growth dependence and its impact on indigenous communities. The study confirms that innovation exemplars must be 'adaptive and dynamic enough to meet the challenges of the future'. He contends that 'the Basque Government can fairly claim to have played a major role in introducing new initiatives – with respect to new sectors like biotech and nano-tech; new innovation and talent-related agencies' (Morgan 2016: 1544). He notes 'the criticism levelled at the Basque Government is not that it failed to introduce change/novelty, but that its policy initiatives have been compromised by a disjuncture between supply and demand in the policy design process because demand side measures have received much less prominence than supply-side measures' (ibid.: 1555). Moreover, he reasons the sharpness of gravitational pull is universal and intrinsic in 'the age of austerity and the challenge of smart specialisation' (ibid.: 1548). As the proliferation of universal competition intensifies, pioneering sovereign local governments pursue smarter methods and economic optimism to drive so called 'smart cities' that can pool resources in the direction of interconnected 'city deals' (DBIS 2013). Smart cities, representative of innovation and technological growth, envisage development policies through city connectivity and competitiveness such as in Amsterdam and Norway and operate in a global network of European 2020 flagship cities – Germany, Denmark and Sweden.

A final point to be made about entrepreneurship relates directly to the kind of entrepreneurship we mean, its motivation and its rationale. As noted earlier in this chapter, although entrepreneurship is essentially risk-taking, it may be co-operative in nature, emphasising mutuality rather than voracious profit-making. In the USA, the Cleveland Model of local economic development has the three elements of local procurement, a co-operative investment fund, and an emphasis upon local employment, comprising an approach in Cleveland which is 'rebuilding their city's economy from the ground up, embedding new forms of ownership that redistribute power and wealth' (Scott and Fortune 2016: 20). Entrepreneurship in the local public sector does not have to be red in tooth and claw. It can be informed by values of cooperation and trust, exemplified in the UK by the work of cooperative councils as a firmly established part of local government.

Conclusion: the challenges to public entrepreneurship theory?

This chapter has explored the challenges faced by local government in initiating and supporting local economic development, together with some of the barriers to the growth of public entrepreneurship. It has been suggested that public entrepreneurship has become ever more important in an era of austerity but, simultaneously, has become ever harder to achieve. The link between entrepreneurship and innovation remains centrally important in local economic development, but there remain considerable challenges to achieving effective innovation and 'unlocking' public entrepreneurship (Ostrom 2005). A matrix consisting of local area and territory, a sense of place, community and tribal governance provides potential solutions to the persistent problems of entrepreneurship and innovation.

Our discussion has been based on published sources, informed by original primary research into patterns of economic development in the UK and Europe. The scope for further empirical work to explore the emergent findings is clear, particularly in mapping the rapidly changing role of local government in relation to economic development. The overall theoretical approach adopted in this chapter develops a framework for understanding public entrepreneurship in an attempt to understand our research question – Is local government necessary to deliver economic development? The public entrepreneurship framework proposed here represents both the prospect and a threat for what happens to local government in developing a path for economic development. In the transformation of local government, Cochrane (2016) points towards the shifting paradigm in rethinking the 'local' in local government as it functions under a climate 'of localism, austerity and dreams of urban entrepreneurialism'. Similarly, Travers (2012, 2015) advises of the need to remove substantial cultural barriers for local government in economic development. Overall public entrepreneurship sets out the value for local government involvement in economic development and the 'promise' of innovation in collaborative and cooperative coalitions. Yet, cooperation in economic development may create new societal conflict and new ideologies of winners and losers.

In terms of place-making and effective local entrepreneurship, significant issues remain. The need to understand indigenous communities and the extent to which local places seek self-governance may impede opportunity, particularly in the UK where central government continues to redefine local 'place', first by abolishing the established regions and currently by establishing larger geographical 'combined authorities' which are curiously deemed to be part of a devolution agenda. There is complexity surrounding mutual relationships at local level, generating contradictory understandings of innovation and where it may lie. This is especially important where reciprocal interactions between industry leaders fail to appreciate public values, accountability structures, and regulation, and are impatient with public sector bureaucratic processes (Johnston and Blenkinsopp 2017). It may be that solutions lie in cooperative and mutual examples of good practice, in understandings of local need, and in a resolute shift of authority from national to local government. Yet reality is unlikely to prove so simple.

Note

1 Feldman et al. (2016) distinguish between the twin concepts of economic development and economic growth.

References

Ackerman, J. (2004) Co-governance for Accountability: Beyond 'Exit' and 'Voice'. *World Development* 32(3): 447–463.

Ács, Z. J., Autio, E. and Szerb, L. (2014) National Systems of Entrepreneurship: Measurement Issues and Policy Implications. *Research Policy* 43(3): 476–494.

Alcantara, C. and Nelles, J. (2013) Indigenous Peoples and the State in Settler Societies: Towards a More Robust Definition of Multi-level Governance. *Publius, The Journal of Federalism* 44(1): 183–204.

Asheim, B.T. and Isaksen, A. (1997) Location, Agglomeration and Innovation: Towards Regional Innovation Systems in Norway? *European Planning Studies* 5(3): 299–330.

Audretsch, D. B. and Link, A. N. (eds.) (2016) *Essays in Public Sector Entrepreneurship*. International Studies in Entrepreneurship. Dordrecht: Springer.

Bartlett, D. (2017) Champions of Local Authority Innovation Revisited, Local Government Studies. *Local Government Studies* 43(2): 142–149.

Bartlett, D. and Dibben, P. (2002) Public Sector Innovation and Entrepreneurship: Case Studies from Local Government. *Local Government Studies* 28(4): 107–121

Benington, J. and Moore, M. H. (2011) *Public Value: Theory and Practice*. Basingstoke, Palgrave Macmillan.

Bernier, L. (2014) Public Enterprises as Policy Instruments: The Importance of Public Entrepreneurship. *Journal of Economic Policy Reform* 17(3): 253–266.

Boyett, I. (1996) The Public Sector Entrepreneur – A Definition. *International Journal of Public Sector Management* 9(2): 36–51.

Broome, J. B. and Christakis, A.N. (1988) A Culturally Sensitive Approach to Tribal Governance Issue Management. *International Journal of International Relations* 12: 107–123.

Cantillon, R. (1973) *Essai sur la nature du commerce en general*. English translation by H. Higgs. New York: Augustus.

Casson, M. (1982) *The Entrepreneur: An Economic Theory*. Oxford: Martin Robertson:

Castells, M. (1977) *The Urban Question*. London: Edward Arnold.

Catney, P. and Henneberry, J.M. (2016) Public Entrepreneurship and The Politics of Regeneration in Multi-Level Governance. *Environment and Planning C: Government and Policy* 13(7): 1324–1343.

Cochrane, A. (2016) Thinking about the 'Local' of Local Government: A Brief History of Invention and Reinvention. *Local Government Studies* 42(6): 907–915.

Cooke, P. and Morgan, K. (1998) *The Associational Economy: Firms Regions and Innovation*. Oxford: Oxford University Press.

Crowley, L., Balaram, B., and Lee, N. (2012) *People or Place? Urban Policy in the Age of Austerity*. London: The Work Foundation.

DBIS (2013) *Smart Cities*. London: Department for Business, Innovation and Skills.

Dellepiane-Avellaneda, S. and Hardiman, N. (2015) Fiscal Politics in Time: Pathways to Fiscal Consolidation in Ireland, Greece, Britain, and Spain 1980–2012. *European Political Science Review* 7(2): 189–219.

Edquist. C. and Johnson, B. (1997) Institutional and Organisations in Systems of Innovation. In C. Edquist (ed.), *Systems of Innovation: Technologies, Institutions and Organizations*, 41–63. London: Pinter.

Edwards, C., Jones, G. Lawton, A. and Llewellyn, N. (2002) Public Entrepreneurship: Rhetoric, Reality, and Context. *International Journal of Public Administration* 25(12): 1539–1554.

Elcock, H. and Fenwick, J. (2012) The Political Leadership Matrix: A Tool for Analysis. *Public Money and Management* 32 (2): 87–94.

Feldman, M., Hadjimichael, T., Lanahan, L. and Kemeny, T. (2016) The Logic of Economic Development: A Definition and Model for Investment. *Environment and Planning C: Government and Policy* 34(1): 5–21.

Fenwick, J. and Elcock, H. (2016) Elected Mayors in England: Leaders or Managers? *International Journal of Public Leadership* 12(4): 289–300.

Fenwick, J., Johnston Miller, K. and McTavish, D. (2012) Co-governance or Meta-bureaucracy? Perspectives of Local Governance 'Partnership' in England and Scotland. *Policy and Politics* 40(3): 405–422.

Foucault, M. (1991) Governmentality. In G. Burchell, C. Gordon and P. Miller (eds), *The Foucault Effect: Studies in Governmentality*, 87–104. Chicago, IL: University of Chicago Press.

Graute, U. (2016) Local Authorities Acting Globally for Sustainable Development. *Regional Studies* 50(11): 1931–1942.

Hambleton, R. (2015a) Place-Based Leadership: A New Perspective on Urban Regeneration. *Journal of Urban Regeneration and Renewal* 9(1): 10–24.

Hambleton, R. (2015b) *Leading the Inclusive City: Place-Based Innovation for a Bounded Planet*. Bristol: Policy Press.

Hambleton, R. and Howard, J. (2013) Place-Based Leadership and Public Service Innovation. *Local Government Studies* 39(1): 47–70.

Hambleton, R. and Sweeting, D. (2014) Innovation in Urban Political Leadership: Reflections on the Introduction of a Directly-Elected Mayor in Bristol UK. *Public Money and Management* 34(5): 315–322.

Hartley, J. (2005) Innovation in Governance and Public Services: Past and Present, *Public Money and Management* 25(1): 27–34.

Harvey, D. (1989) From Managerialism to Entrepreneurialism: The Transformation in Urban Governance in Late Capitalism. *Geografiska Annaler, Series B Human Geography* 71(1): 3–17.

Hibbard, M. (2006) Tribal Sovereignty, The White problem, and Reservation Planning. *Journal of Planning History* 5(2): 87–105.

Imrie, R. and Thomas, H. (eds.) (1999) *British Urban Policy and the Urban Development Corporations* (2nd edition). London, Paul Chapman.

Jessop, B. (1999) Narrating the Future of the National Economy and the National State: Remarks on Remapping Regulation and Reinventing Governance. In G. Steinmetz (ed.), *State/Culture: State Formation After the Cultural Turn*, 378–385. Ithaca, NY: Cornell University Press.

Johns, C. M., O'Reilly, P. L. and Inwood, G. J. (2006) Intergovernmental Innovation and the Administrative State in Canada. *Governance: An International Journal of Policy, Administration and Institutions* 19(4): 627–649.

Johnston, L. and Blenkinsopp, J. (2017) Challenges for Civil Society Involvement in Civic Entrepreneurship: A Case Study of Local Enterprise Partnerships. *Public Money and Management* 37(2): 89–96.

Johnston, L. Robinson, S. and Lockett, N. (2010) Recognising Open Innovation in HEI-industry Interaction for Knowledge Transfer and Exchange. *International Journal of Entrepreneurial Behavior and Research* 16(6): 540–560.

Kirzner, I. M. (1973) *Competition and Entrepreneurship*. Chicago, IL: University of Chicago Press.

Kirzner, I. M. (1997) Entrepreneurial Discovery and the Competitive Market Process: An Austrian Approach. *Journal of Economics Literature* 35(1): 60–85.

Kirzner, I. M. (2000) *The Driving Forces of the Market: Essays in Austrian Economics*. London: Routledge.

Klein, P. G., Mahoney, J. T., McGahan, A. M. and Pitelis, C. N. (2010) Towards a Theory of Public Entrepreneurship. *European Management Review, The Journal of the European Academy of Management* 7(1): 1–15.

Lawless, P. (1981) *Britain's Inner Cities: Problems and Policies*. London: Harper & Row.

Lee, Y. (2016) From Competition to Collaboration: Intergovernmental Economic Development Policy Networks, *Local Government Studies* 42(2): 171–188.

Leyden, P. D. and Link, A. N. (2015) *Public Sector Entrepreneurship: US Technology and Innovation Policy*. New York: Oxford University Press.

Liddle, J. (2016) Introduction: Public Sector Entrepreneurship: Key Issues, Challenges and Developments in Theory and Practice. In J. Liddle (ed.), *New Perspectives on Research, Policy & Practice in Public Entrepreneurship*, Contemporary Issues in Entrepreneurship Research vol. 6. Emerald Group. Retrieved from http://ebookcentral.proquest.com/lib/northumbria/detail.action?docID=4560164.

Lindroth, M. (2011) Paradoxes of Power: Indigenous Peoples in the Permanent Forum. *Cooperation and Conflict* 46(4) 543–562.

Llewellyn, N. and Jones, G. (2003) Controversies and Conceptual Development: Examining Public Entrepreneurship. *Public Management Review* 5(2): 245–266.

Loney, M. (1983) *Community against Government: The British Community Development Project 1968–78. A Study of Government Incompetence*. London: Heinemann.

Lundvall, B. Å.(1999) National Business Systems and National Systems of Innovation. *International Studies of Management and Organisation* 29(2): 60–77.

Marks, G. and Hooge, l. (2004) Contrasting Visions of Multilevel Governance. In I. Bache and M. Finders (eds), *Multi-level Governance*, 15–30. Oxford: Oxford University Press.

Mazzucato, M. (2015) *The Entrepreneurial State: Debunking Public vs. Private Sector Myths*. London: Anthem Press.

Mintrom, M. (1997) Policy Entrepreneurs and the Diffusion of Innovation, *American Journal of Political Science*, 41(3): 738–770.

Moore, M. (1994) Public Value as the Focus of Strategy. *Australian Journal of Public Administration* 53(3): 296–303.

Moore, M. and Hartley, J. (2008) Innovations in Governance. *Public Management Review* 10(1): 3–20.

Morgan, K. (2016) Collective Entrepreneurship: The Basque Model of Innovation. *European Planning Studies* 24(8): 1544–1560.

Moulaert, F., Rodriguez, A. and Swyngedouw, E. (eds) (2003) *The Globalized City: Economic Restructuring and Social Polarization in European Cities: Economic Restructuring and Social Polarization in European Cities*. Oxford: Oxford University Press.

Myerson, R. B. (1991) *Game Theory: Analysis of Conflict*. Cambridge, MA: Harvard University Press.

Nelles, J. and Alcantara, C. (2011) Strengthening the Ties that Bind? An Analysis of Aboriginal-Municipal Intergovernmental Agreements In British Columbia. *Canadian Public Administration* 54(3): 315–334.

Nelles, J. and Durand, F. (2014) Political Rescaling and Metropolitan Governance in Cross-Border Regions: Comparing The Cross Border Metropolitan Areas of Lille and Luxembourg. *European Urban and Regional Studies* 21(1): 104–122.

Niezen, R. (2003) *The Origins of Indigenism: Human Rights and the Politics of Identity*. Berkeley, CA: University of California Press.

Olsen, M. (1965) *The Logic of Collective Action: Public Goods and The Theory of Groups*. Cambridge, MA: Harvard University Press.

Ongaro, E., Massey, A. Holzer, M. and Wayenberg, E. (2010) *Governance and Intergovernmental Relations in the European Union and the United States: Theoretical Perspectives*. Cheltenham: Edward Elgar.

Ó Riain, S. (2014) *The Rise and Fall of Ireland's Celtic Tiger: Liberalism, Boom and Bust*. Cambridge: Cambridge University Press.

Ortiz, J, (2002) Tribal Governance and Public Administration. *Administration and Society* 34(5): 459–481.

Osborne, D. (1993) Reinventing Government. *Public Productivity and Management Review* 16(4): 349–356.

Ostrom, E. (1990). *Governing the Commons: The Evolution of Institutional Forms of Collective Action*. Cambridge, UK: Cambridge University Press.

Ostrom, E. (1998) A Behavioral Approach to the Rational Choice Theory of Collective Action: Presidential Address. *American Political Science Association, American Political Science Review* 92(1): 1–22.

Ostrom, E. (2005) *Unlocking Public Entrepreneurship and Public Economies*. Discussion Paper 2005/01. United Nations University (UNU)/World Institute for Development Economics Research (WIDER). Retrieved on 8 February 2017 from www.econstor.eu/bitstream/10419/52899/1/480453004.pdf.

Ostrom, E. (2014) Collective action and the Evolution of Social Norms. *Journal of Natural Resources Policy Research* 6(4): 235–252.

Papillon, M. (2011) Adapting Federalism: Indigenous Multilevel Governance in Canada and the United States. *The Journal of Federalism* 42(2): 289–312.

Perkmann, M. (2007) Policy Entrepreneurship and Multilevel governance: A Comparative Study of European Cross-Border Regions. *Environment and Planning C: Governance and Policy* 25(6): 861–879.

Phillipson, N. (2010) *Adam Smith: An Enlightened Life*. London: Penguin.

Pike, A., Rodríguez-Pose, A., and Tomaney, J. (2017) Shifting Horizons in Local and Regional Development. *Regional Studies* 51(1): 46–57.

Rhodes, R. A. W. (1996) The New Governance: Governance Without Government. *Political Studies* 44(4): 652–667.

Rodrigo, D., Allio, L. and Andres-Amo, P. (2009) *Multi-Level Regulatory Governance: Policies, Institutions and Tools for Regulatory Quality and Policy Coherence*. OECD Working Papers on Public Governance no. 13. Paris: OECD.

Rodriguez-Pose, A. and Di Cataldo, M. (2015) Quality of Government and Innovative Performance in the Regions of Europe. *Journal of Economic Geography* 15(4): 673–706.

Schneider, M., Teske, P. and Mintrom, M. (1995) *Public Entrepreneurs: Agents for Change in American Government*. Princeton, NJ: Princeton University Press.

Schnellenbach, J. (2007) Public Entrepreneurship and the Economics of Reform. *Journal of Institutional Economic* 3(2): 182–202.

Schumpeter, J.A. (1934) *The Theory of Economic Development: An Inquiry into profits, Capital, Interest, and the Business Cycle*. Cambridge, MA: Harvard University Press.

Scott, J. and Fortune, J. (2016) *By Us, For Us: A Co-operative Party Agenda for Enhanced City and County Regions*. London: Co-operative Party

Shaw, K. (2008) *Indigeneity and Political Theory: Sovereignty and the Limits of the Political*. London: Routledge.

Smith, A. (1976) *The Theory of Moral Sentiments*. Indianapolis, IN: Liberty Fund.

Smith, E. (2014) Entrepreneurship at the Local Government Level: Stimulating and Restraining Forces in the Swedish Waste Management Industry. *Public Management Review* 16(5): 708–732.

Stoker, G. (2005) Joined Up Government for Local and Regional Institutions. In V. Bogdanor (ed.), *Joined Up Government*, 156–174. Oxford, Oxford University Press.

Swyngedouw, E. (2006) Governance Innovation and the Citizen: The Janus Face of Governance – beyond the State. *Urban Studies* 42(11): 1991–2006.

Swyngedouw, E., Moulaert, F. and Rodriguez, A. (2002) Neoliberal Urbanization in Europe: Large-Scale Urban Development Projects and the New Urban Policy. *Antipode* 34(3): 542–577.

Tilly, C. (1999) Epilogue: Now Where? In G. Steinmetx (ed.), *State/Culture: State formation after the cultural turn*, 407–419. Ithaca, NY: Cornell University Press.

Travers, T. (2012) *Local Government's Role in Promoting Economic Growth: Removing Unnecessary Barriers to Success*. London: Local Government Association.

Travers, T. (2015) A Near Federal UK Requires a Constitutional Settlement. *Local Government Chronicle* (20 May). Retrieved from www.lgcplus.com/politics-and-policy/a-near-federal-uk-requires-a-constitutional-settlement/5085157.article.

Uyarra, E. (2008) Key Dilemmas of Regional Innovation Policy. *The European Journal of Social Science Research* 20(3): 243–261.

Valdaliso, J., Magro, E., Navarro, M. Aranguren, M. J. and Wilson, J. R. (2014) Path Dependence in Policies Supporting Smart Specialisation Strategies: Insights from the Basque Case. *European Journal of Innovation Management* 17(4): 390–408.

Vecchi, V., Brusoni, M. and Borgonovi, E. (2014) Public Authorities for Entrepreneurship: A Management Approach to Execute Competitiveness Policies. *Public Management Review* 16(2): 256–273.

Wollmann, H. (2014) The Directly Elected Mayor in the German Lander – Introduction, Implementation and Impact. *Public Money and Management* 34 (5): 331–337.

Zerbinati, S. and Souitaris, V. (2005) Entrepreneurship in the Public Sector: A Framework of Analysis in European Local Governments. *Entrepreneurship and Regional Development* 17(1): 43–64.

15
THE WIDE RANGE OF LOCAL GOVERNMENT PUBLIC SERVICES

Elisabetta Mafrolla

Looking for an international definition of local government services

Exploring and explaining local government public services (LGPSs) across national borders is a great opportunity, because the topic is generally siloed in sub-disciplinary empirical analyses undertaken in one national context, or comparing a few national contexts. It is difficult to define the form and possible extension of LGPSs in a cross-country perspective, as though national legislatures should be irrelevant in providing such a definition. Nevertheless, in most countries a law-based definition of public services (including LGPSs) has dominated for a long time. From such a perspective, the definition of public services has changed over time from a narrow subjective concept that considered public service to be the services provided by a public organisation towards a wider objective definition in which the range of public services includes every service provided with the aim of producing a public benefit, regardless of which agency provides the service.

Under the construct of bounded rational agents (Simon 1947), it is difficult to find a stable categorisation for the various features of services that can be considered within the concept of LGPS. It is not a static concept, as the needs of citizens and organisations change over time and across countries, within different time frames. The local community and political representatives scrutinise the benefits and costs of each service and acknowledge the importance of a specific set of public services that better fit the requirements of the community, taking into account the need to maintain and enhance the socio-economic conditions of life in the local jurisdiction.

Following a long established theoretical approach, the so-called median-voter's approach (Downs 1957), the provision of a specific LGPS in a territory is determined by citizens' collective demands for such services. The level of local public expenditure in the production of LGPSs could determine the citizens' satisfaction and the attraction (departure) of citizens towards (from) a territory (Tiebout 1957). Even though critics argued that such an approach neglects the influence of bureaucratic threats and institutional settings (Romer and Rosenthal 1979), no alternative theoretical approach has since dominated the literature. Hence, the definition of LGPS delivery seems to be demand-driven (De Groot 1989) and contingent, similar to what generally occurs in the service delivery industry (Ponsignon et al. 2011).

This makes the possible range of LGPSs extraordinarily wide and its organisation contingent on environmental circumstances (Pennings 1975). City governments in the US, for example, typically provide:

> about forty distinct services, ranging from public works (street repair and garbage collection), to public safety (police and fire), to animal control and maintenance of public recreation areas.
>
> *(Levin and Tadelis 2010: 511)*

To understand the relationships between the two main perspectives of our definitional analysis, we could rely on stakeholder theory, in which the government (hence, also the local government) has a dominant but still unclearly defined role. Government is typically seen as either a non-stakeholder in the background of the community (Buchholz and Rosenthal 2004) or merely one among many stakeholders (Freeman 1984; Neville and Menguc 2006), with no consideration of its unique roles and place in the business–government–society nexus (Dahan et al. 2015).

However, in this chapter, government in various spheres is considered the main actor in the public policy process, which offers a solution to the collective wishes of the community for public goods and services (Buchholz and Rosenthal 2004). The public policy process, then, is the appropriate way for society (where the government and the community work together) to determine the allocation of resources for solving social problems through LGPS provision, thus accurately discerning stakeholders' interests and needs (Dahan et al. 2015).

Overall, the supply of LGPSs is contingent, and the decisions depend on the pressure of the stakeholders' claims that are diffused throughout the policy environment, with political and economic constraints. Stakeholders' claims let human needs emerge (Freeman 1984), both when they are basic needs (i.e. essential to the survival of the community) or when they are sophisticated and non-basic needs (Osborne and Brown 2005). Public policies are drawn to satisfy the human needs from most to least compelling (Mafrolla and D'Amico 2016). LGPS delivery, in such a framework, is the central part of the public policy process, where considering the inputs (i.e. resources) invested at a specific purpose, the output of the process is the LGPS provision, which itself is expected to produce an outcome, generally in terms of citizens' satisfaction (Brusca and Montesinos 2016). Performance measurement will determine the efficiency (inputs–outputs relationship) and effectiveness (outputs-outcomes relationship) of LGPS supply and, therefore, the quality of the public policy adopted by the (local) governments (Pollitt and Bouckaert 2011). Below re discussed three different perspectives adopted to define and classify LGPSs, also offering some empirical analysis to better describe the relevance of space and time contingency in LGPS studies. Subsequently this chapter critically reflects on the potentials for a clear scheme to classify LGPSs across-nations, because although the list of services provided generally mirrors the policy enacted in each jurisdiction, the need for a supra-national field of analysis is particularly acute in relation to the contemporary call for critical global studies in economics and political science.

A classification of the wide range of LGPSs

To manage diversity, there is a need to distinguish various services by classifying them according to the various perspectives and unravelling the contingency knot. Hence, in the absence of an existing dominant categorisation of LGPSs in the literature, in this chapter the concept of LGPS is categorised under three main perspectives. These include:

(i) the subjective-community perspective, which explains how LGPS are *local*, (i.e. useful to those who are settled in a specific jurisdiction);
(ii) the subjective-government perspective, which shows who in the *governments* is responsible for supplying LGPSs, analyses the distribution of responsibilities on LGPSs among different tiers of government, and studies how the government can mandate the operative functions of LGPS to third parties; and
(iii) the objective or functional perspective, which explains what tasks can be considered of *public* interest and/or responsibility.

The subjective-community classification: who benefits from LGPSs?

A LGPSs classification considering what are the community benefits of public action is located in the broader field of a traditional body of literature seeking to categorise and circumscribe public goods. In any manual of public finance (e.g. Stiglitz 2000: 128), the mainstream definition of a public good that could be extended to public service focuses on two main circumstances dealing with the action of consumption (by whom and how such goods are consumed). These are joint consumability or non-rivalrous character (Blümel et al. 1986: 242) and non-excludability (Brown and Jackson 1978: 29) in consumption. These two distinctions (rivalrous and excludable) provide for four types of goods:

(i) Private goods, that are excludable and rivalrous (e.g. a soft drink).
(ii) Common goods, that are non-excludable but rivalrous (e.g. fishing grounds).
(iii) Toll goods, that are excludable but non-rivalrous (e.g. train service, and most of natural monopolies).
(iv) Pure public goods, that are non-excludable and non-rivalrous (e.g. fireworks and national defence).

Public goods are either non-rivalrous or non-excludable. Pure public goods, also called collective goods, bear both characteristics. Private goods are the only category of goods that are not typically provided through public services, although it is feasible to predict that the production of some typically private goods might also be of public interest[1] thus extending the governmental sphere of production to all 'worthy' goods (Savas 1987).

Notwithstanding the existence of the stable limits of excludability and rivalry in consumption, there is much debate among researchers about how public services benefit the community beyond the typical benefits of public goods because the provision of a public service might involve private goods, such as providing food (that is typically a private good) to poor people produces externalities to the whole community where the poor people are living, as it reduces inequalities and generally enhances the quality of life. Probably, due to the blurred boundaries of what is a public service, controversies generally dominate the decision to provide additional services to poorer households. For example, the alleged provision of preferential access to social housing to immigrants in the UK (Battiston et al. 2014), or for EU support of Wi-Fi services in refugees' camps (*Economist* 2017). Hence, the concept of public service is more complex than the one of easily agreed public good, and every activity that is able to enhance the welfare of the community might constitute a public service.

The subjective-government classification: who provides the service?

The subjective-government perspective aims at classifying LGPSs based on the subject that is responsible for supplying the service. Two main issues should be considered for the analysis of this classification.

First, several levels of responsibility might be defined, and different governmental bodies might be charged for the different elements of the LGPS supply chain. Generally, responsibilities for LGPS supply are distributed among the various tiers of government; hence, there is a need to evaluate the mutual relationships between the central and more the localised governments and how the distribution of powers produces a distribution of service duties.

Second, being responsible for the LGPS supply does not necessarily imply that the concrete operational activities of service delivery would be undertaken directly by the government. Generally, the government should evaluate whether and to what extent the service should be provided directly or demanded by a third party that will operate on the behalf and under the directions and regulations defined by the government.

The various tiers of government in LGPS provision

LGPSs can be classified under the subjective-government perspective based on the number of tiers of government that would be involved in the LGPS provision, ranging from services provided by the regional, county, and municipality governments, and possibly to even more localised bodies. The analysis of which government tier is charged with such service delivery raises the overarching question of the decentralisation of authority (i.e. the devolution of power and responsibility over policies from central to local governments; De Vries 2000). Most of the literature from the late 1980s supports the idea that the relationship between the central and local government is grounded on the dominant role of the central government, which can rely on greater human and financial resources (Ranson and Walsh 1985; Marsh et al. 2001) and can utilise legislation to enforce its decisions (Ranson and Walsh 1985). From such a perspective, the central government also enforces the local government's actions and adopts a particular role of controller over local governments' performance in service delivery (Loughlin 1996). Nevertheless, more recent arguments reject this view and support the relevance of a central-local relationship grounded in policy networks (Rhodes 1999), where duality in the central-local relationship creates a multi-level governance model (Sullivan and Gillanders 2005) that is pervasive from the neighbourhood to the EU (Peters and Pierre 2001). Clearly, the world of LGPSs has changed over the last several decades, and the national sovereignty and centralised government dominance of the twentieth century left enough room for a 'multiple sphere government' typical of the twenty-first century (Galligan 2006: 262). For example, in much of Europe during early years of the twenty-first century, the government model turned into a decentralised multi-level model. Some traditionally centralised countries, such as Italy and Spain, strengthened their regional level of government. In the United Kingdom, there was legislative devolution in respect of Scotland, Wales and Northern Ireland, and Belgium formally became a federal state. This also occurred in the former often highly centralised Eastern European countries, where decentralisation created localised bodies, although with weak powers (Bertrana and Heinelt 2011). Moreover, since the 1990s, at peripheral very localised level, inter-municipal cooperation, amalgamation and mergers were seen across Northern, Central, Eastern and Southern Europe reducing the territorial fragmentation of local government

(Wollmann 2008; Allers and de Greef 2018; Swianiewicz 2018). Generally, there is a tendency to decentralise some national powers, thus strengthening the second and third tiers of government and simultaneously reducing fragmentation throughout the amalgamation or co-operation of 'too small' entities, which suggests that the 'meso' level of local government (Sharpe 1993) should be pursued as the best scale of governance model in the provision of services (Bertrana and Heinelt 2011).

The degree of devolution of political powers generally mirrors a devolution of duties in LGPS delivery. To assert how the devolution of powers are translated into a devolution in service delivery, three main elements of autonomy of the localities should be considered (Zangrandi 1994):

- autonomy in organizational functions (i.e. in the use of human resources);
- autonomy in decision making (i.e. in the choice of a governance model and the use of assets); and
- autonomy in financial provision (i.e. the ability of the peripheries to provide for financial needs through revenue collection and service pricing).

The higher the degree of autonomy is in these three spheres of competence, the higher the degree of devolution of powers from the central government towards local governments and the higher the ability of local governments to manage the provision of public services autonomously.

The public-private-partnership governance structure and system

LGPSs can also be classified from a subjective-government perspective based on the service governance structure that is adopted to deliver the service (i.e. whether the government provides the LGPS directly or through a delegated body). This classification relies primarily on analysing the contracting of public services, which occurs when a public manager chooses to rely on external parties in public service delivery. The make-or-buy decision is analysed in the literature mainly by adopting the framework of economic transaction costs (Williamson 1981), and through potential competitive efficiencies and economies of scale (Brown et al. 2006).

The choice of a service governance structure involves the analysis of three main contracting steps (Brown et al. 2006):

(i) choosing whether to make or buy the services;
(ii) selecting vendors to produce them; and
(iii) monitoring the implementation of the contract.

Moreover, three different elements related to the possible contracting process will be significant:

(a) the characteristics of the service;
(b) a set of external constraints (i.e. the political environment); and
(c) the availability of alternative production models.

The characteristics of the service that determine the contracting arena include the specificity of the assets involved in the production of the service and the complexity of the service. Generally, it is argued that economic transaction costs increase when the assets are highly specific and the service is highly complex. The other element that determines the characteristics of a service is the complexity of the service, which is often assessed by its measurability. When services are less measurable, it is difficult (on the side of the vendor) to evaluate the feasible outcome of the production and its foreseeable profits. Moreover, it is difficult (on the side of the government) to monitor the performance of the agent and the quality and efficiency of the production of the services, which might enhance the political incentives dominating in the public sector (Frant 1996). Complexity creates a disincentive for the externalisation of the services and favours the 'make' choice by the government (Brown and Potoski 2003; Levin and Tadelis, 2010). Overall, complex services involving highly specific assets are less likely to be provided by market mechanisms. In such a situation a hierarchical governance model dominates, where local governments manage the service supply autonomously through in-house production. In the opposite situation, in the absence of complexity and with low asset specificity, the market mechanisms would dominate in the supply of services through the contracting-out governance model. Finally, a third governance model may occur, in which the service is complex. Nevertheless, there are evident feasible outcomes in the production of services that are outside the sphere of profit maximisation (Frant 1996) and favour the creation of not-for-profit networks to manage the service supply (Rodrigues et al. 2012).

The make-or-buy decision is settled under bounded rationality (Simon 1947), which is the dominant rationale in social science in which several external constraints misallocate public resources from the comprehensive choice (Jones 2003). In the context of LGPS production, the political environment generates the most relevant constraints. Early studies in the 1980s found that political factors, such as public service constituency groups and governance structures, are significant determinants of local government contracting (e.g. Ferris 1986). Over the last decade, a fervent debate arose between the supporters of the thesis that government contracting-out is more pragmatically oriented (Warner and Hebdon 2001; Brudney et al. 2005) than politically oriented (Fernandez et al. 2008; Ni and Bretschneider 2007; Price and Riccucci 2005) and it was argued that the different relevance of political concerns in contracting-out depends on the different types of goods and services that these researchers examined (Lu 2013). For example, providing public services in the sphere of human health care is more political in nature than is providing tourist information services.

The last element that determines the contracting decision is whether alternative production models are available. The variety of governance mechanisms (i.e. the possibility to undertake the make-or-buy choice) might be reduced by several constraints, primary among which are financial constraints. The issue was widely debated in the literature, with divergent results from conceptual and empirical research. Theoretically, adverse financial conditions should lead to the adoption of external contracting rather than hierarchical solutions because of the need to provide LGPSs at reduced costs, as long as the market service procurement is expected to be more innovative and cost-effective (Ferris 1986; Brown et al. 2006). Nevertheless, empirical research provided opposite results, finding that in-house retention is more prevalent during economic downturns (Rodrigues et al. 2012) and that contracting-out is more prevalent during economic upturns (Pallesen 2004). This argument shows that rationality is bounded in a situation of economic austerity; on the one hand, the aims of technical efficiency and cost savings and the postulates of transaction costs economics are ignored (Nelson 1997). However, the leverage of local governments is elastic to the contingent downturn because contracting out increases the indebtedness of the local government in favour of external providers and involves the risk of higher political concerns (Rodrigues et al. 2012).

The wave towards external contracting of LGPSs that have invested European countries in the Nineties, apparently suffered a cyclical reverse in the aftermath of the 2008 financial crisis

Table 15.1 The subjective-government classification of health care services in 15 countries

		Australia	Canada	Denmark	UK	France	Germany	Iceland	Italy	Japan	Netherlands	New Zealand	Norway	Sweden	Switzerland	US
Organisational and decisional functions	Primary care I															
	II	*		*	*	*	*	*	*	*	*	*	*	*	*	*
	III		*	*	*								*	*		
	Secondary care I															
	II	*		*	*	*	*	*	*	*	*	*	*	*	*	*
	III		*										*			
Financial function (tax revenues collection and funds provision)	I	*		*	*	*	*	*	*		*	*	*	*	*	*
	II						*						*	*	*	
	III												*			
Provider ownership	Primary care SE	*														
	PrE				*	*	*				*	*	*		*	*
	PubE							*								
	Hospitals PrO	*	*				*		*	*	*	*	*	*	*	*
	PubO	*		*	*	*	*					*	*	*	*	

Source: OECD (2016). If information is not available in the OECD database, Thomson et al. (2012) is the alternative source.

In the table I, II, and III stand respectively for the I, II, and III tiers of government; SE, PrE, and PubE stand respectively for self-employed, private employee, and public employee; PrO and PubO respectively stand for privately owned and publicly owned.

(Wollmann 2016), bringing about the re-municipalisation of LGPSs, which differently involved LGPS, although the absorption of such process was (and is currently) contingent upon specific countries and sectors. The response to the crisis was contingent, and took various forms in different countries and sectors. For example, a clear re-municipalisation invested German energy sector policy (Bönker et al. 2016); whereas 'inter-municipalisation', rather than 'convincing signs of re-municipalisation', similarly involved the waste management sector both in Norway and in the Netherlands. The harsh financial crisis favoured a step back to a 'pre-welfare state' in Italy, where not-for-profit (especially church-affiliated) networks dominate public social services (Wollmann 2016: 198).

The provision of health care services: cross-country evidence

The health care sector offers a good natural arena to test the categorisation of LGPSs from the subjective-government perspective. In a health care system, a devolution of powers and responsibilities occurred recently, in favour of the second and third tiers of government in a wide range of states in the developed economies.

Table 15.1 compares the spheres of autonomy at the various tiers of government and outlines how health care service is provided across 15 different OECD countries.

The data show, from the perspective of health care service provision, how the organisational, decisional and financial spheres of autonomy are differently attributed to the various tiers of government across countries (top section of Table 15.1) and whether the government acts mostly as a provider or a commissioner of the service (bottom section of Table 15.1). At a first glance, it seems that most of the powers are in the hands of the second tier of government, whereas the provision of the service is mainly attributable to private operators. The organisational and decisional functions are generally held at the second government tier. Nordic countries (Sweden, Finland, Norway and Denmark) had the most decentralised system, as the primary healthcare system is fully or partially controlled by the municipalities. Almost everywhere, hospitals and specialist care are under the responsibility of the regional authorities, except for Canadian, Norwegian and (a few) German hospitals, which are managed by municipalities. In a few countries (Iceland and Japan), the organisation and decision-making processes remain in the hands of the central government. The central government is responsible almost everywhere for the general collection of tax revenues that are transferred to the second (and occasionally third) tier of government to cover health care investments and expenses. In almost all countries analysed, the central government provides to the more localised entities financing collected through national tax revenues. The second tier is responsible for collecting taxes that fund health care only in Canada, Norway (where the third tier might also collect revenues when appropriate), and Switzerland and in Italy and Germany, though to a very limited extent. Some children's health services are peripherally covered in Germany, whereas in Italy, the second tier is allowed (within a maximum tax cap) to collect revenues that are aimed to provide a level of health service that is higher than the minimum national requirements.

The bottom part of Table 15.1 shows whether the local government acts as a heath care service provider or commissioner. Most of primary health care is provided to the outpatient through a private system, where most of the general practitioners are self-employed, reimbursed by the government on the basis of a per-capita and/or fee-for-service agreement. In Canada, Japan and the United States, they are employees of private organisations. Only the systems in Sweden and Iceland are based on the public employment of physicians for primary care. Secondary and specialist care is provided mainly through hospitals, almost all of which are public. A relevant percentage of private hospital beds operate in Canada, Australia (33%), Germany (50%), Japan (55%) and the United States (85%). Most of the private supply of inpatient healthcare is provided by not-for-profit organisations in Canada, France, Germany, the Netherlands and the United States. Very often, the regional (Australia, Denmark, Italy, Sweden, Switzerland) or municipal (Germany) governments own public hospitals. In France, Iceland and Norway, the hospitals are owned by the central government. In some countries, private contracting is fundamental. This is the case of insurance-based health care systems, such as the long-lasting system of the United States and the newly reformed Netherlands and German systems. In those countries, the insurers levy mandatory (e.g. in Germany and the Netherlands) or voluntary (e.g. in the United States) contributions from citizens and arrange private agreements to define the service cover and reimbursements to the providers.

The health care sector example shows the various organisational forms that LGPS can take, devolving the spheres of authority and making the more localised tiers of government more or less autonomous (and responsible) in the organisational, decisional and financial functions. The advocates of the devolution reform supported the claim that a peripheral arrangement of the service had the opportunity to improve the performance of the service delivery and better satisfy the different needs of the population (Bossert and Beauvais 2002; Jimenez-Rubio et al. 2008). Similarly, the advocates of privatisation reform were supported by a claim for efficiency (Smith et al. 1981; Stone 2002).

These arguments both gradually changed the health care system towards a broad arrangement that today seems mainly state financed, publicly managed at a meso level and privately provided to citizens. No doubts are raised about whether health care should be considered a public service, not even in countries where the role of private providers' and insurers' role is dominant.

The objective classification: can we list LGPSs?

The classification of the range of public services from an objective or functional perspective consists of listing the LGPSs, focusing on which functions should be included (or excluded) in the category of LGPSs and looking at the aspect of public functionalities attributed to the local governments. The term 'public' is ambiguous, so it is difficult to circumscribe it objectively and list what exactly local governments' tasks should be in providing public services. The definition problem is so contradictory that international bodies and organisations also eschewed the term 'public services' in favour of different language (Martin 2004). For example, in 2003, the European Commission first wrote a Green Paper dealing with public services, naming them 'services of general interest', which suggests a categorisation of public services that is based on the benefits (namely, interests) covered by the services. The Green Paper provoked a long debate on what should be included in the category of services of general interest and evolved into several documents aimed at providing a universal European framework.[2] Finally, recognising a lack of clarity on terminology as well as its dynamic and evolving nature, the Commission, proposed a definition of the concept of services of general interest as 'services that public authorities of the Member States classify as being of general interest and, therefore, subject to specific public service obligations'.

This definition still leaves uncertainty about the boundaries of the concept of general interest, although the literature concluded that either the legislators had no interest in better defining the concept or had no room to do so, as the concept is changeable over time and space (Sauter and Schepel 2009). Conclusively, the services of general interest cover a broad range of services, characterised by the existence of a public responsibility for their provision (Martin 2004).

The European Commission (2003, 2011, 2013) suggests a classification of the services of general interest into two main categories:

i) services of general economic interest: i.e. 'economic activities which deliver outcomes in the overall public good that would not be supplied (or would be supplied under different conditions in terms of quality, safety, affordability, equal treatment or universal access) by the market without public intervention' (European Commission 2011: 5). A wide range of services might be included in this category, like postal services, energy, transport, telecommunications, social services, cultural services and other services (Ølykke and Møllgaard 2016).

ii) social services of general interest:
these include social security schemes covering the main risks of life (e.g. services for health, ageing, occupational accidents, unemployment, retirement and disability) and a range of other essential services provided directly to the person that play a preventive and socially cohesive/inclusive role (European Commission 2011); that is, assistance to persons faced by personal challenges or crises, such as debt, unemployment, rehabilitation, language training for immigrants and social housing, which provides housing for disadvantaged citizens or socially less advantaged groups (European Commission 2011, 2013).

This categorisation is often erroneously confused with the classification between the economic and non-economic nature of the service. Upon further investigation, the social nature of a service is not sufficient in itself to classify it as non-economic, and the term social service of general interest covers both economic and non-economic activities that have an aid purpose. An interesting and much-discussed conclusion of the long legislative process of the European Commission is the definitive absence of a closed definition for the concept of service of general interest, as the deferred to the right of single Member States the decision on what to include in (or exclude from) this category (Sauter and Schepel 2009; Ølykke and Møllgaard 2016).

Municipalities currently are by far the biggest agents in local services as either providers or commissioners (Wilson and Game 2006). In various nations, public services are specifically regulated, and local governments thus face legislative mandates of LGPSs for which they must allocate resources and others where they may be allowed discretion to provide. National legislatures typically identify such functional responsibilities along with requirements related to LGPSs' quality and standard (World Bank 2004). So the list of LGPSs that are provided by a local government in an industrial country would be much broader than that provided in a developing country. In most countries of the EU the list of duties of various tiers of local governments is much greater than in South Africa, which is a reference point for developing countries (World Bank 2004). Here the functional list of activities includes 'water supply, sewerage purification, electricity . . . refuse removal, roads and storm-water drainage, health services, emergency services, financial administration . . .'.

As expected, the list of services fulfils basic needs in developing countries, where LGPSs are focused on meeting basic needs (Collins 2012), while covering progressively larger, although discretionary (Wilson and Game 2002, 2011), non-basic needs, such as arts, sports and recreation, in advanced economies (Mafrolla and D'Amico 2016). Discussing the resilience of LGPS provision, debates have ranged from whether enough water was supplied to a large enough share of citizens in Africa, Asia and Latin America (World Bank 2004) to whether the government should strengthen the free availability of municipal schools for music and the arts in Sweden (Government Offices of Sweden 2014).

The case of the objective classification of municipalities' LGPSs in the European Union

The range of public services that are under the responsibility of the first tier governments European Union countries is wide but various. This section suggests an example of how width and various would be an objective classification of municipalities' public services provided in various European Union countries today.

There is an ample variety in the lists, and a 'geography' of European Union LGPSs can be feasibly carved out looking at the differences and similarities in service delivery. The Nordic countries offer a comprehensive range of services, as municipalities provide for almost all of their citizens' needs.

Health care is almost all provided by municipalities in Nordic countries. In contrast, several services, including health care services, are not supplied by French, Italian, Spanish, Polish and British municipalities. Health care is in those countries a responsibility of the central and regional tiers, although wider social services such as elderly care are shared between different spheres of government. Similarly, pre-school service is not provided by public administrations in France, Germany, Poland, Spain and the United Kingdom, where municipal schools do not teach children aged 1–3 years old. However, there are countries in the European Union where municipalities are not involved in children's education at all, although public education is universal. For example, in Spain, the entire school system is arranged at the state level (second tier), providing efficient infant services (starting at 16 weeks old), nurseries, primary and secondary schools, free until the age of 18 (Tremlett 2008). Library services are available at the municipal level in most of EU countries. For example, in the United Kingdom, the tasks attributed to libraries recently expanded to include the organisation of holiday camps and reading groups for children beginning in the first year of life (Wilson and Game 2011). Among leisure services, arts and sports are available at almost all EU countries, although there are differences in the accessibility and extent of the service across nations. For example, schools of music and art for children are provided by municipalities for free in Denmark, Finland, Germany, Sweden and the United Kingdom, but not in France, Italy, Greece, Spain and Poland. In terms of the provision of sports, the commitment of the (local) governments is very different across countries. For example, in the United Kingdom, municipalities offer a wide range of sporting activities for all ages, for some groups without charge (Wilson and Game 2011). In contrast, sports provision in Italy is generally managed by private not-for-profit associations that arrange a contract with the local government for using public infrastructure and offer the service to citizens, including elderly and children, for a fee.

Amenity services (i.e. road construction and maintenance and public transportation) are provided by municipalities almost everywhere in EU. In some places, the municipal activity in public transportation is particularly advanced; for example, municipalities in France arrange private car-sharing and bike rentals as a typical municipal task. The electricity networks are arranged at a municipal level in Denmark, Finland and France, whereas water supply and water waste are supplied by municipalities in many parts of the EU, with few exceptions, like Italy and Germany, where independent supra-municipal agencies are charged with such duties. Police services are in part organised by municipalities, like in France, Italy and Spain, whereas the fire brigade and emergency services are organised at the municipal level almost everywhere in EU, with a few exceptions (e.g. France and Italy) where the fire and rescue services are national bodies.

Conclusion

This chapter suggests overview to explore and examine the wide range of activities that can be considered within the notion of LGPS, and suggested some pillars for their classification and analysis, following the contingency theory and supporting a stakeholder-based perspective in the selection of the subjective and objective definitions of LGPS.

Despite various attempts by policy making bodies and academics to create a clear taxonomy of local government public services, there is no agreed definition of public service that could transcend national borders, because the extent of such services is often determined by national legislations, based on different ideologies and political drivers (i.e. contingent upon time and space). Moreover, supra-national bodies have failed to address a clear definition of public service, including a definition of LGPS. Nevertheless, a discussion on the appropriate cross-national definition of LGPS could feasibly be welcome, because LGPSs exist to satisfy citizens' needs, which change over time and across countries, and the supply or lack of a service will impact on citizens' quality of life (Mafrolla and D'Amico 2016). Hence, the continuing enlargement and harmonisation of the width and variety of LGPSs is in the agenda of humanitarian supranational bodies, aimed at reducing inequalities in citizens' quality of life (e.g. United Nations Development Programme 2016). In the era of innovation and borderless development, LGPSs are increasingly sophisticated (Osborne and Brown 2005), and it has been argued that additional effort is required to reduce the unequal provision of LGPSs around the world (World Bank 2004).

Another feature of LGPS has strengthened their association with local government internationally: almost all OECD countries have undergone some form of devolutionary process in recent decades, which has shifted several responsibilities and powers of public service provision to the second and third tiers of local government. Nevertheless, it can be observed that this process was incomplete, and in some countries, especially due to the harsh times of financial crisis, many public services were recently re-municipalised, or even reduced to a 'pre-welfare' situation, where the public sector fails to provide an appropriate service and citizens rely on private cooperative initiatives to satisfy their needs (Citroni et al. 2016).

Local governments today provide a wide range of services and have the opportunity to arrange their management as either providers or commissioners. Nevertheless, at the same time, they are tightly constrained in their strategic planning because today, they are subject to greater direction and control by the upper tiers of government. The decentralisation of LGPS suggested great possibilities for political scientists and public management theorists and practitioners, as it was supposed to favour a higher quality of services and better performance, along with more responsive and informed decision-making at the peripheral levels. Nevertheless, decentralisation has prompted an extension of the localised provision of LGPS, which will continue to vary between different countries, as development policies should carefully consider the needs of the citizens, which differ over time and between different countries.

Notes

1 E.g. Alcohol in some countries with a historic legacy of excessive consumption
2 A Green Paper, a White Paper and two Framework Documents (2011 and 2013) illustrate the development of 'services of general interest'.

References

Allers, M. A. and de Greef, J. A. (2018) Intermunicipal Cooperation, Public Spending and Service Levels. *Local Government Studies* 44(1): 127–150.
Battiston, D., Dickens, R., Manning, A. and Wadsworth, J. (2014) *Immigration and the Access to Social Housing in the UK*. Centre for Economic Performance (CEP) – Discussion Paper No 1264

Bertrana, X. and Heinelt, H. (2011) Introduction. In H. Heinelt and X. Bertrana (eds), *The Second Tier of Local Government in Europe. Provinces, Counties, Départments and Landkreise in Comparison*, 1–26. Abingdon: Routledge.

Blümel, W., Pethig, R. and von dem Hagen, O. (1986) The Theory of Public Goods: A Survey of Recent Issues. *Journal of Institutional and Theoretical Economics* 142: 241–309.

Bönker, F., Libbe, J. and Wollmann, H. (2016). Re-municipalization Revisited: Long-Term Trends in the Provision of Local Public Services in Germany. In H. Wollmann, I. Kopric and G. Marcou (eds), *Public and Social Services in Europe. From Public and Municipal to Private Sector Provision*. Basingstoke: Palgrave Macmillan.

Bossert, T. and Beauvais, J. (2002) Decentralization of Health Systems in Ghana, Zambia, Uganda and the Philippines: A Comparative Analysis of Decision Space. *Health Policy and Planning* 17(1): 14–31.

Brown, C. V. and Jackson, P. M. (1978) *Public Sector Economics*. Oxford: Martin Robertson.

Brown, T. L. and Potoski, M. (2003) Transaction Cost and Institutional Explanations for Government Services Production Decisions. *Journal of Public Administration Research and Theory* 13(4): 441–468.

Brown, T. L., Potoski, M. and Van Slyke, D. M. (2006) Managing Public Service Contracts: Aligning Values, Institutions, and Markets. *Public Administration Review* 66(3): 323–331.

Brudney, J. L., Fernandez, S., Ryu, J. E. and Wright, D. S. (2005) Exploring and Explaining Contracting Out: Patterns among the American States. *Journal of Public Administration Research and Theory* 15(3): 393–419.

Brusca, I. and Montesinos, V. (2016) Implementing Performance Reporting in Local Government: a Cross-Countries Comparison. *Public Performance and Management Review* 39: 506–534.

Buchholz, R. A. and Rosenthal, S. B. (2004) Stakeholder Theory and Public Policy: How Governments Matter. *Journal of Business Ethics* 51(2): 143–153.

Citroni, G., Lippi, A. and Profeti, S. (2016) Local Public Services in Italy: Still Fragmentation. In H. Wollmann, G. Marcou and G. Koprič (eds), *Public and Social Services in European Countries*, 103–117. Basingstoke: Palgrave Macmillan.

Collins, P. D. (2012) Governance and the Eradication of Poverty: An Introduction to the Special Issue. *Public Administration and Development* 32: 337–344.

Dahan, N. M., Doh, J. P. and Raelin, J. D. (2015) Pivoting the Role of Government in the Business and Society Interface: A Stakeholder Perspective. *Journal of Business Ethics* 131: 665–680.

De Groot, H. and Pommer, E. (1989) The Stability of Stated Preferences for Public Goods: Evidence from Recent Budget Games. *Public Choice* 60: 123–132.

De Vries, M. (2000) The Rise and Fall of Decentralization: A Comparative Analysis of Arguments and Practices in European Countries. *European Journal of Political Research* 38: 193–224.

Downs, A. (1957) *An Economic Theory of Democracy*. New York: Harper & Row.

Economist. (2017) Migrants With Mobile. Phones Are Now Indispensable For Refugees. *The Economist* (11 February). Retrieved on 3 September 2017 from www.economist.com/news/international/21716637-technology-has-made-migrating-europe-easier-over-time-it-will-also-make-migration.

European Commission. (2003) *Green Paper on Services of General Interest*. COM(2003) 270 final – Official Journal C 76 of 25 March. Brussels: European Commission.

European Commission. (2011) *Communication From The Commission To The European Parliament, The Council, The European Economic And Social Committee And The Committee Of The Regions – A Quality Framework for Services of General Interest in Europe*. COM(2011) 900 final, 20 December 2011. Brussels: European Commission. Retrieved from http://ec.europa.eu/archives/commission_2010-2014/president/news/speeches-statements/pdf/20111220_1_en.pdf.

European Commission. (2013) *Commission Staff Working Document – Guide to the Application of the European Union Rules on State Aid, Public Procurement and the Internal Market to Services of General Economic Interest, and in Particular to Social Services of General Interest*. SWD(2013) 53 final/2, 29 April. Brussels: European Commission. Retrieved from http://ec.europa.eu/competition/state_aid/overview/new_guide_eu_rules_procurement_en.pdf.

Fernandez, S., Ryu, J. E. and Brudney, J. L. (2008) Exploring Variations in Contracting for Services among American Local Governments: Do Politics Still Matter? *American Review of Public Administration* 38(4): 439–462.

Ferris, J. (1986) The Decision to Contract Out: An Empirical Analysis. *Urban Affairs Review* 22(2): 289–311.

Frant, H. (1996) High-Powered and Low-Powered Incentives in the Public Sector. *Journal of Public Administration Research and Theory* 6(3): 365–382.

Freeman, R. E. (1984) *Strategic Management*. Boston, MA: Pitman/Ballinger.

Galligan, B. (2006) Comparative Federalism. In R. A. W. Rhodes, S. A. Binder and B. A. Rockman (eds), *The Oxford Handbook of Political Institutions*, 261–280. New York: Oxford University Press.

Government Offices of Sweden. (2014) The Government Invests in Culture and Democracy. Retrieved on 10 March 2017 from www.government.se/press-releases/2014/10/the-government-invests-in-culture-and-democracy.

Jimenez-Rubio, D., Smith, P. C. and Van Doorslaer, E. 2008. Equity in Health and Healthcare in a Decentralised Context: Evidence from Canada. *Health Economics* 17(3): 377–392.

Jones, B. D. (2003) Bounded Rationality and Political Science: Lessons from Public Administration and Public Policy. *Journal of Public Administration Research and Theory* 13(4): 395–412.

Levin, J. and Tadelis, S. (2010) Contracting for Government Services: Theory and Evidence from US Cities. *Journal of Industrial Economics* 58(3): 507–541.

Loughlin, M. (1996) *Legality and Locality*. Oxford: Clarendon Press.

Lu, J. (2013) How Political are Government Contracting Decisions? An Examination of Human Service Contracting Determinants. *Public Administration Quarterly* 37(2): 182–207.

Mafrolla, E. and D'Amico, E. (2016) Does Public Spending Improve Citizens' Quality of Life? An Analysis of Municipalities' Leisure Supply. *Local Government Studies* 42(2): 332–350.

Marsh, D., Richards, D. and Smith, M. J. (2001) *Changing Patterns of Governance in the United Kingdom: Reinventing Whitehall*. Basingstoke: Palgrave.

Martin, B. (2004) *What Is Public About Public Services?* Working Paper Commissioned by the World Bank as a background paper for the World Development Report, *Making Services Work for Poor People*. Retrieved from www.publicworld.org/files/WhatIsPublic.pdf.

Nelson, M. A. (1997) Municipal Government Approaches to Service Delivery: An Analysis from Transactions Cost Perspective. *Economic Inquiry* 55(1): 82–96.

Neville, B. A. and Menguc, B. (2006). Stakeholder Multiplicity: Toward an Understanding of the Interactions between Stakeholders. *Journal of Business Ethics* 66(4): 377–391.

Ni, A. Y. and Bretschneider, S. (2007) The Decision to Contract Out: A Study of Contracting for E-government Services in State Governments. *Public Administration Review* 67(3): 531–544.

OECD. (2016) Health Systems Characteristics Survey. Retrieved on 10 March 2017 from http://qdd.oecd.org/subject.aspx?Subject=hsc.

Ølykke, G. S. and Møllgaard, P. (2016) What is a Service of General Economic Interest? *European Journal of Law and Economics* 41(1): 205–241.

Osborne, S. P. and Brown, K. (2005) *Managing Change and Innovation in Public Service Organizations*. New York: Routledge.

Pallesen, T. (2004) A Political Perspective on Contracting Out: The Politics of Good Times: Experiences from Danish Local Governments. *Governance: An International Journal of Policy Administration and Institutions* 17(4): 573–587.

Pennings, J. M. (1975) The Relevance of the Structural-Contingency Model for Organizational Effectiveness. *Administrative Science Quarterly* 20(3): 393–410.

Peters, G. B. and Pierre, J. (2001) Developments in Intergovernmental Relations: Towards Multilevel Governance. *Policy and Politics* 29(2): 131–136.

Pollit, C. and Bouckaert, G. (2011) *Public Management Reform: A Comparative Analysis* (3rd edition). Oxford: Oxford University Press.

Ponsignon, P. A., Smart and Maull, R. S. (2011) Service Delivery System Design: Characteristics and Contingencies. *International Journal of Operations and Production Management* 31(3): 324–349.

Price, B. E. and Riccucci, N. M. (2005) Exploring the Determinants of Decisions to Privatize State Prisons. *American Review of Public Administration* 35(3): 223–235.

Ranson, S. and Walsh, K. (1985) Introduction: Understanding the Crisis. In S. Ranson, G. Jones and K. Walsh (eds), *Between Centre and Locality*, 1–18. London: George Allen & Unwin.

Rhodes, R.A.W. (1999) *Control and Power in Central–Local Government Relations* (2nd edition). Aldershot: Ashgate.

Rodrigues, M., Tavares, A. F. and Araùjo, J. F. (2012) Municipal Service Delivery: The Role of Transaction Costs in the Choice between Alternative Governance Mechanisms. *Local Government Studies* 38(5): 615–638.

Romer, T. and Rosenthal, H. (1979) The Elusive Median Voter. *Journal of Public Economics* 12(2): 143–170.

Sauter, W. and Schepel, H. (2009) *State And Market In European Union Law: The Public And Private Spheres Of The Internal Market Before The EU Courts*. Cambridge: Cambridge University Press.

Savas, E. S. (1987) *Privatisation: The Key To Better Government*. Chatham, NJ: Chatham House.

Sharpe, L. J. (1993) *Rise of Meso Government in Europe*. London: Sage.
Simon, H. A. (1947) *Administrative Behavior: A Study of Decision-Making Processes in Administrative Organizations*. New York: Free Press.
Smith, H. L., Fottler, M. D. and Saxberg, B. O. (1981) Cost Containment in Health Care: A Model for Management Research. *The Academy of Management Review* 6(3): 397–407.
Stiglitz, J. E. (2000) *Economics of the Public Sector*. New York: W. W. Norton.
Stone, M. (2002) How Not to Measure the Efficiency of Public Services (and How One Might). *Journal of the Royal Statistical Society: Series A (Statistics in Society)* 165(3): 405–434
Sullivan, H. and Gillanders, G. (2005) Stretched to the Limit? The Impact of Local Public Service Agreements on Service Improvement and Central–Local Relations. *Local Government Studies* 31(5): 555–574.
Swianiewicz, P. (2018) If Territorial Fragmentation is a Problem, is Amalgamation a Solution? – Ten Years Later. *Local Government Studies* 44(1): 1–10.
Thomson, S., Osborn, R., Squires, D. and Jun, M. (eds). (2012) *International Profiles of Health Care Systems 2012*. New York: Commonwealth Fund.
Tiebout, C. M. (1957) A Pure Theory of Local Expenditures. *The Journal of Political Economy* 64(5): 416–424.
Tremlett, G. (2008) *Ghosts of Spain: Travels Through Spain and Its Silent Past*. New York: Walker & Company.
United Nations Development Programme. (2016) *Human Development Report 2016. Development for Everyone*. New York: UNDP. Retrieved from http://hdr.undp.org/sites/default/files/2016_human_development_report.pdf.
Warner, M. and Hebdon, R. (2001) Local Government Restructuring: Privatization and Its Alternatives. *Journal of Policy Analysis and Management* 20(2): 315–336.
Williamson, O. (1981) The Economics of Organization. *American Journal of Sociology* 87(3): 548–577.
Wilson, D. and Game, C. (2002) *Local Government in the United Kingdom* (3rd edition). Basingstoke: Palgrave Macmillan.
Wilson, D. and Game, C. (2006) *Local Government in the United Kingdom* (4th edition). Basingstoke: Palgrave Macmillan.
Wilson, D. and Game, C. (2011) *Local Government in the United Kingdom* (5th edition). Basingstoke: Palgrave Macmillan.
Wollmann, H. (2008) Decentralisation and Territorial Local Government Reforms between Local Democracy and Operational Efficiency – Some Comparative Observations and Conclusions in the European Context. In Council of European Municipalities and Regions (CEMR), *Balancing Democracy, Identity and Efficiency: Changes in Local and Regional Structures in Europe*, 82–91. Brussels: Council of European Municipalities and Regions. Retrieved on 22 February 2017 from www.ccre.org/docs/changes_in_local_and_regional_structures_web_EN.pdf.
Wollmann, H. (2016) Provision of Public and Social Services in European Countries: From Public Sector to Marketization and Reverse – or, What Next? In S. Kuhlmann and G. Bouckaert (eds), *Local Public Sector Reforms in Times of Crisis. National Trajectories and International Comparisons*, 187–204. Basingstoke: Palgrave Macmillan.
World Bank. (2004) *World Development Report 2004: Making Services Work for Poor People*. Retrieved from https://openknowledge.worldbank.org/bitstream/handle/10986/5986/WDR%202004%20-%20English.pdf?sequence=1.
Zangrandi, A. (1994) *Autonomia ed economicità nelle aziende pubbliche*. Milan: Giuffrè Ed.

16
PUBLIC SERVICE DELIVERY IN TODAY'S GEORGIA

Giorgi Vashakidze

Introduction

After the collapse of the Soviet Union, a decentralisation policy prevailed in Georgia. Since 2004, however, the government has reversed the trend of decentralisation by reducing the autonomy of local authorities in delivering services and by embarking on the creation of a centralised service delivery model based on the 'one-stop-shop' principle. Today, the government of Georgia uses this model to deliver more than 300 public services at regional and community levels. Justice Houses serve as public service hubs at regional level while Community Centres deliver public services to citizens in communities. This chapter focuses on community centres to analyse governance and public service delivery at the local level in Georgia today.

Arguably, in many former Soviet, now independent states, public administration and particularly public service delivery has experienced major crises. The collapse of the Soviet Union saw not only the relationship between governments and citizens deteriorate, but also that between state agencies. This observation is not surprising as most former soviet societies lived under corrupt and non-accountable authoritarian regimes; inclined to subjugate individual interests and needs to those of the government (Mishler and Rose 1997). The legacy of the Communist public administration continues to influence the performance of most post-Soviet governments, and thus their ability to improve the economic and social well-being of citizens. Among those states that nonetheless launched reforms more or less successfully are the three Baltic States (Estonia, Latvia and Lithuania) along with Kazakhstan, Azerbaijan and Georgia.

The three Baltic states quickly began the transformation of their public administration and public service delivery system in the early 1990s. Kazakhstan, Azerbaijan and Georgia followed in the past decade. Traditionally the decentralisation of authority and resources from the central government to local governments is considered to be an essential element for effective public service delivery. In recent years, this notion has been challenged by the evolution of a new type of public service delivery models in some former constituents of the Soviet Union. One such model is the one-stop-shop in Georgia and other countries, where integration and centralisation of resources and responsibilities became the main ingredient for the central authorities to effectively deliver public services nationwide.

Kazakhstan started reforming public services based on the one-stop-shop (OSS) principle in the mid-2000 and developed a system that delivers a large number of public services to citizens via a state-owned corporation, Government for Citizens. Azerbaijan started reforming its public service delivery by implementing OSS principles in 2012 under the concept of ASAN xidmət ('Easy Service'). The central government of Georgia initiated its public administration reform in 2004 with the aim of triggering economic growth and tackling massive corruption in the public sector. The core of this reform was to centralise the delivery of public services using the OSS principles. Initially, many of the competences for delivering public services were the responsibility of local authorities. The central government did not purposely intend to disempower local authorities. However, they also realised that it was not realistic to quickly reform local capacity to deliver public services effectively and efficiently. It would have taken more time, financial and human resources than were available at that time. Therefore, the central government decided to counterbalance local authorities' inability to serve citizens in a timely, effective and customer friendly manner by creating a network of Justice Houses and Community Centres that deliver public services at regional and at the village/community levels.

Historic background of public service delivery in Georgia

The transition of Soviet Georgia to an independent state was accompanied by violence. The inexperienced political movement that developed during Perestroika led to mass demonstrations – one of which was violently repressed by the Soviet military in April 1989. Public reaction against Soviet power led to the election of a new leadership in Tbilisi and the declaration of independence in April 1991 (Nodia 1998). During this chaotic period, Georgia experienced devastating economic decline as assets and authority were transferred from Soviet to Georgian structures under the control of a newly elected government. The country also experienced considerable political and civil strife as a result of the secessionist tendencies of several ethnic groups. In addition to these conflicts, the weakening of central authority and a dysfunctional state apparatus led to broader disintegrative processes throughout Georgia. The almost complete collapse of trade and industrial linkages with the former Soviet Union and the resulting economic dislocation, led to extreme fragmentation of Georgian society. Amidst the crisis, the central government ruled by decree until a constitution was finally adapted in 1995.

Alongside with the constitution the government started elaborating the legal basis for public service delivery nationwide. The important framework was developed in 1997 when the Parliament adopted the Organic Law on Local Self-Government and Government. The law defined four levels of governance. The first level consisted of village, agglomeration of villages, village/town, and city. The second level comprised rayons or districts and republican or special status cities. The third one was defined as region. There were nine regions, plus the capital city, Tbilisi, and two autonomous republics: Abkhazia and Adjara. The last and forth level was the state.

However, the law lacked clearly defined structure to regulate for instance, issues related to ownership of property or to administrative responsibilities. The expenditure responsibilities as well as the public service delivery structure of local governments and local self-governments were not clearly defined by law, and many provisions of the legislation overlapped. Local self-governments at village level did not have significant and meaningful public service functions; most of these functions were undertaken by the rayons/districts (Ministry of Justice 1997). Basic public services such as the issuing of passports or IDs, registration of citizens or registration of civil acts fell under the responsibilities of regional bureaus of the Ministry of Interior and technical bureaus of local government. This heavily fragmented system created a lot of confusion and overlap in delivering public services. As a consequence, the system became dysfunctional and corrupt. None of the organisations possessed complete data on citizens. The organisational human resource management systems were weak and ineffective, the system could not generate financial resources, and the services were delivered through extremely dilapidated infrastructure. Technical basics such as software and hardware infrastructure that could have helped in securely providing services did not exist. The workflows were completely paper based (Gagnidze 2009).

The functions of land management and registration were controlled by the State Land Management Department. Identical responsibilities were given to technical bureaus under the local self-government. A lack of cooperation between the department and the technical bureaus as well as the overlap in terms of their administrative responsibilities proved solid ground for corruption to prosper. Mismanagement and massive bureaucracy at both central as well as local levels further damaged the reputation of the administration in the eyes of citizens. Public service delivery became to be associated with ineffective bureaucracy, aggressive and non-accountable bureaucrats, bribes, a depressing soviet infrastructure and nerve-shattering processes.

In 2004, the government of Georgia initiated a massive administrative reform that eventually changed the nature and form of public service delivery. The reform aimed at improving bureaucracy through the introduction of legislative changes to simplify procedures and to deregulate the traditionally heavily regulated administrative sphere of governance. The ultimate purpose was to eradicate corruption from the system and to support rapid economic growth in the country. By implementing the policy of OSS public service delivery, the government managed to dismantle the heavily bureaucratic and ineffective public service delivery structure and replaced it with semi-independent, usually centrally operated, small sized agencies that are instructed to tightly work together to deliver public services in a timely, effective and customer friendly manner.

Public service delivery in Georgia now

There are two main channels for the delivery of public services in Georgia. The first, most intensive channel is managed by the centrally operated, state-owned, semi-independent agencies. These agencies are usually under the subordination of various ministries and use the One-Stop-Shop principle of public service delivery. Citizens receive these public services from central government through Justice Houses and Community Centres (CC).

The Justice House is also known as the Public Service Hall (PSH); it is a semi-independent agency and a legal entity of the Ministry of Justice of Georgia (MoJ). It has rights to represent itself vis-à-vis third parties, has its own budget, identification code, accounts in commercial banks and in the state treasury as well as other characteristics necessary for a legal entity of public law.

PSH arrangements were established in 2012 and the main purpose is to provide services offered by public as well as by private agencies through the One-Stop-Shop model of service delivery. The MoJ instructs the agency to support government service delivery, to design and to offer public services through innovation and diversity. PSH is expected to provide consultation to other state or non-state actors in order to improve services delivery with the purpose of effectively offering services to citizens as well as organisations (Ministry of Justice 2015). In essence, it serves as a front office for a number of back office agencies that design and produce public services.

As a result, the public service delivery structure as designed by the central authorities in Georgia can be split into two, front office and back office agencies. The former are customer-oriented and service-minded and responsible for offering services to citizens in a timely and customer-friendly manner while the letter is expected to design and produce public services offered by the front office. Hence, close cooperation between front and back office state agencies is vital to ensure the smooth operation of OSS public service delivery chain in Georgia. Today, PSH delivers more than 300 public services to citizens at regional level.

On the village level public services are delivered by the CCs. CCs operate under the Public Service Development Agency of Georgia (PSDA) which is yet another legal entity of public law established in 2012 under the subordination of the Ministry of Justice.

PSDA is the former Civil Registry Agency of Georgia, with a more extended mandate and responsibilities. In addition to civil registration tasks inherited by the agency, it is expected to innovate and generate new approaches for public service modernisation and development. The issues related to immigration, document legalisation and apostil services fall under the mandate of the agency. The Ministry of Justice empowered the agency to create mechanisms for the implementation of strategically important projects and to initiate reforms in the public sector. The development of Community Centres could be considered as a strategically important project as it reaches previously untapped part of society while delivering public service at village level.

In parallel to these centrally operated services, the second, more fragmented channel of service delivery is under municipal management. Since 2014, the law on local self-government recognises two forms of municipality. The first form is a settlement such as a self-governing city which has clearly defined administrative borders. The second form is an agglomeration of settlements with administrative borders and an administrative centre. In addition, the municipality must have an elected representative and executive branches of government. Today, there are 71 municipalities in Georgia: 12 self-governing cities and 59 agglomerations of settlements (Svanishvili et al. 2014).

The organic law on local self-governance proposes two types of competencies for municipalities: exclusive competencies and delegated competencies. The latter is given to the municipality either by the central authorities or by the authorities of the autonomous republic. It should be based on an agreement between the parties, and a delegating authority must ensure that it supplies material and financial resources for it to be implemented.

The exclusive competences of municipalities cover a whole range of services and can be tentatively grouped under administrative, financial, economic, education and culture and social competences.

Development and functional capacity of the community centres

In 2011, the Government of Georgia approved a project for the 'Introduction of E-governance in Local Governments' that was initiated by the Civil Registry Agency and the European Union Mission in Georgia. The project aimed at improving the management at municipality centres, improving the interaction between municipal centres and trustee offices, providing public services to the local population more effectively, designing easily adaptable software solutions for service delivery and designing a legal framework as well as developing technical infrastructure for the operation and introduction of e-governance.

As of 2012, the Service Development Agency of Georgia succeeded the Civil Registry Agency in supporting and further developing the project through the introduction of CCs. Today, there are 51 Community Centres nationwide and more centres are planned to be inaugurated in 2018.

A typical CC is a multi-functional physical space in a village that is equipped with modern infrastructure and technology. As the functional extension of PSDA, CCs offer civil registration services to citizens and serve as its front office. Besides that, CCs offer front office services to several other state agencies that operate in the back office. Namely, centres offer citizens public services provided by the National Agency of Public Registry (NAPR), the National Archive of Georgia (NAG), the

Social Service Agency (SSA) under the Ministry of Labour, Health and Social Affairs of Georgia (MoLHSA) and Mechanizatory, a limited liability enterprise that acts as a provider for agriculture services under subordination of the Ministry of Agriculture (MoA).

Overall, it provides more than 250 public services to the local population and includes (see the annex II for a non-exhaustive list of public services offered at CCs):

- **Civil registry services**: e-ID, passport, birth registration, secondary education attestation, residence permit, repeated issuance of any civil acts, divorce registration etc.
- **Public registry services**: property right registration, extract on real-estate, registration of a right to build an estate on a land parcel, debtor pledge registration etc.
- **National archive services**: a letter from archive about divorce, death, birth, award, evacuation, information on registration of physical and judicial entities etc.
- **Social services**: a letter confirming that a family is registered in a social assistance database, accepting citizens request for the need of an auxiliary technical assistance etc.
- **Agriculture services**: paving and cleaning of water canals, land mulching, excavation work, vineyard care and protection, mowing, pressing of hay etc.

Most of the services available at the centres fall under the responsibility of the Ministry of Justice, except for social and agriculture services. Citizens can also receive services offered by private companies in the centres. For instance, Magticom offers telecommunication related services while Liberty Bank helps ensure that the population receives financial services.

Interaction between Community Centres, National Agency of Public Registry and National Archive of Georgia

In order to deliver public services nationwide, the back office agencies responsible for service design and production enter into an agreement with the PSDA to delegate competences to deliver public services through centres. PSDA has the right to define the number of centres that will offer services to citizens, but has an obligation to provide the back office agency with the exact number and location of those centres. The back office agency has the unrestricted right to monitor public service delivery in centres to ensure that standards and the quality of the provided services meet its expectation. The back office agency also has the right to demand PSDA should introduce sanction against employees who violate or jeopardise public service delivery or to propose awards for those who perform well. It can perform monitoring at centres anytime.

Back office agencies make sure that the centre operators have the up-to-date knowledge necessary to provide services. For that reason, they are obliged to provide training and support or any other necessary assistance for the operators. For instance, the NAPR takes the responsibility to train operators at centres via the Educational Centre of the Ministry of Justice. Moreover, the agency must consult upon the request of operators and must grant them access to its data centre. To raise awareness about service delivery standards and to solve any pertinent issues, NAPR must ensure that inter-agency meetings are organised to strengthen cooperation between the agencies. It must inform PSDA of any new legislative or administrative changes to ensure the uninterrupted delivery of public services. PSDA has the right to demand NAPR to provide any necessary software solution and instructions to operate its services.

PSDA must ensure that its employees do not abuse the rights granted by NAPR and guarantee that the citizens' personal data protection is respected. In case of violation of personal data protection, the agency takes responsibility to pay penalties to NAPR as well as to any third parties if necessary. The agency does not have rights to demand financial resources or financial support from NAPR while delivering services. It does not have the right to introduce additional fees for the services delivered. The agreement grants each party the right to suspend or terminate the agreement if the parties violate the terms and conditions.

PSDA also has an agreement signed with the National Archive of Georgia (NAG) to provide services through centres. Similar to NAPR, the National Archive takes the responsibility to provide consultation to operators as well as to ensure that they have unrestricted access to its database. NAG should periodically train PSDA personnel to meet its service delivery standards. To deliver services timely and without delays, NAG must provide the necessary equipment to centres. Particularly, it needs to ensure that the archive stamp necessary for the verification of archive documents is timely delivered. PSDA does not have rights to either demand financial resources from NAG or to introduce any additional fees for delivered services.

The National Agency of Public Registry, the National Archive of Georgia as well as the Public Service Development Agency fall under the direct subordination or the Ministry of Justice of Georgia. This fact most likely helps agencies to coordinate their efforts while delivering services via the centres. However, in parallel to these agencies, there are two more actors who deliver their services to citizens via the centres: the Social Service Agency of Georgia (SSA) and Mechanizatory Ltd. The first operates under the Ministry of Labour, Health and Social Affairs of Georgia and the latter is a sub-agency of the Ministry of Agriculture of Georgia. This has implications for how such organisations interact with the PSDA to deliver their public services to citizens through the centres.

Interaction between Community Centres, Social Service Agency and Mechanizatory Ltd

An agreement signed by the agencies stipulates the rights and the obligations of each party and delegates competencies to PSDA to deliver Social Service Agency services through the centres. The Social Service Agency has the right to perform monitoring anytime and demand that the centres meet the set service standard. SSA assigns its regional branches to respective Community Centres to streamline inter-agency interaction. Operators are expected to intensively communicate with representatives of SSA in respective regional branches to keep proper accountability of paper work and to ensure that the operators pass on the acquired original documents on a weekly basis. SSA ensures proper training for the centre personnel and provides all necessary technical equipment for the delivery of public services.

The agreement also gives detailed instruction to operators what kind of documents they must request to provide services. For instance, for the operator to launch the procedure for granting the right to state pension or to a package of state pension, it is necessary to request ID documents from a citizen. If the request is from a third party, then the operator must request appropriate documents to prove that the requestors is a legal representative of the beneficiary. The operator must follow several procedures. A special form provided by SSA needs to be completed, and the operator must assist the citizen to fill the form if necessary.

As soon as the request is processed, the operator must provide the citizen with proof that the request is accepted. The proof needs to have a date, the name of the requestor, the number of pages, the code granted by the system and it needs to be verified by an official stamp. As soon as the request is in the SSA database, it is processed by the agency. Once the decision is made, it is obligatory for the operator to use the SSA database to print the document. The written response to the beneficiary must be verified by the operator with a stamp of the agency on the document. Each service that falls under the agreement is followed by thorough instructions on how to operate it. These social services are provided free of charge to citizens via the centres.

Likewise, the agreement signed by PSDA and Mechanizatory Ltd stipulates the responsibilities and the rights between the parties. Mechanizatory grants the right to the agency to offer agriculture services (agro-services) such as tractor services, processing crops by herbicides, soil treatment, soil watering etc. via the centres. The agency has the right to perform unannounced visits in the centres to assess the front office service quality and standard. It takes responsibility to provide trainings to personnel as well as makes sure that printers, cartridges or any other special forms to ensure effective operation of its services are delivered. It ensures that the price list for the agriculture services is up to date. The agency requests the right to access the Mechanizatory database, but it does not have rights to introduce any additional fees for the services provided.

The price of the service is calculated using the agro-service fee, the area of the customer's ground that is to be serviced and the distance that service providers and equipment (technical means) have to travel to reach the customer. A customer is defined as any physical person or legal entity interested in receiving services. The services can be requested either individually or as a group. In case of a group request, customers have the opportunity to make savings as transportation costs for the technical means will be lower. If there is work to be done in a neighbouring area or the land parcels are next to each other, then the costumers can place a special neighbour request and save time and money for the services requested.

Effective interaction between the back office and front office agencies is crucial while delivering public services via the centres. The role that the operators play in the process has a tremendous influence on how the quality of the service is perceived either by internal or external customers. To uphold the quality of services delivered as well as to achieve high satisfaction of customers, the operators must follow certain rules and standards to meet the demands.

Public service delivery standards in the Community Centres

Usually, the quality of service depends on two major variables. The first variable is the expected service quality in terms of the specific/tangible outcome of the public service. The second variable is the perceived service quality which responds to how it is delivered i.e. it focuses on the process of service delivery (Grönroos 1984). The quality standard introduced by the Public Service Development Agency for the Community Centres puts high emphasis on the process of the service delivery. It requires operators to meet strict standards of behaviour that are intended to improve the customer experience. This code of conduct contains unusually detailed instructions. For instance, when welcoming a customer, the operators are instructed to:

- smile as naturally and as pleasantly as possible;
- remain polite when interacting with customers and must not use affirmative phrases;
- be proactive and should listen to customers without interrupting them;
- not use complicated terminology during the interaction and should offer various options to receive a requested service;
- avoid negatively perceived non-verbal behaviour (e.g. employees are advised not to behave impatiently or stand with their arms crossed, and they may not want to lean back while sitting or lean on the table while standing); and
- not use social media, or send messages or read literature that are not related to their immediate work.

If a customer is not satisfied with the service and his/her complaint is related to the work of the centre, then the operator must immediately engage the customer to understand the issue and to assist in solving it. Also, the operator should thank the customer after the service is finished and wish him/her a pleasant day.

As soon as all documents are collected and filed, the operator deals with the next customer. Employees are expected to take care of their work place by tidying up their desks and are required to adhere to the requirements of a strict dress code. They need to make sure that their identification badge is clearly visible to customers. It appears likely that such a strict code of conduct and adherence to it is the reason for continuous high customer satisfaction as shown in the results of surveys conducted by research organisations and which will be discussed in greater detail in the next chapter.

In parallel to the strict corporate standards, operators must regularly undergo trainings to better deliver public services. The PSDA in cooperation with the back office agencies train operators in topics such as:

- granting or cancelling citizenship, type of resident permits and how to issue them;
- registration procedure of civil acts and their issuance, registration of citizens and issuance of identification documents such as passport or IDs;
- issuance of travel document and registration of citizens on an address;
- use e-document software and e-registration of an enterprise;
- produce extracts from state property registry; and
- registration of citizens for purposeful social assistance program and offering social insurance packages.

Operators receive relevant materials either electronically or hard copies or both and are expected to pass an exam after a training period.

This highly intensive service delivery system requires all actors in the front and back offices to work together to establish a service deliver chain. It allows central authorities to interact with the citizen directly as well as to cooperate with the local authorities in respective regions and communities to better deliver public services. Therefore, it is important to look through the findings of customer satisfaction surveys to analyse the impact of this system on authorities and customers.

The impact of service delivery on customers and authorities

In 2013, ACT, a local research and consulting company, conducted a customer satisfaction survey on behalf of the PSDA of Georgia. The survey focused on those communities where the centres operate and asked citizens about their knowledge of and satisfaction with their work. Overall, ACT engaged randomly selected respondents in 13 communities. The majority of respondents (61%) were aware of the existence of such a centre in their village. Others (39%) knew about the centre, but identified is as a local bank or associated it with a local council. This is less surprising than it may seem considering that the Community Centre is a multi-functional space where citizens can receive not only public services but also financial services. Less than half (43%), however, had received public services in their village at the time of the survey, and a mere fraction of those who had received services (10%) had not used the centres for that purpose. Figure 16.1 shows the percentage of citizens who knew the type of services they could receive in the centres.

We can note that the vast majority of respondents (82%) expressed satisfaction with the services received. In particular, citizens appreciated the quality of services, the rapid response of operators, the comfortable environment, cheap prices and proximity of the locations.

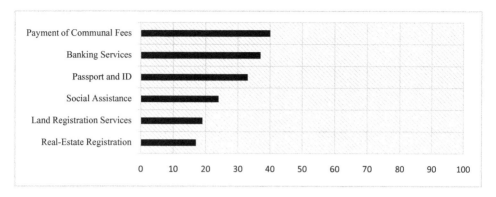

Figure 16.1 Types of services citizens knew could be received in the centres, 2013

Some very significant factors that help define customer satisfaction were the competency of operators, affordable prices for services and the kindness of staff, and notably the absence of long waiting lines and simple as well as clear language of communication between operators and citizens. These survey results reflect well on the extensive code of conduct for operators and how it is being implemented.

90% of respondents would use the services offered in centres again in the future. However, the majority of citizens did not know the centres also offer public space for free (Figure 16.2).

A similar survey was carried out by IPM, a local research organisation, to assess the satisfaction of customers with the public service offered in local municipalities without Community Centres.

This 2013 study focused on six municipalities. Questions touched on customer knowledge, attitude, perceptions and behaviour. Similar to the results of the centre study, the majority of users (74%) and non-users (75%) of municipal services received information about the municipality from their acquaintances. Figure 16.3 illustrates the type of services that citizens were aware of, and how often citizens used the services in the past.

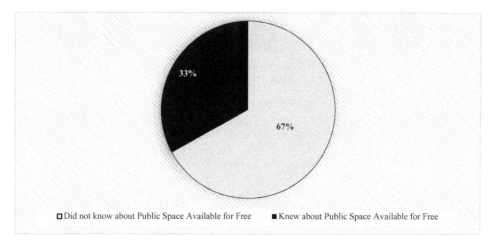

Figure 16.2 Knowledge about public space available for free in centres, 2013

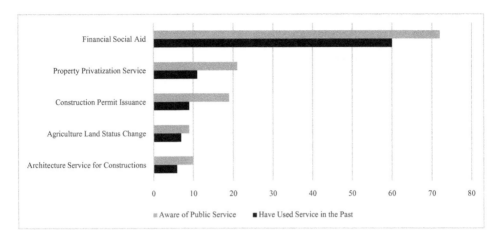

Figure 16.3 Types of services citizens are aware municipalities offer and usage of those services by citizens, 2013

IPM also asked citizens to assess how well municipalities perform their functions and how well personnel at municipalities respond to citizens (Figure 16.4). The majority was not generally satisfied with the performance of municipalities and their personnel.

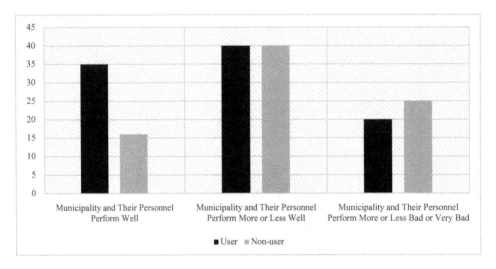

Figure 16.4 How well municipalities perform their functions and how well personnel responds to citizens, 2013

Customers expect municipalities to respond to citizens' demands in a timely manner, to provide precise and clear information, and to improve the quality of advice and the kindness of personnel. The questions aiming to assess how fairly municipalities treat citizens indicated that citizens doubted the fairness of municipalities (Figure 16.5). This fact does not reflect well on the extent to which citizens generally trust the local authorities.

Public service delivery in today's Georgia

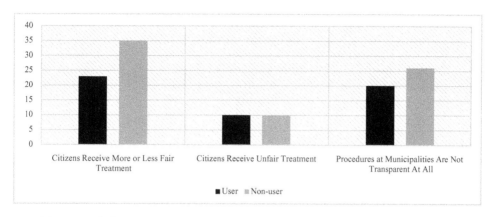

Figure 16.5 How fairly municipalities treat citizens, 2013

Despite this, almost half (47%) of those using local municipalities for obtaining public services were satisfied with the work of local municipalities. A mere 11% of users were completely dissatisfied. By comparison, among non-users these proportions were reversed with only a fifth (21%) expressing satisfaction compared to more than half (57%) being more or less satisfied, and another fifth (20%) being completely dissatisfied. The survey showed that on the Likert scale from 1 being the worst and 5 being the best, almost all municipal services received either average or lower than average score in terms of service quality as perceived by citizens, and that non-users suspect service delivery to be worse than perceived by those using them.

In 2016, ACT repeated its customer satisfaction survey to assess potential changes in the level of satisfaction with the performance of centres compared to the 2013 results. This study almost doubled the number of communities surveyed, covering 25 villages. The survey results showed that the majority of the population (97%) had heard about the centres in their respective communities and more than half among those (59%) had heard about at least one of the service provided by CCs. In terms of service ranking, the majority of citizens (62%) had heard about passports and identity cards services, almost half of them (41%) had heard about land registration services, and a third of them (27%) had heard about birth certificates issuance.

Similar to the 2013 survey, the survey in 2016 showed that the main source of information about CCs remained neighbours or friends. More than 80% of citizens received the information from those sources. The most commonly used services as mentioned by citizens are shown in Figure 16.6.

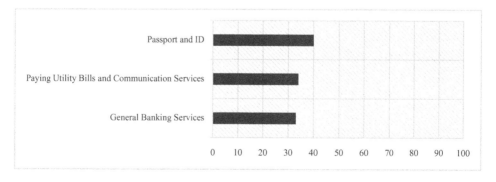

Figure 16.6 Most commonly used services in the centres, 2016

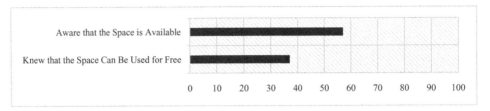

Figure 16.7 Knowledge about public space available for free in centres, 2016

It should be noted that the overwhelming majority of the population were satisfied with the quality of services received. Citizens positively assess the location and accessibility of the centres. In general, customers (98%) did not face obstructions or other difficulties when approaching the centres and they usually are consulted by a representative upon arrival. 19% of customers received services by paying certain fees and 91% of those who paid fees for services believe that the price of the service was acceptable.

The only points of criticism are the occasional waiting lines or queues. 31% of customers believe that the centres must introduce better line management to meet the citizens' demands. It is important to note that the issue of waiting lines was not mentioned by the customers in the survey conducted in 2013. The most likely reason for the occurrence of waiting lines is the popularity of the community centres among customers and that ever greater numbers of citizens use a CC to receive services.

The survey also reviewed the utilisation of public space offered by the Community Centres to citizens for free. In contrast to the results in 2013, more citizens mentioned that they are aware that the free space is available (Figure 16.7). However, it is not clear whether they use it frequently or not.

In parallel to exclusive services offered by the centres, citizens can receive so-called additional or specific services (Figure 16.8). For instance, customers are aware that they can receive assistance to submit an electronic application for the programme 'Produce in Georgia' or use notary services available in the centres.

The comparison of two surveys conducted in 2013, clearly shows that customers praise the services at Community Centres for the same reasons that they criticise the performance of local municipalities. In particular, citizens are highly satisfied with the quality of response of operators. They value the kindness of staff as well as the clarity of procedures and the time they save while interacting with the personnel. In contrast, citizens are not satisfied with the level of

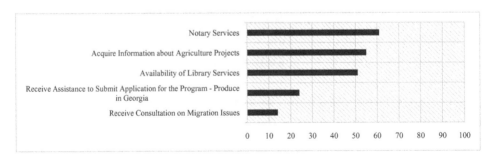

Figure 16.8 Awareness about additional services available in the centres, 2016

transparency of municipal procedures. In particular, the ambiguous response they often receive from personnel and the frequency of being redirected to other institutions to receive services.

The survey conducted in 2016 affirmed once again that a clear majority of costumers is satisfied with the services provided by the Community Centres. The main factors that determine customer satisfaction is the territorial proximity, high-quality and fast provision of services. Citizens praise the customer-oriented personnel and service-minded environment.

The surveys also identified neighbours and friends as the main source of information about the public services that either centres or municipalities offer. While this proves that satisfied customers are important to attract others, it also shows that more needs to be done to disseminate information about public services and to communicate directly with citizens to continue improving.

The one aspect on which both Community Centres and municipalities scored poorly, however, is the engagement of citizens in decision making. The biggest challenge for both central and local authorities still remains the genuine engagement of citizens in decision making. The studies conducted on behalf of state agencies and international organisations continually showed that citizens feel that they are not properly consulted in the process of public service policy design and implementation.

Conclusion

With the current administrative and procedural structure of public service delivery, Georgia can be considered to operate a mixed model of public services. The large number of public services that previously belonged to local municipalities are today provided by the central authorities. However, there are a set of important public services that still fall under the exclusive competencies of local authorities. It is evident that the existing model of service delivery creates competition and sometimes tension in the relationship between central and local authorities. The central authority uses the OSS model of public service delivery and the surveys show that the citizens are satisfied with the quality of services.

In contrast to the central government, the local authorities need to improve the quality of services delivered and to ensure that they technological base is not lagging behind. To avoid misconception among the population and to portray the customer friendliness of authorities, both layers of government might consider the possibilities of greater co-operation in developing and delivering public services.

Community Centres can serve as good examples of cooperation between central and local authorities as it brings the central services to local communities and simultaneously helps local authorities to improve their image vis-à-vis citizens. However, this is not enough as citizens demand more genuine engagement in decision making while designing and implementing the state policies.

The centrally operated agencies could co-operate more effectively with local authorities to share their experience and knowledge on how to transform the public service delivery structure in local municipalities. It would be wiser for local authorities to model their public service delivery structure according to the One-Stop-Shop principles which have been effectively used by the central agencies.

The central authorities' concern with local governments success should logically extend to making sure that local government services are provided in a timely and customer-friendly manner. Local governments and local services are where most citizens interface with government. Therefore, increasing citizens participation in local decision making while developing local government public service reform will help central and local government to make future public service delivery structures more effective and sustainable.

Glossary

ACT – research and consulting company
CC – Community Centre
CRA – Civil Registry Agency of Georgia
GoG – Government of Georgia
ID – identification card
IPM – research and consulting company
Mechanizatory Ltd – a limited liability enterprise under subordination of MoA
MoA – Ministry of Agriculture of Georgia
MoLHSA – Ministry of Labour, Health and Social Affairs of Georgia
MoJ – Ministry of Justice of Georgia
NAG – National Archive of Georgia
NAPR – National Agency of Public Registry of Georgia
OSS – one-stop-shop model
PSH – Public Service Hall (also known as Justice House)
PSDA – Public Service Development Agency of Georgia
SSA – Social Service Agency

References

Gagnidze, N. 2009. Civil Registry Reform. In *Policy Paper: Challenges to the Effective Governance in Georgia*, pp. 11–19. Washington, DC: USAID.

Grönroos, C. 1984. A Service Quality Model and its Marketing Implications. *European Journal of Marketing* 18(4): 36–43.

Ministry of Justice. 1997. Organic Law of Georgia, Local Governance and Self-Government Code. Retrieved on 10 November 2016 from https://matsne.gov.ge/ka/document/view/33436.

Ministry of Justice. 2015. Order 85. Retrieved on 20 November 2016 from https://matsne.gov.ge/ka/document/view/2923513.

Mishler, W. and Rose R. 1997. Trust, Distrust and Skepticism: Popular Evaluations of Civil and Political Institutions in Post-Communist Societies. *Journal of Politics* 59(2) (May): 418–451.

Nodia, G. 1998. Dynamics of State-Building in Georgia. *Demokratizatsiya* 6(1): 6–13.

Svanishvili, A., Losaberidze, D., Kandelaki, K. and Kiguradze K. 2014. *Local Governance and Elections, Guidance for Political Parties* (ადგილობრივი თვითმმართველობა და არჩევნები. დამხმარე სახელმძღვანელო – გზამკვლევი პოლიტიკური პარტიების წარმომადგენლებისათვის). Tbilisi: International Centre for Civic Culture.

17
THE PROVISION OF PUBLIC AND PERSONAL SOCIAL SERVICES IN EUROPEAN COUNTRIES

Between marketisation and the return of the public/municipal and third sector

Hellmut Wollmann

Introduction

The chapter discusses the provision of public and personal social services. The former are infrastructural services, often also labelled public utilities and now called 'services of general economic interest' (European Commission 2011), such as water supply, sewage, public transport and energy. Personal services describe the services and care provided to meet individual needs, such as child care, elderly care, care for the disabled, education and similar services.

The range of organisations and actors involved in the provision of these services includes the public, the private and the third sector. Within the public sector a distinction is made between the central state, regional or provincial bodies and local governments which also includes public/municipal companies. The private sector is essentially composed of private (primarily commercial) organisations and companies. There is no settled definition of the third sector (Salamon and Sokolowski 2016) but it can be argued to include established non-profit (NGO-type) organisations and a wide range of informal societal organisations and actors, such as cooperatives, self-help organisations and initiatives and social enterprises. This broad and differentiated understanding of public, private and 'third sector' actors will allow us to capture the varied institutions and actors involved in the provision of public and social services.

In its country coverage the article is based on a selection of European countries which, on the North–South axis, include the UK, Sweden and Germany, on the one side, and Italy and Greece, on the other. On the West–East axis, the ex-Communist transformation countries such as Hungary and Poland figure prominently in this analysis.

This chapter builds on the author's own work, on available research, particularly on work conducted by the members of an international working group that was formed between 2013 and 2015 within the European Union-funded COST Action 'Local Public Sector Reforms' (see Bouckaert and Kuhlmann 2016). Reports of their findings have been published in Wollmann,

Kopric and Marcou (2016; for a summary see Wollmann 2016) and will be used and quoted below. In addition, this chapter draws on Wollmann (2014, 2016, 2018).

Developments up to the 1980s

It will be helpful to set the recent phase of development in the context of an overview of the institutional development in the period from the pre-welfare state period of late 19th century up to the 'neo-liberal' 1980s.

In the mid to late 19th-century period, under the dominant ('Manchester Liberal') doctrine of minimal government, emerging public services were carried out by various forms of local government, while the developing personal services were rendered by societal, voluntary and charitable organisations

The developed welfare state reached a high point in the 1970s, and in key European countries was marked by a 'social democratic welfare state regime' (Esping-Andersen 1990). At that time, the institutional development of service provision was in some countries guided by the political assumption that public and social services were best provided by the public/municipal sector, while service provision by not for profit organisations found their role diminished. After 1945, under the Labour government the U.K. epitomised the public sector-centred delivery of public and social services, with the nationalisation of the energy and the water sectors as well as the introduction of the National Health Service. There were different approaches from this public sector-centred pattern in countries with a 'conservative welfare state regime' (Esping-Andersen 1990). Based on the traditional 'subsidiarity principle' (for example in the then West Germany), personal social services were primarily provided by third sector non-profit organisations.

In the majority of Central and Eastern European countries after the Communist take-over post-1945, the *centralist Socialist ('late-Stalinist') State model*, public and personal social services were carried out by the central State administration proper or through centrally controlled local units.

Since the late 1970s, under the impact of *neo-liberal market liberalisation policy and New Public Management (NPM) principles* the preponderance of public/municipal provision was in many countries reduced or even dismantled by corporatising, outsourcing and privatising service provision. After 1979, under the neo-liberal Conservative Government led by Margaret Thatcher, the UK became the leading example of promoting the neo-liberal policy agenda both nationally and internationally. From the mid-1980s,, the EU increased the impact of its 'Europeanising' market liberalisation policy throughout its member countries. The extent of this drive was manifested in Germany by the abolition of the historical ('path-dependent') privilege of the third sector non-profit organisations. In Central and Eastern European countries, after 1990, with widespread and turbulent transformation of centralist states and propelled by successive waves of accession to the EU and its market liberalisation regime, the institutions of public and social service provision developed in a similar fashion.

Development in service provision since the early 21st century

Since the early 2000s the development of the institutions and actors involved in service provision has followed trajectories that have varied from country to country. There has been a divergence and bifurcation between the continuing thrust of market liberalisation and privatisation with the advances of private sector provision, on the one hand, and a 'comeback' of the municipal sector (re-municipalisation) and the strengthening and (re-)emergence of the third sector, on the other.

Continuing market liberalisation and privatisation in service delivery

The market liberalisation of service provision which has been triggered since the 1980s has continued and even gained further momentum since the 2000s with further corporatisation, outsourcing and privatisation of service provision.

The persistent drive of the EU for market liberalisation materialised in the EU regulation of public procurement, in particular on the tendering of concession contracts for the outsourcing of service provision. In a first move the European Commission, in late 2012, proposed a draft Directive on concession contracts pertaining to all types of 'services of general economic interest', including water services (see Marcou 2016: 18). The draft directive was criticised particularly by local authorities (with the German authorities being especially vociferous) for virtually nullifying the 'wide discretion' that the EU, in the Lisbon Treaty of December 2009, accorded to local authorities in their autonomy to decide how to organise local service provision (see below). In the water sector the draft Directive was suspected by the local authorities as 'opening the door to privatisation with negative consequences for the population' (Deutsche Städtetag 2013). After prolonged controversial discussions the directives were modified so that the general market liberalisation thrust was in part mitigated. The provision by municipal organisations and companies which operate entirely under the control of the local authorities (in the so called 'in house' variant) are exempt from the (EU-wide) tendering process. Moreover, in a separate directive (2014/25 EU; see Marcou 2016: 23) water provision was explicitly excluded from the application of the general rules on concession contracts. However, notwithstanding these procedural variations the EU procurement directives and their transposition into national legislation have become significant drivers of further market liberalisation.

The 'Europeanisation' of market liberalisation has received further international and global impulses from the recent international negotiations on TIPP (Transatlantic Trade and Investment Partnership) and TISA (Trade in Services Agreement). Particularly from the point of view of local governments and their associations, such international agreements have been critically assessed as a potential menace of their local 'discretion' and as giving access to powerful international private sector providers (Deutsche Städtetag 2014).

Against this backdrop, since the mid-late 1990s the trend towards corporatising service provision, particularly in the form of municipally owned enterprises (MOEs), has gained further momentum in the NPM-inspired search for greater operational flexibility and economic efficiency. In countries with a fragmented network of – usually small – municipalities the formation of *inter-municipal companies* has progressed. At the same time the number of mixed (public-private or municipal-private) companies (with an increasing share of private sector, including international, companies) and the number of organisational and contractual public–private partnerships (PPPs) have multiplied (see Grossi and Reichard 2016).

Within this general trend towards *corporatisation*, however, some significant variance due to country- and service-specific factors can be observed. In Sweden, public services 'such as municipal housing, water and sewage services, energy distribution, public transport have to large extent been transformed into municipal companies . . . with a new push for corporatisation since 2007' (Montin 2016).

Such MOEs tend to have a *hybrid* perspective. Because they are exposed to competition from private sector companies they tend to be guided by an entrepreneurial, profit-seeking economic rationality; however, being embedded in the political context of local government, they are also influenced by a political rationality insofar as they also have non-economic goals, and take account of social and ecological concerns and so on (see Montin 2016; Wollmann 2014).

In Germany, too, the trend towards such MOEs has extended to almost all sectors (see Bönker et al. 2016; Grossi and Reichard 2016). The centrifugal dynamics of MOEs have posed a serious challenge to the steering capabilities of local authorities, which the latter have tried to meet by establishing specific administrative *steering units*.

In Italy, NPM-inspired national legislation in the early 1990s was designed to reduce the number of MOEs (*municipalizzate*) engaged in the water and waste services – at that time about 5000 – by establishing a nationwide network of districts of 'optimal territorial size' (*ambito territoriale ottimale*, ATO) each comprising several municipalities and stipulating that only one provider should be commissioned (through an open tender process) to provide a given service in each ATO district. The aim of the legislation was to open the service market up to private competition, including international competition. However, in 2011 the legislation on ATOs was repealed, leaving it to the regions to define their own systems with the result that, as has been noted pointedly, the 'situation is now more chaotic and uncontrolled than ever' (Citroni et al. 2016).

Greece embarked on a different strategy for regulating the corporatisation of service provision. Beginning in the early 1980s, under the socialist Pasok government, there has been a mushrooming in the number of MOEs. They were created as a political instrument for expanding local responsibility for service provision via a process labelled 'corporatised municipal socialism' or even 'clientelist corporatisation' (see Tsekos and Triantafyllopoulou 2016). National legislation passed in 2002, stipulating that thenceforth only *companies of public benefit* could be established, was intended to slow down the rampant growth in MOEs.

After 1990, in Central and Eastern European countries, public and social services which had been in the hands of the social state were largely transferred to the local authorities (municipalised) and subsequently often hived off or corporatised categorised as *budgetary institutions*. As in Western European countries, this paved the way for the involvement of private, including international, companies.

Similarly, outsourcing of services continued to be widely, even increasingly, employed well into the late 1990s and beyond. This is particularly true in the case of Central and Eastern European countries where the transfer of public functions to outside providers can, in part, be regarded as deferred stage of the still 'unfinished' transformation of the previous 'socialist' state (see Mikula and Walaszek 2016).

In Western European countries asset privatisation of services has recently been extended as well, both through private investors taking stakes (usually minority stakes) in MOEs and through organisational PPPs. For instance, in Germany and Austria private investors hold shares in some 40% of MOEs (see Grossi and Reichard 2016). An additional push towards privatisation has been triggered by the budgetary ('sovereign debt') crisis which particularly affected South European countries (see Tsekos and Triantafyllopoulou 2016 on Greece; and Magre Ferran and Pano Puey 2016 on Spain).

Moreover, in Central and Eastern European countries marketisation and privatisation has been additionally propelled by their wish and need to 'catch up' with the in part still 'unfinished business' of their secular post-communist transformation.

Hence, to sum up, the institutional development of service provision has been marked since the mid-2000s, under the persistent impact of EU-driven 'Europeanisation', by a continuing trend, with variance between countries and sectors, towards further corporatisation, outsourcing and privatisation.

The return of the public/municipal sector in service provision

In contrast, and in in a divergent trend, a 'comeback' of the public/municipal sector as a provider of public services has developed for a number of reasons.

Less enthusiasm for neo-liberal beliefs

Since the late 1990s is has become more and more evident that the ambitious neo-liberal expectation that (material or functional) privatisation would entail better quality of services at lower prices has not materialised. This political and conceptual disillusionment has been globally prompted by the financial crisis of 2008 which significantly contributed to reassessing and recalibrating the role of the state and of the public sector to rectify private sector and market failures.

The pros and cons of private vs. public sector provision

Well into the 1990s, it was all but taken for granted in the political and academic discourse that the privatisation of service provision would lead to 'better quality at lower costs'. This assumption has been seriously called into question both through practical experience and in academic research. Recent internationally comparative studies plausibly suggest that the provision of public utilities by public enterprises is on a par with, if not superior to private sector providers (Mühlenkamp 2013: 18). Research does not support the conclusion that privately owned firms are more efficient than otherwise-comparable state-owned firms'). The balance sheet turns out even more favourable for public/municipal provision if the transaction costs of outsourcing of services (costs of tendering, monitoring, contract management etc.) are taken into account, leave lone positive 'welfare effects' (social, ecological etc. benefits) of public/municipal provision.

Changing values in political culture and popular perception

This reappraisal of the merits of public sector-based service provision is also reflected in and supported by a growing popular perception and sentiment which tends to value service provision by the public/municipal sector higher than that by the private sector. This trend is evidenced by a growing number of local referendums in which the privatisation of public services and facilities was rejected or their remunicipalisation was demanded (Kuhlmann and Wollmann 2014: 199). On the national level one significant example was the national referendum held in Italy on 8 June 2011 in which the privatisation of water provision was overwhelmingly rejected (Kuhlmann and Wollmann 2014: 205). The international, if not global, dimension and perspective of this development shows in the emergence and actions of social and political movements of which *Attac* is exemplary (see www.attac.org/node/3727).

The enhanced role of local governments in the intergovernmental setting

The readiness and motivation of local authorities to engage themselves and their municipal companies in the provision of public utilities has recently been fostered by remarkable changes in their intergovernmental setting.

For one, in the EU context the status of the local government level has recently been strengthened, for example in the Treaty of Lisbon of December 2009 'local government' has been explicitly recognised – for the first time ever in EU constitutional law.

> The Union shall respect the equality of Member States before the Treaties as well as their national identities, inherent in their fundamental structures, political and constitutional, inclusive of regional and local self-government.
>
> *(Treaty of Lisbon, Art 3, S 2)*

In a protocol to the Treaty of Lisbon (which has the same legal status as the Treaty itself) it has been stipulated that regarding 'services of general interest' the EU explicitly recognises:

> . . . the essential role and the wide discretion of national, regional and local authorities in providing, commissioning and organizing services of general economic interest as closely as possible to the needs of the users . . . the diversity between various services of general economic interest and the differences in the needs and preferences of users that may result from different geographical, social or cultural situations.

The binding force of EU norm-setting has been significantly mitigated in favour of country by country choices (see Bauby and Similie 2016: 102). However, as afore-mentioned, this stands in noticeable contrast with subsequent moves of the European Commission to promote the regulation of procurement of service provision and to constrain the discretion of local authorities (Marcou 2016: 19).

Furthermore, in certain policy fields, the local government level has been recognised as an important actor both by the EU and by the national governments. This applies prominently to environmental protection and energy saving. So, at their summit held in March 2007 the European heads of State agreed on an Energy Policy for Europe in which local governments have been recognised as crucial actors.

Renewed self-confidence and action orientation of local government

So various local authorities in different countries have 'rediscovered' the provision of public utilities under their own responsibility and in their own operation as a strategy and way to generate revenues of their own instead of leaving them to the 'profit making' of private sector providers. Moreover, they seek and use this an opportunity to regain political control over the quality and price-setting of service provision and to pursue social, ecological etc. objectives welfare effects, for instance by way of cross-subsidising structurally and inherently loss making service sectors such as public transport. In doing so, they act upon and play out a 'political rationality' which in principle is guided by the common good of the local community.

A grid-specific window of opportunity

As in the field of grid-based services, such as energy and water, concession contracts are usually awarded on a time-limited basis and hence expire after the set time span This opens a 'window of opportunity' for municipalities to renegotiate the concessions contracts and to possibly remunicipalise the services.

The comeback of the public/municipal sector has emerged essentially along two tracks. Either municipal companies have been established from new or have expanded; there have also been developments in merging and forming intermunicipal companies. In some cases municipalities have proceeded to remunicipalise facilities and services by re-purchasing shares previously sold to private companies or by insourcing previously outsourced services after the end of the respective concession contracts.

Some good examples of this can be seen in energy and water provision.

Energy

In the *UK*, since the (asset) privatisation of the energy sector in 1989, the country's energy market has been dominated by private energy companies, while the local authorities were left with an all but marginal role, for instance, in the operation of district heating services. However in a recent conspicuous policy turn, in 2010, the then Conservative–Liberal Democrat coalition government explicitly encouraged local authorities to resume a responsibility in the energy sector particularly by engaging in the generation and utilisation of energy saving and renewable energy generation technologies The national goal has been set to supply 15% of the country's energy consumption from renewable energy by 2020. Enabling legislation has followed suit. In the meantime a considerable number of local authorities have initiated local projects, particularly pertaining to power and heat coupling (in conjunction with district heating) and in solar energy. Sheffield, Leeds and Bradford are leading the UK in renewable energy installations. However, the local level initiatives appear to have since slackened. 'The climate change work has narrowed, is very weak or absent in 65% of local authorities' (Scott 2011).

In *France*, the electricity market continues to be dominated by EdF, which is still in 80% State ownership. It generates 75% of the country's energy production from its 24 nuclear power stations and is encouraged by government policy to be a 'champion' on the national as well as international energy markets. Some 230 municipal energy companies which were exempted in 1946 from nationalisation continue to provide energy services to not more than 5% of the households. Their generation of electricity is, to a considerable degree, based on renewable (particularly hydro) sources. So far, notwithstanding their potential in renewable energy, the role of the municipal companies has apparently remained limited also because they continue to be legally restrained to only serve their respective local market (see Allemand 2007: 40; Allemand et al. 2016).

While ENEL (which is in 30% state ownership) and other institutional and individual (largely private sector) currently play a major role in Italy's energy market, the municipal energy companies (*municipalizzate*) which, in 1962, were exempted from the nationalisation continue to hold a fairly strong position in the energy sector (see Prontera and Citroni 2007). This applies particularly to big cities. In 2008 the municipal companies of Milano (1.2 million inhabitants) and Brecia (190,000 inhabitants) merged to form a consortium-type stock company called *A2A* which is listed on the stock market and generates 3.9% of the country's electricity, while a multitude of other small municipal companies generates another 10% (see AEEG 2001: 51). As Italy has politically and legally committed herself to do without nuclear power, the municipal energy companies whose power generation traditionally has a strong alternative and renewable (hydro) energy component (see AEEG 2001: 52) appear poised for an expanding role.in the country's energy sector.

In Germany into the late 1990s, the Big Four private sector energy companies (E.on, RWE, EnBW, Vattenfall) did significantly better in the energy market, than municipal companies (*Stadtwerke*) (Wollmann et al. 2010). As the *Stadtwerke* have traditionally focused on energy-saving technologies (such as heat and power coupling, HPC), they have become crucial local actors in the eyes of the federal government. This is important in the policy change, in reaction to the nuclear disaster in Fukushima, to terminate the country's nuclear power generation by 2022. At the same time, the European Commission, in recognising the competitive potential that the local energy companies have in the local and regional energy markets, proceeded to strengthen their competitive 'muscle' by exerting pressure on the 'Big Four' to sell local grids and give up previously acquired minority shares in *Stadtwerke*. Hence, many municipalities have turned to re-purchase local grids and shares of the *Stadtwerke*. The dynamics of this development is evidenced also by a growing number of newly founded *Stadtwerke*

Water provision

Although, in England and Wales, the privatised water services have come to be severely criticised for high tariffs and high operating profits, a serious discussion about returning water services back to public (state or local) operation has so far not developed. In Scotland, in contrast the supply of domestic water is within the control of Scottish Water, a publicly owned company.

In France, the privatisation of water services, through the traditional route of 'outsourcing' (*gestion déléguée*), to private companies, particularly the 'Big Three', has further progressed, a process of remunicipalising water services has gained momentum since the late 1990s. First of all steep price and tariff increases have increasingly discredited the privatisation of water provision. Where left-wing council majorities and mayors gained power, they have sought to undo the privatisation effected by their right-wing predecessors and to make use of the expiration of concession contracts in order to remunicipalise water services (Lieberherr et al. 2016).

In Italy, the large-scale privatisation of Italy's water sector at which the Ronchi Decree of 2009 targeted was conspicuously stopped by the national referendum held on 11 June 2011 in which the Ronchi Decree was rejected by 96% of those who voted. The political mobilisation against water privatisation was largely carried by the (left-leaning) Forum Italiano dei Movimenti per l'Acqua which was founded in 2006 and was composed of some 150 municipalities and political organisations.

In Germany, well into the early 2000s, private water companies, including major players such as Veolia, Suez, RWE and E.on made significant advances in the municipally dominated water sector. However, recently a counter-trend has set in, as municipalities make use of upcoming expiry of concession contracts to renegotiate the contracts and to regain control over the local water services. This development has been prompted not least by demands of the local citizens, as expressed in a growing number of binding local referendums. Thus, in the City of Stuttgart where, in 2003, water provision was completely sold to a large German provider (EnBW), the city council, in responding to a local referendum, decided in June 2010 to repurchase water facilities at the conclusion of the contract (Kuhlmann and Wollmann 2014: 199).

Remunicipalisation in the wider country and sector perspective

Variations the in rate and intensity processes of remunicipalisation can also be observed in other service sectors, such as waste management, public transport, as well as in other countries (see Hall 2012; Dreyfus et al. 2010). An intriguing example of the dynamics of a local 'multi-utilities' operation is offered by the German city of Bergkamen (50,000 inhabitants) which, under the innovative leadership of a committed mayor, has become a pilot in remunicipalising public services in a broad multi-utility mix that includes energy, waste management and public transport) (Schäfer 2008).

A cautious summary

However, in order to realistically and cautiously assessing the potential of further remunicipalisation, some other factors need to be considered. So, when considering to remunicipalise once the concession expires municipalities typically face difficult negotiations (on compensation etc.) with the outgoing private provider (on France see Bordonneau et al. 2010: 136). Moreover, they often lack skilled personnel to take the operation back in their own hands. So, for instance in Germany only in a small percentage of expired concessions the municipalities have chosen to remunicipalise the service provision, while in most cases deciding to renew the expired contracts with the previous providers (see Grossi and Reichard 2016: 303).

The (re-)emergence of the third sector

Although there is continuing debate on definitions, in this chapter the 'third sector' is understood as comprising (NGO- type) non-public non-profit organisations (such as the traditional not-for-profit organisations in Germany and Sweden) as well as the broad array of informal social actors (such as cooperatives, self-help organisations, social enterprises and the like; Salamon and Sokolowski 2016).

As discussed above, in the late 19th century ('pre-welfare state') setting 'informal' societal organisations and actors were significantly engaged in local level provision of personal social services and care, and in some countries during the period of the advanced welfare state such organisations prevailed (particularly in Germany and Sweden) although under more recent neo-liberal regimes they lost ground to private sector (commercial) providers.

Public utilities

In the provision of public utilities energy cooperatives have recently made remarkable advances. Founded typically by local citizens they join the cooperative movement which, historically dating back to the 19th century, is made up of a multitude of very mixed organisations that primarily focus on agricultural, housing, banking and consumer matters (Cooperatives Europe 2015).

In Germany, since the late 1990s, the founding of energy cooperatives has been prompted by the growing environmental engagement of citizens and this has been incentivised by the Federal Renewable Energy Act of 2000 that guarantees fixed feed-in tariffs for anyone generating renewable power for a 20-year period (see Bönker et al. 2016: 80). The, as of now, some 1,000 energy cooperatives (out of a total of some 7,500 cooperatives) typically operate solar parks and wind turbines, have some 200,000 members and generate electricity for some 160,000 households (see Borchert 2015). It is worth recalling that energy cooperatives sprang up in Germany first in the late 19th century when rural dwellers founded cooperatives typically in self-help initiatives as the private sector electricity companies refused to connect such remote areas. In the 20th century however, 'energy cooperatives' had almost disappeared until their recent revival.

In a similar vein, in France, since 2005 some 10 energy cooperatives have been established as well as in the UK (see Co-operatives UK 2016). In 2011 an EU Network of Energy Cooperatives has been founded with 20 members from 12 EU countries.

While the emergence of energy cooperatives is, no doubt, a remarkable example of a 'societal' initiative which, in view of the growing importance of local level renewable energy generation and supply they are likely to have further growth potential. However such forecasts need to be cautious since until now the overall quantitative contribution of cooperatives to overall energy generation is quite modest. In Germany, for instance, where so far, in international comparison, the largest number of energy cooperatives has been founded the electricity generated by them amounts to just 0.5% of the country's total electricity production. Moreover, it should be borne in mind that the existence of energy cooperatives until now depends markedly on tax benefits and the guarantee of feed-in tariffs.

Social services and care

Third sector organisations and actors have also (re-)appeared in the provision of personal social services and care for the needy. This development has emerged on two tracks.

For one, in the wake of the world-wide financial crisis post 2008 European governments have resorted to fiscal austerity and retrenchment policies. These included policy initiatives designed to relieve the public sector of its direct financial and operational responsibility for the provision of social services and to 'top-down' activate and 'tap' the financial and operational potential of third sector organisations and actors.

The top-down track is exemplified by the policy initiative inaugurated by the EU in 2011 that was targeted at the creation of social enterprises. These typically rest on a 'hybrid' concept of combining an entrepreneurial orientation with a 'common good' commitment (European Commission 2014). In Greece, in responding to, and benefiting from this EU program, social enterprises have recently been founded 'in a wide spectrum of services mostly in the social sector (childcare and care for the elderly)' (Tsekos and Triantafyllopoulou 2016: 145).

Some national policies have aimed at shifting the provision of personal social services and help for those in need back onto the affected individuals, their families and their peers or, more broadly, shifting such services to the societal or civil sphere.

In Italy the municipalities have traditionally played a relatively minor role in delivery of personal social services, which has largely been left – in line with the subsidiarity principle – to not-for-profit, mainly church-affiliated organisations and the families.

> Recent Italian government policies have had the direct effect of further reducing public provision of social services and forcing people to rely ever more heavily on private provision . . . including informal, and sometimes cheaper, solutions such as 'grey' care by migrants.
>
> *(Citroni et al. 2016)*

Societal organisations and actors have from local roots come to life in reaction to the neo-liberal policy-inspired financial cutbacks in personal social services and to the socio-economic needs engendered by the impact of shifting the financial and operational burden back to the needy and their families and peers.

The cooperatives that focus on providing personal social services and care can historically be traced back to the self-help organisations of the 19th century. Italy is the prime example of this long and continuous development. While in Italy the total number of cooperatives currently amounts to some 40,000 with a broad scope of agricultural, housing etc. cooperatives, as of now about 1,400 social cooperatives (*cooperative sociali*) exist half of which are engaged in children, elderly and disabled care (see Thomas 2004: 250; Bauer and Markmann 2016: 288).

In Germany, about 330 social cooperatives (*Sozialgenossenschaften*) have emerged compared to a total of some 7,500 cooperatives. Most of them have been founded since the early 2000s, half of them as self-help cooperatives and one third 'solidary' cooperatives, that is, with an altruistic orientation (see Alscher 2011). In the UK, cooperatives 'have spun out of a wide scope of local government services including adult social care . . . children's services . . . and social care' (UK Government, 2013, quoted in Bauer and Markmann 2016: 288).

Moreover, in reaction to fiscal austerity measures and to the ensuing cutback of social services provision 'societal' self-help initiatives have come to life which aim at providing services and care for themselves as well as for others (see Warner and Clifton 2013). For instance in Greece voluntary groups have sprung up, at first in big cities, such as the 'Atenistas' in Athens, and subsequently 'all over the country' (Tsekos and Triantafyllopoulou 2016: 144).

In Poland 'the dynamic activity of NGOs is often seen as a form of 'social capital' and is regarded as a remarkable symbol of the positive shift which has taken place since the end of the socialist period' and reforms have 'encouraged citizens to organise many new social associations whose aim was to complement (or even replace) the role of state institutions in addressing social problems' (Mikula and Walaszek 2016).

A cautious summary

Notwithstanding the remarkable (re-)emergence of third sector initiatives, organisations and actors, their future course and expansion should be assessed with caution. A major challenge lies in their precarious financial potential. Although they have proved to be able to mobilise additional financial resources (donation money, membership fees, also user charges), personnel resources (volunteers) as well as entrepreneurial and organisational skills (particularly in the case of social enterprises) their durable and long-term engagement and growth depend crucially on the availability of sufficient public funding. The salience of this financial aspect has been highlighted in a recent major international study on the third sector (Enjolras et al. 2016: 9). At the same time, it is this very financial dependence and the ensuing need to compete for such (if available) public funding that compels the third sector organisations in the current NPM-shaped administrative environment to accept and adopt 'contract based management procedures . . . where the terms of delivery are strictly defined by public agencies (including) the permanent bureaucratic stress to report to their funders' (Enjolras et al. 2016: 9); this, however, may run counter to core beliefs and mores of such societal actors that (ideally) hinge on autonomy, trust, intrinsic motivation and 'informal' relations. Besides, small societal actors are liable to encounter difficulties, because of their small size and unfamiliarity with the formalised and 'bureaucratic' tendering procedures linked with public funding, when it comes to successfully compete with the larger and operationally more skilled and adapted private sector, but also the larger and longer established non-profit organisations (see Henriksen et al. 2016: 230).

Conclusion

While, in a historical developmental and cross-country perspective, the institution and actor setting of service delivery have demonstrated largely convergent trends, the recent phase is marked by divergent and 'bifurcated' trajectories.

Under the advanced welfare state that peaked in the 1970s the delivery of public and social services was characterised, in a largely convergent manner, by the ('social democratic') preponderance of the public (state or municipal) sector. The exception was in those countries with a 'conservative welfare state regime' (such as Germany and Italy) in which third sector (NGO-type) providers had a privileged position.

Under the neo-liberal policy shift since the 1980s and the EU's market liberalisation drive, the previous social democratic primacy of the public/municipal sector in service provision has given way, in an again largely convergent manner, to the marketisation and pluralisation of service providers with a growing salience of private sector companies and actors.

By contrast, the most recent phase since the early/mid-2000s is marked by a divergence and, as it were, 'bifurcation' of trends. On the one hand, marketisation and privatisation of service delivery has continued, if not intensified by the EU's regulation of competitive service contracting and, driven by the EU's regulation by the fiscal pressure to privatise public/municipal assets. On the other hand, the municipal sector has seen a 'comeback' in the provision of public services mirroring a re-appraisal of the performance and merits of the public/municipal sector in service provision; at the same time the (re-)emergence of societal third sector type cooperatives, social enterprises and self-help groups has occurred against the backdrop of the rising of social and personals needs caused by neo-liberal fiscal austerity measures. The 'comeback' of the municipal sector reminds us of the role which the local authorities played under the advanced welfare state, as well as their 19th century pre-welfare state engagement, as the (re-)emergence of societal organisations and actors may be seen reminiscent of the crucial role such 'informal' organisations played in social service and care provision in the late 19th century 'pre-welfare state' period.

In the historical perspective another striking features is apparent. During the phase of the advanced welfare state the decision-making regarding the institutional setting of services can be seen as largely taking place within and influenced by respective *national* arenas. By contrast, during the neo-liberal policy and New Public Management inspired phase the institutionalisation of service provision appears shaped by an *internationalisation* and more specifically by an '*Europeanisation*' of the pertinent arena.

Finally, the recent phase appears, in either of its 'bifurcated' trajectories, taking on a '*globalised*' dimension. Hence, further privatisation has been significantly prompted, as a long-range effect, by the financial fallout of 2008. At the same time, the 'comeback' of the municipal sector has been considerably triggered by a disenchantment with the 'private sector' and the 'market forces' revealed by 2008.

Similarly, the stepped up engagement of the local authorities in local level (renewable) energy provision (and the related national policy shifts) have been strongly impinged upon by the Fukushima disaster of 2011. Moreover, the re-emergence of 'social actors' in the provision of social services and care as resulting from fiscal austerity measures can be traced back as long-range consequence of the financial crisis. Thus, the divergent and 'bifurcated' institutional trajectories of the recent developmental phase can, through possibly multi-phased 'causal loops', be traced back firmly and essentially to global influences.

References

AEEG (Autorità per l'Energia Elettrica ed il Gas) 2001, *Annual Report on State of Services*, AEEG, Milan.

Allemand, R. 2007, Les distributeurs non-nationalisés d'electricité face à l'ouverture de la concurrence, in *Annuaire 2007 des Collectivités Locales*, pp. 31–42, CNRS, Paris.

Allemand, R., M. Dreyfus, Magali, M. Magnusson and J. McEldowney 2016, Local government and the energy sector: a comparison of France, Iceland and the United Kingdom, pp. 233–248, in H. Wollmann, I. Kopric and G. Marcou, eds, *Public and Social Services in Europe: From Public and Municipal to Private Sector Provision*, Palgrave Macmillan, Basingstoke.

Alscher, M. 2011, Genossenschaften – Akteure des Markt s und der Zivilgesellschaften, retrieved from www.fes.de/bürgergesellschaften/publikationen/dokumente.

Bauby, P and M. Similie 2016, What impact have the European Court decisions had on local public services?, pp. 27–40, in H. Wollmann, I. Kopric and G. Marcou, eds, *Public and Social Services in Europe: From Public and Municipal to Private Sector Provision*, Palgrave Macmillan, Basingstoke.

Bauer, H. and F. Markmann 2016, Models of local public service delivery: privatization, publicisation and renaissance of the cooperatives?, pp. 281–296, in H. Wollmann, I. Kopric and G. Marcou, eds, *Public and Social Services in Europe: From Public and Municipal to Private Sector Provision*, Palgrave Macmillan, Basingstoke.

Bönker, F., J. Libbe and H. Wollmann 2016, Re-municipalisation revisited: long-term trends in the provision of local public services in Germany, pp. 71–86, in H. Wollmann, I. Kopric and G. Marcou, eds, *Public and Social Services in Europe: From Public and Municipal to Private Sector Provision*, Palgrave Macmillan, Basingstoke.

Borchert, L. 2015, Citizens' participation in the Energiewende, retrieved from www.cleanenergywire.org/factsheets/citizens-participation-energiewende.

Bordonneau, M.-A., G. Canneva, G. Orange and D. Gambier 2010, Le changement de mode de gestion des services d'eau, pp. 131–147, in *Droit et Gestion des Collectivités Territoriales, Annunaire 2010*, Editions le Moniteur, Paris

Bouckaert, G. and S. Kuhlmann 2016, Comparing Local Public Sector Reforms: Institutional Policies in Context, pp. 1–20, in S. Kuhlmann and G. Bouckaert, eds, *Local Public Sector Reforms in Times of Crisis*, Palgrave Macmillan, Basingstoke.

Citroni, G., A. Lippi and S. Profeti 2016, Local public services in Italy: still fragmentation, pp. 103–118, in H. Wollmann, I. Kopric and G. Marcou, eds, *Public and Social Services in Europe: From Public and Municipal to Private Sector Provision*, Palgrave Macmillan, Basingstoke.

Cooperatives Europe 2016, Key figures 2015, retrieved from https://coopseurope.coop/sites/default/files/The%20power%20of%20Cooperation%20-%20Cooperatives%20Europe%20key%20statistics%20 2015.pdf

Co-operatives UK 2016, UK energy sector goes co-operative, retrieved from www.uk.coop/newsroom/uk-energy-sector-goes-co-operative.

Deutsche Städtetag (2013) Privatisierung der kommunalen Wasserversorgung verhindern, hohe Qualität und stabile Preise sichern, retrieved from www.staedtetag.de/presse/mitteilungen/064444/index.html.

Deutsche Städtetag (2014) Kommunale Daseinsvorsorge nicht durch Freihandelsabkommen einschränken – transparent verhandeln, retrieved from www.staedtetag.de/presse/mitteilungen/071767/index.html.

Dreyfus, M., A. E. Töller, C. Iannello and J. McEldowney 2010, Comparative study of a local service: waste management in France, Germany, Italy and the UK, pp. 146–166, in H. Wollmann and G. Marcou, eds, *The Provision of Public Services in Europe: Between State, Local Government and Market*, Edward Elgar, Cheltenham.

Enjolras, B., L. Salamon, K. H. Sivesind and A. Zimmer 2016, The third sector: a renewal resource for Europe, Summary of main findings of the Third Sector Impact Project, retrieved from www.thirdsectorimpact.eu.

Esping-Andersen, G. 1990, *The Three Worlds of Welfare Capitalism*, Princeton University Press, Princeton, NJ.

European Commission 2011, *Communication from the Commission to the European Parliament, the Council, the European Economic and Social Committee and the Committee of the Regions: A Quality Framework for Services of General Interest in Europe*, retrieved from http://ec.europa.eu/services_general_interest/docs/comm_quality_framework_en.pdf

European Commission 2014, *A Map of Social Enterprises and Their Ecosystems in Europe*, European Commission, Brussels.

Grossi, G. and C. Reichard 2016, Variance in the institutions of local utility services: evidence from several European countries, pp. 297–312, in H. Wollmann, I. Kopric and G. Marcou, eds, *Public and Social Services in Europe: From Public and Municipal to Private Sector Provision*, Palgrave Macmillan, Basingstoke.

Hall, D. 2012, *Re-municipalising Municipal Services in Europe: A Report Commissioned by EPSU for Public Services International Research Unit (PSIRU)*, retrieved from www.epsu.org/IMG/pdf/Redraft_DH_remunicipalization.pdf.

Henriksen, L. S., Smith, S. R., Thoegersen, M. and Zimmer, A. 2016, On the road towards marketization? A comparative analysis of non-profit sector involvement in social service delivery at the local level, pp. 121–136, in S. Kuhlmann and G. Bouckaert (eds), *Local Public Sector Reforms in Times of Crisis*, Palgrave Macmillan, Basingstoke.

Kuhlmann, S. and H. Wollmann 2014, *Public Administration and Administrative Reforms in Europe: An Introduction in Comparative Public Administration*, Edward Elgar, Cheltenham.

Lieberherr, E, C. Viard and C. Herzberg 2016, Water provision in France, Germany and Switzerland, and divergence, pp. 249–264, in H. Wollmann, I. Kopric and G. Marcou, eds, *Public and Social Services in Europe: From Public and Municipal to Private Sector Provision*, Palgrave Macmillan, Basingstoke.

Magre Ferran, J. and E. Pano Puey 2016, Delivery of Municipal Services in Spain, pp. 119–134, in H. Wollmann, I. Kopric and G. Marcoou, eds, *Public and Social Services in Europe: From Public and Municipal to Private Sector Provision*, Palgrave Macmillan, Basingstoke.

Marcou, G. 2016, The impact of EU law on local public service provision: competition and public service, pp. 13–26, in H. Wollmann, I. Kopric and G. Marcou, eds, *Public and Social Services in Europe: From Public and Municipal to Private Sector Provision*, Palgrave Macmillan, Basingstoke.

Mikula, L. and M. Walaszek 2016, The evolution of local public services provision in Poland, pp. 169–184, in H. Wollmann, I. Kopric and G. Marcou, eds, *Public and Social Services in Europe: From Public and Municipal to Private Sector Provision*, Palgrave Macmillan, Basingstoke.

Montin, S. 2016, Local government and the market: the case of public services and care for the elderly in Sweden, pp. 87–102, in H. Wollmann, I. Kopric and G. Marcou, eds, *Public and Social Services in Europe: From Public and Municipal to Private Sector Provision*, Palgrave Macmillan, Basingstoke.

Mühlenkamp, H. 2013, From State to Market Revisited. *Empirical Evidence on the Efficiency of Public (and Privately-owned) Enterprises, MPRA paper*, retrieved from http://mpra.ub.uni-muenchen.de/47570.

Prontera, A. and G. Citroni 2007, Energie et administrations locales en Italie: Dénationalisation, libéralisation et concurrence, pp. 191–208 in *Annuaire 2007 des Collectivités Locales*, CNRS, Paris.

Salamon, L. M. and S. W. Sokolowski 2016, Beyond nonprofits: re-conceptualizing the third sector, *Voluntas* 27(4): 1515–1545.

Schäfer, R. 2008, Privat vor Staat hat ausgedient: Rekommunalisierung: Modetrend oder neues Politikphänomen?, pp. 3–10 in *Öffentliche Finanzen*, Sonderbeilage, Sonderbeilage zur Frankfurter Allgemeinen Zeitung vom 19.6.2008.

Scott, F. 2011. Is localism delivering for climate change? Emerging responses from local authorities, local enterprise partnerships and neighborhood plans, Executive summary, retrieved from www.green-alliance.org.uk/grea_p.aspx?id=6100

Thomas, A. 2004, The rise of social cooperatives in Italy, *Voluntas* 15(3): 243–255.

Tsekos, T. and A. Triantafyllopoulou 2016, From municipal socialism to the sovereign debt crisis: local Services in Greece 1980–2015, pp. 135–150, in H. Wollmann, I. Kopric and G. Marcou, eds, *Public and Social Services in Europe: From Public and Municipal to Private Sector Provision*, Palgrave Macmillan, Basingstoke.

Warner, E. and J. Clifton 2013, Marketization, public services and the city: the potential for Polanyan ounter movements, *Cambridge Journal of Regions, Economy and Society* 7(1): 2–17.

Wollmann H. 2014, Public services in European countries: between public/municipal and private sector provision – and reverse?, pp. 49–76, in C. Nunes and J. Bucek (eds), *Fiscal Austerity and Innovation in Local Governance in Europe*, Ashgate, Farnham.

Wollmann H. 2016, Public and social services in Europe: from public and municipal to private provision – and reverse?, pp. 197–312, in H. Wollmann, I. Kopric and G. Marcou, eds, *Public and Social Services in Europe: From Public and Municipal to Private Sector Provision*, Palgrave Macmillan, Basingstoke.

Wollmann, H. 2018, Public and personal social services in European countries from public/municipal to private – and back to municipal and 'third sector' provision?, *International Public Management Journal* (forthcoming).

Wollmann, H., H. Baldersheim, G. Citroni, G. Marcou and J. McEldowney 2010, From public service to commodity: the demunicipalization (or remunicipalization?) of energy provision in Germany, Italy, France, the UK and Norway, pp. 168–190, in H. Wollmann and G. Marcou, eds, *The Provision of Public Services in Europe: Between State, Local Government and Market*, Edward Elgar, Cheltenham.

Wollmann, H., I. Kopric and G. Marcou, eds 2016, *Public and Social Services in Europe: From Public and Municipal to Private Sector Provision*, Palgrave Macmillan, Basingstoke.

PART IV

Citizen engagement

18
PRACTICES AND CHALLENGES OF CITIZEN PARTICIPATION IN LOCAL GOVERNMENT

Case studies of mid-sized cities in Russia and the United States

Sofia Prysmakova-Rivera, Elena Gladun, Thomas Bryer, Andrey Larionov, Dmitry Teplyakov, Olga Teplyakova and Natalia Nosova

Introduction

Citizen participation is a vital tool of democratic governance. It not only communicates citizens' interests and preferences to governmental officials but improves government legitimacy, responsiveness, transparency, and accountability. According to Arnstein (1969), citizen participation is citizen power. The degree of public participation varies from the absence of power, where citizens are excluded from participating in public affairs, to full inclusion of citizens in social, economic and political processes.

Under the influences of new public management and new public governance, public administration in some societies has shifted from highly bureaucratic, hierarchical, impersonal structures to horizontal systems that are open to the external environment and public participation systems. However, tensions between bureaucracy and democracy, closed versus opened systems, and expertise versus citizen participation remain.

Although governments around the world have made significant steps forward in promoting public institutions to be more responsive and open for civic engagement, citizen participation does not seem to be substantially increased. This can be explained by a lack of citizen trust in government (Hardin 1998; Yang 2005; Blind 2007; Wang and Wart 2007), or the poor quality of communication between public officials and citizens (Arnstein 1969; McLeod, Scheufele and Moy 1999).

The objective of this chapter is to explore challenges facing local governments in promoting civic engagement, and the practices used to try and do this. We apply a theoretical framework for civic engagement adapted from Cooper, Bryer and Meek (2006). The framework addresses five dimensions of citizen participation: size, scope, purpose, location, and processes of public engagement. The study focuses on the context and environment of local governments in the United States and Russia and explores the following questions:

- How do local governments in mid-sized cities build a meaningful dialogue with citizens?
- How do they promote citizen participation?
- What challenges do such cities face when encouraging civic engagement?

The focus for exploration is through case studies of some mid-sized cities in Russia and the United States. As case studies, these represent examples from two societies that are vastly different in institutional design and socio-cultural context. The exploration sheds light on similarities and differences, reflecting both common concern at the most localised levels of government and addressing the perceived gaps in mutual respect and understanding that plague both societies despite difference political environments.

Theoretical perspectives

Under the umbrella of new public management and new public governance are a set of theoretical and practical tensions that prioritise expert-based decision-making or mass participation, reliance on rules for fair treatment or inclusion of diverse views and interests of stakeholders in communities. These are reflected in the dynamic balance between maintenance of bureaucracy and enhancement of democracy, between stabilisation of a closed system and the uncertainties introduced in an open system, and between negotiated responsiveness to diverse interests and commitment to technical guidance and expertise. These tensions are explored in the following pages and are then discussed within the context of Russia and the United States.

Bureaucracy v. democracy

The concepts of bureaucracy and democracy have many definitions and interpretations. However, generally scholars agree that bureaucracy is constituted of hierarchical impersonal institutions, with seniority and legitimacy based on expertise. In contrast, democracy represents horizontal institutions based on the values of equality, freedom, pluralism, openness, citizen participation, and legitimacy based on free elections and representation.

Some scholars believe that bureaucratic absolutism, which is characterized by unlimited centralized authority, is prevented by democracy (van Waarden 2015). Van Waarden (2015) suggested that the 20 century scholars like Mosca, Marx and Engels, and Michels saw bureaucratic government as a necessary tool to regulate ignorant and incompetent masses that exclude the possibility of full democracy. In their view, an efficient public institution is highly centralised and expert-oriented (ibid.)..

At the same time, van Waarden (2015) argued that a second group of scholars believe that democratic values are threatened by bureaucratic norms and thus seek more participatory bureaucracy. Rights and equity in the interaction between the public sector agency and its clientele and the quality of its relationship, expressed in accountability responsibility, and responsiveness are the basis of democratic governance (Harmon and Mayer 1986). According to Hughes (2013), bureaucracy abrogates the power of citizens or the politicians and stifles creativity and innovation. Harmon and Mayer (1986) assume that 'legal, political and bureaucratic sanctions induce competent and conscientious administrative performance' (as cited in Berkley and Rousse 2004: 103).

Nevertheless, many contemporary scholars believe in the reconciliation of bureaucratic expertise and democracy. As indicated by van Waarden (2015), bureaucratic expertise is necessary for 'implementing and specifying policies, enforcing laws, and reducing socio-economic inequalities' (van Waarden 2015: 628). Bureaucracy is a necessary tool for democracy; it exists to accomplish tasks (Hill and Lynn 2009; Berkley and Rousse 2004) and bureaucracy can be enhanced by democracy.

Closed v. opened systems

Closed systems experience little or almost no access from external forces and fail to understand and develop the processes of feedback that are essential for survival (Harmon and Mayer 1986). Although open systems bring structural and cultural changes, uncertainty and interdependence (ibid.), Salancik and Pfeffer (1978) believe that public sector organisations are not intrinsically self-sufficient. They 'must engage in exchanges with their environment in order to survive' (Shafritz, Ott and Yang 2015: 343). Social and cultural pressures make public institutions change their structures and values based on efficiency and effectiveness (ibid.).

Participative administration and civic engagement

In recent years, various Western societies have witnessed the rise of populist movements, which favour personal power, strong leadership, direct forms of majoritarian democracy, expression of people's voice through referenda, opinion polls and representative bureaucracy (Albertazzi and McDonnell 2008). Such populist movements sees the 'virtue of ordinary people (the silent majority) over the 'corrupt' establishment', which includes big businesses and banks, 'elected officials, government officials, intellectual elites and scientific experts' (Inglehart and Norris 2016: 6).

Hughes (2013) argues there is a trend to reform government structures into participative administrations, when governmental systems become open in their relations to the citizenry. The role of managers is 'to involve the public to manage public responses to new initiatives' (Hughes 2013: 245). There are multiple functions of public participation tools (Arnstein 1969; Rosener 1975). However, the manner and the feasibility of implementation to achieve desired results relies on:

- local political culture;
- administrative culture; and
- citizen trust, efficacy and competence (Cooper, Bryer and Meek 2006).

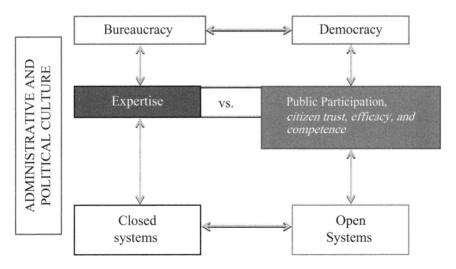

Figure 18.1 Conceptual framework

Figure 18.1 summarises the relationships across these concepts. As the above cited literature shows, populist movements push against bureaucratic structures and expertise and give impetus to governance change at all levels of government.

Governance, characterised by a high demand for open systems and participative administration, allows citizen participation in decision-making processes, protection of minority rights, and promotion of horizontal checks and balances. However, the tension between bureaucracy and democracy still exists and is reflected in different societies, such as those of Russia and the United States.

Conceptual application to Russia

The dynamic development of recent Russian society has brought with it multiple and complicated tasks and objectives for public authorities (Kozbanenko 2006: 323). In 2000, public administrative reforms were started in Russia aiming to introduce the model of 'new governance', a development borrowed from the experience of administrative reform in western countries. The idea of reforms is to change models of interaction between the state and civil society (Osborn and Gaebler 1992). The basic attributes of the new governance (or as it is often named in the research literature, 'state or public management'), are the following:

- Evaluation of governance efficiency by its results.
- Competition between governmental organisations and between governmental and commercial organisations in providing services to citizens.
- Allocation of state functions to private organisations, usually under contract.
- Decentralisation of powers based on the principle of subsidiarity which makes it possible for local authorities and nongovernmental organisations to participate in developing state policy (Bukhard 1998).

However, in Russia, a 'new public management' model has generally failed. The western experience does not translate to Russia effectively. The Russian model of public administration is characterised by strong executive power and can predominantly be described as the bureaucratic type where all political decisions are made by public authorities. As a result, the role of civil society and business is minimised, and the changes and reforms are designed by political elite (i.e. officials of the upper levels of authorities). They are primarily interested in exact and rapid implementation of their own decisions by the lower levels of the administrative hierarchy.

In these conditions, there is a conflict between the present political and administrative system and new public management technologies borrowed from the Western experience. The effective functioning of these technologies is based on a well-structured mechanism of internal and external control over the activities of officials at different levels. Some researchers believe that such a conflict occurs because Russia is unable to accept new institutions of modern public management. A new public management system might be possible in Russia only if the state system implements the basic administrative mechanisms of the traditional bureaucratic model (Polterovich 2007). Various empirical studies show that rational bureaucracy can contribute to the successful modernisation of society. A comparative analysis of the activities of state bureaucratic bodies in a number of developing countries has shown the connection between the modern rational bureaucracy and the economic growth of these states (Evans and Rauch 1999).

In Russia, many public authorities have recently achieved a certain level of rational bureaucracy. However, the basic principle of the Russian public management remains 'top-down' and, generally, the interest of the bureaucracy prevails. Some horizontal links are noticeable, but in most cases they are artificial and are used mainly to create a positive image of state power. In these circumstances, the inclusion of representatives of business and civil society in the process of reform and decision-making is becoming a key factor.

Local authorities and the private sector have the potential to become the driving force of administrative reforms. They can motivate public authorities to be more flexible and innovative in their decision-making. Russia needs new laws on public service, new approaches to the budgetary process, and reforms of regional and local government that will become the foundation for a new state administration aimed not at the interests of bureaucrats and oligarchs but on the social and economic needs of ordinary people. However, these new approaches have not yet developed in a single and clear action plan. They have not become a coherent strategy for public administration reform in Russia.

Conceptual application to United States

The dynamic balance between bureaucratisation and democratisation has spurred numerous reform and counter-reforms in the United States. The first governance approach can be classified as a 'government by gentlemen' system, whereby only elite men ruled, debated issues through official institutions, and set policy. This gave way to the 'spoils system' that opened government offices to the masses, so long as appointees supported the party and the politicians in power. Rule by elite was considered to be undemocratic as such; opening the spoils of victory – government offices – to the common man was a response to this elitism. However, the spoils system led to corruption and also to violence, including the assassination of President James Garfield by a supporter disappointed by his failure to benefit from the system. Thus emerged administrative reforms that placed emphasis on technical merit and experience as the mechanism to, as John Rohr (1986) puts it, 'run the Constitution'.

Merit systems were developed and embedded within bureaucratic systems that are stereotypically framed within Weber's ideal-type bureaucracy and typified by Taylor's scientific management procedures. These are decidedly not systems that are conducive to engagement with citizens in democratic discourse; they also are considered as antithetical to innovation and achievement of results. Thus emerged three governance reform efforts that maintained different foci: new public management focused on reducing bureaucracy, treating the public as customer, and encouraging innovation and entrepreneurship akin to private sector models; new public administration similarly sough to reduce bureaucracy but sought to redirect administrative practices towards socially good outcomes such as social justice and equity; new public service did not specifically seek to reduce bureaucracy but to formalise roles for citizens within bureaucratic systems. Each of these reform efforts remain a part of current administrative procedures across levels of government.

With reforms built on top of each other, the resulting governance systems consist of a cacophony of competing goals and objectives for the administrative system as a whole and for individual public administrators. Administrators have conflicting objects of their responsiveness: to their political bosses (dictated responsiveness), the rules of their agencies (constrained responsiveness), to customers of government (entrepreneurial responsiveness), their own policy goals (purposive responsiveness), and to any agreements they develop in consultation and deliberation with citizens and other stakeholders (collaborative responsiveness). The result is a need to negotiate responsiveness to potentially conflicting and equally legitimate demands (Bryer 2007).

Methodology

Although there are a large number of theoretical articles identifying the correlation between open governments and citizen participation and empirical studies on specific programmes in large cities that promote civic engagement, there is little of empirical research on civic participation in mid-sized cities that lack the financial support and resources as their larger peers.

The aim of this study is to compare and contrast different approaches to public participation in mid-sized cities and communities, within and across the United States and Russia. We seek to answer the following questions: How do local governments in mid-sized cities promote citizen participation? What are the challenges the municipalities face when they encourage civic engagement? Responses are compared across countries.

The current research is a qualitative multiple case study. Case studies provide a deep understanding of the phenomenon, events, people or organisations. The comparison of cities in Florida, United States, and the Tyumen Region of Russia is introduced in order to understand public participation in local government decision-making processes. Locations were selected for convenience as well as theoretical interest, given different population sizes and geographic locations.

The data were collected through semi-structured interviews with purposively selected government leaders in the towns. Interviews addressed five dimensions of civic engagement, based on the framework developed by Cooper, Bryer and Meek (2006):

- Who is involved?
- Who initiatives the engagement?
- Why are citizens involved, or not involved?
- How are citizens involved?
- Where does the engagement happen?

According to the authors, these five factors, which include the size, scope, purpose, location, and process employed to engage citizens, identify the government's ability to 'maximize citizen efficacy, competence, and trust, as well as government trust, responsiveness, and legitimacy' (Cooper, Bryer and Meek 2006: 84).

Interviewees identified the challenges that such local governments face and lessons they have learned based on their past experience when promoting civic engagement practices. The research also used secondary data sources, such as websites and government reports in order to provide the demographic information, identify the form of government, and access details on initiatives and programmes that promote civic engagement. The study applied qualitative thematic content analysis, which inductively determined themes of commonalities and contrasts across the cities.

Case selection and introduction

Russia

In the Russian Federation, there are several types of local governments.
The Russian Federation is divided into 6 types of federal units that are:

- Republics: 23.
- Territories: 9.

- Regions: 45.
- Autonomous region: 1.
- Autonomous districts: 4.
- Federal cities: 3.

The Russian municipal jurisdictions are divided across two levels and seven types:

- Municipal cities with intra-urban districts: 3.
- Intra-urban districts: 19.
- Municipal cities (urban okrugs): 560.
- Municipal districts: 1,788.
- Urban settlements: 1,592.
- Rural settlements: 18,177.
- Intra-urban territories of federal cities (Moscow and St Petersburg): 267.

Federal Law No 131-FZ (2003) 'On General Principles of Local Self-Government in the Russian Federation' in Chapter 5 specifies forms of public participation. However it has a special provision allowing citizens to choose any additional form of participation provided their activities do not contradict the Constitution of the Russian Federation, or federal and regional laws. The same legislation specifies the duty of public authorities and their officials to assist citizens to implement their rights of participation in local self-government. Many forms of public participation related to local issues have been developed in Russia, which require to be based on two core principles on. The principle of legality means that the procedure for citizens' participation in the decision-making on local affairs should not contradict any law. The principle of voluntary participation requires that people are not coerced to any form of participation, and there are no sanctions for those who do not participate.

Nevertheless, local governments in some cases are obliged to organise citizens' participation in certain forms: regular elections and public hearings, for example. Most forms of citizen participation are mandatory only if they are initiated by an organisation, a group of people or one person (referendum; voting on the recall of a deputy or an elected official of local government; citizens' appeal to public bodies and to officials of local government). There are also forms of citizens' participation that are not necessarily required; they are conducted at the discretion of local authorities, or in rare cases, initiated by state authorities (for example: a survey of citizens' opinions when making decisions on changing the purpose of the municipal land for objects of regional and interregional value).

Only a few forms of public participation lead to a mandatory decisions – elections, referenda, recall of a deputy or an elected official of local government, or a citizens' forum exercising the powers of a representative body of the municipality. All other forms can be defined as public consultation. Forms of public participation do not differ in the mid-sized cities of the Russian Federation with the exception of one form – that is the citizens' forum exercising the powers of a representative body of the municipality. This form is used in the municipalities with a population of fewer than 300 people. However, in practice, there is a significant difference in the forms of public participation used in larger settlements

In 2014–2015, amendments to the Federal Law No 131-FZ delegated most powers related to local government to the regional level. The consequences were considerable and four of them should be pointed out: (1) a significant loss of local powers in small towns, (2) a strengthening of the executive power at the local level, (3) a weakened role of the citizens in the process of local executive branch formation in favour of the executive authorities of the regions, and (4) an increased capacity of regional authorities to exert influence on local governments.

United States

In the United States governmental jurisdictions are divided across seven distinct units. According to the most recent census of governments, there are approximately 87,900 unique governmental units across the country, as follows:

- Federal government: 1.
- State governments: 50.
- County governments: 3,034.
- Municipalities: 19,431.
- Towns: 16,506.
- School districts: 13,522.
- Special districts: 35,356.

These numbers change incrementally quite regularly particularly for governmental units that are subordinate to that of the state. County governments are akin to municipal districts in Russia; municipalities are generally akin to the urban okrugs, and towns are akin to the villages or hamlets. School districts are sometimes established in full alignment with the boundaries of a district/county or city municipality, but they can also across these boundaries to encompass multiple district or city municipalities. Special districts often span district and city municipalities and are focused on specific functions and services, such as water districts, fire districts, or library districts. The districts thus formed permit multiple municipal governments to pool scarce resources and achieve economies-of-scale while providing needed services to populations across multiple geographical and jurisdictional boundaries.

Tiers and spheres of government

The relationship between different levels of government is based on the principles of federalism, which establish and sustain a formally clear though sometimes ambiguous set of responsibilities between each level of government. This division of powers has multiple motivations, such as protection against oppressive government that might readily be found within a heavily centralised authority structure, enablement of policy experimentation that can lead to innovation that might be replicated or scaled up, and provision of more opportunities for direct citizen participation in affairs that affect citizens quality of life.

For our case studies in Russia we selected two different types of municipalities. Both are located in Tyumen Region, which is the third largest region in the country. As in Russia, the cases selected represent jurisdictions of different sizes. All are located in the State of Florida, the second largest State in the United States by population. Two mid-sized cities are Gainesville and St Augustine.

Case introductions

Russia

The city of Tobolsk was founded in 1587. For several centuries it was the administrative center of Siberia (Siberian, Tobolsk province, Tobolsk governorship). Tobolsk is the second largest town in the Tyumen Region. The population is 102,000 people; the territory is 23,920 hectares (59,108 acres).

Tobolsk is governed by the city administration with one Head of Administration who is elected for five years by the representative authority of the Tobolsk urban district – 'Tobolsk city Duma' which comprises 25 commissioners/deputies elected for 5 years from candidates chosen by competitive commission of the regional Governor.

Zavadoukovsky urban okrug is located in the south-eastern part of the Tyumen region. The total area of the municipal city is 295.9 hectares (731.2 acres).

The territory of the Zavodoukovsky urban okrug includes the city of Zavodoukovsky, as well as surrounding areas, consisting of twenty big villages, twelve hamlets, and eleven rural settlements. The total population is 46,400 in the urban population, 21,000 in the rural area.

The type of government is the same as in Tobolsk: the city administration with a Head who is elected for five years by the representative authority of the Zavodoukovsky urban district – 'city Duma'. Zavodoukovsky city Duma consists of 20 commissioners/deputies elected for 5 years.

United States

St Augustine (www.citystaug.com) is the oldest city in the United States, founded in 1565. The city is located in northeastern Florida with a population of 13,676 for the year 2016. The population density is relatively low, at 1450 people per square mile. It is governed by a commission-manager form of government. Five elected commissioners are responsible to enact policies and ordinances, and approve spending. The city manager is appointed by the commission and responsible for administrative functions and day-to-day operations of the city. One of the city's commissioners serves a two-year term as a mayor, while the other four have a four-year term. Every two years, the elections are held for the two four-year seats and for the mayor's seat.

The City of Gainesville (www.cityofgainesville.org) was founded in 1896. The city is located in North Central Florida. The population is 128,460. The population density is average, accounted for 2,666 people per square mile. It is governed by a Council-Manager form of government. The city council and mayor make policy decisions, and the city manager implements them.

Findings

Russia

In many parts of Russia, the public does not have many opportunities to significantly influence the executive bodies of local government. Nevertheless, the authorities are interested in civil society with checks and balances system, allowing for participatory actions by local governments and municipal employees. Local authorities are becoming more and more dependent on the regional executive authorities, mostly on the Governor who demands they build a dialogue between local authorities, business and civil society.

In our interview in the research sites, the majority of respondents mentioned that the relationship between business and public authorities has been improved in the last 2–3 years. Also, respondents from both the local authorities and the public and business named several forms of public participation which can help to find solutions to local issues and better interactions between authorities, civil society and business. The most successful participation occurs through the large public organisations, such as:

- veterans' organisations;
- public chambers;

- territorial public self-government;
- business councils (for interaction of power and business); and
- public hearings.

Each of these types of organisations are described below and the manner in which they assist public participation.

Veterans' organisations are public organisations uniting active pensioners. Originally, such organisations were formed in the USSR by veterans of the Second World War to assist the authorities in solving various kinds of issues, including control over officials. The initial structure was the councils of veterans, which determined the traditions, the forms of work, and the scope of their interests.

Representatives of veterans' organisations mentioned the very successful, constant and effective interaction in organising mass cultural events, joint events for young people and the elder generation, and patriotic meetings with schoolchildren (for example, 'courage lessons' or topical events such as 'a persona is famous for his work').

The Public Chamber is one of the forms of public engagement. This is a fairly young institution that has become active with the adoption on 21 July 2014 for the Federal Law No 212-FZ 'On the Basics of Public Control in the Russian Federation'. Public chambers (councils) of municipal entities are regulated by regional laws.

The representatives of the local authorities say that citizens still lack confidence in the authorities. When addressing civil servants, citizens feel as if the interests and objectives of the population and the officials are totally different. This opinion is provoked by the intricacies of Russian legislation, as well as by the high cost of legal assistance. Public chambers help to overcome this situation. Ordinary people can come to the public chamber and feel better able to engage in discussion. The public chambers consult the citizens, assist in drawing up an appeal, and also monitor the consideration of the appeal in the local government bodies. Public chambers organise their work in the form of discussions on various kinds of local issues; they invite representatives of local bodies to the meetings, and, in turn, representatives of public chambers participate in the commissions of both the local administration and the representative body of the municipality. In our research sites, local government bodies provide public chambers with rooms for meetings and receptions of citizens.

For example, the response of the public chamber of the Zavodoukovsky urban okrug to the citizens' requests was a questionnaire on issues related to poor quality of medical care. As a result, a number of problems were identified, an appeal was submitted to the Head of the municipality, who organised the meeting and invited the Chief physician of the Zavodoukovsky City Hospital, as well as representatives of the public chamber. The existing problems were voiced and admitted. The Chief physician asked the public chamber to draw up a roadmap for solving the identified problems. The map was compiled and sent to the Chief physician, who did not act on it. The Head of the municipality was informed and later dismissed the Chief physician. The representatives of the public chamber have acknowledged that the new administration of the Zavodoukovsky City Hospital is implementing the new roadmap.

The network of the local administration and the public chamber of the Zavodoukovksy urban okrug is very efficient; the public chamber even participates in the certification commission for municipal employees. The certification commission evaluates the professional and personal qualities of the candidates for municipal service. The procedure of evaluation includes professional and psychological testing, interviews, a questionnaire, after which the commission recommends the applicant and the city manager makes the final decision on the employment.

The third type of large public organisation is territorial self-government (TSG). Territorial self-government, in contrast to veteran organisations and public chambers, is regulated by the Federal Law 'On General Principles of Local Self-Government in the Russian Federation'. According to this law, territorial self-government means the self-organisation of citizens at the place of their residence.

The Federal law vests TSG with the right to initiate legal acts in local government bodies. The Statutes of some municipalities provide for the participation of TSGs' representatives in commissions of a municipal representative body with the right to a consultative vote. In the case study locations such a provision is not legally fixed, nevertheless TSGs use it in practice. The respondents – representatives of the legislative branch of the considered middle towns – explained that representatives of TSGs are provided with all materials by the legislature of middle towns in advance, and they can freely participate in the discussions and meetings of the legislature. In Zavodoukovsky urban okrug, the vice mayor holds regular meetings with active TSG members. In the city of Tobolsk, some training is organised for TSG members, and local authorities sponsored a meeting of TSG members with their colleagues from Tyumen to share experiences.

The main interest of TSG is townscaping. In Zavodoukovsky urban okrug, the townscaping can be funded by budgetary sources. However, very often TSGs collect money from citizens residing on their territory, and invite the municipality to finance additional works. In this case, local governments co-finance the townscaping works in the following way: three rubles from the local budget to match the funding of each ruble from residents. Another example of cooperation is public space cleansing. In this case, TSGs provide their members' participation, and the local government provides transport for garbage disposal, working tools and supplies. The joint activities have improved the relations between the local authorities and TSGs, and they reached the next level of efficient interaction – regulatory.

In the city of Tobolsk, two of the existing territorial self-governments are very active in townscaping issues – for example, planting flowers and organising 'flower competitions'; representatives of the authorities point out that such events involving people of all ages make a link between generations and teach attentiveness to the problems of another generation. The administration and local businesses also join such events giving organisational, informational and financial support.

Another peculiarity of the city of Tobolsk is a large number of students living there, with branches of two universities (the Basic Regional Industrial University and Tyumen State University, a member of the leading Russian universities group). Young people living in the city of Tobolsk are very active and many of them are involved in the work of the Youth Parliament of Tobolsk. Among other things, young people conduct moot sessions of the Parliament, and they are allowed to participate in the meetings of the municipal representative body.

Entrepreneurs can be involved in all the organisations mentioned above and in addition, issues related to business are resolved in other forms of participation. The main mechanism of interaction between the local government and business are the advisory councils of entrepreneurs created under the auspices of the local administration in our study sites. In these, the Councils for the Development of Small and Medium-sized Enterprises have been established. These councils are initiated and supported by the head of the municipality; nevertheless, the majority of their members are business people. The business councils also include representatives of federal authorities exercising control functions over entrepreneurs who are permanently located in middle towns. The work is conducted in the form of meetings. The agenda is formed according to the proposals of entrepreneurs and the local administration, as indicated by interviewees about 50/50. The municipal administration is the main organiser of the meetings. The business community is interested in issues of changing federal legislation, business development issues, land issues, and development of communal infrastructure.

The two study locations (Tobolsk and Zavodoukovsky) resolve issues related to changes in legislation differently. In Tobolsk there is a strong branch of the all-Russian public organisation of small and medium-sized business 'OPORA RUSSIA/ Reliance of Russia' and legislative initiatives of the regional and federal level are transferred to the top-level management of this organisation. In Zavodoukovsky urban okrug, the same issues are resolved by giving powers to the members of the regional parliament (the regional parliament has the right of legislative initiative to the Federal Parliament). It is interesting to note that the presence of the business organisation 'OPORA RUSSIA/ Reliance of Russia' in one of the case sites determined the special forms of public participation that are unavailable in the other locations. One of the efficient forms both for the public authorities and business society is 'business lunch' sponsored by the 'OPORA RUSSIA/ Reliance of Russia' every two weeks.

In Zavodoukovsky urban okrug there is not such a strong organisation of entrepreneurs, and the public authorities have made efforts to organise a platform for communication with entrepreneurs. A successful form of interaction between representatives of business and government is weekly meetings with the mayor. Any business person can come to such a meeting without warning and ask a question or ask for help. However, respondents from both sides consider pre-determined questions for discussion are more effective – in this case, the authorities can get prepared, for example, to invite representatives of state authorities and municipal corporations.

All respondents admit that the relation between public authorities and business society is good, becoming even better over the last 2–3 years. One respondent described his case; he addressed the local administration several times with one and the same issue. In 2013, his request was rejected; the background of this rejection was a lengthy and bureaucratic procedure for resolving his issue. In 2016, he attended a meeting with the mayor, and the organisers helped him to write down a well-structured appeal letter. Thereafter the administration helped with the issue.

United States

The City of St Augustine is widely known for its historic architecture. In 2016, together with citizens and experts from the National Alliance Preservation Commission (NAPC), the Planning and Building Department has developed the Historic Preservation Master Plan. Citizens have participated in the survey, which identified strengths and weaknesses of the historic preservation of properties, and citizen suggestions on improvements, followed by public workshops and presentations held by the experts from the NAPC.

However, according to the city's mayor, such large numbers of visitors leads to parking and traffic congestion. In addressing this problem, the city's government created a Mobility Initiative, which engaged different stakeholders, government departments, local businesses and NGOs. City officials gathered information through citizen surveys about mobility issues in the city and developed strategies for addressing concerns based on feedback. Currently, the Neighbourhood Mobility programme allows residents to meet and walk with city staff and discuss specific concerns. This is a highly personal process that has given officials the opportunity to literally walk in the shoes of their citizens, and for citizens to get to know city officials more.

Among other urban planning issues, citizens show a high interest in the issues of stormwater drainage. Every year the city conducts a citizens' survey that identifies these and other mobility and infrastructure issues. As the mayor identified, in addition to the state-mandated public hearings, the city initiates a large number of meetings and programmes organised through the Planning and Building Department open for public participation. Public forums and workshops, neighbourhood councils, and online surveys using Survey Monkey are the main tools to engage citizens.

The city staff reached out to citizens mainly through social media: website, news, notes. However, people who live outside the city and the elderly population receive flyers that encourage citizen action. The mayor considers their governmental website very responsive and encouraging of electronic participation. However, city officials report they get more feedback through their personal Facebook and Twitter pages.

However, the number of people participating is relatively low, which makes public meetings not very representative. In case of the Mobility Initiative, the city government hired a consultant, who was responsible for advertising the event. Only 100 people participated in the Mobility workshop, which aimed to help in understanding planning issues. The consultant, who was not a full-time member of city staff, demonstrated a lack of ability to connect with citizens. According to the mayor, one of the barriers to such engagement is 'poor ability to communicate the way people understand. People in the government cannot devolve to jargon. The hardest thing to do is to simplify the hardest issue' (N. Shavers, mayor of St Augustine, personal communication, 4 April 2017).

The situation in Gainesville is not significantly different. As in St Augustine, city officials have experimented with different approaches to engaging citizens. However, in similar way, the desired outcomes for quality, quantity and responsiveness of engagement have not been met.

In 2015, the City of Gainesville created a uniquely named Department of Doing. The department, formerly known as the Planning and Development Services department, has shifted its focus from policy-orientation to service-orientation. According to the director of the department, its responsibility is to provide helpful and transparent information in a timely manner to residents, focus on accomplishments, assist residents in establishing new businesses in the city and engage citizens in decision-making processes related to urban planning and building services.

The issues that attract citizens' attention include construction of very tall buildings, creation of adult-oriented businesses such as strip clubs, and location of gas stations. Also the city government requires that residents be invited to participate in neighbourhood workshops prior to a development application being approved. Review and advisory boards make decisions on development applications according to state requirements.

The citizens are informed about meetings through newspaper advertisements, plastic signs, and flyers. When city staff have a specific concern they communicate to people through neighbourhood email lists. When it comes to broader issues, emails are sent to all citizens. Also residents have access to the city's Facebook and Twitter pages, and Facebook Live is often used to broadcast meetings online.

The city government created the Open Government platform, initiated by the mayor to make government 'as open and transparent as possible'. The platform improves access to city data and encourages citizens to participate in local decision-making processes. According to the mayor, residents use city data for economic purposes, modelling their economic analysis and establishing new business enterprises. The platform is available for computer and mobile devises. Residents can also submit their concerns online via a virtual City Hall. For example, 311GNV portal allows submission of complaints on a variety of issues including graffiti and damaged or missing signs. Then the issue is channelled to the relevant department. The city also creates open discussions with the community through the EngageGNV portal. In more traditional in-person meetings, the City organises public hearings and neighbourhood councils.

Despite the successful efforts of the city to increase citizen participation, both the mayor and the director of the Department of Doing still indicate a small number of residents engaged in public decision-making processes. The City is struggling to engage a true cross-section of residents with socio-economic diversity. Similarly, the mayor stated that 'the area is not represented. Citizen activists do not always represent populations around the city' (N. Shavers, personal communication, 4 April 2017). The mayor suggests that the City should find better ways to reach out to the community, and for models they look to bigger jurisdictions such as Boston or San Francisco.

Although the cities differ according to their location, population size and density, racial makeup and poverty level, both cities are home to a low level of civic engagement and significant challenges in reaching out to the population. City officials of both cities indicate the lack of proper means of communication on the part of government and lack of interest on citizens' part. As was indicated in interviews, these factors lead to a low representativeness of population.

Discussion

Our findings show that attempts to create open systems and processes do not necessarily lead to open outcomes. Although there are notable capacities developed and being implemented to increase civic engagement, the lack of tools to measure the outcomes of participation and to ensure robust and representative participation limit the good intentions of the ideas. According to Nichols-Barrer and colleagues:

> although citizen participation is often cited as a principal or ancillary objective in governance reform initiatives, outcomes related to civic participation are rarely evaluated rigorously.
>
> (Nichols-Barrer et al. 2015: 1)

Officials from both Gainesville and St Augustine in the United States observed that low non-representative civic participation leads to a very weak input in decision-making processes. McLeod and colleagues (1999) believe that the willingness to participate depends on information and motivation. As indicated by both cities, one of the main reasons of low participation is lack of appropriate communication with citizens. Although the city governments facilitate a variety of tools for online and in-person engagement, the same groups of people come to meetings. McLeod et al. (1999) argue that both media and interpersonal communication are crucial in incentivising citizens participation. As was mentioned by the mayor of St Augustine, that the best way to reach out to residents is to go directly into the community to talk to them. This suggests that City staff should pursue more interpersonal communication when media fails to incetivise public participation.

The cities are forced to more closed systems and expertise because of a small number of citizens engaged. However, Kalu (2017: 83) suggests that 'citizens are already participating in government through their elected representatives'. Citizens do not necessarily seek direct participation; rather, they expect depoliticisation of the bureaucratic system, representation and accountability. In this case the open system is not necessary, if elected officials show a high level of representativeness and expertise. This is the standard 'loop model' of democracy (Bryer and Sahin 2012).

In contrast to Kalu's (2017) argument, the findings show that citizen participation in both Russia and United States does improve policies and programmes enacted by government. As Irvin and Stansbury (2004: 55) indicate, 'with citizen participation, formulated policies might be more realistically grounded in citizens' preferences, and the improved support from the public might create a less divisive, combative populace to govern and regulate'. This suggests that citizen participation can lead to increases in citizen efficacy and competence and trust in government (Cooper, Bryer and Meek 2006).

Nicholas-Barrer and colleagues (2015) explain the decrease in civic participation, due to the fact that open governance reforms and transparency raise public awareness about governmental issues and reduce people's satisfaction with government performance. Consequentially, perceived administrative performance decreases public trust in government (Vigoda-Gadot and Yuval 2003). According to van Ryzin (2007: 532), citizen satisfaction can indeed predict future behaviour and attitudes of interest, such as 'staying in a jurisdiction or trusting local government'.

However, Olken's (2010) study provides empirical evidence, that citizens, who do not directly get involved in decision-making processes, are less likely to be satisfied with outcomes. In this case, if government officials initiate the engagement of citizens in administrative decision-making processes on specific community issues in order to gain information or get assistance from the public, that can increase trust and lead to positive outcomes in government performance and citizens' satisfaction (Yang and Holzer 2006; Stumbraitė-Vilkišienė 2012). Eventually, citizen satisfaction is more likely to improve trust in government. Furthermore, public trust strengthens the quality of governmental responsiveness (Yang and Holzer 2006).

The preceding themes suggest commonalities between Russia and the United States. There are also potentially important differences. Overlaid across the bureaucracy–democracy 'divide', we can suggest differences in the centre of control of participatory processes. As Cooper et al. (2006) suggest, 'who' develops and implements the participation is a central question of concern for understanding the efficacy of participatory processes.

At least in the cases examined herein, we might label Russian participatory processes as 'state-centred' and the American cases as 'market-centred'. By that we mean the participation at the local level in Russia is heavily influenced by State actors performing State-mandated functions. Though there are state-level (Florida) laws that establish parameters for participation at the local level, there are no national level mandates. Further, the parameters established in Florida law tend to be ambiguous and thus open to diverse interpretations (Bryer 2010).

This ambiguity opens the door to private actors managing public participation processes in the United States, rather than State-level actors. These are For-Profit consulting firms that have established profitable models 'selling' participatory processes in packaged formats to cities. Such market-oriented mechanisms are not seen in Russia, and they represent perhaps a third element of the bureaucracy–democracy divide – that of marketability (Lee 2015; Walker 2014).

Conclusion

The study found that citizen participation is an important tool that enhances representativeness, transparency and responsiveness of local governments. We identified potentially successful practices in promoting civic participation in mid-sized cities. Among them are the participation of citizens in surveys, workshops for development applications, development of cities' historical preservation plans and planning code, engagement with diverse stakeholder groups, public chambers, territorial public-self-government, and business councils. However, together with cities' successes, the study discovered that lack of communication is one of the main challenges that prohibit a high level of participation. The literature suggests that interpersonal communication between city officials and residents can incentivise their participation. Interviewees also indicated the lack of citizen interest as a reason for low engagement. Although the study supported that idea with the literature review, further empirical study is needed to identify the genuine reason for low participation on citizens' part and the barriers to utilising the full capacity of state and market mechanisms to enhance local democratic practice across these two cultures. This will provide a broad perspective on the reasons for and benefits of civic engagement in government decision making processes – processes that are important across societies as different as the United States and Russia.

References

Albertazzi, D. and McDonnell, D. (2008) Introduction: The Sceptre and the Spectre. In D. Albertazzi and D. McDonnell (eds), *Twenty-First Century Populism: The Spectre of Western European Democracy*, 1–11. Basingstoke: Palgrave Macmillan.

Arnstein, S. R. (1969) A Ladder of Citizen Participation. *Journal of the American Institute of Planners* 35(4): 216–224.

Berkley, G. and Rousse, J. (2004) *The Craft of Public Administration* (9th edition). Boston, MA: McGraw Hill.

Blind, P. K. (2007) Building Trust in Government in the Twenty-First Century: Review of Literature and Emerging Issues. In *7th Global Forum on Reinventing Government Building Trust in Government*, June, 26–29. Vienna: UNDESA.

Bryer, T. A. (2007) *Negotiating Bureaucratic Responsiveness in Collaboration with Citizens: Findings from Action Research in Los Angeles*. Los Angeles, CA: University of Southern California.

Bryer, T. A. (2010) Living Democracy in Theory and Practice: Getting Dirty in a Local Government Incorporation Process. *Public Administration and Management* 15(1): 259–304.

Bryer, T. A. and Sahin, I. (2012) Administrators as Deliberative Representatives: A Revised Public Service Role. *International Journal of Public Administration* 35(14): 925–933.

Bukhard, G. (1998) Retrospective Analysis of Performance in the Public Sector [Ретроспективный анализ производительности в государственном секторе]. In *Effectiveness of Public Administration* [Эффективность государственного управления]. Moscow.

Cooper, T. L., Bryer, T. A. and Meek, J. W. (2006) Citizen-Centered Collaborative Public Management. *Public Administration Review* 66(S1): 76–88.

Evans, P. and Rauch, J. E. (1999) Bureaucracy and Growth: A Cross-National Analysis of the Effects of 'Weberian' State Structures on Economic Growth. *American Sociological Review* 64(5): 748–765.

Farazmand, A. (2002) *Modern Organizations: Theory and Practice*. Westport, CT: Greenwood.

Federal Law No 212-FZ (2014) *On the Basics of Public Control in the Russian Federation*. Legislative Archives of the Russian Federation, 28 July. 30 (I), 4213. Retrieved from http://base.garant.ru/70700452.

Federal Law No 131-FZ (2003) *On General Principles of Local Self-Government in the Russian Federation*. Legislative Archives of the Russian Federation, 6 October. 40, 3822. Retrieved from http://base.garant.ru/186367.

Fry, B. R. and Raadschelders, J. C. N. (2013) *Mastering Public Administration: From Max Weber to Dwight Waldo* (2nd edition). Washington, DC: CQ Press.

Hardin, R. (1998) Trust in Government. *Trust and Governance* 1: 9–27.

Harmon, M. M. and Mayer, R. T. (1986) *Organization Theory for Public Administration*. Boston, MA: Little, Brown.

Hill, C. and Lynn, L. E. Jr. (2009) *Public Management: A Three Dimensional Approach*. Washington, DC: Congressional Quarterly Press.

Hughes, O. E. (2013) *Public Management and Administration: An Introduction* (4th edition). Basingstoke: Palgrave Macmillan.

Inglehart, R. F. and Norris, P. (2016) *Trump, Brexit, and the Rise of Populism: Economic Have-Nots and Cultural Backlash*. RWP16-026. Cambridge, MA: Harvard Kennedy School.

Irvin, R. A. and Stansbury, J. (2004) Citizen Participation in Decision Making: Is it Worth the Effort? *Public Administration Review* 64(1): 55–65.

Kalu, N. K. (2017) *Citizenship: Identity, Institutions, and the Postmodern Challenge*. New York: Routledge.

Kozbanenko, V. A. (2006) Modernization Management Resources: Traditions and Innovations [Модернизационные ресурсы управления: традиции и инновации]. In *State Management in XXI Century: Traditions and Innovations* [Государственное управление в XXI веке: Традиции и инновации]. Moscow: Moscow State University.

Lee, C. W. (2015) *Do-It-Yourself Democracy: The Rise of the Public Engagement Industry*. New York: Oxford University Press.

McLeod, J. M., Scheufele, D. A. and Moy, P. (1999) Community, Communication, and Participation: The Role of Mass Media and Interpersonal Discussion in Local Political Participation. *Political Communication* 16(3): 315–336.

Nichols-Barrer, I., Protik, A., Berman, J. and Sloan, M. (2015) Impacts of Supporting Civic Participation in Local Governance: Experimental Evidence from Rwanda (No. 2536ddc8fdea407fb27b2d41a53407fa). *Mathematica Policy Research*. Retrieved from https://ideas.repec.org/p/mpr/mprres/2536ddc8fdea407fb27b2d41a53407fa.html.

Olken, B. A. (2010) Direct Democracy and Local Public Goods: Evidence from a Field Experiment in Indonesia. *American Political Science Review* 104(2): 243–267.

Osborn, D. and Gaebler, T. (1992) *Reinventing Government: How the Entrepreneurial Spirit is Transforming the Public Sector*. New York: Penguin Group.

Polterovich, V. M. (2007) *The Strategy of National Reforms as the Art of Reform* [Стратегия национальных реформ, как искусство реформ], Moscow: GU VSE.

Rohr, J. (1986) *To Run a Constitution: The Legitimacy of the Administrative State*. Lawrence, KS: University of Kansas Press.

Rosener, J. B. (1975) A Cafeteria of Techniques and Critiques. *Public Management*, 57(12), 16–19.

Salancik, G. R. and Pfeffer, J. (1978) A Social Information Processing Approach to Job Attitudes and Task Design. *Administrative Science Quarterly* 23(2): 224–253.

Shafritz, J. M., Ott, J. S. and Yang, Y. S. (2015) *Classics of Organization Theory*. Boston, MA: Cengage Learning.

Stumbraitė-Vilkišienė, E. (2012) *Citizen Participation in the Local Public Service Provision and Quality Improvement*. Moscow: UMDCIPE.

Van Ryzin, G. G. (2007) Pieces of a Puzzle: Linking Government Performance, Citizen Satisfaction, and Trust. *Public Performance and Management Review* 30(4): 521–535.

Van Waarden, B. (2015) John Stuart Mill on Civil Service Recruitment and the Relation between Bureaucracy and Democracy. *Canadian Journal of Political Science* 48(3): 625–645.

Vigoda-Gadot, E. and Yuval, F. (2003) Managerial Quality, Administrative Performance and Trust in Governance Revisited: A Follow-Up Study Of Causality. *International Journal of Public Sector Management* 16(7): 502–522.

Walker, E. T. (2014) *Grassroots for Hire: Public Affairs Consultants in American Democracy*. Cambridge: Cambridge University Press.

Wang, X. and Van Wart, M. (2007) When Public Participation in Administration Leads to Trust: An Empirical Assessment of Managers' Perceptions. *Public Administration Review* 67(2): 265–278.

Yang, K. (2005) Public Administrators' Trust in Citizens: A Missing Link in Citizen Involvement Efforts. *Public Administration Review* 65(3): 273–285.

Yang, K. and Holzer, M. (2006) The Performance–Trust Link: Implications for Performance Measurement. *Public Administration Review* 66(1): 114–126.

19
THE URBAN GOVERNANCE OF AUSTERITY IN EUROPE

*Adrian Bua, Jonathan Davies, Ismael Blanco,
Ioannis Chorianopoulos, Mercè Cortina-Oriol,
Andrés Feandeiro, Niamh Gaynor, Steven Griggs,
David Howarth and Yuni Salazar*

Introduction

The 2008 financial crash and ensuing austerity policies (Blyth 2012) have impacted profoundly on European political economies (Streeck 2013). While Northern economies such as Germany have fared relatively well, the impacts in the Mediterranean countries as well as in France and Britain has been deep (Streeck 2013, 2016). Peck (2012: 651) highlights the importance of the urban sphere for understanding austerity politics, 'as cities become beachheads and staging grounds for both tax revanchism and progressive forms of counter-politics'.

Furthermore, the intensity, propinquity and densities characteristic of the urban level make it an ideal terrain on which to engage with the actors and strategies that define, govern and resist austerity as well as mediate structures and institutions.

This chapter describes the urban governance of austerity in Europe, focusing on which actors are involved in the advancement of and resistance to austerity; how they are doing it; through which alliances between state and non-state actors. It outlines the strategies developed by different actors as well as the outcomes produced by the correlation of forces at the urban level. In doing so we draw on research carried out in five European cities – Athens, Barcelona, Dublin, Leicester and Nantes. In doing so our project contributes to literatures that since the crash have brought critical political economy forcefully back in to academic debates on democratic theory (Streeck 2013, 2016), public administration (Davies 2011) and urban governance (Peck 2012; Davies and Blanco 2017).

The main question addressed in our analysis of these cases is that which the research originally set out to answer- what happens to the ideology and practice of 'network' and 'collaborative' forms of governance under conditions of capitalist crisis and austerity (Ansell and Gash 2008; Stoker 2004; Sullivan et al. 2013). Prior to the crash, collaborative and network forms of governance were widely advocated as substitutes to outmoded state and market based governance forms. We call this tendency the 'collaborative moment',[1] built around the notion of an epochal shift from competition and vertical hierarchies to trust-based association and horizontal networking. We set out to investigate the durability of the 'collaborative moment' in times of austerity.

In this chapter we outline the main findings in our European cases of Athens, Barcelona, Dublin, Leicester and Nantes in relation to this question. In essence concluding that the harsh realities of austerity policies and politics have, one way or another, eroded collaborative governance, belying it as a governance ideology that seems functional only in 'good times'. We proceed as follows. First, we historically situate austerity politics in Europe as a further wave of neo-liberal re-structuring, and examine some of the current literature on austerity politics and governance to elicit our main themes of inquiry. The second and third sections respectively describe our comparative method and introduce our cases. The fourth, most substantive part discusses our findings, organised according to the main themes already identified. Finally, we outline our comparative findings before concluding along the lines above.

Urban austerity governance

As Fordism and the Keynesian compromise unravel, cities around the world have been central to the neoliberal drive to re-establish capitalist profitability through budget squeezes, administrative rationalisation, de-regulation and (re)commodification (Harvey 2012). These policies are part of the broader historical process of 'unleashing' (Glyn 1994) capitalism from the constraints of Keynesian social democracy, including reduced state fiscal capacity, increased public and private debt-dependence and the manipulation of public policy agendas to appease creditors (Crouch 2004, 2011; Streeck 2013). We understand the austerity agenda following the 2008 crash as a further wave of neo-liberalisation (Davies and Blanco 2017), which accelerates the trajectory towards technocratic governance (Swyngedouw 2009) and the development of 'market-conforming democracy' (Angela Merkel cited in Streeck 2014: 44) encapsulated in Streeck's (2015) concept of the 'consolidation state'.

Despite these powerful forces, scholars have established that the embedding of neoliberalism and austerity policies within urban administrations interacts with local contexts and institutional legacies (Brenner et al. 2010; Blanco, Griggs and Sullivan 2014). Indeed, recent empirical research reported by Davies and Blanco (2017) has established the variegated nature of urban regimes and public policies under austerity. The depth and modalities of austerity policies are complex. Not all countries, or cities within countries, are equally affected. National states and transnational institutions such as the EU exert more or less influence depending on the level of integration in transnational institutions, notably the Euro itself. Moreover, there is greater or lesser space for political choice at local and urban state levels, depending on the configuration of central–regional–local relations. For example, our case study city of Nantes was far more favourably positioned than Athens; the former growing robustly with a strong tax base, the latter bearing the brunt of waves of EU mandated austerity. Thus, we will introduce our cases by considering the priorities and public policies pursued and the degree to which austerity is embedded and / or contested within them. Our cross case findings are summarised in Table 19.1 below, and 'austerity embeddedness' constitutes the first row.

Second, we tackle the central theme – how practices of networked and 'collaborative governance' (Ansell and Gash 2008) are affected by and operate under austerity. One of our key premises in the study in this respect is that of a 'collaborative moment' of the late 20th and early 21st century. This was characterised by widespread enthusiasm about the potential for networks to improve governance (Stoker 2004). Intellectuals reasoned that prosperity had broken down old cleavages based on class, race and gender, allowing social relations based on trust to flourish (Beck et al. 1994). Networks made up of capable agents could overcome the shortcomings of public hierarchies and market mechanisms (Newman 2004; Stoker 2004), and revitalise forms of participatory democracy (Griggs and Howarth 2007; Hirst 2000; Torfing and Sorensen 2014).

In public administration 'collaborative governance' was institutionalised through new forms of public participation in policy making (e.g. Bua 2017; Gaynor 2011), statutory partnerships and co-production of public services (Durose, Justice and Skelcher 2013). We set out to ask what impact the financial crash and ensuing austerity policies would have upon the ideology and practice of collaborative governance – would the collaborative moment endure, or be unravelled by, post-crash exposure to austerity and distributional conflict? Would it prove to only be suitable for times of relatively high growth, or to be insulated from the volatilities and iniquities that come so strongly to the fore in crises? Thus, our second theme (and the second row in Table 19.1 below) is that of 'governance trajectories', where we summarise the lineage of governance practices across our cases.

At the same time, we know that austerity has led to a phenomenal expansion of protest movements (Ortiz et al. 2013), leading urban commentators to identify the animation of resistance as one of the 'double movement contradictions' of austerity (Peck 2012: 649). In response, states have policed and sought to criminalise protest, leading scholars to identify an authoritarian phase of neoliberalism (Albo and Finnelly 2014). That these social responses bear the genesis of counter-hegemonic projects has been borne out by the development of the 're-politicising city' (Dikeç and Swyngedouw 2017) – a space where the political rationality of neo-liberalism is challenged and alternatives that begin to arise through organisational and political experimentation. The intensity, modalities and effects, of resistance vary locally (Davies and Blanco 2017) and we can expect the nature and extent of resistance to have an important influence on the governance trajectories in our cities. Thus, our third theme (and third row in table one) of 'resistance politics' includes the strength and prevalence of anti-austerity movements in our cities, their aims and repertoires of action.

Resistance movements and social responses are widely varied. Although there is significant overlap, a rough distinction can be made between activisms led by traditional organisations such as political parties and trade unions, usually geared towards specific goals or policy demands; pre-figurative forms of protest that articulate more general grievances and demands, often calling for a new kind of politics; and social innovation that responds to crises of social reproduction bought about by marginalisation from state provision and market exchange (Della Porta 2015; Mayer 2013; Pares et al. 2017; Tormey 2015). We will explain how these, as well as more muted forms of protest, have interacted with austerity governance in our cities, and to what effect. The final row in table one summarises the outcomes we have identified across the cases.

Methods

The broader research project focussed on eight cities (Athens, Baltimore, Barcelona, Dublin, Melbourne, Montreal, Leicester, Nantes, see ESRC Final Report 2017) and considers the broader question of the urban governance of the rolling crises of Fordism and Welfarism. In this contribution we focus on the five European cases because our scoping research revealed that it is here that the 'collaborative moment' was most relevant and we can thus most clearly trace the impact of varying degrees of austerity upon it.

Research in each case was based on interviews and focus groups with key stakeholders, as well as observations at relevant collaborative encounters. We prioritised fidelity to our cases over a strict comparative framework (Robinson 2016) and thus case researchers had considerable freedom to develop the thematic focus of the study, which varies across our cases, within the overall problematic of collaborative governance under austerity.

Findings

Table 19.1 summarises our provisional findings across the themes above.

Table 19.1 Austerity governance in European cities

	Athens	Barcelona	Dublin	Leicester	Nantes
Austerity embeddedness	Embedded at central and local scales	Centrally embedded but locally resisted	Embedded at central and local scales	Embedded at central and local scales	Centrally embedded since 2014, deferred locally with strong local tax base.
Governance trajectory	History of clientelism – formation of 'elite–pluralist' collaborative regime under austerity	Collaborative moment, collaborative retrenchment under austerity, radicalisation post-2015	Collaborative moment, collaborative retrenchment under austerity	Collaborative moment, to collaborative retrenchment under austerity	Collaborative moment; accelerated collaborative infrastructure under austerity, but mediated by the French Republican tradition
Resistance politics	Widespread. Resistance disengaged from policy making following defeats.	Widespread; engaged in policy making; strong counterpower; state-social movement alliance	Ascending following recent waves of protest; generally disengaged from policy making; emerging counterpower	Limited and contained; disengaged from policy making; little counterpower	Some resistance; disengaged from policy making; seeks to avoid state co-option; exerts some counterpower
Outcomes	Elite pluralist regime, with legitimacy crisis; volunteerism, atomisation	Radicalisation of collaborative moment; re-politicisation	Pro-austerity regime, collaborative retrenchment, nascent re-politicisation	Collaborative retrenchment Austerian Realism, boosterism	Attempted radicalisation of 'collaborative moment'; legitimacy challenges

Source: Author's elaboration from qualitative data

The embeddedness of austerity governance

All our cases operate in a context of austerity measures being imposed by higher tiers of authority. In Barcelona (Spain), Dublin (Ireland), and Athens (Greece), such measures were prescribed by transnational institutions such as the European Union and the International Monetary Fund, in order to ensure repayment on bailouts and loan programmes. As noted above, France and the UK have had more freedom of manoeuvre, but austerity is also adopted at the national level despite recent adoption of anti-austerity policies by the British opposition Labour Party and a recent softening of austerity measures by the UK Conservative government. In France, the election of president Emmanuel Macron in 2017 signifies a potential deepening of pro-Austerity, neoliberal governance, though the city of Nantes remains the least directly affected of all the five EU case studies.

At city level there is more variation. Policy makers in Athens, Dublin and Leicester have followed a strict austerity agenda. For example, in Leicester the Local Authority budget is forecast to be cut by almost half by 2020, from the 2010 baseline. In Athens, the national economic contraction has also led to a fall in tax receipts and the City has been ruled by a pro-Austerity mayor who has implemented austerity over and beyond EU bailout conditions. Given the extremity of economic recession in Greece and poor prospects of economic revival in the near future, attracting large philanthropic investment to invest in programmes that can attenuate the severe social fallout and engender economic development is a significant priority in the City (Chorianopoulos and Tselepi 2017). Leicester and Dublin also implement austerity measures, whilst focussing on attracting inward investment to increase local employment and commercial rate intakes. Dublin seeks to build on its success in establishing itself as a global hub for IT companies, and Leicester continues to regenerate the city centre and build up its tourist and service sector industries. The City council has followed a policy of faithfully implementing nationally mandated austerity measures. However, it aims to mitigate impacts by using discretionary funding to help the most vulnerable, and, demonstrating remnants of a welfarist logic (Pierre 2011), co-ordinating local welfare services to maximise welfare benefit receipts and preserve municipal services as far as is compatible with austerity budgeting.

The cases of Barcelona and Nantes testify to the variegated and contestable nature of neoliberalism and austerity (Brenner et al. 2010; Davies and Blanco 2017). The impacts of the crash and austerity in Barcelona have been deeply felt, especially through sharp increases in poverty, social exclusion and social inequalities, with the unemployment rate rising to 18.6% in 2012 (23.8% in Catalonia; 25% in Spain), and the at-risk-of-poverty rate reaching 18.2 in 2011 (20.5 in Catalonia; 20.6% in Spain). In response, the City's first Conservative administration (2011–2015) since the 32-year period of rule by the Socialist Party followed a conventionally neoliberal approach of cutting services, developing budget surpluses and building on competitive advantage in the tourism industry. However social impacts such as rising inequality, touristification and gentrification led to an anti-austerity left coalition taking office in 2015, developing a more interventionist social, fiscal, economic policies, that seek to invest surpluses accrued by the previous administration and regulate businesses more closely, especially in tourism where the City seeks to develop a more sustainable model. It is fair to say that Barcelona's 'new municipalism' (Observatorio Metropolitano 2014) and pro-democracy ambitions have made it a global reference point for left-wing, anti-austerity urbanism with socially transformative aspirations.

Nantes is affected by national impacts of austerity such as increased unemployment and cuts to local government funding, but has arguably managed to avoid severe impacts due to a growing population and economic performance that is positive relative to other French cities. However, poor neighbourhoods have been harshly hit by the crisis, with much higher rates living in poverty and sharp decreases in household income. There is therefore an issue of inequality despite continued economic growth. Policy makers in Nantes frame the most important problem facing the city as one of 'dechrochage', whereby certain communities have become disconnected from the economic motor that is Nantes. In the words of one policy officer: 'for people, the financial crisis is more about décrochage and isolation, and it is that which we are worried about, that is to say people exiting [what we might see as] the community of residents'.

Whereas the Barcelona administration has more socially transformative aspirations, the main consensus in Nantes is for a more reformist agenda, based on often technocratic solutions that do not fundamentally question the (broadly neo-liberal) growth model of the city. As we will see, however, local resistance movements and some more critical officials argue such problems cannot be resolved within the existing growth model.

Governance trajectories

Our cases vary in terms of governance trajectories and specifically how practices of networked and collaborative governance have fared. We found variance in, first, the existence of and institutional make-up of the 'collaborative moment' and second the forms of post-crash austerity governance and the role of collaboration within these.

Athens is a city with a strong history of clientelism, which, combined with legacies of authoritarianism arrested the development of local collaborative dynamics (Chorianopopulos 2012). However, more recently a range of state-led collaboration initiatives were developed in response to Greek state and EU directives. In response, municipalities set up deliberative forums, and launch partnership schemes with businesses and civil society groups. These forums are driven by state, corporate and third sector elites. They are also substantially animated by the prospect of attracting investment by large philanthropic funders, focussed especially on urban regeneration, economic development and social policy. For example the most prominent municipal social policy scheme is a venture with an NGO called Solidarity Now, established in 2013 by George Soros's Open Society Foundations (OSF) and 'Innovathens', a municipal economic development initiative in the tech sector, is funded by Samsung.

Thus, the post-austerity 'collaborative turn' in Athens has occurred mainly among a limited range of 'elite' corporate and NGO partners. This 'elite pluralist' regime excludes grassroots groups, which have been sidelined by large national and transnational charities and in any case do not wish to participate. It is also strongly rejected by the multitude of fragmented anti-austerity groups, which, as we shall expand upon below, have proliferated since the crash but turned in on themselves following the capitulation of the national Syriza government when attempting to confront the EU and develop an anti-austerity agenda.

The history of collaborative public administration in Barcelona predates that of the 'collaborative moment'. Public-private and public-community collaboration had a key role in the governance of the City at least since Spain's transition to democracy. Commentators even talk of a 'Barcelona Model' of collaborative public administration (Blanco 2009). The only Conservative administration (2011–2015) to have governed in recent history was critical of this approach, but was unable to fundamentally change it due its high degree of embeddedness. The Conservative administration led by Xavier Trias followed a strongly neoliberal policy programme, aiming to develop a budget surplus including, cutting social provisions, privatising public assets and building on the city's competitive advantage in tourism. It succeeded in all three, and generated considerable social fallout in doing so. Combined with the already significant effects of austerity, this animated resistance movements, which led to the election of anti-eviction leader Ada Colau to the City administration on a Municipalist platform in 2015.

Colau's administration adopts a more radical participatory and collaborative rhetoric that seeks to reclaim public goods, and create new ones often in partnership with the many social movements that exist in the city. In contrast to Athen's 'elite-pluralist' regime, Barcelona seeks to develop bottom-linked (Garcia 2006) forms of collaboration, characterised by strong organic links between to-down state-led practice and policies and bottom-up social movements. The co-production of public policy, public-commons partnerships and transformative forms of social innovation (Pares et al. 2017) are all collaborative concepts that the city administration is attempting to operationalise. One city official, for example, spoke of the emancipatory potential of the 'commons' (as in resources held in trust for, belonging to or affecting a whole community, but not under direct state control):

> The Commons aren't spaces owned by the public sector, but they represent a shared and common wealth. The attributes of universality, redistribution, accessibility . . . characteristic of the Public are missed in many public administration projects. This is why I think that the Commons are more capable of acting as the Public than the public administration itself.

This could be said to amount to a radical revival of the ethos of the 'collaborative moment'. However, unlike the collaborative consensus in the golden years of neo-liberalism, this more radical approach accepts, and seeks to address, the iniquities of the neo-liberal political economy and bring back into the realm of politics much that has been kept at arm's length by it (Dikeç and Swyngedouw 2017).

Dublin and Leicester share some similar traits in governance trajectories. The 'collaborative moment' of the late 20th and early 21st century was strong in both cities (e.g. Gaynor 2011), which went with the grain of public policy trends in Ireland and the UK (described by Davies 2011 as the 'paradigm case' of collaborative governance) and developed a thicket of collaborative infrastructures. Both cities experienced collaborative retrenchment with the onset of the crash and austerity policies, as central government imposed cuts on local administrations, which reacted with a centralisation of authority, as well as funding for civil society groups and collaborative partnerships. In Dublin retrenchment had begun before the crash and ensuing austerity policies, which then firmly consolidated it.

In Leicester the Mayor's agenda is strongly focussed on cutting whilst attracting inward investment and boosting growth. This approach is underpinned by what we have called 'austerian realism' (ESRC Final Report 2017) – that is, regretful, but diligent, compliance with austerity for perceived lack of alternatives. This austerian realist logic inflects policy throughout the City council. It leads, for example, to accepting market led economic development as the only way out of the crisis. Collaboration is still alluded to by local policy actors, but the emancipatory rhetoric of the collaborative moment is gone, replaced with a strongly 'functionalist' logic, whereby collaboration becomes a tool to confront and manage scarcity, as one policy officer put it:

> So there is an acceptance that to get things done in a positive way here, private and public sector and indeed the voluntary sector have to work together, that we can't fight with each other because that's wasted energy and wasted resource.

In Dublin, collaborative governance continues along a similar path – in retrenched, rationalised and bureaucratised form and focussing mainly on coping with austerity. Moreover, in both cities service rationalisations and cut backs to third sector funding have deeply impacted upon small locally based voluntary organisations, and favoured large national and international organisations. For example, one respondent (a community activist) in Dublin explained:

> there were about 55,000 people working in the community sector, and, after austerity, there were about 20,000 that were taken out of the mix. So, there was just a massive cull, if you like, at that level.

The voluntary sector has been decimated by cuts, undermining civil society networks. The result is a hollowed out voluntary and community sector engaged more in competition than in collaborative relationship-building, and with a diminished ability to voice the needs of citizens or, importantly, speak truth to power.

Our fifth and final case, the city of Nantes, has a tradition of participatory governance most immediately rooted in the last Mayoral administration of Jean Marc Ayrault (1989–2012). The City's collaborative approach is explained in reference to the '*jeu à la Nantaise*', in reference to the City football team's slick passing game. The current Mayor, Johanna Rolland, also made citizen engagement a policy priority committing to a 'constant dialogue' between local councillors and citizens. Out of all our cases, Nantes is the one in which the rationale remains closest to that of the 'collaborative moment'. Collaborative governance is deemed to go beyond the merely managerial objectives of improving services and efficiencies, to harnessing the expertise of citizens, countering political disengagement and building social cohesion within the contours of a pro-business, relatively boosterish growth model.

Critics question the authenticity of the City's collaborative forums, arguing that they are strongly influenced by the state, warranted by the French Republican tradition, and provide little else than window dressing for decisions that have already been made. They also label City sponsored participation initiatives as forms of incorporation, with little real influence. In this vein one respondent commented on the '*jeu à la Nantaise*' analogy:

> who do you look for when building a team, and when [do] you pass the ball? . . . You may pass the ball, but in the final instance you are obliged to follow . . . because the project is too advanced.

The criticism here is that the policy process advances irrespective of citizen dialogue, which is bought into line with it through information giving and pedagogy. Indeed, critics charge the kinds of groups represented at collaborative forums with being 'apolitical', 'non-adversarial' and deeply embedded in top down governance practices. At the same time, elected representatives and policymakers question the legitimacy, and 'political' motives of critical actors, associating them with narrow party political or ideological interests, rather than those of the general citizenry – an accusation often made by traditional political actors against new forms of participatory governance in the 'collaborative moment' (Baiocchi and Ganuza 2017). Indeed, a common response to the charge that power remains firmly in the hands of politicians as 'no bad thing', as 'it is [the local politicians'] job after all'. In this rationale, the basis for judgements about the governance of the city shifts from input to output forms of legitimacy. This is a vision of the purpose of citizen dialogue that sits uneasily with the 'renewal of public action' rhetoric advanced by the Mayor in her participatory policy making programmes. It is also questionable to what extent this kind of collaborative governance can generate inclusion and overcome the challenge of 'dechrochage' without developing a more socially transformative agenda.

Resistance politics

Our cases cover a range of responses to austerity and forms of resistance. First, Athens was a key site of anti-austerity struggles after 2010, mainly centred around trade unions and the rise of Syriza, a party of the left that has governed since 2015 and which anti-austerity popular movements helped bring to power. However, the capitulation by Syriza to creditors and the EU and adoption of austerity measures in July 2015 deeply affected the anti-austerity movement, rooted in traditional forms of working class organisation. Since then a diffuse network of grassroots organisations has emerged. This network is made up of predominantly small-scale schemes, mainly focussed on managing the human crisis – but with a strongly anti-austerity identity.

The diverse organisations share a few common traits, such as informality, a focus on meeting human needs, rejection of cooperation with the state and a profound aversion to state institutions associated with austerity. Strongly influenced by the disappointment at Syriza's capitulation, their rebellious political stance feeds on the marginalisation from formal structures and institutions. As local activists put it:

> there's this growing realisation that we're on our own, under no protective umbrella of any formal authority or institution. Not only that, but that we're actually against them. Hence the shift towards self-organisation . . . The election of SYRIZA and the great disappointment that followed it shattered any remaining illusions that there's a chance for a way out via formal politics and institutions.
>
> . . . volunteerism is a form of resistance. It's a statement, exposing the absence of the authorities from where they are needed; it's a way to show and deal with the problems the city is facing.

Despite the proliferation of initiatives, this movement remains diffuse and has not developed the kind of synergies necessary to develop a transformative politics at scale. This is perhaps because recent disappointments loom large, leading to a rejection of more organised forms of struggle at city or national level.

Like Athens, Barcelona has witnessed a proliferation in grassroots projects that aim to mitigate the fallout from austerity. However, the trajectory of the protest movement has been different, essentially because it connected with a pre-existing tradition of co-operativist and left-wing activism and also fed into a national wave of protest politics that has led to a project of reform in the City and also significantly influenced national politics (Feenstra et al. 2017). The immediate roots of this phenomenon lie in the Spring of 2011, with the eruption of the indignados movement (also known as the 15M) which began a process of resurgence of the left, that led to the election of the 'Barcelona en Comu' administration led by Ada Colau in 2015 on a 'new municipalist' platform (Observatorio Metropolitano 2014). This process gave a political platform for the small-scale self-help initiatives that proliferated in the years following austerity (Davies and Blanco 2017).

This confluence of movements has made Barcelona arguably Europe's most significant site of political resistance to austerity in Europe. The Barcelona experience is rightly taken to demonstrate that urban social movements can spearhead broader processes of political reform. Significant challenges are of course faced. To name a few by advancing policies that contradict the preferences of local and national elites, the existence of a hostile national state that aims to centralise authority in order to dutifully implements austerity measures. As one respondent put it:

The tools are very tiny and the expectations are great. How can the City Council of a city that is globally located on the map of the relevant cities in the world, which attracts migratory flows, capital flows . . . how can it manage a power that it does not have? The City Council does not have the power of the city. It is a very small portion of power.

Moreover, 'Barcelona' en Comu faces a significant political challenge in negotiating cleavages between separatist and non-separatist forces, though these do overlap to an extent. The municipalist movement, as well as the broader Catalan and Spanish left, is split in terms of support for and opposition to separatism, as well as on strategic questions related to the nature of its response to the centrality of the Catalan independence struggle in the Spanish political agenda (e.g. Miley 2017; Navarro 2017).

This reality means that while Barcelona represents an important beginning, it cannot be the end of the process. Urban struggles must gain traction on the national and international stages. The City administration and protest movements are aware of this, and have developed a broadly complementary relationship which might be summarised as the social movements giving the City government political support and legitimacy in exchange for representation, and the City administration using the political capital of social movements to make transformative demands at higher tiers of authority.

Our third case, Dublin, has recently experienced something of a political renaissance as communities become involved in diverse practices of resistance, resilience, solidarity and support. As the austerity measures above ratcheted up, public opposition grew in scale with protests catalysed by the introduction of new water charges in 2014. The so called 'water protests', however, developed into a broader process of resistance to austerity policies in general that attracted significant parts of the population. This broad-based support for anti-austerity politics was highlighted by respondents from the city council. In the words of one councillor:

People are just incensed. Not because they are the left-wing. Not because they are radical revolutionists. It's because they've been shafted. They can see that they do not have pensions. They see no future for their kids.

A movement with a relatively wide repertoire has developed, that is perhaps unique in the history of the Irish state for the diversity of the people involved and its 'bottom-up' nature, largely by-passing formal political institutions. Thus, a survey carried out in 2015 of 2,556 people involved found that 54 per cent were 'new activists' (Hearne 2015) that had never protested before, and many of our respondents highlight the high levels of female participation. Thus, the movement cuts across class and gender divides and largely involves people that are new to activism, perhaps signalling the rise of a new political class. The challenge now for emancipatory social movements is to engage these new political actors in innovative and non-traditional ways that can also articulate an effective and genuinely transformative political process.

Above we noted that Dublin and Leicester share similar traits in terms of austerity governance. However, the extent and nature of contentious politics in both cities is very different. Cultures of resistance to austerity in Leicester have been seriously undermined by waves of de-industrialisation, and the decline of militant trade unionism. As one official suggested 'that confrontation thing is . . . that's just not the British spirit anymore'. Thus, unlike Dublin, austerity in Leicester has not led to sustained city-wide resistance. Resistance is led by traditional institutions such as trade unions, is relatively sporadic and defensive in nature, seeking to prevent cuts to specific services. Moreover, local politics are deeply influenced legacies of defeat of municipal socialist resistance to Thatcherite reforms in the 1980s – and waves of centralisation under Thatcher and Blair governments. Thus, recent calls by local trade unions for the council to implement a no cuts budget were dismissed out of hand by the city council, whose lesson from history is that resistance to the centre is futile and counterproductive. The spectre of disobedience leading to rule from Westminster looms large.

In this vein, one councillor we interviewed argued that 'drama and conflict are not in the best interests of the City'. This is certainly true from the perspective of attracting external investment and generating economic growth – which has become the main, and perhaps the only, strategy being pursued to improve the situation. However, some of our respondents lamented the lack of contentious politics, arguing that it could serve for democratic revitalisation and social justice. There is also a sublimated yearning for social democratic solutions amongst many politicians, public officials and parts of the voluntary sector, but this has not yet materialised into sustained protest. The 'austerian realist' (ESRC Final Report 2017) logic is at play here, undermining resistance for lack of perceived alternatives.

Despite these limitations, there have been some instances of successful resistance to cuts. A campaign to save a local library from being cut managed to mobilise citizens, organised groups and found allies within the council – showing what a vigorous campaign can do. Yet, as is the case throughout the UK, austerity has been delivered with few signs of any sustained revolt. Beyond the legacies of defeats and the austerian realist logic, some argue this is also due to the severity of the social impacts of austerity measures such as cuts and punitive welfare reforms that keep people preoccupied with managing acute personal crises, as per one respondent:

> They say to us 'why aren't the English kicking off like the Greeks?'
> I think it is precisely around the issue of everyone is being made to look at their own individual crisis . . . they are so ensnared in looking at the latest change affecting them, that it's a full-time job sorting out these issues.

In Nantes there are resistance movements. Opposition to the building of an airport became an issue that tied together demands against national and local policies including urban boosterism. However they generally had little to do with formal politics and institutions, despite the involvement of some groups of interest and direct action protestors. There is also scepticism towards the top-down form of participatory governance described in the section above, which creates an opportunity for resistance. As one respondent put it: 'each time that you put a debate into the public arena, there are always those people who seize it and manage to construct some counter-power'.

Thus, despite its constraints, there is room to use the collaborative process to construct challenges and contest the municipality. Forms of resistance are therefore part and parcel of participatory governance and citizen dialogue in Nantes, a dynamic found by analysts of comparable exercises in participatory governance in other cities (Baiocchi and Ganuza 2017). However, on the whole, in similar fashion to Athens, civil society actors who advance anti-austerity politics, such as unions, choose not to engage in formal politics, including the structures of citizen dialogue across the city, mainly because they see little value in investing in arenas that they see as tokenistic, with little chance of influencing policy and certainly no prospect of advancing the socially transformative agenda that inspired them. Equally, actors engaged in contentious politics are not 'welcome' in the participatory governance arena. As a consequence, collaborative governance in Nantes tends to be marked by parallel systems of participation and protest, whose actors have different goals and view each other with considerable scepticism.

Finally, one of the reasons why an anti-austerity resistance project is not articulated from the City institutions is because they have articulated austerity within a broader discourse of the social and political crises facing Nantes. At the same time, they have arguably sought to deploy local investment and taxation powers to ward off the impacts of the global financial crisis. Thus, foregrounding the agency of the local authority in governing the city, a local official told us that 'we are Keynesian here!'. This links a discourse which views poverty and inequality as problems that are resolvable through the City's policy interventions. However, these policies are coming under increasing pressure since 2015.

Comparative insights

Our cases portray a range of differences and similarities across the three central themes that concern us. These include the degree of which austerity is embedded, through which policies and the social and political effects, the impact of austerity on the ideology and practice of collaborative governance and the development, and nature, of resistance, understood as one of the 'double movement' (Peck 2012) effects of austerity.

All our cities have at some point engaged in substantial cuts and service rationalisations and privatisations. Thus, cuts are a general feature of urban austerity across the board, but its depth and continuity varies across our cases. The measures have been softest in Nantes which is an outlier in terms of its sustained, relatively positive economic performance in the post-2008 period. Moreover, Nantes has experienced spending pressures but governing elites do not see themselves as engaging in significant austerity cuts, proclaiming instead that 'we are Keynesians here'. Athens, Dublin, Barcelona and Leicester, on the other hand, have implemented swingeing cuts. Political change in Barcelona, however, has recently challenged this agenda, developing a more expansionary economic policy (within the limits of authority of the local government) and seeking to reclaim public assets and generate public goods.

Austerity has gone hand in hand with processes of state re-scaling and reconfiguration. A degree of centralisation has occurred everywhere because local austerity targets are set by national governments. In the case of Spain, centrally driven local government reforms such as the 2013 Montoro law have overtly sought to recentralise power. French municipal reorganisation in 2015 displays a complex interplay between centralising and decentralising dynamics, which scholars have explained in terms of new forms of 'steering' (Ghorra-Gobin 2015). In England and Ireland this process has also been nuanced. In Ireland, local government reforms that accompanied austerity and were putatively intended to empower localities are deemed to have had the reverse effect. Local Government in England, the case with perhaps the highest levels of pre-existing centralisation, has been in a more or less constant state of churn since 2010, with successive national governments engaging in putatively decentralising reforms such as those contained in the Localism Act of 2011 and the devolution drive of David Cameron's Conservative administration of 2015–2016. However, the general consensus is that the direction is one of centralisation, with even nominally decentralising reforms leading to greater central control over local government (Bailey and Wood 2017; Bua et al. 2017; Davies 2008). Centralisation is not limited to public institutions, but also to civil society, where austerity conditions lead to a retraction of funding from small, locally based VCO organisations, and an empowerment of large, national and multi-national charities, called 'super-majors' in the UK context.

Forms of urban economic boosterism are a popular response to austerity, which often leaves city policy makers thinking that of economic growth is the only way out of crisis and into a better future. Branding and place marketing is central to urban growth strategies for coping with and moving beyond austerity. Cities integrate context-specific features, such as cultural and ethnic diversity, or specialisation in luxury tourism, into their branding. However, growth alone cannot compensate for austerity. There is an ever-present tension between the realities of urban development and the idea of a socially just, inclusive city. In fact, as might be expected, austerity cuts, welfare reforms and housing foreclosures hit the worst-off hardest of all. In some cases, austerity hits the middle classes too.

In terms of austerity and collaborative governance, our analysis suggests that the ideology and practices associated with the 'collaborative moment' appear to wither on the vine in conditions of fiscal stress, low growth and intensified distributional conflicts. The only place where we see discourse and practices approaching that of the collaborative moment is Nantes, a city that has avoided many of the impacts of austerity through relatively positive economic performance – and even here, the authenticity of collaboration is frequently questioned. A very different story applies to other cities. In the cases of Leicester and Dublin, the collaborative ethos was profoundly affected by austerity, from one aiming to create social cohesion and improve policy-making by harnessing the capacities of networks, to a consolidation of a shift towards retrenched and rationalised networks firmly focussed on survival, and closely aligned with the economic boosterism of the local state. Athens differs in that the 'collaborative moment' did not penetrate the political culture of Greece, despite attempted reforms. A more determined effort has been made to establish collaborative institutions in the austerity period, but with high levels of grass roots alienation, a participatory governance culture seems untenable. Rather, post-Austerity collaboration can be described as an 'elite-pluralist' model, heavily focussed on philanthropic funding, exclusive of small VCOs and anti-austerity actors. The marginalisation of small VCOs and anti-austerity actors is also evident in Dublin and Leicester, where austerity has served as a tool to discipline and control civil society as well as leading to the collapse of many organisations. This empowers large NGOs over organisations with more organic local links, which fundamentally undermines the capacity to carry out collaborative governance.

Barcelona's trajectory differs in the key respect that it has resulted in the recasting of a collaborative ethos that is more critical vis-à-vis the neoliberal system, and based on alliances with organisations and social movements that espouse a socially transformative agenda. This highlights the re-politicising (Dikeç and Swyngedouw 2017) potential of anti-austerity urban movements. Whilst resistance to austerity features in all our cases, Barcelona is the only case where a significant anti-austerity and broader agenda of resistance to neoliberalism has developed in state institutions. Anti-austerity movements of comparable dimensions developed in Athens, linked to a national movement. However, since the 2015 defeat at the hands of creditor interests and the EU, the urban resistance has disengaged from state institutions, while organised working class resistance has also diminished. The challenge here is similar to consolidating the politicising potential of the anti-austerity movement in Dublin – to engage these actors in ways that maintain and collectivise their critical energy.

Conclusion

Our study highlights the importance of the urban context for austerity governance – what happens in cities matters and cities affected by crisis and austerity respond in varied ways, with local histories, economies, traditions, struggles, conflicts and geographies making a big difference. Forms of collaborative governance vary widely on a continuum from those concerned with radicalising participatory democracy to those preoccupied mainly with managing austerity and maintaining state control. However, in relation to the 'collaborative moment' it seems that austerity policies have significantly diminished it. Austerity clearly weakens the prospect for building strong, inclusive and equitable social partnerships between governments and citizens. It leads governments to demand greater levels of citizen activism, while making it harder to achieve. At the same time, austerity concentrates government resources in large third sector organisations, often with little connection to locality. The capacity of these larger organisations to campaign and influence policy is itself reduced. Austerity governance therefore tends to be either hierarchical and state-centred, or rooted in 'elite' partnerships involving governments, business leaders and NGOs. Conversely, the evidence from Nantes suggests – as Davies and Blanco (2017) also argued of Donostia – that it is much easier to sustain a participatory collaborative governance apparatus, however flawed or inadequate, when fiscal pressure on municipalities is limited and public services are sustained. Thus, far from being the expression in public administration and democratic practice of an epochal shift from competition and vertical hierarchies to trust and horizontal networks, collaborative governance is belied as a governance ideology, which is functional, in its ideal-typical sense, only in the 'good times' when boom and bust were supposedly abolished (Summers 2008). The 'collaborative moment' is thus weakened by post-crash exposure to scarcity and intensified distributional conflict – the rose-tinted spectacles of democratic theory are shattered by the harsh realities of political economy.

Anti-austerity movements do, however, abound – and cases such as Barcelona demonstrate the potential they have to turn into a project for democratisation and profound institutional reform and change. Resistance to austerity is clearly very uneven. However, given a felicitous alliance between electoral and grass-roots anti-austerity forces, change is possible. As the recent suspension of Catalan autonomy highlights, attempts to challenge austerity governance orthodoxies will encounter much hostility from embedded forces with immense power. In response, emancipatory politics must aim to link opposition movements, build alliances between cities, social movements, workplace and community organisations capable not only of winning urban power, but also of challenging higher tiers of government.

Acknowledgements

We are very grateful to the UK Economic and Social Research Council for funding the research discussed in this paper: *Collaborative Governance under Austerity: An Eight-case Comparative Study* (Ref: ES/L012898/1), led by Professor Jonathan Davies. See http://cura.our.dmu.ac.uk/category/austerity-governance.

Note

1 The term 'collaborative moment' was coined by our colleague, Professor David Howarth, at a project team meeting in June 2015.

References

Albo, G. and Finnelly, C. (2014) *Austerity against Democracy: An Authoritarian Phase of Neoliberalism?* Centre for Social Justice. Retrieved on 26 January 2018 from www.socialjustice.org/uploads/pubs/AustDemoc.pdf.

Ansell, C. and Gash, A. (2008) Collaborative Governance in Theory and Practice. *Journal of Public Administration Research and Theory* 18(4): 543–571.

Bailey, D. and Wood, M. (2017) The Metagovernance of English Devolution. *Local Government Studies* 43(6): 966–991.

Baiocchi, G. and Ganuza, E. (2017) *Popular Democracy: the Paradox of Participation*. Stanford, CA: Stanford University Press.

Beck, U., Giddens, A. and Lash, S. (1994) *Reflexive Modernization: Politics, Tradition and Aesthetics in the Modern Social Order.* Stanford, CA: Stanford University Press.

Blanco, I. (2009) Does a 'Barcelona Model' Really Exist? Periods, Territories and Actors in the Process of Urban Transformation. *Local Government Studies* 35(3): 355–369.

Blanco, I., Griggs, S. and Sullivan, H. (2014) Situating the Local in the Neo-liberalisation and Transformation of Urban Governance. *Urban Studies* 51(15): 3129–3146.

Blyth, M. (2012) *Austerity: The History of a Dangerous Idea.* New York: Oxford University Press.

Brenner, N., Peck, J. and Theodore, N. (2010) Variegated Neoliberalization: Geographies, Modalities, Pathways. *Global Networks* 10(2): 182–222.

Bua, A. (2017) Scale and Policy Impact in Participatory and Deliberative Democracy: Lessons from a Multi-Level Process. *Public Administration* 5(1): 160–177.

Bua, A., Vardakoulias, O. and Laurence, R. (2017) *Understanding Devolution: A Critical Appraisal of the Greater Manchester Devolution Deal.* London: New Economics Foundation.

Chorianopopulos, I. (2012) State Spatial Restructuring in Greece: Forced Rescaling, Unresponsive Localities. *European Urban and Regional Studies* 19(4): 331–348.

Chorianopoulos, I. and Tselepi, N. (2017) Austerity Urbanism: Rescaling and Collaborative Governance Policies in Athens. *European Urban and Regional Studies* 1–17.

Crouch, C. (2004) *Post-Democracy.* Cambridge: Polity Press.

Crouch, C. (2011) *Strange Non-Death of Neoliberalism.* Cambridge: Polity Press.

Davies, J. S. (2008) Double Devolution or Double-Dealing? The Local Government White Paper and the Lyons Review. *Local Government Studies* 34(1): 3–22.

Davies, J. S. (2011) *Challenging Governance Theory: from Networks to Hegemony.* Bristol: Policy Press.

Davies, J. and Blanco, I. (2017) Austerity Urbanism: Patterns of Neoliberalisation and Resistance in Six Cities of Spain and the UK. *Environment and Planning A* 49(7): 1517–1536.

Della Porta, D. (2015) *Social Movements in Times of Austerity: Bringing Capitalism back into Protest Analysis.* Cambridge: Polity Press.

Dikeç, M. and Swyngedouw, E. (2017) Theorizing the Politicising City. *International Journal of Urban and Regional Research* 41(1): 1–18.

Durose, C., Justice, J. and Skelcher, C. (2013) *Beyond the State: Mobilising and Co-producing with Communities: Insights for Policy and Practice.* Birmingham: University of Birmingham.

ESRC Final Report (2017) *Governing in and Against Austerity: International Lessons from Eight Cities.* Leicester: De Montfort University. Retrieved from http://cura.our.dmu.ac.uk/files/2017/08/Governing-in-and-against-austerity.pdf.

Garcia, M. (2006) Citizen Practices and Urban Governance in European Cities. *Urban Studies* 43(4): 713–718.

Gaynor, N. 2011. Associations, Deliberation and Democracy: The Case of Ireland's Social Partnership. *Politics and Society* 39(4): 497–520.

Ghorra-Gobin, C. (2015) *La Métropolisation en Question.* Paris: Presses Universitaires de France.

Glyn, A. (1994) *Capitalism Unleashed: Finance, Globalization and Welfare.* Oxford: Oxford University Press.

Griggs, S. and Howarth, D. (2007) Airport Governance, Politics and Protest Networks. In M. Marcussen and J. Torfing (eds), *Democratic Network Governance in Europe,* 66–88. Basingstoke: Palgrave Macmillan.

Harvey, D. (2012) *Rebel Cities: From the Right to the City to the Urban Revolution.* London: Verso.

Hearne, R. (2015) *The Irish Water War, Austerity and the 'Risen People': An Analysis of Participant Opinions, Social and Political Impacts and Transformative Potential of the Irish Anti-Water Charges Movement.* Retrieved from www.maynoothuniversity.ie/sites/default/files/assets/document/TheIrishWaterwar_0.pdf.

Hirst, P. (2000) Democracy and Governance. In J. Pierre (ed.), *Debating Governance: Authority, Steering, and Democracy,* 13–35. Oxford: Oxford University Press.

Mayer, M. (2013) First World Urban Activism: Beyond Austerity Urbanism and Creative City Politics. *City* 17(1): 5–19.

Miley, T. J. (2017) The Perils and Promise of Self-Determination. *Roar Magazine* (21 October). Retrieved on 26 January 2018 from https://roarmag.org/essays/self-determination-kurdistan-catalonia-thomas-jeffrey-miley/?utm_source=feedburner&utm_medium=email&utm_campaign=Feed%3A+roarmag+%28ROAR+Magazine%29La.

Navarro, V. (2017) Porque las derechas y muchas izquierdas españolas no entienden o no quieren entender lo que pasa en Catalunya. *Publico* (18 October). Retrieved on 26 January 2018 from http://blogs.publico.es/vicenc-navarro/2017/10/18/por-que-las-derechas-y-muchas-izquierdas-espanolas-no-entienden-o-no-quieren-entender-lo-que-pasa-en-catalunya.

Newman, J. (2004) Modernizing the State: A New Form of Governance? In J. Lewis and R. Surender (eds), *Welfare State Change: Towards a Third Way?* Oxford: Oxford University Press.

Observatorio Metropolitano (2014) *La Apuesta Municipalista: La Democracia Empieza por lo Cercano*. Madrid: Observatorio Metropolitano. Retrieved on 26 January 2018 from www.traficantes.net/sites/default/files/pdfs/TS-LEM6_municipalismo.pdf.

Ortiz, I. Burke, S. Berrada, M. and Cortes, H. (2013) *World Protests*. Working Paper. New York: Initiative for Policy Dialogue and Friederich-Ebert-Stiftung. Retrieved on 26 January 2018 from www.cadtm.org/IMG/pdf/World_Protests_2006-2013-Final-2.pdf.

Pares, M. Ospina, S. and Subirats, J. (2017) *Social Innovation and Democratic Leadership: Communities and Social Change from Below*. Northampton: Edward Elgar Publishing.

Peck, J. (2012) *Austerity Urbanism: the Neoliberal Crisis of American Cities*. New York: Rosa Luxembourg Stiftung. Retrieved on 26 January 2018 from www.rosalux-nyc.org/wp-content/files_mf/peck_austerity_urbanism_eng.pdf.

Pierre, J. (2011) *The Politics of Urban Governance*. Basingstoke: Macmillan.

Robinson, J. (2016) Comparative Urbanism: New Geographies and Cultures of Theorizing the Urban. *International Journal of Urban and Regional Research* 40(1): 187–199.

Stoker, G. (2004) New Localism Progressive Politics and Democracy. *Political Quaterly* 75(1): 117–129.

Streeck, W. (2013) *Buying Time: the Delayed Crisis of Democratic Capitalism*. London: Verso.

Streeck, W. (2014) How Will Capitalism End? *New Left Review* 87 (May–June).

Streeck, W. (2015) *The Rise of the European Consolidation State*. MPIfG Discussion Paper 15/1. Cologne: MPIfG.

Streeck, W. (2016) *How Will Capitalism End?* London: Verso.

Sullivan, H., Williams, P., Marchington, M. and Knight, L. (2013) Collaborative Futures: Discursive Realignments in Austere Times. *Public Money and Management* 33(2): 123–130.

Summers, D. (2008) No Return to Boom and Bust: What Brown Said When He Was Chancellor. *The Guardian* (11 September). Retrieved on 16 November 2017 from www.theguardian.com/politics/2008/sep/11/gordonbrown.economy.

Swyngedouw, E. (2009) Antinomies of the Post-Political City: In Search of a Democratic Politics of Environmental Production. *International Journal of Urban and Regional Research* 33(3): 601–620.

Torfing, J. and Sorensen, E. (2014) The European Debate on Governance Networks: Towards a New and Viable Paradigm? *Policy and Society* 33(4): 329–344.

Tormey, S. (2015) *The End of Representative Politics*. Cambridge: Polity Press.

20

REDRESSING THE TRUST DEFICIT

Local governments and citizen engagement

Jonathan Carr-West

Introduction: local governments in crisis

Local governments have developed over time to serve a dual function. They are democratic bodies that give citizens and communities a voice and a way to exercise political agency to shape the places they live in. They are also the institutions responsible for the commissioning and delivery of many public services delivered at a local level, and with some localised discretion on what form and volume those services take. Currently, both these functions of local government are under severe pressure and this makes it harder, not easier, to develop and scale up the sorts of innovation needed to relieve the pressures on public services.

Globally public services, often provided through local governments, have been under severe financial pressure. In the United Kingdom, particularly in England, local government has received deep and sustained cuts in its levels of funding since 2010. The Institute for Fiscal Studies estimates excluding school education with government financial support largely transferred directly to schools, the core funding for English local governments has reduced by an average of 26 per cent between 2009/10 and 2016/17 (Institute for Fiscal Studies 2017: 9). The Local Government Association (LGA) further estimates that from 2015 to 2020 local government in England and Wales will lose 77 pence out of every pound it recedes in grant funding and that by the end of the decade local government could face an aggregate budget deficit of £5.8 billion annually (LGA 2017).

Alongside reductions in overall funding the period 2010 to 2020 in England there has been a major change in the way local government is funded with a reduction in grant from central government and an emphasis on locally raised resources. The shift from direct grant funding emphasises increased reliance on local revenues, especially business rates. It is intended that revenue support grants to local government will be entirely replaced by local business rate retention by 2020.

This creates a position of profound uncertainty for local governments. The Local Government Information Unit (LGiU) conducts an annual local government finance survey targeting key decision makers within councils in England and Wales. The 2017 survey featured the views of 157 senior people in 126 councils. Eighty-four per cent of them reported that the current system of local government finance was not fir for purpose; 42 per cent thought that their financial position would require them to make cuts to services that would directly impact the public and only 23 per cent felt they would be better off with complete local business rate retention (LGiU 2017).

The financial pressures are also present in jurisdictions across the world. This is apparent even in countries sometimes thought to be less affected by the financial crisis of 2008. It has been estimated recently that up to 30 per cent of councils in Australia may be financially unsustainable (Drew and Ryan 2016) and a UN-Habitat report on finances for local government service in the developing world found that inadequate funding was a key constraint (UN-Habitat 2017).

So there are severe pressures on local government expenditure. However, at the same time demand in key service areas for local governments has been rising sharply, driven by the immediate challenge of fiscal austerity and by the profound questions raised by long-term challenges such as an ageing population, a fluid and highly competitive global economy, population movement, climate change, rapid urbanisation and technological development.

To take just two indicative examples, there are currently around 10,000 people in the UK over the age of a hundred. On current trends, by 2070 that figure will have risen to over one million people and this increase is of course paralleled by increases in the numbers of people in their seventies and eighties (Brown 2008). In health care, the cost of tackling diabetes, already 10 per cent of the National Health Service (NHS) budget, could rise to 17 per cent within 20 years (LGiU 2013).

The broad outline of public service reform is becoming clear. We need to move from a system that is geared towards acute interventions and remedial action to one that is characterised by demand management, prevention, integration of services, multi-agency working and which is co-produced with, and designed around, the needs of service users. That means recognising that the real challenges we face cannot be solved by the state alone. Instead they require collaborative engagement from all parts of the public realm and civic society – a new relationship between citizen, civil society and the local state in which each supports the other in their respective contributions to the common good.

That requires a consideration of the total asset base of a community and the value in social networks and civic energy. That also requires greater early intervention, not just in terms of 'invest to save' but also as building capacity and resilience in communities. We need to review how we structure incentives for action: for the market and most importantly for citizens. It means understanding the networks of social action already present in every community and aligning public services with them. We can only meet the profound challenges posed to our current model of local public services through a new relationship between local governments and the communities they serve and through a vastly increased element of citizen participation in the design and delivery of those services.

That requires a very different vision of what local government do. Local governments need to become a convener, a facilitator, a catalyst of civic action. Various developments in different local governments in different countries give examples of innovation best practice. There are examples of citizens juries, participatory budgeting, digital engagement platforms, and refreshed examples of town hall meetings. The case studies in this chapter give an indicative sample of these sorts of initiative.

However, it is essential to recognise that local government is not simply a delivery body for public services. Copus, Wall and Roberts have argued that we must distinguish between local government and local democracy (Copus et al. 2017). Local government is the body that delivers (or commissions) public services at a local level. While local democracy is a process of governance which gives political expression to the views of people in a locality such that they may shape the places they live in, there is a rich and diverse body of thought that sees this ability to exercise local autonomy as an essential precondition of liberty and well-being. Many observers normally conflate these two functions but, the authors argue, are in reality distinct and, indeed, may be in tension with one another. An elected council is a representative democratic institution: a way of giving people within communities, voice and agency through elected members. On the other hand, it is a technocratic machine designed to deliver public services at a local level.

These are not at all the same thing. Both of these separate functions are under severe pressure and in each case, these pressures drive a need for enhanced citizen participation while simultaneously and paradoxically making such participation harder to achieve. This creates a trust deficit whereby a collapse in trust in local governments as democratic institutions makes it harder to achieve the types of reform we need for effective public service provision in the future.

In this chapter we examined the broad background to this changing climate of trust and distrust and then report on some instances where local governments have developed initiatives to try and encourage citizen engagement and rebuild trust between residents and local governments.

The trust deficit

The sort of public service reform we need in order to respond to both the fiscal pressures on local government and the rise in demand on key services requires more interaction between citizens and the state. This requires trust between citizens and the institutions of local service delivery. Unfortunately, we are currently experiencing an increasing crisis in levels of trust, which makes the sort of reform local government needs harder to achieve.

Globally we are witnessing an increasing collapse of trust in established institutions of all forms. This is often related to the emergence of the phenomenon of 'post-truth' news and campaigning strategies. The argument can be outlined as follows: propaganda, spin, and downright mendacity have always been part of political discourse. But in the past these phenomena existed with a certain relationship to truth. There was concern about whether political statements were true or not; now there appears to be declining public concern about whether such campaigning claims and statements are even correct. Truth is no longer the key criterion; instead, people appear more concerned with how statements make us feel and how far they reinforce what we already think (D'Ancona 2017). President Trump provides the most obvious example of this phenomenon. His claim that crowds at his inauguration were bigger than those at Barack Obama's, for instance, was quickly shown to be false but, to the surprise and dismay of many of his detractors, this evidence falsity didn't appear to make any difference to the views of his supporters. This is linked to a continuing wave of technological change and the ways in which social media change how we consume and, crucially, share information about the world. A growing number of people access news though social media – two thirds of adults in the US (Pew Research Center 2017) – but social media is structured in a way that reinforces existing assumptions and attitudes. The manner in which algorithms are structured creates channelled sharing within our networks of belief and preference: generally with like-minded people. Thus many consumers of such social media channels are not exposed to views that challenge and the analytical muscles that weigh up, and adjudicate between, different claims about the world are diminished.

Overall, the collapse in trust has many sources. Some are general: the changing nature of employment in post-industrial economies; the differential effects of globalisation; rapid population changes in some communities. Some are more specific such as the financial crisis of 2008, or in the UK the MP expenses scandal of 2009, or the Grenfell Tower fire of 2017. All feed a sense that decision-making elites are detached from, and no longer represent the interests of, the people they are meant to serve.

So citizens who consider themselves neglected and left behind by globalisation, or contemporary culture, or capitalism, or the way in which their society is changing are rejecting politics as usual in favour of populist parties and campaigners. Politics is now often contested in the spaces between a new set of oppositions: open vs closed; rooted vs cosmopolitan; local vs global; evidence vs emotional resonance; and, institutions vs networks. What Goodhart (2017) has recently described as a culture war between 'anywheres' and 'somewheres.' That is, the difference between geographically and socially mobile people with 'achieved' identities created by careers and education and people who derive their sense of identity from where they come from and the communities and institutions within which they are embedded. The referendum result on Brexit; the election of President Trump; turmoil in Italian politics are all, in different ways, symptoms and causes of a 'post institutional' politics: a politics in which trust in established institutions is reduced.

To date local government in the United Kingdom has retained a higher degree of trust than national government, and is generally regarded more favourably than is central government (Ipsos MORI 2017); it cannot stand apart from these broader social changes. For local governments there is a direct democratic mechanism by which the concerns, needs and aspirations of communities are hardwired into decision making by their elected representatives. Where this is not working, local government loses its practical and ideological raison d'être. Local democracy relies on trust when that trust is diminishing.

How local government can rebuild trust

If this analysis is correct, local governments need to nurture more citizen participation while simultaneously facing a trust deficit that makes it hard to make that participation happen, then it becomes an urgent priority to begin to encourage participation in a way that reinforces or rebuilds trust.

We need to recognise that local government's track record in encouraging participation is not as good as it might be. In the first decade of this century, there was an initiative from the Department for Communities and Local Government (DCLG) embed the 'community empowerment' agenda (DCLG 2008), but this met with some resistance. LGiU were commissioned by the IDeA (the Improvement and Development Agency) to produce a toolkit for councillors on community empowerment. Preparatory research found elected members committed to an ideal of representation based on the principles of Burke, and mainly indifferent, or even actively hostile, to more participatory methods of government (LGiU 2010).

In any event, within two or three years, when UK local government began to come under severe fiscal pressure from 2010/11 and with a change of government, that strategy was abandoned. However, as ideas of increased participation have re-emerged, the case studies described below provide some key lessons on how these themes develop in a way that supports trust rather than undermining it further.

There are three crucial steps local government needs to take to begin and extend this process of rebuilding trust between institutions and communities:

- Start real conversations about place.
- Engage the community in the council's decision-making.
- Make local governments catalysts for civic action.

These are described further in the following sections.

Start real conversations about place

There is an urgent task for political leaders to reframe the narrative – internally and externally. This is not a problem with communities not getting what institutions are trying to do; it's as if people feel let down by institutions that is at least to some extent because institutions have let them down. Local government needs to take the community's concerns and aspirations seriously even if they do not mesh neatly with corporate priorities. Trust begins in a dialogue about the places citizens and residents live. What do the people who live here now aspire to? How can we live together effectively? What is the relation of this place to the wider world? What are our priorities and what compromises are we willing to make to achieve them?

Engage the community in the council's decision-making

There is a need for an uncompromising focus on participation and dialogue in everything local government does. There are many tools for this: citizens juries, participatory budgeting, online engagement platforms, town hall meetings, intensive outreach. The important thing is that local governments invest in these processes and commit to treating their outputs seriously.

Make local governments catalysts for civic action

Local governments needs to develop organisationally and function more like a network; focused more on connections and outcomes and less defined by process and hierarchy.

Elected representatives have a crucial role to play in this and a study by LGiU and the Local Trust identified four key ways in which they could support enhanced participation (LGiU and Local Trust 2017). They can identify need and capacity in communities and spread the word that the council is open to working with residents. They can encourage community ownership, reflecting voices that aren't usually heard. They should advise residents how to navigate the council's processes, acting as advocates and facilitating connections and access to resources. Finally, they can ensure a constant dialogue between council and residents and between different groups of residents. All of that requires councillors to exercise a different form of representative leadership, taking a backseat in projects and offering advice and support rather than strong direction.

These are the three crucial steps to the sort of engagement that will design trust back into local government. The case studies below illustrate what each of these steps might look like in practice.

Case studies

Starting real conversations about place

If we are to overcome challenges around public trust, we need to develop genuine dialogue between public institutions and citizens. There are many ways to do this including traditional face to face public meetings. There's also potential, however, to use digital technology to expand the range and speed of these conversations. A good example is provided by the Madrid Decides portal.

Madrid Decides

'Madrid Decides' (https://joinup.ec.europa.eu/document/madrid-decides-gives-madrilenians-voice-municipal-governance) is a new citizen participation portal created by the City of Madrid and launched in September 2015. It is a good example of how a local authority can create a new platform to enable an open conversation about the place the community lives in and their aspirations for it. Madrid Decides allows citizens to forward proposals to improve the city, comment on them, debate issues, and vote for proposals that citizens would like the Town Hall to implement as policies. Anyone can register and post on the site but only registered residents of Madrid can vote on proposals and they have to verify their accounts on the platform in order to be able to do so.

If a proposal attracts supporting votes equivalent to, or higher than, 1 per cent of all registered Madrid residents (around 27,000 votes) within 12 months it is automatically passed to the city council and is fast tracked to popular consultation. This provides a direct route from the online platform into the established governance processes of the city.

The portal was developed within about seven weeks and at very low cost (approx. €100,000) by using open source coding which was open to volunteers. It replicates the look and feel popular sites such as Reddit and the Spanish site Menéame so that it seems familiar to users and is easy to navigate. In 2017, the platform ran popular consultations on the regeneration of the Gran Plaza, mobility on the Gran Via, and the remodelling of public spaces in eleven districts. Citizens also proposed a 100 per cent sustainability target for the city and an initiative to introduce a single integrated ticked for all public transport in the city and these initiatives are passed forward for consideration by the council who are consulting on how to achieve them.

Engaging the community in the council's decision-making

Madrid Decides provides an example of engagement with citizens that is wide but shallow: citizens are able to propose projects and to vote on them but the level of detail is inevitably limited. There are other engagement techniques, however, that allow far more in depth examination of the issues and bring citizens right into the heart of an institution's decision-making.

Participatory budgeting was developed in Porto Allegre Brazil in 1989 as a method of involving the community in budget and spending decisions. It took place within the context of a democratising country emerging from authoritarian control and with very disparate levels of public service provision in different parts of the country. It used local direct voting, neighbourhood meetings and regional assemblies to decide on budgets and to provide oversight of spending. Over the last thirty years, it has become common in South America, Europa and recently in the UK. It is seen as an effective way of engaging the whole community in one of the most important and often dauntingly technical functions of local government.

Two examples from different states illustrate how local authorities can engage members of the community in complex decision-making, helping to build trust both by making visible the complexity of the issues involved and by helping the community to feel that decisions are being made by them, not done to them.

Participatory budgeting in Melbourne

In Australia, the practice was adopted much later with the first experiments taking place in 2012. A recent assessment in the Australian Journal of Public Administration outlines analysed six examples of participatory budgeting in the Australian context (Christensen and Grant 2016). These ranged from very small scale initiatives such as AUS$ 100,000 on community grants over a single year in Melville in Western Australia to large scale initiatives such as in Canada Bay, New South Wales in 2012, or Melbourne in 2015 in which all services and operations were reviewed through a participatory budgeting perspective.

In Melbourne's case, this involves a budget of AUS$ 5.9 billion over 10 years. A citizens' jury of 43 randomly chosen citizens was convened, known as the Melbourne People's Panel which has access to the council's financial data and was briefed by council officers, councillors and relevant experts. The Panel presented their recommendations to the council and this formed part of the council's 10-year financial plan. The People's Panel sat alongside a broader Participate Melbourne initiative launched in 2013 to provide an online portal for the community to engage with the council.

The Melbourne People's Panel (as with five of the six Australian initiatives examined) used randomly selected citizens in deliberative processes designed to allow participants to work through questions in some detail, testing assumptions, formulating criteria and developing consensus.

This sort of deliberative process was not a feature of the initial and earlier South American iterations of participatory budgeting that tended to favour direct voting; however, this can be a more effective method of establishing a representative sample of people for the process and for working through more controversial political issues. The disadvantage is they require significantly more investment of time and resource to make them work effectively and local government actors sometimes lack the skills required to implement these initiatives successfully.

There are concerns about the sustainability of these forms of participatory budging initiative, and whether they can be scaled up beyond the current discussion of relatively modest project finances. Additionally, it is not clear what happens if they make recommendations that clash with State and Federal policies, especially given the primacy of State government over local government within the Australian system. Nonetheless the authors conclude that the ability of participatory budgeting to bring the community into difficult decisions and build support for them, means that within a tightening fiscal landscape for Australian local government they are likely to remain an important tool for encouraging citizen engagement (Christensen and Grant 2016).

Antwerp

The City of Antwerp has been undertaking a participatory budgeting initiative developed since 2013 in the central area, where the population is approximately 190,000. The project was initiated by a politician, Willem Fredrik Schiltz, who has now moved on from the council and has a seat in the Flemish regional parliament, where he has been pushing for participatory budgeting to be used more widely throughout Flanders.

The Antwerp participatory budgeting model is based on consensus rather than voting. The available budget is €1.1 million provided by a 10 per cent top slice of council budgets. The most recent cycle of budgeting encouraged participation from approximately 1,000 participants. The process is consensus-based across three rounds. This method was chosen over voting because it was seen to be important that people talk to each other and listen to each other. Consensus gives people a challenge – listen to each other and reach consensus, it pushes people to involve themselves in a different way from traditional position advocacy.

The events bring together people in large-scale public meetings arranged in multiple tables of six or seven. This number was developed by the friends and family of the city council team spending an evening in a bar and testing what was the biggest size of table discussion that kept everyone involved without sparking side-conversations. It also has validation through long established work on optimal participation for group educational discussion and decision-making.

Each table reaches its own consensus, and follows a three-stage process. In the first round, participants choose the five topics that they think are most important, from a list of more than 90 nominated by the city council. The twelve most popular topics across all tables go on to the next stage.

In the second stage, money is distributed across the twelve priority issues. Participants have background information on typical costs of this kind of project in the local area, and what the council is already doing. Using poker-style chips, they can move money around and distribute it between the different issues. At least four people have to agree that money should go on a topic, and the final distribution has to be by consensus around the group.

The third and last stage is asking for finalised projects; in 2016, project bids totalled € 4 million and participants make a collaborative ranking of the projects. They can choose to prioritise several smaller projects or one bigger project. The council take the collective ranking of projects and allocate the budget until it is exhausted. Once the point is reached where a project is too big for the remaining funds, it is skipped, and the next project that fits within the funds available receives money; this continues until available funds are exhausted.

The participants are self-selecting, but the council assesses representativeness. In the first year, underrepresented groups included under-25s; people in poverty; people with lower educational attainment; and, those with migrant backgrounds. The council therefore started to work on targeted outreach with those groups of people to prepare them to participate.

This outreach work reviewed why underrepresented groups didn't come, and worked together with partner organisations. They found that potential participants were uncertain what would be expected of them if they became involved, so the city council gave them training, explained the process and facilitated a discussion in stakeholder organisations about what was important to them. The council organised development courses in personal skills so that potential participants could express themselves on the topics that were important to them. Following the training, at the main event, the participants who had received special support were valued by other self-nominated participants because of their expertise and capabilities. Such support has led to a higher degree of repeat participation in subsequent years.

Making the council a catalyst for civic action

The case studies above show how councils can create broader conversations with their communities and bring those communities into the decisions that the council makes. They still rely, however, on a model in which the council is the primary agent. The final step identified towards building trust is to move to a scenario in which the council is not the sole or primary actor but is the catalyst for social action within the community. This is much more ambitious and much harder to achieve. As argued above, local elected politicians can be a crucial go between in this endeavour. Two examples from the UK indicate what form this might take.

Big Local and Every One Every Day

Big Local is an initiative funded by the Big Lottery Fund that commits £1m of long-term funding committed and an intensive programme of training and support to 150 areas across England to enable residents to make their areas a better place to live. Communities identify local needs and work together to develop initiatives to deliver on these priorities.

Crucially this process is independent of local government but in many of the places where the process has worked best it has been actively supported by local councillors. A study by the Local Government Information Unit identified some of the most striking examples of local government, and local councillors in particular working to support the participatory agenda within Big Local areas (LGiU and Local Trust 2017).

Bringing back a sense of pride and ownership in Chatham

The Luton Arches Big Local project was set up as part of Local Trust's Big Local programme to support residents to make their area a better place to live. The project was led by residents who set their own priorities and plans and local councillors have helped provide the group with the confidence, resources and knowledge they needed to get started and to earn the support of fellow councillors.

Many residents had a low opinion of their area, and part of the project's work focused on trying to engender more pride and ownership within the community. The Big Local group put in three bids for a Pocket Park project (including one to central government) and won all three. When the group started working on planting new trees in a park, local residents dismissed the scheme, believing that the park would only be vandalised. However, because the project got residents involved in this process of designing the park, people were willing to volunteer to maintain it as they felt ownership of the space in a way that they may not have if it had been a council-initiated project.

Initially councillors and officers in Medway had strong ideas about how the Big Local project should work, but in time they came round to the idea that the power dynamic should be based on residents leading the way. It also helps them to know that they have a willing group of residents that they can call upon to test ideas or discuss projects. Councillors have become advocates for the work being done and provided additional support by linking the project coordinators with a variety of local public and civic organisations. Big Local initiatives are distinct from the host local governments; are community led; and are relatively small scale. The final case study highlights an attempt to transform a whole council into a civic enterprise.

London Borough of Barking and Dagenham: Every One Every Day

Every One Every Day is an ambitious new participation project launched in the London Borough of Barking and Dagenham in east London. It is a partnership between the council and the civic action organisation Participatory City and the largest project of its kind in the UK when in late 2017.

The ambitious scheme works with 25,000 residents across the borough to create over 250 neighbourhood-led projects and form more than 100 new businesses over a five-year period. The project has £6.4 million funding from The Big Lottery Fund; the Esmée Fairbairn Foundation; the City Bridge Trust; the City of London Corporation's charitable funding and from the Borough Council.

As part of the initiative, residents are invited to share ideas for projects and community businesses they would like to see happening into their neighbourhoods. This could include new shared maker – spaces, incubator spaces for new community businesses, urban patch farms; and other project ideas that are identified by the community.

Participatory City employs facilitators to help generate ideas, make connections and enable people to follow through but the key agency lies with organised residents to suggest the kinds of projects that make sense to them and which they feel will improve their lives and prospects

For the council the value lies in the creation of economic activity but also, perhaps more importantly, of social capital: ties within the community that enable people to help each other more effectively and to fulfil their own aspirations.

This creates a stronger civic economy that acts as a first line provider of public services, building resilience and capacity within the community and reducing the need for expensive, reactive retrieval interventions from the council.

Conclusion

Globally, local governments remain in extremely challenging situations. Local public services remain under huge fiscal pressure just as demand for them is increasing exponentially. The fiscal pressures on local governments are more particularly in some countries, but are present to some degree in many parts of the world. There is an extensive literature and practice around public service reform, centred on preventative strategies, demand reduction and integrated multi-agency commissioning, but none of these ideas will work unless local people support them, engage with them and help deliver them. Local governments can therefore only respond to the dual challenge of diminishing resource and increasing demand if it is able to draw on the civic energy of the people it represents. This requires a high level of trust between local government institutions and their local communities. At the same time, however, such institutions are experiencing a crisis in trust in institutions, which makes it harder to engage people. This need not be an insuperable dilemma. It is possible to develop a direction that encourages participation in a way that rebuilds trust.

The case studies gathered here give an indication of the sorts of actions that local governments can take to make progress in rebuilding trust. Crucially, these case studies illustrate steps in a progressive process that restores trust and builds a foundation for reform. First, we need to create a space for open dialogue between communities and local authorities. Second, we need to develop processes that allow the community to have a genuine role in shaping decisions by the council. Finally, and most ambitiously, we need to move away from seeing the council simply as a body that delivers services on behalf of citizens and see it instead as a body that catalyses and supports autonomous action by the community.

However, while our case studies illustrate each of these elements, they remain isolated examples of innovation rather than a wholesale process of transformation. How to disseminate awareness of and develop such initiatives elsewhere should form the focus of thinking about improvement and development in local government. As well as technical expertise, it is likely to depend both on political leadership and on substantial culture change as various stakeholders within local governments reconceptualise their role and attempt to change their practice. Supporting this cultural shift will be challenging. The forms of organisational and personal development required should be the subject of further study.

We have become accustomed over the last decade to discussing a fiscal deficit, and local government has been shaped by the austerity through which various central governments have tried to tackle it. However, the real deficit we should be worrying about now is the trust deficit. Eliminating that is the greatest priority for local government around the world.

References

Brown, G. (2008) *The Living End*. Basingstoke: Palgrave Macmillan.
Christensen, H. E. and Grant, B. (2016) Participatory Budgeting in Australian Local Government: An Initial Assessment and Critical Issues. *Australian Journal of Public Administration* 75(4): 457–475.
Copus, C., Roberts, M. and Wall, R. (2017) *Local Government in England: Centralisation, Autonomy and Control*. Basingstoke: Palgrave Macmillan.
D'Ancona, M. (2017) *Post-Truth: The New War on Truth and How to Fight Back*. London: Ebury Press.
DCLG (2008) *Communities in Control: Real People, Real Power*. London: Department for Communities and Local Government.
Drew, J. and Ryan, R. (2016) *Giving Local Governments the Reboot*. Sydney: McKell Institute.
Goodhart, G. (2017) *The Road to Somewhere: The Populist Revolt and the Future of Politics*. London: C. Hurst.
Institute for Fiscal Studies (2017) *The Local Vantage: How Views of Local Government Finance Vary Across Councils*. London: Institute for Fiscal Studies.

Ipsos MORI (2017) *2017 Veracity Index*. Retrieved from www.ipsos.com/ipsos-mori/en-uk/politicians-remain-least-trusted-profession-britain.

LGA (2017) *Local Government Association Briefing: Local Government Finance and Arrangements beyond 2020*. London Local Government Association.

LGiU (2010) *Community Empowerment What Is It and Where Is It Going?* London: Local Government Information Unit.

LGiU (2013) *Connected Localism*. London: Local Government Information Unit.

LGiU (2017) *2017 State of Local Government Finance Survey*. London: Local Government Information Unit.

LGiU and Local Trust (2017) *Community Collaboration: A Councillor's Guide*. London: Local Government Information Unit and Local Trust.

Pew Research Center (2017) *News Use Across Social Media Platforms 2017*. Washington, DC: Pew Research Center.

UN-Habitat (2017) *The Challenge of Local Government Financing in Developing Countries*. Nairobi: UN-Habitat.

21
DOES MODE OF PUBLIC OUTREACH MATTER?

Sheldon Gen and Erika Luger

The concern over modes of public outreach

Public participation in policy-making and implementation is a cornerstone of democratic governance (Arnstein 1969; Cornwall 2008). Normative and descriptive research point to the many advantages of engaging the public to strengthen the processes and outcomes of local government policies and services. To fulfil these advantages, government agencies have developed a plethora of modes to engage the public. These range from more passive modes – from the perspective of the public – such as newsletters and surveys, to highly active modes such as public hearings and citizen panels (McLaverty 2011; Roberts 2008).[1] Evidence clearly shows that public outreach has become a normal part of government decision making (e.g. Shaw 2000). However, despite the ubiquity of public participation, and the diversity of modes of engagement, the various modes are not employed equally. One study (Shaw 2000) found that just one mode of outreach was commonly used by agencies: public hearings. Leighninger (2014) described the consequences of limited modes of outreach when he wrote:

> The outdated laws on public participation – and the failed public meeting formats they perpetuate – represent one of the key obstacles to improving the relationship between citizens and government. If we want to stem the rising tide of incivility, mistrust, and policy gridlock, we need to reexamine the official processes for engaging the public.
> *(Leighninger 2014: 305)*

Such narrow outreach efforts can lead to 'participatory inequality' (Schlozman, Verba and Brady 1999: 431), when levels of participation and expressed interests adhere 'closely to the fault lines of social class'. Instead, given the wide range of available modes, government agencies should be concerned with their selections of modes, to ensure that they attract representative participation and broad public interests (Carnes et al. 1998). The assumption is that different modes of engagement induce different segments of the community to participate, which might bias the public input toward the preferences of those participating. This is particularly concerning in communities with socioeconomically diverse populations that have diverse policy preferences. But so far, this assumption has not been empirically tested. This study answers the question,

'Does mode of public outreach matter?' by developing the theoretical link between mode of public outreach and policy outcomes, and testing the link in a case of environmental planning in a diverse US city.

Linking modes of outreach to policy outcomes

The academic literature on public participation is vast, but lacks direct examinations of a link between modes of public outreach and policy outcomes. Instead, we review here three segments of the literature from which we develop that theoretical link: (1) the theoretical and descriptive purposes of public participation in policy-making, (2) a continuum of various modes of public outreach used in policy development, and (3) preferences for different modes of outreach.

Purposes of public participation

The literature identifies several purposes of public participation. One way in which these purposes can be organised is through categories adapted from policy and programme logic models: processes, outputs, and outcomes.[2] After all, participation in policy-making processes can be thought of as an intervention meant to affect some desired policy outcome. First, public participation is widely said to be a *legitimate process* of decision making in a democracy, though the reasons for legitimisation are varied. DeLeon (1992) claims that in the policy formulation stage, public participation incorporates public input to make-up for the shortcomings of the purely rational framework for policy analysis. Frederickson (1982) and Nalbandian (1999) explain that it is government responsiveness to the public that legitimises the process. By incorporating public input, agencies' decisions can respond to explicit preferences of the citizenry, thereby justifying those decisions. The American Society for Public Administration has codified this prescription in its code of ethics (Svara 2014), calling for the promotion of participation to empower citizens in democratic processes. Denhardt and Denhardt (2000) go further by reasoning that legitimacy stems from the collaboration formed between government and the public to solve public issues together. Additionally, the public support that is gained through public participation is addressed by a few empirical studies. The building of public commitment (Bryson and Anderson 2000) and consensus (Xu 2005) to the problems and solutions identified justify the process of public inclusion. As varied as these authors' views are, they would agree that when public input is included in policy-making processes, the legitimacy of those processes are improved.

Complementing this view are perspectives that focus on the outputs and outcomes of public participation. Here, *outputs* are the immediate and direct effects of public participation, and they focus on the exchange of ideas between the public and the government. In what Sanoff (2000) calls 'pseudo participation,' the purpose of engaging the public is to transfer information and rationales from the government to the public, in efforts to educate the public and persuade it to support the government's pre-established position. It is clearly a pessimistic view of participation, existing at the bottom of Arnstein's ladder of participation as 'tokenism' (Arnstein 1969). On the other hand, King, Feltey and Susel (1998) claim that the purpose of 'authentic public participation' is the transfer of information and preferences from the public to the government, in order to better inform government decisions. It increases relevant information for decision-making (Bryson and Anderson 2000) including the identification of public needs (Xu 2005).

Outcomes are more distant effects of public participation, and are often indirect and moderated by confounding variables. Several authors claim the purpose of public participation lies in the many outcomes they produce. Smith and Huntsman (1997) reason that public participation creates value for the public. Using the metaphor of citizens as shareholders in the community enterprise, they argue why citizens are willing to invest personal effort, on top of taxes, toward government efforts that personally affect them. In this metaphor, government agencies are trustees of the enterprise's assets and must use the public investments (i.e. inputs) to create value for the public. The forms of that value might include the responsiveness to public concerns described earlier, more effective implementation of policy (Kastens and Newig 2008), and wider distribution of benefits (Gallagher and Jackson 2008). Others also note that public participation results in an important positive outcome for government agencies: adaptation to their changing environments. Taking a systems theory view of public organisations (Easton 1965), Frederickson (1982) and Koenig (2005) find that citizen participation helps local governments adapt to, and be successful within, their changing environments. The participation becomes the inputs from the environment to which organisations can adapt.

Despite this long list of positive potential purposes for public participation, its impact on policy making is moderated by the government agencies' intents for outreach. As mentioned above, critics have argued that public outreach is used by government officials to sell to the public decisions already made; while others argue that it is genuinely used to shape decisions. In his study of welfare reform in the 1990s, Shaw (2000) found that these two perspectives on public outreach were nearly equally split among government officials. Furthermore, when identifying the most influential sources of input, interest groups and the general public ranked in the middle of a list of sources, with government officials taking the top spots. His study and others' (e.g. Handley and Howell-Moroney 2007) significantly dampen the promised benefits of public participation, making them contingent upon government intent.

Modes of outreach

Adding to the complexity of the issue are the many modes of public outreach. In perhaps the broadest study of public participation in US cities to date, Wang (2001) found that the most common modes were public hearings, citizen advisory boards, and neighbourhood meetings. Others included individual citizen representatives, surveys, focus groups, telephone hotlines, and the internet. Shaw (2000), focusing on welfare reform across the US, made similar findings. While many modes of participation were used, the most common were public hearings, task forces, focus groups, surveys, meetings with community leaders and groups, public-initiated calls, and news media.

A few studies have focused on the niches that have developed around specific modes of outreach. In their case study of local policy-making processes, for example, Watson, Juster and Johnson (1991) concluded that surveys are useful in helping set budgetary and policy priorities. Crosby, Kelly and Schaefer (1986) found that citizen panels – characterised by a jury-like process of discovery and deliberation – are effective in engaging the public in highly complex issues. Drawbacks of these deliberative modes, however, include their potential to alienate less articulate persons and their vulnerability to indecision (Roberts 1997). Kakabadse, Kakabadse and Kouzmin (2003) concluded that electronic modes of public outreach can efficiently deliver information and register citizens' views, but they might alienate those without access to electronic media, and they may potentially individualise democracy rather than increasing public discussion and community interaction. Indeed, Merry (2010) found that organisational blogging has high potential for public engagement, but evidence suggests that few in the public actually engage in discussion through blogs. Of course, these modes of participation are not mutually exclusive, and a combination of them might maximise the potential of achieving broad public input (Weeks 2000).

Overall, the literature on the different modes of participation is under-organised. For the purposes of this current study, an initial, simple categorisation of modes of participation

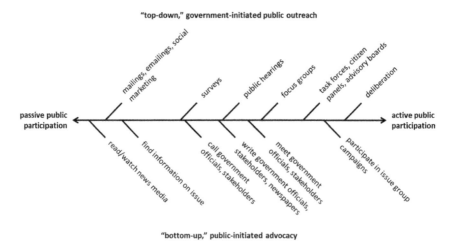

Figure 21.1 Modes of public participation

helps us develop a testable hypothesis about whether different modes of participation affect who participates.

Figure 21.1 organises commonly cited modes of public participation along two dimensions. The horizontal line represents a continuum of public participation ranging from passive to active, from the public's perspective. Purely passive participation is characterised by receiving information, while purely active participation is marked by the production of information and policy decisions. Those entries above the line are 'top-down' government-initiated public outreach modes, which are the focus of this study. Those below the line are 'bottom-up' or 'citizen driven' advocacy modes initiated by public individuals and groups (Buckwalter 2014; McLaverty 2011). Thus, basic information dissemination is on the left side of the line, with government mailings and emailings on the top side and public attention to the news on the bottom side. At the right side of the continuum are modes far more demanding of the public's energy, such as citizen panels on the top side, and issue group advocacy activities on the bottom. The figure is not meant to be comprehensive in listing and locating modes of public participation. Rather, it simply provides a framework for categorising the modes that is useful for the current study.

Preferences for modes of outreach

Even when government agencies genuinely seek public input to shape decisions, and even with the broad variety of modes of participation, achieving wide public participation is challenging, and those who actually participate are not necessarily representative of the general public. In fact, Glicken (1999) argues that the diversity of cultures and perspectives in US society represents the greatest *impediment* to wide participation. These different cultures in the US, she claims, define the process of democracy or the role of public participation differently. While a few empirical studies have contradicted this claim (e.g. Greenberg and Lewis 2000; Laurian 2004), more have generally supported it (e.g. Williams and Florez 2002; Xu 2005). The broad support, however, is mixed in specifying how different cultures – often operationalised by ethnicity or race – are affected. They generally find that whites participate at the highest rates, followed in order by African-Americans, Latinos, and Asian-Americans (e.g. Leighley and Vedlitz 1999; Uhlaner, Can and Kiewiet 1989; Verba et al. 1993).

The mixed findings on the effects of race and ethnicity may be due to the dynamic nature of these social constructs. Junn (2000) eloquently argued that race is an unreliable predictor of political participation because of its changing meaning over time and its widely varying meaning among people. Still others argue why it remains an important predictor of public participation. Verba et al. (1993) reasoned that different resources – such as education level, income, religion, and job – facilitate and encourage participation, but these resources are not distributed equally among ethnic groups. Therefore, ethnicity remains a predictor of public participation. Xu (2005) and Junn (2000) added that the varied participation levels also reflect different levels of assimilation to the dominant culture. Overall, these researchers would agree with Nelson's earlier claim (1979: 1025) that ethnicity is an 'enduring and important element of social division' that is a strong predictor of political participation.

Other demographic correlates of public participation have also been examined. Studies looking at economic class have generally found that those with higher socio-economic status participate at higher rates than others (e.g. Larson and Lach 2008; Laurian 2004). The assumption is that it is more difficult to get participation from lower-income groups because of their competing demands on time and resources coming from basic needs (Sen 2008). Furthermore, modes of outreach that demand high involvement (i.e. those toward the right of Figure 21.1) have been found to skew participation by economic class (King, Feltey and Susel 1998). Higher education levels are also commonly found to increase participation rates (e.g. Larson and Lach 2008; Williams et al. 2001; Xu 2005), though some evidence does contradict this claim (e.g. Laurian 2004). Also, Ebdon (2000) found that the political cultures of cities were significant predictors of participation. In essence, citizens are more active if their communities already hosted active community organisations (Austin 1972). Other examined demographic characteristics that have not widely affected participation rates include gender, age, household size, employment status, and years of residence (e.g. Greenberg and Lewis 2000; Larson and Lach 2008; Laurian 2004).

These numerous studies make broad conclusions on the demographic predictors of general public participation in government decision-making. However, when we focused on studies comparing preferences for different modes of participation, we found very few. In their examination of public participation in decisions regarding chemical weapons stockpile sites, Williams et al. (2001) found that civic functions and signing petitions were the most popular modes of participation overall. Looking even more specifically at the demographic determinants of preferences for different modes of participation yielded few and conflicting studies. In her study of public participation in budgetary processes, Ebdon (2000) found no clear pattern in preferences for different participation modes by different races. Still, Hampton (1999) reasoned that some ethnic groups prefer to express their views privately within their own cultural group. Additionally, verbal modes of participation such as public hearings may exclude those whose first language is not English or those who are undereducated.

A theoretical link

Even with these mixed findings on the demographics of preferences for outreach modes, an unanswered question remains: does it matter? That is, would different demographics of participation lead to different public input and, ultimately, different policy decisions? Carnes, Schweitzer, Peelle, Wolfe and Munro's (1998) case studies on the Department of Energy's public outreach found that successful stakeholder participation only needs to be full and active. The department did not find representativeness as a criterion of success. Indeed, from an agency's perspective, the attributes of successful public participation have more to do with process and opportunity for participation than outcome. But from the public's perspective,

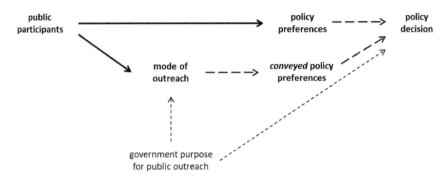

Figure 21.2 Hypothesized effect of mode of outreach on policy decision

The public may have varied preferences for both policies and modes of outreach. These are represented by the solid arrows, and they are the relationships observed in this study. Policy preferences can affect policy decisions (long dashed arrows), depending upon the government's purpose for public outreach (short dashed arrows).

Source: Author.

it is reasonable to expect that those opportunities to participate do not systemically alienate certain stakeholders, especially if those alienated have substantially different policy preferences. As Cornwall (2008: 281) prescribed, public outreach must account for 'who is involved *and who is absent*' (emphasis added). Some have clearly argued that representativeness of those participating is key to ensuring that the preferences of community are accurately presented (McComas 2001) and political power is equitably distributed among competing segments of the community (Strange 1972). But empirical evidence is lacking.

This study begins to fill this gap in the literature by testing hypothesised links between modes of public outreach and policy preferences conveyed to the government. The overall model we hypothesise is summarised in Figure 21.2 and is derived directly from the literature reviewed above. In the upper path of this model, public participants have policy preferences that would ideally affect policy decisions. In the lower paths, to measure those policy preferences government agencies select modes of outreach, which has the potential of biasing participation if different segments of the public have varied preferences for modes of engagement.

The profile of those participating is then hypothesised to affect the policy preferences conveyed to the government because of differences in policy preferences among the segments of the public. For example, different ethnic groups have broadly different environmental policy preferences because of their widely differing experiences with the environment (Taylor 2002). Those conveyed policy preferences are then hypothesised to influence the ultimate policy decisions. However, that influence is moderated by the government's purpose for public outreach. Under 'pseudo' participation, (Sanoff 2000) conveyed public preferences would have no effect on policy decisions. On the other hand, under authentic public participation (King, Feltey and Susel 1998) the conveyed public preferences would greatly affect policy decisions.

This study focuses on two links in this model, between participants and mode of participation, and between participants and conveyed policy preferences. In Figure 21.2 they are represented by solid arrows. We limit our analysis to these parts of the model because we adopt the normative prescription for authentic public participation whereby public participation is *meant* to affect policy decisions in a democracy. As such, the link between conveyed policy preferences and policy decision is assumed, or at least prescribed.

Empirical Method

These hypothesised links were tested with data from an environmental planning effort in San Francisco, USA. The San Francisco Public Utilities Commission (SFPUC) recently developed a new 30-year master plan for the city's wastewater system. Having met all environmental regulatory requirements under the prior master plan, SFPUC chose to focus the new master plan on improving levels of service and attending to public preferences for the system. For example, SFPUC weighed the relative importance of competing principles to guide the master plan, such as promoting public health, environmental protections, environmental justice, customer service, etc. At the same time, it wished to prioritise major capital improvement projects and options, including sewer replacements, diversion of effluent discharge from the bay to the ocean, separating the sewer and storm drain systems, and redistribution of treatment facilities and capacities.

To balance and prioritise these competing demands, SFPUC sought public input through authentic public participation (King, Feltey and Susel 1998) representing the diverse communities of San Francisco. It commissioned an initial study that examined, among other things, how the public would like to provide input to SFPUC and what values and policy preferences should guide the master planning process. Its purpose was to use the information to develop an extensive public outreach programme that would yield representative participation from the diverse communities. This is a particularly difficult challenge for San Francisco because of the wide-ranging demographics within the city. These include the ethnically based neighbourhoods of Chinese, Japanese, Russians, and Hispanics; a wide range of economic strata from the affluent Marina District to the poorer Bayview/Hunters Point District; as well as wide variance in education levels and immigration status. This challenge for the city presented an optimal setting to test the hypothesised linkages in Figure 21.2: the city has a diverse population, was considering a broad range of public outreach modes, and was considering competing policy priorities.

The data used in this study came from a representative household survey conducted from December 2005 through January 2006. The survey instrument, developed from the results of four focus groups, measured preferences for a variety of participation modes (limited to those considered by SFPUC at the time), and broad policy preferences and priorities regarding the wastewater system. Select questions used in our study are summarised in Appendix A. For all questions on preferences, a four-point Likert scale was used where '1' indicated strong preference and '4' indicated weak preference. To enhance representativeness, the computer-assisted telephone survey was conducted in English, Mandarin, Cantonese, and Spanish. While more languages are spoken in San Francisco, these four are the most commonly spoken by monolingual residents. Each number in the household sample was called up to 15 times to recruit participation. A stratified random sample of 803 households were surveyed, representing a 37 per cent cooperation rate.[3] Post-stratification weights were applied to the responses to both account for probability of selection and match US Census Bureau statistics on ethnicity and numbers of households in each neighbourhood. The resulting data allowed us to test whether the modes of participation employed by SFPUC might yield differences in conveyed policy preferences.

The demographic variables tested in this study included ethnicity (white, African American, Asian, Hispanic, and other), education level (up to a high school diploma, some college, BA/BS degree, graduate degree), six income categories, gender, home ownership, and number of children. Additionally, three confounding variables were included to account for biases associated with the wastewater context of the survey: membership in any environmental group, paying for the sewer bill, and familiarity with the wastewater system.

Respondents were asked about their likelihood of participation in 11 different modes of public participation. Most of these were government-initiated outreach modes, reflecting the original purpose of the survey to develop an effective outreach campaign. From most passive to most active (from the public's perspective) the modes were: reading mailed information, reading emailed information, reading website information, signing a petition, responding to a mailed survey, responding to an online survey, writing letters to officials, calling officials, educating neighbours about issues, attending neighbourhood meetings, and attending city hall meetings. Respondents' preferences for each of these modes were regressed on the demographic variables to determine if different modes attracted different participants.

Similarly, respondents were asked 24 questions about specific policy options and priorities related to the wastewater system. The specifics of these questions are not important to our current study because of their uniqueness to the context of the original study (i.e. wastewater master planning in San Francisco). Instead, this set of questions simply represents a range of competing policies to test whether preferences for them vary significantly by demographic characteristics.

Findings

The resulting sample of respondents represented the population of San Francisco well in terms of ethnicity, age, and sex. Furthermore, respondents' preferences for modes of participation and specific policies exhibited sufficient variance for regression analysis. Thus, we first regressed preferences for the 11 public participation modes on the set of demographic variables. Table 21.1 summarises five of those regressions, representing the range of findings. All 11 regression equations were statistically significant, with $p < 0.01$ in all cases, confirming prior research that generally demonstrated that preferences for modes of outreach vary by demographic variables. However, our findings were able to compare the variance in preferences among competing modes of participation. Among these 11 modes, the adjusted R^2s ranged from a low of 5.1 per cent for signing petitions, to a high of 25.5 per cent for reading website information. Thus, in the context of this environmental planning effort, if only one mode of outreach were to be used, petitions would result in the most demographically representative set of participants since these demographic variables explain only 5.1 per cent of the variance in preference, while relying solely on reading website information would result in more demographically biased set of participants.

Looking more deeply at the regression equations, the significant demographic predictors clearly varied across the modes of participation analysed, but a few clear patterns did emerge. The most robust pattern is the predictive value of ethnicity. Specifically, African American respondents reported greater likelihoods of participating in all 11 modes than white respondents. (The coefficients are negative because lower numbers in the Likert scale indicated stronger preferences for participation.) The same pattern existed for Hispanic respondents for 10 of the modes. These findings appear to contradict earlier studies that found lower levels of participation for ethnic minority groups (e.g. Gallagher and Jackson 2008; Hampton 1999; Sen 2008). However, this may be due to the specific policy context of our data. African American and Hispanic residents in San Francisco might simply be more concerned with wastewater issues because of the location of the main treatment plant in a predominantly minority neighbourhood. Asian respondents, on the other hand, were not distinguishable from white respondents except for reading emailed information, and they generally scored low on all participation modes. The more important pattern to notice in the context of this study is simply that ethnicity is a robust predictor of preference for different modes of participation.

Another fairly robust pattern is the relationship between education level and mode of participation. In general, for more passive modes of participation (e.g. read mailed/emailed information, respond to surveys), those with higher levels of education reported higher likelihoods of

Table 21.1 Select regression analyses of preferences for specific modes of public outreach (for clarity, only significant coefficients are reported)

Dependent variables: preferences for modes of participation	Read mailed info b	Read mailed info t	Read website info b	Read website info t	Sign petition b	Sign petition t	Respond to mailed survey b	Respond to mailed survey t	neighbour-hood meetings b	neighbour-hood meetings t
Ethnicity: reference group = white										
Other			−.35	−2.21^						
African Am.	−.16	−1.70*	−.51	−3.32~	−.47	−3.34~	−.33	−2.84~	−0.28	−1.91*
Asian										
Hispanic	−.21	−2.22^			−.46	−3.33~	−.42	−3.64~	−0.31	−2.13^
Education level: reference group = up to HS diploma										
Some college	−.40	−4.25~	−.93	−6.83~	−.28	−2.27^	−.60	−5.84~		
BA/BS	−.38	−4.25~	−.59	−4.24~			−.47	−4.39~		
Grad. degree	−.38	−3.92~					−.23	−1.98^	0.30	2.01^
Household annual income: reference group = <$25,000										
$25–49.9k					−.29	−2.34^				
$50–74.9k					−.31	−2.38^				
$75–99.9k			−.41	−2.57~	−.35	−2.35^			−0.50	−3.27~
$100–149.9k					−.25	−1.70*				
$150k +	.27	2.53^								
Age			.02	6.23~	−.01	−1.83*	−.01	−2.07^	−0.01	−2.19^
Years in SF			−.01	−2.02^			−.01	−2.39^		
Years current res.										
Female	.17	3.19~	−.24	−2.96~			.19	2.90~		
Owns home							.15	1.66*		
No. of children	.06	1.87*								
Env. group										
Pays sewer bill			−.29	−2.82~						
Att. to sewer sys.			.10	2.24~					0.20	4.40~
n	567		555		557		564		561	
F	4.04~		10.01~		2.43~		5.76~		4.64~	
Adjusted R^2	0.102		0.255		0.051		0.151		0.120	

*$p < 0.10$
^$p < 0.05$
~$p < 0.01$

Other modes of participation analysed: read emailed information ($F_{(21,554)} = 7.74$, $p < 0.01$, adj.$R^2 = 0.204$), respond to online survey ($F_{(21,547)} = 7.10$, $p < 0.01$, adj.$R^2 = 0.190$), educate neighbours on issues ($F_{(21,556)} = 6.39$, $p < 0.01$, adj.$R^2 = 0.169$), write letters to officials ($F_{(21,555)} = 6.37$, $p < 0.01$, adj.$R^2 = 0.169$), and call officials ($F_{(21,551)} = 8.22$, $p < 0.01$, adj.$R^2 = 0.216$).

participating than those with lower levels of education. For more active modes of participation (e.g. meetings in neighbourhoods and city hall), those with higher levels of education reported lower likelihood of participation than those with lower levels of education. These findings provide a deeper understanding of the previously found trends associating education with participation. Rather than being a simple linear relationship in which higher levels of education result in higher levels of participation (e.g. Larson and Lach 2008; Williams et al. 2001; Xu 2005), our findings suggest a nonlinear relationship in which the mode of participation moderates the relationship.

Age and sex were also frequently significant predictors of preference, but their patterns among the 11 modes are not clear. Income level and years in residency (i.e. in San Francisco and in current residence) were not significant in more than half of the regression equations.

Next, we regressed preferences for the 24 policy options and priorities on the same set of demographic variables. Table 21.2 summarises five of these regression equations. All 24 resulting

Table 21.2 Select regression analyses of preferences for policy options and priorities (for clarity, only significant coefficients are reported)

Dependent variables: preferred policy options and priorities	Redistribution of sewage to treatment plants		Willingness to pay for redistribution		Fewer fines from federal government		Improve reliability		Minimise costs	
	b	t	b	t	b	t	b	t	b	t
Ethnicity: reference group = white										
Other									.23	1.87*
African American	.35	3.20~	−.76	−5.11~	−.21	−1.67*				
Asian	−.15	−1.73*					−.15	−2.14^		
Hispanic	.29	2.62~	−.53	−3.45~			−.42	−4.76~		
Education level: reference group = up to HS diploma										
Some college							−.31	−3.93~		
BA/BS	.37	3.57~					−.29	−3.50~		
Grad. degree							−.20	−2.17^	.37	3.32~
Household annual income: reference group = <$25,000										
$25–49.9k	−.18	−1.87*	.25	1.81*						
$50–74.9k	−.43	−4.17~	−.26	−1.77*						
$75–99.9k	−.28	−2.37^					.19	1.94*	.23	1.98^
$100–149.9k	−.40	−3.52^								
$150k +									.35	2.86~
Age	−.01	−4.50~			−.01	−2.37^				
Years in SF	.01	3.27~			.01	2.01^	−.01	−3.27~		
Years current res.			.01	2.53^					−.01	−3.14~
Female	−.19	−2.99~					.09	1.75*	.12	1.97^
Owns home			.35	2.87~	−.20	−2.08^	.13	1.93*		
No. of children	−.18	−4.46~	.19	2.85~			.05	1.69*		
Env. group member			−.49	−4.55~	.29	3.34~	−.15	−2.42^	.23	3.11~
Pays sewer bill									.22	2.97~
Att. to sewer sys.	.09	2.67~								
n	494		404		523		561		561	
F	7.19~		5.36~		1.88^		4.72~		6.96~	
Adjusted R^2	.209		.186		.034		.122		.183	

*p < 0.10
^p < 0.05
~p < 0.01

19 other specific policy options and priorities were also regressed (see Appendix A for relevant survey questions). All were statistically significant, with p < 0.01. Adjusted R^2 ranged from 0.051 to 0.206.

regression equations were statistically significant (23 of them with $p < 0.01$, and 1 with $p < 0.05$). The amounts of variance in preference explained by the regression equations (i.e. the adjusted R^2s) ranged from 3.4 per cent to 20.9 per cent. In other words, up to a fifth of the variance in policy preferences can be explained by the demographic variables. Among these regression equations, the most prevalent variables were ethnicities. In 16 of the 24 equations (67 per cent), Hispanic respondents held different policy preferences than white respondents. In roughly half of the equations the same was true for African American and Asian respondents. After ethnicity, the next most prevalent demographic variable was age, which was significant in 42 per cent of the equations. Each of the rest of our demographic variables was significant in at least four of the 24 equations, but none was significant in more than 9 (37 per cent).

Overall, our analysis confirms the observed portion of the model hypothesised in Figure 21.2. Within this specific policy context, the selected modes of participation would affect the demographic make-up of who participates, and these different demographic groups have significantly different policy preferences. Table 21.3 summarises the significance of our demographic variables across the 11 regression equations on modes of participation and the 24 regression equations on policy options and priorities. It shows that the demographic variables that are most frequently related to *both* mode of participation and policy preferences are ethnicity, age, and gender. Specifically, African American and Hispanic respondents preferred different modes of participation

Table 21.3 Frequency distributions of significant independent variables in 35 regression analyses

	Preferences for 11 modes of participation			Preferences for 24 policy options, priorities	
	no relationship	negative relationship	positive relationship	no relationship	relationship
Ethnicity: reference group = white						
Other	7 (64%)	0	4 (36%)	20 (83%)	4 (17%)
African American	0	0	11 (100%)	13 (54%)	11 (46%)
Asian	10 (91%)	0	1 (9%)	12 (50%)	12 (50%)
Hispanic	1 (9%)	0	10 (91%)	8 (33%)	16 (67%)
Education level: reference group = up to HS diploma						
Some college	3 (27%)	0	8 (73%)	16 (67%)	8 (33%)
BA/BS	4 (36%)	2 (18%)	5 (45%)	15 (63%)	9 (37%)
Grad. degree	5 (45%)	2 (18%)	4 (36%)	18 (75%)	6 (25%)
Household annual income: reference group = <$25,000						
$25–49.9k	9 (82%)	0	2 (18%)	18 (75%)	6 (25%)
$50–74.9k	9 (82%)	0	2 (18%)	18 (75%)	6 (25%)
$75–99.9k	5 (45%)	0	6 (55%)	15 (63%)	9 (37%)
$100–149.9k	8 (73%)	0	3 (27%)	18 (75%)	6 (25%)
$150k +	8 (73%)	1 (9%)	2 (18%)	17 (71%)	7 (29%)
Age	2 (18%)	3 (27%)	6 (55%)	14 (58%)	10 (42%)
Years in SF	7 (64%)	0	4 (36%)	17 (71%)	7 (29%)
Years current res.	10 (91%)	1 (9%)	0	15 (63%)	9 (37%)
Female	4 (36%)	2 (18%)	5 (45%)	15 (63%)	9 (37%)
Owns home	9 (82%)	2 (18%)	0	17 (71%)	7 (29%)
No. of children	8 (73%)	3 (27%)	0	15 (63%)	9 (37%)
Env. group member	8 (73%)	0	3 (27%)	14 (58%)	10 (42%)
Pays sewer bill	9 (82%)	0	2 (18%)	20 (83%)	4 (17%)
Att. to sewer sys.	4 (36%)	7 (64%)	0	16 (67%)	8 (33%)

than white respondents in over 90 per cent of the equations, *and* they preferred different policies than white respondents in 46 per cent and 67 per cent of the equations, respectively. Similarly, age predicts preferences for 82 per cent of the modes analysed, *and* it predicts preferences in 42 per cent of the policies analysed. Gender predicts 63 per cent of mode preferences and 37 per cent of policy preferences. These all suggest that a specific mode of outreach chosen is likely to affect the demographics of who participates and the policy preferences conveyed to public agencies.

Conclusion

The clearest limitation of this empirical analysis is the scope of its claim. We collected data within the context of wastewater issues in a unique city to measure residents' preferences for modes of participation and policy priorities. Our conclusion for this study, however, is neither a specification of the demographic preferences for modes of participation, nor a ranking of policy preferences. Those conclusions are the SFPUCs, for their specific purpose of developing a master plan for wastewater services. Instead, our purpose in this study is to test the general hypothesis that mode of participation *can* indeed affect conveyed policy preferences by moderating who engages the process. SFPUC's case provided the experiment to test the hypothesis, and our findings confirm the hypothesis. The mode of public outreach does matter.

Another limitation is in its data collection method. Because our data were collected by survey, it is reasonable to expect our findings to be biased toward the use of surveys as a mode of participation. We made substantial efforts to minimise this source of bias, as described earlier, but with a 37 per cent cooperation rate we cannot be sure of our success. But again, our purpose is not to establish a ranked preference for these modes of participation, which surely vary with issues and locales. Instead, we draw the general conclusion that demographic predictors of preference for each mode must be accounted when conducting public outreach.

While these may be broad claims, they are nonetheless critical to the practice of public outreach, and this study adds an important empirical contribution to an overlooked topic. Local governments seeking public input to inform decisions must select modes of outreach that attract representative participation. This is a clear way for public agencies to meet the American Society for Public Administration's code of ethics on representative participation, which has evolved from a limited defensive standard to 'eliminate all forms of illegal discrimination,' to the current proactive directive to 'reduce disparities in outcomes and increase the inclusion of underrepresented groups' (Svara 2014).

Bryson, Quick, Slotterback and Crosby (2013) warn, however, that a specific generalizable design for public participation does not exist, because participation does vary considerably with local conditions and issues. Instead, they prescribe a general approach to designing participation campaigns that evolves as it is implemented. They note that 'successful public participation requires designing iteratively, in response to specific purposes and contexts' (Bryson et al. 2013: 24). So, a local government official designing an outreach plan might start by relying on past experiences in their specific policy context, then adjust the plan according to demographic responses to the plan. In our current case, ethnicity, age, and gender were the most predictive characteristics of preferences for modes of participation, so the SFPUC would select an initial set of modes based on these linkages, then adjust the outreach as they measure the representativeness of participants.

Indeed, our findings suggest that relying on just one or a few modes of public outreach would bias participation and likely misrepresent the full community's true policy preferences.

Unfortunately, government agencies do tend to limit their outreach practices to one dominant mode (Bartels 2014). Our findings show that this undermines the purposes of authentic public participation, which are to give representative voice to the public, in order to make policies that reflect public preferences. As Timney noted (2011: 87), 'For most citizens, the reality of public participation process rarely meets the promise of democracy.'

The inertia behind this organisational habit is rooted in that central tension found in public agencies today (Neshkova 2014). On the one hand, a bureaucratic ethic that values efficiency and expertise seeks nominal outreach while maintaining control of the decision-making processes. On the other hand, a democratic ethic that values public preferences reflected in policies and services seeks partnerships with the public (Buckwalter 2014). Applied to public outreach, this tension manifests itself as a drive for more of the same limited outreach (e.g. public hearings) versus a drive for broader outreach that draws representative participation. Our research finds that more is not necessarily better, if the greater numbers of participants do not accurately represent the ranges and distributions of policy preferences. In such cases, the biases in conveyed preferences may be exacerbated by greater quantities of the same outreach. As McLaverty (2011: 415) notes in his review of recent innovations in public outreach, 'The fear that democrats have about the mechanisms [i.e. the modes of public outreach] is that, rather than dealing with the issue of under-representation by some social groups, they will accentuate inequalities in participation.' Indeed, our findings demonstrate that instead of focusing on the *quantities* of participation, a greater focus must be placed on the strategic deployment of outreach modes to yield *representative* participation.

Notes

1 Even without solicitation from a government body, the public has many access points to the policy making process, should they decide to use them (e.g. providing direct feedback, advocacy work).
2 Logic models include the inputs, activities, outputs, and outcomes of programmes. In this study, the purposes of public participation can be categorized in the latter three elements, where legitimate processes essentially are the activities.
3 The cooperation rate is the ratio of all completed surveys to the total of all households contacted (completes + refusals).

References

Arnstein, S. 1969. A Ladder of Citizen Participation. *Journal of the American Institute of Planners* 35: 216–224.
Austin, D. M. 1972. Resident Participation: Political Mobilization or Organizational Co-optation? *Public Administration Review* 32: 409–420.
Bartels, K. P. R. 2014. Communicative Capacity: The Added Value of Public Encounters for Participatory Democracy. *American Review of Public Administration* 44(6): 656–674.
Bryson, J. M. and S. R. Anderson. 2000. Applying Large-Group Interaction Methods in the Planning and Implementation of Major Change Efforts. *Public Administration Review* 60(2): 143–153.
Bryson, J. M., K. S. Quick, C. S. Slotterback and B. C. Crosby. 2013. Designing Public Participation Processes. *Public Administration Review* 73(1): 23–34.
Buckwalter, N. D. 2014. The Potential for Public Empowerment through Government-Organized Participation. *Public Administration Review* 74(5): 573–584.
Carnes, S. A., M. Schweitzer, E. B. Peelle, A. K. Wolfe and J. F. Munro. 1998. Measuring the Success of Public Participation on Environmental Restoration and Waste Management Activities in the U.S. Department of Energy. *Technology in Society* 20(4): 385–406.
Cornwall, A. 2008. Unpacking 'Participation': Models, Meanings and Practices. *Community Development Journal* 43(3): 269–283.

Crosby, N., J. M. Kelly and P. Schaefer. 1986. Citizen Panels: A New Approach to Citizen Participation. *Public Administration Review* 46(2): 170–178.

DeLeon, P. 1992. The Democratization of the Policy Process. *Public Administration Review* 52(2): 125–129.

Denhardt, R. B. and J. V. Denhardt. 2000. The New Public Service: Serving Rather than Steering. *Public Administration Review* 60(6): 549–559.

Easton, D. 1965. *A Framework for Political Analysis*. Englewood Cliffs, NJ: Prentice-Hall.

Ebdon, C. 2000. The Relationship Between Citizen Involvement in the Budget Process and City Structure and Culture. *Public Productivity and Management Review* 23(3): 383–393.

Frederickson, H. G. 1982. The Recovery of Civism in Public Administration. *Public Administration Review* 42(6): 501–507.

Gallagher, D. and S. Jackson. 2008. Promoting Community Involvement at Brownfields Sites in Socio-Economically Disadvantaged Neighbourhoods. *Journal of Environmental Planning and Management* 51(5): 615–630.

Glicken, J. 1999. Effective Public Involvement in Public Decisions. *Science Communication* 20(3): 298–327.

Greenberg, M. and M. J. Lewis. 2000. Brownfields Redevelopment, Preferences, and Public Involvement: A Case Study of an Ethnically Mixed Neighbourhood. *Urban Studies* 37(13): 2501–2514.

Hampton, G. 1999. Environmental Equity and Public Participation. *Policy Sciences* 32(2): 163–174.

Handley, D. M. and M. Howell-Moroney. 2007. Ordering Stakeholder Relationships and Citizen Participation: Evidence from the Community Development Block Grant Program. *Public Administration Review* 70(4): 601–609.

Junn, J. 2000. The Significance of Race and Class for Political Participation. Paper presented at the conference, Political Participation: Building a Research Agenda, 12–14 October, Center for the Study of Democratic Politics, Princeton University, Princeton, NJ.

Kakabadse, A., N. K. Kakabadse and A. Kouzmin. 2003. Reinventing the Democratic Governance Project through Information Technology? A Growing Agenda for Debate. *Public Administration Review* 63(1): 44–60.

Kastens, B. and J. Newig. 2008. Will Participation Foster the Successful Implementation of the Water Framework Directive? The Case of Agricultural Groundwater Protection in Northwest Germany. *Local Environment* 13(1): 27–41.

King, C. S., K. M. Feltey and B. O. Susel. 1998. The Question of Participation: Toward Authentic Public Participation in Public Administration. *Public Administration Review* 58(4): 317–326.

Koenig, H. O. 2005. Empowerment in Local Government Administration: The Case of Elgin, Illinois. *The Innovation Journal: The Public Sector Innovation Journal* 10(1).

Larson, K. and D. Lach. 2008. Participants and Non-Participants of Place-Based Groups: An Assessment of Attitudes and Implications for Public Participation in Water Resource Management. *Journal of Environmental Management* 88(4): 817–830.

Laurian, L. 2004. Public Participation in Environmental Decision Making. *Journal of the American Planning Association* 70(1): 53–65.

Leighley, J. and A. Vedlitz. 1999. Race, Ethnicity, and Political Participation: Competing Models and Contrasting Explanations. *The Journal of Politics* 16(4): 1092–1114.

Leighninger, M. 2014. Want to Increase Trust in Government? Update Our Public Participation Laws. *Public Administration Review* 74(3): 305–306.

McComas, K. A. 2001. Public Meetings about Local Waste Management Problems: Comparing Participants with Non-Participants. *Environmental Management* 27(1): 135–147.

McLaverty, P. 2011. Participation. In M. Bevir (ed.), *The Sage Handbook of Governance*, 402–418. Los Angeles, CA: Sage.

Merry, M. 2010. Blogging and Environmental Advocacy: A New Way to Engage the Public? *Review of Policy Research* 27(5): 641–656.

Nalbandian, J. 1999. Facilitating Community, Enabling Democracy: New Roles for Local Government Managers. *Public Administration Review* 59(3): 187–197.

Nelson, D. C. 1979. Ethnicity and Socioeconomic Status as Sources of Participation: The Case for Ethnic Political Culture. *The American Political Science Review* 73(4): 1024–1038.

Neshkova, M. 2014. Does Agency Autonomy Foster Public Participation? *Public Administration Review* 74(1): 64–74.

Roberts, N. 1997. Public Deliberation: An Alternative Approach to Crafting Policy and Setting Direction. *Public Administration Review* 57(2): 124–132.

Roberts, N. (ed.). 2008. *The Age of Direct Citizen Participation*. Armonk, NY: Sharpe.

Sanoff, H. 2000. *Community Participation Methods in Design and Planning*. New York: Wiley.

Schlozman, K. L., S. Verba and H. E. Brady. 1999. Civic Participation and the Equality Problem. In T. Skocpal and M. P. Fiorina (eds), *Civic Engagement in American Democracy*, 427–459. Washington, DC: Brookings Institution Press.

Sen, S. 2008. Environmental Justice in Transportation Planning and Policy: A View from Practitioners and Other Stakeholders in the Baltimore–Washington, D.C. Metropolitan Region. *Journal of Urban Technology* 15(1): 117–138.

Shaw, G. M. 2000. The Role of Public Input in State Welfare Policymaking. *Policy Studies Journal* 28(4): 707–720.

Smith, G. E. and C. A. Huntsman. 1997. Reframing the Metaphor of Citizen–Government Relationship: A Value-Centered Perspective. *Public Administration Review* 57(4): 309–318.

Strange, J. H. 1972. Citizen Participation in Community Action and Model Cities Programs. *Public Administration Review* 32: 655–669.

Svara, J. H. 2014. Who are the Keepers of the Code? Articulating and Upholding Ethical Standards in the Field of Public Administration. *Public Administration Review* 74(5): 561–569.

Taylor, D. 2002. *Race, Class, Gender and American Environmentalism*. General Technical Report PNW-GTR-534. Portland, OR: US Department of Agriculture, Forest Service, Pacific Northwest Research Station.

Timney, M. M. 2011. Models of Citizen Participation: Measuring Engagement and Collaboration. In C. S. King (ed.), *Government is Us 2.0*, 86–100. Armonk, NY: M. E. Sharpe.

Uhlaner, C. J., B. E. Can and D. R. Kiewiet. 1989. Political Participation of Ethnic Minorities in the 1980s. *Political Behavior* 11(3): 195–231.

Verba, S., L. K. Schlozman H. Brady, and N. H. Nie. 1993. Race, Ethnicity, and Political Resources: Participation in the United States. *British Journal of Political Science* 23(4): 453–497.

Wang, X. 2001. Assessing Public Participation in US Cities. *Public Performance and Management Review* 24(4): 322–336.

Watson, D. J., R. J. Juster and G. W. Johnson. 1991. Institutionalized Use of Citizen Surveys in the Budgetary and Policy-Making Processes: A Small City Case Study. *Public Administration Review* 51(3): 232–239.

Weeks, E. C. 2000. The Practice of Deliberative Democracy: Results from Four Large-Scale Trials. *Public Administration Review* 60(4): 360–372.

Williams, B. L. and Y. Florez. 2002. Do Mexican Americans Perceive Environmental Issues Differently than Caucasians? A Study of Cross-Ethnic Variation in Perceptions Related to Water in Tucson. *Environmental Health Perspectives* 110(Supplement 2: Community, Research, and Environmental Justice): 303–310.

Williams, B., L. Suen, H. K. Brown, S. Bruhn, R. DeBlaquiere and S. E. Rzasa. 2001. Hierarchical Linear Models of Factors Associated with Public Participation Among Residents Living Near the US Army's Chemical Weapons Stockpile Sites. *Journal of Environmental Planning and Management* 44(1): 41–65.

Xu, J. 2005. Why Do Minorities Participate Less? The Effects of Immigration, Education, and Electoral Process on Asian American Voter Registration and Turnout. *Social Science Research* 34: 682–702.

Appendix A

Select relevant survey questions

Below are the substantive, verbatim questions on the survey that were used in this analysis. Those not listed here (in the interest of saving space) are the demographic questions. Words in ALL CAPITAL LETTERS were instructions to the interviewer, and were not read to the respondents.

22. Now, I'll read you a list of benefits associated with a well-running sewer system. For each, please tell me how important this benefit is to you. How important is . . . READ ITEM THEN READ RESPONSE OPTIONS

	Very important	Somewhat important	Not very important	Not at all important	NO OPINION/ DON'T KNOW	REFUSE
Less pollution in the bay and ocean	☐	☐	☐	☐	☐	☐
Better public health	☐	☐	☐	☐	☐	☐
Fewer fines paid to the Federal government	☐	☐	☐	☐	☐	☐
Convenient disposal of household sewage	☐	☐	☐	☐	☐	☐
Less frequent flooding of streets	☐	☐	☐	☐	☐	☐

30. Would you support a redistribution of sewage treatment so that the Southeast plant, the Oceanside plant near the zoo and the North Point plant would share the volume of sewage more equally?

Yes

No

Maybe

DON'T KNOW

REFUSE

32. Would you support a state-of-the-art upgrade to the Southeast sewage treatment plant that would reduce the size and visibility of the plant and reduce odor and other negative impacts in that neighbourhood?

Yes

No

Maybe

DON'T KNOW

REFUSE

34. Now I'll read you some specific ideas for improving the City's sewer system. For each, please tell me your level of support or opposition of it as a part of the City's Wastewater Master Plan. How about . . . .
READ ITEM THEN RESPONSE OPTIONS

	Definitely would support	Maybe would support	Probably would not support	Definitely would not support	DEPENDS/ DON'T KNOW	REFUSE
Having more plants, trees and permeable pavement on streets to allow stormwater flow into the ground	☐	☐	☐	☐	☐	☐

Building a pipeline that would discharge all treated into the ocean rather than the Bay	☐	☐	☐	☐	☐	☐
Recycling and treating water for no-drinking uses like landscaping and industry	☐	☐	☐	☐	☐	☐
Separating the sewer and storm drain systems so that stormwater would flow straight into the ocean and Bay without being treated, which would reduce the amount of sewage needing to be treated	☐	☐	☐	☐	☐	☐

35. As the SFPUC updates this master plan, it will consider social, environmental, and economic priorities. I'm going to read a list of priorities to be considered in developing the master plan. For each, please tell me how important this priority is to you. How about . . . . READ ITEM THEN RESPONSE OPTIONS

	Very important	Somewhat important	Not very important	Not at all important	NO OPINION/ DON'T KNOW	REFUSE
Promoting public awareness about the sewer system	☐	☐	☐	☐	☐	☐
Promoting public health and safety	☐	☐	☐	☐	☐	☐
Reducing impacts of the sewer system on neighbourhoods	☐	☐	☐	☐	☐	☐
Promoting equity or environmental justice	☐	☐	☐	☐	☐	☐
Managing future growth and demands on the system's capacity	☐	☐	☐	☐	☐	☐
Preparing for natural disasters such as earthquakes	☐	☐	☐	☐	☐	☐

(continued)

(continued)

	Very important	Somewhat important	Not very important	Not at all important	NO OPINION/ DON'T KNOW	REFUSE
Improving the reliability of the system	☐	☐	☐	☐	☐	☐
Using the latest technologies	☐	☐	☐	☐	☐	☐
Minimising costs	☐	☐	☐	☐	☐	☐
Minimising impacts on the Bay and ocean	☐	☐	☐	☐	☐	☐
Minimising the use of natural resources such as energy, chemicals, etc.	☐	☐	☐	☐	☐	☐

38. *The SFPUC is considering many ways of getting public input for the wastewater master plan. I am going to read to you a list of potential ways you could provide your input. Considering all the things you already do in your daily life – including obligations of family, work, school, etc. – how likely would you participate in each of the following events regarding the wastewater master planning process? How likely would you be to . . . . READ ITEM THEN RESPONSE OPTIONS*

	Very likely	Somewhat likely	Not very likely	Not at all likely	DON'T KNOW	REFUSE
Attend meetings in your neighbourhood	☐	☐	☐	☐	☐	☐
Attend meetings at City Hall	☐	☐	☐	☐	☐	☐
Read information sent to your home	☐	☐	☐	☐	☐	☐
Read emails sent to you	☐	☐	☐	☐	☐	☐
Read information on a website	☐	☐	☐	☐	☐	☐
Respond to a survey sent to your home	☐	☐	☐	☐	☐	☐
Respond to a survey online	☐	☐	☐	☐	☐	☐
Write letters to officials	☐	☐	☐	☐	☐	☐
Call officials	☐	☐	☐	☐	☐	☐
Educate your neighbours about the issues	☐	☐	☐	☐	☐	☐
Sign a petition	☐	☐	☐	☐	☐	☐

# 22

IMPROVING SOCIAL DEVELOPMENT IN BRAZIL THROUGH AN OPEN BUDGET PERSPECTIVE

Does collaborative stakeholder engagement matter?

Welles Abreu and Ricardo Gomes

Introduction

This chapter discusses the importance of external collaborative stakeholders as drivers of open budgets intended to assist social development. Its main purpose is to test whether external collaborative stakeholders are engaged in developing open budgets in order to affect better social development. The presence of a collaborative environment around external stakeholder influence and initiatives with open budgets could be a key element in facilitating social gains.

In this context, social development means an improvement in the individual quality of life and the welfare of society's members (Davis 2004). Governments that prioritise people's opinions in their decision-making processes should include them in the development process of socially progressive policies (Department for International Development 2006).

Governance theory proposes that multiple stakeholders need to be gathered in forums with public agencies in order to promote consensus-oriented decisions. According to Osborne (2006), this is the core of the pluralistic nature of institutional relationships between government and society. Hence, governance relates to the public administration decision-making process, which is based on institutions and procedures related to citizens' voice and public concerns (Bovaird 2005).

Such open budget discussion facilitates collaboration in public policy decision-making process, whatever the budgetary phase – drafting, approval, execution, or auditing (Ling and Roberts 2014). The definition of an open budget is the provision of societal and citizen access to public policy information and participation, with accountability as a key perspective (Khagram, Fung and De Renzio 2013). The foundations of open budgeting involve the disclosure of budgetary information as well as free access to government procedures by citizens, engagement of the community in public policy decisions, and holding public authorities accountable by enforcing budget controls (Jinguang and Xianyong 2011).

According to Emerson, Nabatchi and Balogh (2012), collaboration in the governance model happens in public policy decision-making processes based on budgetary actions that are transparent, participatory and accountable in their structural arrangements. In these government processes, external stakeholders with a collaborative attitude are likely to drive decisions about governance outcomes by including social commitment in the budgetary process (Department for International Development 2006).

Collaborative stakeholders influence the strategic management process (Keijzers 2003) by contributing to the improvement of the delivery of public products and social services (Svendsen 1998). Therefore, support from external collaborative stakeholders is likely to induce government actions for delivering social policies focused on responsiveness to the aims of the society (Gomes, Liddle and Gomes 2010).

This study uses structural equation modelling as a methodological tool to help test the complex links formed between external collaborative stakeholders, open budgets, and social development. The availability of budgetary resources moderates the governance process by constraining the capacity to meet social policy needs. Brazil has a great deal of relevant data available for municipalities (economic and geographic statistic surveys, and government agencies' databases). Moreover, the position of Brazil in the 2012 Open Budget Survey indicates it is an important and influential actor worldwide in such developments.

The chapter is structured as follows. First, in order to provide a better understanding of the case of Brazil, a brief history of its public administration, public service budgeting, and social development is presented. Some theories that support the thesis that social development is likely to be explained by these types of relationship between government and society are presented. The methodological aspects are presented in the next section, and the research design described. Results and discussions are then presented, where empirical evidence is gathered. In the conclusion, different aspects supporting the idea that the engagement of external collaborative stakeholders is a core element of the open budget approach for social development are recapitulated.

The Brazilian context

The recent institutional changes in public administration that were designed to implement the governance model are related to the introduction of open initiatives in budgetary processes to achieve better social policy results (Ferreira et al. 2016). In the following sections, a short historical account of Brazil is presented.

Brazilian public administration

Brazilian Public Administration is a complex institutional system that focuses on the governance model for government reforms at all levels: federal; state; and municipal (Abrucio 2005). However, less than a century ago, Brazil had a patrimonial model, based on privilege and private interests in the public policy processes (Bresser-Pereira 2009). Only in the 1930s did Brazil start reforms to reform such historic arrangements, with the purpose of establishing formal, impersonal, and meritocratic control over procedures, with a formal hierarchy acting in the public interest (Bresser-Pereira 1996).

In the 1990s, the Brazilian government introduced reforms based on the ideas underpinning new public management or NPM (Osborne 1994). These reforms concentrated on: (a) resource decentralisation – allocation to local levels; (b) administration; (c) decentralisation – empowerment; (d) reducing levels in the hierarchy; (e) management by results; and (f) administration focused on service to citizens. This process was steered by a Brazilian Master Plan, which was modelled upon the United Kingdom's state management reforms carried out by Margaret Thatcher (Bresser-Pereira 2010).

The Fiscal Responsibility Act of 2001 (Constitutional Law No. 101) is one result of this process, which, together with complementary institutional changes, culminated in Brazilian Budget Management Reform (Core 2004), which was significant new development in terms of public administration.

The enthusiasm for NPM did not last, in various of the adopting countries and in Brazil. In the 2000s, concerns about governance turned toward institutional changes focused on the advance of social democracy (Peci, Pieranti and Rodrigues 2008). According to Knopp (2011), Brazil is still in a consolidation process. It is following an international trend to focus on issues related to the creation of:

- more inclusive policy spaces, with transparency, participation, and accountability initiatives;
- setting a legitimate public policy agenda to build trust between government and society; and
- modifying government procedures to make the decision-making process more flexible and efficient.

The recent adoption of transparency, participation, and accountability initiatives in the public policy arena as part of an open budget approach is an attempt to strengthen democracy in order to promote social progress (Abreu and Gomes 2016; Ferreira et al. 2016). This has followed the new public governance wave when society received more attention from public managers and politicians in order to increase education and health quality, as well as to reduce corruption and to improve budgetary institutions and processes.

Brazilian public budgeting

The budgetary process is central to the formulation of a strategy for public policy results. The total budget commitment will depend on the costs of the alternatives chosen. This complex process of calculation takes into account several variables, and there is little theory that helps predict the consequences for social development (Davis, Dempster and Wildavsky 1966).

According to March (2009: 5), 'the most common and best-established elaboration of the pure theories of rational choice is that which recognizes uncertainty about future consequences of present actions'. Bounded rationality presupposes that budget decisions occur with a limited range of alternatives in the context of a stochastic process (Padgett 1980). Individuals want institutions to make their decisions logically (North, Wallis and Weingast 2009). This process is often complex, systematic and rationally limited, and aims to establish identities, finding rules for recognised situations (March 2009).

Social institutions play an important role in the organisation and application of budgetary rules to stimulate a collaborative environment. Social institutions encourage individual action by making available the content of identities and rules, supporting certain behaviours in identifiable situations. These institutional structures are not static, and may change in the face of external pressures, resulting in reforms (March 2009).

In Brazil, as Sanches (2007: 190) noted, the 1988 Federal Constitution introduced a number of significant institutional changes in the public budgeting process. It emphasises the obligation to prepare the following budgetary acts: PPA (medium-term planning, four years,), LOA (short-term planning, annual), and LDO (goals fiscal-term, annual). Brazil's Budgetary Acts are available on the Senate's website (see www12.senado.leg.br/orcamento).

The 2000 Brazilian Budgetary Reform was developed based on strong international influences – due to the financial crisis in the 1990s – with the purpose of giving governments more effective and efficient results, improving public policy delivery and reducing state costs (Core 2004). The changes to budgetary institutions from Decree 2829/1998 impacted all mentioned instruments (PPA, LOA and LDO), focusing on: (a) more flexibility in budgetary programming; (b) increased responsibility of programme managers for the delivery of public policy results; and (c) the establishment of multi-year fiscal goals focused on debt control.

Recently, Abreu and Gomes (2013) found evidence in Brazil of emancipatory budget processes, including parliamentary adjustment, public meetings, public policy councils, the influence of non-government organisations, citizen participation in the elaboration of PPA, priorities set by public policy specialists, citizens' budgets (documents that summarise the public budget for society), actions towards fiscal education, and data disclosure.

Brazilian social development

Social development concerns better delivery of social goods and services, as well as an increase in the capacity to generate jobs and redistribute national income for a better individual quality of life (Gentil and Michel 2009). On the road to social development, a budget strategy has inevitable social consequences (Abreu and Gomes 2010; Ferreira et al. 2016).

According to Ramos (1983: 149–150), 'There is notable progress, in the field of economic theory, if the analysis of the development progress occurs from a systematic strategic view' (translated by the authors). The budgetary allocation decision-making process must be associated with social development strategies, based on ethical conditions for the reduction of poverty as the preferred public policy consequence (Ramos 1946, 1981).

The budgetary strategy should take into account the risk analysis and plan reliability, in order to increase government capacity for public policy implementation (Siccú 2009). The fiscal policy must stimulate tax revenue, on a progressive basis, focused on social justice and equity, as well as building citizens' awareness (Abreu and Gomes 2010). Sicsú (2008) states that budgetary strategies are only effective if the government involves society. Therefore, the formulation of the budgetary strategy for Brazilian social development should not be a cabinet plan, but a joint process constructed with the society (Abreu and Gomes 2013).

According to Abreu and Gomes (2013), in order to achieve social development, the budgetary strategy should promote social inclusion, democratic representation, authentic dialogue, and collective knowledge. This strategy is aligned with the open budget approach.

According to the 2012 Open Budget Survey, Brazil leads on this process in Latin America in the, and its participation in the Open Government Partnership and in the Global Initiative of Fiscal Transparency recognise the Brazilian position as one of the most important countries in this field. As a result, the Brazilian government proposal to the United Nations General Assembly was adopted in 2012, that recognising transparency, participation, and accountability in fiscal policies can, (a) enhance financial stability, poverty reduction, equitable economic growth and the achievement of sustainable development; and (b) should be promoted in a manner that is consistent with diverse circumstances and national legislation (Abreu, Gomes and Alfinito 2015).

The *Human Development Report 2014* of the United Nations Development Programme (UNDP) highlighted recent social improvements in Brazil, including reduced racial disparities for Afro-Brazilian and mixed-race populations, by implementing affirmative action policies in education. Brazilian social progress suggests that the influence of civil society on people-friendly

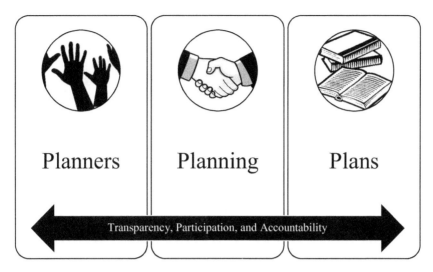

Figure 22.1 Brazilian budgetary governance model
Source: Authors

policies and outcomes is a key aspect of state and civil society interaction. The Brazilian open initiatives in budgetary processes are possible factors in social gains, by increasing participation in budgetary allocation, disclosing budgetary data, and strengthening spaces for social influence (UNDP 2014).

The profile of the public administrator in the governance model focuses on the process of decision-making in public policy, and not only on producing more and better quality using fewer resources. Brazil is recognised for its implementation of governance tools and its moves toward better governance, although there is still a long way to go (Peci, Pieranti and Rodrigues 2008; Knopp 2011). After changes in 2000, the Brazilian budgetary process followed a trend which seeks to increase the strategic dimension and integrate planners, plans, and planning (Figure 22.1). Recent developments advanced in the governance model promote transparency, participation, and accountability (Abreu and Gomes 2010).

Despite the relatively short time since the introduction of these changes, and cultural inertia, social gains associated with the current governance reforms can already be seen (Abreu and Gomes 2013). In order to continue development into a social democracy, it is important that non-government planners engage with the planning process even more to produce equitable plans (Knopp 2011; Abreu and Gomes 2013).

Non-government planners play a fundamental role in carrying out collaborative actions, given that the open budget process is related to the collective behaviour of strategic planners as a core component of social progress (Abreu and Gomes 2013; Ferreira et al. 2016). Brazil considers that the open budget approach is a possible strategy to obtain social gains, and there is an opportunity to study it in order to have a better understanding of the open budget consequences.

Our wider literature review presents a wider context for the open budget approach, and considers the literature on governance, stakeholders, and public budgets, to support the empirical examination of the Brazilian context.

The wider context: open budget knowledge

According to Bovaird (2005), governance results are brought about by democratic decision-making, open government processes, social inclusion, and equality. Good governance is associated with a better capacity to prevent conflicts, to meet human rights obligations, help business growth, and deliver essential public services to citizens to achieve social progress (Department for International Development 2006). In the governance model, multiple stakeholders gather in forums with public agencies to engage in consensus-oriented decisions (Ansell and Gash 2008).

The governance decision-making process is based on citizen engagement with collaborative involvement (Emerson et al. 2012). In this case, leadership and resources are crucial for setting, and maintaining the clarity of the rules, in order to build trust and support negotiations for better social development (Khagram, Fung and De Renzio 2013; Ansell and Gash 2008).

Social development is considered to be a result of governance (Ling and Roberts 2014; De Renzio and Wehner 2015). The UNDP uses the Human Development Index as a measure of social development (Noorbakhsh 1998), based on 'The expansion of people's freedoms to live long, healthy and creative lives' (Klugman 2010: 12).

The open budget approach and our hypotheses

The open budget approach relies on actions of transparency, participation, and accountability in a strategic manner, from planning and forecasting revenues and expenditures to executing public policies (Jinguang and Xianyong 2011). From direct democracy to indirect delegate models, the adoption of an open budget approach is subject to an ongoing debate about the people who should represent civil society (Mansuri and Rao 2004).

Budgetary transparency involves full disclosure of all relevant fiscal information in a timely and systematic manner (OECD 2002). Transparency means making information publicly available through institutions (Meijer 2013, 2009). Participatory budgeting gives otherwise marginalised and excluded people the right to have their voices heard and to influence public decision-making (Kasymova and Schachter 2014). Participation creates incentives to articulate and aggregate citizens' interests, providing linkages between the ruler and ruled, policymakers and citizens (Shah 2007; Fung and Wright 2003).

Budgetary accountability involves procedures for public hearings to investigate spending, public audits and an independent judiciary (Alt and Lowry 2010). Accountability is the responsiveness and responsibility exercised by state authorities during the period between political elections in democratic environments (Friis-Hansen and Cold-Ravnkilde 2013; Gaventa and McGee 2013).

Due to its complexity, accountability should be classified through both public and social approaches, which link with transparency and participation initiatives, respectively (Yilmaz, Beris and Serrano-Berthet 2010). This relationship gathers transparency, participation, and accountability in a mutually integrated and reinforced open budget framework toward social development (Ling and Roberts 2014; Khagram, Fung, and De Renzio 2013).

Hypothesis 1: More open budget actions stimulate gains in social development results.

De Renzio and Masud (2011) state that the Open Budget Index has a rigorous methodology, independence, and comparability, making it a useful addition to existing tools. Moreover, there is statistical evidence of a positive relationship between the Open Budget Index and the Human Development Index in resource-dependent countries (De Renzio, Gomez and Sheppard 2009).

Nevertheless, the Open Budget Index focuses on the transparency perspective. The development of a complete index for open budgeting remains a challenge. A measurement that gathers transparency, participation and accountability should be the key to identifying the level of open budget. According to Ling and Roberts (2014), an index for the open budget can be composed of selected survey items. The items included should relate to access to information, mechanisms of inclusion, and responsiveness and responsibility.

Budgetary resource

Budgeting means the allocation of scarce resources in the government decision-making process (Rubin 2009). The budget process happens stochastically in a bounded rationale, since decision-makers have limitations in studying possible alternatives (Padgett 1980).

The public budget is more than a document with words and figures that contain targets for government expenditures and justifies them. It is the translation of public policy priorities into financial resources (Davis, Dempster and Wildavsky 1966). According to Hyde (2002), the public budget is an instrument of management, development, control and allocation.

Traditionally, as Rubin (2009: 17) states: 'One of the major characteristics of public budgeting is that those who pay the bills are not the ones who make the decisions on how the money is to be spent'. Although budget-makers never have enough revenue to meet the requests of all spending agencies, the budget 'represents a judgment upon how scarce means should be allocated to bring the maximum return in social utility' (Key 1940: 1138).

As a powerful instrument for the implementation of democracy, the public budget needs to broadly reflect citizens' preferences to influence the economy and to focus on social outcomes (Foster and Fozzard 2000). On the other hand, the availability of budgetary resources determines the limits within which the government will execute public policies (Hughes 2003). According to Emerson et al. (2012), resources are part of the governance model as elements of joint action capability. Hence, the availability of budgetary resources moderates the governance process by the constraints on the budget's capacity to promote social progress.

Hypothesis 2: The availability of more budgetary resources provides for greater delivery of social development.

The literature provides some indexes for measuring the level of budgetary resources. These are almost all related to public expenditures and per capita revenues. Elson and Cagatay (2000: 1351) argue that 'When restrictive macroeconomic policies are needed, it is important to adjust the composition of fiscal expenditure and revenue so as to protect the people who are worst off.'

However, the association between budgetary resources and social development is only recently begun to be examined in specific empirical studies. Therefore, there is a window of opportunity to test new theories and check the link between the traditional budgetary view (focused on resource availability) and the recent open budget approach.

Collaborative stakeholders

A stakeholder can be any organisation, group or individual (Freeman 1984). Stakeholders are those who have power, urgency, and legitimacy, based on demands and expectations, that can affect or be affected (Mitchell, Agle and Wood 1997). The potential for stakeholder cooperation is particularly relevant since it can facilitate collaborative efforts between an organisation and its stakeholders, which can result in better management performance (Savage et al. 1991).

According to Koontz (2005: 460), 'Collaboration is characterised by diverse stakeholders working together to resolve a conflict or develop and advance a shared vision'. Stakeholders that are more dependent on a given organisation usually demonstrate greater commitment to cooperation (Freeman 1984). Unfortunately, the importance of stakeholder cooperation is commonly ignored because the analysis requires a sophisticated understanding of the types and magnitudes of stakeholder influence (Gomes and Gomes 2008).

Emerson et al. (2012: 14) propose that 'quality interaction through principled engagement will help foster trust, mutual understanding, internal legitimacy, and shared commitment, thereby generating and sustaining shared motivation'. The relationships of collaborative stakeholder are based on public and organisational values, by which collective social rules support shared gains (Freeman 1984).

The participation of external collaborative stakeholders can influence government actions to help deliver social policies (Gomes, Liddle and Gomes 2010). For instance, external collaborative stakeholder support for addressing health problems in South Africa influenced the relaxation of intellectual property protection for HIV/AIDS medications in 2003 (Doh and Guay 2006).

External collaborative stakeholders typically use strategies to promote government actions in a communicative manner with a collective, collaborative and cooperative environment (Khagram and Ali 2008). Poverty reduction in social development processes is focused on collaboration among various stakeholders (Bowen 2005).

The influence of community cooperation on social development represents a collective endeavour toward social change, whereby external collaborative stakeholders lead actions that directly address social needs (Bowen 2005; Khagram and Ali 2008). Therefore, the literature suggests that social development relates to the open budget, the budgetary resources, and external collaborative stakeholders.

Hypothesis 3: More external collaborative stakeholders' influence promotes better social development outcomes.

Collaborative stakeholders act in a strategic manner focused on collective and cooperative causes, based on community values (Svendsen 1998). The coordination of external collaborative stakeholders' influence is concentrated on collective interests (strategies and habits), as well as on social agreements, conventions, and regulations (Keijzers 2003). The engagement of external collaborative stakeholders ought to facilitate communication about potential influence on government decision-making processes.

Hence, the open budget approach suggests that external stakeholders who act collaboratively push the actions of open budgeting toward social commitment (Khagram, Fung and De Renzio 2013). A Korean case study suggested that external stakeholders (of the Citizens Coalition for Economic Justice) who acted in a strongly collaborative environment drove transparency, participation, and accountability initiatives in order to stimulate social policy debate in public forums (You and Lee 2013).

Hypothesis 4: An increase in the external collaborative stakeholders' influence has a positive impact on open budget actions.

A collaborative stakeholder can act by assessing the political inducements for relevant interest groups in terms of public perceptions of legitimacy (Mitchell, Agle and Wood 1997). In this process, the resource and lobbying strategies of external collaborative stakeholders turn toward collective issues related to public interests from a budgetary perspective (Doh and Guay 2006). For example, a social fund is an institution typically set up as an autonomous agency of a national government that involves external collaborative stakeholders, through which government agencies create social mechanisms to channel budgetary resources to meet social demands (De Haan, Holland and Kanji 2002). The engagement of external collaborative stakeholders increases the availability of budget resources to finance social projects designed to improve living standards and help empower vulnerable and poor populations.

Although the literature suggests that external collaborative stakeholders also act by inducing an increase in the budgetary resource, further empirical investigations are needed to check the link between collaborative stakeholders and budgetary resources. Collective action in community settings is, by itself, a relevant opportunity to develop knowledge to make available the resources required in the government decision-making processes (Bowen 2005).

Hypothesis 5: An increase in the external collaborative stakeholders' influence positively affects the availability of budgetary resources.

Gomes and Gomes (2008: 265) suggest that a starting point that can help in stakeholder measurement is to recognise that stakeholders can be either people (or categories of people) or organisations. Stakeholder influence should be focused on the identification of who has the power and interest in government decision-making processes (Gomes, Liddle and Gomes 2010). However, the literature is not clear on how to measure the level of external collaborative stakeholder involvement, although some theoretical considerations support its measurement.

Non-governmental organisations are identified as entities that mobilise communities to influence government's social actions (Bowen 2005). Gomes et al. (2010) state that external collaborative stakeholders should join together in a non-governmental organisation, to influence public policies, including the possibility of receiving budgetary transfers.

According to Doh and Guay (2006), the variation among non-governmental organisations in Europe and the USA shows different levels of collaborative influence in these two regions. Therefore, the number of non-governmental organisations could be a proxy to determine the level of external collaborative stakeholder engagement in a region, always in relation to the overall population, to allow for the limited capacity of non-governmental organisations to mobilise people.

Based on our literature review, the logical deductions from the collaborative budget model are:

- External collaborative stakeholders are non-government and government actors working for collaborative and social budgetary commitments.
- Open budget involves the disclosure of budgetary information, free access by citizens to government, engagement of budgetary stakeholders, giving society a voice to support policy decisions, answerability of public authorities, and enforceable social budget controls.
- Budgetary resources are the available resources that guide the levels of expenditure.
- Social development means governance outcomes in a cooperative approach for the improvement of quality life and the welfare state.

Empirical considerations

To check the theoretical hypotheses, this study is based on an objectivist perspective, using a quantitative strategy to check elements that may be involved in the open budget process. In line with Shadish et al. (2002), we use an ex-post-facto method formulated from complex links between the elements identified above in the literature.

Following Williams, Vandenberg and Edwards (2009), we argue that the use of structural equation modelling can support an expansion of the literature. Structural equation modelling and goodness-of-fit statistics help to test the theoretical suggestions related to the open budget approach. Furthermore, we tested the model's stability, the effects of variables, and the power of endogenous variables to predict the exogenous variable, as well as observing the covariance and residual matrices.

We collected data from official governmental surveys and financial databases, as well as from the UNDP index. In the following section, we describe each of the variables.

Exogenous variable

Social development

The UNDP formulates the Human Development Index (HDI) as a proxy for social development. HDI has three aspects (income, longevity, and education), which cover points theoretically considered for the definition of social development. For Brazil, this index is based on national census data consolidated at the municipal level. The data are available on the UNDP website (available at www.undp.org/content/brazil/pt/home.html/).

Endogenous variables

MUNIC open budget index

The Brazilian Institute of Geography and Statistics conducts a yearly survey to collect municipal data on public administration and policies called MUNIC. The selection of the MUNIC survey items had the purpose of determining the open budget level and was based on the identification of transparency or participation actions, which linked with accountability view. In this process, we identified 20 items related to government communication initiatives to provide transparency and 20 items associated with citizen engagement to promote participation (see Appendix). Therefore, the composition of this innovatory index considers that each of the 40 selected items has the same weight to gauge the open budget level. The data are available on the Brazilian Institute of Geography and Statistics website (ww2.ibge.gov.br/english).

External collaborative stakeholders

The Brazilian Institute of Geography and Statistics also carries out a municipal survey to collect data on non-governmental organisations. We used the per capita number of non-governmental organisations in a municipality as a proxy for the external collaborative stakeholder power to influence social development results, taking into account the importance of the population in increasing effect. In this sense, the density of non-governmental organisations indicates the influence level of external collaborative stakeholders in order to mobilise people over a public policy decision-making process.

Budgetary resource

The Brazilian National Treasury consolidates municipal accounts in a database. We used per capita municipal public expenditure as a proxy for the budgetary resource. In this case, as in the case of external collaborative stakeholders, we scale this to the population. The data are available on the Brazilian National Treasury website (www.tesouro.fazenda.gov.br).

Most of the data pertain to 2010, so we decided to adopt a cross-sectional analysis because of the broad sample of Brazilian municipalities – 96.4% of municipalities and 96.2% of the

Table 22.1 Sample of Brazilian municipalities in numbers

Geographic region	Number of municipalities	Region population	Municipality population		
			Mean	Minimum	Maximum
Northeastern	1,706	53,011,607	31,074	1,253	2,675,656
Southeastern	1,653	78,242,310	47,334	805	11,253,503
Southern	1,158	27,538,451	23,781	1,216	1,751,907
Middle-western	434	10,934,484	25,195	1,020	1,302,001
Northern	413	13,721,741	33,225	1,037	1,802,014
Sum	**5,364**	**183,448,593**			

Source: Brazilian Institute of Geography and Statistics

population (Table 22.1). We used the 2009 data from the MUNIC survey, because of the prioritisation of the national census in 2010 precluded conducting the MUNIC survey that year.

We used the 2010 national census data to obtain the municipal populations, to operationalise the per capita indexes. All data are in a 0–1 standard scale. We used the STATA 13 software for all statistical tests. Figure 22.2 depicts the tested structural equation modelling. The variables are in boxes and arrows indicate their relationships. Each of the hypotheses was tested in isolation and from an integrated perspective, and the compound of the five hypotheses represents the structural equation modelling.

Finally, as Mikut and Reischl (2011) suggest, we used comparative analyses with the support of a data mining tool (Rapidminer software) to help test the results. Following the suggestions of Monteiro (1995), we used the regional classification of Brazilian Institute of Geography and Statistics to aggregate the municipalities into two groups: the equatorial (northern and northeastern regions); and the tropical (southern, south-eastern and middle-western regions).

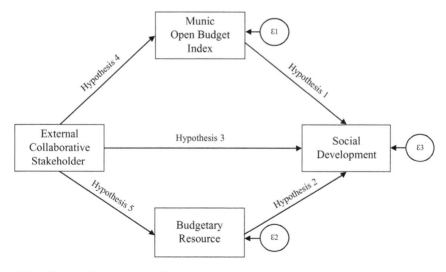

Figure 22.2 Structural equation modelling
Source: Authors

Results

Based on the literature review, we examined the relationship among external collaborative stakeholders, MUNIC open budget index, budgetary resources, and social development. These variables are combined in three structural equations. The data of this cross-sectional study come from 5,364 (96%) of the 5,566 Brazilian municipalities in 2010. Social development is the exogenous variable, and external collaborative stakeholders, MUNIC open budget index, and budgetary resources are the endogenous variables. Table 22.2 reports the summary of the statistical results of structural equation modelling.

We used the maximum likelihood estimation method. The three structural equations have coefficients and constants which are statistically significant at the $p < 0.001$ level. The equations explain 30%, 2% and 10%, and of social development in terms of external collaborative stakeholder involvement, MUNIC open budget index, and budgetary resources, respectively. The overall explanation is 15%. Therefore, all the structural equations make a relevant contribution to explaining social development.

The result of the Chi-squared test (model v. saturated) is 2.55 (p-value $= 0.1103$), meaning that the difference between the covariance matrices is not statically significant at the 0.05 level. Moreover, all residuals of covariance and observed variables are less than 0.001, and the structural equation modelling satisfies the stability condition (stability index $= 0$). Hence, according to the recommendations of Hair et al. (2006), these tests suggest sufficient goodness of fit.

Figure 22.3 presents the estimated model with the coefficients and errors, which we call the collaborative budget model. The relationships between the variables are those that are represented by the theoretical hypotheses in Figure 22.2.

Table 22.2 Structural equation modelling: statistical summary results

Social development (SD)	Structural equations		
	1st CS; OB; BR => SD	2nd CS => OB	3rd CS => BR
Intercept	0.5204363 ***	0.3956755 ***	0.1305619 ***
	(0.0030983)	(0.0028387)	(0.0016253)
External collaborative stakeholders (CS)	0.166952 ***	0.226319 ***	0.3222374 ***
	(0.0111584)	(0.0230644)	(0.0132056)
MUNIC open budget index (OB)	0.2164679 ***		
	(0.0062236)		
Budgetary resource (BR)	0.2087836 ***		
	(0.0108699)		
R-Squared	0.3006103	0.0176337	0.0999146
Fitted	0.0050924	0.0174581	0.0062463
Variance predicted	0.0015308	0.0003079	0.0006241
Residual	0.0035616	0.0171503	0.0056222
N	5364		
Overall R-Squared	0.149655		
Chi² (test of model v. saturated)	2.55		
Prob > Chi²	0.1103		

Significance levels: *$p < 0.05$; **$p < 0.01$; ***$p < 0.001$

Source: Authors

Improving social development in Brazil

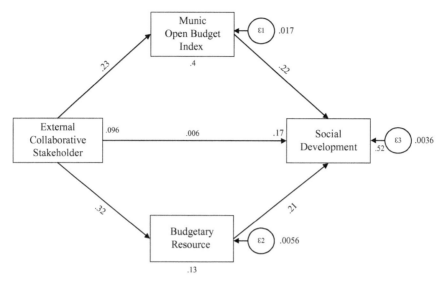

Figure 22.3 Estimated structural equation modelling: the collaborative budget model
Source: Authors

From the analysis of the levels of significance of the coefficients, we can infer that the five theoretical hypotheses are confirmed by the empirical results of the three structural equations employed in the tests. In other words, MUNIC open budget index, external collaborative stakeholders, and budgetary resources relate to social development, and external collaborative stakeholders relate to an open budget and budgetary resources. In combination, these results produce the model.

Table 22.3 shows the direct, indirect and total effects of external collaborative stakeholders, MUNIC open budget index, and budgetary resources on social development. Adding direct and indirect effects of the external collaborative stakeholders' variable, we have a coefficient of 0.28 and that means: adding one unity in this variable is likely to increase social development in nearly 30% of instances. The effect sizes in the model help to identify which independent variable has the strongest effect on the exogenous variable.

The empirical evidence indicates that the MUNIC open budget index has the strongest direct effect on social development, followed by budgetary resources and external collaborative

Table 22.3 Direct, indirect and total effects of the structural equation modelling

Variables of the structural equations	Effects on social development		
	Direct	Indirect	Total
External collaborative stakeholder	0.166952 ***	0.1162687 ***	0.2832207 ***
	(0.0111584)	(0.006824)	(0.0119583)
MUNIC open budget index	0.2164679 ***		0.2164679 ***
	(0.0062236)		(0.0062236)
Budgetary resource	0.2087836 ***		0.2087836 ***
	(0.0108699)		(0.0108699)

Significance levels: $*p < 0.05$; $**p < 0.01$; $***p < 0.001$

Source: Authors

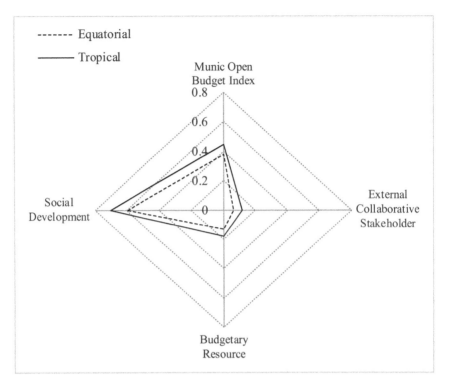

Figure 22.4 Municipal open budget means
Source: Authors

stakeholders. However, considering the indirect effect of external collaborative stakeholders, this ranking changes considerably, since external collaborative stakeholders move into the first position, followed by MUNIC open budget index and budgetary resources.

In Figure 22.4 we present comparative results for aggregations of Brazilian municipalities in equatorial (northern and north-eastern regions) and tropical (middle-western, south-eastern, and southern regions) groups. It shows the means of MUNIC open budget index, external collaborative stakeholders, budgetary resources, and social development for both groups. According to Abreu, Gomes and Alfinito (2015), we should expect higher social development in the tropical group than in the equatorial group.

However, the fact is that this phenomenon (higher mean in the tropical group than the equatorial group) occurs for all the independent variables (MUNIC open budget index, external collaborative stakeholders, and budgetary resources), and the lines for the two groups do not intersect in Figure 22.4. The variation of these means is directly related, which agrees with the results of structural equation modelling.

Conclusion

Poor social conditions continue to be a problem throughout the world, and point to the need to study the determining factors in achieving better social development. This chapter contributes to this field by testing the consequences for social development by applying statistical tests from a theoretical framework, which we call the collaborative budget model of public sector governance.

The main contributions of this study are to extend the governance literature focused on collaborative citizen engagement:

- social development is promoted by open budget, external collaborative stakeholders, and budgetary resources; and
- external collaborative stakeholders have a greater overall effect on social development than open budget and budgetary resources.

Not only are an open budget and budgetary resources crucial to explaining social development, but also the engagement of external collaborative stakeholders can be regarded as an innovative element of the open budget approach. Therefore, collaborative participation assumes great importance in the literature, due to its ability to produce direct and indirect effects on social development. Finally, budgetary resources contribute to the model, ensuring that all variables are significant and the equations are relevant.

The comparative tests of the means of variables indicate that the variation of the open budget, external collaborative stakeholders, budgetary resources, and social development are directly related. According to the hypotheses, the variation in collaborative engagement is likely to affect the other variables. Hence, a concentrated effort to increase external collaborative stakeholder participation might be a strategic method to improve not only social development but also a greater measure of openness in budgeting and budgetary resources.

The collaborative budget model is based on cooperative processes. Shepsle and Bonchek (1996) state that social results become more similar over time, due to the elimination of inconsistencies in a collective environment. The external collaborative stakeholder is associated with the collective behaviour of non-government organisations, which should produce gains in leadership performance in order to promote social progress.

However, stakeholder conflict is typically a problem, which could result in a condition described as 'the tragedy of the commons'. Such conflicts can arise because of different identities, insatiable desires, and competitions for primacy among stakeholders (Hardin 1968: 1243). In this process, it is very important to consider democracy-strengthening to build social commitment and remove stakeholder conflicts. In this context, inclusive initiatives in the civic community based on citizen engagement should activate society with equity and opportunities for trust and cooperation with social policy.

We can therefore answer the question of our chapter title: does collaborative stakeholder engagement matter? We conclude that creating bridges for citizens' participation in decision-making is likely to influence social development in a great deal. External stakeholders influence open budget directly and indirectly. By influencing the other elements of the equation and influencing the way local government deals with social development, one increase of one unity in the stakeholder influence is able to increase social development in nearly 30% (see Table 22.3). That means, it is a good investment of resources to promote ways for making stakeholder influences come through.

With that intention, the Brazilian Government adopted a new act to stimulate citizen engagement from non-government organisations in order to promote social public policies. Published in 2014, the law No. 13.019 (MROSC) established forms of partnership between government agencies and non-government organisations, to form a mutually cooperative regime to execute public policies with reciprocal interests. This new Brazilian institutional initiative is based on the premise of increasing citizen engagement, based on transparency, participation, and accountability. In the coming years, a broad range of panel-data will be produced and create an opportunity for a panel-data study to check whether the institutional changes brought about by the MROSC result in better social development for Brazil.

Altogether, the open budget approach remains a fruitful field for research, needing further investigation. For instance, although this study highlights the importance of the external collaborative stakeholders in order to achieve social development, the understanding of how nongovernment organisations act in collaboration remains unclear. We do consider that the critical challenge of reducing global poverty can be aided by citizen engagement in the public policy decision-making process.

References

Abreu, Welles Matias, and Ricardo Correa Gomes. 2016. Do Open Budget Institutional Changes Improve Social Development? *Contabilidade, Gestão e Governança* 19(3): 422–439.

Abreu, Welles Matias, and Ricardo Corrêa Gomes. 2010. Public Budget: Analysis of the Strategies' Formulation Under the Perspective of the Emancipatory and Developmentist Planning. *Revista do Serviço Público* 61(3): 269–286.

Abreu, Welles Matias, and Ricardo Corrêa Gomes. 2013. The Brazilian Public Budget and the Emancipatory Perspective: Is There Any Empirical Evidence supporting this approach? *Revista de Administração Pública* 47(2): 515–540.

Abreu, Welles Matias, Ricardo Corrêa Gomes, and Solange Alfinito. 2015. Can Fiscal Transparency Explain Social Development in Brazilian States? *Revista Sociedade, Contabilidade e Gestão* 10(2): 54–69.

Abrucio, Fernando Luiz. 2005. Reforma do Estado no federalismo brasileiro: a situação das administrações públicas estaduais. *Revista de Administração Pública* 39(2): 401–422.

Alt, James E, and Robert C Lowry. 2010. Transparency and Accountability: Empirical Results for U.S. States. *Journal of Theoretical Politics* 22(4): 379–406.

Ansell, Chris, and Alison Gash. 2008. Collaborative Governance in Theory and Practice. *Journal of Public Administration Research and Theory* 18(4): 543–571.

Bovaird, Tony. 2005. Public Governance: Balancing Stakeholder Power in a Network Society. *International Review of Administrative Sciences* 71(2): 217–228.

Bowen, Glenn A. 2005. Local-Level Stakeholder Collaboration: A Substantive Theory of Community-Driven Development. *Community Development* 36(2): 73–88.

Bresser-Pereira, Luiz Carlos. 1996. Da Administração Pública Burocrática à Gerencial. *Revista do Serviço Público* 47: 7–40.

Bresser-Pereira, Luiz Carlos. 2009. Nação, Sociedade Civil, Estado e Estado-Nação: Uma Perspectiva Histórica. *Textos para Discussão* 189: 1–23.

Bresser-Pereira, Luiz Carlos. 2010. Democracia, estado social e reforma gerencial. *Revista de Administração de Empresas* 50(1): 112–116.

Core, Fabiano Garcia. 2004. Reformas orçamentárias no Brasil: uma trajetória de tradição e formalismo na alocação dos recursos públicos, Trabalho apresentado ao IX Congreso Internacional Del CLAD sobre la Reforma del Estado y de la Administración Pública, Madrid, Spain.

Davis, Gloria. 2004. *A History of the Social Development Network in The World Bank, 1973–2003.* Washington, DC: World Bank.

Davis, Otto A, Michael Alan Howarth Dempster, and Aaron Wildavsky. 1966. A Theory of the Budgetary Process. *The American Political Science Review* LX(8): 529–547.

De Haan, Arjan, Jeremy Holland, and Nazneen Kanji. 2002. Social Funds: An Effective Instrument to Support Local Action for Poverty Reduction? *Journal of International Development* 14(5): 643.

De Renzio, Paolo, Pamela Gomez, and James Sheppard. 2009. Budget Transparency and Development in Resource-Dependent Countries. *International Social Science Journal* 57(1): 57–69.

De Renzio, Paolo, and Harika Masud. 2011. Measuring and Promoting Budget Transparency: The Open Budget Index as a Research and Advocacy Tool. *Governance* 24(3): 607–616.

De Renzio, Paolo, and Joachim Wehner. 2015. *The Impacts of Fiscal Openness: A Review of the Evidence.* Retrieved from www.internationalbudget.org/publications/the-impacts-of-fiscal-openness-a-review-of-the-evidence.

Department for International Development. 2006. Governance, Development and Democratic Politics. In *DFID's Work in Building More Effective States.* London: Department for International Development.

Doh, Jonathan P, and Terrence R Guay. 2006. Corporate Social Responsibility, Public Policy, and NGO Activism in Europe and the United States: An Institutional-Stakeholder Perspective. *Journal of Management Studies* 43(1): 47–73.

Elson, Diane, and Nilufer Cagatay. 2000. The Social Content of Macroeconomic Policies. *World Development* 28(7): 1347–1364.

Emerson, Kirk, Tina Nabatchi, and Stephen Balogh. 2012. An Integrative Framework for Collaborative Governance. *Journal of Public Administration Research and Theory* 22(1): 1–29.

Ferreira, Marco Aurélio Marques, Anderson de Oliveira Reis, Gislaine Aparecida Santana Sediyama, and Ambrozina de Abreu Pereira Silva. 2016. Integration of Planning and Budgeting at the State Level of Public Administration: the Case of Minas Gerais. *Contabilidade, Gestão e Governança* 19(1): 3–22.

Foster, Mick, and Adrian Fozzard. 2000. *Aid and Public Expenditure: A Guide*. London: Overseas Development Institute London.

Freeman, R Edward. 1984. *Strategic Management: A Stakeholder Approach*. Boston, MA: Pitman.

Friis-Hansen, Esbern, and Signe Marie Cold-Ravnkilde. 2013. *Social Accountability Mechanisms and Access to Public Service Delivery in Rural Africa*. Copenhagen: DIIS Reports, Danish Institute for International Studies.

Fung, Archon, and Erik Olin Wright. 2003. *Deepening Democracy: Institutional Innovations in Empowered Participatory Governance*, vol. 4. London: Verso.

Gaventa, John, and Rosemary McGee. 2013. The Impact of Transparency and Accountability Initiatives. *Development Policy Review* 31(s1): s3–s28.

Gentil, Denise Lobato, and Renaut Michel. 2009. Estratégia de Desenvolvimento e Intervenção Fiscal do Estado. In João Sicsú and Armando Castelar (eds), *Sociedade e Economia: Estratégias de Crescimento e Desenvolvimento*, 131–142. Brasília: IPEA.

Gomes, Ricardo Corrêa, and Luciana de Oliveira Miranda Gomes. 2008. Who is Supposed to Be Regarded as a Stakeholder for Public Organizations in Developing Countries? *Public Management Review* 10(2): 263–275.

Gomes, Ricardo Corrêa, Joyce Liddle, and Luciana Oliveira Miranda Gomes. 2010. A Five-Sided Model of Stakeholder Influence: A Cross-National Analysis of Decision Making in Local Government. *Public Management Review* 12(5): 701–724.

Hair, Joseph F, William C Black, Barry J Babin, Rolph E Anderson, and Ronald L Tatham. 2006. *Multivariate Data Analysis*, vol. 6. Upper Saddle River, NJ: Pearson Prentice Hall.

Hardin, Garrett. 1968. The Tragedy of the Commons. *Science* 162(3859): 1243–1248.

Hughes, Owen. 2003. *Public Management and Administration: An Introduction*: Basingstoke: Palgrave Macmillan.

Hyde, Albert C. 2002. *Government Budgeting: Theory, Process, and Politics*: Belmont, CA: Wadsworth.

Jinguang, Hu, and Zhang Xianyong. 2011. On the Value and Path of Open Budget. *Nankai Journal (Philosophy, Literature and Social Science Edition)* 2: 011.

Kasymova, Jyldyz T, and Hindy Lauer Schachter. 2014. Bringing Participatory Tools to a Different Level. *Public Performance and Management Review* 37(3): 441–464.

Keijzers, Gerard. 2003. Creating Sustainable Directions: Evolving Stakeholder Approach in Seven Multinationals. *The Journal of Corporate Citizenship* 10: 79–89.

Key, Vladimer O. 1940. The Lack of a Budgetary Theory. *American Political Science Review* 34(6): 1137–1144.

Khagram, Sanjeev, and Salim Ali. 2008. Transnational Transformations: From Government-Centric Interstate Regimes to Cross-Sectoral Multi-Level Networks of Global Governance? In Jacob Lark, Ken Conca and Matthias Finger (eds), *Globalization and Environmental Governance: Toward a New Political Economy of Sustainability*, 132–160. London: Routledge.

Khagram, Sanjeev, Archon Fung, and Paolo De Renzio. 2013. *Open Budgets: The Political Economy Of Transparency, Participation, and Accountability*. Washington, DC: Brookings Institution Press.

Klugman, Jeni. 2010. *Human Development Report 2010: The Real Wealth of Nations: Pathways to Human Development*. Basingstoke: Palgrave Macmillan.

Knopp, Glauco. 2011. Governança social, território e desenvolvimento. *Revista Perspectivas em Políticas Públicas* 4(8): 53–74.

Koontz, Tomas M. 2005. We Finished the Plan, So Now What? Impacts of Collaborative Stakeholder Participation on Land Use Policy. *Policy Studies Journal* 33(3): 459–481.

Ling, Cristina, and Dawn K Roberts. 2014. *Evidence of Development Impact from Institutional Change: A Review of the Evidence on Open Budgeting*. World Bank Policy Research Working Paper. Washington, DC: World Bank.

Mansuri, Ghazala, and Vijayendra Rao. 2004. Community-Based and -Driven Development: A Critical Review. *The World Bank Research Observer* 19(1): 1–39.

March, James G. 2009. *Primer on Decision Making: How Decisions Happen*. São Paulo: Leopardo.
Meijer, Albert. 2009. Understanding Modern Transparency. *International Review of Administrative Sciences* 75(2): 255–269.
Meijer, Albert. 2013. Understanding the Complex Dynamics of Transparency. *Public Administration Review* 73(3): 429–439.
Mikut, Ralf, and Markus Reischl. 2011. Data Mining Tools. *Wiley Interdisciplinary Reviews: Data Mining and Knowledge Discovery* 1(5): 431–443.
Mitchell, Ronald K, Bradley R Agle, and Donna J Wood. 1997. Toward a Theory of Stakeholder Identification and Salience: Defining the Principle of Who and What Really Counts. *Academy of Management Review* 22(4): 853–886.
Monteiro, Carlos Augusto. 1995. A dimensão da pobreza, da fome e da desnutrição no Brasil. *Estudos Avançados* 9(24): 195–207.
Noorbakhsh, Farhad. 1998. A Modified Human Development Index. *World Development* 26(3): 517–528.
North, Douglass, John Wallis, and Barry Weingast. 2009. *Violence and Social Orders*. Cambridge: Cambridge University Press.
OECD. 2002. *OECD Best Practices for Budget Transparency*. Paris: OECD.
Osborne, David. 1994. *Reinventando o Governo*. Brasília: MH Comunicação.
Osborne, Stephen P. 2006. The New Public Governance? *Public Management Review* 8(3): 377–387.
Padgett, John. 1980. Bounded Rationality in Budgetary Research. *American Political Science Review* 74: 354–372.
Peci, Alketa, Octavio Penna Pieranti, and Silvia Rodrigues. 2008. Governança e New Public Management: convergências e contradições no contexto brasileiro. *Organizações & Sociedade* 15(46): 39–55.
Ramos, Alberto Guerreiro. 1946. Administração e Política à Luz da Sociologia. *Revista do Serviço Público* 3: 5–11.
Ramos, Alberto Guerreiro. 1981. *A Nova Ciência das Organizações: Uma Reconceituação da Riqueza das Nações*. Rio de Janeiro: Fundação Getúlio Vargas.
Ramos, Alberto Guerreiro. 1983. *Administração e Contexto Brasileiro: Esboço de Uma Teoria Geral da Administração*. Rio de Janeiro: Fundação Getúlio Vargas.
Rubin, Irene S. 2009. *The Politics of Public Budgeting: Getting and Spending, Borrowing and Balancing*: Chicago, IL: CQ Press.
Sanches, Osvaldo Maldonado. 2007. O Cliclo Orçamentário: Uma Reavaliação à Luz da Constituição de 1988. In James Giacomoni and José Luiz Pagnussat (eds), *Planejamento e Orçamento Governamental*, 187–217. Brasilia: ENAP.
Savage, Grant T, Timothy W Nix, Carlton J Whitehead, and John D Blair. 1991. Strategies for Assessing and Managing Organizational Stakeholders. *Academy of Management Executive* 5(2): 61–75.
Shadish, W R, T D Cook, and D T Campbell. 2002. *Experimental and Quasi-Experimental Designs for Generalized Causal Inference*. New York: Houghton Mifflin.
Shah, Anwar. 2007. *Participatory Budgeting*. Public Sector, Governance and Accountability Series. Washington, DC: World Bank.
Shepsle, Kenneth, and Mark Bonchek. 1996. *Analyzing Politics*. New York: W W Norton.
Siccú, João. 2009. A Construção de Uma Estratégia de Desenvolvimento. In João Sicsú and Armando Castelar (eds), *Sociedade e Economia: Estratégias de Crescimento e Desenvolvimento*, 19–28. Brasília: IPEA.
Sicsú, João. 2008. Planejamento Estratégico do Desenvolvimento e as Políticas Macroeconômicas. *Texto para Discussão* 1346: 7–25.
Svendsen, Ann. 1998. *The Stakeholder Strategy: Profiting from Collaborative Business Relationships*. San Francisco, CA: Berrett-Koehler.
UNDP. 2014. *Human Development Report*. Retrieved from www.br.undp.org/content/brazil/pt/home/library/relatorios-de-desenvolvimento-humano/relatorio-do-desenvolvimento-humano-200013.
Williams, Larry, Robert Vandenberg, and J R Edwards. 2009. Structural Equations Modeling in Management Research: A Guide for Improved Analysis. *The Academy of Management Annals* 3(1): 543–604.
Yilmaz, Serdar, Yakup Beris, and Rodrigo Serrano-Berthet. 2010. Linking Local Government Discretion and Accountability in Decentralization. *Development Policy Review* 28(3): 259–293.
You, Jong-sung, and Wonhee Lee. 2013. A Mutually Reinforcing Loop: Budget Transparency and Participation in South Korea. In *Open Budgets: The Political Economy of Transparency, Participation, and Accountability*, 105–129. Washington, DC: Brookings Institution Press,

Appendix

Items that comprise the new Brazilian Municipality OB index

Code	Description
A130	Communication to general public: mail
A132	Communication to general public newspapers
A133	Communication to general public: internet
A134	Communication to general public: telephone
A135	Communication to general public: ombuds offices
A145	Communication by internet (egov initiative): newsletter
A146	Communication by the internet (egov initiative): document public access
A147	Communication by the internet (egov initiative): procurement
A148	Communication by the internet (egov initiative): ombuds offices
A149	Communication by the internet (egov initiative): electronic trading
A150	Communication by the internet (egov initiative): electronic processes
A151	Communication by the internet (egov initiative): electronic licensing
A152	Communication by the internet (egov initiative): government journals, legislation, and finance
A153	Communication by the internet (egov initiative): civil servant selection
A154	Communication by the internet (egov initiative): school enrolment
A155	Communication by the internet (egov initiative): certificate issuance
A156	Communication by the internet (egov initiative): medical appointment scheduling
A158	Communication by the internet (egov initiative): friendly disability
A159	Communication by the internet (egov initiative): suburbs with free public access points
A160	Communication by the internet (egov initiative): government agencies with free access points
A197	Education policy: participative management in schools
A211	Education policy: existence of a council
A212	Education policy: the council has community participation
A214	Education policy: the council is advisory
A215	Education policy: the council is deliberative
A216	Education policy: the council is normative
A217	Education policy: the council is investigative
A218	Education policy: the council had a meeting last year
A223	Education policy: private partnership
A224	Education policy: community support
A391	Health policy: existence of a council
A393	Health policy: the council has community participation
A394	Health policy: the council is advisory
A395	Health policy: the council is deliberative
A396	Health policy: the council is normative
A397	Health policy: the council is investigative
A398	Health policy: the council had a meeting last year
A401	Health policy: Government planning
A417	Health policy: private partnership
A418	Health policy: community support

Source: 2009 MUNIC Survey (www.ibge.gov.br)

23
CIVIC ENGAGEMENT IN LOCAL POLITICS IN CENTRAL EUROPE

Oto Potluka, Judit Kalman, Ida Musiałkowska and Piotr Idczak

Introduction

Over the last twenty-five years, fundamental changes have occurred in the Visegrad countries. These changes have had a clear impact on the democratic development of these societies. In particular, these changes have affected both the process of shaping local governance and the role of civil society.

Civil society and civic engagement have become vibrant and essential factors for preserving democracy. Before the 1990s, civil society in the Visegrad countries manifested as various forms of anti-state opposition. Civil society was seen as a key factor in bottom-up initiatives against totalitarian regimes. Since the beginning of this systemic transformation, membership in democratic parties reflected increasing democratic development. Later, the political decision-making process became detached from civil society. Although the political parties became more professionalised, they also became brokers between civil society and the state. This had the effect of diminishing civil society's participation in political processes (Katz and Mair 1995).

The distortion and suppression of characteristic civil-society attitudes and values under previous regimes resulted in deficient civic engagement. Restrictive rules relating to freedom of association and participation in public matters during the communist period eroded the foundations of a viable civil society (Petrova 2007). The legacy was a high level of social distrust, a perception of the state as a force hostile to society, and the elimination of traditions and patterns of civil society (Adam et al. 2005; Paldam and Svendsen 2001). Therefore, it was not easy for civil society to regain its lost position, improve new democratic structures, and contribute to transparency. The persistence of the dominating role of public authorities and central governments in political representation has been disillusioning for many civil-society organisations (Potluka and Liddle 2014). This is particularly important at the local level, where civil society helps to deepen and sustain democratic local governance. Moreover, it strengthens social participation in political decision-making and enhances the local political system's credibility by promoting transparency and accountability. Nevertheless, according to recent studies (Potluka and Liddle 2014), partnership is reasonably strong at the local level. However, this is not the case for all Central European countries. The data at the local level show that even if local civil-society organisations have higher acceptance levels with respect to local political decision-making, this is not generally the rule (Potluka 2009; Potluka and Liddle 2014).

In longer-established European states, civil society and public authorities exist as two inherent elements of the social system. When considering the Visegrad countries' historical experience and consequences of the systemic transformation, it is therefore important to consider the current state of civil society in those countries. Civil society highlights issues of importance for incentives and actions undertaken by local communities. It is composed of committed citizens who share common interests and responsibility for the common good (Calhoun 2011; Laine 2014). This reasoning is relevant because it provides an overview of how civil society engagement affects local politics and shapes its performance to focus on the common good.

The chapter discusses the development and current structure of local political systems in the Visegrad countries. The primary focus is on the role of the local political system, social capital, civic engagement and civil society organisations (CSOs: defined as trade unions, professional associations, civic associations, religious organisations, foundations, endowment funds, and public benefit corporations) in political decision-making.

Political and regional structure of the Visegrad countries

Since 1989, changes in the legal framework regarding decentralisation and the delegation of competencies to the regional and local levels have been introduced in all of the Visegrad countries. While preparing for EU membership, these countries had to bring into force a common Nomenclature of Units for Territorial Statistic (NUTS) (see http://ec.europa.eu/eurostat/web/nuts/overview) which subdivided their territory into regions at three different levels (NUTS 1, 2 and 3 respectively, ranging from bigger to smaller territorial units). A system of local administrative units (LAU) was also introduced. It is a component of the NUTS system and corresponds to the level of counties/micro- regions (LAU 1) and the level of municipalities or equivalent units (LAU 2). Not all NUTS areas have administrative and political self-governing bodies (see Table 23.1). However, competencies were delegated at the regional and local levels and to the local authorities of the lowest level (municipalities – LAU 2) to provide public services and perform tasks in the areas of education, social and health services, and basic infrastructure (water, sewage, solid waste, road maintenance, lighting, etc.). During the transition period, the decentralisation process seemed successful. In some countries, however, especially after the crisis of 2008, further evolution of the functioning of local entities was seen as reversing prior achievements (see Hungary below for example).

The Czech system

Local elections occur every four years (Act No. 491/2001 Coll. of the Czech Republic on Elections to Municipal Councils) according to the governance system in the Czech Republic (The Czech National Council's law 367/1990 on municipal statutes and Act No. 128/2000 Coll. of the Czech Republic on Municipalities). The Czech local election system at the municipal level enables local governments to decide (within the legal framework) on the size of their assembly for the following election period. Local governments may also divide city districts into several election districts. Political parties that have received a higher share of votes get better results as the election apply the d'Hondt system of calculating votes into seats.

The elected municipal assembly is responsible for electing the mayor. Mayors must be elected members of the assembly. Similarly, the regional assemblies are responsible for electing regional presidents. This system differentiates the Czech Republic from other Visegrad countries, in which mayors are elected directly.

Table 23.1 Characteristics of administrative division and election systems at the local level in the Visegrad countries

		Czech Republic		Slovakia		Hungary		Poland	
		No.	self-governed	No.	self-governed	No.	self-governed	No.	self-governed
NUTS 1 (macroregion)	(1)	1		1		3		6	
NUTS 2 (region)	(2)	8	No	4	No	7	No	16	Yes
NUTS 3	(3)	14	Yes	8	Yes	20	Yes	72	No
LAU 1	(4)	77	No	79	No	197	No	380	Yes
LAU 2 (municipality)	(5)	6,253	Yes	2,927	Yes	3,155	Yes	2,478	Yes
Election system at the municipal level	(6)	Proportional		Proportional, plurality for mayoral elections		Mixed system: proportional, with compensatory lists in larger places, Plurality block voting in municipalities with fewer than 10,000 residents (number of mandates reduced since 2010)		Mixed system: Proportional plurality voting (municipalities that do not enjoy the rights of a county)	
Term of elected municipal authorities (LAU 2 level)	(7)	4 years		4 years		4 years		4 years	
Elected bodies at the municipal level	(8)	Municipal councils; district councils		Mayors; municipal councils; district councils including district mayors		Mayor and city government(s) directly elected; district local councils + city council and mayor general (in the capital city)		Mayor; municipal council; district local councils + city council and mayor general (in the capital city)	
Turnout in 2014 municipal elections (in %)	(9)	44.5		48.3		44.3		47.2	
Country population (million)	(10)	10.5		5.4		9.8		38.0	

Source: Adapted from Eurostat (2016b) (rows (1)–(5)), National election commissions of the Visegrad countries (rows (6)–(9)), Eurostat (2016a) (row (10))

Self-governed: Regions or municipalities governed by an elected assembly. In the annex, we translate the territorial classifications from the national language; NUTS: Nomenclature of Units for Territorial Statistics; LAU: Local administrative unit.

The 2014 local elections show both that established political parties (and political movements) lost ground and that the electorate is moving towards independent candidates and new political movements. It would be risky for incumbent politicians to establish a system that is advantageous for election parties with a high share of the votes in such a situation because it is unclear who will win.

The Slovak system

The municipal governance and municipal election systems are different in the Czech Republic and Slovakia, although both countries had a long common history in Czechoslovakia. In Slovakia, municipal governance is established by Act no. 369/1990 Coll. of the Slovak Republic: the Act on Municipal Administration. Municipal elections are regulated by the Act of the Slovak National Council no. 346/1990. City districts can be further divided into smaller electoral districts. In each electoral district, up to 12 council members can be elected depending on the proportion of the population living in that area. The individual candidates with the highest number of votes win the seats and become council members.

Additionally, as part of the municipal elections, citizens of large cities elect a city mayor, members of the city council, a local mayor, and the local council. Unlike local council ballots, for city council ballots, the city districts correspond to electoral districts as required by Article 9(2) of the Act of the Slovak National Council. 346/1990 Coll. on elections to municipal bodies, as amended.

The Hungarian system

Until the early 2000s Hungary was widely considered a successful case of decentralisation, having made great progress on legal, institutional, regulatory and financial frameworks that enabled truly local decisions (Soós and Kálmán 2002). The new system of fully autonomous, elected local governments established by Act LXV of 1990 on Local Governments was considered a major cornerstone of democracy, counterbalancing any authoritarian central government and effectively representing local interests. Until recently, municipalities have had very broad responsibilities for service provision, similar to Nordic countries' much larger local governments. Localities enjoyed autonomy in their spending preferences related to these responsibilities, although they were constrained in specific service standards by various sectoral laws. This in effect constrained some aspects of local governments' decisions and performance. Since 1990, the Hungarian system of local elections has involved a compromise between 'bottom-up' and 'top-down' politics. In settlements with fewer than 10,000 inhabitants, a plurality formula with a block vote system was used. Larger localities used a mixed formula with compensatory lists. The plurality block vote system helps to select individual candidates, and the compensatory lists 'let in' national political actors at the local level (Kákai 2004) because the list system forces politicians to establish organisations to compete in elections (Dobos 2014). Approximately 60–80% of elected representatives and mayors run as independent candidates in the under-the-limit municipalities, whereas only a few (approximately 8–10%) independent candidates run in the larger cities (Pálné Kovács 2008). The separation of 'locality' and 'national party politics' clearly determines local governments' political profiles (Swianiewicz and Mielczarek 2005). Thus, national parties focused on organisation building at the local levels, especially in larger cities (Soós and Kálmán 2002; Soós 2005). Bottom-up political representation of local civil-society organisations was also present, in part because of the lack of any regional or local parties. Recent public administration reform and changes in the local electoral system give local governments less room to manoeuvre and facilitate re-centralisation tendencies.

The Polish system

In 1990, a new law on Polish local self-government was introduced that provided local authorities with the power to ensure local development conditions (Act on Local Self-government 1990 of 8 March 1990, Dz. U. 1990 no. 16 item 95).

In Poland, local, regional and national elections are held every four years. Poland's first democratic local elections occurred on 27 May 1990. According to Polish law, municipalities that do not enjoy the rights of a county have used the plurality voting system since 2014, whereas in cities that enjoy the rights of a county (and in the counties and voivodships/regions), the d'Hondt proportional election system has been applied (Act on 5 January 2011 – Election code, Dz. U. z 2011 r. No 21, item 112).

The citizens elect members of the councils of municipalities, counties, and regions. Since 2002, they have also elected representatives of the municipalities, such as presidents (in larger cities)/mayors of the cities and chiefs of non-urban municipalities. In the capital city, there are also district council elections.

Current development and dynamics at the local level in the Visegrad countries

In the Czech Republic, a shift from established political parties to local initiatives and movements characterises recent developments in local politics. In 2010, 43.0% of candidates were from parliamentary political parties. Among the candidates elected, the share of members of these political parties was 30.4%. In 2014, the situation changed: only 35.3% of candidates and only 23.5% of those elected were from parliamentary political parties. A similar development is evident in Slovakia. On the one hand, this development is a sign of democratic decision-making. On the other hand, this development demonstrates a crisis in a political system based on political parties. Moreover, the development is causing some political disconnection at the local, regional and national levels.

In Hungary, a major reorganisation of the territorial governance system has been carried out since 2010. First, the local electoral system was changed (Act LXV of 2010) between the national and local elections in 2010, mostly away from proportional representation and towards a majority system. While this was occurring, the requirements for participating in proportional elections (by establishing a party list in the bigger municipalities and regional/capital elections) became more difficult to meet.

The reform, which was introduced together with major changes in public administration, came into effect in three phases. First, county government became responsible for maintaining certain institutions, with newly established, deconcentrated government offices at the county level legal supervision rights over municipalities and changing the rules of asset management (from January 2012) to constrain the ability of local governments (LGs) to become indebted. Second, LGs' financing and tasks changed significantly beginning in January 2013, when the formerly local government task of providing public education and health care was shifted back to state administrative organisations financed from the national budget. At that time, it was also observed that LGs' autonomy in providing social services was decreased. Third, the incompatibility of national and local political positions was announced (from October 2014). One possible conclusion is that local governments overall have become less significant actors, and their leadership has been assumed by national party politics. This trend reverses the decentralisation process that was in place in the period after the 1989 transition.

Current political changes in Poland have not substantially affected regional and local politics. In the 2014 local election, the majority of elected candidates came from established parties. New politicians (either independent or from the city movements) also entered Poland's local (urban) councils (PKW 2016). The next elections are planned for 2018, and it can be expected that reactions to the changes observed at the national level will be expressed in citizens' political preferences. Moreover, there has been discussion about changes to the election code. One of the main challenges regarding the provision of public services by Polish self-governments involves budgeting; for example, the planned reform of education and the elimination of one level of the post-primary schools will generate additional costs at the local level.

With regard to CSOs, no major legal changes have been introduced. However, there are plans to legitimise the centralised system of supervising and granting subventions to CSOs within the National Centre for Civil Society. This idea has been strongly criticised by both CSOs themselves and the Polish ombudsman, who argues that the creation of such a body contradicts the idea that the roots of civil society are found at the bottom (Bodnar 2016).

Development of civic engagement and opinions about the likelihood of influencing policies

Knowledge of people's actual needs is a crucial aspect for the successful long-term design and implementation of any public policy. If this aspect is neglected, problems with local ownership of programmes and projects will hamper the sustainability of projects and programmes as well as perceptions of the policy itself. The limitations of a centralised top-down approach without knowledge of local needs are an important issue (EC 2004). Thus, civic engagement helps to increase awareness of needs at all levels of policy-making.

Citizens engage in local political decision-making not only through elections and direct participation but also through indirect participation in civil-society organisations. These three methods differ in their tools and approaches.

Direct political participation in elections

Civic engagement is seen as a crucial issue for established democracies. Therefore, the literature on political participation argues that this concept is one form of action through which citizens seek to influence social or political outcomes (Brady 1999). Political participation refers to citizens' attempts to influence public representatives' decisions that concern societal and economic issues (Adler and Goggin 2005; Berger 2009; Brady 1999; van Deth et al. 2007; Parry et al. 1992). In this sense, voting turnout has been described as the most commonly used measure of citizen participation. Voting is the principal way that people make their voices heard in the political system.

The selection of options by voting is a principle of democracy. Although this right is guaranteed, there is a question about how people apply it. All four Visegrad countries have witnessed scepticism about the influence of voting at all levels. Electoral participation is below the EU average (OECD 2016). In comparison, some countries have voting mandatory voting (Belgium and Luxemburg) which ensures high levels of turnout; other countries (Malta and Italy) habitually have high voter turnout. Nevertheless, there is a significant difference, as estimated by a sample of 155 regions in 15 Western European countries and 42 regions in six Central and Eastern European countries (see Figure 23.1). On average, the gap in regional turnout between the groups of investigated countries is 18.6%.

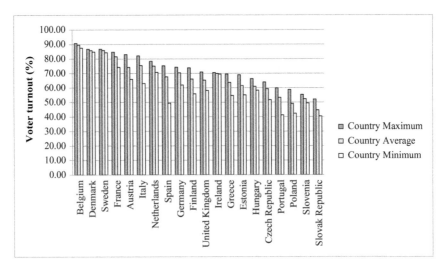

Figure 23.1 Differences in participation in general elections among European regions

The figure displays the regional maximum, minimum and average of voter turnout in the last national election in each country is considered. Data relate to regional level.

Source: Adapted from OECD (2016)

The difference in the level of electoral participation is often described as the legacy of communism in Central and Eastern European countries. Citizens of Western European countries generally have had more, and longer, experience in civic participation and political engagement. Consequently, they have more opportunities to express their desires and views (Coffé and van der Lippe 2010). In established and stable democracies, voting norms are supported by internalised feelings of guilt, shame or even fear of external judgements by friends, family or community members (Bolzendahl and Coffé 2013). In turn, citizens in newer democracies have had to confront democratic transition and learn civic attitudes. Thus, norms about not only voting rights and opportunities but also expressing one's opinion in general influence political participation, but only weakly (Armingeon 2007). Moreover, voters in Central and Eastern European countries see regional elections as less important than national or local elections.

Not only is participation in general elections lower in regions in Central and Eastern European countries, but there are also differences within this group of countries (see Figure 23.1 for regional maximum, minimum and average in each country). The Czech Republic and Hungary have generally higher participation, although some Czech regions have low participation. Polish and Slovak regions are the opposite. In post-transition countries, political interest does not correlate with participation (Petrova and Tarrow 2007). This means that although people may be interested in political life, that interest is expressed by means other than voting. This practice reflects activism without participation. Moreover, citizens in Central and Eastern Europe are more sceptical about democracy and more dissatisfied with democratic performance (18% and 62%, respectively, compared to 6% and 33% in Western Europe) (Karp and Milazzo 2015). On the one hand, scepticism about democracy may discourage citizens from participating in elections; on the other hand, people who are unsatisfied with the results of democracy may withdraw from political participation (Karp and Milazzo 2015).

Direct participation – individual engagement

Civil society is strongly based on the value of trust. This is in line with not only social capital and its essential components, such as interpersonal trust, but also citizens' trust in public institutions (Putnam 2008). Fukuyama (1997, 1999) suggests that social capital means people's ability that results from the prevalence of trust within society to ensure the respect of instantiated norms that lead to cooperation in groups. In turn, those norms relate to traditional advantages such as honesty, honouring commitments, reliably performing one's duties, and reciprocity. In practical terms, this means that trust is the willingness to permit the decisions of others to influence society's welfare (Sobel 2002). In this sense, social activity stimulates the development of civil society structures that choose local elites and leaders from within. Furthermore, the development of civil society leads to the identification of individuals who possess the collectivity, internalisation of the common good and social, economic and political empowerment that result in the intensification of both social and individual actions (Durkheim 1999).

Trust in other people is much lower in the Visegrad countries than in other EU member states. According to the European Social Survey (ESS Round 7: European Social Survey Round 7 Data 2014), in terms of general trust, all four Visegrad countries occupy the last places among the European countries covered in the survey (see Figure 23.2). In 2014, the responses in Visegrad countries to the statement 'Most people can be trusted' varied from 20.8% agreement in the Czech Republic to 18.3% in Slovakia, 18.2% in Hungary and 16.4% in Poland. This means that the average level of trust in those countries (18.4%) was more than three times lower than in Denmark, Norway and Finland (which averaged 65.7% agreement). Despite a noticeable increase in interpersonal trust during the analysed period, a large portion of society expressed uncertainty about dealing with other people.

The figure also shows that Poland, which achieved the highest increase in the level of trust during the past decade, takes last place in this respect among all Visegrad countries. The reasons for this result are historical and relate to Poland's past experiences. Poland's partitions in the eighteenth and nineteenth centuries, its experience of World War II and the imposition of a communist regime created a negative image of authorities. Current attitudes reflect a negative perception of the government, institutions, political rules and regulations and principles of social life (Lewicka-Strzałecka 2007).

Although there are many reasons for this phenomenon in the Visegrad countries, the most relevant reason is primarily derived from the systemic transformation, particularly in the Czech Republic and Poland (Bartkowski and Jasińska Kania 2004; Hausner 2014; Fidrmuc and Gërxhani 2008; Czapiński and Panek 2015). Czechoslovakia's Velvet Revolution was a relatively quiet upheaval without large revolutionary actions and crises. After its dissolution into the Czech Republic and Slovakia, an important role in the systemic transformation of both countries was played by local democratisation (i.e., the new local councils, local political parties and grassroots organisations) and by specific traditions of self-help rooted in the culture (Bartkowski and Jasińska Kania 2004). It seems that the Czech and Slovak structures of civil society could have begun to develop very early. However, because of a low societal mood caused by a considerable economic decline and unmet expectations, this did not occur (Císař 2013).

In Poland and Hungary, the transformation programme was based on the 'shock therapy' approach. Negative socio-economic effects quickly appeared. These effects included the following: a rapid rise in unemployment and social inequality, the destabilisation of governments, the rapid implementation of institutional reforms that were not always properly prepared and introduced and a decrease in the economic growth rate. This led to dissatisfaction with democracy

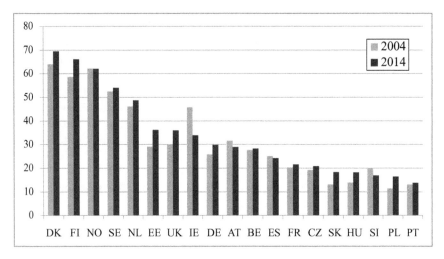

Figure 23.2 Percentage of people trusting others in Europe (age 16+)

Results were calculated as a cumulative value of percentage of answers from 7 to 10 on the following scale: 0 ('You can't be too careful in dealing with people') to 10 ('Most people can be trusted').

Source: Adapted from ESS Round 2: European Social Survey Round 2 Data (2004); ESS Round 7: European Social Survey Round 7 Data (2014), for Slovakia; ESS Round 6: European Social Survey Round 6 Data (2012)

and political elites (Nový 2014; Bartkowski and Jasińska Kania 2004). In addition, it should be stressed that both countries' cultural traditions feature strong family ties, especially in Poland. Trust is limited to immediate family members and employees of family-run businesses.

These attributes hinder citizens from increasing trust in themselves and their level of social capital because these feelings are deeply rooted in society and are difficult to overcome in the short term. As a result, the lack of trust in other people negatively affects or complicates the development of civil participation and activity. This seems particularly true if one considers the other feature of social capital – people's ability to cooperate in the form of an informal or formal partnerships and a simple willingness to help other people. Results show that only 17.1% of the Visegrad population fully agreed with the opinion, 'People mostly try to be helpful'. The more formal people's activities are for the benefit of the others, the less different the findings are from the general view of social capital in Visegrad countries. This is expressed by people's willingness to be involved in improving and preventing deterioration in society. The data demonstrate that only 4.8% of respondents answered 'yes' to the question, 'Have you worked in an organisation or association last 12 months' on their own initiative to improve/prevent something. These results show that people in Visegrad countries are unwilling to initiate or join activities for the benefit of their own community. Moreover, interesting insights arise from analysis of the interdependence between the above-mentioned aspects. As shown in Figure 23.3, one common feature of the Visegrad population is a low level of trust and a small number of people willing to help others and work in their community. This is confirmed by this population's distant rankings compared to other European countries, particularly in Scandinavia.

The low level of trust and willingness to act together are closely related to the low level of general civic engagement expressed by both involvement in organisations and electoral participations. The literature on social capital suggests that a higher level of citizen trust leads to stronger social and political involvement (Coffé and van der Lippe 2010). Therefore, citizens

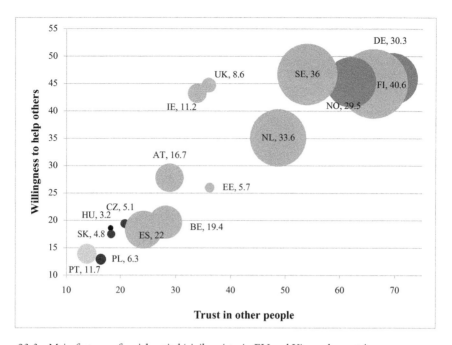

Figure 23.3 Main features of social capital/civil society in EU and Visegrad countries

Three features of social capital/civil society were considered: (1) trust in other people, calculated as in Figure 23.2; (2) willingness to help others.

Source: Adapted from ESS Round 2: European Social Survey Round 2 Data (2004); ESS Round 7: European Social Survey Round 7 Data (2014); for Slovakia ESS Round 6: European Social Survey Round 6 Data (2012)

who display a very low level of trust in either themselves or their national institutions are less likely to vote or engage in civic activities. Howard and Gilbert (2008) argue that active citizens are more likely to be trusting than inactive people are. They have found that the share of inactive people is the highest in Eastern Europe (nearly 70% according to their civic involvement index) and is more than double that of Western Europe. Although an authoritarian history has a strong negative effect on civic involvement levels in newer democracies (Hooghe and Quintelier 2014), low income levels, a lack of good governance and high levels of corruption can also strongly affect participation (Tavits 2008; Neundorf 2010). As Hooghe and Quintelier (2014) argue, the timing of the democratic transition can shape the political system's capacity to provide good governance, but it does not directly affect citizens' attitudes and participatory habits.

Indirect participation through civil society organisations

Public perceptions of the role of civil society organisations (CSOs) differ across the EU countries. Studies are inconclusive regarding the role of civil society agents' participation in political decision-making. Some see this approach as beneficial because of better-targeted policies that bring new knowledge and skills to political processes, shared knowledge among involved actors, transparent decision-making, and the efficient use of public resources (Lowndes and Skelcher 1998; Leonardi 2006; Bache 2010). However, other studies note the risks of involving

Table 23.2 Opinions about the likelihood of influencing political decision-making in Central Europe

	CSOs are capable of influencing political decisions at the:			An effective method of influencing political decisions is:			
	Local and regional level	National level	EU level	Voting in local/ regional elections	Voting in national elections	Voting in European elections	Membership in a CSO
CZ	74	55	37	68	60	39	44
HU	71	57	50	63	58	49	50
PL	82	68	51	65	56	48	53
SK	71	62	54	69	67	55	53
EU27	75	70	53	73	70	54	54

All values are % of responses.

Source: Adapted from EC (2013)

lobbying groups, including CSOs, the low skills of stakeholders outside the political mechanism, the destabilisation of existing systems through obstruction, and low accountability (Scharpf 2007; Geissel 2009; Peters and Pierre 2004).

According to 41% of European citizens, CSOs are unnecessary (EC 2013). However, this result is influenced by responses from five Member States – Romania, Greece, Bulgaria, Portugal and Cyprus – in which a majority of the population tends to reject the role of CSOs in political decision-making. It is important for our study that the respondents in Visegrad countries view CSOs as a necessary element in society (higher frequency of responses supporting the role), although these countries are spread around the average (CZ and HU above and SK with PL below the EU-27 average).

At the local level, Slovakia and Hungary provided the lowest rate of agreement to the statement that CSOs can influence policies at local level within the EU (for details and comparison with other Visegrad countries, see Table 23.2). The Czechs do not believe that CSOs are capable of influencing policy at the national or EU level, only at the local level. Of all the EU countries, the CSOs in the Czech Republic have the lowest perceived ability to change public policies (EC 2012).

The causes of this situation are CSOs' low financial and advocacy capacities (Frič 2004; Rose-Ackerman 2007) and general post-communism mistrust of organisations, the persistence of friendship networks, and post-communist disappointment with political development (Howard 2011). Moreover, the Czech Republic experienced a long-term dispute about the role of the civil society in public life (Potůček 1999).

The importance of CSOs as partners for the public sector is illustrated by the fact that 6% of EU citizens see membership in or support of a CSO as a method of influencing the political decision-making process (EC 2012). Only 12% of EU citizens perceive joining a political party as a means of influencing policies, although the only purpose of a political party is participation in political decision-making. Moreover, respondents see these two segments as having an equal influence on decision-makers in Hungary (9%), and Poland (7%) (EC 2012). This finding underlines the importance of CSOs' role in political decision-making.

Advocacy by CSOs

CSOs need financial and personnel capacities to fulfil their advocacy role. Professionalised non-profit organisations have sufficient skills and funding to be successful in their advocacy activities. Increasing employment follows their professionalism (Frič 2015). They establish a relationship with the public sector, to which they deliver public services, and they increase their transparency and credibility to obtain funding from benefactors. However, professionalisation means engaging in managerial decision-making and may result in less internal democracy and civic participation together with a decreasing advocacy role. In the extreme case, professionalisation can lead to the application of purely managerial approaches without advocacy. Moreover, a civil society sector with few financially sustainable organisations increases the risk of sudden changes and diminishes the long-term viability of the entire sector.

The EC (2013) study notes that Czech citizens do not see CSOs as effective political agents and that only 47% of Czechs share the values or interests of some CSOs and trust that CSOs influence political decision-making appropriately. Slovakia (51%) reports a slightly higher level of shared values with CSOs. Poland (62%) and Hungary (67%) are positioned above the EU-27 average (59%) (EC 2013). The Czech position is the lowest among the EU member states, a position shared by Spain and Estonia.

Moreover, the Czech Republic and Latvia are the only two countries where membership in a CSO is perceived as an ineffective way to influence political life, with a share of agreement at 52% and 54%, respectively (EC 2013).

The long-term development of the advocacy role of civil-society organisations is decreasing in the Visegrad countries. The Slovak and Hungarian cases show an especially decreasing trend in recent decades (note the scores in Figure 23.4). Poland is the only case of a visible positive trend throughout the observed period.

In 1999, Hungarian CSOs participated in regional debates before the passage of comprehensive CSO legislation. The ineffective centralised model persisted in CSOs. Thus, CSOs' identification of their target groups' needs was very weak and primarily based on a top-down approach (USAID 2015).

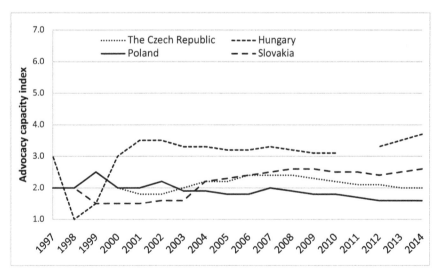

Figure 23.4 Development of advocacy capacity of CSOs in the Visegrad countries

An index value of 1–2 means 'Enhanced Advocacy', a value of 3–5 means 'Evolving Advocacy', and a value of 6–7 means 'Advocacy Impeded'. We do not display missing values for Hungary in 2011 and the Czech Republic in 1997–1999.

Source: Adapted from USAID (2015), calculations of the authors

Conclusions

This chapter considers the various factors that determine civic engagement through electoral participation and the role and position of civil society in the Visegrad countries. It describes the development and current structure of local political systems along with certain inherent difficulties and features. After 1989, all four countries introduced fundamental changes that shaped their democratic and economic transition, including new institutions such as a legal and financial framework for decentralisation and the delegation of competencies to the regional and local levels, along with strengthening their civil society.

Before joining the EU, the Visegrad countries reshaped their territorial governance system and introduced administrative units at the regional and local levels. This was in line with the basic idea of the effectiveness of decentralisation: the best knowledge of local needs and preferences leads to the successful design and implementation of public policies. During the transition period, the decentralisation process seemed successful. In some countries, however, the reversal of prior achievements and re-centralisation is observable through recent reforms in territorial administration and changes in the scope of municipalities' power (Hungary), especially after the 2008 crisis and fiscal austerity. These changes are consistent with recent political ideologies and a contested neoliberal democratic vision of development.

Citizens can engage in local political decision-making not only through elections and direct participation but also through indirect participation in civil-society organisations. In all of the Visegrad countries, citizens participate in the direct elections of local assemblies and mayors (although not the latter in the Czech Republic), and there is usually a high share of independent candidates. Elections are held every four years. Election systems are proportional in the Czech Republic and Slovakia and mixed in Hungary, Poland and Slovakia (mayoral elections). However, all Visegrad countries experienced lower than the EU average and declining voter turnout rates, especially in regional or local elections. There are differences within this group. The Czech Republic and Hungary have generally higher participation, whereas Polish and Slovak regions are lower. The lower and declining turnout rates in these post-communist countries re attributed to institutional, political and economic aspects.

The picture is more discouraging for indirect forms of civic participation. The civil sector remains fairly weak, and low participation rates in civil-society organisations are visible in the Visegrad countries compared to their Western European counterparts. The reason for this situation lies in social norms and trust. One general feature of the Visegrad countries is a low level of trust, confirmed by their last places compared to other European countries, especially Scandinavia. The average level of trust in the Visegrad countries amounted to 18.4% in 2014, whereas for all European countries it stood at approximately 33.8% (ESS Round 7: European Social Survey Round 7 Data 2014). Poland, despite a regular growth in trust since 2004, was ranked last among the Visegrad countries.

In addition to low general trust, there is a high level of uncertainty and untrustworthiness in these countries with respect to dealing with other people along with a passive attitude and low willingness to help others or act for their communities. Some of these features are a legacy of the communist past, whereas others are attributable to the negative socioeconomic consequences of the transition process and disillusionment with democratic development. As a result, the development of civil participation and activity seems much slower and more difficult. Activity in civil-society organisations remains significantly lower than in Southern European countries with similarly low levels of trust (Portugal, Spain).

Respondents in Visegrad countries view CSOs as a needed element in society, although they view membership in them as an ineffective form of participation and seem to attach more value to voting in elections despite demonstrating low actual turnout rates. Visegrad respondents perceive CSOs to be weaker than Western European respondents do. CSOs are considered capable of exerting some influence on local- and regional-level politics in all Visegrad countries (although HU and SK are the lowest in the EU in this respect), but less at the national level (CZ and HU) and especially at the EU level (CZ). Czech citizens do not consider CSOs effective political agents; only 47% of Czechs share the civic values or interests of some CSOs. These figures are slightly higher and comparable to EU averages in the other three Visegrad countries.

The advocacy capacity of CSOs within the Visegrad countries seems to have been fairly stable throughout the past fifteen years, showing a strong relationship with those countries' financial capacities. Instead of any improvement, however, a decrease is visible in the overall index measuring the advocacy capacities of Hungarian and Slovak CSOs, with Poland showing a somewhat positive trend. The factors that contribute to these decreasing capacities and other measurement tools that would better demonstrate the nuanced details of CSO capacities remain to be explained by future research.

Much research has been conducted on the transition experience of Central and Eastern European countries, especially on the institutional, political and economic aspects at the national level. Less research has focused on the local or regional levels and on civic engagement or civil-sector development. This chapter has highlighted only certain details with regard to these issues in the Visegrad countries. However, local-level data generation, the measurement of civil society's capacities and strength and, especially, tracking progress across time remain important tasks for future research as the Visegrad countries travel further down the path towards democratic and open local governance.

References

Act No 128/2000 Coll. of the Czech Republic, on Municipalities (the Municipal Order).
Act No. 367/1990 of the Czech National Council of 4 September 1990 on the municipal statutes.
Act No. 369/1990 Coll. of the Slovak Republic, the Act on Municipal Administration.
Act No. 491/2001 Coll. of the Czech Republic, on Elections to Municipal Councils.
Act No. LXV/1990 Republic of Hungary, On Local Governments.
Act of the Slovak National Council. 346/1990 Coll. on elections to municipal bodies as amended.
Act on 5 January 2011 – Election code, Dz. U. z 2011 r., no. 21, item 112.
Act on local self-government 1990 of 8 March 1990, Dz.U. 1990 no. 16, item 95.
Adam, F., Tomsic, M., Ronecevic, B. and Makarovic, M. 2005. *The Challenges of Sustained Development: The Role of Socio-cultural Factors in East-Central Europe*. Budapest: Central European University Press.
Adler, R. P. and Goggin, J. 2005. What Do We Mean By 'Civic Engagement'? *Journal of Transformative Education* 3: 236–253.
Armingeon, K. 2007. Political Participation and Associational Involvement. In Van Deth, J. W., Montero, J. R. and Westholm, A. (eds) *Citizenship and Involvement in European Democracies: A Comparative Analysis*. London: Routledge.
Bache, I. 2010. Partnership as an EU Policy Instrument: A Political History. *West European Politics* 33: 58–74.
Bartkowski, J. and Jasińska Kania, A. 2004. Voluntary organizations and the development of civil society. In Arts, W. and Halman, L. (eds) *European Values at the Turn of the Millennium*. Leiden: Brill.
Berger, B. 2009. Political Theory, Political Science and the End of Civic Engagement. *Perspectives on Politics* 7: 335.

Bodnar, A. 2016. Powstanie Narodowe Centrum Społeczeństwa Obywatelskiego. Bodnar komentuje. *Portal Samorządowy*. Retrieved on 22 December 2016 from www.portalsamorzadowy.pl/polityka-i-spoleczenstwo/powstanie-narodowe-centrum-spoleczenstwa-obywatelskiego-bodnar-komentuje, 86998.html.

Bolzendahl, C. and Coffé, H. 2013. Are 'Good' Citizens 'Good' Participants? Testing Citizenship Norms and Political Participation across 25 Nations. *Political Studies* 61: 45–65.

Brady, H., E. 1999. Political Participation. In Robinson, J. P., Shaver, P. R. and Wrightsman, L. S. (eds) *Measures of Political Attitudes*. San Diego, CA: Academic Press.

Calhoun, C. 2011. Civil Society and the Public Sphere. In Edwards, M. (ed.) *The Oxford Handbook of Civil Society*. New York: Oxford University Press.

Císař, O. 2013. A Typology of Extra-Parliamentary Political Activism in Post-Communist Settings: The Case of the Czech Republic. In Jacobsson, K. and Saxonberg, S. (eds) *Beyond NGO-ization: The Development of Social Movements in Central and Eastern Europe*. Farnham: Ashgate.

Coffé, H. and Van Der Lippe, T. 2010. Citizenship Norms in Eastern Europe. *Social Indicators Research* 96: 479–496.

Czapiński, J. and Panek, T. 2015. Social Diagnosis 2015: Objective and Subjective Quality of Life in Poland. *Contemporary Economics* 9: 106–115.

Dobos, G. 2014. Changing Local Relations: Effects of Political and Administrative Reforms in Hungary. *8th ECPR General Conference*. Glasgow: ECPR.

Durkheim, É. 1999. *O podziale pracy społecznej*. Warsaw: PWN.

EC 2004. *Project Cycle Management Guidelines*. Brussels: EC.

EC 2012. *Standard Eurobarometer 77: European Citizenship*. Brussels: EC.

EC 2013. *Flash Eurobarometer 373: Europeans' Engagement in Participatory Democracy*. Brussels: EC.

ESS Round 2: European Social Survey Round 2 Data 2004. Data file edition 3.5. NSD – Norwegian Centre for Research Data, Norway – Data Archive and distributor of ESS data for ESS ERIC.2.

ESS Round 6: European Social Survey Round 6 Data 2012. Data file edition 2.3. NSD – Norwegian Centre for Research Data, Norway – Data Archive and distributor of ESS data for ESS ERIC.

ESS Round 7: European Social Survey Round 7 Data 2014. Data file edition 2.1. NSD – Norwegian Centre for Research Data, Norway – Data Archive and distributor of ESS data for ESS ERIC.

Eurostat. 2016a. Demographic Balance 2015 (Thousands). Retrieved on 9 December 2016 from http://ec.europa.eu/eurostat/statistics-explained/index.php/File:Demographic_balance,_2015_%28thousands%29_YB16.png.

Eurostat. 2016b. NUTS: Nomenclature of Territorial Units for Statistics: National Structures (EU). Retrieved on 9 December 2016 from http://ec.europa.eu/eurostat/web/nuts/national-structures-eu.

Fidrmuc, J. and Gërxhani, K. 2008. Mind the Gap! Social Capital, East and West. *Journal of Comparative Economics* 36: 264–286.

Frič, P. 2004. Politický vývoj ve střední Evropě po r. 1989 a jeho dopad na neziskový sektor. Prague: UK FSV CESES. Retrieved on 15 May 2015 from http://www.ceses.cuni.cz/CESES-20-version1-sesit04_03_fric.pdf.

Frič, P. 2015. Občanská společnost a definice NNO, vývoj, stav a trendy. Retrieved on 10 June 2016 from www.vlada.cz/assets/ppov/rnno/dokumenty/studie_fric_pro_web.pdf.

Fukuyama, F. 1997. *Zaufanie. Kapitał społeczny a droga do dobrobytu*. Warsaw: Wydawnictwo Naukowe PWN.

Fukuyama, F. 1999. *Social Capital and Civil Society: IMF Conference on Second Generation Reforms*. Washington, DC: IMF.

Geissel, B. 2009. Participatory Governance: Hope or Danger for Democracy? A Case Study of Local Agenda 21. *Local Government Studies* 35: 401–414.

Hausner, J. 2014. Dokąd idziemy? In Sroczyński, G. (ed.) *Gazeta Wyborcza*. Warsaw: Gazeta Wyborcza.

Hooghe, M. and Quintelier, E. 2014. Political participation in European countries: The effect of authoritarian rule, corruption, lack of good governance and economic downturn. *Comparative European Politics* 12: 209–232.

Howard, M. M. 2011. Civil Society in Post-Communist Europe. In Edwards, M. (ed.) *The Oxford Handbook of Civil Society*. New York: Oxford University Press.

Howard, M. M. and Gilbert, L. 2008. A Cross-National Comparison of the Internal Effects of Participation in Voluntary Organizations. *Political Studies* 56: 12–32.

Kákai, L. 2004. *Önkormányzunk értetek, de nélkületek! Pártok és civil szervezetek a helyi társadalmakban*. Budapest: Századvég Kiadó.

Karp, J. A. and Milazzo, C. 2015. Democratic Scepticism and Political Participation in Europe. *Journal of Elections, Public Opinion and Parties* 25: 97–110.

Katz, R. S. and Mair, P. 1995. Changing Models of Party Organization and Party Democracy: The Emergence of the Cartel Party. *Party Politics* 1: 5–28.

Laine, J. 2014. Debating Civil Society: Contested Conceptualizations and Development Trajectories. *International Journal of Not-for-Profit Law* 16: 59–77.

Leonardi, R. 2006. Cohesion in the European Union. *Regional Studies* 40: 155–166.

Lewicka-Strzałecka, A. 2007. Korupcja i zaufanie. *Annales: etyka w życiu gospodarczym* 10: 211–219.

Lowndes, V. and Skelcher, C. 1998. The Dynamics of Multi-Organizational Partnerships: An Analysis of Changing Modes of Governance. *Public Administration* 76: 313–333.

Neundorf, A. 2010. Democracy in Transition: A Micro perspective on System Change in Post-Socialist Societies. *The Journal of Politics* 72: 1096–1108.

Nový, M. 2014. Electoral and Non-Electoral Participation in the Visegrad Countries: Complements or Substitutes? *East European Politics and Societies and Cultures* 28: 863–886.

OECD 2016. *OECD Regional Well-Being*. Paris: OECD.

Paldam, M. and Svendsen, G. T. 2001. Missing Social Capital and the Transition in Eastern Europe. *Journal for Institutional Innovation, Development and Transition* 5: 21–33.

Pálné Kovács, I. 2008. *Helyi kormányzás Magyarországon*. Pécs: Dialóg Campus Kiadó.

Parry, G., Moyser, G. and Day, N. 1992. *Political Participation and Democracy in Britain*. Cambridge: Cambridge University Press.

Peters, B., G. and Pierre, J. 2004. Multi-Level Governance and Democracy: A Faustian Bargain? In Bache, I. and Flinders, M. (eds) *Multi-Level Governance*. New York: Oxford University Press.

Petrova, V., P. 2007. Civil Society in Post-Communist Eastern Europe and Eurasia: A Cross-National Analysis of Micro- and Macro-Factors. *World Development* 35: 1277–1305.

Petrova, T. and Tarrow, S. 2007. Transactional and Participatory Activism in the Emerging European Polity: The Puzzle of East-Central Europe. *Comparative Political Studies* 40: 74–94.

PKW 2016. *Wybory Samorządowe 2014*. Warsaw: PKW. Retrieved on 8 December 2016 from http://pkw.gov.pl/434_Wyniki_wyborow.

Potluka, O. 2009. *Impact of Partnership on Political Decision-Making. Leading Citizen-Driven Governance: Collective Regional and Sub-regional Leadership in the UK and Beyond*. Bristol: RSA.

Potluka, O. and Liddle, J. 2014. Managing European Union Structural Funds: Using a Multilevel Governance Framework to Examine the Application of the Partnership Principle at the Project Level. *Regional Studies* 48: 1434–1447.

Potůček, M. 1999. Havel versus Klaus: Public Policy Making in the Czech Republic. *Journal of Comparative Policy Analysis* 1: 163–176.

Putnam, R., D. 2008. *Samotna gra w kręgle: Upadek i odrodzenie wspólnot lokalnych w Stanach Zjednoczonych*. Warsaw: Wydawnictwo Akademickie i Profesjonalne.

Rose-Ackerman, S. 2007. From Elections to Democracy in Central Europe: Public Participation and the Role of Civil Society. *East European Politics and Societies* 21: 31–47.

Scharpf, F., W. 2007. The Joint-Decision Trap Revisited. *Journal of Common Market Studies* 44: 845–864.

Sobel, J. 2002. Can We Trust Social Capital? *Journal of Economic Literature* 40: 139–154.

Soós, G. 2005. Local Party Institutionalization in Hungary. DPhil, Central European University.

Soós, G. and Kálmán, J. 2002. Country Report – Hungary: Report on the State of Local Democracy in Hungary. In Soós, G., Tóka, G. and Wright, G. (eds) *The State of Local Democracy in Central Europe*. Budapest: Open Society Institute.

Swianiewicz, P. and Mielczarek, A. 2005. Parties and Political Culture in Central and Eastern European Local Governments. In Soós, G. and Zentai, V. (eds) *Faces of Local Democracy: Comparative Papers from Central and Eastern Europe*. Budapest: Open Society Institute.

Tavits, M. 2008. Representation, Corruption, and Subjective Well-Being. *Comparative Political Studies* 41: 1607–1630.

USAID. 2015. *The 2014 CSO Sustainability Index for Central and Eastern Europe and Eurasia*. Washington: US Agency for International Development. Retrieved from www.usaid.gov/sites/default/files/documents/1863/EuropeEurasia_FY2014_CSOSI_Report.pdf.

Van Deth, J. W., Montero, J. R. and Westholm, A. (eds) 2007. *Citizenship and Involvement in European Democracies: A Comparative Analysis*. London: Routledge.

Appendix 1

Glossary of acronyms

CSO	civil society organisation
CZ	Czech Republic
EU	European Union
HU	Hungary
LAU	local administrative unit
LG	local government
NUTS	Nomenclature of Units for Territorial Statistics
OECD	Organisation for Economic Co-operation and Development
PL	Poland
SK	Slovakia
USAID	The US Government agency that works to end extreme global poverty and enable resilient, democratic societies to realize their potential

Appendix 2

Translation of territorial classification in national languages

	Czech Republic	Slovakia	Hungary	Poland
NUTS 2	*region soudržnosti*	*oblast*	*régió*	*województwo*
NUTS 3	*kraj*	*kraj*	*megye*	*podregion*
LAU 1	*okres*	*okres*	*járás*	*powiat*
LAU 2	*obec*	*obec*	*helyi önkormányzat*	*gmina*

PART V

Multi-level governance

24
AUSTRALIA
Challenging institutional constraints

Chris Aulich

Introduction

As a relative latecomer to the family of federations, the founders of the 1901 Australian federation were able to draw inspiration and experience from the federations of Canada and the United States. While the new Australian constitution reflected numerous examples of policy learning from the North American models, the political reality was that the federation initiative came from the former colonies which were reluctant to surrender significant powers to national and local governments. As a result, the final iteration of the Australian constitution firmly entrenched power with the colonies (to be called 'states'), ceding a narrow set of functions to the national ('Commonwealth') government, and not even referring to the existence of local government. Full control over the third sphere of government was retained by the states, with the basis of local government functions and powers to be clarified under state-based local government acts.

Contrary to the preferences of the states, twentieth century Australian political history was dominated by the steady accretion of Commonwealth powers at the expense of the state level of government, especially with respect to securing control over revenue raising. For example, in 1901 the states collected 87 per cent of all government revenue but by 2004–2005 that proportion had decreased to 18 per cent (Robinson and Farrelly 2013). Vertical fiscal imbalance has resulted from the significant expansion in the Commonwealth's powers to collect revenue and distribute finances to state and local governments. At the same time, however, the position of local government in the constitution remains unchanged from the arrangements made in 1901.

Local government remains formally a 'creature of the states', subject to state government legislation for its existence and for the exercise of its functions and powers. Many researchers have focused on the institutional weakness of Australian local government and on the constraints that bind the local sector. As one noted: 'it is clear that Australian local government has not won for itself that place in our polity which a long history has given it in Britain' (Finn 1990: 49).

Stoker (2011) has, however, urged researchers to look beyond institutional perspectives in comparative studies of local governance as these often yield enormous variation and complexity within countries, let alone between countries. Instead, he suggests that comparisons might better be made in terms of a number of fundamental societal roles played by local government. Stoker argues that a study of these basic societal roles adds a further benefit when international comparisons can be more easily made and made in a more nuanced way.

Stoker's approach resonates well in the Australian context with institutional arrangements, functions and local authority (or 'council') capabilities varying markedly between, and within, local government systems in six states, two mainland territories and three external territories. In this chapter, Stoker's framework of societal roles is adapted – governance at a local level in Australia is considered in relation to three primary societal roles: expressing local identity, generating local economic development and providing welfare and services for local citizens. Examining Australian local government in this way leads to the conclusion that identity does matter to local communities, many of which have developed robust forms of local governance in spite of the institutional constraints they face.

Before considering the three societal roles, the next section of this chapter details some of the institutional issues that influence the extent to which councils are able to advance their local governance roles.

Institutional issues in Australian local government

Institutional weakness has been a pervading characteristic of local government in Australia, which remains subservient to the states,[1] its legitimacy and operations dependent upon state government legislation – the state Local Government Acts. These acts prescribe arrangements that confine local government to a relatively narrow range of functions, among the weakest range of any developed country (Aulich 1999).

Recognition of local government was not provided in the Australian constitution of 1901 and later attempts to rectify this have been unsuccessful – the first attempt failing at a referendum in 1988, and a second referendum scheduled for 2013, did not proceed. In the latter case, an expert panel recommended that constitutional recognition be put to a referendum, but the panel acknowledged that 'fewer than 30 per cent of Australians had a sufficiently strong commitment to the idea of recognising local government' (Expert Panel 2011). Proposals were withdrawn when it became clear that the referendum had no realistic prospect of success.

While there has been some devolution of functions to the local sphere in the past two decades, the historic reality of administrative subordination of local government continues to be a primary feature of central-local relationships in Australia. There is limited inclination to engage in significant redistribution of authority across levels, particularly downwards. There are strict limitations on local government powers to raise their own revenues beyond the application of taxes on the unimproved value of property (or 'rates'). This leads to a major transfer role for the centralised revenue collector (the Commonwealth) to state and local governments and leaves local government with limited revenue raising capacity. Since the late 1970s the Commonwealth has been the largest external provider of funding for local government, though local government does raise about 85 per cent of its own revenues (ACELG 2011).

There is considerable diversity in the local sector, reflected in the range and scale of functions, councils' fiscal positions, their physical, economic, social and cultural environments, the varying state government legislative frameworks within which councils operate, and the differing attitudes and aspirations of local communities. This diversity includes variations in size with almost a half of the councils having populations of less than 10,000 with others having more than half a million. About 75 per cent of the total number of councils are classified as 'rural' or 'regional' (Commonwealth of Australia 2012: 245)[2] with the urban–rural divide representing one dimension of uneven resources recognised by the provision of national government grants to those councils most in need. This process of 'horizontal equalisation' provides additional funding based on 'disadvantage factors' such as the length of roads to be maintained or the limited capacity to generate income through local taxes and rates. Table 24.1 underlines

Table 24.1 Characteristics of selected Australian councils, 2000–2001

Council	State	Classification[a]	Population	Area	Road length	Rate Income	Rate Income per capita	2007–2008 financial assistance grant entitlement			
								General purpose	Local road	Total	Total grant per capita
			no.	sq km	km	$'000	$	$	$	$	$
Armadale	WA	URM	33,364	4,804	1,602	18,431	348.55	1,441,715	1,374,981	2,816,696	43.21
Banana	Qld	RAV	14,596	15,755	3,324	12,107	829.47	3,212,212	1,558,086	4,770,298	220.07
Brisbane[b]	Qld	UCC	989,152	1,327	5,491	916,300	926.35	17,881,408	11,764,886	29,646,294	18.08
Bulloo	Qld	RTS	468	73,805	4,654	2,538	5 423.59	2,154,852	1,039,038	3,193,890	4 604.38
Burnside[b]	SA	UDM	42,986	27	234	21,345	496.56	774,036	374,675	1,148,711	18.01
Capel	WA	RSG	10,517	554	450	2,483	236.09	725,364	1,344,644	2,070,008	68.97
Cardinia	Vic.	UFM	60,276	1280	1,349	25,868	429.16	5,081,275	1,806,949	6,888,224	84.30
Devonport	Tas.	URS	25,122	111	241	28,027	1,115.62	626,614	842,941	1,469,555	24.94
East Gippsland	Vic.	URM	42,075	20,931	2,846	25,114	596.89	7,526 118	3,917 726	11,443 844	178.87
Flinders	Tas.	RAS	879	1,994	385	1,750	1,990.71	517,367	495,921	1,013,288	588.59
Forbes Shire	NSW	RAV	10,003	4,720	1,803	4,960	4 95.85	2,533,970	1,474,621	4,008,591	253.32
Gosford City	NSW	UFV	163,469	940	1,046	48,834	298.73	6,401,006	1,784,583	8,185,589	39.16
Goyder Regional	SA	RAM	4,085	6,688	3,247	3,056	748.15	1,747,143	520,273	2,267,416	427.70
Jabiru	NT	URS	1,174	13	31	1,422	1 210.87	137,579	85,604	223,183	117.19
Marrickville	NSW	UDL	76,524	16	190	32,318	422.32	2,667,780	458,287	3,126,067	34.86
wiluna	WA	RTS	969	184,000	1,879	279	288.11	905,681	619,516	1,525,197	934.66

Source: Commonwealth of Australia (2010)

[a] In this column, rural councils are designated by the first letter 'R' and urban councils by 'U'. The second and third letters provide a more fine-grained classification, not relevant to this chapter

Table 24.2 Number of councils in Australia, 1910–2017

	1910	1967	1982	2000	2009	2017
NSW	324	224	175	174	152	126
VIC	206	210	211	78	79+	79
QLD	164	131	134	157^	73	77+
SA	175	142	127	68	68	68
WA	147	144	138	142	139	139
TAS	51	49	49	29	29	29
NT	0	1	6	69	16	17
TOTAL	1067	901	840	717	556	535

Sources: Compiled by the author from state and territory government websites

Notes: +De-amalgamation. ^Queensland numbers before 2000 exclude Indigenous community councils established under separate legislation. By 2008 these had been included in the 'mainstream' system.

the range and diversity within Australian local government and emphasises the relative significance of grants and subsidies for some councils, especially those in rural areas.

Over the past three decades, the number of councils has fallen significantly due to consolidation of local government areas through amalgamation. The average population of Australian councils is now around 40,000 – small by comparison with the United Kingdom or South Africa, but considerably larger than across much of Europe (Aulich et al. 2014) (see Table 24.2). Some state governments have managed the process of amalgamation collaboratively with local government but others have used their legislative powers to force consolidation policies, often against the wishes of local communities.

In recent times, local government and its supporters have mounted vigorous challenges to the amalgamation processes and have been successful in retaining, or significantly moderating, state government proposals in the states of Tasmania, Queensland and New South Wales. While there has not been institutional change in terms of redistribution of power or functions, voter action has challenged the view of most state governments that council size has been the primary cause of inefficiencies. This newly found local confidence underlines emerging changes in the relationship between state and local governments and suggests that any evaluation of local government should acknowledge the changing role of local government within communities and include factors such as the role it plays in developing and sustaining local identity, in economic development, in the provision of welfare services and in its contribution to developing the lifestyle of a community.

Expressing identity

That local government means something to its citizens because it expresses where they were born or where they live is arguably one of its longest established roles. This represents the notion of 'identity' though its precise extent is difficult to determine with few direct measures available. In this chapter, two proxy indicators of identity have been used: first, the extent of local reactions to external pressures for consolidation (that is, a measure of how the local community is valued by its members), and second, engagement in the local political process gauged through voter turnout and participation.

Local government consolidation

Over the past three decades, local government has been included as an important part of the nation's economic reform agenda. This agenda has often been expressed at local level through pressures from state governments to consolidate the number of local governments through amalgamation, typically citing benefits of economies of scale that are claimed to result. For the most part, restructuring of local government has been initiated by state governments in the belief that larger units will be more efficient and effective, better suited to the needs of a modern economy, and better able to deliver services and provide sound governance. Predictions of cost savings, and hence reduced property taxes, were a particularly common justification for local government amalgamations especially during the 1990s, when Australia experienced a period of wide-ranging micro-economic reform at all levels in the federation. In the case of sweeping changes made in the state of Victoria for example, it was claimed that savings of about 20 per cent were to be achieved (Moore 1996: 65), although the extent to which any real savings were made in that state and elsewhere remains highly doubtful (Aulich et al. 2014; Bell, Dollery and Drew 2016).

Enquiries into local government amalgamation have typically been focused on efficiency to the exclusion of other issues – such as the importance of good governance and effective local democracy and representation – and rarely included any evaluation of the post-reform experience. There have been questions raised about whether the structural reforms thus far have paid too little attention to the democratic dimension of local government, and concerns have been expressed in some quarters that communities face a growing 'democratic deficit'. Approaches to reform have often been technocratic or top-down (Aulich 1999) with limited opportunities for councils and their communities to have their objections heard. In some cases, established advisory bodies have been by-passed and final decisions made by state ministers responsible for local government. In other cases, state governments waited until *after* major rounds of amalgamations had been completed before establishing advisory bodies, and some states have yet to establish a continuing advisory body even after major structural reforms have been concluded.

Local government has increasingly resisted many of these structural reforms, more often with considerable local support. For example, in Tasmania in 1997, only three years after a collaborative agreement had reduced the number of councils from 46 to 29, the state government unilaterally proposed a further reduction from 29 to 14. Amid 'turbulence and controversy', local governments fought back, led by a group of metropolitan councils which described the state government as 'coercive' and their approach as a 'total affront to democratic principles' (Joint Response 1997). Three smaller councils challenged the forced amalgamations in the Supreme Court of Tasmania, while seven of nine elector polls overwhelmingly opposed amalgamations. Against this backdrop, the state government lost the 1998 elections, in part because of voter reaction to proposals for local government amalgamation (Ruzicka 2016).

In 2008, the number of councils in Queensland was reduced from 157 to 73, generating a community backlash with the establishment of groups such as 'Free Noosa' and 'Capricorn Coast Independence Movement', 'resentful' about the lack of consultation. An incoming conservative government in 2012 gave amalgamated councils the right to apply for de-amalgamation, which was granted to four councils, with others subsequently preparing submissions. The incoming government argued that 'Local Governments need to be autonomous, sustainable, efficient, responsible, accountable and responsive to local needs, with a clear role in enhancing economic, social and environmental quality of life in local communities' (LNP 2011: 2). This focus on community building represented a changing trajectory of reform away from the traditional concerns about efficiency and economies of scale.

In New South Wales in 2015 an attempt was made to reduce the number of councils from 152 to 112, despite a report from the Independent Local Government Review Panel that 'most people are opposed to amalgamations and that only 35 per cent agree that bigger councils could provide better services' (Grennan 2013). The Local Government Minister argued that that 'local government reform is not just about proposed mergers. It's about wider changes to the system to strengthen and improve the ability of councils to deliver the services and infrastructure the community deserves' (ABC News 2015) – no reference being made to local governance or representation. The proposal was widely criticised by voters and councils and a subsequent by-election in a state electorate saw a swing of 35 per cent unseat a government member whose party had held the seat for 70 years. Voters cited objections to forced amalgamation as a key issue for them (SBS News 2016). Other cases in that state were referred to the courts for resolution (Stuart 2017), applying further pressure on the state government to reconsider its amalgamation policies. With the coalition partner in government announcing that it would no longer support forced council amalgamations in rural areas, the state Premier finally announced the abandonment of its amalgamation policies in 2017 (Saulwick 2017).

In the past three decades, the number of councils in Australia has been reduced by nearly a half. While some of these consolidations have been collaborative and have allowed local communities to be engaged in the process of redefining the size and scope of their communities, more often state governments have approached the issue with policies of forced amalgamation. Of late, these policies have been resisted successfully, with arguments based around the need to maintain community identity, even in circumstances where financial viability has been problematic.

Local political engagement

Amalgamations have reduced the number of local representatives with the ratio of population to councillors in Australia now exceeding typical ratios in Europe. In addition, there has been a widespread tendency for amalgamated councils to have fewer elected councillors than the combined total of previous councils, sometimes as few as seven or nine for a population of 150,000. At the same time, the New South Wales state government has instituted a deliberate policy of reducing councillor numbers within *existing* councils. Similarly, legislation in South Australia required councils with more than 12 members to consider reducing their number (Kiss 1997). Significantly, the creation of larger local government units has not been matched by the establishment of subsidiary bodies, such as 'community boards' that exist in parts of New Zealand – although some councils have established informal neighbourhood committees or forums.

At the same time as opportunities for representation have been reduced, voter turnout and 'active participation' has remained low. Research in the 1990s showed that voter turnout at local elections ranged from 12–65 per cent with averages in the low 30s. For most rural local governments only a minority (about 30%) of all seats were contested at elections although this figure was higher in urban elections (about 60%) (Gerritsen and Whyard 1998: 42). More recent research data concerning 'active participation' reveals that little has changed over the past five years from a base of 19 per cent actively participating in civic or political groups (ABS 2013).[3] This finding is perhaps surprising, given that most of the state local government acts legislated during the 1990s introduced mandatory mechanisms for providing greater transparency in local decision-making and for establishing formal mechanisms for enhancing community participation.

It has also been noted that 'Australian citizens are observers rather than participants in formal politics, well over half (54.7%) could not remember conducting any political activity in the last two or three years beyond the practice of voting' (Evans et al. 2013). Voting is not compulsory in local government as it is at state and Commonwealth elections, so it is hardly surprising that voter turnout at local elections remains low. In spite of this, surveys reveal that more people feel that they have greater influence over local decision-making than over national decisions. At the same time, those living in regional communities show less trust in their local governments than their metropolitan counterparts, though this is in the context of declining trust overall for government and politicians (Evans et al. 2016).

One explanation for the apparent passive response to local engagement might be found in the comprehensive Australian Constitutional Values Survey in 2008, which reported that around 40 per cent of Australians do *not* currently have trust in local government performance. Many citizens did not believe local government to be performing well, and blamed lack of resources and weak political status as significant contributing factors (Brown 2009). The report concluded that while a majority of Australians favour some further decentralisation of responsibilities to sub-national governments, there is a 'widely perceived incapacity of any existing subnational level of government to deliver quality local or regional democracy' (Brown 2009: 46). Brown noted that greater attachment to the local area was correlated, albeit fairly weakly, with *less* support for local government. However, he qualified this by arguing that this may be an indicator of the extent to which Australians are 'critical citizens' at a local level, as well as at other levels of governance. People who are more attached to their local area may be more likely to take a closer interest in local politics, and thus be more critically evaluative of the quality of local services and decision-making than others who are not.

The issue is nuanced to the extent that some respondents might support the retention of local government as an important dimension of the national governance system, even if less than satisfied with the performance of particular councils. Brown (2009) concludes:

> Those who value the work of local government appear to do so with a consciousness that it is, indeed, local government which they are valuing, rather than simply being satisfied by the outcomes of services without caring who delivers them. These results confirm that citizens' judgments of local government are not simplistic or ignorant, but based on real interactions with the system.

There is a continuing tension between centrifugal and centralising pressures, which has been captured in a major survey of public opinion about the Australian federation. In his paper on the survey, Brown notes that 'there is majority support (52%) for decentralisation within the system, in the form of the principle of subsidiarity. However, there is also still substantial support (41%) for the principle that decisions are better centralised (Brown 2009: 39). Perhaps this underlines an uncertainty about the roles of the various players in the Australian federation though it may also reflect 'the perceived low performance of local government, which in federal countries such as Canada and the United States commands significantly higher confidence' (Brown 2009: 37).

While there is some ambivalence among communities about the role and performance of local government, it is clear that Australians are resisting municipal consolidation. In particular, pushback is stronger when reform programs are technocratic and do not engage communities in redefining the boundaries of their local areas. The need for sustainable financial and economic reform has been argued by state governments for generations, yet there is still resistance from local communities when proposals for boundary reform arise. Attempts to ameliorate any democratic deficits that may accompany structural reform appear not to have moderated community objections and messages have been sent to state governments that political and legal action are likely to follow unilateral state government proposals to reform council boundaries.

Council consolidation has generated community responses which reflect on the growing appreciation of local government as a major force in expressing local identity and in increasing demands from local communities to be engaged when changes to that identity are being considered. State governments have the formal power to unilaterally reform council boundaries but the resistance from local communities and the demands for local voice are moderating the willingness of state governments to exercise that power. Similarly, there is growing evidence that state governments are more likely to work with local authorities with respect to the economic development of local areas aiming to provide greater coherence in economic development policy and programs.

Economic development

Local government in Australia has a primary role in managing planning and regulation matters especially in the provision of water, sewerage, roads and transport planning. However, the extent of economic development activities and the choice of policy options differ markedly between local governments because of size and capacity. Metropolitan and urban councils typically have a greater capacity to raise revenues than rural and sparsely populated local government areas which are more dependent on assistance from other spheres of government (Twomey 2013: 45; see Table 24.1). As a consequence of this, diversity in capacity and variation in the broader frameworks for economic development established at state level, 'local and regional economic development in Australia is highly complex and lacks coherence' (Pugalis and Tan 2017: 4).

While local government may account for only seven per cent of total public sector outlays, this translates into expenditure of over AUD$16 billion per year or 2.5 per cent of GDP, the collection of four per cent of the total taxation revenue, employment of about 170,000 staff or almost 10 per cent of the total government civilian workforce, and responsibility for more than a quarter of the public sector capital formation, including 30-40 per cent of all construction on electricity distribution, roads and highways, water distribution and sewer systems (Commonwealth of Australia 2012). State and national governments have recognised the importance of this contribution to the national economy and local government reform has been inextricably tied to the national economic reform agenda. At times this has meant a significant narrowing of the reform agenda to issues and programs that advance efficiency rather than on programs and policies that enhance traditional local government democratic values such as participation, responsiveness and representativeness.

Developing new economic roles for local government

The microeconomic reforms of the 1990s were largely driven by state government responses to the national reform agenda, reflecting the strong influence of new public management across all levels of government in Australia (Dollery and Robotti 2008: 93–96). There have been two quite distinct goals of structural reform at local level in Australia – a search for economies of scale and more efficient and effective service delivery on the one hand; and the need for financial viability and strategic capacity to meet emerging challenges on the other. While these goals are inter-related, they do reflect significantly different policy agendas relating to perceptions of the changing role of local government in Australia's federal system.

In relation to local economic development, the abandonment of the *ultra vires*[4] basis of state legislation meant freeing up restrictions on councils to pursue alternative revenue raising and expenditure opportunities and to enable them to operate both more flexibly and more independently of state government – a *limited* form of general competence powers. There is evidence that councils are operating more strategically and utilising the wider powers given under the new local government legislation to broaden their approaches to local economic development.

The more recent emphasis on building strategic capacity (see LGRC 2007), highlights a growing consensus that local government should play more of a developmental role, responding to the varied needs and circumstances of different regions and communities. This applied particularly to areas experiencing rapid economic and population growth, such as South-East Queensland, where the Queensland Local Government Reform Commission favoured larger, more robust units arguing that this would generate economies of scope. The counter argument, advanced by many councils and others, is that resource sharing through strategic alliances, regional organisations of councils or other modes of consolidation apart from amalgamation can achieve the same result, although this may depend on the scope and durability of those cooperative arrangements (see Dollery and Marshall 2003; Aulich et al. 2014).

Taking a similar approach, the New South Wales government has allocated AUD$1.5b from the sale of electricity assets to a Regional Growth Fund aimed at improving local infrastructure such as parks, community centres, data connectivity and building arts and cultural venues with additional special funds made available for mining communities. The projects are designed to tie in with the government's 30-year regional development framework (Sansom 2017), recognising regional diversity and providing greater coherence to economic development in the state.

Enterprise powers to enable councils to engage in business activities were also granted to councils in several states (although they included financial ceilings above which approval by state governments was required) and in other states the new local government acts enabled local government to become involved in entrepreneurial activities and seek membership of unlisted companies, partnerships and associations or undertake land development and trading undertakings as commercial activities.

The move towards general competence powers appeared to be a sincere attempt to strengthen local values by enabling councils to engage more in commercial and community activities free of the limitations imposed by the old, prescriptive local government legislation. State governments encouraged a conception of councils operating as local businesses, and have often drawn analogies between councils and their representatives and a company's Board of Directors and its shareholders. The motivation for this shift has been described by some more cynically as an attempt by state governments to reduce their financial responsibilities for local government. For instance, in introducing some of most radical local government reforms into his state, the then Victorian Minister for Local Government noted that,

> while the Victorian Government was able to take up some of the slack in local government funding through the mid 1980s it can no longer do so because of the significant real terms in reduction in state general purpose grants.
>
> *(LGDV 1990: 2)*

Notwithstanding these views, many councils accepted the challenge to become entrepreneurial and operate more commercially, and as a result there are numerous examples of business ventures and commercial activities developed at local level (for a comprehensive list, see Lewis and Bateson 2013).

Activities which encourage locally led economic development face a number of impediments. First, 'enhanced' responsibilities assumed by local government have been circumscribed by various over-rule provisions contained in state local government legislation. For example, some state governments, impatient with delays in local planning approval, have instituted alternative mechanisms through state government offices or particular developments have been fast tracked or, even, disallowed, under state government over-rule provisions. Further, state government activity has sometimes captured functions that have traditionally been provided by councils, such as the establishment of regional water bodies in Tasmania (Aulich et al. 2014).

Second, given the narrow range of possible revenue sources available to local governments, it is difficult for most councils to meet the increasing demands of their communities for services let alone enhance their economic development roles. In New South Wales for example, it has been estimated that 36 per cent of council income is spent on employees, 24 per cent for materials and contracts (refuse collection, pothole filling, pavement maintenance, lawn mowing, drains cleaning) and 22 per cent for depreciation of infrastructure. This leaves the 'average NSW council with just 18 per cent of current budgets to shape the community at a time when parents call for more childcare centres, cyclists want bike paths, businesses want parking and kids want sports fields' (Campion 2012). Some councils with capacity have, however, made significant progress in promoting the economic health of their communities and programs such as the New South Wales Regional Growth Fund have assisted.

Australian local government no longer has *prime* responsibility to provide physical infrastructure such as main roads, bridges, water supplies and sewerage, as they did during the first half of the twentieth century. Though local government in Australia is operating in the economic development space, its restricted powers and the limits to those powers has meant that it has been difficult for many councils to assume the roles as 'the organiser of a growth machine' (Harding in Stoker 2011). There are signs, however, that the primary focus of local government is shifting from 'roads, rates and rubbish' or 'services to property' more towards 'services to people' (Dollery and Robotti 2008), as local government assumes increasing responsibilities for a wider range of service such as libraries, community health, housing and recreation. In other words, local government has developed a stronger role in welfare provision and community development.

Welfare provision and lifestyle coordination

Councils in the states of Victoria and South Australia pioneered the provision of human and community services at local government level from the 1960s. However, since the reforms of the past three decades, councils in most communities have assumed wider responsibilities in these areas (Lowell 2005) so that it has become one of the basic roles of almost all councils. Of course, the major differences in capacity account for wide variations in the types and level of services that can be offered by councils.

Improved governance and service coordination

With significant funding and programs provided by state and Commonwealth governments, councils have increasingly been required to develop coordinating mechanisms to ensure better integration of services to their communities. These funds and programs are often related to welfare matters such as housing, aged care, employment and services to people with disabilities.

One response has been to develop 'place management' as a guiding basis of governance for many councils. Although this concept may be interpreted variously, it retains some commonality with many international jurisdictions as a 'model for re-casting governments' approach to managing the problems of disadvantaged people and places' (Walsh 2001: 4). In most states, there are examples of place management initiatives targeting disadvantage (see, for example, NSW Premier's Department 2002; ASIB 2011), especially locational disadvantage (Bourke 2003) or neighbourhood renewal initiatives in states like Victoria. The Australian Social Inclusion Board notes that place-based approaches to addressing disadvantage are now a key element of the Australian Government's social inclusion agenda (ASIB 2011).

The concept of place management has also been developed to include mechanisms that transform the way councils are organised and how they operate. It is seen as 'a means of shifting the structure and design of public governance and management from *functional* or *output* units to a focus on *outcomes*' (Zappala and Green 2001: 1). This concentration on outcomes (for example, a sustainable community) distinguishes it from project management, which focuses on outputs (for example, a building). The concept of 'place' in the Australian context has been described variously as 'the process of making places better' (LGRC 2007: 4); or as 'building strategic partnerships between Council, property owners and local businesses, agencies and community groups' to 'get strategic results and coordinate key projects and initiatives in the city centre and neighbourhood centres to achieve the best outcomes' (Parramatta City Council 2012: 2); and as a means for effective community governance by enabling councils to understand what people in their communities are thinking, and as a result take better decisions (McKinlay et al. 2011).

As a framework for structural reform, many councils are pursuing place management (see Mant 2002; Parramatta City Council 2008; Liverpool City Council undated). McKinlay noted that in interviews with local government representatives, a common theme was organisational change, with councils transitioning from 'being functionally structured organisations to organisations designed around place-based management' (McKinlay et al. 2011: 25).

Place-based management is arguably a powerful tool for local governments. Benefits include the ability to operate more holistically, while providing an enabling platform to offer communities and citizens a greater say in how their localities are managed. This view has been reflected in the recent New South Wales Regional Growth Fund, where 'infrastructure' has been more broadly interpreted to include developing arts and cultural venues, community centres, palliative care services and other social capital enhancing ventures. In introducing the program, the state Treasurer noted that the regions require improved infrastructure to service those moving to the regions 'looking for a better lifestyle away from the big cities' (Sansom 2017). The program also recognises that local areas have differing needs, priorities and capacities and the preparation of funding 'bids' enables them to prioritise their local infrastructure needs.

The centrality of place, and the use of place management approaches are increasingly dominating the provision of services by councils to their communities, especially to those citizens facing disadvantage. It has also become a powerful tool to enable some councils to focus attention on important governance issues such as whole-of-local-government approaches to service delivery, more informed targeting of programs, outcomes focused programs and clearer identification of local needs. There are numerous examples of the approach in action, though no fully comprehensive survey has been undertaken, nor has the effectiveness of such approaches been robustly examined. At this stage, it can be concluded that councils in Australia have taken seriously the role of enabling and providing services and strategies designed to meet the broader needs of their communities, although the public value that they create and their effectiveness have yet to be fully assessed.

Conclusions

In the past three decades in Australia, issues such as the distribution of functions and powers, vertical fiscal imbalance, intergovernmental protocols and concerns for overlap and duplication of functions have been the subject of discussion between representatives of the three spheres of government. Despite this opportunity to radically reform intergovernmental relations, the nexus between state and local governments has not been altered to any marked degree, and local autonomy and community governance has not been pursued with the vigour given to programs designed to enhance local government efficiency. The fundamental institutional weaknesses of local government are yet to be addressed: the range of local government functions is comparatively narrow, principles of subsidiarity have not been fully embraced, and effective community governance is only just emerging as an issue.

Nevertheless, local government still retains much of its traditional focuses of concern and has strengthened its sense of local identity by taking firmer and more confident action to identify, promote and protect their local identities. Local government has also added to its traditional roles a wider range of human services which aim to enhance welfare and improve lifestyle of their communities. It is demonstrably leaner, more efficient and better managed with the culture and management practices within individual councils almost unrecognisable from that of a generation ago. Statutory change has mandated more robust community consultation and participation as well as stronger strategic and business planning. Other impacts have variously been reported as providing a more service-orientated culture, a more comprehensive approach to service standards and outputs that reflect community needs, and a focus on service outcomes more than on administrative process.

There are some who raise concerns that economic and managerialist goals have dominated the reform process and given rise to an instrumental perspective that will change fundamentally the role of councils. While the democratic deficit, in particular, has been lamented by some commentators, the reform processes have led to enhancement of democratic practices such as increased accountability, more equitable representation, stronger community engagement, and greater access and transparency.

Two emerging influences may add new challenges to the managerialist focus of reform. First, state government pressure for greater efficiency has yielded fewer, but financially strengthened, local authorities. This may have the unintended consequence of reducing state government leverage over local government and further enhance claims for increased local autonomy (Aulich et al. 2014). Second, the local reaction in states that have approached local government reform in a technocratic way serves to remind state governments that local government is perceived by many in the Australian community as more than a set of instruments for the efficient delivery of local services. Successful resistance to unilateral state reform is emboldening local communities. A more educated and capable citizenry is increasingly using political and legal mechanisms to challenge state governments. This suggests that local power is being flexed despite the clear institutional constraints that it faces.

Notes

1 In this chapter, the term 'state' also includes the Northern Territory. Like all six states it has a system of local government established by Territory legislation making local government a creation of the state government. The Australian Capital Territory and the three external territories were established under Commonwealth legislation giving over-rule powers to the Commonwealth government.
2 Column 3 in Table 24.1 classifies councils as rural (beginning with 'R') or urban ('U'). Compare, for example, the rural Shire of Banana with total annual grants of AUD$220.07 per capita and the nearby urban council of Brisbane with AUD$18.08 per capita.
3 This indicator relates to participation through attending community groups, talking or writing to politicians, signing partitions, voting in elections and in many other ways.
4 Under the *ultra vires* regime, councils were restricted to performing only those activities specifically nominated under *their state* local government legislation.

References

ABC News (2015) NSW Councils to Merge Under State Government Plan for Forced Amalgamations. *ABC News*, 18 December.
ABS (Australian Bureau of Statistics) (2013) 1370.0 Measures of Australia's Progress, 2013: Participation. Retrieved from http://abs.gov.au/ausstats/abs@.nsf/Lookup/by%20Subject/1370.0~2013~Main%20Features~Participation~44.
ACELG (Australian Centre for Excellence in Local Government) (2011) *Consolidation in Local Government: A Fresh Look*. Report. Retrieved from http://acelg.org.au/news-detail.php?id=156.
ASIB (Australian Social Inclusion Board) (2011) *Breaking Cycles of Disadvantage, Part of the Social Inclusion Agenda*. Report. Department of the Prime Minister and Cabinet. Retrieved from www.voced.edu.au/content/ngv45843.
Aulich, C. (1999) From Convergence to Divergence: Reforming Australian Local Government. *Australian Journal of Public Administration* 58(3): 12–23.
Aulich, C., McKinlay, P. and Sansom, G. (2014) A Fresh Look at Municipal Consolidation in Australia. *Local Government Studies* 40(1): 1–20.
Bell, B., Dollery, B. and Drew, J. (2016) Learning from Experience in NSW? *Economic Papers* doi 10.1111/1759-3441.12136
Bourke, P. (2003) *Place Management and Social Capital: What We Are Learning in Brisbane*. Retrieved from www.lgcdsaa.org.au/docs/574199.pdf.
Brown, A. J. (2009) Thinking Big: Public Opinion and Options for Reform of Australia's Federal System. *Public Policy* 4(1): 30–50.
Campion, V. (2012) Patchwork City Comes Undone. *Daily Telegraph*, 8 December.
Commonwealth of Australia (2012) *2008-09 Local Government National Report*. Department of Regional Australia, Local Government, Arts and Sport. Retrieved from www.regional.gov.au/local/publications/reports/2008_2009/LGNR_2008-09.pdf.
Dollery, B. and Marshall, N. (2003) Future Directions. In B. Dollery, N. Marshall and A. Worthington (eds), *Reshaping Australian Local Government*. Sydney: UNSW Press.
Dollery, B. and Robotti, L. (eds) (2008) *The Theory and Practice of Local Government Reform*. Cheltenham: Edward Elgar.
Evans, M., Stoker, G. and Nasir, J. (2013) *How Do Australians Imagine Their Democracy?* Canberra: ANZSOG Institute for Governance, University of Canberra.
Evans, M., Halupka, M. and Stoker, G. (2016) *Who Do You Trust to Run the Country?* Canberra: Institute for Governance and Policy Analysis, University of Canberra.
Expert Panel on Constitutional Recognition of Local Government (2011) *Final Report*. Retrieved from www.rdapilbara.org.au/resources/site1/General/Publication%20Reports/ExpertPanel-FinalReport%20-%20Constitutional%20Recognition%20of%20Local%20Government.pdf.
Finn, P. (1990) Myths of Australian Public Administration. In J. Power (ed.), *Public Administration in Australia: A Watershed*, 41–56. Sydney: Hale and Iremonger.
Gerritsen, R. and Whyard, M. (1998) The Challenge of Constant Change: The Australian Local Government CEO. In K. Klausen and A. Magnier (eds), *The Anonymous Leader*, 31–48. Odense: Odense University Press.
Grennan, H. (2013) Survey reveals most people opposed to council mergers, *The Sydney Morning Herald*, 1 October, p. 30.
Joint Response (1997) *Joint Response to the 1997 Tasmanian Local Government Review Exposure Draft Report*. Hobart: Hobart City Council, Glenorchy City Council and Clarence City Council.
Kiss, R. (1997) Governing Local Communities: Top Down or Bottom Up? The Case of Victoria. In R. Chapman, M. Howard and B. Ryan (eds), *Local Government Restructuring in Australasia*, 45–73. Hobart: Centre for Public Management and Policy, University of Tasmania.
Lewis, C. and Bateson, P. (2013) *Recent Economic Innovation by Australian Local Government*. Discussion Paper. Canberra: ANZSOG Institute for Governance, University of Canberra.
LGDV (Local Government Department of Victoria) (1990) *Microeconomic Reform in Local Government*. Melbourne: LGDV.
LGRC (Local Government Reform Commission Queensland) (2007), Report (Vol. 1). Retrieved from www.dip.qld.gov.au/resources/report/commission-recommendation/vol-01/volume-1-report.pdf.
Liverpool City Council (nd) CBD Place Manager. Retrieved from http://liverpool.nsw.gov.au/our-city/liverpool-city-centre/accessing-planning-controls.

LNP (Liberal-National Party of Queensland) (2011) *LNP CANDO Action: Empowering Queensland Local Government*. Retrieved from http://qldcrs.Igaq.asn.au/c/document_library/get_file?uuid=05073f5-15fc-47b5-9e35-dc1a093aa0d7andgroupId=10136.

Lowell, R. (2005) *Localising Human Services*. Melbourne: Australian Scholarly.

McKinlay, P., Pillora, S., Tan, S. and von Tunzelmann, A. (2011) *Evolution in Community Governance: Building on What Works*. Report. Sydney: ACELG, University of Technology.

Mant, J. (2002) Place Management as an Inherent Part of Real Change: A Rejoinder to Walsh, *Australian Journal of Public Administration* 63(3): 111–116.

Moore, D. (1996) The Financial Benefits of Local Government Reform. In P. Johnston and R. Kiss (eds), *Governing Local Communities – The Future Begins*, 63–72. Melbourne: Centre for Public Policy, University of Melbourne.

NSW Premier's Department (2002) *Local Government Place Management and Community Renewal: An Inventory of Initiatives*. Sydney: NSW Premier's Department.

Parramatta City Council (2012) Place Management. Retrieved from www.parracity.nsw.gov.au/your_council/council/wards_and_place_management.

Pugalis, L. and Tan, S. (2017) *The Role of Local Government in Local and Regional Economic Development*. Sydney: University of Technology.

Robinson, P. and Farrelly, T. (2013) The Evolution of Australia's Intergovernmental Financial Relations Framework. *Australian Journal of Public Administration* 72(3): 304–315

Ruzicka, E. (2016) A Political History of Tasmanian Local Government. PhD thesis, University of Tasmania.

Sansom, M. (2017) NSW Budget: The Impact on Local Councils. *Government News*, 23 June. Retrieved from www.governmentnews.com.au.

Saulwick, J. (2017) NSW Government Abandons Remaining Council Amalgamations. *The Sydney Morning Herald*, 27 July. Retrieved from www.smh.com.au.

SBS News (2016) Orange Bi-election Results Terrible: Baird. *SBS News*, 14 November.

Stoker, G. (2011) Was Local Governance Such a Good Idea? A Global Comparative Perspective. *Public Administration* 89(1): 15–31.

Stuart, R. (2017) Council Amalgamations: Woollahra Heading to High Court. *ABC News*, 6 January.

Twomey, A. (2013) *Local Government Funding and Constitutional Recognition*. Report No. 3, Constitutional Reform Unit, University of Sydney. Retrieved from http://sydney.edu.au/law/cru/documents/2013/CRU_Report_3_%20Local_Government.pdf.

Walsh, P. (2001) Improving Governments' Response to Local Communities – is Place Management the Answer? *Australian Journal of Public Administration* 60(2): 3–12.

Zappala, G. and Green, V. (2001) *Addressing Disadvantage Through Place Management: Is There a Role for Non-profit Organisations?* Working Paper No. 3, The Smith Family Research and Advocacy Team. Retrieved from http://orfeusresearch.com.au/web_images/workingpaperNo3.pdf.

25
LOCAL GOVERNMENT OUTSIDE LOCAL BOUNDARIES

Rescaling municipalities, redesigning provinces and local-level Europeanisation

Koenraad De Ceuninck, Tony Valcke and Tom Verhelst

Introduction

For many decades the traditional picture of local government in most European countries included a three-tier territorial structure and line-of-command. This structure included a first-tier government (i.e. municipalities) defining place-bound local policy, a second-tier government (e.g. provinces, counties, *départements*) overseeing and assisting the latter and central government acting as the over-riding authority. Our chapter discusses a number of evolutions and reforms that have challenged this classic pattern, and ultimately provoked local government to step outside its traditional boundaries.

Denters and Rose (2005: 1) distinguished between macro-level and micro-level trends to denote the 'brave new world' of 'major transformations in the contexts within which local governments operate in most contemporary democracies'. While macro-level trends refer to ongoing processes of urbanisation, globalisation and Europeanisation, their micro-level complements signify the enhanced substantive demands of citizens towards local government as well as their formal quest for participation in the decision-making process. The micro-level trends have been commonly addressed by reforms aiming to improve the efficiency of local government (i.e. output legitimacy) on the one hand and its democratic quality (i.e. input legitimacy) on the other (Kersting and Vetter 2003: 11–26). And although such reforms are by no means a new phenomenon (Rose 2005: 397–399) the rise of local government reorganisation in recent decades signifies a major wave of reform across the European continent.

Starting from the notion of the classic threefold local government structure and line-of-command, this chapter specifically focusses on the macro-level Europeanisation trend and substantive micro-level reforms that have modified traditional local government boundaries. They mainly represent a territorial and / or functional reorganisation of the locality. The former aspect is related to the question how sub-national boundaries are drawn. These boundaries have been subjects of change for many years and this evolution continues. The latter, on the other hand, deals with the allocation of responsibilities and competences among different layers of government. Indeed, a shift of competences through the last decades in many countries has challenged 'old' structures and divisions across the different layers of local government.

At the first tier, these evolutions mainly come down to a redesign of local boundaries with municipal amalgamations, decentralisation and inter-municipal cooperation as the most visible examples of reform – an evolution that goes hand in hand with a shift of competences towards the municipal level. In many countries the municipal level has therefore gained in importance, both in terms of size, financial means and competences. That evolution is taking place against the backdrop of second-tier government being challenged by a continuing search for the most efficient and effective way of coordinating supra-local issues. Traditional structures have subsequently been re-designed, abolished or complemented by new ones (e.g. city regions). Lastly, the ongoing Europeanisation process is challenging national (or in some cases regional) governments as the ultimate supervisory authorities for local government. This has resulted in a new functional design where local authorities comply with EU policies (as mediated by their national government). At the same time, however, the institutional structures of the EU offer them a new functional opportunity to promote local interests at an additional upper-government level.

Within each of these dimensions the chapter first presents an overview of the current situation and its main challenges. Secondly, it outlines the implications for traditional local government in terms of the emergence of new local actors, overlapping responsibilities and spheres of competences, scale and redistribution issues, etc. Finally, within each dimension it presents an assessment of current academic challenges in order to provide students with inspiration for future research activities.

Rescaling municipalities: a story with many facets

The element of scale is very important when talking about local government. Scale is the base for all administrative activities. In that sense, it has always been a part of the debate and discussions on local government reform in past decades in Europe. In the most simple terms, this debate comes down to a discussion between advocates of small versus large local authorities. Both options do have their own rationale (Baldersheim and Rose 2010: 7–10). The first vision argues for small local authorities. In this 'public choice' vision the local political elite is able to deliver local services that provide an answer to specific local needs. If local authorities are not responsive, then it is up to the people to vote them out of office, or to 'vote with their feet' to another local authority were their needs and preferences are better met (Tiebout 1956). This vision also values the idea that local politicians are very accessible for citizens. That access is possible precisely due to the small scale of the local government level. In contrast there is the school that advocates larger local authorities, also called the consolidationist position (Baldersheim and Rose 2010: 8). In this vision, municipalities should merge in order to reach a certain level (and scale) so that they can overcome fragmented, costly and duplicated functions that arise with tighter local boundaries. Larger local authorities are deemed to be more efficient as they can take up more functions and they benefit from economies of scale. That last argument is partly drawn from the private sector, where corporate mergers to achieve scale advantages are a well-known phenomenon.

This discussion comes down to what was already described by Dahl and Tufte (1973). They argued that the search for the optimal scale will always be a trade-off between arguments of efficiency and arguments of very localised democracy. A choice for large scale local authorities will have to be weighed against the advantages of small local authorities. In the same way will the argument of efficiency be balanced against the argument of local democracy. According to both authors, 'no single unit size will be optimal for every purpose' (Dahl and Tufte 1973: 28). In an ideal world, size should be an adaptable and flexible concept, so that units can: 'change in size and scope as technology, communications, values, identifications and other factors alter the balance of gains and costs' (ibid.). The consequence of this dilemma is that every scale decision will always be a compromise. A compromise which essentially involves a political decision about how to structure and organise the local government level.

The current scale debate

Scale reforms, and municipal amalgamations in particular, have been implemented in post-war Europe in the quest for the optimal scale on the local level. These reforms were implemented in two waves. The first wave started in the 1950s and lasted till the 1970s. A second wave started in the 1990s and continued into the current century. It is interesting however to see that both waves differ substantially, not only geographically, but also in the rationale behind their implementation.

The first wave of scale reforms took place in northern and western European countries. Several Scandinavian countries conducted large-scale mergers. Most dramatically, this occurred in Sweden, where the number of municipalities was reduced by 87%. Belgium is also situated in this group thanks to the reform legislation in 1976, which reduced the number of Belgian municipalities by 76%. In the majority of southern European countries scale reforms were limited or even completely absent (Rose 2005: 400). In that period, the focus of these reforms was to put an end to the extensive fragmentation that existed and to implement a minimum or optimal scale for the municipalities so that they could exercise their assigned tasks. Much had to do with the expansion of the welfare state, which in several countries, was an important task for the local level (De Ceuninck, Steyvers, Reynaert and Valcke 2010). The second wave of scale reforms was more focused in central, eastern and southern European countries. For example both Latvia and Greece implemented large scale reforms. Latvia conducted in 2009 a merger by which the number of municipalities was reduced from 524 to 119 (Dexia 2011: 5). In Greece, the same happened in two movements (Getimis and Hlepas 2010). Yet the motivation to implement such scale reforms was not the same during the two waves (Marcou and Wollmann 2008: 133–134). In some eastern European countries, a period of territorial fragmentation started after 1990, often as a reaction against earlier territorial consolidations introduced by former communist governments in an undemocratic manner (Swianiewicz 2010). Quite soon it became clear that this territorial fragmentation was one of the major barriers to the decentralisation and effective functioning of the local government system. As a reaction several countries in eastern Europe introduced some form of scale reform at the local government level, such as the Former Yugoslav Republic of Macedonia and Georgia.

Despite these two waves of scale reforms, the issue of scale did not disappear from the political agenda in the new century. That echoes the arguments of Dahl and Tufte. Existing arrangements are constantly questioned as the socio-economic reality is subject to constant change. Under certain conditions, social changes bring about administrative reforms. In this respect local government has always been the subject of reform in one way or another. The most striking example in this context is Denmark, where a real revolution in local government took place (Mouritzen 2010). The number of Danish municipalities was reduced from 275 to 98. The process was unusual; central government played a vital and dominant role, change moved very quickly, and this left little room for resistance. This brought Mouritzen to the conclusion that 'contrary to received wisdom, the Danish case demonstrates that politics can sometimes achieve the impossible' (Mouritzen 2010: 40).

The 'Danish case' serves as an example for other countries and regions that consider possible scale reforms, for example in Flanders, the Dutch speaking part of Belgium. Both the previous (2009–2014) and the current (2014–2019) Flemish government initiated a debate about internal state organisation. The central elements in their discourse include the reinforcement of local government. Several measures were therefore introduced, such as greater financial autonomy, a decentralisation movement towards the local level and the encouraging of voluntary mergers. The last is remarkable, given the fact that amalgamations have always been a difficult and highly sensitive instrument to implement (De Ceuninck 2009). After all, it affects existing power relations and it can generate new conflicts. Nevertheless, in order to stimulate those mergers, several instruments were created, such as juridical and administrative support with financial incentives. It is also clear that in different German regions and in The Netherlands scale is again under discussion (Walter-Rogg 2010; Boedeltje and Denters 2010). However, in both countries this is a continuation of an existing policy, given that the issue of scale has always been on the political agenda.

Implications of scale discussions for traditional local government

This continuing scale debate and its consequences, an enlargement of the local government level in terms of scale that is often combined with more competences, has strengthened the position of local government across Europe. In several European countries these amalgamations are seen as an instrument in a broader picture, namely as a way to strengthen the local government level, before decentralising extra competences towards the local level. A study from the Council of European Municipalities and Regions (CEMR 2013) points out that a major wave of decentralisation of competences is being prepared in Europe. The question is whether this must be seen as a political commitment towards the local level or as a withdrawal of the central state in a times of crisis? This evolution towards a stronger local government level generates two important consequences for that last, which we will briefly address. First, what are the alternative approaches to deal with the scale issue and second, what about other layers of (supra local) government?

When we talk about the alternatives for municipal amalgamations, the first and foremost alternative is inter-municipal cooperation. Teles (2015) makes the rightful claim that inter-municipal cooperation, despite its relevance, has been less discussed in academic fora than many other local government related themes. The above mentioned study of CEMR (2013: 11) indicates that, despite the many disadvantages associated with municipal amalgamations, this option still remains popular with policy makers. However, the CEMR asserts that amalgamations should be carried out on the basis of well-founded studies. They also argue inter-municipal cooperation can also represent an interesting alternative allowing for more efficient management of competences without losing proximity to the citizens.

A second consequence rises from the fact that the number of European people living in cities and their metropolitan surroundings has rapidly increased during the last decades (Loughlin, Hendriks and Lidström 2011: 10) and those areas have expanded physically. As a result, city-regions (and metropolitan areas) have become more important, both as habitats but also as centres for economic activities. The way these regions are governed touches upon the essence of the debate on scale. However, the reality shows a huge diversity in the way these regions are governed. There are directly elected metropolitan governments (London), but in many instances the development of a city-regional structure resulted in a proliferation of inter-municipal cooperation. As a consequence, local government finds itself in a context in which it has to deal with a multitude of supra local players, in many different forms. Local governments, or independent city-regional structures, will have to deal with that complex reality.

France can serve as an example to illustrate both tendencies. The country did not generally pursue amalgamations, but organised its local level in such a way that inter-municipal cooperation (quite formalised in independent structures) became dominant over the municipalities (Cole 2011: 324). Cole points out that though citizens display more trust in local government institutions, these non-elected structures are responsible for a fast growing part of local expenditure. The challenges this generates have different dimensions. An increasing scale of the local government level demands a different approach towards inter-municipal cooperation. On the other hand, a fast growing landscape of inter-municipal cooperation implies a different approach from the local level in terms of management and democratic accountability. France also witnessed a prolonged debate about the creation of a specific statute for large metropolitan areas (Pasquier 2015).

Current and prospective academic research

The scale debate has reached something of a paradoxical situation. Despite the success of many amalgamation policies in different European countries, many questions can be asked concerning the effects of that policy. The most important effect of amalgamations seems to be an improved service quality, which however does not always seem to go hand in hand with a reduction of costs as proponents of change have hoped for (Steiner et al. 2016). Many other studies have shown that the quality of local democracy suffers as a result of those reforms (Swianiewicz 2010; Kjaer, Hjelmar and Olsen 2010; Lassen and Serritzlew 2011; Denters et al. 2014). In smaller jurisdictions the link between the elected and the citizens is closer. As a result, there is a better flow of information, there is more mutual trust and local governments are more accountable towards the local population. Swianiewicz also points out that several studies show that citizens of small municipalities are more satisfied with local government performance than their counterparts in larger municipalities. As part of research in Denmark after the structural reform in 2007, Kjaer et al. (2010) revealed that local councillors from amalgamated municipalities reported lower levels of influence. A substantially larger proportion of councillors found it more difficult in 2009 (after the structural reform) than in 2003 (before the reform) to realise their political ideas if these were not in agreement with the ideas of the leading administrative officers in the municipality. In that sense their research indicated that political influence shifted, from the elected local council to the local administration.

However, the consequences for local democracy are not the only concern when talking about the results of scale reforms. The question also arises whether the argument holds true that these reforms generate economies of scale. This can be approached from a financial perspective. So the questions are: is spending decreasing? Are costs decreasing? The answers to these questions are crucial for several reasons. Mergers are very often justified and implemented as a purported means of achieving savings. The argument goes that after a municipal merger, things will be organised much more efficiently, and at lower cost than before the operation. A second approach is broader than the first and is about the quality of public services. Usually the latter improve after a municipal merger, which is often due to a more efficient organisation of the local government unit. We do, however, also see here mixed results from studies in this regard. A good example is the study of Allers and Geertsema (2014) from the Netherlands. Based on fifteen years of boundary reforms, they studied the effects of amalgamations on public spending and service levels. In their conclusion Allers and Geertsema are clear:

First, we found no robust evidence of an effect of amalgamation on aggregate municipal spending. Neither an increase nor a decrease of spending can be observed either before or after amalgamation. Secondly, we find no evidence that economies of scale do in fact occur, but only for amalgamations of small jurisdictions, or jurisdictions with homogeneous preferences. Thirdly, we find no evidence supporting the hypothesis that amalgamations generate economies of scale, but that these are used to raise service levels, not to reduce spending.

(Allers and Geertsema 2014: 29)

The authors conclude their research however with a nuanced qualifying statement. Amalgamations of municipalities remain a valid instrument, but it is important to know that economies of scale should not been taken for granted, budgetary savings may be elusive and public services do not automatically improve after a merger. These findings are remarkable, given the fact that the country has a long tradition of amalgamating its municipalities and has a long tradition in evaluating the functioning of the local level (Korsten, Abma and Schutgens 2007). To some extent, similar findings as the one by Allers and Geertsema, were also done in Sweden (Hanes 2015) and in Australia (Aulich et al. 2014). These examples show that there still is a comprehensive research agenda about scale reforms in general and municipal amalgamations in particular to develop.

The demise of the second tier of local government?

Looking at the second tier of local government in Europe (provinces, counties, *départements* and the like) three main features must be taken into account. First, there is a gradual shift from a simple three layer government system into a complex and multi-level institutional landscape. Second, there is the institutional reality that provincial government only plays a modest role within this system. Third, while it is very rare to discern a debate focused on the second tier of local government, most of the time such a debate is part of a broader attempt to reform local government as a whole. Moreover, in the current era of regionalisation the second-tier level has become the weakest link in the chain of multilevel government systems in Europe, which makes it easy to 'target' this level as the main subject of reforms aiming at efficiency and a more simplified institutional architecture (Bertrana, Egner and Heinelt 2016).

Evolution: from territorial rescaling to functional redistribution

Reforms affecting the second level of local government followed the different waves of territorial and structural reforms as described above and affecting the first (municipal) tier of local government. Territorial reforms are mainly intended to optimise the scale for local services and provisions (often framed as enhancing government effectiveness and efficiency) albeit guaranteeing local identities and the democratic inclusion of the local citizenry, functional reforms aim to 'improve' the allocation and division of responsibilities to the different layers of government, including the (re)assignment of tasks and competencies with differing degrees of discretion to the 'local' level (Denters, Goldsmith, Ladner, Mouritzen and Rose 2014). It is often difficult to disentangle functional from territorial reforms, the former often followed the waves of territorial reform.

The aforementioned reform processes also affected the second tier of local government, which frequently is squeezed between the powers of upper levels of government and the municipalities. In some countries it has been up-scaled or even abolished in the context of wider regionalisation processes, in others it has been completely revised to become a proper institutional structure for governing fragmented urban areas by upscaling municipal powers or decentralise tasks of upper government levels (Bertrana, Egner and Heinelt 2016: 1). The only exceptions to this multi-level reform processes can be found in most of the Eastern European countries where decentralisation took place quite recently and - since the democratisation of the second tier of local government over the last thirty years - it has only experienced minor institutional changes.

Northern countries like Denmark, Sweden or the United Kingdom share a long tradition of continuous structural reforms of local government, which has continued during the last decade. Denmark, for example, abolished the 14 existing counties in 2007, shifting most of the tasks to municipalities (which were amalgamated) and creating 5 new regions responsible mainly for health care and hospital provisions (Mouritzen 2011).[1] In Sweden, there is an on-going review of the second tier of local government towards amalgamation which should be complemented by the allocation of more functions of the deconcentrated central state administration at this level of government (Bäck 2011). England is in a continuing process towards the creation of the so-called 'unitary authorities', merging the former counties and districts; in Wales and Scotland unitary councils were created in the mid-1990s.

As opposed to the so called 'North European Strategy', characterised by its coercive top-down approach, the 'South European Strategy' has retained not only the historically based small-size format of the municipalities, but also a highly stable second tier of local government (Bertrana, Egner and Heinelt 2016). One of the most striking features of the reform processes on local government during the last decade in Southern European countries like France, Italy or Spain is their impact on the second tier of local government. In almost all of these cases the economic and financial crisis played a crucial role in the reforms deviating from the 'South European Strategy'.

In France, the *départements* and the regions have been renewed under the government of President Hollande. Sub-national levels of government above the municipalities are experiencing a significant reform of their electoral system, their powers and competences (with a probable abolishment of the general clause of competence) and their territorial structure. In January 2015, for example, different '*métropoles*' were created with both municipal and departmental competences. This applied for cities like Rennes, Bordeaux or Strasbourg. And after the creation of the *métropoles* of Paris and Marseille in 2016, the former 22 regions have been replaced by 13 new regional units.[2]

In Italy in 2015 different provinces have been transformed into ten metropolitan cities. They will also combine the competences of the former municipal and provincial levels of government. These metropolitan cities are led by a 'metropolitan mayor', who is the mayor of the biggest city, and a council consisting of 'metropolitan councillors', elected among and by the municipal councillors and mayors. Furthermore, a transitional regime for the remaining provinces has been proposed and they may be abolished if there is a successful Constitutional reform (Baccetti and Magnier 2016). However, general political uncertainty in Italy leaves it unclear what further specific changes might occur.

The plans of the Dutch cabinet to reduce the number of provinces through mergers have failed.[3] Moreover the existing law on inter-municipal structures (the so-called 'Wgr+' arrangement) was abolished and the provinces became the first and most important government level for spatial planning. Nevertheless, ideas about city-regions, the ongoing amalgamation of municipalities and the development of new cooperative arrangements between municipalities and provinces are still central to an ongoing process of reform (Castenmiller and Herweijer 2015).

Since the regionalisation of the competences regarding the organisation of local government in Belgium (in 2001), the reform plans in Belgium differ in the two main regions of the country (Valcke and Verhelst 2015: 70). After the 2014 regional elections, the Walloon government consolidated the provinces. They remain important at the intermediate government level to support municipalities in partnership with the regional government. The Flemish government that came into power in 2014 in contrast, planned a far-reaching functional reform, altering the role of the provinces. From 2018 onwards Flemish provinces will only be responsible for territory-related competences (and no longer for person-related competences).

The Czech Republic illustrates the exception to the multi-level reform process in Eastern European countries. Since 2000 the country is divided into 14 regions (called 'kraje') acting as the second tier of local government (CEMR 2016: 22–23). And while there is virtually no debate on the abolition of the regions, neither is there debate or reform trying to establish a metropolitan government.

These examples not only show that the democratic quality as well as the effectiveness of the second tier of local government is increasingly contested in the ongoing re-scaling of statehood, but also that reform processes are opening up even in countries where until now this level of local government has shown a high capacity to resist any attempt to impose far-reaching structural reforms.

The implications for traditional local government

In most large and medium sized European countries, local government functions are divided between a municipal and a second tier. Among the European Union member states such units are present in 19 of 28 states (Loughlin, Hendriks and Lidström 2011). Some common functions of the second tier include responsibility for secondary education, health care and specialised social services which typically require larger populations. In addition, the second tier may also have supervisory and coordinating functions vis-à-vis municipalities and other actors (Heinelt and Bertrana 2011).

The recent CEMR report 'Local and Regional Governments in Europe' states that the number of local entities in Europe has decreased by approximately 15% while the number of regions has increased by approximately 10% (CEMR 2016: 3). Although issues of structural reform always are embedded in pre-existing (and shifting) central–local relations, the regionalisation and amalgamation processes have altered the context. Indeed, the need for a second tier level may diminish when amalgamations create larger municipalities with equally increased functions and capacity.

Moreover, there is a further structural development in the background. Traditional forms of place-bound government (national states, provinces and municipalities) are under pressure and are replaced or at least supplemented by government organised through interests. This development is sometimes reflected in functional regions but also in virtual interest or pressure groups. Hence, the relevance of place-bound government is challenged by the network society where dynamic scale levels and 'daily urban systems' could take over from traditional government levels (Castenmiller and Herweijer 2015). While in some countries metropolitan areas are already created, in other countries the city-regional debate is gaining ground. One important question however always needs to be addressed and that is how to guarantee the democratic aspect of decisions in such a network environment.

Current and prospective academic research

Specific scholarly attention to the second tier of local government is rather scarce. Theoretical and empirical observations can be found in the literature concerning government reform in general and publications dedicated to reforms at the municipal level. This should not come as a surprise given the relative weak position of the second tier and the multi-level dimension of 21st century (local) government.

Sadioglu and Dede (2016a, 2016b) edited two volumes, the first of which addresses the effects of recent reforms on local government and politics as well as future innovations. The second volume presents relevant perspectives from comparative research and case studies regarding the structure, process and policymaking aspects of local government.

Schwab, Bouckaert and Kuhlmann (2017) edited a volume on the future of local government in Europe. Their starting point is the wave of political and administrative reforms European local government had to cope with in recent decades. Not only is local government responsible for efficient administration, high-quality services and a legally correct execution of laws, but also for ensuring legitimacy, democratic participation, accountability and trust. Moreover, severe conditions of austerity have been implemented in the aftermath of the economic and financial crisis. The volume presents research findings of an international project on local public sector reforms in 31 countries and tries to give advice to policymakers to shape the future of local government in Europe, addressing key features of local governance like autonomy, performance and participation.

A rare example of a study dedicated solely to the second tier of local government is the volume edited by Heinelt and Bertrana (2011). The book takes a comparative approach to local government across 14 European countries, looking at processes of decentralisation, regionalisation and reforms of local government. The combination of a comparative analysis of institutional trends and reforms of local government with an examination of country-specific features and analysis of recent reform debates, leads the book to argue that the democratic quality and effectiveness of this territorial level of government is in the focus of on-going debates about the rescaling of statehood and a shift from 'government to governance'.

The more recent volume by Bertrana, Egner and Heinelt (2016) had a different approach. It provides a thematic and cross-national analysis of the key actors in local government. Still focussing on the second tier of local government, it examines new empirical data on councillors in 15 European countries and integrates important variables such as party politics, notions of democracy, finance, multi-level settings.

Apart from these rare general approaches there are some authors with country specific focus on the second tier of local government. In these publications two main concerns emerge: first, what is the optimal scale of intermediate government (do we need smaller or larger entities?) and second, how can democratic quality be guaranteed (Baccetti and Magnier 2016; Castenmiller and Herweijer 2015; Valcke and Verhelst 2015).

Future research could on the one hand focus on the effects of the ongoing regionalisation and amalgamation processes for the future role of the second tier level (can it adapt or is it becoming redundant?). On the other hand research is still short on the meaning and importance of identity politics at the intermediate government level. Despite the dawn of network society and daily urban systems, in many countries in at least some of the provinces there is some form of territorial connectedness at the intermediate level that citizens experience – although in other parts of the same countries this is totally absent. Research on how the polis deals with this could explore many aspects of how to build a qualitative government structure for the future of network society.

The Europeanisation of local government: central–local relations revisited?

A third fundamental transformation of local government boundaries concerns the increasing impact of the EU as an additional upper-government layer. Traditionally, local government has been defined by the central state in terms of its functions, discretion, underlying ethos, autonomy, constitutional status and access to higher government levels (Page and Goldsmith 1987; Hesse and Sharpe 1991). Yet in the wake of the European integration process in the 1980s–1990s, and the completion of the Single Market and development of EU regional policy in particular, local government has become increasingly subject to European legislation as well (Goldsmith and Klausen 1997; John 2000). Particularly in policy fields such as the environment, the Single Market and cohesion, the impact of European legislation is substantial nowadays (Guderjan 2015). Regarding the latter, the EU also aims to promote its significance and policies in an indirect way via programmes and financing opportunities for which local authorities can compete (Schultze 2003). At the same time, the top-down regulatory impact of the EU has been matched by proactive bottom-up involvement of local authorities contributing to the EU decision-making process that will affect them later on and/or promote local interests at a higher level (de Rooij 2002) (e.g. individually, or via local networks such as EUROCITIES or associations such as CEMR).[4]

Europeanisation: challenging central–local relations within the state

The dynamic, multifaceted relationship between local government and the EU is commonly defined as the 'Europeanisation of local government'. For Hamedinger and Wolffhardt (2010: 28), this concept denotes:

> the interplay between actors and institutions on the European and the city level, which leads to changes in local politics, policies, institutional arrangements, discourse, actors' preferences, values, norms and belief systems on both levels.

Given its comprehensive impact on local authorities, Europeanisation has been singled out as one of the most fundamental developments in local governance during the past decades (John 2001; Denters and Rose 2005). The new intergovernmental relationship between local government and the EU is moreover part of a broader system of multi-level governance (MLG), in which policy is shaped by non-hierarchical networks of interdependent state and non-state actors (Bache and Flinders 2004).[5] With the acknowledgement of local self-government and subsidiarity in the Lisbon Treaty (2009), the Commission White Paper on European Governance (2001), the Committee of the Regions White Paper on Multilevel Governance (2009) and, more recently, the EU urban agenda and the Pact of Amsterdam (2016), the EU has also (and increasingly) sought to formalise this multilevel concept and the role and structural involvement of local government therein.

There is no doubt that the Europeanisation of local government has changed existing central–local relations in the Member States. Bomberg and Peterson (1996: 1) argue in this regard:

> it has become impossible to understand relations between local and central government in Europe without considering the impact of the European Union (EU) decisions and decision-making. European Union policies . . . have yielded complex relationships between sub-national, national and supranational levels of governments.

Although the characteristic intra-state relations have not become obsolete (Goldsmith 2011), they are affected by Europeanisation in several ways. The top-down impact of EU rules, for instance, reduces the legislative grip of central government, but puts an additional strain on local autonomy and self-government instead (Fleurke and Willemse 2006). Besides, the EU's legislative impact is also mediated to some extent by existing central–local relations since the latter still define the competences and functions of local authorities generally (Jeffery, in de Rooij 2002). Indeed, the impact of EU rules is felt more strongly when local authorities have more competences in the first place. Some Member States also try to find a way to manage the anticipated consequences of the Europeanisation of local government – for instance when they are fined for the non-compliance of local authorities with EU law. In this respect, for example, new acts in the Netherlands and the UK allow central government to pass the cost of European fines on to non-complying local authorities, or to intervene in local policy-making which is perceived to go against EU rules (Backes and van der Woude 2013; Varney 2013).

As regards the bottom-up mobilisation of local government towards the EU, Hooghe and Marks (1996: 73) refer to the new European multilevel polity as a potential 'multiplication of extra-national channels for subnational activity'. Such 'para-diplomacy', however, comes in different forms in practice (Callanan and Tatham 2014). Whereas by-passing the central state to contact EU decision-makers might simply go unnoticed, it can also result in direct conflict when opposite positions are advocated by the central and local level. Cooperative para-diplomacy, on the other hand, where local government uses national government to approach EU-institutions, might be more effective. Besides, the very choice between the different forms of para-diplomacy is often moulded by existing central–local relations and party political contacts in the state as well (Tatham 2010) while it affects those relations in return (Goldsmith 2005). In fact, direct access to European decision-makers might enhance the autonomy of local government vis-à-vis the central state.

The impact on traditional local government

Europeanisation not only affects the central–local relations in the Member States, it also impacts upon local authorities' internal organisation and functioning. Basically, Europeanisation has an impact on nearly the entire range of local government functions (e.g. employer, licensing body, purchaser, planner, etc.) and policy domains (energy, economy, environment, culture, tourism, education, health and safety, etc.). Klausen and Goldsmith (1997) discern three types of impact. First, EU rules directly affect local authorities in their daily operation (e.g. public procurement rules, liberalisation of the energy market). Second, an indirect impact refers to the increased harmonisation of local policy as result of European rules (e.g. working conditions, environmental policy, consumer affairs). Third, Europeanisation has altered the technical, institutional and political context of local government. Competition between local authorities has drastically increased in the quest for European funding or stimulating local trade and industry. Internally, the organisation and behaviour of the local authorities have changed as well. New policy expectations, innovative forms of cooperation and negotiation, adjustments in the organisation (e.g. establishing a department for EU affairs) and task division (e.g. allocating personnel to EU affairs) are common third-order consequences of the Europeanisation process.

Several authors have created a typology or classification to depict the internal Europeanisation of local government. John (2001) uses the image of a ladder with ascending degrees of internal Europeanisation and the corresponding discretion of the local authority to engage with Europe. In the minimal phase, local authorities merely seek to meet the EU's legal requirements. The second phase is financially orientated as the authorities aim at maximising their efforts in the competition for European funding. When local governments enter the third phase, they engage in networking with other authorities in the EU. In the final phase local governments are fully Europeanised; they incorporate EU policies in their internal policy agenda and enter in the process of EU decision-making.

Goldsmith and Klausen (1997) distinguish between counteractive, passive, reactive and proactive local authorities. The first category refers to those authorities which are sceptical about EU affairs and deliberatively choose not to participate in Europeanisation processes. Passive authorities more often engage with Europe as a coincidence than as the result of a deliberative policy choice. Reactive governments, on the other hand, do have an interest in Europeanisation dossiers and are keen on learning, even though their engagement usually builds further upon the initiatives from other actors. Finally, the proactive group is a fairly small one. It consists of those authorities which have a clear vision on their place in Europe and consequently take the lead in Europeanisation processes. These four categories largely coincide with the four general outcomes of Europeanisation that Radaelli (2000) has described: retrenchment, inertia, absorption and transformation.

Irrespective of the typology used to study Europeanisation, it is clear that there is only a small minority of cities and municipalities that belongs to the pioneering group of fully Europeanised governments. Moreover, a closer look at the possible determinants of this internal Europeanisation process reveals a complex and compound reality as well. The list of determinants includes local government size and structural position in the state, national culture, available resources (e.g. finance, personnel, expertise and knowledge), but also eligibility for funding, intrinsic motivations and perceptions, and the presence of political and administrative policy entrepreneurs (e.g. de Rooij 2002; Hamedinger and Wolffhardt 2010; Goldsmith 2011).

Current and prospective academic research

The academic state of the art has grown in parallel with the Europeanisation process from the 1990s onwards. Following from the multifaceted nature of this process, Europeanisation research is quite diverse. Some general lines of inquiry in this large body of empirical research are outlined below.

A first group of studies tackles Europeanisation in a comparative fashion. In 1997, Goldsmith and Klausen edited a book titled *European Integration and Local Government*, which took stock of the Europeanisation of local government in 12 countries at the end of the century. In addition to the different country chapters, which provide useful benchmarks to scrutinise the Europeanisation process over time, the comparative summary yielded a classification of local authorities (see previous section) and an overview of national disparities and underlying mechanisms. One decade later, two comparative edited volumes (Hamedinger and Wolffhardt 2010; Van Bever et al. 2011b) combined thematic in-depth studies at city and/or country level with a theoretical and conceptual overview of the state of the art and a research agenda. The edited volume of Panara and Varney (2013) presents an overview of the position of local government in the multilevel system in 13 European countries on the basis of several themes such as the constitutional framework, local autonomy, organisation and elections, supervision and collaboration, functions, funding, reforms and the European dimension to local government.

The academic state of the art is further comprised of a wide range of studies focusing on particular elements of our research subject. Some examine the diverse aspects of the Europeanisation of local government in a particular country context (e.g. de Rooij 2002; Van Bever et al. 2011a; Guderjan 2015). Others deal with one particular element or dimension of Europeanisation in a given setting. The latter group includes among others implementation studies dealing with

EU compliance at the local level (e.g. Bondarouk and Liefferink 2017), studies of the interest representation of local government (and its associations) in the EU (e.g. John 1994; Heinelt and Niederhafner 2008; Callanan 2012), networks of local authorities at EU level (e.g. Huggins 2013), and the financial mobilisation of local government targeting EU subsidies and programmes (e.g. Schultze 2003; Zerbinati 2012; Verhelst et al. 2015).

In summary, there is an emerging research agenda focusing on the Europeanisation of local government from different perspectives. Future comparative research could build on the work that has been done thus far, while including new (above all East and Central-European) Member States in the analysis and using a common framework of research. Thematic in-depth analyses are recommended to complement the existing research agenda (see e.g. Hamedinger and Wolffhardt 2010; Goldsmith 2011).

Conclusion

This chapter addressed the shifts in the boundaries of traditional local government during the past decades across Europe. This evolution was characterised by a transformation from the typical three-layer structure in which the local level, the second tier government and national authorities played a leading role, towards a more diffuse landscape with shifting boundaries and competences. Furthermore, the contribution identified the main consequences of this evolution for traditional local government and drafted a research agenda responding to it.

With regard to first tier government, the shifting boundaries imply important territorial and functional evolutions. On the one hand, we notice an ongoing search for the optimal scale of local authorities, which in reality comes down to an enlargement of the latter by municipal amalgamations. In many European countries these amalgamations go hand in hand with transferring competences from higher government levels towards the local level. We can therefore conclude that across Europe, the local level is often strengthened during this wave of reform. The research agenda accompanying this evolution is dominated by research into the effectiveness of those reforms. Many recent studies questioned the acclaimed positive outcomes of scale reforms in general and amalgamations in particular.

In contrast with the reinforcement of first tier government, a second transformation of the local boundaries involves major change in the second tier of local government. Most remarkably, this evolution can be observed even in countries where this government level has always shown a high capacity to resist any attempt to impose far-reaching structural reforms. In the current era of regionalisation (with an increase of the number of regions by 10%) the second tier level has become the weakest link in the chain of multilevel government systems in Europe, which makes it easy to 'target' this level as the main subject of reforms aiming at efficiency and a more simplified institutional architecture. Moreover the need for a second tier level diminishes when amalgamations create larger municipalities with equally increased functions and capacity. Finally the relevance of place-bound government is challenged by the network society where dynamic scale levels and 'daily urban systems' could take over from traditional government levels. While specific scholarly attention to the second tier of local government is rather scarce, future research could focus on the effects of the ongoing regionalisation and amalgamation processes for the future role of the second tier level. In addition research lacks on the meaning and importance of identity politics at the intermediate government level.

Finally, local government's central line-of-command has shifted as a result of the ongoing Europeanisation of the local level. Nowadays European rules co-determine many functions and policies of traditional local government. For local government, however, the EU offers as much an additional arena to promote local political interests at a higher political level (in some cases even via by-passing the central state) as it can place a further strain on local autonomy. The relationship between the EU and local authorities is therefore challenging (but not completely replacing) traditional central–local relations in many European member states. Furthermore, the Europeanisation process has impacted upon the internal organisation and activities of local authorities as well (e.g. establishing an EU-department, participating in EU-programmes). Given the recent establishment of local-level Europeanisation as an academic discipline, future comparative and thematic in-depth research could significantly contribute to our understanding of this complex and challenging process.

Notes

1 The new government structures at the Danish regional level also have certain responsibilities regarding regional development, environmental protection and public transportation. These regions do not have the right to impose taxes on their inhabitants, thus relying on transfers from the municipalities and the state.
2 It is unclear if this will proceed. According to the official government website www.gouvernement.fr/action/la-reforme-territoriale (updated on 4 October 2017; last consultation on 22 October 2017) the reform was still on track.
3 The plan was to create 5 or 7 larger entities (called 'landsdelen' or regions) replacing the 12 existing provinces.
4 Additionally, the European context provides new opportunities and incentives for horizontal (often transnational) cooperation between local authorities.
5 For a broader reflection on the connection of intergovernmental relations and MLG, see Ongaro et al. (2010).

References

Allers, M. A. and Geertsema, J. B. (2014). *The Effects of Local Government Amalgamation on Public Spending and Service Levels. Evidence from 15 Years of Municipal Boundary Reform*. Groningen: University of Groningen.
Aulich, C., Sansom, G. and McKinlay P. (2014). A Fresh Look at Municipal Consolidation in Australia. *Local Government Studies*, 40 (1), 1–20.
Baccetti, C. and Magnier, A. (2016). The Italian 'Second Level' in Search of Identity: the Elimination of the Provincia and the Birth of the Metropolitan City. In *Revista Catalana de Dret Públic*, 52 (June 2016), 1–21.
Bache, I. and Flinders, M. (2004). *Multi-Level Governance*. Oxford: Oxford University Press.
Bäck, H. (2011). Sweden. In H. Heinelt and X. Bertrana (eds), *The Second Tier of Local Government in Europe. Provinces, Counties, Départements and Landkreise in Comparison*, 243–268. Abingdon: Routledge.
Backes, C. and van der Woude, W. (2013). The Netherlands. Local Authorities in the Polder-Dutch Municipalities and Provinces. In C. Panara and M. Varney (eds), *Local Government in Europe. The 'Fourth Level' in the EU Multilayered System of Governance*, 231–254. Abingdon: Routledge.
Baldersheim H. and Rose L. E. (eds) (2010). *Territorial Choice. The Politics of Boundaries and Borders*. Basingstoke: Palgrave Macmillan.
Bertrana, X., Egner, B. and Heinelt, H. (eds) (2016). *Policy Making at the Second Tier of Local Government in Europe: What is Happening in Provinces, Counties, Départements and Landkreise in the On-going Rescaling of Statehood?* Abingdon: Routledge.
Boedeltje, M. and Denters, B. (2010). Step-by-Step: Territorial Choice in the Netherlands. In H. Baldersheim and L.E. Rose (ed.), *Territorial Choice. The Politics of Boundaries and Borders*, 118–137. Basingstoke: Palgrave Macmillan.
Bomberg, E. and Peterson, J. (1996). *Decision-Making in the European Union. Implications for Central–Local Government Relations*. Layerthorpe: York Publishing.
Bondarouk, E. and Liefferink, D. (2017). Diversity in Sub-national EU Implementation: The Application of the EU Ambient Air Quality Directive in 13 Municipalities in the Netherlands. *Journal of Environmental Policy and Planning* 19 (6), 733–753.

Callanan, M. (2012). Subnational Collective Action: The Varied Patterns of Mobilisation of Local Government Associations. *Local Government Studies*, 38 (6), 753–775.

Callanan, M. and Tatham, M. (2014). Territorial Interest Representation in the European Union: Actors, Objectives and Strategies. *Journal of European Public Policy*, 21(2), 188–210.

Castenmiller, P. and Herweijer, M. (2015), De Nederlandse provinciën. In H. Reynaert (ed.), *Uitdagingen voor de lokale besturen 2015–2019*, 87–102. Brugge: Vanden Broele.

CEMR (2013). *Decentralisation at a Crossroads. Territorial Reforms in Europe in Times of Crisis*. Brussels: Council of European Municipalities and Regions.

CEMR (2016). *Local and Regional Governments in Europe. Structures and Competences*. Brussels: Council of European Municipalities and Regions.

Cole, A. (2011). France: Between Centralization and Fragmentation. In J. Loughlin, F. Hendriks and A. Lidström (ed.), *The Oxford Handbook of Local and Regional Democracy in Europe*, 307–330. Oxford: Oxford University Press.

Dahl, R. and Tufte, E. (1973). *Size and Democracy*. Stanford: Stanford University Press.

De Ceuninck, K. (2009). *De gemeentelijke fusies van 1976. Een mijlpaal voor de lokale besturen in België*. Brugge: Vanden Broele.

De Ceuninck, K., Reynaert, H., Steyvers, K. and Valcke, T. (2010). Municipal Amalgamations in the Low Countries: Same Problems, Different Solutions. *Local Government Studies*, 36(6), 803–822.

Denters, B., Goldsmith, M., Ladner, A., Mouritzen, P.-E. and Rose, L. (2014). *Size and Local Democracy*. Cheltenham: Edward Elgar.

Denters, B. and Rose, L. (2005). Local Governance in the Third Millennium: A Brave New World? In B. Denters and B. L. Rose (ed.), *Comparing Local Governance: Trends and Developments*, 1–11. Basingstoke: Palgrave.

De Rooij, R. (2002). The Impact of the European Union on Local Government in the Netherlands. *Journal of European Public Policy*, 9 (3), 447–467.

Dexia (2011). *Financiën van de infranationale overheden in de Europese Unie*. Paris: Dexia Editions.

Fleurke, F. and Willemse, R. (2006). The European Union and the Autonomy of Sub-national Authorities: Towards an Analysis of Constraints and Opportunities in Sub-national Decision-making. *Regional and Federal Studies*, 16 (1), 83–98.

Getimis, P. and Hlepas, N. (2010). Efficiency Imperatives in a Fragmented Polity: Reinventing Local Government in Greece. In H. Baldersheim and L.E. Rose (ed.), *Territorial Choice. The Politics of Boundaries and Borders*, 198–213. Basingstoke: Palgrave Macmillan.

Goldsmith, M. (2005). A New Intergovernmentalism? In B. Denters and L. Rose (ed.), *Comparing Local Governance: Trends and Developments*, 228–245. Basingstoke: Palgrave.

Goldsmith, M. (2011). Twenty Years On: The Europeanization of Local Government. In E. Van Bever, H. Reynaert and K. Steyvers (ed.), *The Road to Europe. Main Street or Backward Alley for Local Governments in Europe?*, 31–48 Brugge: Vanden Broele.

Goldsmith, M. and Klausen, K. K. (1997). European Integration and Local Government: Some Initial Thoughts. In M. Goldsmith and K.K. Klausen (ed.), *European Integration and Local Government*, 1–15. Cheltenham: Edward Elgar.

Guderjan, M. (2015). Theorising European Integration of Local Government – Insights from the Fusion Approach. *Local Government Studies*, 41 (6), 937–955.

Hamedinger, A. and Wolffhardt, A. (2010). *The Europeanization of Cities. Policies, Urban Change and Urban Networks*. Amsterdam: Techne Press.

Hanes, N. (2015). Amalgamation Impacts on Local Public Expenditures in Sweden. *Local Government Studies*, 41 (1), 63–77.

Heinelt, H. and Bertrana, X. (eds) (2011). *The Second Tier of Local Government in Europe. Provinces, Counties, Départements and Landkreise in comparison*. London: Routledge.

Heinelt, H. and Niederhafner, S. (2008). Cities and Organized Interest Intermediation in the EU Multi-Level System. *European Urban and Regional Studies*, 15 (2), 173–187.

Hesse, J. J. and Sharpe, L. J. (1991). Local Government in International Perspective: Some Comparative Observations. In J. J. Hesse (ed.), *Local Government and Urban Affairs in International Perspective. Analyses of Twenty Western Industrialized Countries*, 605–608. Baden-Baden: Nomos-Verlagsgesellschaft.

Hooghe, L. and Marks, G. (1996). 'Europe with the Regions': Channels of Regional Representation in the European Union. *Publius: The Journal of Federalism*, 26 (1), 73–91.

Huggins, C. (2013). Motivations Behind Local Government Transnational Networking. *Regional Insights*, 4(1), 9–11.

John, P. (1994). Local Government and the European Union Lobbying. *Contemporary Political Studies*, 2, 906–921.
John, P. (2000). The Europeanisation of Sub-national Governance. *Urban Studies*, 37 (5–6), 877–894.
John, P. (2001). *Local governance in Western Europe*. London: Sage.
Kersting, N. and Vetter, A. (eds), (2003). *Reforming Local Government in Europe: Closing the Gap between Democracy and Efficiency*. Opladen: Leske + Budrich.
Kjaer, U., Hjelmar, U. and Olsen, A. L. (2010). Municipal Amalgamations and the Democratic Functioning of Local Councils: The Case of The Danish 2007 Structural Reform. *Local Government Studies*, 36 (4), 569–585.
Klausen, K. K. and Goldsmith, M. (1997). Conclusion: Local Government and the European Union. In M. Goldsmith and K. K. Klausen (ed.), *European Integration and Local Government*, 237–254. Cheltenham: Edward Elgar.
Korsten, A. F. A., Abma, K. and Schutgens, J. M. L. R. (2007). *Bestuurskracht van gemeenten. Meten, vergelijken en beoordelen*. Delft: Eburon.
Lassen, D. D. and Serritzlew, S. (2011). Size and Equal Opportunity in the Democratic Process: The Effect of the Danish Local Government Reform on Inequality in Internal Political Efficacy. *World Political Science Review*, 7 (1), 145–162.
Loughlin, J., Hendriks, F. and Lidström A. (eds) (2011). *The Oxford Handbook of Local and Regional Democracy in Europe*. Oxford: Oxford University Press.
Marcou G. and Wollmann H. (eds) (2008). *Annuaire 2008 des Collectivités Locales*. Paris: CNRS.
Mouritzen, P. E. (2010). The Danish Revolution in Local Government: How and Why? In H. Baldersheim and L. E. Rose (ed.), *Territorial Choice. The politics of Boundaries and Borders*, 21–41. Basingstoke: Palgrave Macmillan.
Mouritzen, P. E. (2011). Denmark. In H. Heinelt and X. Bertrana (eds), *The Second Tier of Local Government in Europe. Provinces, Counties, Départements and Landkreise in Comparison*, 56–72. Abingdon: Routledge.
Ongaro, E., Massey, A., Holzer, M. and Wayenberg, E. (2010). *Governance and Intergovernmental Relations in the European Union and the United States: Theoretical Perspectives*. Cheltenham: Edward Elgar.
Page, E. and Goldsmith, M. (1987). Centre and Locality: Functions, Access and Discretion. In E. Page and M. Goldsmith (ed.), *Central and Local Government Relations. A Comparative Analysis of Western European Unitary States*, 3–11. London: Sage.
Panara, C. and Varney, M. (2013). *Local Government in Europe. The 'Fourth Level' in the EU Multilayered System of Governance*. Abingdon: Routledge.
Pasquier, R. (2015). *Regional Governance and Power in France: The Dynamics of Political Space*. Basingstoke: Palgrave Macmillan.
Radaelli, C. (2000). Whither Europeanization? Concept Stretching and Substantive change. *European Integration online Papers (EIoP)* 4(8). Retrieved from http://eiop.or.at/eiop/texte/2000-008a.htm.
Rose, L. (2005). Territorial and Functional Reforms: Old Wine in New Bottles or a New Vintage? In H. Reynaert, K. Steyvers, P. Delwit and J. B. Pilet (eds), *Revolution or Renovation? Reforming Local Politics in Europe*, 397–419. Brugge: Vanden Broele.
Sadioglu, U. and Dede, K. (eds) (2016a). *Theoretical Foundations and Discussions on the Reformation Process in Local Governments*. Hershey: IGI Global.
Sadioglu, U. and Dede, K. (eds) (2016b). *Comparative Studies and Regionally-Focused Cases Examining Local Governments*. Hershey: IGI Global.
Schultze, C. J. (2003). Cities and EU Governance: Policy-Takers or Policy-Makers? *Regional and Federal Studies*, 13 (1), 121–147.
Schwab, C., Bouckaert, G. and Kuhlmann, S. (eds) (2017). *The Future of Local Government in Europe. Lessons from Research and Practice in 31 Countries*. Baden-Baden: Nomos.
Steiner, R., Kaiser, C. and Thor Eythorsson, G. (2016). A Comparative Analysis of Amalgamation Reforms in Selected European Countries. In S. Kuhlmann and G. Bouckaert (eds), *Local Public Sector Reforms in Times of Crisis*, 23–42. Basingstoke: Palgrave Macmillan.
Swianiewicz, P. (ed.) (2010). *Territorial Consolidation Reforms in Europe*. Budapest: Open Society Institute.
Tatham, M. (2010). 'With or Without You'? Revisiting Territorial State Bypassing in EU Interest Representation. *Journal of European Public Policy*, 17 (1), 76–99.
Teles, F. (2015). *Local Governance and Intermunicipal Cooperation*. Basingstoke: Palgrave Macmillan.
Tiebout, C. M. (1956). A Pure Theory of Local Expenditures. *Journal of Political Economy*, 64(5), 416–424.

Valcke, T. and Verhelst, T. (2015). Functionele en territoriale hervormingen van het decentraal bestuur. Op zoek naar visie en draagvlak bij provincieraadsleden. In H. Reynaert (ed.), *Uitdagingen voor de lokale besturen 2015–2019*, 59–86. Brugge: Vanden Broele.

Van Bever, E., Reynaert, H. and Steyvers, K. (2011a). Lokale besturen en Europa: Een verkennend onderzoek naar de invloed van Europa op de lokale besturen in Vlaanderen. *Burger bestuur en beleid*, 7 (4), 271–287.

Van Bever, E., Reynaert, H. and Steyvers, K. (2011b). *The Road to Europe. Main Street or Backward Alley for Local Governments in Europe?* Brugge: Vanden Broele.

Varney, M. (2013). United Kingdom. Local Government in England: Localism Delivered? In C. Panara and M. Varney (ed.), *Local Government in Europe. The 'Fourth Level' in the EU Multilayered System of Governance*, 330–368. Abingdon: Routledge.

Verhelst, T., Van Bever, E. and Reynaert, H. (2015). Europese programma's en subsidies voor Vlaamse gemeenten: een surveyanalyse van de activiteit en determinanten tijdens de programmaperiode 2007–2013. In H. Reynaert (ed.), *Uitdagingen voor de lokale besturen 2015–2019*, 131–158. Brugge: Vanden Broele.

Walter-Rogg, M. (2010). Multiple Choice: The Persistence of Territorial Pluralism in the German Federation. In H. Baldersheim and L. E. Rose (ed.), *Territorial Choice. The Politics of Boundaries and Borders*, 138–159. Basingstoke: Palgrave Macmillan.

Zerbinati, S. (2012). Multi-level Governance and EU Structural Funds: An Entrepreneurial Local Government Perspective. *Local Government Studies*, 38 (5), 577–597.

26
LOCAL GOVERNMENT IN THE EUROPEAN UNION'S MULTILEVEL POLITY

Marius Guderjan

Introduction

Public authorities on different levels are engaged with EU Member States in a complicated system of shared jurisdiction. Over the last three decades, European integration has led to emerging patterns of interaction between the local and European levels of government. As part of this dynamic, local authorities have entered the European *Politikverflechtung* – a compound, blurred governance arrangement under which actors and institutions from multiple levels cooperate formally and informally to conduct political and administrative tasks (Derenbach 2006: 77–78).

Two developments are particularly relevant. First, during the 1990s, the movement towards the 'completion' of the Single Market created a number of directives and regulations that affected the practices of local governments and prompted them to increase their engagement with EU policies (Münch 2006: 127; Rechlin 2004: 16ff.). EU directives and regulations have a direct impact on local activities, particularly in the fields of public procurement, state aid, human resources management, the provision of public services, housing, building and spatial planning. This puts local authorities in a position as both executing and shaping actors in Europe's multilevel system.

Second, the EU's regional and cohesion policy has provided local actors across Europe with a formal role in building proactive relationships with supranational institutions (Conzelmann 1995: 134–135; John 2001: 69; Bache 2004: 166ff.; Bache 2008: 23; Goldsmith and Klausen 1997: 1ff.). As the cohesion policy for 2007–2013 was made subordinate to the Lisbon Agenda and the subsequent 'Europe 2020' strategy, the ideas of partnership and dialogue also entered the EU's economic strategies. As a consequence, the local level has gradually developed a greater role in the delivery of policy goals (Van Bever, Reynaert and Steyvers 2011: 236ff.).

As a result of these processes, more and more local authorities have adapted their politico-administrative structures by, for example, opening offices in Brussels, participating in networks, and developing strategies to promote their preferences on the European stage (Fleurke and Willemse 2006: 85; Marshall 2005: 669; Martin 1997: 63; Schultze 2003: 135; Sturm and Dieringer 2005: 282). The interaction between local and European actors has fostered the development of a compound polity that is commonly referred to as multilevel governance (Bache et al. 2011: 125–126). With national governments still in control over local government and their ability to participate effectively in European affairs (Atkinson 2002: 785ff.), the question arises as to what extent, and in what ways, is local government part of the European 'multilevel compound' (Guderjan 2015: 951).

In order to enhance our understanding of the status of local government within Europe's multilevel polity, this chapter begins by examining the role of local government as implementers of EU legislation and policies. It goes on to track local government's constitutional status in European multilevel governance, particularly in relation to the principles of local-self-government and subsidiarity. Finally, the chapter focuses on the relevant institutional structures at different levels through which local governments participate in EU policy-making.

Local government as an implementer of EU legislation and policy

Guderjan (2015: 941) suggests that 'the implementation of European legislation is the strongest link between local and European institutions.' The EU depends on the administrative capacity of its Member States, which in turn depend heavily upon local authorities in order to implement EU policies. The European legislator frequently uses framework legislation that requires a division of responsibility between the EU as a policy initiator, central government as a 'transposer' and local government as an implementer. In this way, local authorities shape EU outputs to varying degrees (Goldsmith 1997: 5ff.; 2003: 121).

In the early 1990s, when the completion of the European Single Market brought a 'flood of directives' affecting local authorities (Alemann and Münch 2006: 17), local authorities became increasingly responsible for the execution of EU directives in the fields of trading standards, environmental standards and public procurement (Goldsmith 1997: 219). EU legislation significantly impacts upon water, gas and electricity supply, water and waste management, public transport, childcare facilities, education, cultural activities, and social and health care. Because the European legislator is often not familiar with the details of practice in local governments across all Member States, EU law causes some confusion and challenges municipal practice by creating a great deal of uncertainty within different local administrations (Fischer 2006: 106).

On many occasions, the European Court of Justice (ECJ) has clarified the application of directives, when existing practices were in conflict with EU legislation. For instance, compensation payment for public service delivery is regulated through Court rulings, such as the judgments on compensation payments Case C–107/98, *Teckal v. Comune di Viano*, [1999] and C–280/00, *Altmark Trans GmbH, Regierungspräsidium Magdeburg v. Nahverkehrsgesellschaft Altmark GmbH*, [2003]. Subsequently, the Commission adopted the 2005 *Monti-Kroes* Package on rules governing compensation for public service obligations IP/05/937 and the 2011 Service of General Economic Interest Package IP/111571, in order to provide more legal clarity.

More recent directives relevant for public service delivery include Directive 2006/123/EC on services in the internal market; Directive 2014/24/EU on public procurement (formerly Directive 2004/18/EC); Directive 2014/25/EU on procurement by entities operating in the water, energy, transport and postal service sectors (formerly Directive 2004/17/EC); and Directive 2014/23/EC on the award of concession contracts. All of these make municipal service delivery subject to European competition law. There are a number of examples that do not exclusively apply to public authorities, but strongly affect municipal practice, such as human resources management (the Working Time Directive 2003/88/EC and the Equal Treatment Directive 2006/54/EC) and social services (Directive 2011/83/EC on consumer rights).

Environmental law has further profound implications for the acquisition of products and services, planning, and municipal building. Examples of these include the Habitats Directive 92/43/EEC on the conservation of threatened or endemic animal and plant species; the Water

Framework Directive 2000/60/EC (and C–461/13) which aims to improve the quality of water bodies; the Environmental Noise Directive 2002/49/EC; the Air Quality Directive 2008/50/EC; the Waste Framework Directive 2008/98/EC on waste management; the Birds Directive 2009/147/EC aimed at protecting of wild bird species; Directive 2010/31/EU on the energy performance of buildings; and Directive 2012/27/EU to improve energy efficiency across the EU by 20 per cent by 2020.

Whereas the above examples concern binding law, there has also been a growing agenda of non-binding policies relevant to the local level. Over time, the EU has become aware of local government's potential role in realising its agenda with regard to social policy, poverty, employment, economic growth, energy, climate change, housing, health, transport initiatives, security and integration of migrants and refugees. The EU has very limited legal competence in these areas and promotes implementation in the context of cohesion policy, Europe 2020 and the new Urban Agenda. In order to qualify for funding, local authorities have to meet the strict requirements of EU policy schemes, and are thus bound to legal provisions. At the same time, the implementation of such policy initiatives requires stronger bottom-up involvement from local authorities.

Local self-government within multilevel governance

The constitutions of many Member States – Austria, Belgium, Bulgaria, the Czech Republic, Denmark, Estonia, France, Germany, Greece, Hungary, Italy, Lithuania, Luxembourg, Portugal, Romania, Slovakia, Slovenia, Spain and Sweden – recognise the right to local self-government or self-administration (CEMR 2007). Except for Monaco, Andorra and San Marino – all of which are too small for a useful subdivision into formalised local authorities – all Member States of the Council of Europe are signatories to the European Charter of Local Self-Government of 1985, Articles 2 and 3 of which state:

> Article 2: The principle of local self-government shall be recognised in domestic legislation, and where practicable in the constitution.

> Article 3: Local self-government denotes the right and the ability of local authorities, within the limits of the law, to regulate and manage a substantial share of public affairs under their own responsibility and in the interests of the local population.

With the Lisbon Treaty, for the very first time the right to local self-government was mentioned in one of the EU's treaties (Art. 4.2 TEU):

> The Union shall respect the equality of Member States before the Treaties as well as their national identities, inherent in their fundamental structures, political and constitutional, inclusive of regional and local self-government.

This reference to local self-government indicates its increasing role in EU affairs, and manifests the constitutional recognition of a 'Europe of four levels' (Hoffschulte 2006: 63). It acknowledges political autonomy and implies that although local authorities are subordinate to regional and/or national governments, they are not merely executing and implementing decisions made at higher levels, but they also take their own governmental action (Panara 2013: 371ff.). In some cases references to local self-government have been used to justify specific actions by local and regional authorities. For instance, C–156/13, *Digibet v. Westdeutsche Lotterie* [2014] (at 34)[1] allowed the *Land* Schleswig-Holstein to temporarily adopt more liberal game-of-chance policies than those of other German *Länder*. Another example is the Opinion of Advocate General Mengozzi on C–115/14, *RegioPost v. Stadt Landau* [2015] (at 82), which clarifies when a contracting authority can require businesses tendering for public services to comply with minimum wage special conditions.

The EU's 'partial' or 'complementary' constitution (Bogdandy 2009: 24) is mainly concerned with the allocation of competencies across European and national institutions. However, constitutional questions are not exclusive to the European and national levels, but reach deep into the political-administrative structures of the Member States. As Panara (2015: 159) puts it:

> Its constitutive elements stem from the combined and coordinated work of the national constitutional system(s) and of the EU. Only a holistic approach, the combined analysis of the domestic system(s) and of the EU, can provide a satisfactory answer in relation to the status of the sub-national authorities in the EU or in relation to the coordination between sub-national authorities and the EU. Multilevel governance is legally and methodologically part of the complex European constitutional space.

Although 'multilevel governance' is a widely acknowledged terminology in EU policies, it is not mentioned in its primary legislation. The acknowledgement of regional and local self-government by the Lisbon Treaty, however, can be interpreted as an implicit constitutionalisation of multilevel governance. The Commission has long recognised that multiple levels are not isolated from each other but are interacting. Throughout the 2000s, a number of initiatives have illustrated the intention of the Commission, and increasingly also the European Parliament (EP), to intensify cooperation with cities and municipalities. The 2001 White Paper on European Governance sought to enforce a true partnership, integrating different levels of government through systematic dialogues with regional and local representatives (Atkinson 2002: 782ff.; Karvounis 2011: 215ff.; Reilly 2001: 1). In 2009, the White Paper on Multilevel Governance, which was issued by the Committee of the Regions (CoR) to draw attention to local and regional government, stated:

> Multilevel governance is not simply a question of translating European or national objectives into local or regional action, but must also be understood as a process for integrating the objectives of local and regional authorities within the strategies of the European Union. Moreover, multilevel governance should reinforce and shape the responsibilities of local and regional authorities at national level and encourage their participation in the coordination of European policy, in this way helping to design and implement Community policies.
>
> *(CoR 2009)*

The state remains a strong gatekeeper for local involvement in European affairs (De Rooij 2002: 448–449; Fleurke and Willemse 2006). Even though subnational actors operate in interconnected policy arenas across different levels (Hooghe and Marks 2001: 3–4, 77ff.), they are set within a national constitutional context which both provides opportunities and defines limits to multilevel governance (Hague and Harrop 2007: 281–282). Whereas the interdependency amongst different levels has grown, this has not necessarily been accompanied by an increase in the actual influence of local governments.

The explicit acknowledgement of local self-government and the implicit recognition of multilevel governance have *de jure* limited the exercise of powers by the EU and by central governments. *De facto*, the application of multilevel governance varies strongly across Member

States. The EU cannot change domestic structures but can adapt existing procedures with the aim of providing subnational authorities with a greater role in making and implementing policies. Even though Union Courts can require an annulment of an EU Act if it infringes local self-government (Art. 4.2 TEU), Panara argues that if domestic litigation on the implementation of multilevel governance is transferred to the Court of Justice, it would have little leeway in the interpretation of multilevel governance:

> given that constitutional arrangements vary asymmetrically across the Union, the ECJ is likely to stick to a minimal notion of multilevel governance whilst applying it to a specific State context, rather than dictating prescriptive solutions for the Member States. The Union notion of 'multilevel governance' must necessarily be minimal and procedural.
> *(Panara 2015: 57)*

Multilevel governance becomes more concrete in the context of cohesion policy, where we can find explicit and legally binding references. Regulation 1303/2013 requires Member States to establish multilevel partnerships with subnational authorities and other societal actors for the delivery of economic, social and territorial cohesion. Article 11 states:

> For the Partnership Agreement and each programme respectively, each Member State should organise a partnership with the representatives of competent regional, local, urban and other public authorities, economic and social partners and other relevant bodies representing civil society, including environmental partners, non-governmental organisations and bodies responsible for promoting social inclusion, gender equality and non-discrimination, including, where appropriate, the umbrella organisations of such authorities and bodies. The purpose of such a partnership is to ensure respect for the principles of multi-level governance, and also of subsidiarity and proportionality and the specificities of the Member States' different institutional and legal frameworks as well as to ensure the ownership of planned interventions by stakeholders and build on the experience and the know-how of relevant actors.

The partnership principle provides the most significant legal communitarisation of multilevel governance and moves beyond the informal patterns of what Benz and Eberlin (1999: 333) called a 'loose coupling'. The Commission monitors compliance with the Code of Conduct on Partnership and may even suspend funding if Member States do not follow its recommendations (European Commission 2014). Governments would hardly want to miss out on the significant amounts of funding they acquire from the Structural Funds. In addition, legal action against Member States is possible if they completely fail to establish multilevel partnerships with subnational authorities and other societal actors. However, Partnership Agreements are designed in accordance with national law practices and leave room for generous interpretations. Various countries in south-east Europe (e.g. Greece, Slovenia, Croatia – see Bache et al. 2011) and central and eastern Europe (e.g. Estonia, Poland, Czech Republic, Hungary, Romania – see Dabrowski 2014) only fulfil the minimal requirements of the partnership principle and produce highly prescriptive operational programme objectives (Van den Brande 2014).

Overall, multilevel governance evolves through negotiations and network-building. Despite its advancement through the recognition of local self-government in the treaties and the legal requirements of the cohesion policy, multilevel governance remains a political rather than a legal principle and thus its implementation is subject to specific contexts.

The relevance of EU subsidiarity for local government

In federal states, subsidiarity has been an established organising principle to guarantee the self-determination of regional and local levels of government. The underlying idea promotes the principle that higher levels of government should only rule over matters that cannot be dealt with by the lower level on its own. Subsidiarity has been an implicit norm for the EU since its early days as the European Coal and Steel Community, and it was later referred to explicitly in the Treaty of Maastricht to regulate the relationship between the EU and Members States. The Treaty of Lisbon extended subsidiarity to the regional and the local level, which, along with the recognition of legal self-government, advances the legal manifestation of multilevel constitutional space. Article 5.3 of the TEU states:

> Under the principle of subsidiarity, in areas which do not fall within its exclusive competence, the Union shall act only if and in so far as the objectives of the proposed action cannot be sufficiently achieved by the Member States, either at central level or at regional and local level, but can rather, by reason of the scale or effects of the proposed action, be better achieved at Union level.

The legislator has to consider the appropriateness, necessity and proportionality of their actions, with Art. 5.4 TEU specifying that '[u]nder the principle of proportionality, the content and form of Union action shall not exceed what is necessary to achieve the objectives of the Treaties'.[2] Consequently, the Commission has to 'take into account the regional and local dimension' within the consultations for legislative acts (Article 2 of the Protocol on the Application of the Principle of Subsidiarity and Proportionality).

Despite these provisions, the possibility for subnational government to challenge EU legislation is limited and is instead mainly reserved to Member State governments which represent their regional and local authorities before the Court of Justice. Regional, but not local, authorities can challenge EU legislation indirectly through the state (Panara 2015: 160), when represented in a federal co-legislating chamber.

Craig (2012: 74) argues that the Court of Justice does not apply a systematic review of subsidiarity in its judgements. It has never annulled a legal act because of an infringement of subsidiarity. First of all, hardly any legal cases have been forwarded on the grounds that the EU has breached subsidiarity. Secondly, in the few cases that have alleged such a breach of subsidiarity, this was not the first or principle plea and he cites fewer than 10 cases in 20 years (ibid.: 80). And finally, in those few cases, the Court decided that the EU was acting lawfully (Panara 2015: 82–83).

The CoR is the designated 'watch dog' of subsidiarity on behalf of local and regional government. It exercises this function through its consultative powers during the legislative stage, as well as through litigation before the Court when subsidiarity is not respected. Article 8 of the Protocol on the Application of the Principle of Subsidiarity and Proportionality states:

> The Court of Justice of the European Union shall have jurisdiction in actions on grounds of infringement of the principle of subsidiarity by a legislative act . . .
>
> In accordance with the rules laid down in the said Article, the Committee of the Regions may also bring such actions against legislative acts for the adoption of which the Treaty on the Functioning of the European Union provides that it be consulted.

Neither the CoR nor national parliaments have yet challenged an act for an infringement of subsidiarity. In 2012, the CoR warned of a violation of the subsidiarity principle by the so-called Monti Package II, which limited the right to strike for posted workers who are sent to provide a service in other Member States on a temporary basis. The CoR thus officially supported twelve national parliaments that used the 'yellow card' mechanism and for the first time threatened to take action for an *ex-ante* appeal before the Court (Piattoni and Schönlau 2015: 97).

Whether the CoR appeals to the Court or not has to be decided by a majority of its appointed members. In 2013, for instance, a plenary session of the CoR voted not to challenge the EU's right to make the acquisition of structural funds conditional on the compliance with the macro-economic objectives of the Stability and Growth Pact. It was believed that macro-economic conditionality in the 2014–2020 cohesion policy was not an infringement of subsidiarity (ibid.: 98).

Two reasons may explain why the CoR has never taken legal action on the grounds of a subsidiarity breach. First, it may be concerned that it risks losing its threat potential if its complaint is not successful. Second, the Commission frequently takes the CoR's views into account when drafting legislation because it prefers to avoid legal disputes. The Lisbon Treaty has allowed the CoR to increase its influence in favour of subsidiarity through monitoring activities and using political leverage. Rather than blocking legislation within the inter-institutional arrangement, the CoR is more effective as an advocate for subsidiarity through propositions, negotiations and consultations (ibid.: 98ff.).

Like multilevel governance, subsidiarity remains subject to political rather than legal interpretation. Subsidiarity is not a 'golden formula' determining the allocation of competences, but a 'useful device' directing attention to national and local diversity and the legitimacy of EU intervention (Syrpis 2004: 334). Thus, cooperation and mutual understanding rather than conflict appears to be a more suitable means of guaranteeing an effective and reconcilable implementation of policies. As Panara (2015: 122) suggests:

> In all the analysed multilevel systems, the appropriate locus for the enforcement of subsidiarity is not the courtroom but participation in the law-making and policymaking processes as required by the principles of 'partnership' and 'loyal cooperation'. Judicial enforcement plays a role only if there is a 'clear' or 'evident' abuse; i.e., where the attribution of a certain power to the central authority is totally illogical or untenable.

Local access to EU policy-making

Formal access for local government actors to EU policy-making is limited. Local authorities are represented through their Member of the European Parliament, and municipal associations have an observer status at meetings of the Council of Ministers but no channels of direct influence. Since the early 1990s, the CoR remains the only formal representation of local government in the EU's institutional set-up. The Lisbon Treaty strengthened its impact on legal proposals that affect subnational government (Neshkova 2010). However, there are three caveats to the CoR being an effective body to promote local policy preferences. First, it has only consultative powers and therefore cannot match the political weight of the EP, the Council or the Commission. Second, its diverse membership dilutes the specific interests of individual local authorities, which consequently prefer to work through European networks that better reflect their own properties and needs, such as EUROCITIES, the European Local Authorities Network (ELAN), the Centre of Employers and Enterprises providing Public Services (CEEP) or POLIS, a network of cities and regions for public transport innovation. Third, depending on the Member State, it is often regional not local delegates who are represented on the CoR. For instance, whilst the UK sends all local councillors, only three of Germany's 24 members are explicitly municipal representatives.

Callanan and Tatham (2014: 191) refer to 'regulatory mobilisation' when local mobilisation addresses EU policies and legislation, and speak of 'financial mobilisation' when local authorities aim to acquire EU funding. It is fair to say that most municipalities do not participate in EU policy-making, and have little influence over policy outcomes (Bache 2008: 31; Catalano and Graziano 2011: 6). A few highly engaged policy-makers and officers bypass the state level and have access to the supranational policy-making cycle on an *ad hoc* basis. But the most effective lobbying is done by domestic and transnational municipal association and networks, who can pool the political weight and expertise of their membership. Member States with particularly strong associations are Denmark, Finland, the Netherlands, the UK, Germany and Estonia (Kettunen and Kull 2009: 122; Eckert et al. 2013: 162; Callanan and Tatham 2014: 199; Guderjan 2015: 947ff.).

While it is up to national governments to create more participation channels for subnational authorities, or to strengthen existing ones (e.g. the CoR), it has become increasingly difficult to exclude local actors from EU policy-making (Schultze 2003: 135). As local authorities are pushing for more responsibilities to deal with European and global challenges, they have learned to deploy a variety of means to engage with EU institutions, either directly or indirectly through domestic channels (Eckert et al. 2013: 157; Van den Brande 2014: 6; Guderjan and Miles 2016: 643). European governance develops not only through a legal constitution, but also through a 'living constitution', and mutually reinforcing learning and practice (Miles 2011: 197). National governments prefer to keep control over local affairs, but they have also started to realise the potential that lies at the local level. As outlined above, the Commission and the EP have long promoted multilevel partnerships and a greater role for local government. This has been with the aim to increase the acceptance, legitimacy and effectiveness of an increasing number of policies that have direct effect within municipalities.

Conclusion

Local authorities are essential for executing EU legislation, and this in turn allows them to shape EU policies. This is particularly the case for laws related to the Single Market, which strongly affect public service provision, procurement and state aid, as well as environmental law. The EU has increasingly acknowledged the right to local self-government and the principle of subsidiarity for the purpose of allowing local authorities to conduct public services according to their domestic structures and politico-administrative traditions. Subsidiarity and multilevel governance have become part of the EU's 'constitutional compound' but remain political rather than 'hard' legal principles.

The realisation of multilevel partnerships (particularly with regard to cohesion and economic policies) vary greatly across Member States. The involvement of subnational government in the implementation and making of EU legislation and policies depends on national governments and the competences of different local authorities. The EU cannot change domestic structures but it can adapt existing procedures to include local government, particularly in terms of the EU's cohesion policy. Even though Member States can be brought before the Court if they completely fail to cooperate with subnational authorities, Partnership Agreements leave room for generous interpretations and may not necessarily empower local government in real terms.

The only institutionalised channel for local government to participate in EU policy-making on a regular basis is the CoR, which holds only consultative powers and is inconsistent in its usefulness to local government due to its diverse membership. The Lisbon Treaty has upgraded the Committee's status and made it a 'watchdog' of subsidiarity, although it has not used its power to bring cases before the Court yet. Like local governments themselves, the CoR has learned to deploy the 'living constitution' and established informal links to more potent EU institutions (primarily the Commission and the EP) to promote subnational concerns.

There is only a minority of local authorities and their associations who seek to influence EU policies directly in Brussels, but the constitutional, legal and political developments over the last two decades indicate an emerging culture of cooperation across local and European levels. There has been an increasing awareness of local practice and attempts to improve the design and delivery of policies through the involvement of local government.

This chapter ends with a brief comment on local government in the light of Brexit. British local government, like that in other Member States, has become interlocked in the EU's multilevel system and disentangling this relationship will not only be challenging for the UK Government but also for local authorities. These are likely to face severe economic, political and social consequences. For British local authorities, the future of funding is the primary issue: how and by whom will they be compensated for a potential loss of Structural and Social Funds and other EU resources? Will the UK Government negotiate future access or make its own commitment to allocate new financial means to the local level? If the UK is partially or completely cut off from the Single Market and trade barriers return, local authorities may further suffer under retreating foreign investment. Yet, local government across the EU will have little say over the conditions of Brexit. The CoR can adopt formal positions and voice local concerns, but it has no binding impact in the negotiations.

The future relationship will determine what European laws continue to apply for British local government. If the UK remains in the Single Market, which the current government rejects, most laws would stay in place. Even in the case of a 'hard' Brexit, the government may not automatically or immediately alter UK legislation implementing EU directives. However, over time it may amend or repeal existing legislation in the fields of procurement, service delivery, employment standards and environmental protection (Sandford 2016). While local councils have already started to demand new legislative freedoms and flexibilities after Brexit, they will be subject to legal uncertainty, and there is no constitutional guarantee or principle preventing a centralisation of powers.

Brexit may affect most local authorities in the EU at best marginally, except for existing cross-border cooperation with UK municipalities. The latter, however, can expect changing obligations, tasks and even powers, after they have left the EU's multilevel polity. The UK's departure from the EU will not only provide a unique occasion to understand European integration from a national perspective but it is also an opportunity to evaluate the status and relations of local government within the EU.

Notes

1 In the present case, the division of competences between the German *Länder*, for instance, cannot be called into question, since it benefits from the protection conferred by Article 4(2) TEU, according to which the Union must respect national identities, inherent in their fundamental structures, political and constitutional, including regional and local self-government.
2 Article 5 further states: 'Draft legislative acts shall take account of the need for any burden, whether financial or administrative, falling upon the Union, national governments, regional or local authorities, economic operators and citizens, to be minimised and commensurate with the objective to be achieved.'

References

Alemann U. Von and Münch C. (2006) *Europafähigkeit der Kommunen: Die lokale Ebene in der Europäischen Union*. Wiesbaden: VS Verlag für Sozialwissenschaften.

Atkinson R. (2002) The White Paper on European Governance: Implications for Urban Policy. *European Planning Studies* 10(6): 781–792.

Bache I. (2004) Multi-level governance and European Union Regional Policy. In Bache I. and Flinders M. (eds), *Multi-Level Governance*, 166–178. Oxford: University Press.

Bache I. (2008) *Europeanization and Multilevel Governance: Cohesion Policy in the European Union and Britain*. Plymouth: Rowan & Littlefield.

Bache I., Andreou G., Atanasova G. and Tomsic D. (2011) Europeanization and Multi-Level Governance in South-East Europe: The Domestic Impact of EU Cohesion Policy and Pre-accession Aid. *Journal of European Public Policy* 18(1): 122–141.

Benz A. and Eberlin B. (1999) The Europeanization of Regional Policies: Patterns of Multi-Level Governance. *Journal of European Public Policy* 6(2): 329–348.

Bogdandy A. Von (2009) Founding Principles. In Bogdandy A. Von and Bast J. (eds), *Principles of European Constitutional Law*, 11ff. Oxford: Hart.

Callanan M. and Tatham M. (2014) Territorial Interest Representation in the European Union: Actors, Objectives and Strategies. *Journal of European Public Policy* 21(2): 188–210.

Catalano S. and Graziano P. (2011) *The Local Usage of Europe*. Comparative Report, Localised Deliverable 5.7, Grant Agreement No: 266768. Oldenburg: Carl von Ossietzky Universität.

CEMR (Council of European Municipalities and Regions) (2007) *Consultation Procedures within European States – An Assessment of the Systems for Consultation between Central Governments and the National Associations Local and Regional Government*. Brussels: CEMR.

Coen D. (2007) Empirical and Theoretical Studies in EU Lobbying. *Journal of European Public Policy* 14(3): 333–345.

Conzelmann T. (1995) Networking and the Politics of EU Regional Policy: Lessons from North Rhine-Westphalia, Nord-Pas de Calais and North West England. *Regional and Federal Studies* 5(2): 134–172.

CoR (Committee of the Regions) (2009) *The Committee of the Regions' White Paper on Multi-Level Governance*. 17 June. Brussels: CoR.

Craig P. (2012) Subsidiarity: A Political and Legal Analysis. *Journal of Common Market Studies* 50(1): 72–87.

Dabrowski M. (2014) EU Cohesion Policy, Horizontal Partnership and the Patterns of Sub-national Governance: Insights from Central and Eastern Europe. *European Urban and Regional Studies* 21(4): 364–383.

Derenbach R. (2006) Die stärkere Einbindung der lokalen Gebietskörperschaften in das europäische Aufbauwerk: Partnerschaft im Modell der 'multilevel governance' statt zunehmender Entfremdung. In Alemann U. Von and Münch C. (eds), *Europafähigkeit der Kommunen: Die lokale Ebene in der Europäischen Union*, 77–101. Wiesbaden: VS Verlag für Sozialwissenschaften.

De Rooij R. (2002) The Impact of the European Union on Local Government in the Netherlands. *Journal of European Public Policy* 9(3): 447–467.

Eckert K., Heuer C., Schubert H., Spieckermann H. and Wessels W. (2013) *Die Stadt Köln als kommunaler Akteur im EU-Mehrebenensystem nach dem Vertrag von Lissabon: Veränderte Opportunitätsstrukturen und Netzwerkpfade zur europäischen Politikgestaltung*. Cologne: Verlag Sozial, Raum, Management.

European Commission (2014) *Investment for Jobs and Growth: Promoting Development and Good Governance in EU Regions and Cities*. Sixth Report on Economic, Social and Territorial Cohesion. Brussels: Directorate for Regional and Urban Policy.

Fischer H. G. (2006) Die Rolle des europäischen Gemeinschaftsrechts in der kommunalen Verwaltungspraxis. In Alemann U. Von and Münch C. (eds), *Europafähigkeit der Kommunen: Die lokale Ebene in der Europäischen Union*, 105–118. Wiesbaden: VS Verlag für Sozialwissenschaften.

Fleurke F. and Willemse R. (2006) Measuring Local Autonomy: A Decision-Making Approach. *Local Government Studies* 32(1): 71–87.

Goldsmith M. (1997) British Local Government in the European Union. In Bradbury J. and Mawson J. (eds), *British Regionalism and Devolution – The Challenges of State Reform and European Integration*, 215–234. London: Jessica Kingsley.

Goldsmith M. (2003) Variable Geometry, Multilevel Governance: European Integration and Subnational Government in the New Millenium. In Featherstone K. and Radaelli C.M. (eds), *The Politics of Europeanization*, 122–133. Oxford: Oxford University Press.

Goldsmith, M. and Klausen, K.K. (1997) *European Integration and Local Government*. Cheltenham: Edward Elgar.

Guderjan M. (2015) Theorising European Integration of Local Government – Insights from the Fusion Approach. *Local Government Studies* 41(6): 937–955.

Guderjan M. and Miles L. (2016) The Fusion Approach – Applications for Understanding Local Government and European Integration. *Journal of European Integration* 38(6): 637–652.

Hague R. and Harrop M. (2007) *Comparative Government and Politics: An Introduction*. Basingstoke: Palgrave Macmillan.

Hoffschulte H. (2006) Kommunen in Europa: Die bürgernahe Basis in einem 'Europa der vier Ebenen'. In Alemann U. Von and Münch C. (eds), *Europafähigkeit der Kommunen: Die lokale Ebene in der Europäischen Union*, 58–76. Wiesbaden: VS Verlag für Sozialwissenschaften.

Hooghe L. and G. Marks (2001) *Multi-Level Governance and European Integration*. London: Rowman & Littlefield.

John P. (2001) *Local Governance in Western Europe*. London: Sage.

Karvounis A. (2011) The Europeanization of the Local Government in the EU Multi-level Governance System: The City Networking Paradigm and the Greek Case. In Van Bever E., Reynaert H. and Steyvers K. (eds), *The Road to Europe: Main Street or Backward Alley for Local Governments in Europe?*, 211–231. Brugge: Vanden Broele.

Kettunen P. and Kull M. (2009) Governing Europe: the Status and Networking Strategies of Finnish, Estonian and German Subnational Offices in Brussels. *Regional and Federal Studies* 19(1): 117–142.

Marshall A. (2005) Europeanization at the Urban Level: Local Actors, Institutions and the Dynamics of Multi-Level Interaction. *Journal of European Public Policy* 12(4): 668–686.

Martin S. (1997) The Effects of EU Regional Policy on Local Institutional Structures and Policies. In Bachtler J. and Turok I. (eds), *The Coherence of EU Regional Policy*, 51–65. London: Jessica Kingsley.

Miles L. (2011) Thinking Bigger: Fusion Concepts, Strengths and Scenarios. In Dietrichs U., Faber A., Tekin F. and Umbach G. (eds), *Europe Reloaded: Differentiation of Fusion*, 187–210. Baden-Baden: Nomos.

Münch C. (2006) *Emanzipation der lokalen Ebene? Kommunen auf dem Weg nach Europa*. Wiesbaden: VS Verlag für Sozialwissenschaften.

Neshkova M. I. (2010) The Impact of Subnational Interests on Supranational Regulation. *Journal of European Public Policy* 17(8): 1193–1211.

Panara C. (2013) Conclusion – The Contribution of Local Self-Government to Constitutionalism in the Member States and in the EU Multi-Layered System of Governance. In Panera C. and Varney M. (eds), *Local Government in Europe: The 'Fourth Level' in the EU Multi-Layered System of Governance*, 369–413. Abingdon: Routledge.

Panara C. (2015) *The Sub-national Dimension of the EU: A Legal Study of Multilevel Governance*. Cham: Springer.

Piattoni S. and Schönlau J. (2015) *Shaping EU Policy from Below: EU Democracy and the Committee of the Regions*. Cheltenham: Edward Elgar.

Rechlin S. (2004) *Die deutschen Kommunen im Mehrebenensystem der Europäischen Union: Betroffene Objekte oder aktive Subjekte?* Discussion Paper SP IV 2004–101. Berlin: Social Science Research Center.

Reilly A. (2001) The EU White Paper on Governance: The Implications of Misguided Assessment for UK Subnational Authorities. *Local Government Studies* 27(4): 1–18.

Sandford M. (2016) *Brexit and Local Government*. Briefing Paper Number 07664 20 July. London: House of Commons Library.

Schultze C. J. (2003) Cities and EU Governance: Policy-Takers or Policy-Makers?. *Regional and Federal Studies* 13(1): 121–147.

Sturm R. and Dieringer J. (2005) The Europeanisation of Regions in Eastern and Western Europe: Theoretical Perspective. *Regional and Federal Studies* 15(3): 279–294. doi:10.1080/10438590500223251.

Syrpis P. (2004) In Defence of Subsidiarity. *Oxford Journal of Legal Studies* 24(2): 323–334.

Van Bever E., Reynaert H. and Steyvers K. (2011) *The Road to Europe: Main Street or Backward Alley for Local Governments in Europe?* Brugge: Vanden Broele.

Van Den Brande L. (2014) *Multilevel Governance and Partnership*. The Van den Brande Report, prepared at the request of the Commissioner for Regional and Urban Policy Johannes Hahn, October.

27
SECOND THOUGHTS ON SECOND-ORDER?

Towards a second-tier model of local government elections and voting

Ulrik Kjær and Kristof Steyvers

Local elections in a multi-level context

An increasing number of election and voting studies scrutinise the local government level (Clark and Krebs 2012). A search in the Social Science Citation Index based on the keywords 'local' and 'elections' in the topic returned 1103 articles in the category of Political Science only and dating back to the beginning of the 1960s (the US and the EU each represent about 43% of all contributions). Most of these studies are empirical and tend to focus exclusively on the level that is allegedly closest to the citizenry in a specific country during a specific period of time. In comparison, there is less theoretical, comparative or longitudinal work to provide an integrated understanding of the tiered dynamics of local elections and voting. Many studies thereby implicitly neglect some of the central aspects of the setting and era in which the local elections are embedded. Therefore Marschall (2010: 471) concludes her review by stating: 'to say that a field of study of local elections exists would be a bit of an overstatement'.

In an increasingly multilevel context, scholars are occupied with analysing different types of elections at different political levels. In regard to local elections this raises questions such as: Is there anything specifically place-bound about these elections and if so, what, to which extent, how, and with what consequences? In other words: How do local elections differ from or resemble elections at the national (or regional and federal) level?

Earlier attempts to answer these questions can be divided into two overall groups. The first group focuses mainly on the European context. It sees local elections as essentially lower ranking and less important than national elections, serving at best a balancing, barometric or mid-term function. This conception is most prominently captured in the notion of second-order elections in Reif and Schmitt's (1980) seminal study, which will be discussed below and serves as the main point of departure for this chapter. The second group argues that local elections differ from national elections. Given the differentiated nature of intergovernmental relations, this tends to figure more prominently in the American literature. According to Oliver (2012), local elections differ from national elections because they pertain to a government level that is smaller in size, has a smaller portfolio of services and functions and is more extreme in its distributive bias (see also Kaufman 2004).

While we acknowledge the merit in both perspectives, we find them equally incomplete when considered separately. Each accounts for only one of the two defining characteristics of almost any local government setting. First, local and national governments co-exist in a vertical relation. This relationship can vary substantially (depending on the level of political decentralisation, for example) but ultimately remains asymmetrical (as local authorities are universally a part of and subordinate to a central state). Second, having by default more than one place-bound authority means that there is horizontal variation at the local level (expressed in multiple entities with separate political institutions and an electoral chain of representation and accountability). Both groups of theories tend to miss one of these characteristics. The lower-rank view clearly incorporates the vertical relation, but overlooks the horizontal variation. The different-kind approach understands horizontal variation (with electoral phenomena differing across localities), but neglects the vertical relation to some extent (failing to situate the local elections appropriately in the contemporary, layered political structure).

This chapter includes both key features (vertical relation and horizontal variation) and therefore draws on insights of both conceptions (lower rank and different kind) in theorising on local elections and voting. Its main aim is to critically engage with the existing frameworks using the predominant second-order perspective as starting point and benchmark (Clark and Krebs 2012). The intention is to reformulate this into an alternative framework denoted as second-tier elections and voting. This notion emphasises the relationship with a first-tier national counterpart (which can be relatively weak or strong) while conceding variation among different local authorities (which can be minor or major). By integrating the insights of both groups of theories, the chapter strives at a more comprehensive understanding of local elections and voting in a multi-level context. Our contribution is thus primarily theoretical pointing out the potential of a comparative (empirical) approach.

The chapter proceeds as follows: The mainstream framework of local elections as second-order national elections is critically assessed; the alternative framework of local elections and voting as second-tier is introduced; and finally, the concluding section summarises the added value of the approach chosen and discusses how future research can further our understanding of the layered and differentiated nature of local elections and voting as second-tier.

Local elections as second-order? A critical assessment of the mainstream framework

Second-order elections: reviewing frameworks and evidence

A longstanding and dominant approach to the study of elections in multilevel systems assumes that they can be ranked in terms of perceived importance as captured in the distinction between first- and second-order elections coined by Reif and Schmitt (1980: 8–9). In their conception, this dichotomy refers to the allegedly decisive national contests with a 'plethora of [. . .] various sorts of elections' subordinate to national elections. Thus, links exists between elections at various autonomous layers with voting behaviour and partisan strategies at the secondary levels affected by conditions and calculations at the main political arena (Reif 1997).

Reif and Schmitt (1980: 8–15) also developed an analytical framework outlining the interrelated dimensions of this linkage. In second-order contests there is supposedly less at stake which systematically affects key electoral dynamics (lower turnout, more invalid votes, better prospects for small and/or new parties and greater potential for loss by governing parties). Party behaviour in the specific arena matters as well, mediated by its political and institutional circumstances (general role of parties and similarities in partisan competition and cooperation). Both are influenced by the institutional-procedural relationship between different types of elections (in terms of timing or system). In addition, campaign efforts of second-order actors aimed at political mobilisation matter (interacting with media interest). Ultimately, the framework acknowledges genuine change in the main political arena as well as in structure and culture.

Originally applied to the first direct election to the European Parliament, the second-order framework has remained an important factor in discussion about the European Parliament. European elections are still seen as lower-salience elections where (dependent on the timing in the national election cycle) the governing and/or larger parties tend to lose votes (Norris 1997; Hix and Marsh 2007). The contemporary literature ranges from encompassing (longitudinal, comparative and/or integrated) assertions (Hix and Marsh 2011) to specific (cross-sectional, country-specific and/or dimensional) variants (e.g. Flickinger and Studlar 2007; De Vries et al. 2011). Despite the general stance 'that the basic second-order model is fairly robust ... [and] quite consistent' (Hix and Marsh 2011: 12), a number of refinements qualify its explanatory power for geographical scope, topical dynamics and party-system configurations (Marsh 1998; Koepke and Ringe 2006; Clark and Rohrschneider 2009).

For regional elections, second-order reasoning is equally commonplace (Dandoy and Schakel 2013). As a convenient prism for scrutinising regional voting and party behaviour, it developed into a default analytical conjecture in a range of contexts (e.g. Hough and Jeffery 2003; Pallares and Keating 2003). Although studies confirm the subordination of regional to national elections (Hough and Jeffery 2006), the subnational translation of the scheme has recently been criticised. The undifferentiated mobilisation of its conceptual heritage induces a nationalisation bias that underestimates effects specific to the regional arena. Hence, a plea to treat these regional elections more on their own terms with potentially distinct voting judgments about regional issues. The national versus regional template of subnational elections may therefore vary depending on the scope of regional authority, the presence and/or success of non-state-wide parties and territorial identity (Schakel 2013). Comparative and longitudinal empirical analysis indeed points at the limited and contingent validity of classic second-order assumptions compared with specific regional conjectures (Schakel and Jeffery 2013). For instance second-order reasoning does not apply when both types of elections coincide. And its explanatory power seems confined to areas where regional authority and regional parties and/or identities are weak. Other country-oriented and/or election-based studies confirm the importance of arena-specific factors (e.g. Jeffery and Hough 2009; Bechtel 2012).

Meanwhile, second-order arguments have long been present and continue to emerge in discussions on local elections as well. In line with their categorisation as part of the plethora in the original framework, some authors have 'a suspicion that ... local elections may be only tenuously related to anything that happens with particular communities' (Gregory 1969: 31), seeing their results as a 'largely accidental by-product of central government's popularity' (Miller 1988: 2). However, this abidingly dominant stance in debates on if and why local elections matter (Clark and Krebs 2012) is more often based on a loose set of a priori assumptions than on systematic empirical grounds.

Second-order elections: a concept applicable to the local level?

Three weaknesses emerge when the second-order framework is applied to local governments. First, as mentioned, the original framework is concerned with comparing the participation in and outcome of an election (as a momentum in a cycle) at a certain level (as a tier as a whole) with those of another one at a different level and point in time. Analytically, the model thus claims that any election is actually a *set of contests* in *different constituencies*. Hence, it focusses more on between-group (i.e. comparing categories of elections) than on within-group variation (i.e. constituencies for one category of elections). While this may be more straightforward when comparing national and European elections, it becomes increasingly difficult when local contests are scrutinised. In most European countries there are hundreds and in some up to thousands of local elections, as there is minimum one for each municipality (more if the electoral districts are wards). The fact that overall national interpretations (e.g. systematically lower turnout in local elections, successful small and new parties, national governing parties tend to lose) have to draw on generalising measures of central tendency inherently leads to an underestimation of place-bound heterogeneity in electoral dynamics.

The claim is that this inherent feature of the local realm should gain prominence when associated elections are analysed. Certain cases (as time-bound contests in specific constituencies) will correspond more to the ideal-typical second-order features than others. Hence, it becomes of analytical interest to discern the factors that explain similarities and differences between localities in that respect. The proposed model explicitly includes possibilities and implications of place-bound variation. However, acknowledging municipal variance within or between countries does not equal ignoring some of the general trends found when characteristics of local elections are compared to similar political phenomena played out at the parliamentary election (Rallings, Thrasher and Denver 2005).

Second, most of the second-order research takes an aggregate perspective. Even though the framework was originally developed to understand individual voting behaviour, many of its dimensions and subsequent indicators draw on ecological characteristics of electoral units such as municipalities (e.g. by comparing local voter turnout with national turnout in proxy constituencies). The available empirical evidence is thus often indirect, evoking additional a priori assumptions on individual voters and subsequent causal logics (e.g. are differences in turnout explained by alternations in absenteeism by the same voter in different elections or do specific voters only turn out at some elections?). Rare individual-level studies of, e.g., the importance voters attach to the local versus other levels and voting motives have challenged the overall second-order nature of the local (Lefevere 2013; Elklit and Kjaer 2013; Marien, Dassonneville and Hooghe 2015).

Thus, more direct and individual-level data are needed to avoid variants of the ecological and individual fallacy. In addition, more distinction should be made between explanations at the municipal and at the voter level (Denters and Mossberger 2006). Hence, to avoid some of the confusion regarding the units of analysis in the second-order framework, a systematic distinction is made between elections (the aggregate level) and voting (the individual level) in the model introduced here. Each is concerned with specific questions: (How) are local elections different from national contests, can be examined at the aggregate municipal level; explaining voting, i.e., why and how do people vote at local elections (compared to national elections), relates to the individual voter level.

Third, the presumption that one type of election is unconditionally superordinate to all others has gradually given way to an exclusively nationalised frame of reference. This can be found in the mainstream interpretation and application of the framework where the less-at-stake dimension has become analytically central. From the original article by Reif and Schmitt, a more balanced reading can be discerned both in terms of the autonomy of each arena and the power relations between them. This is captured in the catch-phrase 'there is less at stake to be sure but there still is something at stake'. It should be noted that while outlining this dimension, Reif and Schmitt (1980: 8–15) refer several times to the local level to illustrate their point. This seems to be neglected in subsequent research that aims to demonstrate the subordinate character of second-order elections.

Overall, this underplays the importance of the political and institutional circumstances of the respective arenas and underestimates effects on voting that are specific to and depending upon the actual arena. So, the model will attempt to treat local elections more on their own terms and assume that distinct judgments about specifically place-bound issues can guide local voting as well without denying the potential influence of national factors. Hence, elections and voting are localised to differing degrees (Rallings and Thrasher 2005: 595). Scant empirical evidence for the UK aligns with this nuanced assertion. Whereas second-order propositions are partly applied, the stakes of local elections were deemed sufficiently high to denote them as 'one-and-three-quarters-order' (Heath et al. 1999). An exploratory account of the Netherlands underlined the vitality to include arena-specific factors to accurately estimate the nature of local elections (Lelieveldt and Van der Does 2014). Therefore, it is postulated that the relationship between the less-at-stake dimension and its counterpart for the specific local arena is a dynamic and discrete balance rather than a static categorisation.

Local elections and voting as second-tier elections and voting? Introducing an alternative framework

Based on these remarks, the alternative conception of local elections and voting as second-tier will now be introduced. It incorporates the default asymmetry in the vertical relations between the various tiers of governance (which is not addressed sufficiently in assertions that local elections are of a different kind) as well as the horizontal variation at each tier (unaccounted for in approaches that rank local elections as a whole to be of second-order).

It is argued that voting and elections are embedded as one feature in the broader dynamics of local politics and government. This context dependency merits consideration as the local tier fundamentally differs from the (supra- or sub-)national, complicating the straightforward application of theories and concepts that allegedly cover all tiers. It also implies a more positive and independent approach to the local beyond it being non-national. The embedding is conceived as such that the framework departs from the broadest dynamics continuing along a non-deterministic chain of causal mechanisms. Hence, the model starts with the specific features of local government. These will in turn affect the way politics is conducted at the local level. How local politics functions will again influence how local elections play out, which ultimately affects if and how people vote in local elections.

The following sections will discuss each block of features conjointly comprising the second-tier framework. In the critical assessment of the second-order model, an alternative argument takes the potential for variation between different cases properly into account. Therefore, within each block, factors will be elaborated upon that may account for variation between as well as within countries leading to one or more hypotheses. A neo-institutional approach for the comparison is adopted (Davies and Trounstine 2012). This stresses the importance of formal political structures as well as more informal norms and routines for scrutinising attitudes and behaviour of (composite) actors (Lowndes 2009). Variation in the institutional set-up will be the starting point to explain cross-national as well as cross-municipal variation, between spaces and over time. As local government and politics features vary, this will also help explain similarities and differences in second-tier elections and voting across local political units and eras. For voting, the potential of cross-individual variation is added.

As the ambition is to reformulate rather than to refute the second-order model, its relevant dimensions and characteristics will be incorporated in the second-tier framework. It is argued that a number of second-order postulates are valid and reliable and can thus be included as premises for the empirical study of local elections and voting. Hence, the first two second-order dimensions make up the backbone for the argumentation. From the less-at-stake dimension, the presumed effects on voting behaviour will be retained and estimated to be most apparent in second-tier voting features. Thus, voters are expected to have less impetus to turn out in second-tier elections. If they do, expressive characteristics of voting prevail (such as – deliberately – casting an invalid vote or punishing established national and/or governing parties). Here the stakes are *nationalised*. It is expected that these voting behaviour features depends on the position in the national electoral cycle of second-tier elections. Regarding the specific arena dimension, the general starting assumption is that something different is at stake in local elections and voting. The idea to analyse these in their own terms evidently runs as a common theme through the framework. It is hypothesised that the extent to which stakes are *localised* depends on various circumstances found in the features of second-tier government, politics, elections or voting explained below.

Moreover, in the critical assessment, the connection between the less-at-stake and the specific arena dimension was rephrased as an evolving equilibrium. It is argued that an inverse relationship exists between the extent to which specific arena characteristics determine local elections and voting and the potential effect of features of the less-at-stake dimension. The default mode of less-at-stake can thus be counterbalanced or even overwritten by characteristics that enhance the specific arena dimension. The institutional-procedural dimension will be most apparent when we discuss the effect of the electoral system as part of the variegated institutional set-up of second-tier elections. The campaign dimension will be included in outlining this feature as well. The second-tier framework is graphically presented in Figure 27.1 and will be elaborated in the next sections.

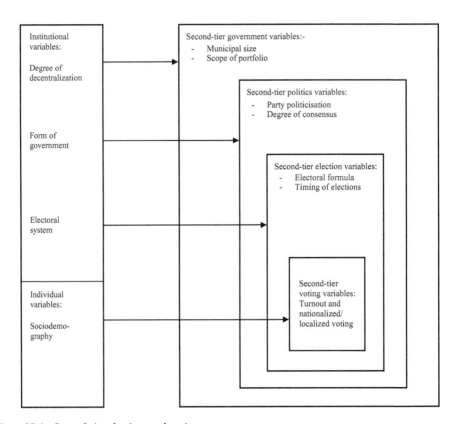

Figure 27.1 Second-tier elections and voting

Second-tier government features

First, it is argued that *government features* at the second-tier level affect elections and voting along the less-at-stake dimension. Therefore, *second-order assumptions will apply* (**P1**). In comparison to the first tier, the second tier is evidently comprised of more and smaller units. This scalar configuration affects the local polity scope (Denters et al. 2015). By default, second-tier elections and voting compose political bodies with relatively less power and/or influence. In many instances, the scope of the second tier is a combination of local self-government (a general competence to address matters of local interest) and multi-level co-governance (the second tier operating as an implementing agency of supra-local regulations and programs with differing degrees of discretion). This dichotomy clearly focusses on the vertical dimensions of polity scope. From a horizontal perspective, it can be noted that in the era of place-bound partnerships between the various spheres of society, local government is identified as the enabler at the nexus (Barnett 2011). Additionally, local government often directly affects the daily life of its citizens. Hence, second-tier elections and voting may be seen as equally relevant albeit in different domains of governance (Lefevere 2013), supporting the something-different-at-stake logic.

For cross-municipal variation, *size* seems a relevant factor but with potentially divergent effects. We may both argue that the *larger* (**H1a**) or *smaller* (**H1b**) a municipality, the more localised second-tier elections and voting. Regarding the former, in larger units more substantial issues might be at stake, generating redistributive political conflicts enhanced by well-developed or renowned partisan and civic actors. Pertinent to the latter, smaller units are associated with less (nationalised) partisanship, closer bonds between politicians and citizens and less ideologically conflictual and more harmonious place-oriented politics (Kjaer and Elklit 2010).

Cross-nationally, divergence in the territorial and functional organisation of second-tier government may matter. Also the functional scope and discretion of local authorities captured in the vertical power relations of intergovernmental arrangements may matter. These have traditionally been grasped in qualitative categorisations that often distinguish between the Southern and the Northern European model (Hendriks, Loughlin and Lidström 2011). In addition, quantitative and discrete measures (using multiple numerical and scalar indicators) have refined and actualised the assessment of cross-national differences in place-bound authority (Sellers and Lidström 2007; Ladner, Keuffer and Baldersheim 2016). The approach and outcome in these typologies differ, but they share that the autonomous position of the second tier may arise through a functional or political rationale. In the first, the municipal ethos is predominantly about the ability to shape and deliver a substantial amount of public services and provisions. In the second, communalism dominates instrumentalism. Local authorities represent different polities with specific identities, providing leverage for vertical interest mediation. It is assumed that both faces of autonomy reduce second-order effects. Thus: *The larger the scope of local authority* (**H1c**) *or the stronger the engraining of political communalism* (**H1d**), *the more localised second-tier elections and voting*.

Second-tier politics features

Second, it is postulated that *politics features* at the second-tier level affect elections and voting along the less-at-stake dimension. Due to these, *second-order assumptions will apply* (**P2**). One crucial local politics feature is the contemporary preponderance of party government in an initially less partisan polity (Copus and Erlingsson 2012). Commonly, organisations associated with the various functions of parties became institutionalised and dominant in place-bound decision-making. Also in the local variant of this governing type, political exchange increasingly galvanises around partisan interests and frames. Ultimately, this stems from the long-term process of politicisation as the '... breakdown of traditional systems of local rule through the entry of nationally organized parties' (Rokkan 1966: 244).

Despite its original teleological assumptions, the end stage of full politicisation has not yet been achieved (Aars and Ringkjøb 2005; Kjaer and Elklit 2010). This echoes the enduring relevance of an alternative conception of place-bound governing as largely outside the political (i.e. partisan) sphere and merely factual and harmonic in which different actors commonly strive for a single best solution to local issues (Copus et al. 2012). Therefore, it is assumed that local party government is a matter of degree and function of cross-municipal variation in politicisation. As the latter is closely associated with national frames of references, it is hypothesised: *the less local party politicisation, the more localised second-tier elections and voting* (**H2a**).

Cross-nationally, the internal form of government and the prevailing mode of local democracy seem to matter. The first refers to horizontal power relations between the legislative and executive branches. Captured in various qualitative typologies (Mouritzen and Svara 2002; Steyvers 2016), these essentially differ between a local presidential (i.e. a directly elected and singular executive as in the strong mayor form) and various subtypes of parliamentarian systems (i.e. non-directly elected and collegiate or managerial executive as in the collective, committee-leader or ceremonial form). This affects the scope of the electoral chain of command and how conflictual or consensual local politics will be (Hendriks, Loughlin and Lidström 2011). Consensual political processes will erode the partisan profiles of politicians, leading to less nationalised voting. Hence, in *local consensus democracies* (**H2b**), *second-tier elections and voting will be more localised*.

The features of second-tier elections

Third, it is assumed, the second tier has some *electoral features* that affect voting along the less-at-stake dimension. Due to these, *second-order assumptions will apply* (**P3**). The nationalisation of the local party system seems key in this respect. This refers to the degree of resemblance in terms of partisan competition and cooperation between local and national levels (Thorlakson 2006). The dominant strand is that national parties are increasingly present and/or obtain more homogenous results in all constituencies (Caramani 2004). The centre of gravity has thereby shifted away from mere place-bound dynamics. When national parties substitute local, second-order voting effects are likely to appear.

Still, others have emphasised the enduring relevance of various non-national lists and/or independent candidates complementing national partisan actors. These tend to maintain a significant supporting part on the municipal scene (Reiser 2008). Party system nationalisation is then not an absolute end-state of contemporary local elections. As a matter of degree, it also remains territorially diverse. Each place-bound party system is a specific mix of local (non-national or independent) and national (local chapters of parties) elements and multilevel correspondence will thus differ across municipalities (Kjaer and Elklit 2010). With the degree to which the same parties are competing identified as a central political circumstance in the original second-order framework, it is therefore argued: *the less nationalised the local party system, the more localised voting* (**H3a**). Additionally, second-tier election campaigns (and municipal variation therein) may matter. Existing mass media logics tend to induce a nationalised bias (with a default focus on supra-local politicians and issues rendering place-bound dynamics subordinate) countervailed by mobilisation efforts by local political actors (Epping, Vos and De Smedt 2014). The specificity of campaigning at this level (more candidate-oriented and community-anchored) also enhances the idea that something different instead of less may be at stake in local elections. Thus: *the more localised the campaign efforts of political actors and/or the framing by the mass media, the more localised voting* (**H3b**).

Cross-nationally, variation in the system and the timing of second-tier elections appears important. The system refers to the rules for conducting local elections and the interplay of districting (one or more constituencies), the ballot structure (closed or open) and the electoral formula and giving way to (subtypes of) proportional, non-proportional (plurality or majority) and mixed systems (Van der Kolk 2007). These are assumed to have (psychological) effects on second-tier voting. Proportionality is associated with multipolar consensus democracy limiting a nationalised electoral frame. It is therefore argued that: *a proportional electoral formula will lead to more localised voting* (**H3c**). However, non-proportional systems are usually not at-large elections as the municipality is often divided into different constituencies (with a comparatively lower district magnitude). This implies candidate-centred voting. Thus: *the more constituencies in the local political unit, the more localised voting* (**H3d**). The timing pertains to the momentum of local elections in relation to that of their national counterparts conditioned by potential differences in length (concurrent or variegated) and/or the tenure (fixed or amendable) of both terms. The second-order literature argues that the size of effects is a function of the position of these elections in the national electoral cycle – the closer to the mid of the national electoral term the more do second-order elections have barometric tendencies (with aggregated interpretations of national parties' failure or success). Therefore: *the less local elections are timed at the mid-point of a national cycle, the more localised voting* (**H3e**).

Second-tier voting features

Finally, actual *second-tier voting features* are incorporated, referring to the motives for turning out and voting for a specific party and/or candidate in the local elections. It is assumed here that *second-order assumptions will apply depending on individual voters' attitudes and behaviour* (**P4**). Essential to the second-tier voting is that this kind of voting is a matter of balancing national and local considerations. Voters may be mobilised along pre-existing national partisan belonging enhanced by nationalised media frames and/or ditto party or candidate strategies (focused on issues, ideology or government participation). At the same time, the proximity and the portfolio of the second tier and the need for parties and candidates to be locally anchored and known (i.e. 'friends-and-neighbour' politics – see Jennings and Niemi 1966) can bring local reasoning to the fore. Another feature concerns the actual alignment of the vote across the various levels (Kjaer and Elklit 2005). Some may split their vote, opting for a different party (or candidate representing it) at local and national elections.

Vice versa, specific individuals will differ in the combination of motives and adjustment along a continuum of localisation and nationalisation of their second-tier voting. Based on the findings of previous research explaining the importance of the local level relative to others (Lefevere 2013) and construing the congruence of local with national voting (Marien et al. 2015), it is argued that *those who are higher educated* (**H4a**), *hold more moderate ideological positions* (**H4b**), *have an outspoken valuation of local policy* (**H4c**) *and are familiar with one or more candidates* (**H4d**) *are more likely to localise their voting*.

Conclusion

Conclusions on local as second-tier elections and voting

In this chapter, the dominant second-order framework to elections at the local level is critically assessed, and substituted with an adapted conception of second-tier elections and voting. While acknowledging the relevance of key second-order postulates, the proposed model starts from

Table 27.1 Local second-tier elections and voting: premises and hypotheses

Second-tier features	Second-order premise	Second-tier localisation
Government	Due to second-tier government features, second-order assumptions will apply (**P1**)	The larger (**H1a**) or smaller (**H1b**) a municipality, the more localised second-tier elections and voting The larger the scope of local authority (**H1c**) or the stronger the engraining of political communalism (**H1d**), the more localised second-tier elections and voting
Politics	Due to second-tier politics features, second-order assumptions will apply (**P2**)	The less local party politicisation, the more localised second-tier elections and voting (**H2a**) In local consensus democracies (**H2b**), second-tier elections and voting will be more localised
Elections	Due to second-tier elections features, second-order assumptions will apply (**P3**)	The less nationalised the local party system, the more localised voting (**H3a**) The more localised the campaign efforts of political actors and/or the framing by the mass media, the more localised voting (**H3b**) A proportional electoral formula will lead to more localised voting (**H3c**) The more constituencies in the local political unit, the more localised voting (**H3d**) The less local elections are timed at the mid of a national cycle, the more localised voting (**H3e**)
Voting	Depending on individual voters' attitudes and behaviour, second-order assumptions will apply (**P4**)	Those who are higher educated (**H4a**), hold more moderate ideological positions (**H4b**), have an outspoken valuation of local policy (**H4c**) and are familiar with one or more candidates (**H4d**), are more likely to localise their voting

the acknowledgment of place-bound heterogeneity, the need to substitute aggregate insights with individual counterparts and the placement of localities and individuals along a continuum of localisation and nationalisation. Given the nested nature of the model (from voters over elections to politics and government) a number of premises were developed with hypotheses to assert variation between voters, municipalities and/or countries in second-tier elections and voting. These are summarised in Table 27.1 below. According to each second-order feature included in our model, second-order premises are opposed to the presumed conditions for the localisation of second-tier elections and/or voting.

Future research into local as second-tier elections and voting

While it should be obvious that the second-tier framework is preferable to the second-order one since it opens up for a much more nuanced understanding of local elections and local voting behaviour, it is also obvious that the main constraint to this approach is the data situation. The hypotheses put forward in this chapter are quite straightforward, and a systematic empirical testing of these hypotheses should be undertaken. However, when it comes to local elections and not least local voting, reliable and comprehensive data are not always available. In the best of all worlds, data – including electoral statistics and survey data on electoral behaviour – would be available for all municipalities in every country (and over time, to be very optimistic). Survey data are available in a few countries, but in most countries a few indicators in the electoral statistics (turnout, number of candidates, votes per party) are the only data available for each municipality and thus for municipal-level analyses. Therefore, this is a call for more and better data. A model to mimic could be the Danish Local Election Study: at the two most recent local elections in the 98 Danish municipalities (in 2009 and 2013), a survey was conducted including several thousand respondents carefully selected to ensure that at least thirty potential voters from each municipality were interviewed to allow for multi-level analyses (see Elklit and Kjaer 2013; Elklit, Elmelund-Præstekær and Kjaer 2017).

As we await the gathering of more data on the local government level, some of the premises and/or hypotheses put forward can already be analysed based on existing data. The variation across municipalities within countries can be analysed for countries where data already exist. Cross-country analyses can be conducted by carefully selecting countries with sufficient data available to pursue some of the hypotheses where sufficient variation cannot be found within a single country. This way some of the hypotheses can be tested. It can also be analysed whether contemporary trends such as municipal consolidation and supra-local centralisation affect the relationships proposed between local government, politics, elections and voting and the variation therein (i.e. along homogenisation or nationalisation of the second-tier).

Putting together datasets from different sources covering different countries to study local elections and voting behaviour within a second-tier framework is laborious and sometimes troublesome, but the rewards should be correspondingly high. As Arend Lijphart advocated almost half a century ago, going local will allow for circumventing the '*many variables, small N*' problem (Lijphart 1971). And it will be possible to say something general about how for instance the party system, the electoral formula, media coverage etc. affect voting behaviour. However, and more to the heart of this chapter, it will be possible to evaluate how 'local' local elections are. To which extent are local elections second-rank or second-kind in the minds of the electorate? And not least: What institutional settings create the degree of interconnectedness between elections at the local and the national/European level?

Such findings would definitely allow a more normative discussion on how connected to (or isolated from) the national election local elections *should* be. To what extent and under which conditions are local elections able to fulfil their essential functions of authorisation, responsiveness and accountability in a place-bound representative democracy? The importance of these mechanisms goes well beyond specific municipalities and offices. Indeed, it remains of first order to the overall health of democracy in contemporary multilevel governance. While some of the more empirical analyses called for in this chapter require compiling of data, these more normative discussions can start right away. So, the chapter not only invites to further discussion of the second-tier framework and empirical testing of the hypotheses proposed within this framework – it also welcomes a more normative discussion about how the knowledge of what factors localise/nationalise local elections should be used when made available.

References

Aars, J. and Ringkjøb, H.-E. (2005). Party Politicization Reversed? Non-Partisan Alternatives in Norwegian Local Politics. *Scandinavian Political Studies 28*(2): 161–182.
Barnett, N. (2011). Local Government at the Nexus? *Local Government Studies 37*(3): 275–290.
Bechtel, M. (2012). Not Always Second-Order: Subnational Elections, National-Level Vote Intentions, and Volatility Spillovers in a Multi-Level Electoral System. *Electoral Studies 31*(1): 170–183.
Caramani, D. (2004). *The Nationalization of Politics: The Formation of National Electorates and Party Systems in Western Europe*. Oxford: Oxford University Press.

Clark, A. and Krebs, T. (2012). Elections and Policy Responsiveness. In K. Mossberger, S. Clarke and P. John (eds), *The Oxford Handbook of Urban Politics*, 87–113. Oxford: Oxford University Press.

Clark, N. and Rohrschneider, R. (2009). Second-Order Elections versus First-Order Thinking: How Voters Perceive the Representation Process in a Multi-Layered System of Governance. *Journal of European Integration* 31(5): 645–664.

Copus, C. and Erlingsson, G. (2012). Parties in Local Government: A Review. *Representation* 48(2): 235–247.

Copus, C., Wingfield, M., Steyvers, K. and Reynaert, H. (2012). A Place to Party? Parties and Nonpartisanship in Local Government. In S. Clarke, P. John and K. Mossberger (eds), *The Oxford Handbook of Urban Politics*, 210–230. Oxford: Oxford University Press.

Dandoy, R. and Schakel, A. (eds) (2013). *Regional and National Elections in Western Europe. Territoriality of the Vote in Thirteen Countries*. Basingstoke: Palgrave.

Davies, J. and Trounstine, J. (2012). Urban Politics and the New Institutionalism. In S. Clarke, P. John and K. Mossberger (eds), *The Oxford Handbook of Urban Politics*, 51–70. Oxford: Oxford University Press.

Denters, B. and Mossberger, K. (2006). Building Blocks for a Methodology for Comparative Urban Political Research. *Urban Affairs Review* 41(4): 550–571.

Denters, B., Goldsmith, M., Ladner, A., Mouritzen, P. and Rose, L. (2015). *Size and Local Democracy*. Cheltenham: Edward Elgar.

De Vries, C., Van der Brug, W, Van Egmond, M. and Van der Eijk, C. (2011). Individual and Contextual Variation in EU Issue-Voting: The Role of Political Information. *Electoral Studies* 30(1): 16–28.

Elklit, J. and Kjaer, U. (2013). (eds), *KV09. Analyser af kommunalvalget 2009*. Odense: Syddansk Universitetsforlag.

Elklit, J., Elmelund-Præstekær, C. and Kjaer, U. (eds) (2017). *KV13: Analyser af kommunalvalget 2013*. Odense: Syddansk Universitetsforlag.

Epping, L., Vos, D. and De Smedt, J. (2014). 'Second-order elections' in de media? Berichtgeving over de lokale verkiezingen van 2012 in België. *Tijdschrift voor Communicatiewetenschap* 42(1): 55–70.

Flickinger, R. and Studlar, D. (2007). One Europe, Many Electorates? Models of Turnout in European Parliament Elections after 2004. *Comparative Political Studies* 40(4): 383–404.

Gregory, R. (1969). Local Elections and the Rule of Anticipated Reactions. *Political Studies* 17(1): 31–47.

Heath, A., McLean, I., Taylor, B. and Curtice, J. (1999) Between First and Second Order: a Comparison of Voting Behaviour in European and Local Elections in Britain. *European Journal of Political Research* 35(3): 389–414.

Hendriks, F., Loughlin, J. and Lidström, A. (2011). European Subnational Democracy: Comparative Reflections and Conclusions. In J. Loughlin, F. Hendriks and A. Lidstroöm (eds), *The Oxford Handbook of Local and Regional Democracy in Europe*, 715–742. Oxford: Oxford University Press.

Hix, S. and Marsh, M. (2007). Punishment or Protest? Understanding European Parliament Elections. *The Journal of Politics* 69(2): 495–510.

Hix, S. and Marsh, M. (2011). Second-Order Effects Plus Pan-European Political Swings: An Analysis of European Parliament Elections across Time. *Electoral Studies* 30: 4–15.

Hough, D. and Jeffery, C. (2003). Regional Elections in Multi-Level Systems. *European Urban and Regional Studies* 10(3): 199–212.

Hough, D. and Jeffery, C. (2006). Germany: An Erosion of Federal–Länder Linkages? In D. Hough and C. Jeffery (eds), *Devolution and Electoral Politics*, 119–139. Manchester: Manchester University Press.

Jeffery, C. and Hough, D. (2009). Understanding Post-Devolution Elections in Scotland and Wales in Comparative Perspective. *Party Politics* 15(2): 219–240.

Jennings, M. and Niemi, R. (1966). Party Identification at Multiple Levels of Government. *American Journal of Sociology* 72(1): 86–101.

Kjaer, U. and Elklit, J. (2005). Are Danes More Inclined to Ticket Splitting than the Swedes and the English? *Scandinavian Political Studies* 28(2): 125–139.

Kjaer, U. and Elklit, J. (2010). Party Politicization of Local Councils: Cultural or Institutional Explanations for Trends in Denmark (1966–2005). *European Journal of Political Research* 49: 337–358.

Koepke, J. and Ringe, N. (2006). The Second-Order Election Model in an Enlarged Europe. *European Union Politics* 7(3): 321–346.

Ladner, A., Keuffer, N. and Baldersheim, H. (2016). Measuring Local Autonomy in 39 Countries (1990–2014). *Regional and Federal Studies* 26(3): 321–357.

Lefevere, J. (2013). Zijn lokale verkiezingen tweederangsverkiezingen? In R. Dassonneville, M. Hooghe, S. Marien and J.-B. Pilet (eds), *De lokale kiezer. Het kiesgedrag bij de Belgische gemeenteraadsverkiezingen van oktober 2012*, 67–92. Brussels: ASP Press.

Lelieveldt, H. and Van der Does, R. (2014). Hoe tweederangs zijn lokale verkiezingen? Een analyse van de Nederlandse gemeenteraadsverkiezingen 2010 vanuit het perspectief van second-order elections. *Res Publica* 56(3): 317–337.

Lijphart, A. (1971). Comparative Politics and the Comparative Method. *American Political Science Review* 65: 682–93.

Lowndes, V. (2009). New Institutionalism and Urban Politics. In J. Davies and D. Imbroscio (eds), *Theories of Urban Politics*, 91–105. London: Sage.

Marien, S., Dassonneville, R. and Hooghe, M. (2015). How Second Order Are Local Elections? Voting Motives and Party Preferences in Belgian Municipal Elections. *Local Government Studies* 41(6): 898–916.

Marschall, M. (2010). The Study of Local Elections in American Politics. In J. Leighley (ed.), *The Oxford Handbook of American Elections and Political Behavior*, 471–492. New York: Oxford University Press.

Marsh, M. (1998). Testing the Second-Order Election Model after Four European Elections. *British Journal of Political Science* 28: 591–607.

Miller, W. (1988). *Irrelevant Elections? The Quality of Local Democracy in Britain*. Oxford: Oxford University Press.

Mouritzen, P. and Svara, J. (2002). *Leadership at the Apex. Politicians and Administrators in Western Local Governments*. Pittsburgh: University of Pittsburg Press.

Norris, P. (1997). Second-order Elections Revisited. *European Journal of Political Research* 31: 109–114.

Oliver, E. (2012). *Local Elections and the Politics of Small-Scale Democracy*. Princeton, NJ: Princeton University Press.

Pallares, F. and Keating, M. (2003). Multi-Level Electoral Competition: Sub-state Elections and Party Systems in Spain. *European Urban and Regional Studies* 10(3): 239–255.

Rallings, C. and Thrasher, M. (2005). Not All 'Second-Order' Contests Are the Same: Turnout and Party Choice at the Concurrent 2004 Local and European Parliament Elections in England. *British Journal of Politics and International Relations* 7: 584–597.

Rallings, C., Thrasher, M. and Denver, D. (2005). Trends in Local Elections in Britain: 1975–2003. *Local Government Studies* 31(4): 393–413.

Reif, K. (1997). European Elections as Member State Second-Order Elections Revisited. *European Journal of Political Research* 31: 115–124.

Reif, K. and Schmitt, H. (1980). Nine Second-Order National Elections – A Conceptual Framework for the Analysis of European Election Results. *European Journal of Political Research* 8(1): 3–44.

Reiser, M. (2008). Conclusion: Independent Local Lists in Eastern and Western European Countries. In M. Reiser and E. Holtmann (eds), *Farewell to the Party Model? Independent Local Lists in Eastern and Western European Countries*, 277–294. Wiesbaden: VS Verlag.

Rokkan, S. (1966). Electoral Mobilization, Party Competition and National Integration. In J. LaPalombara and M. Weiner (eds), *Political Parties and Political Developments*, 241–265. Princeton, NJ: Princeton University Press.

Schakel, A. (2013). Congruence between Regional and National Elections. *Comparative Political Studies* 46(5): 631–662.

Schakel, A. and Jeffery, C. (2013). Are Regional Elections Really 'Second-Order' Elections? *Regional Studies* 47(3): 323–341.

Sellers, J. and Lidstroöm, A. (2007). Decentralization, Local Government, and the Welfare State. *Governance: An International Journal of Policy, Administration and Institutions* 20(4): 609–632.

Steyvers, K. (2016). A Knight in White Satin Armour? New Institutionalism and Mayoral Leadership in the Era of Governance. *European Urban and Regional Studies* 23(3): 289–305.

Thorlakson, L. (2006). Party Systems in Multilevel Contexts. In D. Hough and C. Jeffery (eds), *Devolution and Electoral Politics*, 37–52. Manchester: Manchester University Press.

Van der Kolk, H. (2007). Local Electoral Systems in Western Europe. *Local Government Studies* 33(2): 159–180.

28
THE ARCHITECTURE OF THE LOCAL POLITICAL COMMUNITY
France, Italy, Portugal and Spain

Jaume Magre and Esther Pano

Introduction

The local government systems of France, Italy, Portugal and Spain are often grouped together and considered under the single heading of 'Southern European countries'. However, the characterisation of this discrete category is problematic and often overlaps with other groupings (e.g. Mediterranean Europe). If we focus specifically on the structure and morphology of their respective municipal maps and associated political features, then France, Italy and Spain present some undeniable similarities. Portugal, on the other hand, does not fit neatly into this broader picture as it is not so clearly characterised by a large number of small units of local government. Yet, despite these differences, the four are usually analysed together on the grounds of the similar traditions that underpin the architecture of their local political communities. In this chapter, we analyse the local systems of government of these four countries and seek to highlight their respective similarities and differences.

To do so, we examine not only the size and number of municipal entities and the direct consequences of these characteristics, but also the overall morphology of the local government map and the position occupied by the municipalities in the broader political system. In the next section, we describe the common trends and dissimilarities presented by the systems of local government in the four countries, and consider the weight tradition has played in the configuration of their local institutions. We then report the distribution of municipalities by number of inhabitants and the percentage of the population residing in them, and monitors changing trends in these figures since 1950. The subsequent section focuses on the political structure of local government and presents typologies of both the mayors and of the operation of local elections. Next we analyse the institutional role played by local government in Southern Europe and contrasts its functions with those conducted by their counterparts in the countries of Northern Europe. Finally, we discuss the concepts of community attachment and the formation of community ties in relation to the forging of municipal identities and their consequences on such aspects as political participation and local loyalties. We conclude by recognising that the role of local institutions extends beyond the simple delivery of services inasmuch as they can be considered a manifestation of an entire political community.

The local system of government of Southern European countries: the weight of tradition

Southern European countries have typically been considered as constituting a single group within the various typologies and classifications provided of local government. Since Page and Goldsmith (1987) drew up their typology – one that has subsequently been employed widely by other scholars – France, Italy, Spain and, eventually, Portugal and Greece have usually been assigned to the Franco-Napoleonic group. Page and Goldsmith's (1987) classification is based on historical, morphological and formal criteria, which means that the specific territorial factor is embedded in the broader concept of historical traditions, which results in different systems of local government. This particular typology groups local government systems into two categories: Northern European and Franco-Napoleonic. Later, Hesse and Sharpe (1991) would add a further category – the Anglo group – employing essentially the same rationale as Page and Goldsmith. Both contributions are marked by a strong idea of path dependency; in other words, they hold that certain historical traditions, grounded in specific territorial areas, will result in a particular model of local government. Although the literature has subsequently revised this classification (Hesse and Sharpe 1991; Heinelt and Hlepas 2006; Goldsmith and Page 2010; Kuhlmann and Wollmann 2014; Bouckaert and Kuhlmann 2016), it remains the classic starting point for any description of local government systems.

Southern European countries do indeed have a number of elements in common that are consistent with a given morphology of local government. Generally speaking – albeit with specific differences that we will return to later – three of these elements can be identified as:

- similar administrative tradition;
- large number of small units of local government; and
- relatively low levels of public service provision allocated to local government.

Taking these characteristics as our starting point, we should recognise that the inclusion of Portugal in this group is somewhat debatable as it presents an interesting mix of Napoleonic tradition and British influence (Corte-Real 2008). That is, while Portugal undoubtedly presents some of the above elements – namely, the common administrative tradition and a relatively low level of direct service provision – its municipalities are decidedly not small in terms of population. Indeed, the total number of municipalities is low (308) and has remained steady for many years.

France and Italy, and by extension Spain, have also typically been classified within this same tradition of public administration. Indeed, if we adopt the framework devised by Peters (2008), all four belong to a tradition of local government characterised by seven dimensions: a particular conception of the state and society, a separate administrative law, a clear distinction between administration and politics, the concept of a career civil service, equality and uniformity as the basic values of public administration, a relation between societal actors and the administration, and the manner in which accountability is conceived within the public sector.

In three of these countries, the map of local government comprises a large number of municipalities, most of which have very small populations. This municipal map has typically been analysed from the perspective of the effects of size on democracy. For example, Denters et al. (2014) explore this relationship in four countries (Switzerland, Norway, Denmark and the Netherlands), none of which, unfortunately, coincides with our Southern European countries. In general, the authors do not identify any clear evidence of the impact of size; thus, the idea that 'small is beautiful' does not find any empirical support. Yet, the link between small municipal size and identity does appear to be present in the conception of the system (Dahl and Tufte 1973; Baldersheim and Rose 2010; Denters et al. 2014). Whatever the case, there is some, albeit limited, evidence of the impact of size on the quality and operation of democracy. A further consideration that arises in relation to size is the level of public service provision in local government. We explore this question in more detail in the following section.

A final element – at least, as far as Italy, Portugal and Spain are concerned – emerged as a side-effect of the 2008 economic crisis, as all three countries were forced to implement economic sustainability programmes. These have included a wide range of austerity measures, some of them involving the reform of the territorial structure and administration. Indeed, a number of longstanding programmes aimed at reducing the number of local governments and amalgamating local entities that could never previously be agreed to. However, a window of opportunity was opened up during the crisis, promoted by the need to reduce expenditure. Yet, the extent to which these measures have finally impacted on the local system is unclear. For the time being, these countries maintain their traditional structure of fragmented local governments, despite the fact that the pressure from upper tiers, above all the European Union, has increased over the last decade.

The shape of the municipal system: fragmentation or consolidation?

As noted, one of the defining traits of the Franco-Napoleonic local government systems is the proliferation of small municipalities, Portugal being the exception (Page and Goldsmith 1987; Hesse and Sharpe 1991; Bouckaert and Kuhlmann 2016). In general, the territory of these countries is divided into small municipalities which enjoy equal legal status. Table 28.1 illustrates the distribution of municipalities by number of inhabitants and shows the percentage of the country's population actually living in each category of municipality defined by these population thresholds. In France, for instance, more than 50% of the municipalities have fewer than 500 inhabitants, so representing just 7% of the population. The situation is very similar in Spain (48% and 2%), but less so in Italy (11% and 0.4%). Portugal, in stark contrast, has just one municipality with fewer than 1,000 inhabitants, in a system that is dominated by medium-sized local structures. Portugal, in fact, operates a twofold system of municipal government, made up of municipalities and parishes (*freguesias*). The *freguesias* constitute a sub-municipal tier of government, also endowed with a political structure and exercising its own powers and functions. The system contrasts sharply with those of the other countries in this group, above all as far as the size of the municipalities is concerned.

The last three rows in Table 28.1 show the percentage of municipalities and the percentage of the overall population above and below the 5,000-inhabitant threshold. The resulting picture is striking. For all the countries, except Portugal, the large majority of municipalities have fewer than 5,000 inhabitants, whereas the majority of their respective populations reside in municipalities with more than 5,000 inhabitants. France and, especially, Spain are clear examples of this situation, both with around 90% of their municipalities below the threshold, but with 62% and 88% of their respective populations resident in larger cities. Table 28.2 presents the main descriptive statistics for the municipal populations of the four countries. As expected, France, Italy and Spain present low population means and high standard deviations, with minimums close to zero and their largest cities exceeding two million inhabitants. In the case of Spain, a combined inspection of Tables 28.1 and 28.2 reveals a situation of marked contrasts between highly populated areas – along the Mediterranean coast, the Madrid area, and various big cities – and wide areas of almost deserted territory.

Table 28.1 Municipalities and population distribution in France, Italy, Portugal and Spain

No. of inhabitants	France [N = 35,885] % of municipalities	% of population	Italy [N = 7,999] % of municipalities	% of population	Portugal [N = 308] % of municipalities	% of population	Spain [N = 8,119] % of municipalities	% of population
0–500	53.51	6.62	10.54	0.40	0.32	0.00	48.00	1.57
501–1,000	19.19	7.39	13.98	1.36	0.00	0.00	12.71	1.58
1,001–5,000	21.38	24.29	45.32	14.82	12.01	1.28	23.28	9.41
5,001–25,000	4.94	26.55	25.20	34.44	55.19	19.77	12.26	23.53
25,001–50,000	0.63	11.74	3.16	14.49	13.31	13.95	1.97	11.57
50,001–100,000	0.23	8.32	1.23	10.93	11.36	21.89	1.02	12.79
100,001–500,000	0.11	9.63	0.50	11.46	7.47	37.92	0.69	23.55
500,001–1,000,000	0.01	2.06	0.05	5.15	0.32	5.19	0.05	5.82
>1,000,000	0.003	3.39	0.03	6.94	0.00	0.00	0.02	10.18
Total	100.00	100.00	100.00	100.00	100.00	100.00	100.00	100.00
0–5,000	94.08	38.30	69.83	16.59	12.34	1.29	83.99	12.56
>5,000	5.92	61.70	30.17	83.41	87.66	98.71	16.01	87.44
Total	100.00	100.00	100.00	100.00	100.00	100.00	100.00	100.00

The information in the table is drawn from several sources, and has been combined and validated by the authors. It is interesting to highlight the changes that have occurred in the number of municipalities of some countries even during the writing of this chapter. N corresponds to the total number of municipalities when the databases were consulted.

Sources: Information drawn from the following websites: France – www.insee.fr (2016) and www.ign.fr (2016); Italy – www.anci.it/ (2016); Portugal – www.ine.pt (2016) and www.pordata.pt /2016); Spain – www.ine.es and www.ign.es (2016)

Table 28.2 Municipalities in France, Italy, Portugal and Spain: population and area

	Country	N	Min	Max	Mean	St. Dev.
Population	France	35,885	0	2,229,621	1,833.01	14,944.708
	Italy	7,999	36	2,864,731	7,584.14	42,728.166
	Portugal	308	430	547,733	34,292.79	56,059.484
	Spain	8,119	5	3,141,991	5,742.63	46,215.350
Area (square km)	France	35,885	0.03	18,647	17.53	145.960
	Italy	7,999	0.12	1,287	37.76	50.410
	Portugal	308	8.00	1,721	299.42	277.879
	Spain	8,119	0.03	1,750	62.17	92.281

Sources: See Table 28.1

Differences in the area of the municipalities are also significant. However, in this case the analysis is less clear given the specific geographical and political structures of some areas. For example, islands or other territories may be considered as single municipalities, and so distort the areal analysis. Nevertheless, the mean values are once again highly illustrative. The combined analysis of Tables 28.1 and 28.2 shows that France has the smallest municipalities in terms of area and mean population, with almost 95% of the country's municipalities accounting for just less than 40% of the population. This situation is even more pronounced in the case of Spain where close to 90% of the population (87.44%) resides in just 16% of the municipalities. The case of Italy seems comparatively more balanced presenting a higher population mean and a lower average area, so that the population distribution appears less disproportionate. In contrast to these extremely fragmented maps, Portugal presents a more compact structure of local government, with larger municipalities and a more even population distributed.

Although the amalgamation of municipalities has been widely debated, implementing such programmes in France, Italy and Spain has always generated great controversy. Such processes have been initiated elsewhere in Europe and, in many European countries the number of municipalities has fallen considerably since the mid-twentieth century. In contrast, these three countries have only been able to make modest reductions, if any. All four countries, in this case including Portugal, present a steady pattern of behaviour in this regard. In the case of Italy, however, the last decade has actually seen an increase in the number of municipalities (Steiner et al. 2016). Table 28.3 shows these variations, or rather, their resolute stability.

Given the complexity of implementing large-scale territorial reforms, inter-municipal cooperation has emerged as a viable alternative that respects the traditional structure of the municipal map. In France, for example, inter-municipal associations are extremely widespread. This approach allows the formation of larger organisations while maintaining the system of municipal

Table 28.3 Changes in the number of municipalities

	1950	2007	2016
France	38,000	36,783	35,885
Italy	7,781	8,101	7,999
Portugal	303	308	308
Spain	9,214	8,111	8,119

Source: De Ceuninck et al. (2010: 809), updated by the authors

distribution. Interestingly, the response to the use of these entities has been diametrically opposed in the two Iberian countries. Thus, while in Portugal these inter-municipal associations have been strongly promoted in response to the austerity measures implemented over the last decade, in Spain they are seen to duplicate functions at this level of government and their use has been restricted. The existence of a second-tier government can also be seen as a compensatory mechanism for municipal fragmentation. Although in the case of Portugal, its two-fold local system (*freguesias* and *municipalidades*) represents an administrative deployment at the sub-municipal as opposed to the supra-municipal level. Elsewhere, the existence of second-tier governments is widespread, constituting an additional layer in the stratified institutional system.

Typologies of mayors and elections

The local government system in operation in most countries of Southern Europe fits quite naturally with the typology proposed by Mouritzen and Svara (2002). As noted in previous sections of the chapter, the systems all share the same administrative tradition, but there are obvious differences in their institutional design. The most obvious involve the operation of the electoral system: namely, that of the election of the mayor and that of the system used to choose council members.

Of the four countries included in the study, Italy is the only one in which the mayor is elected directly. In the other three, the election is indirect based on the votes of the council members. In fact, after Italy initiated the direct election of the mayor with the enactment of Law 81 of 25 March 1993, the system was extended to a considerable number of European Union countries. The Portuguese case is exceptional in comparative terms, since voters do not directly elect the mayor but rather they directly choose the municipal executive (or *câmara municipal*). Indeed, in this case, the voters simultaneously and separately choose the municipal assembly and the executive.

In general, in recent years the strong-mayor model has evolved towards the direct election of the mayor (the case of Italy and, although it lies outside the specific scope of this chapter, Greece) or towards a strengthening of the executive powers of the government or of the figure of the mayor (the case of Spain and, to some extent, France). While this is a general trend within local government in Europe, it acquires a special significance in the strong-mayor model, as it means the whole political-institutional system revolves around this figure.

Table 28.4 Elements of the electoral system

	Spain	*France*	*Italy*	*Portugal*
Election of mayor	Indirect	Indirect	Direct	Indirect
Election of council members	Proportional	Majority	Majority*	Proportional
Type of lists in the general[1] system	Closed list system	Closed list system	Semi open list system	Closed list system
Type of lists in municipalities in the general system	Open	Open	Semi-open list system	Non-existent

* In the Italian case, the system for appointing council members foresees various possibilities that take into consideration the election of the mayor in the first or second round and the results obtained by the lists linked to the candidature of the mayor. Either way, the probability of the result being determined by a majority solution is the most likely outcome.

There is no common denominator characterising the election of council members. Spain and Portugal continue to apply the d'Hondt formula when allocating the number of seats; France continues to use a two-round system, with the winning party being granted a majority bonus; and, Italy, in parallel with the introduction of the direct election of the mayor, foresees various possibilities that, in general, result in members being elected on a majority basis.

The greatest similarity occurs in the type of electoral lists used in all four Southern European countries. In the case of municipalities under the general system, most have opted not to open the lists and, therefore, not to accept the possibility of preferential voting. Even in the case of Italy after the 1991 abrogative referendum, voters decided to reduce the number of preferential votes from three to two. This is one of the most striking differences with respect to the countries of Northern Europe, all of which incorporate, to a greater or lesser degree, open electoral lists. The fact that municipalities are much larger in the countries of Northern Europe probably accounts for the need to enhance the community value associated with preferential voting. In contrast, the size of the municipalities in the South makes its introduction unnecessary in most of them.

Despite the differences and similarities in the essential elements of the electoral system, the strong-mayor model emphasises the principle of political leadership, personified in the figure of the mayor, as opposed to the professional management offered by other local government systems. The countries of Southern Europe share a similar model of political organisation and of local government, in which the elected mayor controls the majority of the city and is *de jure* and *de facto* in full charge of all executive functions. The mayor is responsible for executing the decisions of the Council and for managing and overseeing the organisation of the local government and its staff, either because it has a majority of seats on the council, or because a clear division of powers and responsibilities has been established between the council and the executive. In this system, the mayor adopts a presidential role, as is clearly illustrated by the cases of Italy and Portugal, where the mayor enjoys wide powers: the political and administrative system of local government revolves around this figure. Finally, in this model, the chief executive officer has traditionally been the municipal secretary, although in recent years this position has been called into question in several countries: municipal fragmentation combined with the growing complexity of municipal management mean that in many municipalities the municipal secretary ends up executing operational tasks, and rather than being neutral, independent technocrats, they perform the functions of political management.

Beyond the politico-administrative characteristics outlined above, the set of countries that form a part of this institutional tradition are all committed to addressing their territorial diversity institutionally by adapting to the characteristics and community values that typify the smallest municipalities. In France, following the passing of Law of 17 May 2013, a population threshold was fixed at 1,000 inhabitants. Below this figure, a double ballot majority system is employed and the interesting thing is that the voters can modify the lists, *panacher*, without their ballot being considered null. In Portugal, although the general system is the same for all municipalities, there is an institutional mechanism that links the *freguesias* – sub-municipal units that date back to mediaeval times – with the municipality's representative bodies: the municipal assembly is composed of members elected by the citizens of the municipality and by the presidents of the different *freguesias* of which they form a part. Finally, to adapt more adequately to the structure of the country, Spain is the European country with the highest number of municipal electoral systems – specifically three: municipalities of fewer than 100 inhabitants operate an assembly-like system; municipalities with between 100 and 250 inhabitants employ a limited voting system, and in the larger municipalities, the general system is employed.

Table 28.5 Territorial thresholds and sub-municipal units

	Spain	France	Italy	Portugal
Electoral System threshold	250 inhabitants	1,000 inhabitants	15,000 inhabitants	Non-existent
Sub-municipal units	EATIM Districts	Districts	Circoscrizione comunale	Freguesia

This conjunction between the idea of the political essence of the local government (see discussion below) and the form of local government that characterises the countries of Southern Europe means the figure of the mayor transcends the municipal boundaries. The mayor stands as a true representative of the territorial community, be it by simultaneously holding two or more elective offices at different levels of government, by means of *cursus honorum*, or by courtesy of their skills of political leadership.

The Institutional role of local government

Although the institutional role of local government can be considered essential within the architecture of state and local systems (here the contribution of Sellers and Lidström 2007 is particularly relevant), in general, it has received little systematic attention from scholars. To explore this subject further, and to characterise the specific profile of local governments in Southern European countries, we propose analysing two closely interrelated dimensions: first, the autonomy of local government and the way this relates to other levels of government, above all central government; and, second, the tasks and functions assigned to the municipalities and the level of public expenditure under their control. In analysing the first dimension, we attach particular relevance to the Local Autonomy Index (Ladner et al. 2015), while in the case of the second element, we draw on information from a range of sources to illustrate the tasks assumed by local government in each country and the amount of resources exploited in so doing.

The literature struggles to define 'local autonomy' and different studies take different approaches in seeking to interpret this term. For example, the classic contributions focus on characteristics of a legal or constitutional nature (Clark 1984; Goldsmith 1995). Likewise, the functions and resources of local government have been the focus of much of the attention of the literature (Goldsmith 1995; King and Pierre 1990; Pratchett 2004), while more recently comparative studies have become quite prevalent (Sellers and Lidström 2007; Hooghe et al. 2010; Do Vale 2015). However, perhaps of greatest utility, is the work of Ladner et al. (2015) in developing the Local Autonomy Index (LAI).[2] This not only offers the possibility of measuring and comparing levels of local autonomy across countries, but also of analysing its evolution over time.

The index has been calculated for the period 1990–2014, but, here, to avoid the impact of specific reforms, we work with the average score for this period. As expected, the four Southern European countries present similar scores, leaving them somewhere in the middle of the ranking. Meanwhile, the Scandinavian countries occupy the top positions in the ranking and Ireland languishes at the bottom. It should be stressed that the index, in common with many definitions of autonomy, emphasises the relevance of service provision and, thus, these comparative outcomes are largely foreseeable. In short, in the Southern European countries, local government systems appear to have a somewhat limited capacity for public service delivery, especially when compared to their Northern European counterparts.

The functions allocated to the municipalities in France, Italy, Spain and Portugal are primarily related to the provision of public utilities, while most other tasks are normally shared with other levels of government. The range of functions therefore comprises a common core, present in all four countries, plus certain specific activities that are only undertaken by some of them (Marcou 2007; Wollmann 2008; CCRE 2008; CEMR 2009, 2012). They can be summarised as follows:

- *Tasks that are municipal functions in all four countries*: town planning, environment- related services (including, waste management and sewer systems), water supply, transport and general authorisations for cultural activities and economic development.
- *Tasks that can only be identified in some of the four countries or under certain conditions*: social welfare, education, local police, paving and maintenance of local roads.

The evolution in local government expenditure is also useful for illustrating the provision and the intensity of that provision. Table 28.6 shows the changes that occurred between 2008 and 2015 in the spending of the Southern European countries as a percentage of GDP. In general, Portugal and Spain present lower levels of local expenditure than the EU-28 and EU-15 means, France traditionally coincides almost exactly with the EU mean, while Italy normally presents a rate of spending three to four points above the mean. Indeed, the gap in spending between Italy, on the one hand, and Spain and Portugal, on the other, is worth highlighting. Moreover, the table clearly reflects the impact of the economic crisis and the austerity measures implemented in some of the countries (Magre and Pano 2016; Citroni et al. 2016; Medir et al. 2017). Thus, expenditure on local government services in Italy, Portugal and Spain rose gradually up to 2010, when an overall downturn was recorded in spending.

These data appear to be consistent with scores on the Local Autonomy Index. To verify this, Table 28.7 presents information about the distribution of spending by level of government and compares the respective rates of expenditure in the countries of Southern and Northern Europe. Despite the considerable variation within these groups of countries, local government expenditure in the South is markedly lower than in the North, and in all cases significantly different from the figure of 61% reported for Denmark.

This general overview leads us back once more to a discussion of municipal size, but we are now in a position to incorporate other elements, such as the role played by local government in the institutional system and the range of tasks and functions undertaken by the local authorities. Figure 28.1 illustrates the relationship between the size of the municipalities (in terms of population) and local government expenditure as a percentage of total public sector spending. The municipalities in the more developed welfare states of Northern Europe, which have

Table 28.6 Percentage of local expenditure as proportion of GDP

	2008	2009	2010	2011	2012	2013	2014	2015
European Union (28 countries)	11.3	12.1	11.9	11.6	11.6	11.4	11.3	11.1
European Union (15 countries)	11.3	12.2	11.9	11.6	11.7	11.5	11.3	11.1
France	11.2	11.9	11.5	11.4	11.7	11.9	11.8	11.4
Italy	15.1	16.5	15.7	14.9	14.9	15.0	14.7	14.5
Portugal	7.1	7.5	7.4	6.8	6.2	6.6	6.0	5.9
Spain	6.5	7.1	7.1	6.8	5.9	5.9	6.1	6.0

Source: Eurostat (http://ec.europa.eu/eurostat, accessed February 2017)

Table 28.7 Public expenditure by sub-sector of government, 2012 (%)

	Central government	State government	Local government	Social Security funds	
France	32.68	0.00	20.67	46.65	100.00
Italy	31.11	0.00	29.44	39.45	100.00
Portugal	59.32	0.00	12.58	28.10	100.00
Spain	27.12	30.16	10.93	31.79	100.00
Denmark	31.47	0.00	61.50	7.03	100.00
Sweden	38.18	0.00	48.86	12.96	100.00
Norway	66.49	0.00	33.51	0.00	100.00

Source: Based on Eurostat data (http://ec.europa.eu/eurostat, accessed February 2017)

responsibility for a significant number of services, are larger and have higher rates of expenditure. With the exception of the municipalities in Portugal, those in the Southern European countries present a similar pattern (i.e. small in population and low rates of expenditure).

In general, the four Southern European countries, as well as presenting relatively low levels of local expenditure, also undertake a relatively small number of activities (mostly related to the provision of public utilities). As such, local government in these countries fulfils the role as supplier of certain services, but it does not act as the principal provider of more sophisticated activities – such as education, health or a broad range of social services. This has a clear impact in budgetary terms and may also be related to their size. The question as to whether these countries have opted to allocate more sophisticated services to other levels of government because of the size of their municipalities or whether they have been obliged to act in this way because of the difficulties they face in rearranging the municipal map remains an open one.

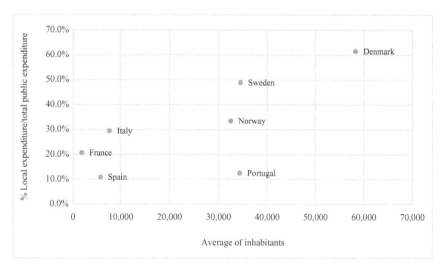

Figure 28.1 Size and local expenditure, 2012

Source: Based on Eurostat data (http://ec.europa.eu/eurostat, accessed February 2017). Population data for France, Italy, Portugal and Spain: see Table XXX. Population data for Denmark: see www.dst.dk/en# (2016). Population data for Norway: see www.ssb.no/en (2016). Population data for Sweden: see www.scb.se/en (2016).

Local community and identity: a complex puzzle

In general, the countries of Southern Europe share the same administrative tradition, which can be characterised by the following features: the universality and uniformity of municipal government; the elective nature of local authorities; the dualism between the municipalities' own and their delegated functions; the *département* (second-tier) constituting the electoral district and local authority, and the will to create a municipality for each human settlement. This last feature explains, in part, the high degree of fragmentation of the territorial structure of the countries of Southern Europe. And it is this very fragmentation that accounts for the existence of strong ties between the members of the community, stimulating higher levels of social relations and participation in community activities and organisations, as well as the development of emotional ties with the municipality – in other words, forging a municipal identity.

The relationship between municipal size and identity has been well established empirically. Two sociologists, John Kasarda and Morris Janowitz (1974) – picking up where Louis Wirth (1938) left off – developed the concept of community attachment by identifying two explanatory models. The first, linear in nature and derived from the studies of Louis Wirth, Ferdinand Töennies and Georg Simmel, claims that the formation of ties with a place depends mainly on such factors as the size, density and heterogeneity of the population. The second model, systemic in nature, and formulated by the likes of Robert Park and Ernest Burgess, seeks the origins of the development of community attachment in factors such as an individual's position in the social structure and life cycle stage.

A territorial structure such as that of the countries of Southern Europe, in which the percentage of municipalities with very few inhabitants has considerable weight in its composition, must necessarily have a direct impact, for example, on electoral turnout rates. This has been captured in the literature by the 'small is beautiful' v. 'bigger is better' debate. Since the first studies published by Verba and Nie (1972) right up to the systematic review undertaken by Blais (2000), the 'small is beautiful' doctrine has obtained greater support from empirical studies of voter turnout (Geys 2006). While there are studies that identify other factors that weaken the effect of the size of the municipality on political participation (Lyons et al. 1992; Kelleher and Lowery 2004 2009), in general, the empirical evidence tends to support the negative effect of increasing size on the number of voters; hence, voters living in smaller municipalities tend to present higher levels of electoral participation, stronger ties with their communities and a higher level of civic participation (Dahl and Tufte 1973; Oliver 2001), above all in metropolitan settings (Oliver 2000).

Having resolved the relationship between size and identity, we need to consider this second variable that characterises local government in the countries of Southern Europe. The Napoleonic model employed by these countries (Hesse and Sharpe 1991) is characterised, as mentioned, by a strong local identity that, to some extent, is gained at the expense of greater municipal autonomy. Thus, the essence of local government of the countries that form part of this model is more political than functional. Local governments are considered the genuine representatives of the territorial community and the holders of elective office are expected to represent the interests of their communities before the other tiers of government. This 'political localism' (Page 1991) explains, to a large extent, the degree of local fragmentation and the determination to uphold the whole system of units of local government, however small they might be. Likewise, it accounts for the fact that all moves taken to amalgamate the municipalities since the 1970s in these countries have been unsuccessful.

This strong sense of identification with the territorial community at the local level has shown itself to be compatible with other attitudinal loyalties held by citizens towards other political and administrative spheres, be they regional (in the case of Spain and Italy) or national (in the case of France). In these countries there exists, therefore, a stratification of identities that are compatible with one another and which provide an added complexity to the institutional fabric.

Conclusion

The institutional tradition of the countries analysed in this chapter is based, with some distinctions, on a specific conception of the territory and of the position of the municipalities within the political system. France, Italy and Spain are the three clearest examples in Europe of highly fragmented local systems, made up of many municipal units with few inhabitants. Moreover, and here we can also include Portugal, they have retained this model unaltered for many years. This is all the more surprising if we consider that they have had to face all kinds of historical turmoil and other transformations of their territorial and political structures that can be considered as being just as traumatic. This is especially true of Spain, which has gone from a centralised unitary state system to a quasi-federal organisation. Yet, the local system in all four cases has shown itself to be highly stable, more so than those of other European countries.

These local systems are founded on identifiable political communities that are recognised as such in a world of plural identities. Moreover, this municipal identity is compatible with other loyalties manifest towards other political and administrative spheres, be they regional (Spain and Italy) or state (France). The result is a juxtaposition of tiers of government that make up a rich tapestry of administrative colours that prove compatible with, and which add complexity to, the institutional fabric. This complexity could have had an impact on other aspects that affect the institutional design including, for example, the implementation of territorial reforms. The major local government reform programmes undertaken by other European countries aimed at redesigning the municipal map so as to create organisational units of an optimal size for service provision proved impossible or enjoyed little success in these countries.

Indeed, faced by the dichotomy between size and autonomy of service provision, it seems that the latter may have suffered the costs of maintaining a fragmented municipal system. The institutional position of the municipalities is often characterised by this conflict: a quite specific local identity and the functionality of service provision. The difficulty in making these two compatible has in some cases been achieved thanks to inter-municipal cooperation, which presents itself as a possible alternative to more drastic reforms. Thus, inter-municipal associations are widespread in France but they also have a presence in the other countries. This solution allows the construction of a solid structure for supplying services while at the same time maintaining the municipal structure. Interestingly, these associations have received quite distinct receptions in Portugal and Spain. Within the framework of the austerity measures introduced over the last decade, inter-municipal associations have been strongly promoted in Portugal but considered a manifestation of the duplication of organisations, and hence restricted, in Spain. The existence of second-tier entities is also seen as a compensatory mechanism for the municipal fragmentation that allows the structure of the municipal map to be maintained. In fact, Portugal, which is the most different of the four models analysed here, operates a two-fold system in which the municipalities operate at a level above the *freguesias*. In the other three countries, the existence of second-tier entities is widespread throughout their territory, constituting a further layer in these stratified institutional systems.

In short, we are dealing with complex institutional systems characterised by plural, yet compatible, identities and which, to date, have resisted all attempts to overhaul their territorial distribution. Their justification lies in the fact that they constitute a model that promotes the strong ties between the formal institution and the citizens' sense of belonging. Indeed, they highlight the fact that the institutions are not simply units for the production of services but rather they reflect the expression of an entire political community.

Notes

1 In this context, the use of the term 'general' refers to the electoral system that is commonly applied to municipalities without taking into consideration any particular characteristic or condition such as volume of population.
2 See http://ec.europa.eu/regional_policy/es/information/publications/studies/2015/self-rule-index-for-local-authorities-release–1-0.

References

Baldersheim, H. and Rose, L. (2010) *Territorial Choice: The Politics of Boundaries and Borders*. Basingstoke: Palgrave Macmillan.
Blais, A. (2000) *To Vote or Not to Vote: The Merits and Limits of Rational Choice Theory*. Pittsburgh, PA: University of Pittsburgh Press.
Bouckaert, G. and Kuhlmann, S. (2016) Comparing Local Public Sector Reforms: Institutional Policies in Context. In S. Kuhlmann, and G. Bouckaert (eds), *Local Public Sector Reforms: National Trajectories and International Comparisons*, 1–20. Basingstoke: Palgrave Macmillan.
CCRE (2008) *L'Europe Locale et Régionale: Chiffres clés 2008*. Brussels: Conseil des Communes et Régions d'Europe.
CEMR (2009) *Balancing Democracy, Identity and Efficiency: Changes in Local and Regional Structures in Europe*. Brussels: Council of European Municipalities and Regions.
CEMR (2012) *Local and Regional Government in Europe: Structures and Competences*. Brussels: Council of European Municipalities and Regions.
Citroni, G., Lippi, A. and Profeti, S. (2016) Local Public Service in Italy: Still Fragmentation. In H. Wollmann, I. Kopric and G. Marcou (eds), *Public and Social Services in Europe. From Public and Municipal to Private Sector Provision*, 103–117. Basingstoke: Palgrave Macmillan.
Clark, G. (1984) A Theory of Local Autonomy. *Annals of the Association of American Geographers* 74(2): 195–208.
Corte-Real, I. (2008) Public Management Reform in Portugal: Successes and Failures. *International Journal of Public Sector Management* 21(2): 205–229.
Dahl, R. and Tufte, E. (1973) *Size and Democracy*. Stanford, CA: Stanford University Press.
De Ceuninck, K., Reynaert, H., Steyvers, K. and Valcke T. (2010) Municipal Amalgamations in the Low Countries: Same Problems, Different Solutions. *Local Government Studies* 36(6): 803–822.
Denters, B., Goldsmith, M., Ladner, A., Mouritzen, P. E. and Rose, L. E. (2014) *Size and Local Democracy*. Cheltenham: Edward Elgar.
Do Vale, Helder F. (2015): Comparing and Measuring Subnational Autonomy across Three Continents. *Lex Localis* 13(3): 741–764.
Geys, B. (2006) Explaining Voter Turnout: A Review of Aggregate-Level Research. *Electoral Studies* 25: 637–663.
Goldsmith, M. (1995) Autonomy and City Limits. In D. Judge, G. Stocker and H. Wolman (eds), *Theories of Urban Politics*, 228–252. London: Sage.
Goldsmith, M. and Page, E. (ed.) (2010) *Changing Government Relations in Europe: From Localism to Intergovernmentalism*. Abingdon: Routledge.
Heinelt, H. and Hlepas, N. (2006) Typologies of Local Government Systems. In H. Bäck, H. Heinelt and A. Magnier (eds), *The European Mayor: Political Leaders in the Changing Context of Local Democracy*, 21–42. Wiesbaden: Verlag für Sozialwissenschaften.
Hesse, J. J. and Sharpe, L. J. (1991) Conclusions. In J. J. Hesse (ed.), *Local Government and Urban Affairs in International Perspective*, 603–621. Baden-Baden: Nomos.
Hooghe, L., Marks, G. and Schakel, A. H. (2010) *The Rise of Regional Authority: A Comparative Study of 42 Democracies (1950–2006)*. London: Routledge.

Kasarda, J. and Janowitz, M. (1974) Community Attachment in Mass Society. *American Sociological Review* 39: 328–39.

Kelleher, C. and Lowery, D. (2004) Political Participation and Metropolitan Institutional Contexts. *Urban Affairs Review* 39: 720–757.

Kelleher, C. and Lowery, D. (2009) Central City Size, Metropolitan Institutions and Political Participation. *British Journal of Political Science* 39(1): 59–92.

King, D. and Pierre, J. (1990) *Challenges to Local Government*. London: Sage.

Kuhlmann, S. and Wollmann, H. (2014) *Public Administration and Administrative Reforms in Europe: An Introduction in Comparative Public Administration*. Cheltenham: Edward Elgar.

Ladner, A., Keuffer, N. and Baldersheim, H. (2015) *Local Autonomy Index for European countries (1990–2014): Release 1.0.* Brussels: European Commission.

Ladner, A., Keuffer, N. and Baldersheim, H. (2016) Measuring Local Autonomy in 39 Countries (1990–2014). *Regional and Federal Studies* 26(3): 321–357.

Lyons, W. E., Lowery, D. and Hooglan DeHoog, R. (1992) *The Politics of Dissatisfaction: Citizens, Services and Urban Institutions*. Armonk, NY: M. E. Sharpe.

Magre Ferran, J., and Pano Puey, E. (2016) Spanish Municipal Services Delivery: An Uncertain Scenario. In H. Wollmann, I. Kopric and G. Marcou (eds), *Public and Social Services in Europe. From Public and Municipal to Private Sector Provision*, 119–134. Basingstoke: Palgrave Macmillan.

Marcou, G. (2007) *Local Authority Competences in Europe. Study of the European Committee on Local and Regional Democracy*. Strasbourg: Council of Europe.

Medir, L., Pano, E., Viñas, A. and Magre, J. (2017) Dealing with Austerity: A case of local resilience in Southern Europe. *Local Government Studies* 43(4): 621–644.

Mouritzen, P. and Svara, J. (2002) *Leadership at the Apex. Politicians and Administrators in Western Local Governments*. Pittsburgh, PA: University of Pittsburgh Press.

Oliver, J. E. (2000) City Size and Civic Involvement in Metropolitan America. *American Political Science Review* 94(2): 361–373.

Oliver, J. (2001) *Democracy in Suburbia*. Princeton, NJ: Princeton University Press.

Page, E. (1991) *Localism and Centralism in Europe: The Political and Legal Bases of Local Self-Government*. Oxford: Oxford University Press.

Page, E. and Goldsmith, M. (eds). (1987) *Central and Local Government Relations: A Comparative Analysis of West European Unitary States*. London: Sage.

Peters, F. (2008) The Napoleonic Tradition. *International Journal of Public Sector Management* 21(2): 118–132.

Pratchett, L. (2004) Local Autonomy, Local Democracy and the 'New Localism'. *Political Studies* 52: 358–375.

Sellers, J. M. and Lidström, A. (2007) Decentralization, Local Government, and the Welfare State. *Governance: An International Journal of Policy, Administration, and Institutions* 20(4): 609–632.

Steiner, R., Kaiser, C. and Eythorsson, G. T. (2016) A Comparative Analysis of Amalgamation Reforms in Selected European Countries. In S. Kuhlmann and G. Bouckaert (eds), *Local Public Sector Reforms in Times of Crisis: National Trajectories and International Comparisons*, 23–42. Basingstoke: Palgrave Macmillan.

Verba, S. and Nie, N. (1972) *Participation in America: Political Democracy and Social Equality*. Chicago, IL: University of Chicago Press.

Wirth, L. (1938) Urbanism as a Way of Life. *American Journal of Sociology* 44(1): 1–24.

Wollmann, H. (2008) Comparing Local Government Reforms in England, Sweden, France and Germany: Between Continuity and Change, Divergence and Convergence. Retrieved from www.wuestenrot-stiftung.de/download/local-government.

PART VI

Getting and spending

29
LOCAL GOVERNMENT ANTI-CORRUPTION INITIATIVES IN POST-SOVIET GEORGIA AND UKRAINE

Another tale of two cities

Terry Anderson

Introduction

When the Soviet Union collapsed in 1991, the former republics faced a future both filled with hope and overshadowed by deep concern. One of the greatest difficulties to have confronted the newly emerging democracies since achieving independence is the continuing presence of corruption. The numerous systemic and pervasive forms of corruption in the region have impeded attempts to create stable and efficient economies and have also given rise to widespread feelings of injustice and cynicism. A further complication is that the same characteristics that make corruption problematic also often negatively affect attempts to address it (Nasuti 2015). One formidable obstacle to efforts to reduce the level of corruption in any society is the interests of powerful and well-connected elite groups who feel personally threatened by such reform efforts. Their immediate reaction is typically to mobilise to prevent changes from occurring. This is even more problematic when, as potential leaders come up through the ranks during their careers, they tend to either become socialised into the norms of the system or completely excluded from power. The result is that those who ultimately hold positions from which they can actively influence policy formulation and implementation are often so compromised they are no longer willing or able to act on reforms. Given these factors, corruption can become remarkably resistant to any reform efforts (Nasuti 2015).

The region of Eastern Europe and the former Soviet Union provide a rich environment in which to study corruption. In large part, common experiences throughout the twentieth century have shaped common experiences since the collapse of the Soviet Union. This has led to the ability to discuss many political, economic, and social issues using a comparative approach that can be supported. This discussion compares efforts at the local level in Georgia and Ukraine to address their respective problems with corruption.

A brief overview of corruption

It would be difficult to examine anti-corruption initiatives across countries without first understanding what corruption is and how it affects governance. Transparency International (TI), a non-governmental organisation promoting transparency and accountability in international development, asserts that transparency is ensured by shedding light on everything government does (see www.transparency.org). It guarantees that public officials in any capacity, together with those in the business community, act visibly and understandably, and report openly and regularly on their activities so that the public can hold them accountable. Such transparency is claimed to be the best way of preventing corruption and helps increase trust in both the institutions and those who work and serve in them.

In the early 1990s, corruption was not something that many were willing to openly discuss, largely because it was so prevalent in the everyday lives of leaders, corporations, other organisations and citizens. For example, globally, many major companies regularly wrote off bribes as business expenses to take advantage of tax breaks; corrupt acts committed by some longstanding heads of state were widely publicised; and many international agencies were resigned to the fact that corruption would steal funding from development projects throughout the world. Despite the magnitude of the problem, prior to the early 1990s, there was no global organisation with a goal to curb corruption, and, perhaps even more importantly, no way to accurately measure corruption at the global level.

Corruption can be defined most simply as 'the abuse of entrusted power for private gain' (from www.transparency.org). To take it further, it often involves allocation of resources and opportunities unfairly and inefficiently. It is usually discussed within the context of specific actions taken by those labelled as being corrupt. Corruption comes in many forms including embezzlement, fraud, collusion, extortion, abuses of discretion, favouritism, gift-giving, clienteles, financing networks of cronyism and patronage, and improper political contributions.

Corruption can be classified in a variety of different ways, where the distinction is most often a function of how much money is lost and where the corruption occurs. Corruption has been around for a very long time and will undoubtedly continue well into the future unless governments can develop effective ways to combat it. It affects virtually every aspect of the relationship between citizens and their governments. It comes with a very high cost and affects societies in many ways. At its worst, corruption can cost lives, as in cases where substantial bribes become the only way to receive health care in an emergency. In other cases, corruption can cost people their freedom.

The effects of corruption can be felt in political, economic, and social matters. From a political perspective, corruption is an obstacle to democracy and the rule of law. As noted by Stockemer et al. (2013), 'There is evidence that corruption is especially disruptive in democracies because it undermines the basic principles of a free state.' Corruption delegitimises the political and institutional systems where it takes root (Rock 2009; Sung 2004). Further, corruption also discourages citizen participation in democratic elections, because lower participation may exacerbate legitimacy problems. This is harmful in established democracies but is even more problematic in newly emerging ones or those in transition where democracy is not fully consolidated. Developing accountable political leadership in a corrupt climate is extremely challenging; understanding political corruption can be even more so.

Perhaps the area most negatively affected by corruption is a country's economy. Mauro (1997) investigated some of the root causes of public corruption, and found that much of it could be traced to 'Government intervention in the economy, where policies aimed at liberalisation, stabilisation, deregulation, and privatisation can sharply reduce the opportunities for rent-seeking behavior and corruption' (Mauro 1997: 8).

Where pervasive government regulations are combined with significant levels of discretion by government officials in applying them, many individuals will offer bribes to officials to circumvent the rules and officials will often accept them. Numerous policy-related sources for corruption have been identified such as trade restrictions, government subsidies, price controls, multiple exchange rate practices and foreign exchange allocation schemes, and low wages in the civil service (Mauro 1997).

Early scholars (Leff 1964; Nye 1967; Huntington 1968) held firmly that corruption could benefit social modernisation in countries with slow or inefficient bureaucracies. More recent research has identified numerous detrimental effects of corruption (North 1990; Ades and Di Tella 1996; Mauro 1997; Gupta, Davoodi, and Alonso-Terme 2002; Fisman and Svensson 1999; Podobnik et al. 2008). Corruption undermines people's trust in the overall political system, and, more specifically, in its institutions and its leadership. When the public becomes distrustful or apathetic, those sentiments can then become yet another hurdle to challenging corruption.

Corruption as an ethical violation

In order for good governance to be practised, there must first be good public servants. In general, corrupt acts by public servants raise serious ethical concerns about the capability of a democratic government to serve all citizens. It is common among contemporary, democratic market-oriented countries to hold public servants to higher ethical standards than other professions. Despite being an obvious double standard, it can be argued that from the standpoint of political and legal philosophy, it seems entirely justifiable, as ethical accountability is essential in keeping the corrupt and opportunistic behaviour of public servants in check.

Successful engagement of corruption requires first knowing its source and cause. Every country seems to have some level of corruption that citizens will tolerate and even expect. Very often, the 'bad apple' explanation serves in identifying the most common source of corruption. But trying to attack corruption by eliminating one bad public servant at a time is usually ineffective since another will take his or her place and the problem simply resurfaces. Experience has shown that unless accountability and transparency policies are implemented in all levels of an operation, corruption continues to be a problem.

Accountability makes public servants answerable through a system of values, actors, expectations, actions, means, and relationships. Anti-corruption initiatives often consist of measures that provide direction, are linked to performance measurement, or establish procedures. But, in fact, accountability in the public sector must go much further to include both external standards that pressure the moral development of public servants and internal virtues that support good administrative judgment (Erakovich et al. undated). There is simply no replacement for individual judgment. Ethical behaviour cannot be guaranteed by creating rules and formulas followed in a mechanical way. In order to behave ethically, public administrators must have their own set of core values and democratic ideals that stand up to changes in their official working environment. An administrator having these qualities has the integrity to take responsibility for their words and actions, even in the face of politics.

What must happen in order to hold officials accountable is that an ethical climate must be established. Central to creating such an environment is developing a means for ensuring transparency. Transparency implies openness, communication, and accountability. In public services, it means that public servants should be as open as possible about all the decisions and actions they take. They should justify their decisions and restrict information only when the wider public interest demands it (Chapman 1993). Extreme transparency in management requires that all decision making should be carried out publicly. Further, it requires that the public have access to information that contributed to the decisions so that they may assess the decisions for themselves.

Transparency and corruption

Corruption most often occurs when there is insufficient openness in state processes and weak administrative controls over the practices and behaviour of government officials. US Supreme Court Justice Louis Brandeis, in 1913, wrote concerning the problems associated with corruption that 'Publicity is justly commended as a remedy for social and industrial diseases. Sunlight is said to be the best of disinfectants; electric light the most efficient policeman' (cited at Brandeis University undated). Brandeis was not speaking of any specific form of corruption, but rather of abuse of power in general. However, his view reflects an important underlying truth – that public knowledge of such behaviour reduces it.

This has led to the assertion by some that transparency can be a solution to corruption (Rose-Ackerman 2004). Transparency can make political institutions more transparent thereby making citizens more aware of which officials may be engaged in corruption. Citizens can then make rational choices about whom to vote for. They will also know who may be taking bribes and be able to assess whether poor performance is due to the taking of bribes or simply indicative of general incompetence.

Transparency, while a necessary but insufficient condition for reducing corruption, can, in fact, have the opposite effect. For example, Bac (2001) asserts that a higher level of transparency in decision-making increases the probability of detecting corruption or wrongdoing. However, he adds that increased transparency might alert outsiders to the identity of key decision-makers and thereby enhance incentives to establish connections for corruption. This can result in reducing the detection effect for generating local transparency improvement and ultimately increasing corruption by increasing opportunities for connecting with those inclined to be corrupt.

Despite the possibility of making the situation worse by increasing transparency, Cuervo-Cazzura (2014) concludes that a high level of transparency can reduce imbalances in information available to government officials and citizens such that citizens can more easily identify those officials who are engaging in corruption and avoid entering into relationships with them. This high level of transparency also keeps corrupt individuals in check for fear they will be denounced for engaging in corruption.

Anti-corruption reforms in Georgia and Ukraine

Anti-corruption reform initiatives have been widely studied. A review of them leads to the conclusion that corruption can be challenged primarily through four sources of control. First is from outside through external organisations such as the IMF, the World Bank and the donor community that have applied substantial pressure on transitioning and developing countries to fight corruption by applying political conditionalities. These organisations encourage the practice of 'good governance', which implies honesty, efficiency, and accountability of the bureaucratic departments, as well as specific political issues like multiparty elections, civil society enforcement and human rights. A second source of control is from above in which control comes from rulers whose reforms target speeches, campaigns, executive reporting systems, institutional reforms, degree of administrative discretion, and size of various departments and offices. Successful reform depends on political will. Third, control can come from inside through administrative and bureaucratic institutions where professionalism and defence of public over private depend

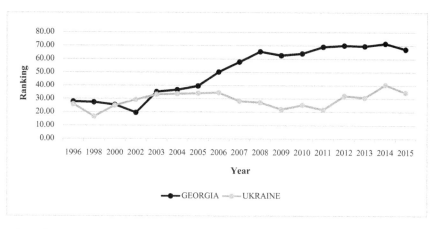

Figure 29.1 Corruption Perception Index ranking for Georgia and Ukraine, 1999–2015

on the internal and institutional administrative controls that rely heavily on various controlling and auditing bodies within the state administration. Finally, control can come from below through the civil society, the business community, and individual citizens, and is based on the principles of democracy. It includes checks and balances, the separation of powers, rule of law, and legislative and judicial independence considered fundamental to democratic systems and necessary to ensure the political responsiveness of politicians and civil servants.

By compiling annual data for the ranking assigned to the two countries by Transparency International in its Corruption Perception Index (CPI) for 1999 through 2015, it appears that Georgia and Ukraine began essentially at the same level of perceived corruption in 1999. But by 2015, Ukraine's ranking was significantly higher than Georgia's (Figure 29.1). This leads to the conclusion that some anti-corruption reforms implemented in Georgia have been successful in addressing the problem. However, in the case of Ukraine, the experience has not been the same.

It might at first be tempting to conclude that Georgia could implement its reforms efficiently just because the population and the territory of Georgia is small, and therefore easier to manage and monitor. But the real reason probably goes well beyond that. In fact, much of Georgia's success in addressing corruption can be credited to the fact that the government demonstrated a deep commitment to face the problem directly by creating a clear and transparent national anti-corruption strategy and action plan of consisting of well-defined reforms that, once implemented, resulted in sanctions against people involved in corruption, including high ranking officials. Within that plan, they reduced the overstaffed and inefficient public administration by abolishing unnecessary functions of state bodies; increased the salaries of public officials, civil servants and the police; privatised state-owned property and identified people who mismanaged state property for their own benefit; improved the custom service and treasury service by selecting competent officials to manage them; and reduced the number of face-to-face transactions in all of those services by implementing various platforms for e-governance. They improved tax administration by reducing the number of taxes, creating a transparent and simplified tax system, significantly reducing limitations and regulations for private business, and creating centres where citizens could receive all necessary information and documents at a single point.

Georgia's approach to corruption is important as it reflects their depth of understanding of the nature of the problem itself. In contrast, changes like those occurring in Georgia after the

Rose Revolution did not take place in Ukraine after the Orange Revolution of 2004, even though that event also brought a new, avowedly reformist leadership to power. Ukrainian President Viktor Yushchenko found that he had to recruit established politicians, many of whom were more supportive of the corrupt status quo, to maintain a viable governing coalition. The Georgian administration could focus on pursuing its reform agenda, but divisions quickly arose in the Ukrainian government that led to gridlock and prevented action from being taken against corruption. Even though the Georgian government was less accountable to the public than was the case in Ukraine, the combination of its composition and its power allowed it to overcome pressures from vested interests and push against corruption in a way that was not possible in Ukraine (Nasuti 2015).

Creating transparency and openness with a new online portal at Tbilisi City Hall

In the years immediately following Georgia's independence from the Soviet Union, citizens questioned the accountability and transparency of the Tbilisi City Hall. The questions were predicated by the fact that citizens did not have financial and other kinds of data about the Tbilisi City Hall and the non-commercial and private legal persons that where under its control. At the same time, journalists and other interested persons were not given the opportunity to evaluate the degree to which decision makers at Tbilisi City Hall were effective in fulfilling their obligations due mainly to the restriction of access to public information. Furthermore, citizens were not equipped with the legal mechanisms and processes that would give them opportunities for full participation in city governance. For citizens of Tbilisi to be fully engaged in local governance, it was very important to inform them and to have maximum transparency in the financial and other key data about the Tbilisi City Hall. In addition, City officials needed to consider implementing services that focused on citizens' activities and what they needed to be involved. Consultants for the City leadership suggested that the answer seemed to lie in the formation of a new web-based solution.

The City hired the Institute for Development of Freedom of Information (IDFI) to develop their proposed solution and so began the project with financial support by the Open Society Georgia Foundation (OSGF). The IDFI is a Georgian non-governmental organisation founded in 2009 to advocate archive transparency by working on openness, transparency, and improvement of access to public information. Initially, IDFI focused on watchdog activities, monitoring government activities, disclosing violations, and informing the public. Beginning in 2012, IDFI gradually started to shift its focus from watchdog to think tank activities. Currently IDFI acts in a hybrid fashion, combining monitoring and analytical skills with evidence-based advocacy, strategic litigation, awareness raising, and consulting activities. It is recognised internationally for its high-quality, independent research and, based on this research, provides innovative, practical recommendations that strengthen democracy in Georgia and neighbouring countries and foster economy and social welfare. It is also known internationally as an organisation that specialises in promoting open and democratic governance.

Working together, the IDFI team, City officials, and other community leaders outlined the objectives of the project that ultimately included the following:

- to increase the level of transparency and accountability of Tbilisi City Hall;
- to promote effective and transparent spending of public funds;
- to support the development of freedom of information by establishing the standards of e-democracy;

- to improve public control over public institutions with the engagement of the citizens, the civil society, and the media; and
- to inform citizens and increase their engagement in the discussion and decision-making processes in the public sector (Open Government Partnership 2015).

To achieve those project objectives, the IDFI team conducted a thorough analysis and study of international practice. Based on that study, the IDFI prepared and presented to Tbilisi City Hall their concept of the structure of the web portal. The concept was discussed publicly with the full participation of officials of the government of Tbilisi and leaders of municipal boards, and was approved by the Mayor of Tbilisi. The resulting portal of Tbilisi City Hall included multiple modules and pages designed to increase civic participation in the activities implemented by the Tbilisi City Hall. To achieve high standards of accountability of local government, portal developers focused on integrating such modern modules as online databases of public information and open data, pages for petition and projects, lists of institutions and companies under Tbilisi City Hall, easily accessible reports and budget, individual pages for municipal boards and other structural subdivisions, and special services for people with disabilities, among others. Once fully implemented, project developers and City officials expected the portal to substantially promote open and participation-based e-governance in Tbilisi.

According to the concept, the plan was to equip the new system with the following features:

- Adaptations to make it accessible for disabled persons.
- Contents to include current information about municipalities, commercial entities, and non-commercial legal persons in a single system.
- A personal page for the mayor that included the mayor's schedule, blog, and opportunities and methods for contact.
- Background information about the mayor, the deputies, and the other administration employees.
- A petition page with a means for petition uploading, and information on how to join various groups and mobilise supporters.
- A site for facilitating the citizens' connection to Tbilisi City Hall addressing such issues as participation in polls, evaluation the work of Tbilisi City Hall including municipalities, how to provide information to officials, and how to upload photos and videos to the web page.
- A list of existing social services for citizens.
- Information for job-seekers.
- Information for those interested in starting a business including how to secure permissions, licenses, and registration, as well as information concerning taxes and fees.
- A site for establishing communication with City officials concerning public meetings or means for participating in local governance processes such as budget planning (IDFI 2014a).

The long-term perspective for the project included creating and implementing a new concept of the web page of Tbilisi City Hall to guarantee proactive access of public information and formation of a citizen-oriented informational web system. What made this project unique was that it would not result in just a single web page. As a portal, it would permit each structural entity within the municipality to create its own content located in its own sub-page, thereby putting all the information for Tbilisi in one central place for easier access by citizens.

The overall strategy for development consisted of a three-pronged approach. First, the IFDI development team planned to study the internal organisation, processes, and procedures of the Tbilisi City Hall. Second, the team worked to determine the current public requirements towards the new web-based portal. Finally, the IDFI team prepared to use those results to create a working prototype.

In the first stage, studying the internal organisation, processes, and procedures of the Tbilisi City Hall, IDFI team members found that, as a system, it was one of the largest and most difficult public bodies in terms of governance. To determine the content of the online system, to unify the standards of the disclosure of the public information, to combine the current information about municipalities, commercial entities and non-commercial legal persons in a single system, and to formulate corresponding procedural documents, it was going to be necessary to work up and research the internal business procedures and information about how it was all managed. To accomplish this, the IDFI team needed to collect and analyse the information about the internal managerial procedures of the Tbilisi City Hall with the collaboration of the corresponding members of the Tbilisi City Hall. Initial studies of the work up, exchange, and publishing of information in the Tbilisi City Hall and its structural or dependent bodies was essential for effective functioning, sharing the responsibilities and obligations, and evaluating administrative resources and technical opportunities for integration and development in current and upcoming electronic service web page.

To address the second prong, determining the public requirements for the new online system, it was important to understand the expectations and the requirements of the consumers, both from the side of service and information recipients, to determine its purpose and required content. On the one hand, availability of public information was important, and on the other, Tbilisi City Hall had to offer various services and programmes to residents of Tbilisi. Thus, both the informational content needs and services, applications, and other activation mechanisms of involvement had to be integrated. At the same time, it was necessary to determine the priorities of the system from the functional point of view. The IDFI team decided that public meetings with the relevant organisations and experts would help them in drawing out the additional indicators that must be considered in creating the technical assignment project. At the same time, it was important to research the best international practices, based on which the modern technical and innovative projects should be offered. The project team felt that analysis of the innovative systems or transparency mechanisms of the web-based systems of foreign countries' municipalities would assist them in considering modern standards, as well as in working out the conceptual documentation and making recommendations based on established arguments and international practice.

The final stage of development, merging the concept and the prototype of the system, involved bringing together administrative and consumer needs and established international practice, to produce a detailed description of the system that included the following:

- Preparation of the description of the structure and navigation of the portal.
- Preparation of the necessary technical instruction for using the portal;
- Designation of the structure of the division of public information and open data and its data management optimisation plan.
- Determination of the structure of citizen involvement applications, e.g., platform of petitions, online platform for defending nature and cultural heritage, public consultations platform, etc.
- Preparation of technical instruction for the systemic requirements of the portal and for necessary cyber-safety regulations.
- Preparation of the content sharing and basic functional and navigation descriptive HTML prototype.

In a presentation by the IDFI team to officials of Tbilisi City Hall on 23 December 2014, David Narmania, Mayor of Tbilisi City Hall, stated:

> Tbilisi City Hall, as a system of public body should be transparent and accountable to every citizen. On the first stage, transparency and accountability could be achieved through creating a modern and citizen-oriented informational web-system. Thus, we fully expressed readiness to commence this project with IDFI and Open Society of Georgia that will enable us to create one of the modern and transparency-oriented portal. We also took the initiative to proactively disclose the information in order to meet the Open Government Partnership commitments. We are committed to disclose information about budget, procurements, and etc.
>
> *(IDFI 2014b)*

On 22 July 2015, the new information portal was launched at Tbilisi City Hall. Officials were generally pleased with the results, but they did recognise that the project did not live up to their expectations in the short term. Almost immediately several shortcomings were identified that suggested future revisions would be needed. Leaders determined that the system as developed was not unified, that is, it was not fully integrated so that citizens could easily navigate through it and maximise its potential (Open Government Partnership 2017). There was little public awareness about the many important projects and services developed by Tbilisi City Hall. Further, Tbilisi City Hall's web page and other sources of information about individual agency or department activities did not ensure the necessary dialogue. Without a unified, simple system in place, the broader public could not be reached.

As a result, the initial project was expanded to include new features and functions to integrate the system so that more information could be provided in a format that was easy for the public to acquire and use. New reform priorities were established aimed at creating a unified system that could increase the level of information available to the public to increase the participation of the civic society and ensure governmental accountability to the public. The planned system includes institutional, electronic, and legislative procedural components based on identified legal and factual conditions for 2017. They are expected to significantly increase the effectiveness of Open Government mechanisms and, if successfully implemented, to potentially produce more democratically oriented change in the governance process in Tbilisi, not only quantitatively, but also qualitatively. This will also probably create support for and increase positive outcomes from existing as well as future innovations (Open Government Partnership 2017).

Creating transparency in budgeting and procurement in Lviv, Ukraine

While Tbilisi City Hall was addressing its problems with citizens' access to public information, municipalities in Ukraine were wrestling with the same issues. Combatting corruption through openness was a critical part of Ukraine's national reform process from the moment of achieving independence. However, Ukraine's attempts to reduce corruption and increase transparency have been more resistant to reform than experienced in many other former Soviet republics. Despite numerous efforts to stem the problem, corruption remains perhaps the most pervasive problem in Ukraine's efforts to consolidate its democracy. An unstable national level government with its growing list of elected officials and national-level career bureaucrats known to be guilty of taking bribes and committing other corrupt acts has deeply marked its first 22 years of independence and served to make transparency extremely difficult.

The issue of budget transparency and use of public funds became particularly important in Ukraine after the Revolution of Dignity during 2013–2014 that culminated in the Maidan protests in February 2014. Demands for openness and accountability of local authorities, especially with regards to financial issues, resulted in legislative promises of these requirements. During 2015, several significant laws were passed that collectively led to more openness and accountability in the budgeting process at the national level. In February 2015, the Law of Ukraine 'On Openness of Public Funds Usage' was adopted, followed by Amendments to Article 28 of the Budget Code of Ukraine regarding access to the information on the budget visualisation in the form of open data in April 2015. This law, when approved by the President of Ukraine, required owners of data on planning and implementation of the state and local budgets to proactively disclose this information in the form of open data. Justification for the new legislation was rooted in an even larger legislative effort to formulate a more comprehensive anti-corruption strategy for Ukraine.

The case of municipal budgeting in Lviv, in Western Ukraine, is one example of how implementation of the national financial reform legislation at the local level suggests that progress is possible. Efforts to implement anti-corruption reforms in Lviv has been an ongoing priority since the current mayor, Andrei Sadovyi, took office in March 2006. While many initiatives have been implemented since that time in Lviv, one that is especially important to the citizens of that city today is one that addresses issues with the City's budget documents. That Lviv should be at the centre of the fight to increase transparency in municipal budgeting is not unexpected, given its history of leadership in reform in post-independence reform in Ukraine. But there are also some broader, more general tendencies among cities in general that make them a logical front line for this fight. It is often easier for citizens at the municipal level to become engaged in understanding how money gets spent and why. And they are often more committed to tracking whether promises are kept.

But ultimate success in increasing openness really depends on how such initiatives are executed. In the matter of public budgeting, making data open would be just the beginning; even more importantly, the data had to also be useful and comprehensible, and this was to be a much bigger challenge (Internews 2015). In Ukrainian cities that had websites, the majority did contain some financial information. Yet, it was generally displayed as long uploaded text files using financial terminology that was unclear to the ordinary citizen and providing little opportunity for interactivity or visualisation. The result was that citizens and local journalists rarely felt that budgeting data was open and thus did not participate in forming or monitoring their city budgets.

According to the International Budget Partnership, in 2014 Ukraine was ranked 54th out of 100 countries in terms of budget transparency and accountability at the national level, opening only a limited volume of budget information. Further, Ukraine stood at 23rd out of 100 in providing the public with opportunities to engage in the budget process (www.international budget.org). Before 2013, under the Yanukovych regime, the idea of a municipal budget available to download was not even a consideration. Much of the information was only available in hardcopy; it was difficult to access and virtually impossible for civil society and local stakeholders to analyse and interpret. Further, when information was available online, finding it was often difficult as it was often buried within other data sets. Even when the information could be located, it was probably presented as a long text document or spreadsheet, containing specialised financial terminology that most citizens would not understand (Internews 2015).

Supporters of reform in Lviv felt that increasing access to budgets and public procurement processes at the municipal level would be a great place to begin their own serious reforms. At that time, if citizens of Lviv wanted to examine the municipal budget they had to be capable of wading through a 637-line municipal budget file available to them only as a paper document that had to be reviewed at the City's budget office. Still, within the context of Ukraine, even this gave Lviv's residents an advantage over their counterparts in other major cities. The result of a few early reform efforts was that more data became available, but it was very hard to find and was not presented in a comprehensible way. Transparency activists and journalists argued that with the budgets still not truly open, citizens could not be active participants in forming and monitoring local government spending. Citizens' groups joined them in pushing for even better access, greater transparency, and effective public control over local spending. They saw this as a part of building healthy democratic communities by being a way to combat corruption.

Very soon help arrived as several open data and open budget laws passed in 2014 and 2015 began to change things. In 2014, the United Nations Development Programme (UNDP) implemented a pilot project called 'Open Budget.' Its goal was to increase local government budget transparency and promote civic engagement. It brought civil servants, civil society workers, IT experts, and journalists together to create ways in which municipal budget information could be better shared with the public. The project began by developing online tools to maximise the communications potential of local governments and incorporated the work of journalists who were intentionally chosen to be among the first participants to learn how to use the digital tools so they could produce data-driven stories that people could understand. Project developers focused on stimulating government–citizen transparency in underserved communities.

Open Budget began with a series of workshops to determine what people wanted from open budgets and to ensure that the delivery method selected would be one that would be right for users from different backgrounds. In these workshops, programme leaders immediately observed that citizens did not understand the budgeting process. This left them unable to effectively provide input for establishing budget priorities. Further, programme facilitators conducted listening sessions with civic activists, local officials, and journalists that revealed two other important points. First, these focus group members wanted to understand how to interpret the numbers and codes in city budget files. Second, they wanted to understand each stage in budget creation and be informed of the status at each milestone so that they could engage in the process (Internews 2015).

Based on information from these interested groups, the Open Budget project team developed a free, user-friendly, online tool for local governments to use in presenting budget information through a variety of graphic data visualisations and launched it in the beginning of 2015. It consisted of two independent components. First, was a graphic visualisation of the budget which could include up to 10 types of visualisation for both revenues and expenses of the city budget. In addition, there was a calendar of the budget cycle to present information concerning the budget estimation and drafting; opportunities and results of public discussion; and notification of approval, execution, and reporting. Second, the programme could interface with official city websites to propose possible visualisations and generate the code to embed the graphics directly into those websites.

The Lviv City Council implemented the Open Budget initiative in 2015 with the full support of UNDP. Compared to other Ukrainian cities, adopting e-governance in Lviv had long been among the priorities for local authorities as a means of facilitating citizens' access to public services through the usage of modern information and communication technologies. By 2015, several e-government tools had already been introduced by City officials. E-applications, online payment for utilities, scheduling appointments with civil servants online, getting on the list for available apartments, examining expenditures at their children's kindergarten classes, monitoring the movement of the public transport, and obtaining information concerning various other public services provided citizens with a head start in the development of e-government and e-democracy. As a result, according to Holub et al. (2014), Lviv ranked 2nd among the 100 largest cities in Ukraine in a UNDP-sponsored assessment of implementation e-tools as the basis for online administrative service provision.

With Lviv as an early adopter of the tool aimed at making the Ukrainian government at all levels more accountable to its citizens, Lina Mykolayiv, Deputy Director of Finance Policy in Lviv City Council was moved to proudly comment that,

> The reports on budget execution were regularly presented through the Lviv city council website. However, the reports were just general figures, such as expenditures on education or communal services. From now on, the citizens will see the detailed expenses – for each school or kindergarten. The citizens can also can participate in budget formation and submit proposals on funds distribution. This builds trust and is another step to maximize the transparency of the budget process in the city
>
> *(Internews 2015)*

To increase citizen review of the budget and use of the new information tool, Lviv conducted a survey asking citizens what information was missing in their budget visualisations. City officials established a plan for further improvement to the presentation of the city budget based on this feedback from the public. The question then was how to continue the reform effort. Helping local government to present their budgets in a more comprehensible way was just the first part of the process of increasing transparency and accountability in budgeting and procurement. The next step was to simplify the data, making it easier to understand so that journalists and transparency activists could unravel what that information revealed about local government competence and trustworthiness. Once they understood it, it would be their responsibility to inform the public who could then begin holding elected officials to greater accountability through a more open political process. Questions concerning what those data told local communities about local government spending on services related to health facilities, schools, and local infrastructure, and how their region compared to other regions with similar or different numbers of inhabitants, could explain how local elected officials decided on priorities, thereby keeping them honest and requiring them to consider more carefully whether they were getting it right for the community they served.

At the time at which Lviv and other Ukrainian cities began using Open Budget, Ukraine ranked 55th on the Open Data Barometer assessed by the Open Data Institute (ODI), making it the lowest among its neighbours in Europe and Central Asia. Ukraine was labelled as 'capacity constrained' as open data initiatives are 'highly dependent upon a small network of leaders and technical experts' (Onyiliogwu 2015). ODI research has shown that the broader challenge was embedding and sustaining open data initiatives across the government. To ensure the sustainability of an open data initiative, a government had to overcome cultural challenges, not just technical ones. Ukraine's long history of a lack of openness around government information was evident; overcoming related cultural barriers to becoming more open could be approached in number of ways.

Future reforms should seek to strengthen and invest in additional government open data initiatives so that officials are able to focus on relationship management within the government. Effective change management within and between government departments is essential. Reforms should also focus on raising awareness of open data and related support mechanisms among different government agencies and departments. Further, reforms should provide decision makers with real opportunities to take part in ongoing learning about open data. Future reforms should aim to produce implementation champions to ensure that the open data initiatives grow from the bottom up. Perhaps most importantly, future reforms must solicit and utilise external sources of financial support, such as international agencies, which invest in solutions resulting in greater transparency and improved service delivery.

In the furtherance of its continuing democratic transition, the Ukrainian government is having to rapidly improve its public image and its service delivery, both of which can be helped by ensuring open data. Keeping up the current momentum is key to ensuring that open data becomes standard government practice and fostering a true open government. The example provided in Lviv clearly demonstrates that reform is possible, and democracy is advanced where people are informed and engaged. Currently, any municipality wishing to use the open-source tool can access it online and upload their data on city expenditures and revenues into the system. By visiting the website and reviewing the information located there, anyone could start their own investigation of public spending. Instead of listening to anecdotal accounts of corruption among public officials, citizens could literally check and retrieve actual information on when government officials were spending the tax payers' money, to whom they were making payments, on what goods or services payments were being made, and the amounts being paid.

Conclusion

When information on government activities is limited, especially budgeting and procurement activities, there are opportunities for corruption to result in the exploitation of public resources for private gain. To build and increase transparency, accountability, and integrity in government, citizens must insist on government policies that lead to increased openness in public data. The challenge for the future is to move progressively toward systematic approach to the release of data of public value. As stated in a report produced by Transparency International in 2015:

> By enabling increased transparency in government activities, budgets and expenditures, open data becomes a critical ingredient in accountability interventions. The argument is clear: not only should open data reduce the mismanagement and misallocation of resources, it should also help secure a transparent, more accountable exchange between governments and citizens. Indeed, public interest in ending corruption and inefficiency in governance has generated a demand for governments to open up more data and to improve information transparency. Governments are under pressure to facilitate public access to and oversight of their work, as well as to produce information that is easier to work with and compare.
>
> *(Transparency International 2015: 8)*

Research into the importance of open data as an instrument for fighting corruption shows clearly that open data is relevant and essential for transparency and accountability; innovation, economic development, and efficiency; and inclusion and empowerment. This leads to the obvious conclusion that open data should contribute to anti-corruption reform, by influencing institutions, processes, and public engagement. These two case studies provide positive examples of major cities in transitioning democracies recognised for high levels of corruption for over two decades having found some success in addressing corruption by creating systems to increase citizen access and utilisation of public financial data.

However, just making information available will not prevent corruption if conditions for publicity and accountability are weak. In fact, in the absence of basic democratic principles and practices such education, media circulation, and free and fair elections, transparency alone will probably not reduce corruption. Furthermore, research has also shown that transparency requirements implemented by government in the form of policy are less effective than non-government-controlled transparency institutions, such as a free press (Lindstedt and Naurin 2003). It is important to note that reforms focusing on increasing transparency should be accompanied by measures that strengthen the capacity of citizens to act on available information.

To be successful, high levels of transparency must be accompanied by complementary systems and punishment that can change the incentives to engage in corruption. A competitive political system is important as the opposition has an incentive to identify and punish those in power and replace them. The government can also increase the likelihood of being caught and of being punished if caught (Cuervo-Cazzura 2014). But it all begins with transparency and the establishment of an informed citizenry.

References

Ades, A. and Di Tella, R. (1996). The Causes and Consequences of Corruption: A Review of Recent Empirical Contributions. *Institute of Development Studies* 27(2): 6–11.

Bac, M. (2001). Corruption, Connections, and Transparency: Does a Better Screen Imply a Better Scene? *Public Choice* 107(1): 87–96.

Brandeis University (undated). Justice Louis D. Brandeis: From The Encyclopedia of World Biography. Retrieved on 11 June 2018 from www.brandeis.edu/legacyfund/bio.html.

Chapman, R.A. (Ed.). (1993). *Ethics in Public Service*. Edinburgh: Edinburgh University Press.

Cuervo-Cazzura, A. (2014). Transparency and Corruption. In J. Forssbaeck and L. Oxelheim (eds), *The Oxford Handbook of Economic and Institutional Transparency*, 323–337. Oxford: Oxford University Press.

Erakovich, R., Carroll, W., Smith, C., Campbell, T. and Wright, L. (Undated). *Corruption, Ethics and Accountability: A Normative Approach to Control*. PA Times Online. Retrieved from http://patimes.org/corruption-ethics-accountability-normative-approach-control.

Fisman, R. and Svensson, J. (1999). *Are Corruption and Taxation Really Harmful to Growth? Firm-Level Evidence*. Policy Research Working Papers #2435. Washington, DC: World Bank. Retrieved from http://documents.worldbank.org/curated/en/205081468759613677/pdf/multi-page.pdf

Gupta, S., Davoodi, H. R., and Alonso-Terme, R. (2002). Does Corruption Affect Income Inequality and Poverty? In G. T. Abed and S. Gupta (eds) *Governance, Corruption, and Economic Performance*, 458–488. Washington, DC: International Monetary Fund. Retrieved from www.imf.org/external/pubs/nft/2002/govern.

Holub, N., Konotoptsev, O., Kuspliak, I., Levchenko, O., Naumenko, T., Serenok, A., and Yaskevych, A. (2014). *100 Cities – a Step Forward: Monitoring of Introducing the Electronic Governing as the Basic Way to Render Administrative Services Electronically*. A project of Podil Agency for Regional Development NGO supported by the UNDP. Retrieved from www.academia.edu/8116194/100_CITIES_A_STEP_FORWARD._MONITORING_OF_INTRODUCING_THE_ELECTRONIC_GOVERNING_AS_THE_BASIC_WAY_TO_RENDER_ADMINISTRATIVE_SERVICES_ELECTRONICALLY.

Huntington, S. P. (1968). *Political Order in Changing Societies*. New Haven, CT: Yale University Press.

IDFI. (2014a). Supporting Establishment of New Standards of Transparency and Accountability at Tbilisi City Hall. Institute for Development of Freedom of Information, 31 October. Retrieved from https://idfi.ge/en/tbilisi-city-hall-web-portal.

IDFI. (2014b). Presentation on the Concept of New Web-Portal of Tbilisi City Hall. Institute for Development of Freedom of Information, 23 December. Retrieved from https://idfi.ge/en/concept-of-a-new-web-portal-of-tbilisi-city-hall-was-presented.

Internews. (2015). Battling Corruption in Ukraine: How Local Government is Opening Up Spending to Public Scrutiny. Internews, 10 August. Retrieved from https://medium.com/local-voices-global-change/battling-corruption-in-ukraine-d17ae8ed263f#.fvvfflbsf.

Leff, N. H. (1964). Economic Development through Bureaucratic Corruption. *American Behavioral Scientist* 8(3): 8–14.

Lindstedt, C. and Naurin, D. (2003). *Transparency against Corruption*. Retrieved from http://info-a.wdfiles.com/local--files/resursi/Catharina%20Lindstedt.%20Daniel%20Naurin%202003%20Transparency%20Against%20Corruption%20_Accepted%20version_.pdf.

Mauro, P. (1997). Why Worry about Corruption? Retrieved on 11 June 2018 from https://projects.iq.harvard.edu/gov2126/files/mauro_1997.pdf.

Nasuti, P. (2015). *The Reformist Leviathan: Centralization of Power and Anti-corruption Initiatives in Georgia and Ukraine*. Unpublished doctoral dissertation, University of Wisconsin, Madison, WI. Retrieved from http://search.proquest.com.libproxy.troy.edu/pqdtglobal/docview/1682495044/full-textPDF/DF401FF6F174551PQ/10?accountid=38769.

North, D. C. (1990). *Institutions, Institutional Change, and Economic Performance: Political Economy of Institutions and Decisions*. Cambridge: Cambridge University Press.

Nye, J. S. (1967). Corruption and Political Development: A Cost–Benefit Analysis. *American Political Science Review* 61(2): 417–227.

Onyiliogwu, K. (2015). *How Ukraine is Embracing Open Data after the 2014 Revolution*. Open Data Institute, 22 September. Retrieved from (https://theodi.org/blog/ukraine-embracing-open-data-2014-revolution.

Open Government Partnership. (2015). *A New Portal of Tbilisi City Hall – The Move Towards Transparent and Open Government*. Open Government Partnership, 22 July. Retrieved from https://idfi.ge/en/tbilisi-city-halls-new-portal-the-move-towards-transparent-and-open-government.

Open Government Partnership. (2017). *Tbilisi Action Plan 2017*. Open Government Partnership. Retrieved from www.opengovpartnership.org/sites/default/files/Tbilisi_Action-Plan_2017_Eng.pdf

Podobnik, B., Shao, J., Njavro, D., Ivanov, P. C., and Stanley, H. E. (2008). Influence of Corruption on Economic Growth Rate and Foreign Investment. *The European Physical Journal* 63(3): 547–553. Retrieved from https://arxiv.org/pdf/0710.1995.pdf

Rock, M. T. (2009). Corruption and Democracy. *Journal of Development Studies* 45(1): 55–75.

Rose-Ackerman, S. (2004). *The Challenge of Poor Governance and Corruption*. A paper produced for the Copenhagen Consensus 2004 project. Cambridge: Cambridge University Press. Retrieved from www.copenhagenconsensus.com/sites/default/files/cp-corruptionfinished.pdf.

Stockemer, D., LaMontagne, B. and Scruggs, L. (2013). Bribes and Ballots: The Impact of Corruption on Voter Turnout in Democracies. *International Political Science Review* 34(1): 74–90.

Sung, H. E. (2004). Democracy and Political Corruption: A Cross National Comparison. *Crime, Law and Social Change* 41(1): 179–194.

Transparency International. (2015). *Connecting the Dots: Building the Case for Open Data to Fight Corruption*. Transparency International. Retrieved from http://webfoundation.org/docs/2017/04/2017_OpenDataConnectingDots_EN-6.pdf.

30
ENHANCING VFM AUDIT IN LOCAL GOVERNMENT
The Best Value initiative

Michela Arnaboldi and Irvine Lapsley

Introduction

Contemporary auditing within governments, internationally, has an emphasis on value for money audit. This focus on value for money audit was initially developed in the UK in the 19th century and subsequently spread throughout the world (Dewar and Funnell 2017: 5). Government auditors seek to find economy, efficiency and effectiveness in the provision of public services. This audit practice conventionally scrutinises specific policies or aspects of programmes. These procedures are so well accepted they can be regarded as routine.

This chapter examines the potential for the diffusion of a *second* UK innovation in public audit: Best Value audit. This is an alternative, more holistic approach to value for money audit. Best Value audit represents the state of the art in performance auditing for local government. While this form of audit has existed in the UK from 1997, and cannot be regarded as an innovation in the UK, it nevertheless would be regarded as a significant innovation in local government audit internationally. This chapter examines the UK experience of Best Value and evaluates the potential for this new form of value-for-money (VFM) audit to be adopted, internationally. Local government Best Value built on, and extended, performance auditing processes and techniques, particularly VFM auditing. At a professional and organisational level, there is a tension around VFM auditing as problematic in practice, which may be accentuated by Best Value.

However, in England the Conservative Minister for local government in the 2010 coalition government blocked the powers of England's audit agency (the Audit Commission) which was responsible for Best Value audit. Subsequently this Minister closed the Audit Commission as a cost saving measure, bringing Best Value Audit in England to an end. However, the Best Value Audit approach remains embedded in local government accountability in Scotland. Successive Scottish Governments of different parties have continued to regard Best Value Audit as an important accountability mechanism and this is our reference point for the possible diffusion of this practice internationally.

When the Best Value initiative was launched in the UK there was considerable research which was critical of the concept. That body of research is too voluminous to be considered in detail in this chapter. However, that early critical research appears to have informed the decision to withdraw from Best Value Audit in England. This chapter offers more recent research to inform this debate. This chapter reports on an investigation of Best Value with a comprehensive survey of all local authorities in Scotland. This study examines the nature, conduct and impact of Best Value audit in Scotland to determine if the critique made in England of Best Value as overly prescriptive (Alwardat et al. 2015) has support. The results in this chapter contrast with that critique of Best Value in England as advanced by the Department of Communities and Local Government (DCLG) (DCLG 2015; Sandford 2013). The survey results reveal support amongst practitioners for the merits of Best Value audit in the enhancement of transparency and accountability in local government. We also identify the portability of these distinctive audit practices to wider, international settings. We examine this phenomenon in the following sections.

The Best Value initiative

The Best Value initiative is discussed here in two stages: first an examination of what the Best Value initiative was intended to achieve and an examination of current policy. This discussion raises issues over the efficacy of Best Value audit for local government. The issues raised by this discussion are addressed in the survey of practice.

The introduction of Best Value

Best Value (DETR 1998) can be seen as transcending what is conventionally regarded as VFM auditing, both in terms of scope and process. With the election of the 'New' Labour Governments of 1997, 2001 and 2005 there have been a number of shifts in policy from the preceding Conservative administrations. The 'New' Labour administration sought to shift this focus of CCT on cost savings to retain notions of efficiency, but combined with consideration of quality. To this end, a new process ('Best Value') was devised for local government services. This new process is wide-ranging: it builds on VFM, but extends into considerations of management systems (the efficiency of management structures, strategies and processes); the relationship of the local authority to its setting (communications with local taxpayers and the electorate and local businesses). However, this audit process also extends into standards setting, management frameworks, local performance plans, self-monitoring and a greater focus on outcomes. Indeed, Best Value has continuity with VFM, but extends to including additional concepts, such as accountability, transparency, continuous improvement and ownership.

It is evident from the above that the 'Best Value' concept extends beyond the conventional boundaries of public sector audit and is intended to pose a fundamental challenge to managers of public services to rethink how best they can deliver their services. The initial Best Value report in Scotland stated that this approach was to be a more fundamental mechanism for change in the operating procedures of local government, rather than a specific focus on the economy, efficiency and effectiveness of services. This report defined Best Value (Scottish Office 1997: 3), as follows:

> a process rather than a product . . . a process of change and of progress . . . [it] promotes changes in attitude, culture and management style within councils . . . [it] requires councils to constantly reflect on what they are doing to measure their successes and shortcomings, and to take action to improve.

The concept of Best Value has gone beyond its initial ideas and its development phase. It achieved statutory backing in England in 1999 and in Scotland in 2003.

Table 30.1 Key milestones in England's new local government audit

Financial year	Key milestones
2010/11	Ending of Assessment and Inspection. Announcement of Disbandment of Audit Commission
2012/13	Outsourcing contracts take effect. Audit Commission staff transfer to private sector
2014/15	Final year of Audit Commission framework. Residual Audit Commission closes before April 2015
2015/16	New regulatory regime is introduced
	Outsourcing contracts are transferred to another body to run their remaining two years
2017/18	Local bodies appoint their own auditors from the start of the financial year

Source: Department of Communities and Local Government, Local Audit and Accountability Bill: Impact Assessment, May 2013, p. 12

Current policy on Best Value

While the Best Value regime continues to thrive in Scotland, it has ceased to exist in England. This cessation was entirely attributable to a political intervention. In the aftermath of the global crisis, the UK Coalition Government of 2010 embarked on a policy of austerity to reduce the scale of public expenditure. The decision to close the Audit Commission was announced in 2010 by the Department of Communities and Local Government (DCLG 2010):

> This decision was taken in line with the coalition Government's commitment to radically scale back centrally imposed, bureaucratic and costly inspection and auditing, saving taxpayer's money. The Audit Commission's responsibilities for overseeing and delivering local audit and inspections will stop; the Commission's research activities will end; audit functions will be moved to the private sector; councils will be free to appoint their own independent external auditors from a more competitive and open market. This will save council tax payers £50 million.

So in 2010, the Audit Commission, which then had responsibility for Best Value Audit, was stripped of its entitlement to undertake Best Value Audits (Sandford 2013). This was a cost saving measure initiated by Eric Pickles, Secretary of State for Communities and Local Government (DCLG); he also, in 2015, subsequently closed the Audit Commission (DCLG 2015). As the institution with the greatest accumulation of VFM expertise, this lead to the demise of Best Value audits in local government, with limited VFM studies in local government by the National Audit Office which audits central government. The key milestones in the closure of the Audit Commission, the cessation of the Best Value framework and the privatisation of local government audit are shown in Table 30.1.

Conceptual perspective: audit as problematic

Auditing – but especially VFM auditing – can be regarded as problematic from a number of dimensions, but here we focus on three:

(1) universality (Power 1994, 1997);
(2) (in)completeness (Mautz and Sharaf 1961); and
(3) (un)intended consequences (Radcliffe 1998; Keen 1999).

On *universality*, Power (1994) has observed that the spread of audit influences and practices have resulted in an 'audit explosion'. Power depicts this 'audit explosion' in a number of ways: the width both of the scope of audit (to include financial audit, environmental audit, value for money audit, management audit, data audit, intellectual property audit, medical audit, teaching audit, technology audit) and of the range of persons subjected to these audit requirements. He later developed this thesis further by advancing the case that we are now an 'audit society' (Power 1997), in which 'inspection' of all manner of activities is the order of the day. This phenomenon of the inspection society also spawns new forms of audit. For example, Prosser (2005) has advocated 'gender audits' which would be compulsory inspections of companies pay policies to detect salary differentials for male and female workers. However, the 'audit society' is not simply a question of more audit. While many people have been left untouched by these new and various forms of audit, Power (1997) contends that this phenomenon of a constant checking of activities undermines trust in this new 'audit society'. This inspection has the aim of cultural change and the introduction of new social norms (depicted as 'managerialism') in activities which were previously bounded by professional discretion and judgment. This *universality* or centrality of the audit function is linked to performance auditing (Arnaboldi and Lapsley 2008) as part of the reforms of the public sector. These views of an irresistible spread of audit, especially performance auditing, is a matter many commentators see as increasingly questionable in terms of enhancement of public services delivery.

(In)completeness, a further dimension, comes from the seminal work of Mautz and Sharaf (1961). This contribution to the literature was an attempt to shift academic thinking about audit from a practical to more conceptual views of auditing. However, within this monograph, Mautz and Sharaf (1961: 240–248) turn to the limits of audit. In developing and extending the scope of audit into other fields of expertise, Mautz and Sharaf point to the need to get beyond the superficial, beyond the working knowledge and to a level of real insight in fields beyond the immediate discipline to investigate with authority or to risk being led astray (ibid.: 241). Mautz and Sharaf also caution against auditing assuming roles and responsibilities for which it has incomplete competencies (ibid.: 243):

> auditing has changed with the times in the past, and there are indications that it should be prepared to change with the times now and in the future. In changing, however, it is important that auditing leadership recognize the limitations and potential of the profession and the field of knowledge with which it is concerned. No profession can afford to spread itself over a number of widely divergent and even conflicting types of activity without careful consideration of the hazards involved.

Most of all, Mautz and Sharaf (ibid.) comment on the (in)completeness of audit's theoretical framework as sufficient to provide a robust foundation for the further development of audit practice. Of course, they were making these comments in 1961. However, they did have the foresight to observe that 'auditing stands at the threshold of service opportunities we can as yet scarcely foresee, even in dim outline' (ibid.: 248). Given the developments in performance auditing generally, and the specific initiative discussed within this paper, this observation can be seen as remarkably prescient. The subject of auditing might be seen as (in)complete on a number of levels, in Mautz and Sharaf terms: an incomplete theoretical foundation; incomplete knowledge and competence bases for forays into wider settings for audit investigation.

The third dimension of *(un)intended consequences* of performance auditing reaffirms earlier observations that the *universality* of audit may be dysfunctional and the *(in)completeness* of audit as a body of knowledge limits its extension to a wide range of activities. The *intended* consequences of performance auditing were to enhance the efficiency and effectiveness of audited activities. However, numerous studies suggest that these declared intentions are not achieved, for a variety of reasons. Radcliffe (1998) writes of the adoption of VFM audit as an act of faith by its proponents and enablers. Fundamentally, the (un)intended consequences of efficiency audits arise because, as Radcliffe (ibid.) puts it: (1) it is not clear how auditors know what efficiency is and (2) it is not evident how auditors classify activities as 'efficient' or 'inefficient'. This observation strikes at the very heart of efficiency auditing. A similar study, in a different setting by Keen (1999) offered the observation that the nature of VFM reports (as accumulations of 'facts') and the approach of VFM teams (pragmatic reviews, highly intuitive) meant that VFM was a 'craft' a highly intuitive process. This finding reveals efficiency auditing as problematic: the challenge of linking specific operational situations to management processes and policy contexts may be beyond the competencies of efficiency auditors – a situation which is highly likely to confound *intended* consequences of efficiency audits.

Overall, we see these three different dimensions: the irresistible spread of the audit explosion (*universality*); the limitations on the theoretical foundations of audit, especially in its forays into new domains (*(in)completeness*) and the difficulties of process, including the definition and measurement of key operational concepts such as efficiency which undermines the simple application of VFM to achieve desired intentions (*(un)intended consequences*) – all combining to make the technology of performance auditing problematic. There is evidence in the literature that VFM auditing can be problematic. Indeed, the routine nature of VFM practices does not mean they are immune from criticism. A number of authors have suggested that VFM audit can be problematic. For example, in Canada, Boothe (2015) criticised VFM auditors for making highly subjective judgements. Also, Alwardat et al. (2015) found considerable conflict within VFM initiatives conducted in the UK. Similarly, Norwegian civil servants were hostile and critical of the conduct and outcomes of VFM audits (Reichborn-Kjennerud 2015). The potential problematic issues of VFM audit are considered further below. Despite these misgivings performance auditing retains its central role in public governance systems. Indeed, this paper examines the Best Value initiative which not only gives primacy to performance auditing, but which gives it a far wider scope and prominence than the conventional practice of VFM audit.

However, much of the critiques of Best Value were made speculatively, or were based on pilot implementations of Best Value. There is a need for more comprehensive findings on actual practices in Best Value, which is addressed next.

Our research approach

Given the early critical literature on Best Value and in the interests of evidence based policy making, a comprehensive survey of contemporary practice is appropriate to detect the scope and range of the Best Value implementation and its implications for governance and audit. This survey is a response to the criticisms of Best Value audit as being overly prescriptive, clumsy and bureaucratic (Alwardat et al. 2015; DCLG 2015; Sandford 2013). The results of this survey contrast with that critique of Best Value in England as advanced by the Department of Communities and Local Government (DCLG). The research approach

Table 30.2 Survey questionnaire structure

		No of questions	Closed questions	Semi-structured questions	Open questions
I	Setting	2	2		
II	Operation of Best Value	5	3	2	
III	Impact of Best Value	4	4		
IV	Conclusion	1			1

adopted was a comprehensive survey among all of the 32 local authorities in Scotland. The questionnaire was targeted at lead officers responsible for Best Value as the officers in local government who would be best informed and have the best overview of the nature and outcomes of Best Value implementation (Higgins et al. 2004). The questionnaire was based on 12 questions; the questions are mainly closed (see Table 30.2); however the format gave respondents the opportunity to add comments to each answer. The questionnaire design was based on earlier case study research into Best Value practices (Arnaboldi and Lapsley 2008).

We seek to explore the different dimensions of Best Value implementation by: (1) focusing on Best Value implementation to determine the receptivity of local authorities and whether this is widespread/universal or not; (2) examining the operation of Best Value, to determine whether the mechanisms to be deployed were operating as intended and (3) to explore whether Best Value had become embedded in the life of local authorities, with the achievement of continuous improvement and cultural change (or 'colonisation', as Power 1997 put it).

There were 32 responses from, 32 Scottish councils – a response rate of 100%. In the analysis below, councils are referred to by a designated number (c1, c2 . . . c32), for reasons of confidentiality.

Results of the survey

The results of this survey are analysed in the three sections: setting (to gauge the receptivity of the context for Best Value); operation of Best Value; and the impact of Best Value.

Setting

We examined the receptivity of Scottish local authorities to the concept of Best Value by exploring their practices *prior* to the introduction of Best Value. Specifically, we focussed on two practices: whether service reviews were commonplace in local authorities before the formalisation of the Best Value initiative, and whether local authorities had used measurable targets or defined outcomes as an integral part of their planning systems. The results of this part of the survey are shown in Table 30.3.

Table 30.3 Practices before Best Value

	Question	Yes	No
Q1	Had your local authority been doing 'Best Value' reviews, before the policy was made official?	22	10
Q2	Did your planning system before Best Value have measurable targets or defined outcomes (example)?	27	5

Table 30.4 Comments on setting and receptivity

Q1 & Q2 (common comments)	Service review (Q1) no. councils	Council reference	Targets/ outcomes (Q2) no. councils	Council reference
Presence of central co-ordinated action	4	c2; c20; c25; c28	14	c2; c4; c7; c9; c15; c17; c18; c20; c22; c25; c27; c28; c30; c31
Differential penetration within the councils	2	c8; c23	9	c3; c8; c11; c12; c13; c16; c23; c26; c32
Q1 (Comments) Value for money reviews	4	c5; c13; c17; c23		

These results show that a very high percentage of Scottish councils (Q1 = 69%; Q2 = 84%) addressed these issues before the introduction of the Best Value framework. This is indicative of a receptive context for the Best Value initiative. Indeed, the extent to which such practices were extant in Scottish local authorities suggests Best Value may have at least partially been a codification of existing practices. The additional comments made by respondents to questions one and two on 'receptivity and setting' are shown in Table 30.4.

However, looking at the comments for both answers (see Table 30.3) what emerges is that not all of the councils, (i.e. those which answered 'yes' to Q1 and Q2), had a central, co-ordinated system for reviewing and defining targets and outcomes. Reviews were often ad hoc and the use of targets and defined outcomes had a diverse penetration in the different service areas. Councils justify this 'patchy' situation on two grounds: (1) the different services across councils and (2) the different skills of managers, which suggests that, before Best Value introduction, service evaluation and reviews were dependent on key people within organisations. The following comment illustrates this:

> Management of a service always requires staffing structures and systems to be reviewed to respond to changing needs but, before Best Value, this was on an ad hoc basis and would rarely include consideration of current procedures etc. to improve efficiency. At most, reviews within sections or departments would be carried out as a response to particular issues or need. There was no systematic and regular consideration within service areas.
>
> *(c8 comment on Q1)*

> ... experience across the council was patchy – some services such as housing, leisure had an expensive array of performance data – other departments were less well developed.
>
> *(c13 comment on Q2)*

It is interesting to note that the number of local authorities which declared that they had measurable targets (see Table 30.3), is greater than the number of organisations having a review system. Indeed, for four of these councils, reviews were essentially VFM studies. This suggests that performance measures have been used for defining targets but not for evaluation

Table 30.5 Operation of Best Value

	Question	Yes	Partially	No
Q3	Is the approach to Best Value as exemplified in the Accounts Commission Management Modules all about form filling?	5	14	13
Q4	Does compliance with Best Value requirements divert your local authority/s resources from front line services? (Examples?)	5	12	15

or decision-making. This is the kind of discontinuity which we would expect to see addressed under the Best Value regime. We can see this as a depiction of the universality of these features of the audit, inspection society (Power 1994, 1997), as all local authorities have to embrace these facets of local government management.

Operation of Best Value

The second section of the questionnaire tackled the Operation of Best Value, including questions on: the form of the Best Value approach (reports, modules, etc.) (Q3 and Q4), and the specific mechanisms advocated by the Scottish Government (three-year budgets, benchmarking, and activity-based costing). Q4 (see Table 30.4) determines if the approach to Best Value adopted by the Scottish Government is simply a bureaucratic task, which diverts resources from front-line services.

Table 30.5 shows the distribution of three categories of response (*yes*, *partially* and *no*) to the questions in this part of the survey. Some authorities set themselves in the middle, affirming that the practices defined in Best Value can become a formal task, diverting resources and staff time from service delivery.

More than 40% of respondents (41% for Q3 and 47% for Q4) affirm that Best Value is *not* about form filling and these tasks are not diverting resources from the front-line services. However the majority of respondents reported that Best Value was or could be a bureaucratic task which displaced core activities.

Recurrent comments are spread over the first two categories (*yes* and *partially*); these comments are reported in Table 30.6. These comments are indicative of an incompleteness in the process of Best Value implementation.

One issue which was commented on, in response to questions 3 and 4 is related to managers' ability to adapt the approach designed for Best Value reviews as a management tool rather than

Table 30.6 Comments on bureaucracy and displacement

Q3 & Q4 (common comments)	Form (Q3) no. councils	Council reference	Benefits (Q4) no. councils	Council reference
Depends on who carries out the review	3	c5; c7; c10	4	c5; c6; c7; c14
Initial cost for setting the system, but long term benefits	3	c13; c23; c25	5	c1; c3; c8; c9; c29
Need to be integrated in the council/manager activity	3	c8; c12; c28	6	c7; c10; c12; c17; c18; c27

as a time-consuming procedure aimed only at satisfying a formal request. The following comment highlights this difficulty of securing commitment to Best Value:

> It depends on how well managers, in particular, understand what Best Value actually means. To some it is seen as a parallel exercise to the real job of managing the service. There has also been an unfortunate link made between Best Value and service review, and consequently cuts, to the extent that some people think they are synonymous. Where this has occurred the knock on effect is undoubtedly the diversion of resources, usually people's time, from front line services. This was because work, particularly review work, was being done twice; once to satisfy Best Value 'bureaucracy' and once to meet 'service needs'.
>
> *(c7 comment on Q4)*

This comment leads to the issue of displacement. The introduction of Best Value has involved new schemes and rules for evaluating and measuring performances; managers may perceive the usefulness of the process of Best Value but the achievement of results is not immediate. There is a high initial cost for putting the system in place that will give benefits only in the medium to long term. This problem is reflected in these comments taken both from Q3 and Q4:

> It was at the start, less so now. It did grow dramatically, three one year, another three the next, with follow up reviews growing in number each year. Appeared sustainable in the longer term.
>
> *(c23 comment to Q3)*

> It can do, officer time spent on review activity diverts limited resources from elsewhere. However, generally viewed as an investment towards overall objectives.
>
> *(c9 comment to Q4)*

Finally, some managers suggested that a possible means of promoting commitment to the implementation of Best Value would come from integrating reviews in the *day to day* management and in the council strategy as this comment shows:

> If best value work is to be seen as part of the day-to-day activity of everyone, then services have to be resourced to be able to adapt to that. Since these levels of resourcing are only ideals, authorities have to look at resource –efficient ways of getting folk involved, such as focussed workshops of short duration, and which have well defined expected outcomes.
>
> *(c23 comment on Q4)*

These findings contrast with the expectations of Power (1997) and Keen (1999) and with the experience at the case study pilot study reported upon by Ball et al. (2002).

Question 5 looks at an important instrument of Best Value, the *three year budget* which marks the potential for a real change in local authority financial planning processes. As shown in Table 30.7, a very high percentage of organisations reported positive benefits from this mechanism: 72% including the first two groups of answers; 91% by adding the councils which consider three year budget to be potentially an effective tool but they are still in the early stages of its implementation.

Table 30.7 Survey response – three-year budgets

Question	Effective	Potentially effective	Needs time to be effective	Ineffective	Don't know
Q5 How effective are three year budgets	17	6	6	2	1

The additional comments of respondents identify the way in which the three year budget can improve local authority performances. Eleven local authorities (c3, c7, c8, c9, c14, c17, c20, c21, c26, c27, c28) affirm that effectiveness has been (or will be) achieved by integrating three year budgeting in corporate and service planning. This practice forces managers and politicians to consider service performances over a longer period of time and to evaluate the resources required. It is interesting to note that councils have different views on the relationship between budgeting and strategic planning. Five organisations had not used three year budgets as part of their financial systems; while the other six authorities see (or have seen) the budget as a trigger for revising their planning process.

Another benefit achieved by the implementation of the three year budget is the reduction of annual allocations made on a political basis, as shown by the following comments:

> Good from a political basis in that the monies are set without political annual changes being made.
>
> (c6 comment to Q5)

> One benefit of this has been in the framing of the capital programme where instead of the annual bun fight Councils can take a longer term view of their investment programmes allowing some projects to be deferred until future years.
>
> (c7 comment to Q5)

Another important instrument advocated by Best Value circulars is *benchmarking*. Earlier research (Arnaboldi and Lapsley 2003; Bowerman et al. 2001) has shown that benchmarking is considered to be an important instrument for improving the service delivery process in local authorities.

The importance of this instrument is reflected by the results of the survey where 84% of the councils affirm that benchmarking is feasible and useful; a further 41% of these organisations consider a rigorous approach is possible. The remaining 43% consider benchmarking to be a valuable exercise, although it can only produce results if tackled carefully. These results suggest an incomplete theoretical foundation for benchmarking in local government which is accentuated by data collection problems. Some respondents suggest the use of clusters to take account

Table 30.8 Survey response – benchmarking

Question	Yes	Not rigorous but feasible	Yes, by cluster	No
Q6 Is rigorous Best Value benchmarking feasible, given the differences in local authorities in Scotland?	13	7	7	5

of the diversity of local authorities in Scotland. This classification can be made according to the object of the benchmarking exercise as suggested by this Best Value officer:

> There are various types of benchmarking and the choice [of the sample] will depend on the information required and the relative differences between each council: Data benchmarking – comparing statistics and indicators; Process benchmarking – comparing processes and procedures; Functional benchmarking – comparing how services are delivered and organised; Strategic benchmarking – comparing strategy or policy implementation.
>
> *(c17 comment on Q6)*

Sample selection is one of the problematic issues identified by benchmarking detractors; further, respondents highlighted two important issues related to the operational process of collecting data. First many, comparable, local authorities are reluctant to share data. When Best Value was first introduced this was a common problem among supporters of benchmarking as shown by this comment:

> A Best Value culture was not embedded within authorities and there was often a reluctance to provide information which might have compared unfavourably with other authorities.
>
> *(c8 comment to Q6)*

Second, performance measurement systems are often not structured to provide the requested data. This implies a time consuming exercise, 'where an external help would be useful' (c30 comment to Q6).

The last specific operational aspect addressed in the second part of the questionnaire is the improvement induced by Best Value in *cost accounting* and its support in the reviewing process (Q7) (see Table 30.9).

The table shows that the distribution between 'yes' and 'no' answers is balanced. Eleven local authorities affirm that Best Value has refined costs, thereby influencing service evaluation. Three organisations, although answering positively, highlight that, again, the penetration of the practice within the council is not homogeneous. 78% of negative answers are definite; in particular some managers consider the use of costs for comparing services is weak, as the following comment shows:

> In a nation with such geographic/physical, social and economic diversity and different policy priorities in councils, the cost of service delivery – even within Audit Scotland family groups is always going to have wide variances. Consideration of cost is irrelevant. Best Value encouraged a cost based approach. Service standards are what's important.
>
> *(c23 comment to Q7)*

Table 30.9 Survey response – costing practices

	Question	Yes		No		Don't know
Q7	Has the arrival of Best Value sharpened up the costs used by your local authority in market testing, benchmarking, options appraisals?	14 11	some areas 3	14 11	improved approach 3	4

The 22% of negative answers includes 3 councils which have adopted the methodologies suggested by Best Value, but this exercise has not resulted in sharper costs or it is difficult to define a direct relationship between costing practice and services improvement.

These three mechanisms – three-year budgeting, benchmarking and refined costing – have been reported upon in fairly positive terms. There is little sign of the ineffectiveness of the technologies underpinning VFM found by Radcliffe's (1998) observations on VFM audit. Although Radcliffe's criticism applied to VFM audit, and these mechanisms are much broader, reflecting the nature of Best Value. However, Radcliffe (1998) depicted the use of VFM as 'an act of faith' by VFM auditors. In this instance, we gather and report the views of the Best Value officers and they are key protagonists of the Best Value regime and may therefore support these kind of mechanisms as an 'act of faith'.

The impact of Best Value

The third part of the survey investigated the impact of Best Value on the organisation. The continuous pressure from central government for new initiatives and methodologies has created a situation in which managers may tend to respond selectively to these requests, and further, if corporate commitment is missing, with a different commitment within the authority. The consequence may be a lack of homogeneity and continuity in managing change. Questions 8, 9 and 10 consider the impact of Best Value from the following perspectives: continuous improvement, culture and depth of penetration in the local authorities.

Question 8 and 9 show a high percentage of positive answers (84% for Q8 and 81% for Q9). Included in the percentage (for Q8) are the fifteen councils which affirmed that Best Value makes a significant contribution, but the translation into operational practice is dependent on other elements.

Effective management is the key factor identified in the survey comments. In particular, a pre-requisite for continuous improvement (Q8) depends on the involvement of people (managers, staff, politicians, and stakeholders) at all levels within these organisations. The following comment is an example of this perception:

> Continuous improvement is a culture, driven by people at all levels within organisations who want to do things better to the benefit of their customers. The corollary is that the organisation must have a culture where change through continuous improvement is the norm. Employees at all levels have to play their part. It is a hearts and minds job, not one driven solely by legislation.
>
> *(c7 comment on Q8)*

Best Value appears to be a tool which may or may not deliver change; this is valid also for cultural change (Q9). However, managers added some comments on this and clarified the manner in which Best Value has contributed to shaping a new culture. Three issues emerge: (1) an

Table 30.10 Continuous improvement and culture change

	Question	Yes	Depends	No
Q8	Does Best Value deliver continuous improvement?	12	15	5
Q9	Has Best Value resulted in, or contributed to a change of culture in your local authority?	26	–	6

Table 30.11 Best Value penetration in local authorities

	Question	Yes		No	
Q10	Has the Best Value regime penetrated all parts and levels of your local authority?	16	Simple no 11	16 Not all areas 3	Not all levels 2

awareness of the necessity to undertake systematic skills development for managers and leaders; (2) acceptance of service reviews as part of management and the awareness of their benefit; (3) capability in adapting to environmental change.

Managers surveyed also highlighted some criticisms of the Best Value framework itself. The most important criticism seems to be the *high frequency* of reviews. The rapid cycle of delivering documents can divert the attention of managers from interpreting data and using them for improving the service, as the following comments show.

> ... the 'cycle time' for continuous improvement means some benefit can be lost as reviews come around again too quickly!
>
> *(c12 comments on Q8)*

> ... there is a down-side to this in that we are constantly being required to do more with less and this can be a problem in terms of morale and continuity.
>
> *(c17 comments on Q8)*

The last question, investigating the impact of Best Value, tackles the issue of the penetration of these practices within councils, both in terms of service areas and levels within services.

The results of the survey (11) support the perception that the Best Value approach has not been embedded homogeneously within all areas and at all levels. However the positive percentage of 50% is surprisingly high. This is justified by the additional comments made by respondents: they reveal that the Best Value approach has been adopted extensively but its impact on service performance and its improvement in the managerial culture did not get equal responses. The three councils that highlighted a differentiation among areas cited education as the most critical service; the depth of penetration is identified as a problem by two councils, which observed the difficulties in going down the organisational levels, beyond middle management.

The last part of the questionnaire addressed the overlapping of Best Value with other government initiatives, which could result in frustrating, time consuming work of filling different forms with similar information, without gaining benefits, and in which Best Value could be overtaken by other initiatives.

Table 30.12 Best Value and other initiatives

	Question	Yes		No	Possible (future)	No answer
Q11	Has the Best Value initiative been overtaken by other Scottish Government initiatives for all/ parts of your local authority?	13 Many areas 6	Some areas 7	14	4	1

Observing Table 30.12 it appears that 44% of the managers who answered the questionnaire do not perceive other initiatives from the Scottish Government as inhibiting Best Value. While 41% observe significant (19%) or a moderate (22%) level of programmes overlapping. The remaining 13% stated a concern for the future.

This nearly equal division between *yes* and *no* shows different attitudes in undertaking the Best Value Review process. Councils who answered *no* to this question are not neglecting other Scottish Government initiatives but they consider them as an integrating part of the modernising agenda, as the following comment explains:

> In many ways, all of these initiatives are linked and work is continuing right now to develop clearer and more deliberate links between these processes. . . . The messages coming out from these initiatives are consistent – identified best practice and the recommendations which are being made in audit reports are not changing, so the end target and the definition of good management practice is clear.
>
> *(c7 comments to Q11)*

However the 42% of local authorities which responded to the survey highlighted a number of initiatives which could overtake Best Value reviews,. A council commented showing particular concern about overlapping with Best Value:

> . . . the burden associated with the various Scottish Government inspectorates (such as for Education (e.g. Quality Management in Education) and for Social Work) compromise the work needed to respond to the needs of Best Value appraisal.
>
> *(c26 comments on Q11)*

Here we see elements of what has been depicted as the potential 'colonisation' of management (Power 1997) and the breadth of Best Value taking this audit regime into areas which may be undermined by the competences of auditors (Mautz and Sharaf 1961). Overall these findings contrast with, for example, Higgins et al. (2004) which depicts Best Value managers as sceptical over the usefulness of the Best Value regime.

Conclusions

The practice of VFM audit is well established, internationally. The VFM approach has most recently focussed on the effectiveness of public-private partnerships in a variety of countries, including Australia, the UK, Hong Kong and Italy (English 2007; Chung 2016; Wu et al. 2016; Santandrea et al. 2016). The VFM approach is evident in a wide variety of projects, internationally. Recent VFM studies include: an assessment of the impact of austerity on US city governments (Jimenez 2016); an assessment of public policy on science parks in Denmark (Nielsen 2016); an assessment of overseas aid in Germany (Holzapfel 2016); an assessment of citizen concerns with environmental issues in Israel (Ben-Porat et al. 2016); and a study of its effectiveness as a device to counter corruption in Nigeria (Agbo and Aruomoaghe 2014). This audit practice conventionally scrutinises specific policies or aspects of programmes.

This research has investigated potential of the UK innovation of Best Value audit for adoption, internationally. The Best Value audit approach represents the state of the art in VFM audit. It offers a more holistic approach to VFM. The explicit purpose of Best Value was to replace a system of cost saving – compulsory competitive tendering (CCT) – with a more refined measure of the value of local authority services. Best Value started as a line in a political manifesto (Labour Party 1997). The Best Value regime is depicted by its proponents as building on, and extending, value for money audits in local government. Our closer inspection of Best Value in the light of the proposed conceptual perspective, allows us to draw some more general conclusions. Best Value reveals, in fact, a much greater, more comprehensive form of audit which resonates with Power's (1994, 1997) ideas of the audit society.

Although the enlargement of scope and the emphasis on processes, there has been criticism along the lines of 'universality' – this is merely the latest addition to Power's audit society. There have been criticisms of the competencies of auditors to 'inspect' not only all local authority services, but to challenge (by their audit) the very nature of the local authority itself. In addition, there have been serious reservations over (in)completeness – over the competencies of auditors to sit in judgement in the manner expected by the Best Value regime. Also, there have been reservations over the (un)intended consequences of the uncertain technology of Best Value. There has been evidence of the adverse effects of Best Value: the displacement of resources from front-line services to compliance with Best Value and scepticism over performance measures and audit and inspection requirements.

However, the findings of the survey in this chapter contrast with the misgivings of expert commentators at the inception of Best Value and on the basis of the pilot implementations of Best Value. In this study, we found positive responses to Best Value on the grounds that it had built on previous practices for service reviews (including the use of measurable targets and defined outcomes). There was some limited evidence in this survey that Best Value had become a form-filling exercise, but the presence of previous experience emerged as relevant in implementation and avoiding displacement of resources from front-line services to Best Value reporting requirements. This situation recalls the problem of universality and the need for a different approach to VFM, accounting for organisational diversity. This is true in the UK but it is evident in other countries where differences are evident in research results (Gildenhuis and Roos 2015; Torres et al. 2016; Desmedt et al. 2017).

The Best Value managers in the survey also responded positively to the new practices introduced with Best Value (such as three year budgets, benchmarking and costing) although with more mixed results on the latter. Most importantly, these Best Value officers responded positively to the suggestion that the Best Value regime had contributed to a culture change in their local authority. This may be interpreted as evidence of the 'colonisation' of managerialism depicted by Power (1997) where the organizational culture is central (Prowle 2016).

In conclusion, this chapter has shown that Best Value has made significant progress over its 20 year existence. There is the reversal in England with the closure of the Audit Commission, the abandonment of Best Value and VFM and the reversion to basic financial regularity audit. But how portable is Best Value as a state of the art practice to other international settings? The political context is crucial. The abrupt demise of Best Value in England can be attributed to the election of a new political party in government. Second, local governments have to be open in their outlook to new practices and ideas. Third, the nature of the change required is for a culture change. This may prove to be an obstacle for certain settings. Fourth, there is the issue of expertise. A high level of expertise in VFM studies can be seen as a necessary precondition of the adoption of Best Value. Most importantly for local governments, their auditors and any central government oversight bodies, there needs to be a recognition of the need for a shift from short term pressures to longer term planning as a focus. These conditions make the adoption of Best Value in local government a ground-breaking reform with considerable potential to improve the management and delivery of services and the experiences of citizens as service users.

References

Agbo, S. and Aruomoaghe, J. (2014) Performance Audit: A Tool For Fighting Corruption in Nigeria's Public Sector Administration. *International Journal of Management and Sustainability* 3(6): 374–383.

Alwardat, Y. A., Benamraoui, A. and Rieple, A. (2015) Value for Money and Audit Practice in the UK Public Sector. *International Journal of Auditing* 19(3): 206–217.

Arnaboldi, M. and Lapsley, I. (2003) Activity Based Costing, Modernity and the Transformation of Local Government: A Field Study. *Public Management Review* 5(3): 345–375.

Arnaboldi, M. and Lapsley, I. (2008) Making Management Auditable: The Implementation of Best Value. *Abacus* 44: 22–47.

Ball, A., Broadbent, J. and Moore, C. (2002) Best Value and the Control of Local Government: Challenges and Contradictions. *Public Money and Management* (April–June): 9–16.

Ben-Porat, G. A., Shamir, O. B. and Yuval, F. A. (2016) Value for Money: Political Consumerism in Israel. *Journal of Consumer Culture* 16(2): 592–613.

Boothe, P. (2015) Not in Their Shoes: The Problem with Value-for-Money Audits. Retrieved from www.macleans.ca/economy/economicanalysis/not-in-their-shoes-the-problem-with-value-for-money-audits.

Bowerman M., Ball A. and Francis G. (2001) Benchmarking as a Tool for the Modernisation of Local Government. *Financial Accountability and Management* 17(4): 321–329.

Chung, D. (2016) Risks, Challenges and Value for Money of Public–Private Partnerships. *Financial Accountability and Management* 32(4): 448–468.

DCLG (2010) Eric Pickles to Disband Audit Commission in New Era of Transparency. Press Release, 13 August. London: Department for Communities and Local Government.

DCLG (2015) *Revised Best Value Statutory Guidance*. March. London: HMSO.

Desmedt, E., Morin, D., Pattyn, V. and Brans, M. (2017) Impact of Performance Audit on the Administration: A Belgian Study (2005–2010). *Managerial Auditing Journal* 32(3): 251–275.

DETR (1998) *Modernising Local Government*. London: Department of the Environment, Transport and Regions.

Dewar, D. and Funnell, W. (2017) *A History of British National Audit: The Pursuit of Accountability*. Oxford: Oxford University Press.

English, L. (2007) Performance Audit of Australian Public Private Partnerships: Legitimising Government Policies or Providing Independent Oversight? *Financial Accountability and Management* 23(3): 313–336.

Gildenhuis, E. and Roos, M. (2015) The Performance Audit: Are There Differences in the Planning Approach and Practices Followed within the South African Public Sector? *Southern African Journal of Accountability and Auditing Research* 17(1): 49–60.

Higgins, P., James, P. and Roper, I. (2004) Best Value: Is It Delivering? *Public Money & Management* (August): 251–258.

Holzapfel, S. (2016) Boosting or Hindering Aid Effectiveness? An Assessment of Systems for Measuring Donor Agency Results. *Public Administration and Development* 36(1): 3–19.

Jimenez, B. S. (2016) Performance Management and Deficit Adjustment in US Cities: An Exploratory Study. *International Journal of Public Administration* 39(10): 729–743.

Keen, J. (1999) On the Nature of Audit Judgements: The Case of Value for Money Studies. *Public Administration* 77(3): 509–525.

Labour Party (1997) *New Labour: Because Scotland Deserves Better*. London: Labour Party.

Mautz, R. K. and Sharaf, H. A. (1961) *The Philosophy of Auditing*. Monograph No. 6, Lakewood Ranch, FL: American Accounting Association.

Nielsen, C. (2016) Getting Value for Money from Your Science Park. *Public Money and Management* 36(7): 539–546.

Power, M. (1994) *The Audit Explosion*. London: Demos.

Power, M. (1997) *The Audit Society: Rituals of Verification*. Oxford: Oxford University Press.

Prosser, M. (2005) Gender Inequalities in Pay. Paper presented at EU Gender Equality Conference, Birmingham, 7–8 November.

Radcliffe, V. S. (1998) Efficiency Audit: An Assembly of Rationalities and Programmes. *Accounting, Organizations and Society* 23(4): 377–410.

Reichborn-Kjennerud, K. (2015) Resistance to Control – Norwegian Ministries' and Agencies' Reactions to Performance Audit. *Public Organization Review* 15(1): 17–32.

Sandford, M. (2013) Local Audit and Accountability Bill. Bill 101 of 2013–14. Research Paper 13/56, 1 October. London: House of Commons Library.

Santandrea, M., Bailey, S. and Giorgino, M. (2016) Value for Money in UK Healthcare Public–Private Partnerships: A Fragility Perspective. *Public Policy and Administration* 31(3): 260–279.

Scottish Office (1997) *Best Value Task Force: Report to Secretary of State and COSLA*. SODD Circular 22=97. Edinburgh: Scottish Office.

Torres, L., Yetano, A. and Pina, V. (2016) Are Performance Audits Useful? A Comparison of EU Practices. *Administration and Society* (7 July). Retrieved from http://journals.sagepub.com/doi/abs/10.1177/0095399716658500.

Wu, J. A. B., Liu, J. C., Jin, X. D. and Sing, M. C. P. E. (2016) Government Accountability within Infrastructure Public–Private Partnerships. *International Journal of Project Management* 34(8): 1471–1478.

31

FINANCING AND TAXING FOR LOCAL GOVERNMENT

Kenneth Gibb and Linda Christie

Introduction

Over time and in most places, the key source of dispute between local and central government usually centres on finance. How much is local government spending, what it is doing to household tax burdens, to what extent are key financial decisions relatively autonomously determined by local government and to what extent are they centralised to higher level tiers of government? As we shall see, there are idiosyncratic and path dependent reasons why different systems of government achieve different local government finance system outcomes. Gallagher et al. (2007) argue that we need to think of local government across multiple dimensions – finance, the allocation of services between different tiers of government and the functional geography of local government. All interact and when central government chooses to reform local government, it normally does so without taking account of the knock-on effects on the other dimensions, which sometimes don't become apparent for years. We explore these interdependencies further in the next section.

In this chapter we argue that a critical element in the wider finance debate is the form of local tax adopted and how it interacts with other forms of finance available to local government. As we shall see, most countries use a mix of property and income taxes to fund a proportion of the cost of local government services but they vary hugely in terms of how they operate and the ways in which specific systems of local government finance adjust them to reduce their perceived political cost. A second theme of this chapter is to make explicit this sense, that local taxes, especially on property, are not as legitimate in the eyes of taxpayers as are some other taxes. This appears to be a sufficient to change the behaviour of government considering local taxes and in particular to constrain their willingness to pursue meaningful reform. In the United Kingdom (and in other states), this has been most clearly shown by the long term and continuing unwillingness to undertake regular revaluations of properties.

This chapter draws extensively on an earlier review of international evidence of property and other forms of the taxation of local government (Gibb and Christie 2015 – written for the recent Scottish Commission on Local Tax Reform), and also from chapters on local government finance by the same authors in Gibb and Christie (2016) and Gibb et al. (2017). The current chapter begins with a brief in-principle account of the key interconnections found between finance and the structure of local government and its critical fiscal and service interconnections with higher levels of government. We then look at Organisation of Economic Co-operation and Development (OECD) data that suggests considerable variety in financing, local autonomy and taxation models internationally. The third main section of the chapter pulls together the main messages from an international review of local taxation. The paper then turns to the highly salient question of property tax reform, its drivers, challenges and possible ways forward. The fifth section is a case study of recent efforts to reform local taxes in Scotland before a short concluding section.

Financing and taxing in local government: general considerations

Different national systems of local government vary hugely around the developed world for historical, political and institutional reasons. Nonetheless, there are a number of common high-level features that apply universally, regardless of whether we are talking about a federal system or a unitary model of government. We outline these strands briefly before turning to national and comparative evidence.

The functional division of public services between national, state and local government is critical. In particular, some countries provide welfare state type services through local government and that may make them more likely to adopt income taxation to pay for them (Hollis et al. 1992). Countries which are more oriented to the provision of amenity and facility type services locally are often more likely to use an element of 'beneficial' taxes such as those based on property (i.e. house values respond to and capitalise beneficial public services so that would on the face of it make an argument for a property-based tax).

The distribution vertically of services is also part of the reasoning behind intergovernmental grants – if local government delivers nationally-driven basic education, then intergovernmental grants may help fund the programme, and this is also the case for the support of other national priorities delivered locally such as emergency services (often called specific grants).

In countries like the UK, the grant system operates in large part as a 'block' and can be used to control and direct local government spending for macroeconomic as well as political reasons. Grant adjustment has implications for local tax levels and the freedom local government has to set and adjust its tax rates. More generally, one can distinguish three types of grant – specific grants tied to a function (as discussed above), grants that compensate for different levels of need across a country (e.g. because of the age distribution locally, different levels of spatial deprivation or economic activity, etc.), and grants that equalise uneven resource or tax bases so that income and therefore expenditure can itself be more consistent across local governments who would otherwise have very different resources and hence require wildly different tax rates to achieve the same spend per head. This also connects to in-principle ideas that local taxation should be as neutral as possible across space, other than through the explicit discretion of local governments who seek to have different tax rates because in some way that reflects local preferences. The grant system is also one way that governments facing fiscal pressures may transfer cuts or resource reductions down the way to local government rather than choosing to cut back national services.

This all means that the choice of local taxes, and willingness to reform them, is not simply a local political question but speaks instead to the wider system of governance in a nation and specifically about the intergovernmental relations, power, treasure and ideology that pertains to different tiers (and of course may often represent different political aspirations and parties). 'Fixing' local government's taxation (e.g. an unpopular tax that is blamed on the national as opposed to the local government) may actually be a multi-level problem associated with those intergovernmental relations, the distribution of powers between different tiers, the interaction of the grant and tax system, the geography of local government (and whether administrative boundaries roughly equate to functional economic geography), as well as the actual taxes being adopted. These factors help explain why inertia may fatally inhibit credible reform in this arena.

OECD analysis of local taxes and sub-central tax autonomy

Table 31.1 summarises the distribution of local taxes across the OECD members in 2010 (Slack and Bird 2014).

Table 31.1 Local taxes in OECD countries, 2010

	Property	Income*	Goods and services	Other**	Local taxes as % of local expenditure
Australia	100	0	0	0	n.a.
Austria	15	61	10	13	59
Belgium	53	37	10	0	32
Canada	91	0	2	7	n.a.
Chile	40	0	60	0	n.a.
Czech	51	0	48	0	40
Denmark	11	89	0	0	34
Estonia	8	90	3	0	45
Finland	6	94	0	0	46
France	54	8	25	12	39
Germany	16	78	6	0	36
Greece	24	0	21	55	12
Hungary	14	0	80	6	19
Iceland	21	77	2	0	67
Ireland	100	0	0	0	13
Israel	95	0	5	0	39
Italy	9	25	33	33	41
Japan	30	49	19	2	n.a.
Korea	16	17	27	40	n.a.
Luxembourg	4	92	1	2	31
Mexico	59	0	2	39	n.a.
Netherlands	48	0	50	2	9
New Zealand	91	0	9	0	n.a.
Norway	5	88	1	5	38
Poland	29	58	8	4	27
Portugal	34	35	26	5	25
Slovak	51	0	49	0	11
Slovenia	12	78	6	3	40
Spain	30	21	39	11	42
Sweden	3	97	0	0	64
Switzerland	1	84	1	13	58
Turkey	11	24	50	14	n.a.
United States	73	5	21	0	n.a
UK	**100**	**0**	**0**	**0**	**12.6**

Source: Adapted from Slack and Bird (2014: table A2, p. 29)

*includes income and payroll taxes; **includes social security contributions, other property-related taxes and other taxes. All figures rounded and may not sum to 100%

Six of the countries rely on property taxes for nine-tenths or more of their local tax revenue (including the UK, Australia, Ireland and Canada). At the same time, ten rely on income taxes for at least three-quarters of their local tax revenue (including the Scandinavian group, Denmark, Germany, Iceland, Luxembourg, Slovenia and Switzerland), though the table does not show the extent to which this incorporates a degree of tax sharing with nationally-derived income taxation. Six countries rely on taxes on goods and services to support at least 48% of local tax revenues (Slovakia, Turkey, Chile, Czech, Hungary and, surprisingly, the Netherlands). Only Greece relies on 'other taxes' to raise 50% or more of its local tax revenue. The UK, Ireland and Australia have just one tax raising all local tax, though it is the case that Sweden, Luxembourg, Israel and Finland all have one tax raising more than 90% of their local tax revenues. On the other hand, twenty countries operate a diverse system with at least two taxes where the smaller contribution is at least 20%.

Blochliger and Nettley (2015) consider the degree of local autonomy or what they call sub-central tax autonomy enjoyed by State and local governments in the OECD (based on 2011 data). For reference, ten of the 34 member states have either: provincial state, regional or Lander governments as well as local government. The authors define tax autonomy in terms of the extent of freedom of lower tiers of government over tax policy in their jurisdiction with special attention given to the specifics of tax-sharing arrangements (which is sometimes difficult to isolate and to contrast from intergovernmental grants).

Blochigler and Nettley also compare change to this degree of autonomy or decentralisation over time, from 1995 to 2011 (though note that OECD membership expanded considerably over this period). The authors report that the share of taxes allocated to the sub-central level actually increased from 13.5% to 15.5% and where tax base and rate-setting was relatively more decentralised, the share of autonomous local tax revenue also increased. The frequency of constitutional rules that maintained relatively more centralised power over local finance also fell. This process of decentralisation was argued to be more marked at the higher sub-national levels of State/Region/Lander level; whereas lower tier local government was more stable in terms of degree of autonomy. This is in strong contrast to the narrowing of autonomy of local government functions and finance in countries like the UK since the end of the 1970s.

Incidence

An important question in matters of local taxation concerns the *incidence* of local taxes (i.e. who does it fall on and can it reasonably be described as progressive?). While the incidence of a local income tax is straightforward (it can be measured directly as a percentage of current income), this is not so for the property tax. This is because there are several quite different perspectives as to the meaning of how local property taxes work and therefore how they impact on people in distributional terms (Bird and Slack 2004):

- As a tax on the consumption of housing services, it is regressive because housing generally constitutes a relatively larger share of consumption by poor people. This perspective is a driver of much property tax reform (e.g. the desire to redesign taxes to be more progressive in terms of current incomes and to protect the asset-rich but cash-poor household).
- As a tax on capital (in the form of housing wealth), it is essentially progressive since ownership of capital as a rule is relatively concentrated within higher income groups. The failure to tax this wealth appropriately may also impair the economy's potential in that light or advantageous taxation leads to incentives to tie up potentially productive wealth in predominantly unproductive second-hand housing.

- Other commentators believe that tax falling on land is in effect paid out of economic rents and that thus it is inherently just or fair to tax such unearned increments arising from public actions. Again, it is argued that failure to levy such a land value or site value tax prevents an opportunity to promote the more efficient allocative use of land.

Slack and Bird (2014) argue that thinking about incidence in terms of tax reform involving property taxation is inherently problematic because we are dealing with the distributional effects of a largely *capitalised* tax[1] on a particular form of wealth and, in addition, property prices are lower than they would be in the absence of the property tax.

Key messages from comparative research

In this section, we draw on an international review of local taxation carried out by the authors (Gibb and Christie 2016) for the recent Scottish local tax commission. Seven broad points are made.

First, both property and income-based systems of local taxation *vary considerably* across the OECD in terms of key features of their design:

- The nature of the tax base and its assessment. Typically, property tax bases are developed based either on rental values, capital values, land values only or area-based measures. (Almost) all are generally required to have some form of regular general revaluation process built-in as well as a system for enforcement and appeal.
- The extent that local governments are free to set tax rates annually. Most countries adopt some form of central influence or control over the size of increase, perhaps through indices link to cost of living or other rules. However, Slack and Bird (2014) suggest that across OECD, on average, local governments only have discretion over about a sixth of their property tax revenues.
- The appropriate balance between local autonomy and higher-level influence or control through tax and grant sharing to achieve national policy objectives or to assist with resource or need equalisation (i.e. national equity issues at a local level to reduce variations in spending need or the local tax base). A wider important conclusion is that, in practice, it is not realistic to wholly separate local tax from the wider system of local government finance or indeed from the tax burden as a whole.

Second, while recurrent local land and property taxes do evidently vary, *key features reappear* in different countries, including why specific nations favour them. Almy (2013) contends that the principal generic arguments for a property tax are that:

1. they are hard to avoid or 'flee';
2. local government services are provided to occupiers/owners;
3. the tax captures some of the uplift in land values following public investment;
4. as a dedicated source of revenue, the property tax provides a degree of local autonomy [true of *any* genuinely local tax];
5. the high visibility of property taxation provides accountability and transparency; and
6. land registration/cadastral systems have wider value and can support the general functioning of property markets.

Blochliger (2015), in addition, points to econometric analysis that property taxes can play a small but significant role in reducing house price volatility. They can also underpin sustainable land use via land valuation taxes by helping to constrain urban sprawl and promoting the development of brown field sites.

However, these positive elements also contain the source of generic problems for property taxation as a source of local revenue (Blochliger 2015). Almy (2013) stresses that property taxes are under-utilised as a source of revenue despite their positive economic merit. The property tax is what Enid Slack calls a *presumptive tax* – it is widely felt by taxpayers to be one imposed on them and its visibility, perceived regressive unfairness and frequent valuation disagreement leads to unpopularity with citizens and politicians. Almy argues that this in turns leads to 'legislative neglect', or the relative unwillingness of legislators and governments to actively renew, update and maintain the property tax in terms of revaluation, tax rate setting and the relationship with the wider local government finance system. The concept of presumption and its political consequences are integral to any discussion of the barriers to tax reform involving property taxes.

Third, governments respond to this heightened *saliency* of property taxes by using a battery of policies designed to ameliorate the perceived unpopularity of property taxes (on the basis of the arguments above). Many of these adjustments have re-distributional and other (arguably) unintended or cumulative consequences. These include:

- Banding, as in the case of the UK council tax, though in principle the weights chosen between each band could be organised in different ways (see discussion of Council Tax reform below).[2]
- Capping tax bills (i.e. putting a ceiling on how much they can increase) is a common way to reduce the cost of living effects of annual increases. This may involve real or nominal freezes, other limits to increases, with more or less discretion for local government within such systems. There are also examples of constitutionally-binding limits on tax bill increases such as Proposition 13 in California.
- Property tax reliefs and exemptions are widely used internationally but are everywhere different in their specifics. Many types of property or land uses have exemptions or other concessions, as do household circumstances in some countries. At the same time, property tax in either (or both) the domestic and non-domestic settings may be allowable for tax deductibility.
- As an attempt to address the well-known *cash-poor, asset-rich* problem, deferrals, rebates and abatements are widely used, again varying in their national specifics. Deferring payments have been widely available in different forms in Denmark, France, Germany, the Netherlands, Spain, Sweden, parts of the United States and Northern Ireland (Almy 2013), usually deferring till the point of sale or as a lien on estates. However, evidence from Northern Ireland and the United States suggest they are not popular with taxpayers who link these ideas to subjective anxieties with paying for older care and inheritance tax (Northern Ireland Assembly 2007).
- Rebate schemes tend to focus on helping households on low current incomes but such schemes typically face the high cost of delivering means-tested benefits, even if they are well-targeted.
- There are also income-related 'circuit-breakers' which are designed to protect households from paying an excessive share of their income on property taxes or do so on some kind of sliding scale. These are common in North America.
- A common option chosen is to simply delay revaluation – this can be argued to be a de facto form of regressive subsidy to the extent that the property tax is a wealth tax and housing wealth is held more by higher income groups who would benefit from the failure to uplift property values through regular revaluation.[3]

Fourth, several countries have nonetheless *embarked on property tax reform* in recent years. Countries reforming property taxes include: Denmark, Estonia, Hungary, Iceland, Latvia, Lithuania, Macedonia, Netherlands, Russia, Sweden, Greece, Ireland and the UK (the introduction of the council tax in 1993 and, separately, the reform of Northern Ireland's rates in 2007 and reform in Scotland in 2016/17) The reasons for the reforms have been related to national tax reforms, local government finance reform, specific changes to local taxation based on principles of reducing inequality, raising revenue or tax simplification. Reform is discussed further below.

Fifth, several countries and provinces or states within countries employ variations on *land value taxation* or *site value taxation* (Dye and England 2010).

Sixth, a number of countries rely primarily or extensively on *local income taxation*. We should, however, distinguish between locally-raised income tax and sharing nationally collected revenue, subsequently assigned to local government. Corporate income tax is also often used locally in a way analogous to non-domestic property taxation (and as well as property taxation). Those countries where the largest source of local tax revenue is income tax (i.e. Denmark, Finland, Germany, Norway, Sweden, Switzerland) tend to have local governments who have significant responsibility for redistributive services (i.e. people related services: social services and housing (Slack and Bird 2014). The UK is an exception in that the local delivery of a national welfare service (state school education) is largely funded out of intergovernmental grants.

Finally, local property taxes have *wider impacts on economies*:

- In the housing market, they may operate to counter-act well known tax biases in favour of home ownership, which may exacerbate market volatility and wider problems resulting from excess favouring of home ownership. Alm et al. (2011) looked at the impact of the US housing market collapse after 2006 and argued that rather than falling house prices damaging the property tax yield, price falls only fed into valuations with a lag and that many local governments were able to compensate through adjusting tax rates.
- Property taxes influence economic decisions more generally as part of the total tax system. Widening the tax base to include more immovable property and land may reduce revenue risk, lower reliance on more mobile (within and between nations), elastic and volatile sources of taxation such as incomes. It may also, on a revenue neutral basis, allow for lowering marginal tax rates on income by shifting tax towards property.
- Recurrent property taxes are often argued to be preferred to taxes on property transactions that may be inefficient because they restrict mobility and that have much more volatile and unpredictable yields (Mirrlees et al. 2011).
- Many countries operate incentives through the local property tax system to encourage investment into specific places, though it is contentious as to what this does for economic efficiency, more generally (Norregaard 2013).
- Local government has an important impact on the overall burden of taxes and this would still be the case if they were 100% funded by central government grants, even if the visibility and saliency were completely altered.

Combining local taxes

The Burt Review (2006) found that in 23 out of 28 countries studied, multiple local taxes were in operation – usually a combination of property and income taxes. However, Burt (2006) argues that public opinion does not support the introduction of new supplementary taxes because it is perceived to be a way of creating more tax revenues rather than redistributing existing levels of revenue (presumption and saliency resurface again). Any effort to introduce such taxes to either supplement a reformed or a new property tax undoubtedly needs to address this particular issue.

There are as many different sets of hybrid systems as countries that run them. Slack (2013) reports seven completely different fiscal arrangements in seven global cities. The income tax element may be a supplement or the core form of local tax; it may be a national surcharge on the national income tax that is then redistributed locally or in some cases it may be a genuinely local contribution. Again, as with property taxes, the rate and the total bill may be capped in different ways by the national government. Slack (2013) found that all cities studied bar London had access to at least five local sources of revenue. London (and UK local government) relies wholly on the council tax for locally-determined revenues (UK business property taxes are levied at a national uniform tax rate and from a local government point of view operate more as a per capita grant than a tax although some changes to this arrangement are currently being considered).

Why combine taxes on a revenue-neutral basis? First, logically, the two taxes would individually have less marginal impact on households introducing a degree of progressivity and limiting the burden of the property tax. This would also alter the distributional outcome of the local tax burden. Second, this would be a simpler alternative to applying one of the various ameliorations to the property tax discussed earlier and may actually allow the authorities to develop a purer property tax albeit with a more modest yield (pragmatically, this may help overcome the residual resistance to property taxes). Third, Hollis et al. (1992) develop a coherent argument in favour of linking local tax type to service provision - services more related to redistributive/need functions could be funded by a combination of national grants and (progressive) local income tax while more local amenity or facility related services would be funded by property taxes. A similar division might logically be applied to non-domestic or business property taxes.

Reforming property tax systems

This penultimate section is in two parts. First, we consider some general principles that promote and constrain the capacity to deliver property tax reform for local government finance. Second, we briefly look at a case study of these questions – the recent experience (2014–2016) in Scotland where the devolved Scottish Government assembled a cross party expert Commission on Local Tax Reform. Once it reported towards the end of 2015, they then encouraged all political parties to bring forward reform proposals at the 2016 Scottish elections.

We have identified the importance of evident challenges and idiosyncrasies found in national local tax systems. We have argued that they also impact on general tax reform questions, and the scope for tax reform, specifically, property tax reform. There continues, as we have seen, to be considerable interest in property tax reform internationally. Many countries and systems of local government wrestle with the potential of property taxes versus the limited political room for manoeuvre they feel they can operate within.

Slack and Bird (2014) distinguish four general issues for property tax reform: establishing the preferred tax base, how to assess the tax base, how to set the tax rate and thus the tax bill, and, how to run the system itself? Almy (2013: 61) concludes: 'unless the tax structure is simple enough to be efficiently administered, and fair enough to gain the confidence of the population, administrative reform by itself will not succeed'.

Table 31.2 below from Slack and Bird (2014) is a helpful analysis of the challenges and possible ways forward with reform. They focus on six themes, several of which have already emerged in this chapter (i.e. saliency, the presumptive nature of the tax, volatility of tax bills and liquidity constraints). Promising approaches have recurring elements such as regular (annual) revaluations of property in the tax base, phasing in change and investing in voter taxation education.

Table 31.2 Strategies for property tax reform

Issues and problems	Promising approaches	Problematic approaches
Salience: property tax is more visible than other taxes	Link tax reforms with improvement in local services Phase-in Withhold tax at source and other payment options	Assessment limits PT capping
Liquidity constraints: imperfect association between taxpayers' incomes and PT especially for seniors	Tax deferrals for seniors More payment options Phase-in	Assessment limits PT capping
Perceived regressivity: taxes higher as a % of income for low income taxpayers	Tax credits deferrals bundle with other tax reforms Bundle with spending changes low-income housing exemptions	Banding Classified tax rates Progressive tax rates Assessment limits PT capping
Volatility: potentially large swings in taxes for some taxpayers	Annual reassessment Index base Taxpayer education Communication in understandable forms Phase-in	Assessment limits PT capping
Presumptive Tax: taxbase is inherently arbitrary	Taxpayer education Consultation Accessible appeals process Phase-in	Self-assessment Classified PT rates Assessment limit PT capping
Inelasticity is problem for LG, not for taxpayers: taxes do not increase with econ growth	Annual reassessment Index base phase-in	

Source: Based on Slack and Bird (2014: table 1, p. 22)

Many of the problematic dimensions of reform relate to efforts to ameliorate property tax incidence (as we also discussed earlier). Overall, reform is multi-dimensional, political and complex:

> property tax reforms could clearly be designed and implemented much more sensibly than appears to have been the case. To do so, however, countries need to recognise clearly both the nature of the task facing would-be reformers and also the complexity of the task they face ... inextricably related to very long-lived assets and often deep-rooted social beliefs and norms.
>
> (Slack and Bird 2014: 26)

Case study: reforming the council tax in Scotland

Our case study of a local tax reform programme, in Scotland in 2015–2016, unearthed many of the technical issues we have examined in this chapter but also clearly demonstrates the importance of politically credible solutions for critical stakeholders and the inertia created by long standing path dependencies.

The long shadow cast by the poll tax

The community charge (or 'poll tax') was launched in Scotland in 1989 as the headline element of the new 'paying for local government' finance system (Department of the Environment 1986). Arguably the contemporary reform debate in Scotland is the direct result and continuing aftermath of this infamous 'mother of all political blunders' (King and Crewe 2013).

The funding system for local government was revolutionised in 1989 when the domestic rate system was replaced because of long standing complaints that had been heard sympathetically by then Prime Minister Thatcher. First, the government introduced a much-simplified grant system primarily determined by demography and by local needs alongside greater freedom to impose service fees and charges. Second, the non-domestic rate was nationalised and turned into a grant. After a Scottish-wide revaluation of eligible business properties, a national tax rate was set and revenues collected centrally before being returned to local government on a common per capita basis. Not only did local government lose rate-setting power but they also no longer received the income in proportion to their business property tax base. Third, the controversy surrounding non-domestic rates was nothing compared to that with the community charge – a flat rate tax charged on all adults which was effectively the residual element of the system and bore all of the (now much larger) gearing consequences of only leaving a small share of tax raising powers locally. A further critical reform was to end the principle of 100% rebates for those on means-tested general income based social security. Instead, everyone had to make a minimum 20% contribution.

The new tax's introduction led to rioting, mass non-payment, local government bankruptcy threats, the downfall of the British prime minister, Mrs Thatcher, in November 1990 and the unseemly race for a politically feasible solution by her successor John Major and the minister responsible, Michael Heseltine. As a result, in 1993, the council tax was introduced. This was to be a form of hybrid property tax based on 1991 capital values but adopting eight bandings wherein each band paid a bill which was a fixed proportion of band D (the reference point set by local government); the Scottish distribution of bands is shown in Table 31.3. The bands' implicit tax rate (the percentage relative to those in the reference band D) were also much 'flatter' than the distribution would have been if taxes were fully proportionate to property values. So high value properties assessed at a minimum of eight times the lowest tax band, only paid a tax of approximately three times that paid the lowest council tax band. Council tax was supposed to be regularly revalued but apart from Wales with a revaluation in 2007, this has not

Table 31.3 Local council tax bands, Scotland, 2013

Band	Percentage of all dwellings (2013)	Value range (1991)	Percentage of band D
A	21	Up to £27,000	67
B	24	£27,001–35,000	78
C	16	£35,001–45,000	89
D	13	£45,001–58,000	100
E	13	£58,001–80,000	122
F	7	£80,001–106,000	144
G	5	£106,001–212,000	167
H	1	£212,001 or more	200

Source: CIPFA presentation made to the Scottish Commission on Local Tax Reform

happened and outside of Wales, 1991 values remain the basis for the tax. The government reintroduced 100% rebates for those on lowest incomes.

Chartered Institute of Public Finance and Accounting (CIPFA) data presented to the Scottish Commission on Local Tax (CLTR) reform provides a snapshot of local government finance in Scotland. In 2013/14, the Scottish local government system spent just over £12.5 billion with the largest components being education (£4.6 billion), social work (£3 billion) and interest payments/other spend (£2 billion). Spending reflects the functional competencies of local government and we should also note that these have significantly changed in recent years with the establishment of national police and fire/emergency services funded directly from Holyrood. On the revenue side, the required £12.5 billion is funded in the following main component parts:

- £7.225 billion from central transfers or grant in aid;
- £2.436 billion in national non domestic rates;
- £1.977 billion from council tax; and
- £877 million from other incomes (fees and charges) and contribution from reserves.

The average band D council tax for 2013/14 was £1,149 and levels varied from £1,024 in the Western isles (Eilean Siar) to £1230 in Aberdeen City, though the distribution of payments is quite compressed across the 32 authorities.

Reforming council tax

What are the principal problems associated with the council tax? First, the council tax has not had a general revaluation since it was set up 1991 – not only do new properties and sales have to be recalibrated to 1991 values and bands, but the assumption is that various segments of housing markets, neighbourhoods and towns remain in the same market hierarchy that was identified in 1991. This is quite implausible, not least because of the extensive tenure and economic change under was in the last 25 years, let along local housing market change. This also means that the council tax base is inelastic technically – it does not increase in size unless either more properties are added to the valuation list or there is some form of revaluation or indexation of the tax base. Instead and in the absence of a revaluation, the tax rate would have to increase.[4] Analysis for the Commission (Commission on Local Tax Reform 2015) carried out by Chris Leishman at Heriot-Watt University suggested that nearly three in five (i.e. 57%) properties today are now in the 'wrong' council tax band (equally split between being too high and too low).

Second, evidence from the English regions suggests that low value housing market regions pay higher shares of capital value in council tax than do high value market regions (Leishman et al. 2014). In addition to this spatial inconsistency that seems intuitively unreasonable, it also appears that council tax is regressive in terms of payments per decile of the income distribution (Burt 2006; Commission on Local Tax Reform 2015). As a proportion of property value, lower valued properties pay a larger proportion of their value in council tax than do higher valued properties. To the extent that the distribution of property values proxy for wealth held by households, this is not progressive. This is a direct consequence of the banding weighting system. In addition, a system of personal discounts (single adult households) and exemptions further attenuate the property tax.

Meanwhile, and for what turned out to be nine years, and as part of a broader deal (or 'concordat') between the Scottish government and its local authority counterparts, there was a council tax freeze paid for out of additional compensation in the Block Grant although local governments were 'fined' by grant reduction if they choose not to continue with the freeze. The Scottish Government promoted the freeze as a way of protecting household disposable income in difficult times, but it should be recognised that the freeze conferred the greatest absolute benefit to those in the higher council tax bands. Overall, the freeze represented a considerable cumulative process of fiscal centralisation. The council tax freeze cost the Scottish budget £70 million in its first year and a further £70 million in each subsequent year on top of previous years' resources required to keep Band D payments constant. This implies that, in order to remain at 2008/09 levels in 2016/17, now required an annual subvention of £630 million (nine times £70 million), which amounts to more than £3 billion cumulatively in cash terms over the nine years – a substantial opportunity cost. Post-election survey analysis in 2011, however, suggested that the freeze was the single most popular policy proposal in the election campaign (Mitchell 2015). Good politics, bad policy?

At the same time, and under the UK coalition government's localism reforms, Whitehall decided to reduce the council tax rebate system (known as council tax benefit) by 10% across the board as part of deficit reduction measures. In England, this involved passing the remaining council tax benefit back to individual local authorities for them to set and manage as they locally thought best (creating in turn a patchwork of local benefit systems). This was not followed in Scotland – instead the 10% shortfall was funded fully by Holyrood and town hall to maintain the level of benefits for low income rebates but a national scheme, now called the Council Tax Reduction Scheme was then introduced, though ostensibly it was much the same as the former national council tax benefit, as least as far as the recipient is concerned.

Finally, the decision was taken to launch a broad based and multiparty commission on local tax reform at the end of 2014. This was carried out through 2015 and reported in November of that year. The intention was that the Commission would provide analysis and options for reform for the political parties to include in their electoral platform for the 2016 Scottish general election.

Reform and the 2015 Commission

The Commission on Local Taxation Reform (CLTR) had as its remit the tasks to look at the reform or abolition of council tax and to address (if it chose to) the council tax freeze. The Commission's brief did not extend to non-domestic taxation, nor did it include the balance between grant in aid and local revenues, or the system of grant allocation and the broader debate between local government autonomy and central government influence and control.

The CLTR was timed to take evidence and report in time for the development of party manifestos for the Spring 2016 Scottish election. It was a broad-based commission featuring all of the major political parties (except the Scottish Conservatives through their choice), independents, relevant professional bodies and it was co-chaired by the local government minister and the convener of the Convention of Scottish Local Authorities (COSLA). The Commission was serviced by a Secretariat drawn from seconded Government and COSLA officials.

Commission recommendations and party responses

The Commission duly reported and was strong on diagnosis of what was wrong with the present system. The Commission recommended that the council tax should be replaced and the freeze ended. As to how it should be replaced, local tax reform ideas remained at a high level of abstraction favouring a (regularly revalued) property tax solution but one that could be augmented by an element of income taxation. The Commission suggested that further work would be required to assess the practical basis for a land value tax as an alternative to a more conventional property tax. The Commission also made it clear that they expected the main political parties to respond in their (Spring 2016) Scottish election manifestos in how they would secure local tax reform and build on the Commission's recommendations.

From February 2016 onwards, political party proposals started to emerge:

- The governing Scottish National Party (SNP) proposed a modest set of reforms entailing a reweighting of the bands so that higher value properties pay more, an additional high value band, an end to the freeze, additional support for low income households in higher value bands, hypothecation of extra revenue from higher bands into education and consultation over localising a proportion of future Scottish income tax receipts. There would be no general revaluation.
- The Conservatives low tax commission proposed broadly similar though less progressive reweighting of bands to the SNP proposal (i.e. a relatively minor reconfiguring of the existing council tax system but also without a general revaluation).
- Scottish Labour recommended a new property tax, one which included a fixed element but with higher percentage tax rates on properties above a certain level. This would operate locally in terms of rate-setting and would retain a national system of rebates. The precise local nature of the tax was, however, under-specified.
- The Liberal Democrats moved from their longstanding support for a local income tax towards a land value tax.
- The Scottish Greens had the most thorough-going reform proposals involving a five-year transition to a property tax with a long term plan to use this as the basis for a future land value tax. The proposal also included a £10,000 allowance, a revaluation (which would distinguish land from buildings) and higher tax yields from more expensive properties.

The SNP were re-elected but only as a minority government. Their proposals concerning increased tax rates for higher value properties and no general revaluation were duly enacted, as was an adjustment to the social security element to protect below median income households from uplift in tax bills created by the higher bands, though they were not able to command a majority in terms of hypothecating extra income to education and as yet have not moved forward with the idea of localising income tax receipts.[5] The freeze was ended but increased tax bills were capped at 3%.

The question of more thorough-going comprehensive reform is, for the time being, on hold. An interesting question is why did the outcome not go further? While it may be considered that there has been progress of a sort – in reducing the flattening effects of the bands and putting an end to the freeze, there is clearly no appetite from within Government for wider reform and reintroducing regular revaluation, although the devolved government in Wales has successfully revalued domestic properties. Some of the proponents of more systemic reform of local government finance are more positive and see the recent experience as progressive and moving Scotland, albeit slowly, in the right direction. In a longer term context, it may turn out to be most instructive that the SNP and the Lib Dems have now both turned away from a local income tax as their preferred solution towards property taxation, and in an even longer time period, it does seem that land value taxation in principle is moving towards wider acceptability and is certainly no longer viewed in Scotland as fringe thinking..

Final reflections

The finance system that governs local taxes and spending is the result of incremental changes over time to elements of grant systems, tax policy and the distribution of services and functions across local and central government. It is also inherently determined by the fundamental degree of autonomy and discretion allowed to municipal government by higher tiers. These factors and also the fundamental geography and scale of local government units are necessary components shaping the form and level of local taxation, and, to an extent, its effectiveness and acceptability to citizens. And that is before we actually look at the design and structure of the local tax system.

There is a dissonance between economic and in-principle arguments about local taxes, and how they are perceived by people and politicians. Academic commentators are widely positively disposed to property taxation as an instrument for doing good but that there is also recognition that as a salient, highly visible, presumptive tax, arguments over incidence can be trumped by the question of ability to pay from current income. Ironically, this has led to many of the difficulties we see with property taxes around the world, as governments attempt to assuage voters by softening the incidence of the property tax through reforms like circuit-breakers, postponing revaluation and by employing other ostensibly progressive measures to alleviate the symptoms. Finding the right way to compensate low income tax payers remains a critical issue. Land and property taxes may have desirable impacts on housing markets, resource allocation and land use but that also depends on their design. There is, undoubtedly, plenty of international evidence suggesting that, all too readily, the best laid reform plans can all go wrong.

Systems of local tax and the inter-governmental finance and distribution of services are highly idiosyncratic. They are the product of long periods of evolution and punctuated periods of reform (and hence exhibit considerable path dependency). With such different contexts, design details and complex interactions with other taxes, one must be cautious about reading too much into the simple transferability of local tax systems across nations with often very different governance institutions. Policy transfer in order to reform local tax problems should not be embarked on lightly.

The recent Scottish experience of attempted tax reform is instructive since it featured many of the issues thought to inhibit purposive property tax reform (Table 31.2 above), for example, as a result of the salience and presumptive nature of council tax, there was clearly an unwillingness to contemplate general periodic regular revaluation, and because of liquidity problems, relatively complex means-testing was introduced to ameliorate the impact of higher band weightings on more expensive property for cash-poor households. Path dependency played two roles, arguably, in terms of the difficulty of moving away from 1991 values or the freeze in tax bills (though this was phased out via an initial cap of 3% maximum increases).

Finally, from a British perspective, it is apparent that cities and national systems of local government elsewhere typically have more than one local tax at their disposal and frequently have *many* taxes at their disposal. More taxes of lower yield but revenue neutral overall may also of course reduce revenue risk as well. In an international context, nonetheless, it remains odd to restrict oneself to one form of domestic local tax.

Notes

1 The cumulative burden of annual property taxes is capitalised into the present value (i.e. the asset value of a property), in this case reducing the property's value in terms of what the bidders in the market are willing to pay compared to a situation without such a tax.

2 And now also used for the new property tax in Ireland.
3 It is commonly argued that revaluation need not adversely affect tax bills for those living in higher value property – if the overall tax bill (value times tax rate) does not change. However, not revaluing is in the interests of those owners of appreciating property values.
4 And common media or commentator criticism about profligate high tax rates set by local government of course ignores the structural causes of high tax rates i.e. the failure to revalue.
5 Nor did they proceed with adding extra high value bands.

References

Alm, J., Buschman, R. and Sjoquist, D. (2011) Rethinking Local Government Reliance on the Property Tax. *Regional Science and Urban Economics* 41: 320–331.

Almy, R. (2013) *Property Tax Regimes in Europe*. Nairobi: UN-Habitat.

Bird, R. and Slack, E. (2004) *International Handbook of Land and Property Taxation*. Cheltenham: Edward Elgar.

Blochliger, H. (2015) *Reforming the Tax on Immovable Property: Taking Care of the Unloved*. Economics Working Paper 1205. Paris: OECD.

Blochliger, H. and Nettley, M. (2015) *Sub-Central Tax Autonomy: 2011 Update*. OECD Working Papers on Fiscal Federalism 20. Paris: OECD.

Burt, P. (chair) (2006) *A Fairer Way: Report by the Local Government Finance Review Committee*. Edinburgh: Local Government Finance Review Committee.

Commission on Local Tax Reform (2015) *Just Change: A New Approach to Local Taxation* http://localtaxcommission.scot/download-our-final-report/.

Department of the Environment (1986) *Paying for Local Government*. London: HMSO.

Dye, R. and England, R. (2010) *Assessing the Theory and Practice of Land Value Taxation*. Washington, DC: Lincoln Institute of Land Policy.

Gallagher, J., Gibb, K. and Mills, C. (2007) *Rethinking Central Local Government Relations in Scotland: Back to the Future?* Glasgow: David Hume Institute.

Gibb, K. and Christie, L. (2015) International Literature Review for the Commission on Local Taxation. Retrieved from http://localtaxcommission.scot/tell-us-what-you-think/international-evidence-review.

Gibb, K. and Christie, L. (2016) Local Tax Reform in Scotland: Fiscal Decentralisation or Political Solution? In D. Bailey and L. Budd (eds), *Devolution and the UK Economy*, 57–78. Lanham, MD: Rowman & Littlefield.

Gibb, K., Maclennan, D., McNulty, D. and Comerford, M. (eds) (2017) *The Scottish Economy: A Living Book*. Abingdon: Routledge.

Hollis, G. et al. (1992) *Alternatives to the Community Charge*. York: Joseph Rowntree Foundation/Coopers Deloitte.

King, A. and Crewe, I. (2013) *The Blunders of our Governments*. London: One World.

Leishman, C., Bramley, G., Stephens, M., Watkins, D. and Young, G. (2014) *After the Council Tax: Impacts of Property Tax Reform on People, Places and House Prices*. York: Joseph Rowntree Foundation.

Mirrlees, J., et al. (2011). *Tax by Design: The Mirrlees Review*. Oxford: Oxford University Press for the Institute for Fiscal Studies.

Mitchell, J. (2015) *State of the Nation – Local Government*. Briefing Paper. September. Edinburgh: Local Government Information Unit Scotland.

Norregaard, J. (2013) *Taxing Immovable Property: Revenue Potential and Implementation Challenges*. IMF Working Paper. Washington, DC: International Monetary Fund.

Northern Ireland Assembly (2007) *An International Comparison of Local Government Taxation*. Research Paper 10/07. Belfast: Northern Ireland Assembly.

OECD (2010) *Tax Policy Reform and Economic Growth*. Paris: OECD.

Slack, E. (2013) *International Comparison of Global City Financing*. Report to the London Finance Corporation.

Slack, E. and Bird, R. (2014) *The Political Economy of Property Tax Reform*. OECD Working Papers on Fiscal Federalism No.18. Paris: OECD.

32
ADAPTING TO THE FISCAL ENVIRONMENT

Local governments, revenue and taxation powers

Mark Sandford

Introduction

The central approach of this chapter is that, following Ambrosanio and Bordignon (2006) and Martinez-Vazquez (2015), the shape of local government revenue sources and taxation systems is best understood through an empirical lens. Taxation, like politics, is the art of the possible, and this is no less true of the choices about structures, the degree of local discretion, and the proportion of local authority finance that is raised locally. An empirical glance at the heterogeneity of local government revenue systems suggests that their shape is driven by public administration heritage, broader political developments and historical contingencies (Caulfield 2000; Loughlin et al. 2011; Blochliger and King 2007). This could, of course, equally be said of local governments themselves.

This perspective contrasts with the literature on the economics of local government finance. The points of consensus of this substantial literature are rarely reflected in real-world practice, either in terms of the taxes available to local authorities, their interaction with other sources of revenue, or the rationales for change. Even where the need for change is accepted among government institutions, historical contingencies are frequently critical in triggering its occurrence (Shah and Thompson 2004: 3). The starting point for understanding local government taxation should therefore be almost anthropological, tracing the qualitative influences driving local government and public finance as *systems*. Local authorities are not, and cannot be, atomised economic actors: they exist in systems of governance, constitutional contexts, and are subject to political and cultural pressures. To deliver public services and respond to local people's economic and welfare concerns, they must maintain relationships with dozens of public bodies (Smoke 2015). These may have their own electoral mandates, cover overlapping or broader geographical territories, or have access to larger sources of funding or broader legal powers.

Thus, this chapter summarises the observable practices of local authorities' taxing and revenue-raising capacities; looks at commonly used taxes; and notes some recent innovations in revenue-raising practice. It can only be a glance at a highly heterogeneous environment. Local sources of revenue includes the familiar (property taxation, fees, shared revenues) alongside more exotic beasts. Their characteristics in different states arise in the context of their environment – principally local government's functions, and the balance between local government as central government agent and as an actor in its own right (Caulfield 2000). Local government finance forms an element of a broader economic system. Its shape is influenced by central funding practice, political priorities, and the national economic outlook; and, as with local government itself, changes to local government finance systems can often be second-order effects of broader political struggles.

On this view, local taxation systems should not necessarily be expected to be coherent or rational. They are best understood as manifestations of the dynamic and ongoing relationship between local and central government within each given state. The economically ideal 'autonomous local government' is elusive in global practice. Much more common is a multi-layered relationship, consisting of a tangled web of past intentions and political convenience. Central government also provides an essential legal and financial management framework for local authorities (DFID 2015).

The relationship is characterised by co-operation *and* conflict on several fronts at any one time. Taking this into account, it is less surprising that most local authorities receive some form of transfer funding (grant) from higher tiers of government. They will often use transfers to carry out functions on behalf of central government. Equally, it is common for local authorities to have access to less funding for these functions than they require ('unfunded mandates') – and/or to face restrictions in their access to sources of revenue. It is this type of 'push factor', arising from dynamic pressures on revenue, that accounts for local authorities' frequent attempts to access innovative or unconventional sources of funds (Martinez-Vazquez 2015; DFID 2015; Glaeser 2011).

Economic theories

Much early scholarly assessment of local government taxation took place through the lens of economics. The lodestone of this perspective is Charles Tiebout's 1956 paper 'A Pure Theory of Local Expenditures'. Tiebout postulates individuals as consumers who select a local government area according to its fit to their preferences for 'public goods'. As such, local authorities are conceived purely as providers of public services, with none of the broader strategic responsibilities that normally characterise a 'government'. Tiebout acknowledges that his model is an ideal type; and he has little to say about appropriate sources of revenue for local authorities (see Oates 1972; Brennan and Buchanan 1980). Richard Musgrave's *The Theory of Public Finance* (1959) balanced this perspective with the 'ability to pay approach', citing a long history of views that the incidence of tax should be progressive. He recommended that only immobile tax bases, and those that were relatively evenly spread between localities and formed a stable source of revenue, should be taxed locally. Redistribution and macroeconomic management should be left to higher tiers of government. This may be cited as a more 'progressive' response to the Tiebout-Oates perspective. Conversely, Brennan and Buchanan advocate taxing mobile factors of production precisely because this incentivises tax competition between localities.

These perspectives all share a weaving of normative factors into proposed economic/constitutional structures. In practice, decisions to decentralise rarely arise from rational economic calculations. They are normally driven by short-term political considerations (Shah and Thompson 2004; Fjeldstad 2015; Smoke 2015). Moreover, effective implementation of changes in fiscal structures require the building of capacity and influencing of attitudes, among central and local governments and taxpayers (Smoke 2015). Fiscal structures normally have some connection with the responsibilities of local authorities; and responsibilities are frequently joint or concurrent between central and local government. This contrasts with the economic literature, which tacitly assumes a 'dualist' approach, where tasks are neatly allocated to one tier or another.

In practice local government systems can rarely avoid interlocking with one another. Even the most dualist approach will include points where different tiers co-operate to increase effectiveness. 'Concurrent functions', where more than one tier of government has a legal responsibility, are commonplace. Local authorities may seek influence over regional or national functions, in response to local electoral pressure. Disputes between tiers regarding jurisdiction may arise, and may be settled in constitutional courts. Local fiscal systems could be expected to reflect these messy patterns (Ambrosanio and Bordignon 2006: 321).

Additional considerations apply in developing countries. There, debates around fiscal decentralisation may be overshadowed by questions over the effectiveness and legitimacy of the state. Bahl and Linn (2014) note that fiscal centralisation is the norm in developing countries. Local governments may face challenges establishing a functioning local administrative apparatus, and local taxation systems may face allegations of corruption or clientelism (Smoke 2015: 43). Fjeldstad suggests that:

> local governments [in Africa] seem to raise whatever taxes, fees and charges they are capable of raising, often without worrying excessively about the economic distortions and distribution effects that these instruments may create.
>
> *(Fjeldstad 2015: 149)*

Popular acceptance of tax systems and visible impartiality in their enforcement are also key to their functioning in such a context. Where effective administration is absent, particularly sharp instances of centralisation can ensue. For instance, property taxes, despite being popular (and theoretically optimal) sources of local authority revenue in OECD countries, are centralised in China and Indonesia, while they are controlled at state level in India, Nigeria and Pakistan (Shah and Thompson 2004).

The obstacles to economic rationality

This is not to say that economic criteria do not matter for the functioning of a taxation system. Indeed, property taxes, licensing and fees, and shared income taxes crop up repeatedly in real world systems, as might be inferred from Musgrave's perspective. But these exist within a broader funding climate. In particular, most local governments receive intergovernmental transfers driven by political imperatives (Martinez-Vazquez 2015). The circumstances giving rise to these imperatives include:

- Variations – sometimes severe – in tax base and wealth between local areas within a single state (UN-Habitat 2015: 11). This would mean, for instance, that a 5% rise in a given tax would raise much more revenue in some areas than others. This might occur because properties are more numerous or valuable, the inhabitants' incomes are higher, or more use is made of chargeable services.
- Varying economic or social need across local areas. How this translates into a funding system depends upon the state's priorities. If local authorities are expected to make nationally mandated public services available on a needs basis, there are likely to be initiatives towards redistributive funding. Some local authorities will receive more funding per capita than others.
- Central governments' use of local authorities as delivery agents for central policies. These may relate to delivering public services (as above), or to more diffuse responsibilities. Often, though not always, such responsibilities will be accompanied by grant funding ('intergovernmental transfers').

These pressures should be taken into account when assessing aspirations towards greater local 'fiscal autonomy'. It is not uncommon for reviews of local government to recommend that local government should raise an increased quantity of its own revenue, without offering any particular rationale for this view (e.g. UCLG 2010; CoE 2004; UN-Habitat 2015). Local fiscal autonomy, and the constraint of central government influence over local authorities, can often be regarded as an absolute good. This aligns with the economic literature on local government finance, and it can often reflect the aspirations of some local governments themselves. But greater local fiscal autonomy could reduce the capacity of local authorities to fulfil the type of tasks outlined above. This is recognised by the European Charter of Local Self-Government, which recommends provisions for horizontal equalisation *as well as* access to a buoyant and diverse range of local revenue sources (CoE 1995).

In practice, the interplay between state-wide priorities and local discretion determines the shape of a local government funding system. This 'interplay' is frequently a conflict. For instance, where a central government prioritises using local authorities as delivery agents, real fiscal autonomy is likely to be low. Where tax bases vary, this may lead to variations in outcomes. Central government may balance this with grant funding, but to a limited extent. Explicitly or implicitly, any local funding system will navigate a balance between these considerations.

Variations in wealth between local government areas, and thus tax bases, are referred to as *horizontal fiscal imbalance* (HFI). HFI may be counteracted by a system of *horizontal equalisation*. This will often be implemented via general, un-ring-fenced grants. This prevents differences in revenue-raising capacity between wealthier and less wealthy areas from translating directly into the level of local public services provided. Alternatively, conditional grants may be allocated on a needs-related basis, and these may be ring-fenced for use on public services that are mandated by a higher tier of government. Needs assessment may be a particular concern if local authorities act as agents for national services; but it can equally feature where this is not the case.

As noted, it is extremely rare for local authorities to raise all of their revenue locally. The phenomenon of *vertical fiscal imbalance* (VFI) indicates the existence of a gap between revenue raised locally and revenue spent by a local authority. Almost all local government systems exhibit some degree of VFI: Blochliger and Kim (2016: 97) describe it as 'probably inevitable'. Indeed, it is common globally for local authorities to obtain a majority of their revenue from sources over which they have no direct control, either in the form of central grants or funds from shared or assigned revenues (see below).

Aspirations towards 'fiscal autonomy' amount to aspirations to reduce VFI. Concepts of 'accountability' are often found at the root of these intentions. The argument in short is that local authorities' accountability to taxpayers is promoted by a direct relationship between local taxation and spending (Martinez-Vazquez 2015; Slack 2009). In addition, Blochliger and Kim (2016) argue that grant systems are more susceptible to political interference, and that localisation of taxes incentivises efficient tax collection and identification of the tax base. Logically, to the extent that VFI – and any system of horizontal equalisation – is present, accountability and its accompanying benefits are reduced. In its pure form, this is the 'benefit model' of local government (Bailey 1999; Glaeser 2011; Musgrave 1959). This sees locally raised taxes as providing a direct relationship between electors and local governments. Electors pay a desired amount in tax for an agreed basket of public services.

There is no room here to explore these debates in detail, except to note that the assumptions of the 'benefit model' disregard the broader location of local government in a system of governance. They also disregard the broader strategic, place-shaping and representation roles that are characteristic of local authorities. Moreover, accountability can be defined more widely than purely fiscal responsibility to taxpayers. Many local authorities tackle accountability in part via transparency, audit, and public consultation mechanisms. Taxation is not the only route through which local preferences may be determined:

> All local governments, however, need to be responsible, accountable, and efficient. To do so, they need to raise their own revenues as much possible, adhere to an open and visible municipal budgetary process, and engage in transparent and prudent financial management.
>
> (Slack 2009: 72)

The tangled web: local government revenue sources

Any empirical local government finance system comprises a dynamic equilibrium between the pressures noted above, subject to external political forces. This reminds us that local government is a form of *government* – a complex organisation facing multiple responsibilities, pressures, incentives, disincentives, legal requirements, financial requirements, and aspirations. Interdependence with other public bodies is high; local capacity is variable; and complex and multi-layered partnerships proliferate. Multiple sources of funding are a source of resilience in such a context (Martinez-Vazquez 2015). Indeed, access to a range of sources of funding could be more valuable than access to only one or two sources, even if the latter offered larger revenue streams.

It is important to view local taxation capacity in the context of other sources of income. It is common for other sources of income to exceed the revenue available from local taxes. The most common sources of income for local authorities are:

- *Intergovernmental transfers* (grants). These are distributed to local authorities by higher levels of government (regional/state or central). They may be (but are not always) associated with particular responsibilities carried out on behalf of those governments, and therefore they may (but need not) include legal limits on what the funds may be spent upon (conditional or 'ring-fenced' grants). Canada's provinces transfer funds to local authorities to the value of some 20% of the localities' total revenues; of these funds, 80% are ring-fenced. Alternatively – or at the same time – grants may be distributed according to some form of assessment of local need for local government services. This type of grant functions as a counterweight to horizontal fiscal imbalance, but without direct legal requirements applying to how the funding is used.
- Distribution of public funding is a highly complex field with its own extensive literature (e.g. Smith 2006; Steffensen 2010). Comprehensive redistribution systems covering local government funding as a whole are rare (UCLG 2010: 16). OECD analysis suggests that redistributive grants reduce disparities between local authorities within states considerably (Blochliger and Kim 2016: 98). Nevertheless, local authorities frequently experience 'unfunded mandates' – legal responsibilities accorded by higher-tier governments but without adequate revenue to carry them out. Some states, such as Poland, have constitutional provisions banning unfunded mandates (Banaszak 2013).
- *User charges*: These exemplify the 'benefit model' of local government. They are charged to individuals or organisations in return for a specified local service. They are popular and relatively politically acceptable in the USA, Canada and Australia (Caulfield 2000) and in some states in Africa (Fjeldstad 2015). Their use can reduce reliance on local taxes (Ambrosanio and Bordignon 2006: 308). Fees may be charged for a broad variety of services, such as licences for specific types of business (e.g. selling alcohol); rents for public housing; construction licensing; vehicle registration; or waste disposal (Boetti et al. 2012).

User charges can be distinguished from trading income (see below) in that they are charged for statutory services or for services over which the local authority has an effective monopoly. Fees do not normally constitute a large proportion of local government income where functioning taxation or intergovernmental transfer systems exist. The power to set fee levels does not necessarily reside with the local authority. A fixed rate, or range, may be set by a higher tier of government.

- *Trading/commercial income.* This relates to local authority services (e.g. leisure, housing, or legal services) that compete with those available on the open market. However, it may also refer to charges for utilities (water, gas and electricity) and for urban transit, which may be either fully publicly owned or dominated by the local public sector. States vary in the degree to which they permit local authorities to practise commercial activity. In many states, local authorities are permitted to derive income from their own property and charge for the provision of local services. Access to revenue from this source is also influenced by the degree of privatisation in the state in question: states which have privatised or deregulated utilities will be unable to directly benefit from revenue from them.
- *Borrowing.* Local authorities frequently have access to money markets, bond markets, or national/municipally owned lending agencies. Borrowing is the most common source of funds for significant capital expenditure. This is normally used for infrastructure investment (urban transit systems, housing, renewal of public utilities, or property). The sums involved frequently dwarf the annual revenue available to an authority, and capital investment allows the cost of an asset to be spread over a longer period of time ('intergenerational equity').

Local borrowing is normally included in any assessment of a nation-state's financial health. This leads central governments frequently to seek to manage local government borrowing levels. This may range from limits on sources of finance or limits on amounts borrowed through to a legal requirement for approval or an outright ban. For instance, Ethiopia, India, Indonesia, Korea, Mexico and Peru require central government approval for local authority borrowing. Lithuania, Poland, Czech Republic and Slovenia forbid borrowing from foreign bodies (Shah and Thompson 2004: 18).

The balance of revenue from each of these sources of income is highly variable. Economic differences generate variations within states and between years. Comparison of the average percentages of revenue that derive from each of these sources *between* states also reveals enormous variation (Blochliger and Kim 2016). This, again, reflects the heterogeneity of local government roles and functions between states.

Financial incentives

The balance between sources of revenue, and the terms on which revenue is obtained from each source, work together to create a unique basket of incentives for local authorities in each state. For instance, where property taxation dominates, local authorities may seek (among other things) to use policy levers to increase the property tax base. Where shared income tax makes a major contribution, we might expect to see a close interest taken in effective tax collection, in debates over the exact share of tax revenues to be passed to local authorities, and in any horizontal redistribution mechanism. Where transfers make up a substantial proportion of funding, local authorities may develop a supplicant relationship with the transferor, emphasising their need levels or alleging the existence of 'unfunded mandates'. Direct financial incentives – as opposed to general demands for efficiency – may also be established by central government. In England, the Business Rates Retention Scheme incentivises growth in the commercial property tax base by allowing growth in tax revenue through the creation of new buildings to be retained over a 7-year period, while subjecting revenue from existing properties to a pooling mechanism.

Where central controls limit the variation in local tax revenue, or real or perceived unfunded mandates are present, local authorities may seek to develop revenue raising capacity in ways that are less subject to central control. The revenue available from such sources may be marginal to an authority's spending requirements, but it can nevertheless offer relief from spending pressures. This approach also allows authorities to avoid the political consequences of raising local taxes. Political pressures against this are no less fierce at local level than at national level.

Alternatively, local authorities may simply deliberately overspend, calculating that central government will come to their rescue at the end of the year with supplementary grants rather than impose spending reductions and suffer political consequences. Local authorities have successfully pursued this course in Brazil and Argentina in recent years (Gordin 2016).

How local is a 'local tax'?

The level of local control over ostensibly 'local taxes' may vary. A local authority with full control of a local tax would expect to:

- set the rate – including any reliefs and exemptions;
- define the tax base – again including any reliefs and exemptions;
- collect the tax, and retain the revenues collected.

Internationally, the number of 'local' taxes that meets each of these criteria is fewer than might be expected (OECD 1999; Blochliger and King 2007). Many limits have developed on local authorities' discretion over 'local taxes'. The power to set the rate may be limited by the central or state government, or it may hold discretionary powers to prevent large rises. Many property taxes are raised and lowered within nationally defined limits. For instance, Estonia's counties may impose a land value tax of between 0.1% and 2.5% of the value of land. Norway's municipalities must set a property tax of between 0.2% and 0.7% of each domestic property's assessed value.

Similarly, the tax base may be defined by central government. Thus, for instance, although revenue and rate-setting is localised, tax bands, exemptions, reliefs and allowances may be fixed nationally. For instance, the bulk of Sweden's income tax revenue is retained by municipalities (24%) and counties (7%); but the bands are set, and the tax base defined, by the central government. This benefits taxpayers by avoiding complexity arising from multiple systems. This means that local authorities' discretion is focused almost entirely on the *rate* of tax. Since the rate of tax is the most critical element in an individual's tax bill, it carries the highest political salience. Political considerations may therefore, in practice, limit local authorities' discretion.

Assigned revenues

Alongside local taxation powers, many states operate 'shared taxes' or *assigned revenue* systems. A proportion of revenue from specified national taxes is allocated to local government. This could be classified as a form of intergovernmental transfer rather than a local tax, the total quantity of which is determined by actual revenue levels. Nevertheless, there is evidence that local access to national tax bases promotes better services (DFID 2015: 25).

Normally shared taxes are collected centrally and distributed to local governments (though the reverse situation does occur in transition economies: see Shah and Thompson 2004: 10). Revenue may then be distributed to the authorities in which they were raised (the 'derivation principle'), or they may be subject to some form of horizontal equalisation (Martinez-Vazquez 2015). This means that some local authorities may only see a limited relationship between the tax collected in their area and the revenue that they themselves obtain.

For instance, in Germany, 15% of income tax revenue is retained by the local government sector, but it is assigned to municipalities via an equalisation system. In Japan, in 2013/14, 32% of 'liquor tax', 25% of 'tobacco tax', 22.3% of 'consumption tax', and 32% of income tax were assigned to the local government sector. The funds are collected by the central government, and local needs are taken into account when distributing them. By contrast, Poland allocates income tax revenues direct to the locality in which they were raised. In 2015/16, the Czech Republic allocated 23.58% of income tax and 21.93% of VAT to local government, and Finland allocated 29% of 'corporate taxation' to local government.

In these systems, the percentage of each source of assigned revenue may change from year to year. The Japanese government took the decision to increase the consumption tax rate from 1% to 1.7% in 2014, and a further increase to 2.2% is anticipated in 2017. Political controversy may therefore surround the decisions on the percentage of revenue assigned, rather than focusing on the sums themselves.

Each of these phenomena can serve to limit the degree to which 'local taxes' act as a source of autonomy for local authorities. In practice, local governments may find that they have little realistic opportunity to alter their revenue levels – or to influence public policy – via sources of revenue described as 'local taxes'. Even a local authority that appears to raise almost all of its revenue locally may actually have little room for manoeuvre regarding tax levels. It may be hedged in by political or legal limits on adjusting tax levels and tax bases. It may also face legal requirements from higher tiers of government that make it impractical to either increase or reduce revenue levels substantially. Journaud and Kongsrud (2003) suggest that the actual 'taxing capacity' of local government in a given state may be different from the actual quantity of revenue arising from own or shared sources. In Germany, for instance, local authorities receive considerable shared revenue from agreed sources but have no control over the tax rates.

Types of local taxation

Stephen Bailey (1999) postulates eight characteristics that a local tax should aim to meet:

- *Equity*: regressive taxes are to be avoided.
- *Efficiency*: promoting voters' awareness of the link between taxation and service provision.
- *Visibility*: encouraging voters to be aware of the level of tax they are paying, hence promoting accountability.
- *Autonomy*: local control over the rates of tax, to maximise local electors' control over the type and degree of service provided by their local government.
- *Economy*: taxes should be easy to collect, with minimal administration.
- *Sufficiency*: a buoyant tax base and flexible rates will help to ensure that revenue keeps pace with inflation and changes in levels of need. This becomes more significant the greater the proportion of revenue that is raised locally.
- *Stability*: tax revenue levels should be stable, affected minimally by economic fluctuations and cycles.
- *Immobile tax base*: it should not be easy to transfer the tax base out of a local authority area if the tax rate changes. This criterion favours property-based taxes – real property being mostly immobile – and disfavours income-based taxes – on the grounds that individuals can move to other jurisdictions. This criterion also points away from sales-based taxes.

No local tax can meet all eight of these criteria fully. A tax can be successfully operated locally if it meets many or most of them. The types of tax that are most frequently used by local authorities globally do demonstrably meet many of these criteria. This section sets out the most common forms of local taxation used.

- *Property taxes.* These most often consist of an annual charge calculated via (1) an assessed value of the property and (2) the tax rate levied on that value. There may additionally be a property transfer tax ('stamp duty'), though it is less common for this to be under the control of local government. Property taxes frequently form the largest source of revenue for local authorities, particularly in English-speaking countries: in Canada, some 50% of local authority revenues are drawn from the local property tax. The assessed value may relate to either the capital or rental value of the property, or some proportion thereof; or it may be based on the property's surface area, or some more complex tax base.

    Some states have a single property tax system applying to both domestic and commercial property, while others distinguish between the two: for instance, Sweden has no local commercial property tax. There may also be discrepancies between rates for, and revenues collected from, a property tax. In Poland, 80% of property tax revenues come from commercial property (Loughlin et al. 2011: 489).

    A small number of states (examples being Estonia and Australia) use forms of 'land value tax' – valuing land distinctly from property upon it (Bahl and Wallace 2008). Land value tax is favoured by economic analysis, on the grounds that it avoids the distortion of incentives.

    The key advantage of property tax is that property is rarely mobile, thus the tax is difficult to avoid (Fjeldstad 2015). It provides a stable and visible revenue stream. Where property values are only assessed on cycles that are several years long, this can serve to insulate local authorities' revenue levels from immediate cyclical effects arising from economic downturns (Alm, Buschman and Sjoquist 2012). By the same token, the visibility of the tax, and of any fluctuations in rates and revenue, can be a source of taxpayer discontent (Caulfield 2000). This explains why property values in many states have not been reassessed for many decades, such as France (1970), Germany (1964; 1935 for the former East Germany), and Austria (1973). This affects the relative incidence of the taxes on different taxpayers, and can erode acceptance of the system. More fundamentally, creating and maintaining a cadastral register can be very challenging in developing countries (Devas and Delay 2006; DFID 2015). It can be challenging to establish the legal owner and/or the occupier, or even the existence, of a property.

- *Income taxes.* Localised forms of income tax are particularly common in Scandinavia and northern Europe, and the former USSR. In most cases, 'local income taxes' constitute a share of a nationally administered income tax. In Sweden, in 2015/16, municipalities raise income tax at a standard rate of 24%, and counties at a rate of 7%. These rates form part of the national income tax and are collected nationally. Higher rate income tax revenues go to the central government.

    Local income taxes are stable and relatively visible, can be collected effectively, and generate significant income. Some countries (e.g. Kazakhstan and Ukraine) distribute the revenues on the basis of an equalisation formula (UCLG 2010). It is relatively rare for local authorities to be able to vary local income tax *rates*. Examples of states in which this power is available to local authorities include Croatia, Brazil and Switzerland.

- *Consumption taxes.* Local sales taxes generate significant revenue in North America, but they are also an ancillary revenue source in states elsewhere. They are easy to collect, visible and relatively stable. They are pro-cyclical (i.e. they rise during periods of economic growth, and fall when the economy falls back).

Sales taxes are not progressive in their incidence, and thus their contribution to 'equity' is ambivalent. As much economic activity is mobile in principle, variations in rates across localities can lead to spillover effects ('cross-border shopping'). The closest equivalent in Europe, Value Added Tax (VAT), may not be varied locally within individual European Union states under European law. Many EU states assign a share of VAT revenues to local authorities (e.g. Greece, Czech Republic, Germany).

- *Transport, environmental and tourism taxes.* Transport related taxes may include parking fees; road pricing (congestion charging); vehicle registration charges; and zones for special emissions levies. Nottingham, in the UK, levies a charge on the provision of workplace parking spaces. Environmental taxes may include fees or levies on waste collection. 'Tourism tax' typically consists of a small levy per night on the occupation of hotel beds. This is common in areas with strong regional tourist economies, such as Spain and Malta, but also in local authorities in other states such as Germany, Belgium, Canada and France.

Table 32.1 Own taxes as percentage of local revenue

	Corporate income tax	Consumption taxes	Personal income taxes	Property taxes	Other
States/regions					
Canada	5.63	22.68	22.24	3.09	7.91
USA	3.84	29.30	17.42	1.30	0
Switzerland	7.19	3.51	32.66	8.32	0
Spain	0.31	3.35	14.78	14.89	0
Belgium	0	4.85	17.93	10.43	0
Australia	0	10.24	0	12.16	9.42
Germany	0	0	0	1.79	0
Austria	0	0	0	0	0
Municipalities					
Sweden	0	0	63.43	0	0
Switzerland	6.13	0.12	39.56	8.32	0
Denmark	0	0	43.58	2.47	0
Finland	0	0	41.54	2.42	0
Norway	0	0	39.55	4.04	0
Japan	10.67	2.61	11.18	13.89	0.07
France	0	2.12	0	19.48	14.15
Luxembourg	30.24	0.28	0	2.27	0
Spain	0	12.28	0	20.09	0
Belgium	0	2.79	22.62	5.74	0
Italy	2.97	8.02	0.77	5.59	11.98
South Korea	2.49	1.90	2.59	14.19	4.03
Germany	8.83	0	7.15	6.32	0
Portugal	4.81	0	3.35	9.31	0
Hungary	0	14.19	0	2.16	0.04
United Kingdom	0	0	0	13.53	0
Netherlands	0	4.27	0	5.34	0
Greece	0	0.43	0	5.33	0
Czech Republic	0	2.10	0	1.42	0
Austria	0	0	0	0	0
Ireland	0	0	0	0	0

Source: OECD (2014)

The importance of each of these types of tax to local governments is dependent on the quantity of money that each raises. Here, again, there is great variation between states. Table 32.1 shows the percentages of revenue raised from each of these sources. In some states, property taxes raise large proportions of local revenue, while in others they raise far smaller proportions. Assigned income tax revenue makes up a substantial proportion of local revenue in some areas, but in many states it is not used at all. Transport-related taxes and environment-related taxes commonly raise far smaller sums of revenue. Revenues from unconventional sources of funding (see below) may be volatile and/or attached to particular projects or localities: they cannot substitute for more 'mainstream' revenues. Thus not all local taxes are equal. A local authority cannot necessarily replace lost revenue from one source with an equal quantity of revenue from any other source at will.

Aside from political considerations, and the size of the available tax base, the degree to which revenues can be raised locally also depends on the state/national tax regime (Martinez-Vazquez 2015: 15). Some states distinguish explicitly between taxes that may be levied by central government and taxes that may be levied by local governments, but more common is the use of 'shared tax bases' – where more than one tier of government will levy a tax rate within a particular tax structure. Either way, the national tax regime is a key constraint on the room for manoeuvre available to local authorities.

Sources of revenue: innovation

We noted above that the fiscal landscape faced by local governments could give rise to incentives to develop particular sources of finance further. Local authorities' activities in this regard are often influenced by 'push factors'. If their revenue-raising power from one source is curbed, they will attempt to compensate by generating more revenue from an alternative source. Often, the attractiveness of such sources is that they are subject to fewer governmental or constitutional restrictions in their particular jurisdiction (Gelfand 1979). Clearly, the constitutional position of local government influences its ability to do this: it will be easier if local authorities have general powers to act unless prohibited from doing so, and harder where specific legal permission is needed for every act. Recent innovative approaches include:

- The United Kingdom has pioneered the use of *social impact bonds* (SIBs). These bring together investors, a public service commissioning body or bodies, and service providers in a contractual relationship. The investors provide capital at the outset of the project. The commissioning body or bodies then agree contractual terms and agreed outcomes for the service providers. The service providers are paid with the investors' money. The investors will then receive a return on their investment, according to success criteria laid out in the contract. This is to be paid from savings arising from efficiencies in the provision of the service. The contract may also provide that a certain share of any savings is to be retained by the commissioning body.

    The performance of SIBs so far has been variable. The world's first SIB, in Peterborough, showed some progress against metrics (RAND Europe 2015). An interim evaluation of the London rough sleepers SIB, in March 2015, found more mixed results (DCLG 2015). Many SIBs in the UK are underwritten by a pool of 'soft money', often supplied by a major charitable funder; this reflects in part that risk levels have been too great to attract large scale commercial funding (Corry 2016).

- The USA has dominated the use of *tax increment financing* (TIF). A TIF scheme borrows money for infrastructure development and uses as collateral the increased tax revenues that will arise when the development is complete. These can be property taxes, sales taxes, or revenues from a broad local deal. Allentown, Pennsylvania agreed a deal with state and other authorities for future local revenues from 14 taxes (controlled either locally or at state level) to be placed in a fund to repay bond finance (Urban Land Institute 2016: 21). TIFs may often make use of financial 'special purpose vehicles', which can allow state or central government borrowing controls to be circumvented (Briffault 2010).

TIFs are a form of 'uplift' or 'betterment' taxation. 'Uplift' refers to the idea that public investment – such as a new transport link or a regeneration scheme – often leads to rises in private property values. Normally these rises in value are retained entirely by property owners, even if they were driven by public funding. If uplift taxation is available to a local authority, this in itself may act as an incentive to pursue development policies, alongside or in place of other elements of its responsibility: 'TIF exemplifies the fiscalization of local development policy. TIF enables local governments to pursue what is often the principal local development goal-increased tax base, while avoiding the political and legal limits on increased local taxation. . . . TIF programs are market-oriented, aimed at inducing or retaining investment by private entrepreneurs. Moreover, local governments use TIF to act as entrepreneurs, formulating and implementing development plans' (Briffault 2010: 66–67).

- Some local authorities in Poland operate property leaseback schemes. They sell properties to private sector entities, with a requirement that the local authority must be permitted to lease the property back for an agreed number of years at an agreed rent. The local authority will then have an option to repurchase the property at the end of the period, with the minimum price set out in statute. These arrangements allow access to capital finance for authorities whose poor financial performance prevents them from accessing municipal bonds or conventional bank loans. The arrangements also do not need to be officially reported as a debt obligation (Kluza 2016).

The existence of these options does not mean that they are open to all local governments. Much depends on the organisational capacity and financial scale of a local authority and the strength of its local economy. For instance, seeking investment via a TIF amounts to participation in a competitive market. Some areas may be unable to find investors; equally, a TIF would fail – leaving substantial debt in the hands of the local authority – if economic growth does not occur and 'uplift' in value fails to materialise. Local authorities that cannot find customers for their properties would be unable to lease them. Social impact bonds that cannot reduce the costs of public services may increase local authority spending instead of reducing it.

A contrasting phenomenon is found in some developing countries. Where a state's local taxation systems are under-developed or non-existent, there have been instances where aid agencies have set up parallel 'taxation' systems to manage the financial dimension of local development. Functionally these may be more effective than local administrative systems. But equally, their existence may undermine the chances of local systems developing (Devas and Delay 2006; Shah and Thompson 2004). 'Tax farming' – where central or regional authorities contract out tax collection privately in exchange for a fee or percentage of the revenue collected – is a distinct phenomenon but one that arises in similar socio-economic circumstances (Shah and Thompson 2004). Smoke (2015: 42) mentions 'constituency development funds', given to parliamentarians in some countries to spend on local matters that may overlap with, and detract from, local government functions.

A final mention should be made of a phenomenon termed 'private government' (Bailey 1999: 162). This phrase refers to the use of 'business improvement districts' and their more common domestic counterpart, 'residential community associations'. These are ad hoc areas established by a local business (or residents') association, within which a tax supplement or a charge is collected and retained by the association for local use. 'Private governments' could be regarded as a further innovative method of raising revenues. They have some of the characteristics of private associations, but with compulsory membership within a particular geographical area. They represent a localised example of the principle of the 'benefits model'. The services they provide are principally consumed by the residents (or businesses) in the geographical area, in their capacity as members.

Conclusion

Local authorities across the world have a broad range of tax and revenue raising capacities. These are normally sufficient to make them significant economic actors locally. This generates a relationship with central government; and it is common for central or state governments to try to minimise the independent fiscal powers and leverage of local authorities (Gelfand 1979). When this happens, local authorities in some areas have responded by being swift on their feet and exploiting previously unnoted opportunities within the financial ecosystem in which they operate.

But this reflects that authorities' taxation powers, and their financial strategies, are expressions of the central-local relationship within which they operate. Some authorities gravitate towards funding sources over which they have greater freedom (using own assets, borrowing) and away from those in which they do not (tax raising). Some retain a strong purchase on a nationally agreed system of financing. In most cases, a broad range of access points to revenue is a good guarantee of local authority financial health. But it is national systems of government, rather than a universal approach of rationality, that explain the approach to sources of revenue that are available to local authorities. Central and state/regional governments are frequently 'jealous gods', and are rarely ready to tolerate the existence of autonomous local entities of the kind favoured by economic theory.

Acknowledgements

My thanks to Andrew Stevens for his assistance.

References

Alm, J., Buschman, R. D. and Sjoquist, D. L. (2012) *Rethinking Local Government Reliance on the Property Tax*. Working Paper. New Orleans, LA: Tulane University.

Ambrosanio, M. F. and Bordignon, M. (2006) Normative versus Positive Theories of Revenue Assignments in Federations. In E. Ahmad and G. Brosio (eds), *Handbook of Fiscal Federalism*, 306–338. Cheltenham: Edward Elgar.

Bahl, R. W. and Linn, J. F. (2014) *Governing and Financing Cities in the Developing World*. Policy Focus Report. Cambridge, MA: Lincoln Institute of Land Policy.

Bahl, R. and Wallace, S. (2008) *Reforming the Property Tax in Developing Countries: A New Approach*. Atlanta, GA: Georgia State University.

Bailey, S. (1999) *Local Government Economics: Principles and Practice*. Basingstoke: Macmillan.

Banaszak, B. (2013) Local Government in Poland: Towards Consolidation? In C. Panara and M. Varney (eds), *The 'Fourth Level' in the EU Multi-layered System of Governance*, 255–276. Routledge: London.

Blochliger, H. and Kim, J. (2016) *Fiscal Federalism 2016: Making Decentralisation Work*. Paris: OECD.

Blochliger, H. and King, D. (2007) *Less Than You Thought: The Fiscal Autonomy of Sub-central Governments*. Paris: OECD.

Boetti, L., Piacenza, M. and Turati, G. (2012) Decentralisation and Local Governments' Performance: How Does Fiscal Autonomy Affect Spending Efficiency? *Public Finance Analysis* 63(3): 269–300.

Brennan, G. and Buchanan, J. (1980) *The Power to Tax: Analytical Foundations of a Fiscal Constitution.* Cambridge: Cambridge University Press.

Briffault, R. (2010) The Most Popular Tool: Tax Increment Financing and the Political Economy of Local Government. *University of Chicago Law Review* 77(1). Retrieved from http://chicagounbound.uchicago.edu/uclrev/vol77/iss1/4.

Caulfield, J. (2000) Local Government Finance in OECD Countries. *Unpublished paper.* Sydney: University of New South Wales.

CoE (1995) *European Charter of Local Self-Government.* Strasbourg: Council of Europe.

CoE (2004) *A Handbook on Finance at Local and Regional Level.* Strasbourg: Council of Europe.

Corry, D. (2016) Some Ifs and Buts about Social Impact Bonds. *New Philanthropy Capital blog*, 15 August. Retrieved from www.thinknpc.org/blog/some-ifs-and-buts-around-social-impact-bonds.

DCLG (2015) *Qualitative Evaluation of the London Homelessness Social Impact Bond.* London: HMSO.

Devas, N. and Delay, S. (2006) Local Democracy and the Challenges of Decentralising the State: An International Perspective. *Local Government Studies* 32(5): 677–695.

DFID (2015) *Urban Finance: Rapid Evidence Assessment.* London: HMSO.

Fjeldstad, O.-H. (2015) When the Terrain Does Not Fit the Map: Local Government Taxation in Africa. In A.-M. Kjaer, L. Engberg-Pedersen and L. Buur (eds), *Perspectives on Politics, Production and Public Administration in Africa: Essays in Honour of Ole Therkildsen*, 147–158. Copenhagen: Danish Institute for International Studies.

Gelfand, M. D. (1979) Seeking Local Government Financial Integrity Through Debt Ceilings, Tax Limitations, and Expenditure Limits: The New York City Fiscal Crisis, the Taxpayers' Revolt, and Beyond. *Minnesota Law Review* 63: 545–608.

Glaeser, E. (2011) *Urban Public Finance.* Cambridge, MA: Harvard University Press.

Gordin, J. P. (2016) Federalism and the Politics of Fiscal Responsibility Laws: Argentina and Brazil in Comparative Perspective. *Policy Studies* 37(6): 236–253.

Journaud, I. and Kongsrud, P. M. (2003) *Fiscal Relations across Government Levels.* Economic Department Working Paper No. 375. Paris: OECD.

Kluza, K. (2016) Financial Innovation in Local Governments as a Response to the Deterioration of their Risk Profile and Legislative Changes: The case of Poland. *Public Sector Innovation Journal* 21(1). Retrieved from www.innovation.cc/volumes-issues/vol21-no1.htm.

Loughlin J., Hendriks, F. and Lidstrom, A. (eds) (2011) *The Oxford Handbook of Local and Regional Democracy in Europe.* Oxford: Oxford University Press.

Martinez-Vazquez, J. (2015) Mobilizing Financial Resources for Public Service Deliver and Urban Development. In UN-Habitat, *The Challenge of Local Government Financing in Developing Countries*, 14–33. Nairobi: UN-Habitat.

Musgrave, R. (1959) *The Theory of Public Finance.* London: McGraw-Hill.

Oates, W. (1972) *Fiscal Federalism.* Cheltenham: Edward Elgar.

OECD (1999) *Revenue Statistics 1965/1998 'Special Feature'.* Paris: OECD.

OECD (2014) *Fiscal Federalism 2014.* Paris: OECD. Retrieved from www.oecd-ilibrary.org/governance/fiscal-federalism-2014/taxing-power-and-the-tax-mix_9789264204577-graph26-en.

RAND Europe (2015) *The Payment by Results Social Impact Bond Pilot at HMP Peterborough: Final Process Evaluation Report.* London: HMSO.

Shah, A. and Thompson, T. (2004) *Implementing Decentralized Local Governance: A Treacherous Road with Potholes, Detours and Road Closures.* World Bank Policy Research Working Paper 3353. Washington, DC: World Bank.

Slack, N. E. (2009) *Guide to Municipal Finance.* Nairobi: UN-Habitat.

Smith, P. (2006) *Formula Funding of Public Services.* London: Routledge.

Smoke, P. (2015) Urban Government Revenues: Political Economy Challenges and Opportunities. In UN-Habitat, *The Challenge of Local Government Financing in Developing Countries*, 34–53. Nairobi: UN-Habitat.

Steffensen, J. (2010) *Fiscal Decentralization and Sector Funding Principles and Practices.* Copenhagen: DANIDA.

Tiebout, C. (1956) A Pure Theory of Local Expenditures. *Journal of Political Economy* 64(5): 416–424.

UCLG (2010) *Local Government Finance: The Challenges of the 21st Century.* Barcelona: United Cities and Local Governments.

UN-Habitat (2015) *The Challenge of Local Government Financing in Developing Countries.* Nairobi: UN-Habitat.

Urban Land Institute (2016) *Reaching for the Future: Creative Finance for Smaller Communities.* Washington, DC: ULI Foundation.

33
FINANCING LOCAL GOVERNMENT IN THE TWENTY-FIRST CENTURY

Local government revenues in European Union member states, 2000–2014

Gerard Turley and Stephen McNena

> Part at least of the financial resources of local authorities shall derive from local taxes and charges of which, within the limits of statute, they have the power to determine the rate.
>
> *(Council of Europe 1985)*

Introduction

This chapter focuses on the funding of local government, and in particular, it examines how local governments are financed across EU member states and over time. Using the EU set of countries allows us to identify both similarities and differences in the financing of local government. The time period chosen is 2000–2014, the first 15 years of the twenty-first century capturing the Great Moderation and years of strong economic growth, the 2008–2009 global financial crisis and the Great Recession, the Eurozone debt crisis, the austerity era and the subsequent years of lacklustre and uneven economic recovery.

The structure of the chapter is as follows: after presenting the economics of local government and the general principles of revenue assignment, the main local government revenue sources of taxes, grants and user charges are outlined. Local government revenue data for the 28 member states of the EU for the first 15 years of the twenty-first century are then reported and analysed. The chapter concludes with a review of some contemporary policy issues and future challenges, namely the inter-related issues of fiscal decentralisation and local autonomy, local government funding measures post-crisis, and, finally, subnational fiscal policy and fiscal rules of local governments.

Local government economics: the theory

Although difficult to define precisely because of cross-country differences in governance and structures, here we define local government as:

> ... a locally elected democratic statutory organisation below the level of the state, province or region, providing public sector services to the populace within the area of its jurisdiction.
>
> (Bailey 1999: 3)

Missing from this definition is the financing of local government and, in particular, the power to levy local taxes. This chapter examines local government funding, and most especially, the different forms of local government revenues in the EU member states, for the period 2000–2014. In terms of coverage, in this chapter we only cover revenue income, namely local taxes, grants/transfers and user charges to finance current or operating expenditure. We do not report capital revenues, loans, income from debt instruments or other forms of external funding.

Underlying subnational government funding are two models of local government finance: the ability-to-pay model and the benefit model. As the title suggests the ability-to-pay model is based on interpersonal distribution of income and wealth, aimed at the equity objective of public policy. In contrast, the benefit financing model focuses on the efficiency objective, with those who benefit from local government services bearing the costs of their provision (Bird 2001). Preference for one approach over the other is related to the potential conflict between equity and efficiency, and the value put on one relative to the other.

A society that uses its scare resources to successfully maximise total welfare must have a mix of expenditures on privately and publicly provided goods and services (Samuelson 1954). With respect to private goods and services, the competitive market system and its pricing mechanism allocates society's scarce resources. In cases of market failure such as public goods, externalities or asymmetric information, outcomes can be improved by government intervention. Once it is decided that provision is by the public sector, the next question that arises is the appropriate level of government, whether that is central, regional or local. Unlike political scientists who emphasise the political or democratic role of local government, economists focus on the economic perspective, namely, in achieving efficiency through local public service delivery.[1] Using the traditional three-pillars or branches of government framework, the main economic functions of government are the allocative, distributive and stabilisation roles (Musgrave 1959).[2] Whereas it is argued that the income redistribution and macroeconomic stabilisation functions are best undertaken by central government, the resource allocation role should primarily be provided by subnational government, and, in cases where the benefits are localised, by local government. Given these normative expenditure assignments, here we concentrate on the allocative function and the efficiency role of local government.

Viewed through the lens of an economist, the argument in favour of local government over national government provision of uniform services is that, given the spatial considerations, local government facilitates, to the extent possible, the matching of public service outputs with local preferences (the so called 'matching' principle of benefits and costs), and in doing so, promotes economic efficiency. Using the benefit taxation model as outlined above, it is desirable that those who benefit from local government expenditure should pay for it (in line with the cost of providing it), and by doing so, maintain the link between taxes paid and benefits rendered. Where benefits do not extend beyond local boundaries, allocative efficiency can be best achieved by providing public services at the lowest level of government possible, i.e. local government units, whether called local authorities, councils, municipalities, etc. The welfare gains that accrue by moving government closer to its constituencies and ensuring that citizens get what they want is the allocative efficiency case for local government and dominates the economic debate in favour of decentralised government. Indeed, the main economic rationale for local government is to improve efficiency.

Due to different preferences for the level and mix of local services and different costs in local public service delivery, there are welfare gains from fiscal decentralisation. Formalised by Oates (1972), this fiscal decentralisation theorem presents the economic case for local government. Alongside Oates's model is the equally famous Tiebout (1956) model of local government finance. According to this theoretical model of choice, if citizens are faced with areas of different type and level of public services, citizens will choose the local area that best reflects their preferences, by 'voting with their feet'. In this case, based on assumptions of perfect residential mobility, absence of spillovers and identical preferences within each area, a political solution is not required as the market is said to be efficient (Loughlin and Martin 2008).

Notwithstanding the economies of scale argument in favour of a more centralised government, functions should be assigned to the level of government whose jurisdiction most closely approximates the geographical area of benefits provided by the function. This indicates that, for example, national defence, foreign affairs, migration and monetary policy should be provided by central government as the benefits and costs are national in scope. In contrast, fire protection, parks and recreation, planning and zoning, and street maintenance, for example, should be, applying the benefits rule, provided by local governments as these are primarily local affairs.[3]

In theory and in practice, spending is much easier to decentralise than revenue. With the limited tax base that local governments have, the inevitable outcome of expenditure and revenue assignments is that local government spending exceeds local government revenue, resulting in vertical fiscal imbalances. In turn, given differences in expenditure needs and fiscal capacities of local governments, assigning local government taxes and revenues will result in horizontal fiscal imbalances. Both of these fiscal imbalances mean that intergovernmental transfers to local governments form an important source of revenue income, to close the fiscal gap but also to narrow the fiscal disparities between local governments using equalisation transfers. In terms of expenditure and revenue assignments, Olson's (1969) principle of fiscal equivalence assigns revenue-generation powers to central and local governments commensurate with expenditure responsibilities and, where possible, aims for a close match between benefit area, tax area, and electoral area.

Any framework for analysis of local government funding should keep in mind a number of key principles of local government financing, including administrative simplicity and efficiency; local accountability, decision making and flexibility; equity, including the ability to pay and the breadth of the revenue base; equalisation; the polluter and user pays principle; and, compatibility with national policies, in particular national taxation strategies (Indecon 2005).

Before outlining the different local revenue sources that countries rely on in practice, we examine the general principles of revenue assignment as presented by the theory of fiscal federalism and intergovernmental fiscal relations.

Revenue assignment: general principles

Economic theory, as outlined above, describes the assignment of expenditure responsibilities or functions to local government. One of the 'rules' of fiscal decentralisation is that finance should follow function; that is, only after expenditures are assigned can revenue assignment be determined, as an estimate of expenditures is needed in order to establish the level of local government revenues, so as to maintain the link between benefit areas and finance areas, and between expenditure responsibilities and revenue resources (Bahl 2002).

Whereas the rationale for which government functions are decentralised to local government is clear, at least in theory, the case for which revenue sources are decentralised is much less straightforward. In terms of local government finance and revenue assignments, for local governments to be accountable to their local residents (whether that is individuals, households or firms), and to ensure that local residents pay for the services received, at least at the margin, there are three conditions that need to be met. First, as far as possible, local government should charge for the services provided, using user charges or fees. Second, if charging is not practical, local governments should impose taxes on local residents, except to the extent that central government is willing to pay. Third, where central government does pay, local governments should, as much as possible, be accountable to central government (Bird 2001). When this involves the payment of intergovernmental grants, they should be designed so that local government recipients are subject to a hard budget constraint with no gap filling or expectation of a bailout (Kornai 1992; Turley 2006). As with user charges, the objective is to, subject to political and economic constraints, 'get the prices right' in the public sector by designing intergovernmental grants in such a way that local governments are fiscally responsible, disciplined and prudent.

User charges

A user charge is a charge per unit of output. Use of the term 'charge' rather than 'price' reflects the administrative rather than market determination of these requited payments. The economic rationale for the use of a user charge is, to the extent possible, to replicate the competitive market system by promoting an optimal level of consumption in charging a price equal to the cost of providing an additional unit of the service. As many local government services are not pure public goods whose characteristics of non-excludability and non-rivalry mean public provision free at the point of use, charges or fees for these local services should apply, with the amount of subsidy dependent on the nature of the good or service, and the degree of externality involved. Because of other factors, such as political constraints and social objectives, user charges are often set below full economic cost, and not aimed at the normal cost recovery. Notwithstanding this reality, and the available exemptions and concessions that are aimed at achieving some degree of equity, the rationale is to promote economic efficiency wherever possible by not giving away local government outputs but by charging for services so that the benefit or utility accruing to residents is linked to public service provision and costs, at least at the margin. Consistent with the polluter/user pays principle, charges, if properly designed, can reduce over consumption, and by doing so, lead to a conservation of scarce resources.

In terms of amounts collected and the effects of user charges, the international evidence is that the yield is less than what economic theory predicts or justifies (and substantially less than income from local taxes or grants), and they seldom produce any significant non-revenue benefits. Indeed, as Bird (2006: 181) concludes:

> In short, user charges are a good idea in principle, but one that appears to be surprisingly difficult to implement well in practice. Such charges therefore seem unlikely to provide anything close to adequate finance for subnational activities in any country.

Local taxes

The next option in funding local government and financing local public services is taxation. This raises the question of what taxes should be levied at the local level, or, more specifically, what makes a good local tax, defined as one where the local government has some control or discretion over the rate (albeit perhaps within limits), the taxable base or both, so as to be adequately responsive to local needs and decisions, while remaining politically accountable to its citizens. As with all taxes, we begin with the premise that local taxes should not unduly distort market conditions or the allocation of resources. Given this, traditional local public finance theory indicates that a good local tax has a number of characteristics: immobile and relatively evenly distributed tax base (so that local governments can vary the tax rate in the knowledge that the taxable base will not move elsewhere, permitting interjurisdictional variation in tax rates, and, at the same time, preventing problems of unnecessary tax harmonisation or harmful tax competition); imposed on local residents (and difficult to export to non-residents); sufficiently buoyant and adequate to meet local needs (expand at least as fast as expenditures but not fluctuate excessively with economic activity as this will cause instability and uncertainty in terms of revenues and expenditures); relatively easy to administer.[4] Other features include visibility (to ensure accountability and reduce evasion) and equity (to ensure fairness and a general acceptance by taxpayers).

Aside from property taxes and broad-based business taxes, other taxes often levied by local government include sales taxes (both general and selective), income taxes and miscellaneous taxes (motor vehicle and fuel taxes, for example). With respect to taxes, some industrialised countries rely primarily on a single tax to fund local government. In the majority of these cases, it is either property tax or income taxes. In some cases taxes are collected at the regional or provincial level (for political, economic or administrative reasons) and subsequently shared, using predetermined formulae, with local government. These revenue sharing arrangements are called shared taxes, and are common in federal countries and many of the former socialist countries. Alternatively, local government can impose a surcharge ('piggy-back') on a tax levied, for reasons of administrative capacity or economies of scale, by an upper tier of government.

Given the different taxes and the different circumstances, history, culture, and institutional capacity of countries, it may be prudent to allow countries find their own most suitable and appropriate local tax system, and, depending on the extent of expenditure assignments, choose a local tax system that is not dependent on a single tax source or a volatile tax base. As with local public finance and intergovernmental fiscal relations, conceptual arguments usually give way to practical reality and, as a general rule, one size does not fit all.

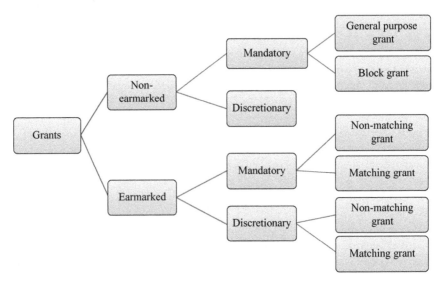

Figure 33.1 OECD taxonomy of grants
Source: OECD/KIPF (2012)

Grants

Regardless of the aforementioned revenue sources assigned to local government, grants or transfers (primarily intergovernmental in nature) will undoubtedly constitute an important source of funding for local government. Apart from a local government revenue source, the issues relating to grants and funding local government usually centre on the design of these grants so as to ensure the desired effects on policy outcomes.

We begin with a classification of intergovernmental grants as there are many different types, with different objectives. An OECD typology of grants is given in Figure 33.1. Aside from these more traditional grants, there are also performance or output-based grants, where the grant payment is conditional on results to be achieved, in terms of local government performance in key areas of, for example, financial performance or service delivery.

As for grant design and best international practice when using intergovernmental transfers as a local government income source, the following principles are useful to apply, namely:

- The basic rule of grant design is that grant programmes be designed to meet grant objectives. The logic here is that the grant objective will determine the grant design and, in turn, the grant programme. There should be different grants for specific objectives pursued, but an excessive number of grant programmes should be avoided as this can often lead to confusion and conflict. As for examples, general non-matching grants or revenue sharing mechanisms to deal with the fiscal gap; general non-matching equalisation grants to address horizontal fiscal imbalances; conditional non-matching grants to ensure minimum standards of services across the nation; and conditional open-ended matching grants to stimulate public expenditures in areas of high national importance but low local priority (Shah 2008).
- No uniform pattern of grants is universally appropriate. Each country's specific circumstances require drawing upon international best practice but, within reason, tailoring and adapting it to suit local circumstances.
- Keep it simple. They should preserve budget autonomy. Grants should be transparent, adequate, stable, predictable, sufficiently flexible, and timely (with respect to annual financial budgeting). Grants should not be negotiable or discretionary, and should not be for the purposes of deficit-filling, due to the problems associated with the soft budget constraint. In the design of a grant system which is both feasible and relevant, quality information and reliable, consistent and comparable data are critical. Given the data requirements sophisticated methodologies may have to be sacrificed for simpler and more workable models.
- In terms of equalisation grants, the formula should be based on quantifiable and objective indicators (*but* also politically acceptable given the nature of equalisation grants, i.e. redistributive, with potential winners and losers), measuring either expenditure needs or fiscal capacity, or both. The formula should be incentive compatible, encouraging local revenue-raising effort and local expenditure restraint.

We now examine the local government revenue sources used in practice, and, in particular, the different local tax sources.

Local government tax sources: in practice

Classification of revenue sources

As seen in Table 33.1, revenues can be classified as current or capital, and own-source or from upper tiers of government.[5] As stated earlier, the focus of this chapter and the coverage of the

Table 33.1 Local government revenue classifications

Categories	Current revenues	Capital revenues
Own-source revenues	User charges	Asset sales
	Local taxes	Betterment levies
	Other (fees, licenses, permits)	Other
Revenues from higher-level governments	Shared taxes	Capital grants
	Grants	

Source: Adapted from Freire and Garzón (2014)

actual revenues reported in Tables 33.3–33.7 are on current revenues, and more specifically, the categories of fees and charges, local taxes and grants. Shared taxes are often classified as grants as the revenue is not considered a local tax revenue.

Here we present the main local tax sources, namely property tax, personal income tax, sales tax and business tax.

Property tax

In general, a property tax is considered a good local tax because the base is immobile, the tax is visible, information required is likely to be available locally, and the yield is considered relatively stable and predictable. However, contrary to conventional wisdom, property taxes are often difficult and costly to administer well (and especially in developing countries where the technical capacity to identify, record, value, assess, collect and enforce is weak), are often politically and electorally unpopular, require regular and visible tax increases due to its inelastic nature (of property values with respect to GDP), and even with these politically difficult increases, produce revenues that are surprisingly low. Property tax in its broadest sense can take various forms, namely a tax on the area or value (assessed or market, capital or rental) of residential or commercial/industrial property, a tax on agricultural land and buildings, a tax on property transactions (in the form of stamp duty, for example), etc. Taxation of unimproved land is often advocated as it minimises any distortionary effects on economic behaviour and activity.

Local taxes on property are the most common local tax source in Europe, and in the EU. Property taxes are particularly popular in countries with a British tradition, including the UK, Ireland, USA, Canada and Australia. This is partly due to traditional and customary factors. In many developing countries, property taxes are less common. As already alluded to, this may be due to a number of reasons, including weak administrative capacity, unclear property rights, absent or insufficient cadastres, difficulty in valuing properties and in revaluations, etc. In sum, property tax is probably a useful and even necessary, but not sufficient, source of local government revenue to finance desirable and adequate local public services.

Personal income tax

Given the role that central government plays with respect to macroeconomic stabilisation and income distribution, personal income taxes, known worldwide for their potential yield, buoyancy and progressivity, are normally not assigned to local government. However, in countries where social services and welfare are the responsibility of local governments, local councils rely on local personal income taxes, either in the form of a locally administered tax, or more likely, a surtax on the national or regional personal income tax. In general, local income taxes are levied at a flat, locally established rate on the same tax base as the national income tax (or, alternatively, on the national tax liability), on the jurisdiction of residence (or, alternatively, of employment) and are usually collected by the central government. The most lucrative local tax source across Europe is sharing or surcharging of individual income tax. In Scandinavian countries where municipalities rely heavily on local income taxes, the local personal income tax is a big revenue raiser, accounts for most of local revenues and can yield revenues up to 15 per cent of GDP. Municipal individual income taxes are also common in other federal-type European countries, including Belgium, Italy and Switzerland.

Sales tax

Local sales taxes are general consumption taxes imposed at the point of sale for certain goods and services. The advantage of a sales tax is the potentially large proceeds of an elastic revenue source. However, its drawbacks include its regressive nature, the loss of substantial revenues to central government (and subsequent loss of macroeconomic control), market distortions arising from interjurisdictional trade, and high administrative costs. The most common sales taxes are retail sales taxes and general sales taxes. The former, once favoured as a regional tax and still common in US states, is still levied as local retail sales taxes in some European countries. As for the latter, the type of general sales tax most commonly used is the Value Added Tax (VAT). Whether levied on an origin basis or a destination basis, most tax analysts consider independent subnational VAT systems to be problematic, and not conducive to a good local tax, for reasons outlined above (i.e. primarily its distortionary impact on cross-border trade). Brazil's ICMS and the Province of Quebec's TVQ are two examples of subnational VATs.

Business tax

Although the case for local business taxation is simply as a form of generalised benefit tax, it is often levied out of convenience or necessity, as an elastic revenue mobilisation instrument, an alternative to user charges on specific public services benefitting specific businesses, or, because

Table 33.2 Local taxes and user charges

Criterion	User charges	Property tax	Personal income tax	Sales tax	Business tax
Revenue adequacy	Yes, for some activities; not in general	Yes, for local government	Unlikely	Yes	Not likely
Revenue buoyancy	No	Not much	Yes	Yes	May be adequate
Correspondence of payers and beneficiaries	Excellent if well designed	Fair if properly done	Not high	Depends on mobility	Depends on design
Local accountability	Excellent	Low	Low (depends on rate discretion)	May be adequate	Usually low
Administrative cost	Sometimes high	Fairly high	Reasonable if imposed as a regional surcharge	Moderate	Sometimes high

(continued)

Table 33.2 (continued)

Criterion	User charges	Property tax	Personal income tax	Sales tax	Business tax
Compliance costs	Irrelevant, in principle	Vary, but not high	Medium	Moderate	Often high
Latitude for corruption	Low	Moderate	Probably high in most countries	Moderate	High
Political acceptability	Not high in most countries	Moderate	Low	Perhaps	High
Distortionary impact	None	Moderate	Moderate	Moderate	Usually high
Progressivity	Irrelevant	Possibly	Largely unknown	No	Usually unknown
Reduces regional disparities	May do so to some extent	No	No	No	No

Source: Adapted from Bird (2006)

of the unclear incidence of tax, as a way of tax exporting by shifting the tax burden on to non-residents. It is also the case that local business taxes are often buoyant and relatively easy to collect. Despite the theoretical arguments against business taxes, in general, and subnational business taxes, in particular, governments all over the world impose local business taxes. Local business taxes are an important source of income in many Central European countries, including Germany, Italy and Hungary. The tax base varies, and can be in the form of corporate or enterprise income, payroll, trade, value added, turnover, etc., can be stock or flow based, and broadly based or narrowly based. Given the popularity of local business taxes, the challenge for local policymakers is to design local business taxes in a way that distorts economic activity the least, while at the same time and in conjunction with other local revenues, raise enough income to pay for essential local services.

Adapted from Bird (2006), Table 33.2 outlines the different non-grant local revenue sources, based on well-established criteria or principles of local public finance.

Local government revenues in EU member states, 2000–2014

Table 33.3 shows that there is wide variation in the size of local government current revenues as a share of GDP across the EU. In 2014 the values ranged from under 1 per cent of GDP in Malta to over 30 per cent of GDP in Denmark. Eight countries had local government current revenues in excess of 10 per cent of GDP. Three Nordic nations (Denmark, Finland and Sweden) have consistently had the largest current revenues, typically over 17 per cent of GDP during the period 2000–2014. Of these countries, Denmark's local government current revenues are by far the largest at between 30–37 per cent of GDP. The smallest current revenues are found in the Mediterranean countries of Malta, Cyprus and Greece, with values typically under 3 per cent of GDP. The four federal or quasi-federal countries (Austria, Belgium, Germany and Spain) have current revenues in the range of 6–9 per cent of GDP during 2013–2014. It is to be expected that local government current revenues are below average in these four countries, due to their sizeable tier of government at the state or provincial level.

Over the time period 2000–2014 local government current revenues as a share of GDP increased in 21 of the 28 countries. The largest increase as measured in percentage points of GDP was in Denmark, where current revenues rose from 30.7 per cent to 36.6 per cent of GDP.

Table 33.3 Local government current revenue as a share of GDP, 2000–2014

	2000	2001	2002	2003	2004	2005	2006	2007	2008	2009	2010	2011	2012	2013	2014
Austria	8.0	8.0	8.0	7.9	7.8	7.7	7.5	7.5	7.7	8.2	8.1	8.0	8.2	8.4	8.5
Belgium	5.9	6.1	6.4	6.8	6.5	6.6	6.6	6.7	6.6	7.2	6.9	6.9	6.9	7.1	7.1
Bulgaria	7.5	6.4	7.5	6.3	6.7	6.6	6.5	6.2	6.7	7.4	7.3	6.7	6.9	8.3	8.9
Croatia	4.5	4.7	4.2	4.2	4.3	4.4	4.5	4.7	4.8	4.8	4.5	4.3	4.4	4.7	4.7
Cyprus	1.2	1.2	1.1	1.2	1.4	1.5	1.6	1.6	1.4	1.5	1.6	1.6	1.4	1.7	1.6
Czech Rep.	7.0	7.0	7.8	9.5	8.9	9.3	9.1	8.8	9.0	8.9	9.2	8.9	8.3	8.7	8.6
Denmark	30.7	31.5	31.9	33.4	33.4	32.7	32.1	31.2	32.0	35.4	35.8	35.9	36.4	36.6	NA
Estonia	7.6	8.8	9.1	8.9	8.7	8.8	8.6	8.6	9.7	10.7	9.8	9.3	9.0	9.1	NA
Finland	17.4	17.1	17.9	18.0	18.1	18.3	18.8	18.7	19.6	21.6	22.1	22.0	22.3	23.0	23.0
France	9.3	9.1	9.4	9.7	9.9	10.1	10.2	10.2	10.2	10.9	10.9	11.0	11.1	11.1	11.1
Germany	6.8	6.5	6.4	6.3	6.4	6.7	6.9	7.0	7.1	7.2	7.1	7.2	7.4	7.4	7.5
Greece	2.7	2.8	2.8	2.3	2.4	2.6	2.6	2.6	2.7	3.1	2.9	2.9	2.9	3.4	3.1
Hungary	10.7	10.7	10.9	11.8	11.6	11.4	11.0	10.7	10.8	11.2	11.2	11.0	9.3	7.7	7.5
Ireland	10.0	10.5	11.1	11.7	11.8	4.6	4.7	4.6	4.6	4.3	3.8	3.6	3.5	3.3	3.0
Italy	12.5	12.9	12.8	12.7	13.3	13.5	13.2	13.4	14.0	15.2	14.6	14.1	14.3	14.1	14.3
Latvia	9.1	8.7	9.1	8.7	9.2	8.6	9.2	9.5	10.4	10.3	10.7	9.6	9.0	8.8	9.3
Lithuania	9.0	9.6	8.8	8.3	8.5	7.8	7.6	6.7	7.6	9.1	9.4	8.1	7.6	7.1	7.3
Luxembourg	5.2	5.3	5.5	5.5	5.1	4.8	4.7	5.0	5.1	5.2	5.1	5.1	5.1	5.1	4.9
Malta	0.8	0.8	0.7	0.6	0.7	0.6	0.6	0.6	0.5	0.6	0.7	0.7	0.7	0.7	0.7
Netherlands	14.0	13.9	14.2	14.8	14.3	13.9	13.6	13.6	13.7	14.8	14.6	14.4	14.2	13.5	13.2
Poland	13.9	14.5	14.8	11.3	12.1	12.3	12.6	12.6	13.2	12.9	12.9	12.3	12.1	12.2	13.1
Portugal	4.7	4.9	5.1	5.0	5.2	5.2	5.5	5.6	5.3	5.5	5.2	5.2	5.2	5.6	5.7
Romania	4.3	6.3	6.2	6.7	6.6	7.0	8.6	9.1	8.6	9.0	9.2	9.1	8.8	8.9	8.5
Slovakia	2.3	2.5	4.9	7.1	7.0	6.1	5.7	5.3	5.5	6.0	5.5	5.6	5.6	6.1	6.2
Slovenia	8.1	8.2	8.1	8.2	8.2	8.2	8.1	7.8	7.8	8.6	9.0	8.9	9.0	9.0	8.6
Spain	5.5	5.4	5.3	5.3	5.3	5.4	5.7	5.7	5.5	5.6	5.5	5.6	5.9	6.2	6.2
Sweden	22.5	22.8	23.1	23.4	23.1	23.5	23.1	23.0	23.5	24.7	24.1	23.9	24.6	24.9	24.6
UK	9.8	10.4	10.6	11.0	11.1	11.2	11.6	11.4	11.6	12.4	12.3	11.5	11.4	10.7	10.5

Source: IMF Government Finance Statistics (www.imf.org/en/Data), with authors' calculations

Note: 2014 data missing for Denmark and Estonia. The 2000–2004 data for Ireland are distorted by the inclusion of intergovernmental grant amounts from central to local government to cover healthcare expenditure. This explains the ratios for the period 2000–2004 in Tables 33.3–33.7, and ending in 2005 with the abolition of the regional health boards and the establishment of the national Health Service Executive.

The second largest increase was in Finland, where current revenues grew by over 5 percentage points, from 17.4 per cent to 23 per cent of GDP. Measured instead as the percentage change in the current revenue ratio, the largest growth was in Slovakia (+265 per cent), followed by Romania (+199 per cent). In the other seven countries, the current revenue ratio fell, although most of the falls were relatively small.

In 12 countries the current revenue ratio peaked in 2008, 2009 or 2010, and decreased between then and 2014. This may be a sign of austerity in public spending during and after the financial crisis. The picture is mixed, however, as nine other countries experienced growth in the current revenue ratio during the same period, with their peaks occurring in 2013 or 2014.

Table 33.4 shows the size of local government current revenues as a share of general government revenues. This figure can be considered as an indicator of the size of the local government sector in each country. Again, there is large variation in this ratio across the EU. In 2013–2014 the values ranged from under 2 per cent in Malta to over 65 per cent in Denmark. Nine countries had ratios in excess of 25 per cent. Again, the three Nordic nations have consistently had the largest ratios, typically between 32–65 per cent during the period 2000–2014. Of these countries, Denmark has always had by far the largest local government sector, with current revenues ranging between 56–66 per cent of general government revenues. Following closely behind these three countries are Poland, the Netherlands and Italy, with ratios in the range typically 30–34 per cent, and the UK, Latvia and Romania, with ratios between 25–29 per cent. The smallest local governments as measured by this ratio are found in Malta, Cyprus and Greece, with ratios under 7 per cent. The four federal or quasi-federal countries have ratios in the range of 13–17 per cent during 2013–2014. Again, these are below average due to the existence of state or provincial governments with significant expenditure and revenue responsibilities.

Over the time period 2000–2014 local government current revenues as a share of general government revenues increased in 20 of the 28 countries. This may be a sign of more decentralisation of government functions. The largest increase was in Slovakia, where the ratio more than doubled, rising from 6 per cent to over 15 per cent. This was followed by Romania, where the ratio doubled, from 12.6 per cent to over 25 per cent. Sweden and Finland, which both had larger than average ratios in the year 2000, saw substantial increases of about 10 percentage points, taking them to 50 per cent and 42 per cent respectively. In the other eight countries, the falls in the ratio were mostly modest, with the exception of Hungary where the ratio fell from 24 per cent to under 16 per cent.[6]

We now consider our three main sources of revenue income, namely taxes, grants and user charges, with the tax, grant and user charge shares of local government revenue data reported in Tables 33.5–33.7. The significance of taxes as a revenue source for local governments is shown in Table 33.5. The ratio is calculated as tax revenue as a percentage of current revenues. This ratio can be used as an indicator of the autonomy of local government, as a lower value may indicate less tax-raising capabilities.[7] Again, there is large variation in this ratio across the EU. In 2013–2014 the values ranged from 0 per cent in Malta to nearly 75 per cent in Croatia. Seven countries have ratios in excess of 50 per cent in 2014. The picture across the EU is mixed, as countries geographically close together with somewhat similar socio-economic characteristics often have very different tax ratios. For example, Latvia's ratio is between 50–60 per cent, but neighbouring Lithuania's is one of the lowest, at 5–7 per cent. Similarly, Sweden's tax ratio has been in the range 55–65 per cent, while Denmark's has been between 33–47 per cent. The lowest tax shares are found in Malta, Lithuania and Bulgaria, with tax ratios under 10 per cent in recent years. The four federal or de facto federal countries have varying tax ratios, from Austria with a below-average 15 per cent, to Spain with an above-average 50–55 per cent.

Table 33.4 Local government current revenue as a share of general government revenue, 2000–2014

	2000	2001	2002	2003	2004	2005	2006	2007	2008	2009	2010	2011	2012	2013	2014
Austria	16.6	15.8	16.3	16.1	16.1	15.9	15.8	15.7	16.0	16.8	16.8	16.7	16.7	16.8	17.0
Belgium	12.0	12.4	12.9	13.8	13.4	13.4	13.7	13.8	13.5	14.7	14.1	13.8	13.4	13.5	13.6
Bulgaria	18.5	15.5	19.6	16.4	16.8	17.5	18.4	16.2	17.3	20.9	21.8	20.8	20.2	22.5	24.6
Croatia	NA	NA	10.8	10.9	11.1	11.6	11.9	12.0	12.3	12.4	12.0	11.6	11.7	12.3	11.7
Cyprus	3.4	3.3	3.2	3.3	3.7	3.6	3.8	3.4	3.5	4.2	4.4	4.4	3.9	4.6	4.0
Czech Rep.	19.9	19.6	22.8	26.5	25.2	25.8	25.7	24.5	24.8	25.9	26.0	25.4	22.7	23.1	23.6
Denmark	56.2	58.3	60.0	62.3	60.6	58.2	58.6	57.2	59.6	65.5	65.8	65.6	66.1	65.3	NA
Estonia	20.9	25.2	25.0	24.1	23.7	25.0	23.5	22.8	25.9	23.7	24.1	23.8	22.9	23.8	NA
Finland	31.8	32.6	33.9	34.7	35.0	35.4	36.0	36.0	37.4	41.4	42.4	41.2	41.2	41.9	42.0
France	18.6	18.2	19.2	19.7	20.3	20.2	20.3	20.5	20.6	22.0	22.0	21.6	21.3	20.9	20.8
Germany	14.9	14.8	14.8	14.5	15.1	15.7	16.0	16.4	16.4	16.3	16.4	16.4	16.6	16.7	16.7
Greece	6.5	6.8	7.0	6.1	6.3	6.6	6.6	6.4	6.7	8.0	7.1	6.7	6.3	6.9	6.6
Hungary	24.2	24.8	26.0	28.0	27.4	27.4	26.0	23.8	23.9	24.3	24.8	24.8	20.1	16.4	15.7
Ireland	28.0	31.4	33.9	34.8	34.2	13.1	12.9	12.8	13.2	12.8	11.6	10.9	10.3	9.7	9.0
Italy	28.3	29.4	29.4	29.1	30.8	31.4	30.1	29.5	31.0	33.1	32.0	30.8	30.0	29.4	29.6
Latvia	26.1	26.3	27.6	27.3	27.5	25.4	25.9	28.5	31.6	29.9	30.0	26.9	25.2	25.1	26.0
Lithuania	24.7	28.6	26.3	25.6	26.0	23.1	22.4	19.5	21.8	25.4	26.4	24.3	23.2	21.5	21.2
Luxembourg	12.7	12.4	13.1	13.0	12.5	11.3	11.6	11.9	12.2	11.9	11.7	11.7	11.4	11.2	10.9
Malta	2.1	2.1	1.9	1.6	1.7	1.5	1.5	1.4	1.4	1.7	1.8	1.7	1.9	1.7	1.6
Netherlands	32.0	32.6	33.9	35.4	34.0	33.1	31.4	32.0	31.2	34.6	33.8	33.7	32.9	30.6	30.1
Poland	NA	35.5	37.2	28.6	31.4	31.0	31.3	31.3	33.0	34.0	33.4	31.2	31.0	31.8	33.7
Portugal	12.1	12.8	12.8	12.5	13.1	13.2	13.6	13.7	13.0	13.9	13.1	12.5	12.4	12.6	13.0
Romania	12.6	19.2	18.7	20.8	20.5	21.6	25.9	25.5	25.4	28.0	27.7	26.7	26.1	26.6	25.3
Slovakia	6.2	7.0	13.6	18.9	19.2	17.4	16.7	16.4	16.6	18.1	17.3	17.0	17.0	16.0	15.2
Slovenia	19.0	19.0	18.7	19.0	18.9	18.8	18.9	18.5	18.5	20.2	20.6	20.5	20.2	19.8	19.2
Spain	14.7	14.3	14.2	14.1	13.9	13.8	14.3	14.2	15.3	16.4	15.5	15.9	16.3	16.7	16.7
Sweden	40.2	42.6	44.6	44.9	44.2	44.0	43.9	44.2	45.9	48.1	48.2	48.3	49.5	49.9	50.4
UK	25.1	26.1	27.9	29.0	28.7	28.5	29.0	28.5	28.0	31.8	31.6	29.3	29.4	26.9	27.1

Source: IMF Government Finance Statistics (www.imf.org/en/Data), with authors' calculations

Note: General government revenue data missing for Croatia (2000, 2001), Denmark (2014), Estonia (2014) and Poland (2000).

Table 33.5 Local government tax revenue as a share of local government current revenue, 2000–2014

	2000	2001	2002	2003	2004	2005	2006	2007	2008	2009	2010	2011	2012	2013	2014
Austria	17.3	15.7	15.4	15.6	15.7	15.5	15.7	15.7	15.4	14.9	15.1	15.1	15.1	15.1	14.9
Belgium	30.7	32.1	32.9	32.5	32.6	32.3	32.2	33.2	29.7	32.4	31.5	31.7	30.1	30.2	29.9
Bulgaria	41.9	52.2	42.2	7.5	7.4	8.1	10.7	13.1	13.5	10.2	10.4	11.5	11.5	10.1	9.6
Croatia	60.8	56.6	61.6	60.6	61.5	58.9	62.1	60.2	60.9	62.3	59.7	61.5	64.1	74.0	74.5
Cyprus	36.8	39.8	35.5	34.9	33.1	29.8	31.6	33.9	34.8	29.8	28.1	28.3	29.0	33.6	30.8
Czech Rep.	60.5	52.1	52.3	44.8	47.5	53.1	52.1	53.1	54.1	49.1	49.4	50.0	54.4	56.2	56.8
Denmark	47.1	47.5	47.0	45.5	44.4	44.7	44.6	35.3	34.7	32.8	33.8	33.7	33.5	34.2	NA
Estonia	56.9	46.1	44.2	44.9	46.4	45.2	47.1	49.8	50.3	47.2	45.3	45.7	46.4	46.2	NA
Finland	56.7	55.9	51.9	49.5	48.1	47.4	47.1	47.2	46.1	44.9	44.8	44.3	43.5	44.3	44.7
France	44.7	44.1	42.4	42.2	44.3	46.2	46.2	47.5	47.3	47.3	38.3	48.7	49.7	49.6	50.4
Germany	40.2	38.9	38.1	38.3	40.1	40.1	42.1	42.2	42.9	39.3	39.2	40.2	40.5	40.4	40.1
Greece	25.0	24.4	24.1	28.3	27.8	27.0	26.5	27.2	26.8	22.5	25.6	26.7	29.4	27.5	28.6
Hungary	35.7	36.8	36.1	36.2	38.3	37.1	38.9	40.9	23.6	23.4	21.6	21.8	25.9	29.1	29.1
Ireland	5.4	5.1	4.9	4.9	4.7	13.2	12.1	13.5	14.7	18.3	20.6	21.4	24.2	23.7	23.5
Italy	46.1	46.1	47.2	50.0	46.1	45.4	46.8	48.8	45.8	39.0	41.3	43.2	46.1	45.9	46.1
Latvia	54.7	56.8	52.6	55.6	52.8	54.3	53.0	53.3	50.4	48.6	53.1	56.8	60.1	60.5	60.7
Lithuania	6.8	5.9	7.3	5.8	5.8	5.5	5.3	5.3	4.8	5.4	5.3	5.5	5.7	6.1	6.4
Luxembourg	41.1	41.0	42.1	41.6	35.5	35.7	33.8	33.4	32.8	33.9	32.7	34.4	30.3	27.3	26.2
Malta	0.0	0.0	0.0	0.0	0.0	0.0	0.0	0.0	0.0	0.0	0.0	0.0	0.0	0.0	0.0
Netherlands	9.2	9.2	9.3	9.3	9.9	10.3	8.9	8.8	8.9	8.9	9.1	9.4	9.8	10.3	10.6
Poland	17.9	18.0	22.0	27.4	33.5	33.5	34.0	36.8	35.3	32.5	31.1	32.4	33.6	34.1	32.9
Portugal	42.0	38.2	38.8	37.2	38.9	39.1	37.9	40.2	42.2	38.3	38.8	40.2	40.6	42.0	43.3
Romania	27.8	17.4	14.1	14.5	13.9	12.5	11.3	12.7	10.5	10.5	11.5	11.8	11.5	11.4	11.7
Slovakia	57.7	55.3	30.8	21.6	20.4	54.2	56.2	57.5	59.9	56.0	50.3	54.5	54.4	50.4	51.2
Slovenia	33.0	33.3	34.1	34.6	34.7	34.0	35.7	43.0	41.4	42.7	44.7	44.4	45.4	44.9	45.2
Spain	54.4	54.0	53.5	52.4	53.3	54.2	53.0	52.4	50.4	47.8	51.7	51.0	50.8	51.7	52.8
Sweden	62.8	63.5	63.7	64.4	64.9	63.6	63.5	59.5	59.8	57.5	55.0	54.8	55.0	55.0	54.3
UK	14.1	13.9	14.1	14.3	14.4	14.3	13.7	14.0	14.0	13.8	13.6	14.2	14.2	15.2	15.2

Source: IMF Government Finance Statistics (www.imf.org/en/Data), with authors' calculations

Note: 2014 data missing for Denmark and Estonia.

During the period 2000–2014, a majority of countries experienced a fall in the tax share of local government revenue. The ratio decreased in 17 countries, and increased in 10 countries. Many of the changes were reasonably small, although the ratio fell by more than 10 percentage points in Romania (–16.1), Denmark (–12.9), Finland (–12.0) and Estonia (–10.7). In 2003 in Bulgaria there were changes to revenue assignment which meant that local income taxes dropped to zero, causing the tax ratio to fall sharply.

Grant transfers as a revenue source for local governments is shown in Table 33.6. The ratio is calculated as current grants from other general government units as a percentage of current revenues. Using IMF data, it excludes capital grants, grants from other countries, and grants from international organisations. This ratio is often used as a measure of the dependence of the local government on higher levels of government. As with the tax ratio, there is large variation in this ratio across the EU, from about 10 per cent in Croatia to over 80 per cent in Lithuania. Countries that have low tax ratios tend to have higher grant ratios. In 2014, there were 10 countries with grant ratios in excess of 50 per cent, indicating large dependence on intergovernmental grants for revenue. The four federal or de-facto federal countries have varying grant ratios, from Germany and Spain with 33 per cent to Austria at nearly 62 per cent, in 2014.

During the period 2000–2014, the general trend was that dependence on grants increased. In eight countries the grant ratio increased by more than 10 percentage points. The four largest increases were in Bulgaria (+42.6), Cyprus (+22.1), Romania (+21.4) and Slovakia (+16.3). The large change in Bulgaria was related to the change in revenue assignment discussed above. The grant ratio fell in seven of the EU countries, and most of the decreases were small. Tax decentralisation has not followed the increasing expenditure decentralisation happening across the EU, so dependence on transfer grants has increased.

The third main revenue source for local governments is user charges and fees, also known as revenue from sales of goods and services. Table 33.7 shows the user charges ratio, calculated as revenue from sales of goods and services as a percentage of current revenues. This ratio varies from about 5 per cent in Denmark, Lithuania and Romania to nearly 30 per cent in Cyprus and Ireland. In 2013–2014, there were four countries with user charges ratios in excess of 20 per cent, while 10 countries had ratios less than 10 per cent, indicating, yet again, the large cross-country variation in local public finance. No particular pattern is evident, with countries like Denmark and Sweden, as well as very different countries such as Malta and Romania all having below-average user charges ratios.

During the period 2000–2014, there was no particular trend, with about half the countries experiencing an increasing reliance on user charges and fees, while the other half saw a fall in the user charges ratio. The change in the ratio was greater than 10 percentage points in three countries: Croatia (–15.8), Cyprus (–13.5) and Ireland (+17.8). Most of the other changes were small.

Given the severity of the 2008–2009 recession, the slow recovery since then, and ongoing fiscal austerity, it might be expected that local governments would increase user charges and fees to improve their budgetary positions. However, the evidence is mixed, as 14 countries did witness an increase in their user charges ratio between 2007 and 2014, with an average increase of 2.6 percentage points. In contrast, local governments in the other 14 countries became less reliant on user charges and fees, with an average reduction of 1.7 percentage points. Again, this is evidence of one of local governments' stylised facts worldwide, namely, large cross-country variation in local government funding.

Table 33.6 Local government grant revenue as a share of local government current revenue, 2000–2014

	2000	2001	2002	2003	2004	2005	2006	2007	2008	2009	2010	2011	2012	2013	2014
Austria	58.4	56.5	54.8	50.9	57.3	56.7	58.9	59.2	61.1	59.9	61.2	62.5	63.2	62.8	61.8
Belgium	42.7	41.6	42.3	43.6	44.3	45.1	44.4	43.8	46.2	44.1	44.7	44.2	44.9	45.7	45.4
Bulgaria	7.9	32.7	41.1	68.4	67.4	51.7	65.6	65.8	66.0	62.3	63.6	57.4	57.9	48.3	50.5
Croatia	NA	NA	12.2	12.7	12.3	12.9	11.0	12.2	11.1	11.6	13.3	11.7	10.0	10.8	10.9
Cyprus	17.0	18.4	18.1	20.9	33.9	39.0	36.5	33.0	33.7	42.2	46.0	47.5	43.7	38.9	39.1
Czech Rep.	19.2	31.1	32.8	43.0	41.2	33.9	35.0	33.8	33.3	37.1	36.5	36.9	31.4	30.0	29.7
Denmark	43.7	43.5	44.0	45.3	46.1	46.1	46.1	55.6	56.2	58.6	58.2	58.4	58.7	57.9	NA
Estonia	33.7	44.3	42.8	41.8	41.7	41.0	38.0	37.4	37.1	36.7	37.7	36.5	35.0	34.7	NA
Finland	21.2	22.0	26.0	27.2	28.1	28.4	28.9	28.5	29.0	29.8	29.8	30.1	30.5	29.9	29.4
France	22.3	24.6	27.0	27.1	27.2	25.7	25.2	24.6	23.9	24.2	38.4	26.4	25.6	25.4	24.8
Germany	28.9	29.0	29.3	28.7	28.0	30.1	28.9	29.5	29.6	31.7	30.6	30.4	30.9	32.3	33.2
Greece	61.6	63.1	63.7	57.0	58.8	60.3	61.5	60.4	60.7	64.7	59.2	63.1	54.3	58.6	58.0
Hungary	45.6	44.7	46.9	48.9	46.1	47.1	44.2	41.9	60.2	57.5	57.0	54.7	50.4	39.6	39.1
Ireland	71.2	73.6	72.4	71.1	71.3	38.5	36.8	33.2	32.8	39.3	40.6	39.8	36.9	37.3	37.6
Italy	36.1	37.3	36.0	33.6	37.8	39.3	38.6	36.5	39.8	46.9	43.9	41.1	38.2	36.9	37.4
Latvia	26.1	27.2	30.1	29.7	27.2	25.9	26.4	31.9	36.0	38.0	36.1	31.5	29.1	27.8	29.4
Lithuania	87.4	81.9	83.4	89.7	83.4	82.9	85.6	87.1	87.3	87.3	85.6	86.3	86.9	86.5	86.0
Luxembourg	37.2	36.5	36.2	36.5	41.6	39.9	43.2	41.5	43.1	43.4	44.5	45.1	47.9	50.6	50.9
Malta	74.7	77.3	79.4	83.2	75.1	77.0	75.0	73.9	75.4	74.1	71.7	69.2	63.5	67.9	63.4
Netherlands	64.9	66.1	67.3	67.8	66.0	65.9	67.1	67.6	68.2	69.5	69.9	70.1	69.9	69.0	69.0
Poland	NA	38.6	36.7	52.4	47.6	49.2	50.1	49.6	49.5	52.0	52.8	52.4	51.3	51.3	46.6
Portugal	21.5	20.9	23.6	24.2	24.4	23.3	22.9	20.5	21.5	23.7	24.8	24.2	23.8	25.8	23.7
Romania	57.6	68.8	76.0	76.2	76.2	79.1	78.1	77.7	81.6	78.1	73.8	69.8	72.0	70.4	79.0
Slovakia	10.4	11.5	NA	NA	NA	29.8	29.5	29.9	27.6	31.7	33.7	29.5	28.9	27.3	26.7
Slovenia	41.1	40.7	40.9	42.2	44.1	45.9	44.3	36.4	36.0	37.2	34.9	35.2	33.7	33.7	33.8
Spain	31.2	31.3	31.1	32.6	32.2	30.9	32.2	32.0	34.0	36.1	32.3	32.9	33.0	33.3	32.6
Sweden	20.5	19.8	19.8	19.4	18.7	20.6	20.9	24.6	24.1	26.8	29.7	29.6	28.5	28.9	30.6
UK	65.7	66.4	66.7	67.4	68.1	68.1	67.7	67.1	66.9	67.9	68.9	68.3	68.3	66.6	66.1

Source: IMF Government Finance Statistics (www.imf.org/en/Data), with authors' calculations

Note: 2014 data missing for Denmark and Estonia. Current grants data missing for Croatia (2000, 2001), Poland (2000) and Slovakia (2002–2004).

Table 33.7 Local government user charges revenue as a share of local government current revenue, 2000–2014

	2000	2001	2002	2003	2004	2005	2006	2007	2008	2009	2010	2011	2012	2013	2014
Austria	14.9	14.6	15.1	15.6	15.8	15.9	15.9	15.7	15.2	15.5	15.7	15.6	15.5	15.4	15.4
Belgium	10.0	9.7	9.7	9.4	10.1	10.2	9.5	9.4	9.6	10.6	10.9	11.1	11.3	11.3	12.0
Bulgaria	8.3	5.7	8.2	9.1	12.9	36.3	6.3	9.3	8.4	10.6	9.0	10.7	8.6	6.8	7.3
Croatia	22.6	25.3	17.7	17.4	17.3	19.1	16.6	17.3	18.1	17.9	18.5	18.8	17.1	6.2	6.8
Cyprus	42.7	39.3	43.9	41.4	30.3	29.6	27.9	28.1	29.1	26.7	24.7	23.1	27.3	27.5	29.2
Czech Rep.	11.2	8.7	6.9	5.2	5.0	6.7	6.6	6.8	6.5	6.8	6.7	6.8	7.6	7.5	7.2
Denmark	6.0	6.0	5.9	5.8	5.9	6.0	5.8	5.5	5.5	5.5	5.3	5.1	5.0	4.9	NA
Estonia	7.8	6.7	8.7	9.2	9.2	9.3	9.2	8.6	8.7	9.3	9.4	9.2	9.6	10.0	NA
Finland	18.5	18.5	18.8	20.0	20.4	20.8	20.7	20.8	21.4	22.1	22.5	22.7	23.2	23.1	23.2
France	16.3	15.9	15.6	15.6	15.7	15.6	15.8	15.8	15.8	15.9	15.9	16.1	16.1	16.3	16.4
Germany	20.7	21.0	21.1	21.7	20.9	20.2	19.7	19.1	18.7	19.6	20.8	20.0	19.7	19.0	18.5
Greece	7.4	7.1	6.6	8.0	7.5	7.6	7.1	7.0	7.1	8.7	10.6	6.1	10.9	10.3	9.9
Hungary	12.1	11.2	10.8	9.9	10.5	10.2	10.3	10.5	9.8	9.7	9.8	9.2	9.3	12.3	9.9
Ireland	11.2	10.5	10.7	11.0	11.7	22.7	21.6	19.9	22.7	23.3	24.7	25.4	26.2	27.2	29.0
Italy	12.5	11.7	11.8	11.5	10.8	10.6	10.0	9.9	9.8	9.7	10.4	10.9	11.2	12.3	12.0
Latvia	6.4	7.8	8.0	8.1	12.4	12.1	11.7	8.9	9.2	10.7	8.8	9.9	9.4	9.6	8.6
Lithuania	4.3	2.5	2.5	2.5	3.2	5.8	3.1	3.3	3.3	3.5	5.1	3.8	4.2	4.7	4.9
Luxembourg	19.5	19.8	19.5	19.9	21.1	22.4	20.9	22.0	20.7	20.8	20.9	18.7	20.2	20.7	21.5
Malta	1.3	2.0	3.5	2.2	3.7	5.9	5.1	6.4	6.7	6.8	7.5	6.1	5.9	5.3	4.0
Netherlands	16.1	15.5	15.0	15.1	15.8	15.9	16.2	15.7	15.3	14.7	14.5	14.2	14.3	14.7	14.7
Poland	16.0	14.6	13.5	16.3	15.1	11.4	10.9	9.1	10.9	11.0	10.8	10.5	10.1	9.7	9.3
Portugal	23.3	21.9	20.0	21.6	18.8	21.8	19.1	19.0	17.9	18.1	18.5	17.9	17.7	16.3	15.7
Romania	7.9	6.3	7.0	6.4	6.4	5.3	3.2	4.5	4.7	5.2	5.5	6.0	4.8	5.9	3.9
Slovakia	11.8	10.3	6.8	15.8	14.4	10.0	8.7	7.6	8.8	8.8	9.6	9.5	11.3	16.3	14.7
Slovenia	15.8	14.9	15.7	15.2	14.4	14.2	14.0	13.5	14.0	13.5	16.0	16.2	17.2	17.1	17.2
Spain	8.7	8.5	9.1	9.0	8.8	9.1	8.9	9.0	9.2	10.1	10.7	10.9	11.1	10.6	10.3
Sweden	11.5	11.6	11.2	10.9	11.1	10.6	10.5	10.3	10.2	10.2	9.9	9.7	9.6	9.5	9.5
UK	12.7	13.4	13.8	13.5	13.2	13.4	14.6	14.4	14.1	14.1	13.7	13.5	13.2	13.7	13.9

Source: IMF Government Finance Statistics (www.imf.org/en/Data), with authors' calculations

Note: 2014 data missing for Denmark and Estonia.

Contemporary policy issues and future challenges

In the context of local government financing, we now discuss some issues that confront all local governments in the twenty-first century, while at the same time, provide the local government academic community with interesting research questions, namely the degree of local autonomy, funding reforms, fiscal rules and subnational fiscal policy.

Fiscal decentralisation and local autonomy

Local autonomy, defined broadly as the power of initiation and immunity, is highly valued in any system of local government (Clark 1984). However specifically defined, measuring and comparing local autonomy is not an easy task. A recent index of local autonomy was developed by Ladner et al. (2015). Using the lowest local administrative units (LAU) of a country as the unit of analysis, the methodology is based on 11 variables, including fiscal autonomy, financial transfer system and financial self-reliance. The 2014 results for these variables and the overall local autonomy index for the 28 EU member states are reported in Table 33.8.

Table 33.8 Local autonomy index, 2014

Country	Fiscal autonomy	Financial transfer system	Financial self-reliance	Local autonomy index
Defined as	the extent to which local government can independently tax its population; on a scale of 0–4	the proportion of unconditional financial transfers to total financial transfers received by the local government; on a scale of 0–3	the proportion of local government revenues derived from own/local sources (taxes, fees, charges); on a scale of 0–3	local autonomy, the aggregate of 11 variables; on a scale of 0–37
Austria	3.00	2.00	1.94	25.17
Belgium	2.00	1.22	3.00	21.79
Bulgaria	1.00	0.00	2.00	23.50
Croatia	1.00	1.71	2.29	20.70
Cyprus	2.00	1.31	2.65	15.73
Czech Republic	1.00	2.00	1.00	24.67
Denmark	3.00	3.00	2.00	27.00
Estonia	1.00	0.00	1.00	23.00
Finland	3.00	3.00	3.00	29.33
France	2.00	3.00	3.00	25.64
Germany	4.00	1.98	1.85	27.50
Greece	1.00	2.00	2.00	19.00
Hungary	1.00	0.00	1.00	17.33
Ireland	2.00	0.00	3.00	12.67
Italy	2.00	2.00	3.00	25.50
Latvia	1.00	2.00	0.00	20.33
Lithuania	1.00	1.00	1.00	23.67
Luxembourg	3.00	3.00	2.00	22.17
Malta	0.00	3.00	2.00	17.67
Netherlands	2.00	2.00	1.00	21.67
Poland	2.00	2.00	2.00	26.71

Portugal	2.00	3.00	2.00	24.33
Romania	2.00	1.00	1.00	20.00
Slovakia	2.00	0.00	2.00	22.00
Slovenia	1.00	0.00	0.00	17.34
Spain	2.00	2.00	3.00	22.06
Sweden	3.00	3.00	3.00	28.67
UK	2.00	1.89	1.00	17.38

Source: Adapted from Ladner et al. (2015)

As outlined by Ladner et al. (2015), the findings across countries and over time are interesting. The degree of autonomy has generally increased since the 1990s indicating greater decentralisation, as found in other studies, including the OECD fiscal decentralisation and tax autonomy indicators (Blöchliger and Nettley 2015). Second, there is large cross-country variation, which can be summarised into three broad groups, with the Nordic countries, Germany and Poland reporting the highest degree of autonomy, as against the UK and its former colonies (Ireland, Cyprus, Malta) and some, unsurprisingly, of the former socialist countries reporting the lowest degree of local autonomy.

Local government funding measures post-crisis

As might be expected given the variation in expenditure assignments and competencies in local governments throughout the EU, the picture with respect to funding options and reforms post-crisis is mixed. After years of revenue growth, the financial and fiscal crisis of the late 2000s resulted in a fall, in real terms, in local government revenues across EU member states. In some EU countries, intergovernmental grants to local governments were cut or frozen in response to the economic crisis and the austerity measures imposed by central governments. In other EU member states, grants were, at least initially, increased (albeit earmarked in many cases), to compensate for the reduction in own-source revenues. Several countries introduced temporary tax measures as a way of stabilising local tax revenue. These included increases in own-source taxes (raising the rate or broadening the base), increases in the share of taxes redistributed to local governments or changes to tax administration and collection so as to, for example, reduce tax evasion. There were also changes to user charges, both in terms of a broadening of services liable for a user fee, and increases in existing fee rates.

With cuts in government spending and local public services so as to balance the budget, fiscal policy at the local level was often pro cyclical, further exacerbating the recession. In other EU countries where the fiscal space was greater, subnational (both regional and local) budgetary policy, in the form of a stimulus package (albeit small) was counter cyclical, offsetting the worst effects of the downturn. Apart from these temporary measures, some countries introduced more structural reforms (for example, changes to tax assignment, local tax systems, grant systems and fiscal rules) aimed at sustaining local revenues and ensuring sound public finances at the local level. Overall, local governments across the EU have had to contribute to the fiscal adjustment and consolidation of the public finances of general government. In many cases, some with a time lag, this has resulted in a shrinking of local budgets, despite the post-crisis (albeit uneven and sluggish in some cases) general recovery in economic activity, and the resilience of local councils in responding to these challenges (Davey 2012; Ahrend et al. 2013; Bailey et al. 2015).

Subnational fiscal policy and fiscal rules of local governments

Related to the two issues above are rules or institutional constraints on the discretionary powers of budget policymakers. Because the vertical structure of government can lead to moral hazard and bailout expectations due to the well-known common pool and soft budget constraint problems, explicit institutional arrangements are often in place to ensure that fiscal policies at the different levels of government are mutually consistent, which, in turn, can help prevent co-ordination problems and deal with the deficit bias considered inherent in fiscal systems, and, ultimately, prevent subnational governments from overspending, under taxing and borrowing excessively. Given this, the purpose of a fiscal rule is to anchor government policy, affect economic agents' expectations, prevent fiscal imbalances, and in doing so, enhance the credibility of public policy and ensure fiscal and debt sustainability. As a commitment device to ensure fiscal discipline, local fiscal rules can take many different forms, including first or second generation, ex ante or ex post, imposed, self-imposed or negotiated, stock or flow, annual or multi-annual, constitutional or legislative, etc.

In broad terms, however, there are two types of fiscal rules. The first sets intermediate objectives that contribute to meeting the overarching fiscal policy goals. These numerical rules include setting requirements for budget balances, constraints on debt accumulation, and limits on the ability to increase spending or the tax burden. Indeed, budgets at local level throughout the EU are commonly subject to balanced budget rules or to borrowing constraints (the golden rule, for example), and, in some cases, subnational governments' power to increase spending or taxes is restricted because of tax and expenditure limits.[8] Another constraint is a no-bailout clause, enshrined in law, explicitly prohibiting upper-tier governments (federal or regional) from taking on or assuming the financial commitments of local governments. The second type of rule, often called procedural rules, is one concerned with the process of implementing objective-setting fiscal rules. These include requirements for accounting transparency, reporting and monitoring, the possible sanctions, and in certain circumstances the establishment of mechanisms that relax the stringency of objective-setting fiscal rules (OECD 2013; Eyraud and Sirera 2015).

Applying international evidence on fiscal rules to local governments throughout the EU member states, the following lessons are worth careful consideration:

- Fiscal rules are rather blunt instruments that in theory are neither necessary nor sufficient to achieve fiscal discipline. They suffer from time inconsistency. When they bind, policymakers are likely to try and evade them. Policymakers can look for loopholes, they can just ignore the rule, or they can change them. Yet fiscal rules can help to have a disciplinary effect. Most of the empirical literature focuses on the US and shows that they can affect the behaviour of subnational governments. These studies also suggest that not only the choice but also the design of constraints matters. Outside of the US, the empirical evidence of the effect of subnational constraints is more limited. However, they cannot substitute for a properly designed system of intergovernmental fiscal relations. While subnational constraints may instil some fiscal discipline, they are not a panacea.
- Fiscal rules need to be well-designed. From reviewing the theory and country practice of subnational fiscal rules, a number of important design issues emerge:

    (i) In summary there is no ideal rule or combination of rules for all countries, local governments and all situations.
    (ii) The coverage, timing, economic cycle, escape clauses, sunset provisions and rainy day funds should all be carefully considered when drafting the rules.

(iii) Rules need to be well-defined, operational, transparent and easy to monitor.
(iv) Trade-offs and side-effects of such rules need to be carefully considered and weighed up against the policy objective and the potential benefits.
(v) Fiscal data on local governments must be available, reliable, comprehensive and timely.
(vi) Importance of communicating the rules and their purpose to local citizens/taxpayers, and of course, the need for consensus (as much as possible) and political support.

- As for international cross-country experience, unduly rigid rules can be unworkable. Fiscal rules that work often rely on the strength of political commitment, monitoring by independent fiscal institutions, as well as clear and effective enforcement procedures for non-compliance. Sanctions and, if required, corrective action need to be credible, automatic, enforceable, non-discretionary and tailored to local circumstances.

Conclusion

The funding of local governments worldwide depends as much, if not more, on political, historical, institutional and cultural factors as it does on sound economic principles and local public finance theory. This is true in the new millennium, and across EU member states. Although the level and mix of local revenue sources, between user charges, grants and local taxes (and within that, between property taxes, personal income taxes, sales taxes, business taxes and other forms of local taxes), may vary as circumstances change and policy choices are debated and implemented, local governments will, despite their adaptability, resilience and record of reform, continue to struggle to adequately and effectively fund local public services, given the nature of intergovernmental fiscal relations, and more specifically, revenue assignment and intergovernmental finance.

EU cross-country local government revenues for the period under review, namely 2000–2014, confirm the large variations between the highly decentralised Northern European countries (Denmark and Sweden, in particular) and the highly centralised countries of Malta, Cyprus, Greece and Ireland. As for changes over time, the local government revenue as a percentage of GDP or general government revenue ratio increased in many countries, with the grant transfers share of current revenues witnessing the largest increase: once again evidence of the importance of intergovernmental grants in financing local government in the twenty-first century.

Notes

1 The most prominent writer in this context is probably the great political economist and philosopher John Stuart Mill. He wrote of local representative bodies, 'It is but a small portion of the public business of a country, which can be well done, or safely attempted, by the central authorities...But after subtracting from the functions performed by most European governments, those which ought not to be undertaken by public authorities at all, there still remains so great and various an aggregate of duties that, if only on the principle of division of labour, it is indispensable to share them between central and local authorities' (Mill [1861]1910: ch. XV). He went on to write, 'It is necessary, then, that in addition to the national representation, there should be municipal and provincial representations: and the two questions which remain to be resolved are, how the local representative bodies should be constituted, and what shall be the extent of their functions' (ibid.).
2 Aside from the efficiency, equity and stabilisation roles, there is also the regulatory function, which often straddles different levels of government.
3 Because of arguments relating to economies of scale, externalities or intergovernmental partnerships, other functions such as health, education, transport and environment may best be provided by regional government, or by multi levels of government, where appropriate.

4 With respect to the immobile tax base, an alternative to the conventional public economics literature is the public choice literature, best espoused by Brennan and Buchanan (1980), who argue that subnational taxes be levied on mobile factors so that inter-jurisdictional competition will restrain the size of government.
5 It is often argued that own-source revenues should ideally be sufficient to enable the richest local governments to finance from their own resources all locally provided services primarily benefiting local residents.
6 The fall in the ratio in the case of Ireland is explained in the note in Table 33.3.
7 Local government tax revenues are not necessarily a sign or guarantee of local autonomy. For more on local taxes and local autonomy, see later sections and Table 33.8.
8 Subnational fiscal rules have increased in importance in Europe over the last two decades. The number of subnational rules adopted by EU member states more than doubled between 1995 and 2012, and in most cases, they were adopted in conjunction with national fiscal rules.

References

Ahrend, R., Curto-Grau, M. and Vammalle, C. (2013) *Passing the Buck? Central and Sub-national Governments in Times of Fiscal Stress*. OECD Regional Development Working Papers, 2013/5. Paris: OECD.

Bahl, R. W. (2002) Implementable Rules of Fiscal Decentralisation. In M. G. Rao (ed.), *Development, Poverty and Fiscal Policy: Decentralisation of Institutions*, 253–277. New Delhi: Oxford University Press.

Bailey, S. J. (1999) *Local Government Economics: Principles and Practice*. Basingstoke: Macmillan.

Bailey, N., Bramley, G. and Hastings, A. (2015) Symposium Introduction: Local Responses to 'Austerity'. *Local Government Studies* 41(4): 571–581.

Bird, R. M. (2001) *Intergovernmental Fiscal Relations in Latin America: Policy Design and Policy Outcomes*. Washington, DC: Sustainable Development Department, Inter-American Development Bank.

Bird, R. M. (2006) Local and Regional Revenues: Realities and Prospects. In R. M. Bird and F. Vaillancourt (eds), *Perspectives on Fiscal Federalism*, 177–196. World Bank Institute Learning Resources Series. Washington, DC: World Bank.

Blöchliger, H. and Nettley, M. (2015) *Sub-central Tax Autonomy: 2011 Update*. OECD Working Papers on Fiscal Federalism, No. 20. Paris: OECD.

Brennan, G. and Buchanan, J. (1980) *The Power to Tax: Analytical Foundations of a Fiscal Constitution*. New York: Cambridge University Press.

Clark, G. L. (1984) A Theory of Local Autonomy, *Annals of the Association of American Geographers* 74(2): 195–208.

Council of Europe (1985) *European Charter of Local Self-Government*. European Treaty Series No. 122. Strasbourg: Council of Europe.

Davey, K. (ed.) (2012) *Local Government in Critical Times: Policies for Crisis, Recovery and a Sustainable Future*. Strasbourg: Council of Europe.

Eyraud, L. and Sirera, R. G. (2015) Constraints on Subnational Fiscal Policy. In C. Cottarelli, and M. Guerguil (eds), *Designing a European Fiscal Union: Lessons from the Experience of Fiscal Federations*, 90–132. Abingdon: Routledge.

Freire, M. E. and Garzón, H. (2014) Managing Local Revenues. In C. Farvacque-Vitkovic and M. Kopanyi (eds), *Municipal Finances: A Handbook for Local Governments*, 147–214. Washington, DC: World Bank.

Indecon (2005) *Indecon Review of Local Government Financing*. Commissioned by the Minister for the Environment, Heritage and Local Government. Dublin: Indecon International Economic Consultants in association with the Institute of Local Government Studies at University of Birmingham.

Kornai, J. (1992) *The Socialist System: The Political Economy of Communism*. Oxford: Clarendon Press.

Ladner, A., Keuffer, N. and Baldersheim, H. (2015) *Local Autonomy Index for European countries (1990–2014)*. Release 1.0. Brussels: European Commission.

Loughlin, J. and Martin, S. (2008) *Local Government Finance: International Experience*. Conference Paper, June. Dublin: Foundation for Fiscal Studies.

Mill, J. S. ([1861]1910) *Utilitarianism, Liberty, Representative Government*. London: J. M. Dent & Sons.

Musgrave, R. A. (1959) *The Theory of Public Finance*. New York: McGraw-Hill.

Oates, W. E. (1972) *Fiscal Federalism*. New York: Harcourt Brace Jovanovich.

OECD (2013) *Fiscal Federalism 2014: Making Decentralisation Work*. Paris: OECD.

OECD/KIPF (2012) *Institutional and Financial Relations across Levels of Government* (ed. J. Kim and C. Vammalle). *OECD Fiscal Federalism Studies*. Paris: OECD.

Olson, M. Jr. (1969) The Principle of 'Fiscal Equivalence': The Division of Responsibilities among Different Levels of Government. *American Economic Review* 59(2): 479–487.

Samuelson, P. (1954) The Pure Theory of Public Expenditure. *Review of Economics and Statistics* 36(4): 387–389.

Shah, A. (ed.) (2008) *Macro Federalism and Local Finance. Public Sector Governance and Accountability Series*. Washington, DC: World Bank.

Tiebout, C. M. (1956) A Pure Theory of Local Expenditures. *Journal of Political Economy* 64(5): 416–424.

Turley, G. (2006) *Transition, Taxation and the State*. Farnham: Ashgate.

INDEX

Locators in *italics* refer to figures and those in **bold** to tables.

ability-to-pay model (taxation) 483, 497; *see also* progressive tax
accountability: corruption 437–438; councillors' role 56; open budgets 327, 330–331; taxation 485–486
active participation *310*, 310
additional member system (AMS) 13
administration 70, 77–79; Australia 364–370, **365–366**; Brazil 326–327; citizen participation 265–277; colonial legacies 99–100; complementarity 71–73; demise of second tier local government 382–385; dichotomy 71–73; distinction from government 6–7; Guyana 168–169; Italy case study 76–77; Latin America 134, 144–145; local, meaning of 3–4; local governance arenas 74–76; local governance era 73–74; rescaling municipalities 378–382; Russia 268–269; Southern Europe 419–423, **421–422**; stakeholder management *75*, 75–77, **78**; Trinidad and Tobago 177; United States 184–186; *see also* multi-level governance
age, citizen participation 316, 318
alternative vote (AV) 13, 14–15, 21–23
amalgamations: Australia 367–368; demise of second tier local government 382–385; rescaling municipalities 378–382; *see also* administration
amenity services, cross-country comparison 228
American Society for Public Administration (ASPA) 92
Anglo group, Europe 419
anti-corruption initiatives 435, 447–448; Georgia 438–443; meaning of corruption 436–438; Ukraine 438–440, 443–447

Antigua, constitution 169–170
Antwerp, Flanders, trust in public services 302–303
architecture of local political communities 418–430
Area Council Development Plans (ACDP) 122
assigned revenues (taxation) 488–489
Athens, Greece, urban governance study 282–292, **283**
Auckland Accord 38
audit *see* Best Value initiative; VFM auditing
austerity in Europe 280, 280–281; case study research 282–292; revenue ratio 506; taxation 513–515; urban governance 280–288, 290–293
Australia: challenging institutional constraints 363–374; electoral systems 21–22; trust in public services 301–302; urban governance study 282–292
Australian Constitutional Values Survey 369
autonomy: local government services 222; local governments 5–6; Southern Europe 425–426; taxation 470, 483, 485, 488, 489, 512–513
Azerbaijan, service delivery 233, 234

Baltimore, US, urban governance study 282–292
Barbuda, constitution of 169–170
Barcelona, Spain, urban governance study 282–292, **283**
Belgium, rescaling municipalities 379
beneficial tax 468
benefit model (taxation) 486–487, 497
Best Value initiative 451–452; audit as problematic 452–454; research study 454–464; United Kingdom 450–451

518

betterment tax 493
Big Local 303–304
Birmingham, UK, local leadership elections 33
block vote 13, 20–21
blogging, as mode of public outreach 309
borrowing (as revenue source) 487
boundaries 377–378, 389–390; demise of second tier local government 382–385; Europeanisation 386–389; excolonialism 99–100; rescaling municipalities 378–382
bounded rationality 223, 327
Bourbon Reforms 132
branding, urban governance 291–292
Brazil: citizen participation 146; electoral systems 141; historical developments 326–329; open budgets 330–340; social development 328–340; trust in public services 301
Britain *see* United Kingdom
budgetary institutions 250
budgetary process: Brazil 327–328, 331; Ukraine's anti-corruption project 443–447; *see also* open budgets
Bulgaria, taxation 509
bureaucracy: administration and politics 71; citizen participation 264–267, 277
bureaucratic absolutism 264
bureaucratic autonomy model 72–73
Burt Review 473–474
business, economic development perceptions United States **89**, 89–90
business improvement districts 493–494
business tax 487–488, 503–504

Canada: electoral systems 18; taxation 490; urban governance study 282–292, **283**
capacity audit (CAPAUD) 175
capital tax 470
Caribbean 163–166, 178–179; Commonwealth 163–164; de-concentration of power 101–102; legal context 177–178; legislative and constitutional change 166–167, 170–176; *see also* Trinidad and Tobago
Central Europe *see individually named countries*; Visegrad countries
centralisation: austerity in Europe 291; Australia 369; taxation 484
central-local relationship: demise of second tier local government 382–385; Europeanisation 386–389; local government services 221–222; Pacific Islands countries 119, 119–120; rescaling municipalities 378–382; taxation 488; *see also* centralisation; decentralisation
chiefs, Pacific Islands countries 39–40, 44, 48–49, 51–52; *see also* traditional leadership
Chile, electoral systems 141
citizen engagement *see* citizen participation

citizen panels, as mode of public outreach 309
citizen participation 9, 263–264, 277–278; Australia 368–370; civic engagement 349–357; collaborative forms of governance 281–282; Latin America 145–146; mid-sized cities and communities case studies 268–277; modes of public outreach 307–318; public entrepreneurship 211–212; purposes of 308–309; service delivery survey in Georgia 240–245; theoretical perspectives 264–267; trust deficit 296–305; *see also* electoral participation
city development *see* economic development perceptions
civic engagement, Visegrad countries 344–345, 349–357
civil service: collaboration 99; corruption 437–438; Latin America 144–145; *see also* administration
civil society organisations (CSOs): austerity in Europe 291; civic engagement 351–352, 353–355, *354*, 357; Visegrad countries 344–345
climate change adaptation, Pacific Islands countries 127
closed systems, citizen participation 265, 276–277
co-consultation 74
co-deliberation 74–75
co-delivery 75, 77
co-design 75, 77
co-evaluation 75
Colau, Ada 285–286
collaboration: colonial legacy states 99–100; Jamaica 171–172; public entrepreneurship 209–211, 212–213
collaborative forms of governance: austerity in Europe 280–282, 285–287, 290, 292–293; open budgets 325–326, 331–333, 334, 336–338
collective decision-making, local leadership elections 27–31
Colombia, electoral systems 18
colonial legacy: administration 99–100; Caribbean 163–166; Latin America 131–133; Trinidad and Tobago 100–101
Columbia, electoral systems 142
commercial income (as revenue source) 487–488, 503–504
Commission on Local Taxation Reform (CLTR) 478–479
common goods 220
Commonwealth: Australia 363; Caribbean countries 163–164; constitutionalism 167–170
communication: councillors' public interaction 57–58; economic development perceptions 92
communism: local government services 248; local leadership elections 28; Visegrad countries 350

community attachment 428–429
community centres, Georgia 236–240
community charge, Scotland 476–477
community context: councillors 60–61; economic development perceptions United States **89**, 89–90; Southern Europe 428–429; trust in public services 300; *see also* citizen participation; modes of public outreach
community mobilization, Pacific Islands countries 48–49
complementarity model, administration and politics 72–73
conflict: citizen participation 145; Pacific Island countries 38, 49, 50, 51; public service delivery in Georgia 234; stakeholders 339; traditional leadership 38, 207; Trinidad and Tobago 100, 104, 107
Conservative Government, UK, May, local leadership elections 33
Conservative Government, UK, Thatcher: local leadership elections 30; poll tax 476; privatisation 65, 248
constituency development funds 125
constitutionalism, Commonwealth 167–170
constitutions: Australia 363, 364, 369; Caribbean 166–170, 178; European Union governance 396, 397–398; Georgia 234–235; Latin America 146; local governments 6; local leadership elections 29; New Zealand 153–155; Pacific Islands countries 42–44, 112, 113, 119–120; Trinidad and Tobago 104–105; United States 183
consumption tax 489, 490–491, 503
continuous improvement 461–462
contracting, local government services 222–225
contracting out, Latin America 137
Cook Islands, decentralisation 120
corporatisation, Europe's local government services 249–250
corruption 436–438; *see also* anti-corruption initiatives
Corruption Perception Index (CPI) *439*, 439
Council of European Municipalities and Regions (CEMR) 380, 384
council tax 472, 476–478; *see also* taxation (local)
councillor-electorate ratio 61–62
councillors 54–55, 65–66; activities 57–61; fundamental role 55–57; institutions 63–64; multi-level governance 64–65; party politics 63–65; workload 61–63
councils: councillors' role 58–59; number of 1–2; reform in Australia **365–366**, 366–370; *see also* administration
county governments, United States 184, 185, 192, **193**, 198
criminal justice, traditional leadership 49–51
Croatia: electoral systems 19; taxation 506, 509

cultural context, economic development perceptions 84–85, 91–92
cultural diversity, Pacific Islands countries 39
customer satisfaction, service delivery in Georgia 240–245
Czech Republic: civic engagement 349–357; demise of second tier local government 384; development and dynamics 348; political and regional structure 345–347, **346**

Dahl, R. 378–379
data, open data initiatives 446–448
decentralisation: austerity in Europe 291; Caribbean 163–166, 173–175, **174**, 178; Latin America 133–134, 139–140, 145–147; local government services 221–222; Pacific Islands countries 119–120, 123–125; public entrepreneurship 208; rescaling municipalities 378–382; service delivery 233; taxation 484, 498, 512–513; Trinidad and Tobago 101–102, 103, 107–108; Visegrad countries 345, 347, 348, 356; *see also* central-local relationship
de-concentration of power 101–102, 164
delegates, representation 55–56
democracy: citizen participation 264–267, 277; civic engagement 349–350, 351–352; collaboration in decision-making 99–100; open budgets 327, 330–331; vs. traditional authority 125–126
democratic deficit, Latin America 140
Democratic Labour Party, Trinidad and Tobago 103
demographics: Caribbean 164, **165**; funding local government 297; modes of public outreach 310–311, 313–318; Pacific Islands countries 110–111, **110–111**; Southern European municipalities 420–423, **421–422**; United States 194; wards 61–62
Denmark: demise of second tier local government 383; rescaling municipalities 379–380; taxation 504, 506, 509
developing countries, taxation 484, 493
development *see* economic development; social development
devolution: Latin America 136; local government services 222; local leadership elections 32–33
D'Hondt system 140–141
dispute resolution, traditional leadership 49; *see also* conflict
double movement, austerity 282, 291
Dublin, Ireland, urban governance study 282–292, **283**

eastern Europe: anti-corruption initiatives 435; local leadership elections 28; *see also* Georgia; Ukraine

520

Index

economic activities, local government services classifications 227
economic crisis *see* financial crisis (2008)
economic development: Australia 370–372; Latin America 131, 133–134; Pacific Islands countries 127–128; public entrepreneurship 203–213
economic development perceptions 82, 92–93; institutional convergence and divergence 83–85, 91–93; United States city development 82–83, 85–92, *95–96*
economic growth: corruption 436; Pacific Islands countries 117–118
economic rationality, taxation 484–486
economic theories: funding local government 496–498; taxation 483–484
education: citizen participation 314–316; cross-country comparison 228; economic development perceptions 92
efficiency: scale 378–379; taxation 489
electoral participation: civic engagement 349–350; English electoral system 29–33; local leadership 25–26
electoral systems 9, 13–14, 23; Latin America 139–142; second-tier model 405–415; Southern Europe 423–425; types of 14–23
e-mail, councillors' public interaction 58
emergency medical services, United States 188–189
energy sector, Europe 253–254, 255–256
England: Best Value initiative 450–452, **452**; councillors 63–64; funding local government 296–297; local leadership elections 29–33; taxation 487–488; *see also* United Kingdom
entrepreneurs: Australia 371–372; citizen participation in Russia 273–274; *see also* public entrepreneurship
environmental law 395–396
environmental tax 491, 492
equity *see* inequality
ethical context: citizen participation 308; corruption 437–438
ethnic context: Caribbean 164; modes of public outreach 310–311, 313–314, 317–318; Trinidad and Tobago 100–101
Europe: architecture of local political communities 418–430; austerity and urban governance 280–293; central-local relationship 386–389; civic engagement 344–345, 349–357; funding local government 504–515, **505**, **507–508**, **510–511**; Lisbon Treaty 252; local government services 221–225, **224**, 228, 247–258; local government services classifications 226–227, 228; local leadership elections 28; market liberalisation 248, 249; multi-level governance 394–402; rescaling municipalities 379–380; second-tier electoral model 407; social enterprises 256; Visegrad countries 345–349, **346**

European Court of Justice (ECJ) 395–396, 399–400
Europeanisation: central-local relations 386–389; market liberalisation 249, 250
Every One Every Day 303–304
excolonialism: collaboration in decision-making 99–100; Trinidad and Tobago 100–101; *see also* colonial legacy
executive elections 16–17; *see also* party executives
executive head, Latin America 142–143
expenditure *see* spending behavior

fake news 298–299
federal institutions: councillors 63–64; economic development perceptions United States 82–83
federalism, United States 270
Fiji: funding local government 121; military 124; place of local government 114; traditional leadership 47, 48; urban governance 117–118
finances *see* austerity in Europe; economic development perceptions; funding; spending behavior; taxation
financial crisis (2008): local government services 223–225; Southern Europe 420; taxation 509, 513–515; *see also* austerity in Europe
financial incentives, taxation 487–488
financial mobilisation 401
Finland, taxation 506
first past the post (FPTP) 13, 14–15, 19, 20–21
fiscal transfers, Latin America 138–139
Flanders, trust in public services 302–303
Florence, Italy, administration 76
France: architecture of local political communities 418–430; austerity governance 284; councillors 63–64; demise of second tier local government 383; energy sector 253, 255; local governments 5, 7; local leadership elections 28; rescaling municipalities 381; urban governance study 282–292, **283**; water services 254
functional perspective, local government services 220, 226–228
funding local government 9; Australia 372; Caribbean 173–175, **174**, 178; contemporary context 296–297, 512–515; economic development perceptions United States 87–89, **88**, 91; economic theories 496–498; Europe 504–515, **505**, **507–508**, **510–511**; Latin America 137–142; New Zealand 153–155; Pacific Islands countries 120–123; revenue assignment 498–501; revenue sources 486–487, 492–494, 499–504; trust initiatives 303–304; *see also* austerity in Europe; taxation (local)

Gainesville, USA, citizen participation 271, 275–276
gemeinschaft relationships 100–101
gender: citizen participation 316, 318; traditional leadership 42–43

geographic context, meaning of local 2–4; *see also* central-local relationship
Georgia (Eurasia): anti-corruption initiatives 438–443; service delivery 233–245
Germany: electoral systems 19; energy sector 253–254, 255–256; municipally owned enterprises 250; social services 256; taxation 489; water services 254
gesellschaft relationships 100–101
global context 1–2; *see also* international context
globalisation: Pacific Islands countries 115–118; trust in public services 298–299
goods, local government services classifications 220–225
governance: anti-corruption initiatives 438–447; austerity in Europe 280–293; citizen participation 264, 266, 267; open budgets 325–326, 329, 330–333; public entrepreneurship 206–208, 211; *see also* multi-level governance
government: distinction from administration 6–7; meaning of 5–6
grant system 468, 486, **500**, 501, 509
Greece: municipally owned enterprises (MOEs) 250; rescaling municipalities 379; social services 257; urban governance study 282–292, **283**
grid-based services 252–253
Gross Domestic Product, taxation 504–505
Grottammare, Italy, administration 76–77
growth *see* economic development perceptions; economic growth
Guyana, constitution of 168–169

health care: cross-country comparison **224**, 225–226, 228; Europe 248
Heseltine, Michael 30–31
horizontal equalisation 485
horizontal fiscal imbalance (HFI) 485
housing: impact of property tax 473; Pacific Islands countries 126–127
housing services tax 470
Hugh Wooding Constitution Commission 104–105
human capital: Jamaica 175–176; Pacific Islands countries 126
Human Development Report 328–329, 334
Hungary: civic engagement 349–357; development and dynamics 348; political and regional structure **346**, 347

identity: Australia's local government 366–370; Southern European community 428–429
immobile tax base 489
income tax: assigned revenues 490, 492; combining tax 473–474; as revenue source 502; Scotland 478, 479

independence: Latin America 133; Trinidad and Tobago 101–104; *see also* colonial legacy
individual decision-making, local leadership elections 27–31
inelasticity, tax **475**
inequality: Caribbean 177–178; Latin America 131, 138–139; modes of public outreach 307–308, 310–311, 313–318; taxation 485, 489
informal settlements, Pacific Islands countries 126–127
infrastructure *see* human capital; physical infrastructure
innovation: public entrepreneurship 203–206, 210–211, 212; revenue sources 492–494
Institute for Development of Freedom of Information (IDFI) 440–441
institutional context: Australia 363; councillors 63–64; economic development perceptions United States 82–92, 85–92; federal 63–64, 82–83; Latin America 144–145; open budgets 327–328; public entrepreneurship 208, 209–210; Southern Europe 425–427; trust in public services 299–300; unitary 63–64
intergovernmental relations: Pacific Islands countries 118–120, 127–128; private vs. public sector 251–252; taxation 468, 486, 501
internal governance, councillors' role 58–59
international context, local leadership elections 26–29; *see also* global context
intra-party choice, electoral systems 16
Ireland, urban governance study 282–292, **283**
Italy: administration and politics 73, 76–77; architecture of local political communities 418–430; demise of second tier local government 383; energy sector 253; municipally owned enterprises 250; social services 256; water services 254

Jamaica: constitution 168; legal reform 171–176
Japan, taxation 489
jurisdictions 3–4, 9; *see also* administration

Kazakhstan, service delivery 233–234
Kiribati: legal context 44–45; place of local government 112, 113–114; traditional leadership 40–41, 51–52, 126; *see also* Pacific Islands countries

Labour Government, UK, local leadership elections 31
laissez faire model, administration and politics 72–73
land distribution, Pacific Islands countries 47–48
land value tax 471, 473, 490
Latin America 131, 146–147; administration 134, 144–145; citizen participation 145–146;

colonial legacy 131–133; decentralisation 133–134; funding 137–142; political system of local government 142–144; post-independence decline 133; poverty 131, 136, 138–139; service delivery 135–137; size distribution of local government 134, **135**

Latvia: rescaling municipalities 379; taxation 506

leadership: *see also* executive head; local leadership; traditional leadership

Lecco, Italy, administration 77

legal context: Brazil budgetary process 327–328; Caribbean 166–178; corruption 436, 437; European Union governance 395–396, 397; Europeanisation 386–389; Pacific Islands countries 120; traditional leadership 44–47, 49; Trinidad and Tobago 176–177; United States 183–184; *see also* constitutions; policy

legitimacy: citizen participation 308; local leadership elections 25, 28, 31

Leicester, UK, urban governance study 282–292, **283**

leisure services, cross-country comparison 228

library services, cross-country comparison 228

lifestyle coordination, Australia 372–373

liquidity constraints **475**

Lisbon Treaty 252, 396–397

Lithuania, taxation 509

local, meaning of 2–4

Local Autonomy Index (LAI) 425–426, 512–513

local boundaries *see* boundaries

local councillors *see* councillors

local democracy 297–298

local elections *see* electoral systems

Local Governance Act, Jamaica 171–172

local governance arenas 74–76

local governance era 73–74

Local Government Bill 2009, Trinidad and Tobago 176–177

Local Government (Financing and Financial Management) Act 2016, Jamaica 173–175

local government services 9; Australia 372–373; citizen participation 297–305; classifications 219–229; Europe 221–225, **224**, 228, 247–258; European Union governance 395; international definition 218–219; and local democracy 297–298; objective/functional perspective 220, 226–228; Pacific Islands countries 123–125; subjective-community perspective 220; subjective-government perspective 220, 221–226; United States 185–189, **187**, 190–197; *see also* funding local government

Local Government (Unified Service and Employment) Act 2016, Jamaica 175–176

local governments' role: importance of 7–8; Pacific Islands countries 112–115; United States 183–184, 186–189

local leadership: economic development perceptions 83–85; economic development perceptions United States 82–83, 85–92; electoral participation 25–26; English electoral system 29–33; international context 26–29; Latin America 139–140, 142–143; public entrepreneurship 209; Southern Europe 423–425

local mobilisation 401

local-centre *see* central-local relationship

London, trust initiatives 304

Lviv, Ukraine 443–447

Madrid Decides 300–301

magnitude, electoral systems 15–16

Malta, taxation 504, 506, 509

Manchester, UK, local leadership elections 33

market liberalisation, Europe 248–250

Marshall Islands 42; *see also* Pacific Islands countries

Master's in Public Administration (MPA) 92

Maud Committee, England 29–30

May, Theresa 33

mayors *see* local leadership

McLeod, J. M. 276

Mechanizatory Ltd 239

media, post-truth 298–299

median-voter's approach 218–219

Melbourne, Australia: trust in public services 301–302; urban governance study 282–292

Micronesia's constitution 43–44; *see also* Pacific Islands countries

migration, Pacific Islands countries 110, **110–111**

military: Fiji 124; Latin America 146

Ministry of Justice of Georgia (MoJ) 235–236, 238

mixed models, elections 13, 14–15, 19

mobilisation, European Union 401

modernism, Caribbean 167–168

modes of public outreach 307–308; policy outcomes 308–318; United States case study 313–318, *321–324*

Montreal, Canada, urban governance study 282–292, **283**

multi-level governance 9; Australia 364–366, **365–366**; councillors 64–65; demise of second tier local government 382–385; European Union 394–402; Europeanisation 386–389; local government services 221–222; second-tier electoral model 405–415; taxation 468–469, 483–485; tribal governance 207–208

multiple non-transferable vote (MNTV) 13

MUNIC open budget index 334, 336–338

municipal codes, Latin America 135–136

Municipal Corporations Act 1990/1991, Trinidad and Tobago 176, 177

municipal corporations, naming conventions 172–173
municipal council, Latin America 143–144
municipal governments, United States 184–185, 186, **187**, 192–195, *195*, 199
municipally owned enterprises (MOEs) 249–250
Musgrave, Richard 483, 484

naming conventions 172–173
Nantes, France, urban governance study 282–292, **283**
National Agency of Public Registry, Georgia 237–238
National Archive of Georgia (NAG) 238
national elections, Latin America 141–142
national government, councillors' role 64–65
national-local *see* central-local relationship
natural resource conservation: Pacific Islands countries 48–49; United States 196
neo-institutional approach 409–414
neoliberalism: austerity in Europe 281, 284, 292; Europe 248, 251; Latin America 137
network forms of governance 280–281, 300
Network of Schools of Public Policy, Affairs, and Administration (NASPAA) 92
Nevis Island Legislature and Assembly (NIL/A) 169–170
new public management (NPM) 71, 73
New Zealand: contemporary context 149–150, 160–161; electoral systems 17–18, 20–21; financial and constitutional model 153–155; implications and impact 158–160; local government model 150–152; reform 155–157
non-proportional voting systems 13, 14–15, 20–23; *see also* alternative vote; block vote; first past the post; second ballot; single non-transferable vote; supplementary vote
North European Strategy 383
Northern Europe, meaning of 419; *see also individually named countries*
Northern Ireland, electoral systems 18

Oates, W. E. 498
objective/functional perspective, local government services 220, 226–228
OECD countries: grant system *500*, 501; health care **224**, 225–226; public entrepreneurship 210; taxation 469–470, 471; *see also individually named countries*
one-stop-shop (OSS) principle 233–234, 235–236
online system, Georgia's anti-corruption project 441–443
open budgets 325–326; Brazil 330–340; social development 326, 328–330; Ukraine's anti-corruption project 443–447
open data initiatives 446–448
open innovation, public entrepreneurship 213

open systems, citizen participation 265, 266, 268, 275, 276–277; *see also* transparency
organisational blogging, as mode of public outreach 309
outreach *see* citizen participation; modes of public outreach
own-revenue 138; *see also* revenue sources

Pacific Islands countries 128; challenges confronting government 118–128; continuing significance of tradition 47–52; global and regional dimensions 115–118; jurisdictions 41–47; place of local government 112–115; societies and government 110–111; traditional leadership 38–41
Pacific Urban Agenda 116–118
Papua New Guinea: decentralisation 119–120; funding local government 122–123; place of local government 112–113, 114–115; service delivery 124–125; traditional leadership 41; urban governance 117–118; *see also* Pacific Islands countries
parish council, naming conventions 172–173
parking services, United States 196
parks and recreational services, United States 188
participation *see* citizen participation; collaboration; electoral participation
participative administration *265*, 265–266
participatory budgeting 76–77, 301–303
partisanship, councillors 62–63
Partnership Agreement, European Union 398
partnerships, public entrepreneurship 209
party executives: councillors' role 64–65; executive elections 16–17
party lists 13, 16, 18–19, 140–141
party politics: councillors 59–60, 63–65; local leadership elections 31–32
party soldier role, councillors 56
passive participation *310*, 310
People's National Movement, Trinidad and Tobago 103
periphery *see* central-local relationship
personal income tax *see* income tax
personal services: Europe 256–258; meaning of 247; *see also* local government services
physical infrastructure: cross-country comparison 228; Pacific Islands countries 126
Piacenza, Italy, administration 77
place management, Australia 373
place marketing, urban governance 291–292
place-bound government, as structure 384, 412
place-making: public entrepreneurship 209; trust in public services 300–301
planning, citizen participation in USA 274–275
pluralistic governance 211
Poland: civic engagement 349–357; development and dynamics 348; political and regional

524

structure **346**, 348; property leaseback schemes 493; social services 257
policy: Best Value initiative 452; Caribbean's reform 166; citizen participation 270–277; European Union governance 395–396, 397, 400–401; modes of public outreach 308–318, *312*; public policy process 219; taxation 514–515; Visegrad countries 349–357; *see also* legal context
political dominance model, administration and politics 72–73
political factors: councillors 62–63; Latin America 142–144; private vs. public sector 251; second-tier electoral model 411–412; *see also* administration; party politics
Politikverflechtung 394
poll tax, Scotland 476–477
Polynesia 39; *see also* Pacific Islands countries
population: Caribbean 164, **165**; funding local government 297; modes of public outreach 310–311, 313–318; Pacific Islands countries 110–111, **110–111**; Southern European municipalities 420–423, **421–422**; United States 194; wards 61–62
Portugal, architecture of local political communities 418–430
post-truth 298–299
poverty: austerity in Europe 284; Caribbean 177–178; Latin America 131, 136, 138–139
power relations: audit as problematic 453; corruption 436; local governments 7–8; local leadership elections 27
presumptive tax 472, 474, **475**
private goods 220
private government (taxation) 493–494
private sector: health care 225–226; and public entrepreneurship 205–206
privatisation: austerity in Europe 291; councillors' role 65; Europe's local government services 248–250; Latin America 136–137; pros and cons 251
procurement, Ukraine's anti-corruption project 443–447
professionalisation, councillors 56–57
progressive tax 470–471, 477, 483; *see also* ability-to-pay tax
property leaseback schemes 493
property tax: assigned revenues 490, 492; beneficial tax 468; benefit model 468; central-local relationship 488; combining tax 473–474; comparative research 470, 471–479; as revenue source 502
proportional voting systems 13, 14–15, 140–141; *see also* party lists; single non-transferable vote (SNTV)
protest movements, austerity in Europe 282, 288–291

public chambers, Russia 272
public engagement *see* citizen participation
public entrepreneurship 203; challenges to theory of 213; international examples 209–213; meaning of 204–208; place-making 209
public goods 220, 227
public interaction, councillors 57–58, 60–61
public outreach *see* citizen participation; modes of public outreach
public participation *see* citizen participation
public policy process 219
public sector 'comeback' trend, Europe 251–255
public servants *see* civil service
Public Service Development Agency of Georgia (PSDA) 236, 237–239
Public Service Hall (PSH), Georgia 235–236
public services *see* local government services; service delivery
public services/utilities: Europe 248–256; historical developments 248; meaning of 247
public value 205
punishment, traditional leadership 49–51
pure public goods 220

quality, service delivery in Georgia 239–245

race: Caribbean 164; modes of public outreach 310–311, 313–314, 317–318; Trinidad and Tobago 100–101
Rarotonga, decentralisation 120
rationality: bounded 223, 327; Latin America 145–146; taxation 484–486
rebate schemes 472
re-election, Latin America 141
reform: anti-corruption initiatives 438–447; Australia 367–370, 371–372, 373; Caribbean 166–168, 170–176; demise of second tier local government 382–385; New Zealand 155–157; rescaling municipalities 378–382; small island states 106–107; taxation 473, 474–479; Trinidad and Tobago 101–106; trust in public services 298–305; Visegrad countries 348–349
Reggio Emilia, Italy, administration 77
regional services: demise of second tier local government 382–385; United States 195–197, *196*
regionalisation, Pacific Islands countries 115–118
regressive tax 470, 472, **475**, 477, 489
regulatory mobilisation 401
Reif, K. 406–407, 408
renewable energy, Europe 253–254
representation, councillors 55–56
residential community associations 494
resilience, Pacific Islands countries 117
resistance movements, austerity in Europe 282, 288–291

resource limitations: Brazil's budget 331, 334–338; economic development perceptions United States 88–89, **89**
resources: Pacific Islands countries 48–49; United States 196
revenue assignment 498–501
revenue ratio 506
revenue sources: common sources 486–487; comparative research 506–509; innovation 492–494; Latin America 138–139; revenue assignment 499–504; *see also* taxation (local)
revenue-sharing 138–139
risk-taking, public entrepreneurship 206, 212–213
roles *see* councillors; local governments' role; local leadership
Romania, taxation 506, 509
Russia, citizen participation 266–267, 268–277

St Augustine, USA, citizen participation 271, 274, 276
sales tax 490–491, 503
saliency, taxation 472, 474, **475**
Samoa: constitutions 43; dispute resolution 49; funding local government 121; legal context 45; place of local government 112, 115; resources 48; traditional leadership 40, 41, 125–126; urban governance 117–118; *see also* Pacific Islands countries
San Francisco, USA, modes of public outreach 313–318, *321–324*
scale: local, meaning of 2–4; rescaling municipalities 378–382; Southern European community 428–429; taxation 498; United States spending priorities 197–200; *see also* devolution; multi-level governance
Scandinavia, rescaling municipalities 379
Schmitt, H. 406–407, 408
school districts, United States 186
Schumpeter, Joseph 205
Scotland: Best Value initiative 451–452, 454–463; taxation reform 475–479; *see also* United Kingdom
Scottish National Party (SNP) 479
scrutiny, councillors' role 56; *see also* accountability; transparency
second ballot 13, 14–15, 22–23
second tier of local government: demise of 382–385; electoral model 405–415; *see also* regional services
self-determination, councillors 62–63
self-governance: European Union 396–398; Georgia 236; tribal governance 208
service delivery: Georgia case study 233–245; Latin America 135–137
services *see* local government services
sewage services, United States 188
sex, citizen participation 316, 318

shared tax systems 488–489
short term of office, Latin America 141
Sinanan Committee 102
single non-transferable vote (SNTV) 13, 21
single transferable vote (STV) 13, 15, 17–18, 21, 22
site value tax 471, 473
size of local government: EU member states 504–506; Latin America 134, **135**; Southern Europe 420–423, **421–422**, **427**, 428–429
Slovakia: civic engagement 349–357; development and dynamics 348; political and regional structure **346**, 347; taxation 506
small states: Caribbean 163–166; independence and reform 101–104, 106–107; *see also* Pacific Islands countries
Smith, Adam 205
social capital, civic engagement 351, 352–353
social development: Brazil 328–340; meaning of 325; open budgets 326, 328–330
social enterprises 256
social equity, Pacific Islands countries 116–117
social exclusion, Latin America 131
social impact bonds (SIBs) 492
social media: citizen participation in USA 275; post-truth 298–299
Social Service Agency, Georgia 238–239
social services: administration and politics 77; Australia 372–373; Europe 256–257; services classifications 227; taxation 468, 497–498; *see also* local government services
socio-economic status, citizen participation 311
Solomon Islands: constitutions 42–43; decentralisation 119, 119–120; land distribution 47; place of local government 113, 115; service delivery 125; traditional leadership 41, 49, 126; *see also* Pacific Islands countries
South Africa: electoral systems 19, 20–21; local government services 227
South European Strategy 383
Southern Europe, architecture of local political communities 418–430; *see also individually named countries*
sovereignty, public entrepreneurship 206–208
Soviet Union: collapse in Georgia 233, 234–235; corruption 435
Spain: architecture of local political communities 418–430; colonial legacy in Latin American 131–133; local leadership elections 28; Madrid Decides 300–301; urban governance study 282–292, **283**
special districts, United States 185–186, 193, 196, 199–200
spending behavior: decentralisation 498; Southern Europe 426–427, **426–427**; Ukraine's anti-corruption project 443–447; United States 189–200, **190**

Index

sport services: administration and politics 77; cross-country comparison 228
stability, taxation 489
stakeholder engagement: management cycle 75, 76, **78**; modes of public outreach 311–312; open budgets 331–333, 334, 336–338
stakeholder evaluation 75, 76, **78**
stakeholder identification 75, 76, **78**
stakeholder interaction 75, 76, **78**
stakeholder management 75, 75–77, **78**
stakeholder mapping 75, 76, **78**
stakeholder theory 219
Stoker, G. 363–364
strategic capacity, Australia 371
structural equation modelling 333–334
subjective-community perspective, local government services 220
subjective-government perspective, local government services 220, 221–226
sub-regional scale, local leadership elections 32–33
subsidiarity, European Union 399–400
sufficiency, taxation 489
supplementary vote (SV) 13, 15, 21–23
surveys, as mode of public outreach 309
Svara, J. 72–73
Sweden: demise of second tier local government 383; rescaling municipalities 379; taxation 506
Syriza, Greece 288

tax increment financing (TIF) 492–493
taxation (local) 467–471, 480, 482–483, 494; assigned revenues 488–489; comparative research 471–474; economic theories 483–484; European Union 504–509, **505**, **507–508**, **510–511**; financial incentives 487–488; Latin America 138; local control 488; obstacles to economic rationality 484–486; Pacific Islands countries 121–123; reform 473, 474–479; revenue sources 486–487, 492–494, 499–504; types of 489–492
Tbilisi City Hall, Georgia 440–443
technology: Caribbean 178; councillors' public interaction 57–58; Georgia's anti-corruption project 441–443
territorial representation, Latin America 140–141
territorial self-government (TSG), Russia 273
Texas, US, economic development perceptions 83–84, 85–92
Thatcher, Margaret *see* Conservative Government, UK, Thatcher
third sector, Europe 255–257
Tiebout, Charles 483, 498
Tobago *see* Trinidad and Tobago
Tobago House of Assembly (THA) 169, 176
Tobolsk, Russia, citizen participation 270–271, 273–274
toll goods 220

Tonga: constitutions 43; funding local government 121–122; land distribution 47–48; legal context 45–46; place of local government 112; traditional leadership 40; urban governance 118; *see also* Pacific Islands countries
Tonnies, F. 100
tourism tax 491
townships, United States 185, 199
trading income (as revenue source) 487–488
traditional leadership: continuing significance in Pacific Island countries 47–52; jurisdictions 41–47; Pacific Islands countries 38–41, 112–115, 125–126; tribal governance 206–208
traditionalism, Caribbean 167–168
training, economic development perceptions 92
transit services, United States 196
transparency: corruption 437–438, 440–447; local leadership elections 25, 28, 31; open budgets 327, 330–331
Transparency International (TI) 436
transport tax 491, 492
tribal governance, public entrepreneurship 206–208
Trinidad and Tobago: constitution 169; decentralisation 107–108; excolonialism 100–101; independence and reform 101–104; law and bill 176–177
Trump, Donald, post-truth 298
trust: citizen participation 296–305; Visegrad countries 351–353, 356
trustees, representation 55–56
Tufte, E. 378–379
Tuvalu: funding local government 122; legal context 46–47, 50–51; place of local government 113; traditional leadership 39; *see also* Pacific Islands countries

UK *see* United Kingdom
Ukraine, anti-corruption initiatives 438–440, 443–447
UNESCAP 116
UN-Habitat 116, 128
unipersonal leadership 142–143
unitary institutions, councillors 63–64
unitary state, Caribbean 167–168
United Kingdom: austerity governance 284; Best Value initiative 450–452, **452**, 463–464; councillor-electorate ratio 61–62; demise of second tier local government 383; electoral systems 19, 20, 21; energy sector 253; funding local government 296–297; local governments 7; local leadership elections 33; social impact bonds 492; taxation 468, 475–479, 487–488; trust in public services 299; urban governance study **283**; *see also* Conservative Government, UK; England; Labour Government, UK; Scotland; Wales

527

United Nations Development Programme (UNDP) 328–329, 334, 445–446
United States: citizen participation 267–277, 270, 271, 274, 275–276; contemporary context 200–201; councillor-electorate ratio 61–62; economic development perceptions 82–83, 85–92, *95–96*; electoral systems 18, 22, 28; local government types 184–186; local governments 5–6; modes of public outreach 313–318, *321–324*; and post-independence Latin America 133; role of local government 183–184, 186–189; service delivery 190–197; spending behavior 189–200; tax increment financing 492–493; urban governance study 282–292
uplift tax 493
Urban Development Community (UDCs) projects 211
urban entrepreneurialism 204
urban governance: austerity in Europe 280–288, 290–293; economic boosterism 291–292; Pacific Islands countries 117–118; public entrepreneurship 211–212
urban regime theory 85
urbanisation: Pacific Islands countries 112, 117, 118, 126; rescaling municipalities 380–381
user charges (revenue sources) 486–487, 499
utilities *see* energy sector; public services/utilities; water services

van Waarden, B. 264
Vanuatu: constitutions 42, 43; decentralisation 119–120; funding local government 122; place of local government 112–113; service delivery 124, 125; traditional leadership 47, 48–49, 51; traditional rights 44; *see also* Pacific Islands countries
Venezuela, electoral systems 140–141, 142
vertical fiscal imbalance (VFI) 485
veterans' organisations, Russia 272
VFM auditing 450–451, 452–454, 463
village level, Pacific Islands countries 112, 125–126; *see also* traditional leadership
violence *see* conflict
Visegrad countries: civic engagement 344–345, 349–357; development and dynamics 348–349; political and regional structure 345–348, **346**
visibility: local leadership elections 25, 28, 31; taxation 489
volatility, tax **475**
voluntary sector, austerity in Europe 287
voting *see* electoral participation; electoral systems

Wales: council tax 476–477; funding local government 296–297; *see also* United Kingdom
ward population 61–62
waste services, United States 188, 196
water services, Europe 254
wealth distribution, local government areas 485
Weber, M. 71, 73, 77
welfare services *see* social services
Westminster Parliamentary System 167
Widdicombe Committee, England 30
Wilson, W. 71, 73, 77
Woonton, central-local relationship 120
World Bank, Pacific Islands countries 41–42, 121

Zavadoukovsky urban okrug, Russia, citizen participation 271, 272, 273–274